Programming and Problem Solving with Ada 95

Second Edition

Nell Dale
University of Texas, Austin

Chip Weems
University of Massachusetts, Amherst

John McCormick
University of Northern Iowa, Cedar Falls

World Headquarters
Jones and Bartlett Publishers
40 Tall Pine Drive
Sudbury, MA 01776
978-443-5000
info@jbpub.com
www.jbpub.com

Jones and Bartlett Publishers Canada
2406 Nikanna Road
Mississauga, Ontario
CANADA L5C 2WG

Jones and Bartlett Publishers International
Barb House, Barb Mews
London W6 7PA
UK

CHIEF EXECUTIVE OFFICER: Clayton Jones
CHIEF OPERATING OFFICER: Don W. Jones, Jr.
V.P., SALES AND MARKETING: Tom Manning
V.P., COLLEGE EDITORIAL DIRECTOR: Brian L. McKean
V.P., MANAGING EDITOR: Judith H. Hauck
V.P., DESIGN AND PRODUCTION: Anne Spencer
NATIONAL SALES MANAGER: Paul Shepardson
SENIOR MARKETING MANAGER: Jennifer M. Jacobson
SENIOR ACQUISITIONS EDITOR: J. Michael Stranz
PRODUCTION EDITOR: Rebecca S. Marks
DIRECTOR OF MANUFACTURING AND INVENTORY CONTROL: Therese Bräuer
COVER DESIGN: Stephanie Torta
TEXT DESIGN: George McLean
COMPOSITION: PageMasters & Company
PRINTING AND BINDING: Courier Companies
COVER PRINTING: Courier Companies

Library of Congress Cataloging-in-Publication Data
Dale, Nell B.
Programming and problem solving with ADA / Nell Dale, Chip Weems, John McCormick.—2nd ed.
p. cm.
Includes index.
ISBN: 0-7637-0792-9
1. Ada (Computer program language) I. Weems, Chip II. McCormick, John (John W.) III. Title.

QA76.73.A35 D36 2000
005.13'3—dc21 99-049488

Printed in the United States of America
04 03 02 01 00 10 9 8 7 6 5 4 3 2 1

Programming and Problem Solving with Ada 95

Second Edition

This book is dedicated to you, and to all of our students, for whom it was begun and without whom it could never have been completed.

N. D.

C. W.

J. M.

To Naomi, wife and best friend.

J. M.

Contents

4 BOOLEAN AND ENUMERATION TYPES, CONDITIONS, AND SELECTION CONTROL STRUCTURES 169

7 TYPES AND SUBTYPES 377

12 PACKAGES, SEARCHING, AND SORTING 685

Preface

The second edition of *Programming and Problem Solving with Ada 95* is a continuation of the best-selling series of books that have been widely accepted as model textbooks for the ACM-recommended curriculum for CS1. It reflects our view of the future direction of computer science education—more rigor, more theory, greater use of abstraction and modeling, and the earlier application of software engineering principles. As always, our efforts are directed toward making the sometimes difficult concepts of computer science accessible to beginning students. The chapters contain numerous figures, short clear examples, and many exercises. Every chapter has one or more complete case studies that guide the reader through the complete specification, design, implementation, and testing steps of software development while promoting a straightforward, disciplined programming style.

Our experience has shown that topics once considered too advanced, such as modeling, Big-O, metalanguages, and testing, can be taught in the first course. We emphasize accurate modeling from the beginning through the use of constraints with all scalar objects. We use EBNF as the formal means of specifying programming language syntax. We introduce Big-O early and use it to compare algorithms in later chapters. We discuss modular design in terms of abstract steps, concrete steps, functional equivalence, and functional cohesion. Preconditions and postconditions are used in the context of the algorithm trace, in the development of testing strategies, and as interface documentation for programmer-written functions and procedures.

Changes in the Second Edition

The second edition incorporates the following changes:

- *The use of Ada 95.* The major impacts of this change on the textbook include longer names for the standard libraries (Ada.Text_IO instead of Text_IO), pre-instantiated packages for the input and output of Integer and Float values, a standard library for elementary mathematical functions, decimal types, the use type clause, changes in the order of declarations (to prevent inadvertent use of global variables), and the ability to "read" values of out mode parameters.

- *An earlier introduction to data modeling.* We introduce range constraints along with variable declarations to encourage accurate modeling of scalar objects. We know that inaccurate modeling of primitive objects is a major cause of faults in software. Early exposure to constraints helps students find such faults in their programs and prepares them for modeling more complicated classes.
- *Attention to length.* In response to feedback from our users and reviewers about the length of the first edition, we have reduced the number of chapters from 17 to 13. We combined and streamlined the material from the three chapters on arrays, sorting and searching, and package writing into two chapters. As it is more appropriate for the data structures course, we eliminated the chapter on elaboration, error handling, and writing generic units. While we also deleted the chapter on numeric data, we included some of this material in our discussions of numeric types in Chapter 7. Finally, we have reduced the number of case studies. Whereas the first edition presented two or three case studies per chapter, most chapters now have one or two case studies.

Chapter Organization

Chapter 1 is designed to create a comfortable rapport between the student and the subject. However, because many students enter the introductory course with some prior exposure to computers, the chapter moves quickly into meaty topics. It includes a section on problem-solving techniques and applies them immediately in a case study. By the end of Chapter 1, students will have a basic knowledge of computer hardware, software, and the techniques used in algorithmic problem solving.

The students first look at syntax in Chapter 2. A section on metalanguages describes the details of EBNF. Because the EBNF for many Ada constructs contains large numbers of choices, we introduce syntax using a *simplified* EBNF definition, one that does not include all the available alternatives. We add alternatives to simplified EBNF definitions as needed. Appendix B presents the complete set of EBNF definitions of the Ada language.

The goal of Chapter 2 is to bring students to the point where they can design a simple program independently. Because there are so many concepts and rules to learn before even the simplest program may be written, the chapter takes a break in the middle to go through a streamlined discussion of program entry, correction, and execution. Then students can reinforce the new concepts by trying them on the computer. The remainder of the chapter fleshes out the details of Ada syntax for more complex expressions and formatting output.

The top-down design methodology is a major focus of Chapter 3. This chapter also covers input and text files other than standard input and standard output. The early introduction of files permits the assignment of programming problems that require the use of sample data files. For those instructors who postpone the use of files, the section is designed to be covered anytime prior to assigning Chapter 9.

Chapter 4 begins with the Boolean data type, but its main purpose is to introduce the concept of flow of control. Selection, using all the forms of Ada's if statement, is used to demonstrate the distinction between physical ordering of statements and logical ordering. We also develop the concept of nested control structures. In addition, Chapter 4 explains enumeration types and enumeration I/O. Enumeration types allow students to write command-driven programs without having to learn the complex rules governing character strings. The chapter concludes with a lengthy Testing and Debugging section that expands on the modular design discussion by introducing preconditions and postconditions. We introduce the algorithm trace and code check as a means of preventing errors and use the execution trace to help locate errors in the code. We also describe data validation and testing strategies extensively in this section.

Chapter 5 concentrates on looping structures. All the structures are introduced using the syntax of the loop and exit statements. Rather than confuse the student with multiple syntactical structures, we teach the concepts of looping using only the loop statement. However, because some instructors prefer to show students the syntax for all of Ada's loops at once, we have written the discussion of the for and while statements in Chapter 8 so that it may be covered optionally along with Chapter 5. In Chapter 5, we first show students the basic loop patterns. We then describe how to select a pattern and design loops using a checklist of seven questions. We introduce the concepts of magnitude of work and Big-O notation at the end of the chapter.

By Chapter 6, students feel comfortable breaking problems into modules and using predefined procedures and packages. They are ready to master writing their own subprograms. Chapter 6 covers flow of control in procedures, formal and actual parameters, parameter modes, parameter association, local variables, scope rules, and interface design. The latter topic includes control abstraction, encapsulation, and conceptual versus physical hiding of an implementation. Finally, we present the function subprogram and discuss when to use functions. In the Testing and Debugging section, we explain how to use stubs and drivers for testing individual modules.

Chapter 7 introduces students to a more formal treatment of scalar types. We use Ada's extensive type model to specify the domain of scalar classes accurately. Ada's strong typing and scalar modeling through programmer specified constraints promote the production of safe programs. Many errors are discovered at compile time rather than during execution, and range checks are performed during execution. In this chapter, we introduce character and decimal types. We discuss the attributes for enumeration, character, float, decimal, and integer types. We treat the details of programmer-defined types and subtypes at a level appropriate for the beginning programmer. We discuss how to choose between using types and using subtypes. The Testing and Debugging section reinforces the use of programmer-defined types and subtypes for passive error detection during program execution.

Chapter 8 features other commonly used control statements such as the case statement, the for loop, and the while loop and lists guidelines for choosing a looping statement. We introduce loop invariants in the Testing and Debugging section.

In Chapter 9 we show students how to write exception handlers so that a program can continue execution after an exception is raised. The most common exceptions raised in students' programs are related to input. Therefore, we begin by expanding on the coverage of text files from Chapter 3. We describe how to use block statements and exception handlers to produce robust input routines and explain the propagation of exceptions in detail. Because many beginning Ada programmers tend to use exception handlers for normal processing or as a quick fix of a run-time error, we discuss when exception handlers are appropriate.

Chapter 9 also covers Ada's sequential and direct files. We use direct files in the solution of problems often given in the array chapters of other texts. We believe that, other than sorting, the majority of introductory "array" problems are solved more realistically with direct files.

We present records in Chapter 10. We introduce records before arrays because students find selecting a component from a structured data type by a *constant* name easier than selecting one by a *variable* index. Although single records can be useful, many applications require a collection of records. We explain how to define a sequential or direct file whose components are records.

We introduce the array data type in Chapter 11. Arrays are the last big conceptual hurdle for the students: a variable to access another variable? Three case studies and numerous small examples assist students in making the jump successfully. We discuss patterns of array access (random, sequential, and as a single object), subarray processing, and indexes with semantic content. We explain how to choose between a multidimensional array and an array of arrays. We introduce Ada's more advanced array features, including unconstrained array types, slices, attributes, catenation, and relational operators.

In Chapter 12 we teach students how to design and implement their own packages. The concepts of information hiding and encapsulation used throughout the previous chapters are stated explicitly in the context of the package. We introduce a simple package taxonomy to help beginning programmers with package design. We explain the Ada program library and the order of compilation. Although we introduced the use package clause in Chapter 2 we did not use it in the first eleven chapters. In Chapter 12 we review the use type and use package clauses and show situations for which the use package clause is appropriate. This chapter also gives students more experience with array processing. We develop searching and sorting algorithms and use Big-O notation to compare them.

Chapter 13 deals with recursion. There is no consensus as to the best place to introduce this subject. Although Chapter 13 is the last chapter, we divide the examples into two parts — those that require only simple data types, and those that require structured data types. You can cover the first part of this chapter after completing Chapter 6. The second part of this chapter contains examples using arrays, which you can treat after or along with Chapter 11.

Pedagogical Features

We incorporate eight different features in every chapter to help students master the concepts.

- **Goals** Each chapter begins with a list of learning objectives for the student. These goals are then reinforced and tested in the end-of-chapter exercises.
- **Special Sections** Four kinds of features are set off from the main text. *Theoretical Foundations* sections present material related to the fundamental theory behind various branches of computer science. *Software Engineering Tips* discuss methods of making programs more reliable, robust, or efficient. *Matters of Style* boxes address stylistic issues in the coding of programs. *Background Information* sections explore side issues that enhance the students' general knowledge of computer science.
- **Problem-Solving Case Studies** Problem solving is best demonstrated through case studies. We include one to three case studies at the end of every chapter. In each case study, we present a problem and use problem-solving techniques to develop a manual solution. Next we expand the solution to an algorithm using modular design methodology, and then we code the algorithm in Ada. We show simple test data and output and follow up with a discussion of what is involved in testing the program thoroughly.
- **Testing and Debugging** Following the case studies in each chapter, this section considers in depth the implications of the chapter material with regard to the thorough testing of programs. The section concludes with a list of testing and debugging hints.
- **Quick Checks** At the end of each chapter are questions that test students' recall of major points discussed in each chapter. Upon

reading each question, students should immediately know the answer, which they can verify by glancing at the answers at the end of the section. The page number on which the concept is discussed appears at the end of each question so that students can review the material in the event of an incorrect response.

- **Exam Preparation Exercises** These questions help students to prepare for tests. The questions have objective answers and are designed to be answered with a few minutes of work. Answers to selected questions are given in the back of the book, and the remaining questions are answered in the *Instructor's Guide*.
- **Programming Warm-up Exercises** This section provides students with experience in writing Ada code fragments or subprograms. The students can practice the syntactic constructs in each chapter without the burden of writing a complete program. Solutions to selected questions from each chapter appear in the back of the book; the remaining solutions may be found in the *Instructor's Guide*.
- **Programming Problems** We have included specifications for problems from a wide range of disciplines in these exercises, which require students to write complete programs.

Ada Options

A programming language as rich as Ada provides many options to the programmer. Our philosophy is not to introduce a new Ada feature until students have reached the point at which they can appreciate its significance. Most people learning Ada as a second language tend to use those options that are familiar to them from their earlier experiences. We use the options that provide the most information to the reader of a program:

- **Early Use of Procedures** Students learn to recognize procedures in Chapter 1 and to use predefined procedures and parameters in Chapter 2. In Chapter 6 they learn how to write their own procedures.
- **Early Use of Packages** We introduce students to the package concept in Chapter 1. They begin using predefined packages in Chapter 2. In Chapter 12, they learn to write their own packages.
- **Prefixing versus Use** The advantage to using a use package clause is that you don't have to type so many characters when entering your Ada program. The advantage of avoiding use package clauses and prefixing all references to package identifiers is the additional documentation provided. Nearly everybody agrees that the benefits of comments and meaningful variable names far outweigh the effort required to type or read the additional characters. We believe that the effort required to prefix all package identifiers is just as worthwhile. Therefore, nearly all of the examples in this text use prefixing rather than the use package clause. However, there are situations in which

the use package clause is preferable to qualification. Such instances are discussed in Chapter 12. We believe that the use type clause improves the readability of Ada code and use it to eliminate the need for prefixed operators in expressions.

- **Parameter Association** In the first five chapters, we employ named association exclusively. As a result, students are made aware of formal parameters from the first time they call an output procedure. They have a much easier time understanding the binding of formal and actual parameters when we use named association. We describe positional association in Chapter 6 and use it in most function calls and single parameter procedure calls in which the formal parameter name supplies no useful information.
- **Exceptions** We introduce exceptions in Chapter 2 when we discuss compile time errors and execution errors. We present exceptions as a powerful passive method of protecting the user; it is better for the program to halt with an exception than to display incorrect results. We show students how to write exception handlers in Chapter 9.
- **Generic Units** There are many advantages to learning about instantiation early. We introduce students to the instantiation of enumeration I/O packages in Chapter 4 in a manner that makes instantiation seem natural. Students can then write command-driven programs without having to deal with the complexities of strings. Early familiarity with instantiation also makes it easier for them to use programmer-defined numeric types and sequential and direct files when they are introduced.

Three major Ada topics not included in this text are tasks, access types (pointers), and inheritance. Although some instructors advocate teaching concurrent programming in the beginning course, we believe that this topic is more suitable after students have a firm grounding in sequential programming. Even though many introductory Ada texts have a chapter on pointers, we have found that very few instructors cover pointers in the first course. Complete coverage of access types is given in our data structures textbook. While object modeling is a recurring theme in the textbook, we take an object-based approach (object-oriented without inheritance) to design. We agree with Pooley and Stevens that "inheritance, which is the icing on the cake… The metaphor indicates that it's nice, and that people often think it is important, but that in fact it's less nutritious than what we've already covered!"[*] A solid grounding in control structures and object modeling through composition are needed before modeling with inheritance.

---

[*] Pooley, R., Stevens, P., p22, *Using UML Software Engineering with Objects and Components*, Addison-Wesley Object Technology Series, Booch, Jacobson, & Rumbaugh, editors, 256pp, 1999.

Supplements

- **Instructor's Guide** The Instructor's Guide features teaching notes, answers to the balance of the exercises, and a carefully worked-out solution and discussion for one programming problem per chapter.
- **Test Item File** The Test Item File, located on a CD-ROM packaged in the Instructor's Guide, includes more than 1,700 possible test questions patterned after those in the Exam Preparation Exercises.
- **Program Code** All the programs are available from the publisher's web site (www.jbpub.com/disks).

Acknowledgments

We would like to thank the many individuals who have helped us with this project. We are indebted to the adopters of the first edition who took the time to send us their comments, the members of the faculty of the Computer Science Departments at the State University of New York at Plattsburgh, the University of Northern Iowa, the University of Texas at Austin, and the University of Massachusetts at Amherst.

The comments, corrections, and suggestions made by our technical reviewers have enormously improved and enriched this book. We are grateful to the following people who reviewed the manuscript under tight deadlines:

John Barnes
  Caversham, England
Gail Miles
  Lenoir-Rhyne College
Edward Okie
  Radford University
Ryan Stansifer
  Florida Institute of Technology

The staff at Jones and Bartlett Publishers have been very helpful. We particularly thank Rebecca Marks, J. Michael Stranz, and Christine Tridente. We also thank Lesley Rock and PageMasters & Company for their assistance.

Anyone who has written a textbook can appreciate the amount of time and effort involved. And anyone related to a textbook author can tell you at whose expense that time is spent. Thanks to all the Dale clan and extended Dale family (too numerous to name). Lisa and Charlie—thanks for your tremendous support and indulgence. Thank you, Naomi, for all of your support and encouragement.

—N. D., C. W., J. M.

CHAPTER 1

Overview of Programming and Problem Solving

GOALS

After reading this chapter, you should be able to

- understand what a computer program is
- describe the major components of a computer and how they work together
- distinguish between hardware and software
- list the basic stages involved in writing a program
- know what an algorithm is
- understand what a high-level programming language is
- describe what a compiler is and what it does

Overview of Programming

com·pu·ter *n. often attrib* (1646): one that computes; *specif:* a programmable electronic device that can store, retrieve, and process data.*

What a brief definition for something that, in just a few decades, has changed the way of life in industrialized societies! Computers touch all areas of our daily lives: paying bills, driving cars, using the telephone, going shopping. In fact, it would be easier to list those areas of our lives *not* affected by computers.

It is sad that a device that does so much good so often is maligned and feared. How many times have you heard someone say, "I'm sorry, our computer fouled things up," or "I just don't understand computers; they're too complicated for me"? Fortunately, the very fact that you are reading this book means that you are ready to set aside prejudice and learn about computers. However, be warned: This book is not just about computers in the abstract. This is a text to teach you how to program them.

What Is Programming?

Much of human behavior and thought is characterized by logical sequences. Since infancy, you have been learning how to act, how to do things. And you have learned to expect certain behavior from other people.

A lot of what you do every day you do automatically. Fortunately, it is not necessary for you to think consciously of every step involved in a process as simple as turning a page of a book.

1. Lift hand.
2. Move hand to right side of book.
3. Grasp top corner of page.
4. Move hand from right to left until page is positioned so that you can read what is on the other side.
5. Let go of page.

Think how many neurons must fire and how many muscles must respond, all in a certain order or sequence, to move your arm and hand. Yet you do it unconsciously.

Much of what you do unconsciously you once had to learn. Watch how a baby concentrates on putting one foot before the other while learning to walk. Then watch a group of three-year-olds playing tag.

On a broader scale, mathematics could never have been developed without logical sequences of steps for solving problems or proving theo-

*By permission. From *Webster's Ninth New Collegiate Dictionary* © 1991 by Merriam-Webster, Inc., publishers of the Merriam-Webster ® Dictionaries.

rems. Mass production would never have worked without certain operations taking place in a certain order. Our whole civilization is based on the order of things and actions.

We create order, both consciously and unconsciously, through a process we call **programming.** This book is concerned with the programming of one of our tools, the **computer.**

Programming Planning, scheduling, or performing a task or an event.

Computer A programmable device that can store, retrieve, and process data.

Just as a concert program lists the actions the players perform, a **computer program** lists the steps the computer performs. From now on, when we use the words *programming* and *program*, we will mean *computer programming* and *computer program*.

Computer programming The process of planning a sequence of steps for a computer to follow.

Computer program A list of instructions to be performed by a computer.

The computer allows us to do tasks more efficiently, quickly, and accurately than we could do them "by hand"—if we could do them by hand at all. In order to use this powerful tool, we must specify what we want done and the order in which we want it done. We do this through programming.

What Is a Computer?

You can learn a programming language, how to write programs, and how to run (execute) these programs without knowing much about computers. However, if you know something about the parts of a computer, you can better understand the effect of each instruction in the programming language.

There are five basic components in most computers: the memory unit, the arithmetic/logic unit, the control unit, input devices, and output devices. Figure 1-1 is a stylized diagram of the basic components of a computer.

The **memory unit** is an ordered sequence of storage cells, each capable of containing a piece of data. It is like an old-fashioned post office with pigeonholes for mail. Each memory cell has a distinct address to which we refer in order to store or retrieve information from it. These storage cells are called memory cells or memory locations.* The memory unit holds data (input data or the product of computation) and instructions (programs), as shown in Figure 1-2.

---

*The memory unit is also referred to as RAM, an acronym for random access memory (because we can access any location at random).

FIGURE 1-1
Basic Components of a Computer

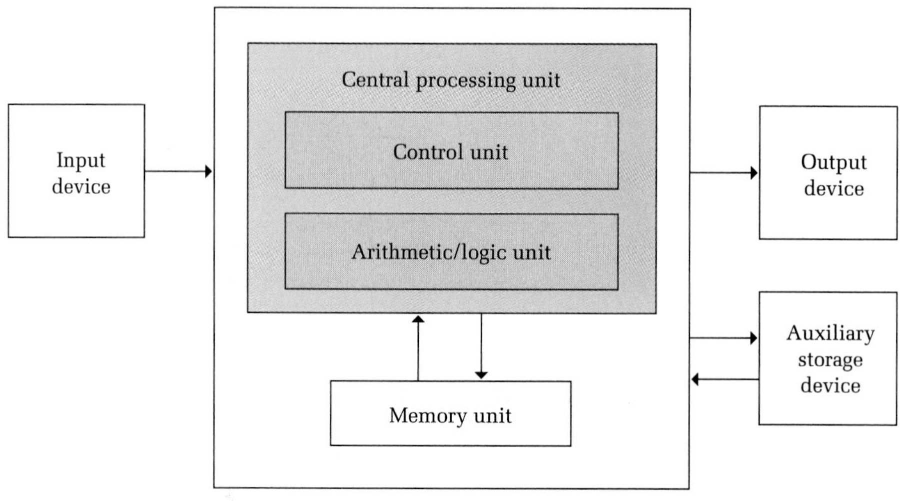

Memory unit Internal data storage in a computer.

The part of the computer that executes instructions is called the **central processing unit (CPU).** The CPU is actually two components: The **arithmetic/logic unit (ALU)** performs arithmetic operations (addition, subtraction, multiplication, and division) and logical operations (comparing two values); the **control unit** controls the actions of the other components so that programs get executed in sequence.

Central processing unit (CPU) The part of the computer that executes the instructions (program) stored in memory; made up of the arithmetic/logic unit and the control unit.

Arithmetic/logic unit (ALU) The component of the central processing unit that performs arithmetic and logical operations.

Control unit The component of the central processing unit that controls the actions of the other components so that instructions (the program) are executed in sequence.

For us to use computers, we must have some way of getting data into and out of them. **Input and output (I/O)** devices accept data to be processed (input) and present data that has been processed (output). A keyboard is a common input device. Another is a mouse, a "pointing" device. A video display is a common output device, as are liquid crystal display (LCD) screens, printers, and speakers.

Input/output (I/O) devices The parts of the computer that accept data to be processed (input) and present the results of that processing (output).

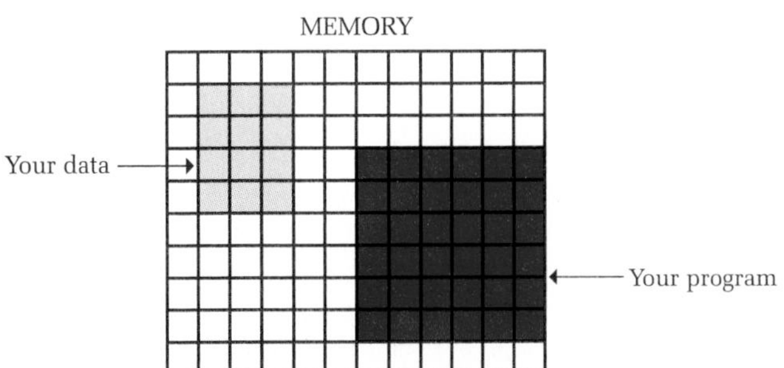

Figure 1-2
Memory

The memory, processors, and I/O devices are connected by a bus. A **bus** is a set of wires and perhaps some minimal electronics that connect multiple subsystems. Communications between subsystems connected to a bus are coordinated by a specific series of steps called a *protocol.*

Bus A set of wires that connect multiple subsystems.

For the most part, computers simply move and combine data in memory. The differences between various computers basically involve the size of their memories and the speed with which they recall data, the efficiency with which they can move or combine data, and limitations on I/O devices.

When a program is executing, the computer proceeds through a series of steps, the *fetch-execute cycle.*

1. The control unit retrieves (*fetches*) the next coded instruction from memory.
2. The control unit translates the instruction into control signals.
3. The control signals tell the appropriate unit (ALU, memory, I/O device) to perform (*execute*) the instruction.
4. The sequence repeats from step 1.

Computers can have a wide variety of **peripheral devices** (see Figure 1-3). An **auxiliary storage device,** or *secondary storage* device, holds coded data for the computer until we want to use the data. Whenever we need to use the data, we tell the computer to transfer the data from the auxiliary storage device to its memory. Typical auxiliary storage devices are magnetic tape drives and disk drives. A *magnetic tape drive* is like a tape recorder. A *disk drive* is a cross between a compact disc player and a tape recorder. It uses a thin disk made out of a magnetic material. A read-write (R/W) head (similar to the record/playback head in a tape recorder) travels across the spinning disk retrieving or recording data. *Compact discs* are an inexpensive medium for storing large amounts of data.

Figure 1-3
Peripheral Devices

Keyboard

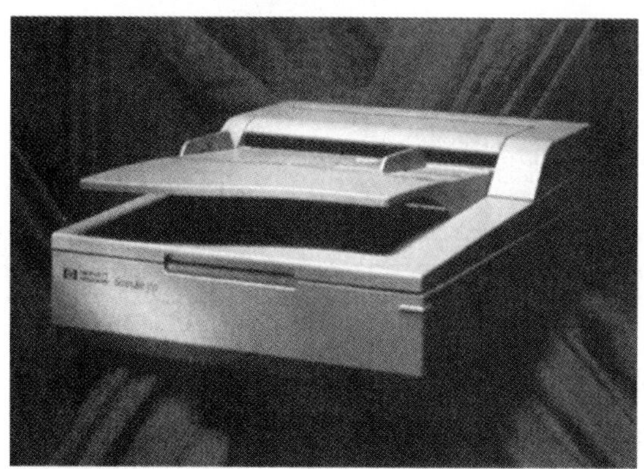

Scanner

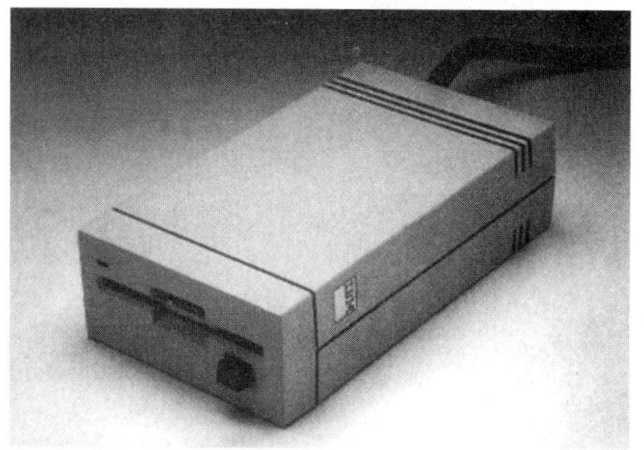

$3\frac{1}{2}$" Disk Drive

Magnetic Tape Drive

Plotter

Figure 1-3
Continued

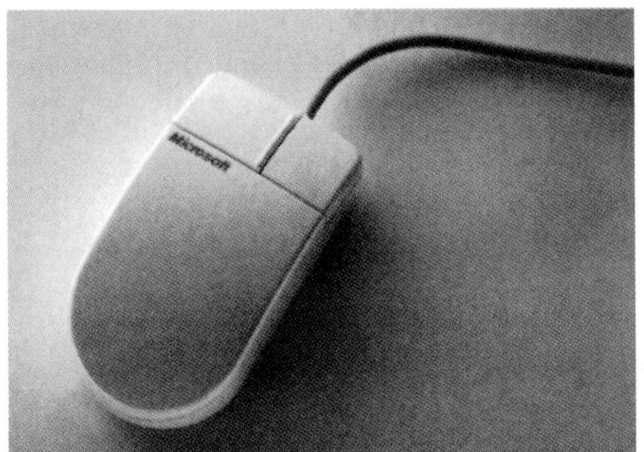

Mouse

Monitor

Laser Printer

CD-ROM Drives

Peripheral device An input, output, or auxiliary storage device attached to a computer.

Auxiliary storage device A device that stores data in encoded form, outside the computer's main memory.

Together, all of these physical components are known as **hardware.** The programs that enable the hardware to operate are called **software.** Hardware usually is fixed in design; software is easily changed. In fact, the ease with which software can be manipulated is what makes the computer such a versatile, powerful tool.

Hardware The physical components of a computer.

Software Computer programs; the set of all programs available on a computer.

In addition to the programs we write or purchase, there are programs in the computer that are designed to simplify the user/computer **interface,** making it easier for us to use the machine. The interface between user and computer is a set of I/O devices—for example a keyboard and screen—that allows the user to communicate with the computer. We work with the keyboard and screen on our side of the interface boundary; wires attached to the keyboard and screen carry the electronic pulses that the computer works with on its side of the interface boundary. At the boundary itself is a mechanism that translates information for the two sides.

Interface A connecting link at a shared boundary, permitting independent systems to meet and act on or communicate with each other.

When we communicate directly with the computer through a keyboard and screen, we are using an **interactive system.** Interactive systems allow direct entry of programs and data and provide immediate feedback to the user. In contrast, *batch systems* require that all the data be entered before a program is run, providing feedback only after a program has executed. In this text we focus on interactive systems, although sometimes we discuss file-oriented programs, which share certain similarities with batch systems. A *file* is a collection of data stored on an auxiliary storage device. The program at the end of this chapter creates a file containing data that may be used by another program, printed, or displayed on a screen.

Interactive system A system that allows direct communication between the user and the computer.

Figure 1-4
User/Computer Interface

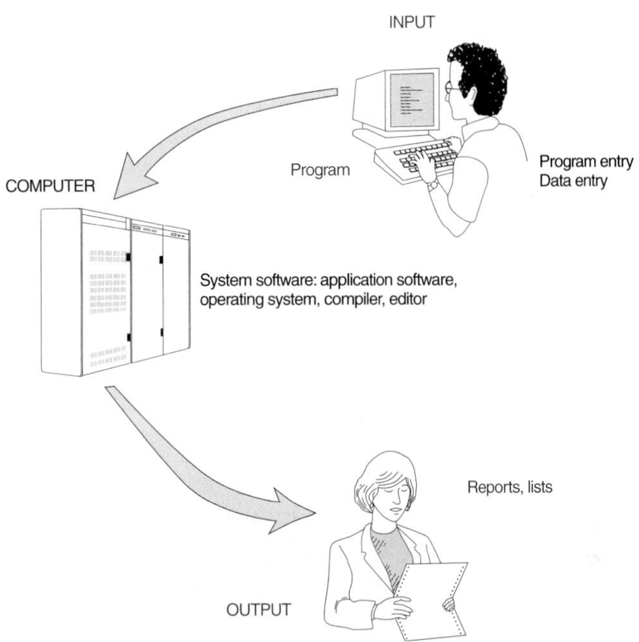

The set of programs that simplifies the user/computer interface and improves the efficiency of processing is called *system software*. It includes the compiler as well as the operating system and the editor (see Figure 1-4). The **operating system** manages all of the computer's resources. It can input programs, call the compiler, execute object programs, and carry out any other system commands. An **editor** is an interactive program used to create and modify programs or data.

Operating system A set of programs that manages all of the computer's resources.

Editor An interactive program used to create and modify programs or data.

Background Information

Mainframes, Micros, and Minis

There are many different sizes and kinds of computers. *Mainframes* are very large (they can fill a room) and are very fast. A typical mainframe computer consists of several cabinets full of electronic components. Inside those cabinets are the memory unit, the CPU, and the I/O devices. It's easy to spot the various peripheral devices: Separate cabinets are labeled "disk drive" and "tape drive." Other units are obviously terminals and printers.

At the other end of the spectrum are *embedded computers:* small computers that are part of a larger piece of equipment whose primary purpose is not computing. A new automobile may, for example, contain a dozen or more small computers that control everything from fuel flow into the engine to the entertainment system.

You are certainly familiar with *microcomputers* or *personal computers* (PCs). It can be difficult to spot the individual parts inside personal computers because of their size. Many PCs are just a single box with a screen, a keyboard, and sometimes a mouse. You have to open the case to see the CPU, which is usually just a large integrated circuit.

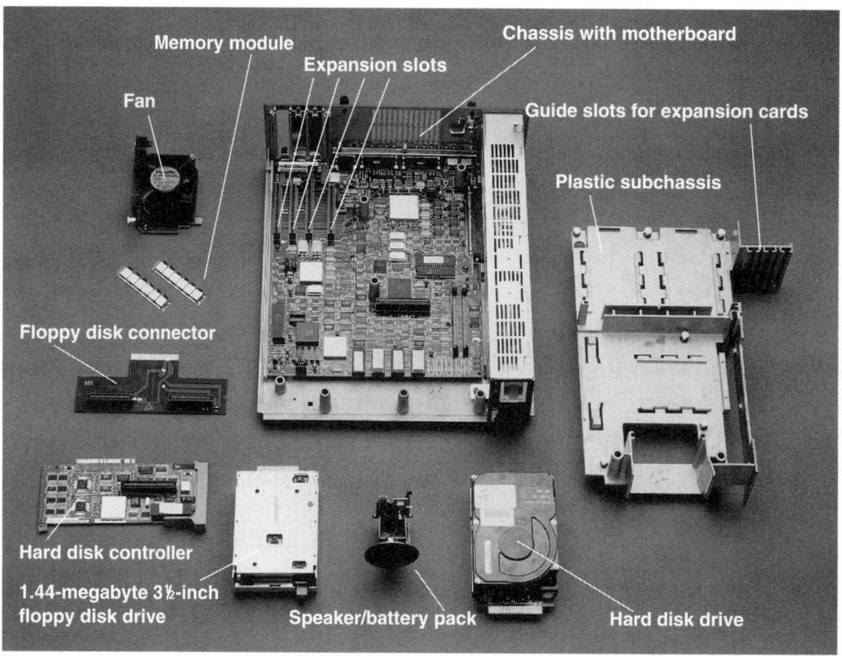

Inside a PC, system unit broken down

Personal Computer, Macintosh

Personal Computer, IBM

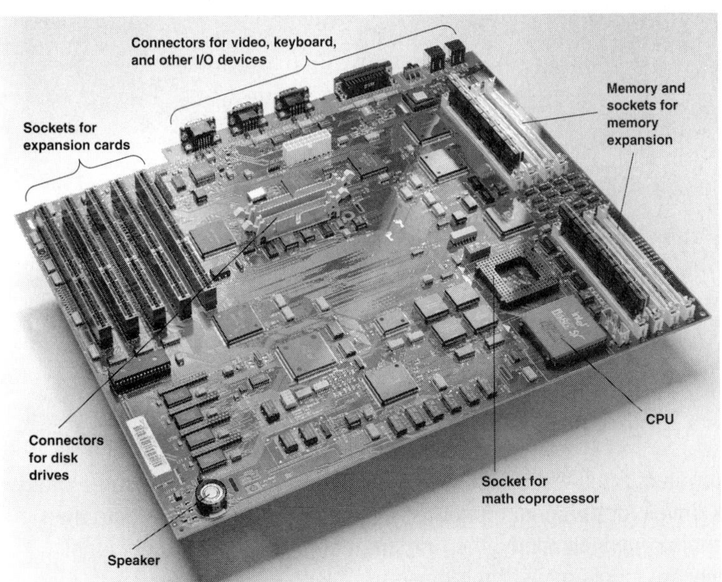

Inside a PC, close-up of a system board

Mainframe Computer

Notebook Computer

Supercomputer

Workstation

Personal computers rarely have tape drives; most operate with disk drives and printers. The disk drives for personal computers typically hold much less data than those used with mainframes. Similarly, the printers that are attached to personal computers typically are much slower than those used with mainframes.

The *supercomputer* is the most powerful class of computer in existence. Supercomputers typically are designed to perform scientific and engineering calculations on immense sets of data with great speed. They are very expensive and so are not in widespread use.

Another class of computer is beginning to rival the supercomputer's great speed but at a significantly lower cost. The *parallel processing computer* contains many, perhaps thousands, of inexpensive central processing units working together to solve a problem. These CPUs may be combined in a single cabinet or spread among several computers connected together in a network.

How Do We Write a Program?

To write a sequence of instructions for a computer to follow, we go through a two-phase process: *problem solving* and *implementation* (see Figure 1-5).

Problem-Solving Phase

1. *Analysis* and *Specification* Understand (define) the problem and what the solution must do.
2. *General Solution* Describe the data and logical sequences of steps (algorithms) to be used to solve the problem.
3. *Verify* Follow the steps exactly to see whether the solution really *does* solve the problem.

Implementation Phase

1. *Specific Solution (Program)* Translate the data descriptions and algorithms into a programming language (code).
2. *Test* Have the computer follow the instructions and then manually check the results. If you find errors, analyze the program and the algorithm to determine the source of the errors, and then make corrections.

Once you have written a program, it enters a third phase: maintenance.

Maintenance Phase

1. *Use* Use the program.
2. *Maintain* Modify the program to meet changing requirements or to correct any errors that occur when using it.

Each time you modify the program, you must repeat the problem-solving and implementation phases for those aspects of the program that change. Together, the problem-solving, implementation, and maintenance phases constitute the program's *life cycle*.

The computer is not intelligent. It cannot analyze a problem and come up with a solution. The programmer must analyze the problem, arrive at the solution, and then communicate it to the computer. What is the advantage of using a computer if it can't solve problems? Once we have a solution for a problem and have prepared a version of it for the computer, the computer can repeat the solution quickly time and time again. The computer frees people from tasks that require great speed or consistency or that are repetitive and boring.

The programmer begins the programming process by analyzing the problem and developing a general model of the problem. This general model describes the objects in the problem and how these objects are manipulated. Understanding and analyzing a problem to build a general

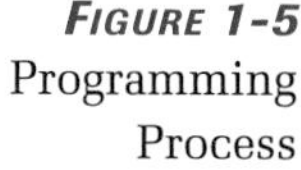

FIGURE 1-5 Programming Process

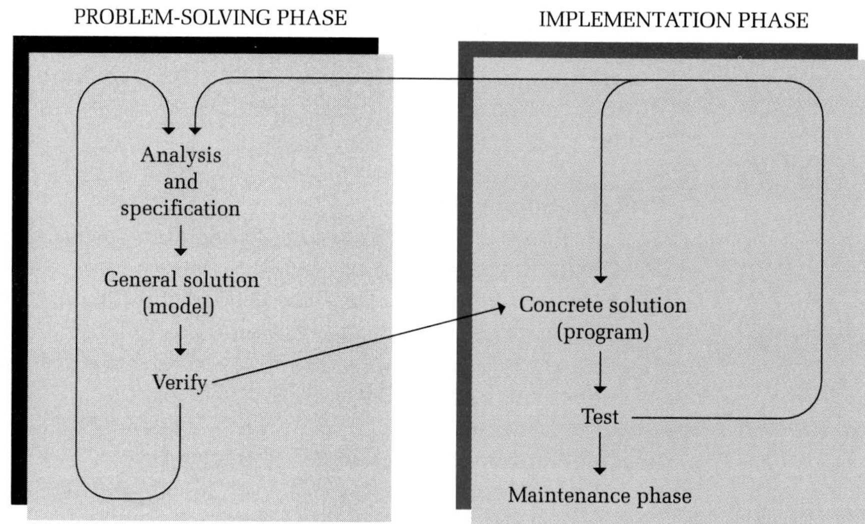

model take up much more time than Figure 1-5 implies. Developing models is the heart of the programming process.

An important part of every model is one or more algorithms. An **algorithm** is a logical sequence of actions. We use algorithms every day. Recipes, instructions, and directions are all examples of algorithms that are not programs. When you start your car, you follow a step-by-step procedure. The algorithm might look something like this:

1. Insert the key.
2. Make sure the transmission is in Park (or Neutral).
3. Depress the gas pedal.
4. Turn the key to the start position.
5. If the engine starts within 6 seconds, release the key to the ignition position.
6. If the engine doesn't start in 6 seconds, release the key, wait 10 seconds, and repeat steps 3 through 6, but not more than five times.
7. If the car doesn't start, call the garage.

Without the phrase "but not more than five times" in step 6, you could be trying to start the car forever. Why? Because if something is wrong with the car, repeating steps 3 through 6 over and over again will not start it. This kind of never-ending situation is called an infinite loop. If we leave the phrase "but not more than five times" out of step 6, the procedure does not fit our definition of an algorithm. An algorithm usually terminates in a finite amount of time for all possible conditions.

Algorithm A step-by-step finite procedure for solving a problem.

Suppose a programmer needed an algorithm to determine an employee's weekly wages. The algorithm reflects what would be done by hand.

1. Look up the employee's pay rate.
2. Determine the number of hours worked during the week.
3. If the number of hours worked is less than or equal to 40, multiply the number of hours by the pay rate to calculate regular wages.
4. If the number of hours worked is greater than 40, multiply 40 by the pay rate to calculate regular wages, and then multiply the difference between the number of hours worked and 40 by one and one-half times the pay rate to calculate overtime wages.
5. Add the regular wages to the overtime wages (if any) to determine total wages for the week.

The steps the computer follows are often the same as those you would use to do the calculations by hand.

After developing a general solution, the programmer tests the model, "walking through" each step of the algorithm mentally or manually seeing how the data objects are modified. If the algorithm doesn't work, the programmer repeats the problem-solving process, analyzing the problem again and coming up with a new model. Often the second model is just a variation of the first. When the programmer is satisfied with the model, he or she translates it into a **programming language.** We use the Ada programming language in this book.

Programming language A set of rules, symbols, and special words used to construct a program.

A programming language is a simplified form of our natural language (with math symbols) that adheres to a strict set of grammatical rules. Natural languages are far too ambiguous a language for computers to follow. Programming languages, because they limit vocabulary, are much more precise.

Although a programming language is simple in form, it is not always simple to use. Try giving someone directions to the nearest airport using a vocabulary of no more than 69 words (the number of words in the Ada language), and you begin to see the problem. Programming forces you to write very simple, exact instructions.

Translating a model into a programming language is called *coding*. The product of that translation—the program—is tested by running (*executing*) it on the computer. If the program fails to produce the wanted results, the

FIGURE 1-6 One Model Can Have Many Different Implementations

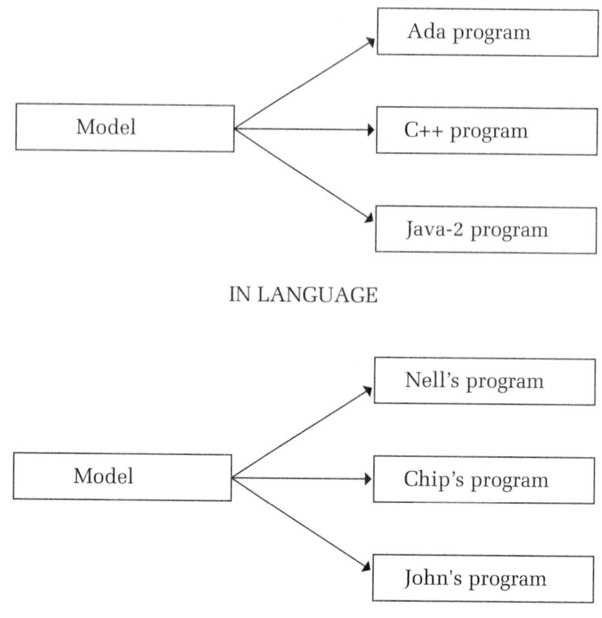

programmer must *debug* it: determine what is wrong and then modify the program or even the model to fix it. The combination of coding and testing a model is *implementation.*

There is no single way to implement a model. For example, a programmer can translate the data objects and algorithms of a model into more than one programming language. Each translation produces a different implementation. Even when different people translate a model into the same programming language, they are likely to come up with different implementations (see Figure 1-6). Why? Because every programming language allows the programmer some flexibility in how a model is translated. Given this flexibility, people adopt their own *styles* in writing programs, just as they do in writing short stories or essays. Once you have some programming experience, you will develop a style of your own. Throughout this book, we offer tips on good programming style.

Some people try to take a shortcut in the programming process by going directly from the problem definition to the coding of the program (see Figure 1-7). A shortcut here is very tempting and from a beginner's point of view seems to save a lot of time. However, for many reasons that will become obvious to you as you read this book, this kind of shortcut actually takes *more* time and effort. Developing a general solution before you write the program helps you manage the problem, keep your thoughts straight, and avoid mistakes. If you don't take the time at the beginning to think out and polish your model, you'll spend a lot of extra time debugging and revising your program later. So think first and code later! The sooner you start coding, the longer it will take to get a correct program.

In addition to understanding the problem, modeling it, implementing the model, and maintaining the program, writing **documentation** is an important part of the programming process. Most programs are used by many different people over a long period of time. Each of those people must be able to read and understand the code. This is especially true for large programs developed by teams of programmers.

Documentation The written text and comments that make a program easier for the programmer and others to understand, use, and modify.

A common difference between beginning and professional programmers is the time they choose to write the program documentation. Experienced programmers create most of the documentation during the problem-solving phase of the programming process. They realize the advantages that writing down explanations has on their own understanding of the problem and its solution. Beginning programmers often write the documentation after completing the implementation phase, just before their programming assignments are turned in to the instructor.

After you write a program, you must give the computer information or data to use to solve the problem. **Information** is any knowledge that can be communicated, including abstract ideas and concepts. **Data** is information in a form the computer can use—for example, numbers and letters.

Information Any knowledge that can be communicated.

Data Information that has been put into a form a computer can use.

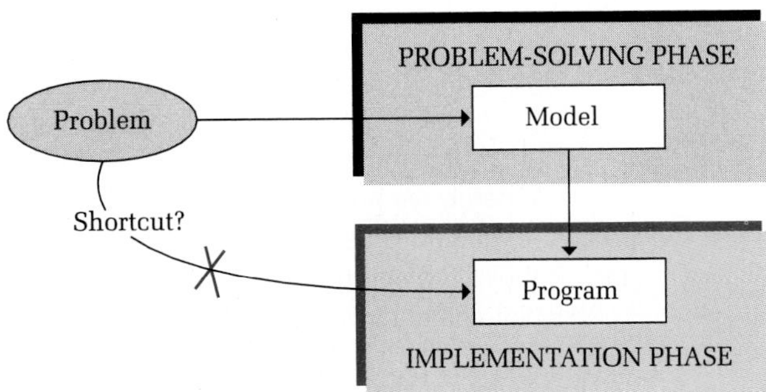

FIGURE 1-7 Programming Shortcut?

THEORETICAL FOUNDATIONS

Data Representation

In a computer, data is represented electronically by pulses of electricity. Digital electric circuits, in their simplest form, are either on or off. Usually a circuit that is on is represented by the number 1, and a circuit that is off is represented by the number 0. Any kind of data can be represented by combinations of enough 1s and 0s. We simply have to choose which combination will represent each piece of data we will be using. For example, we could arbitrarily choose the pattern 1101000110 to represent the name "Ada."

Data represented by 1s and 0s is in *binary form.* The binary (base 2) number system uses only 1s and 0s to represent numbers. (The decimal [base 10] number system uses the digits 0 through 9.) We often use the word *bit* (short for binary digit) to refer to a single 1 or 0. So, the pattern 1101000110 has 10 bits. A binary number with 10 bits can represent 2^{10} (1024) different patterns. A byte contains 8 bits; it can represent 2^{8} (256) patterns. Inside the computer, each character usually is represented by a byte. Groups of 16, 32, and 64 bits generally are referred to as *words* (although the terms *short word* and *long word* sometimes are used to refer to 16-bit and 64-bit groups, respectively).

The process of assigning bit patterns to pieces of data is called *coding*—the same name given to the process of translating a model into a programming language. In the early days of computers, programming meant translating an algorithm into patterns of 1s and 0s because the first computers could work only with language that was binary in form.

You can use binary coding schemes to represent both the instructions that the computer follows and the data that it uses. For example, 16 bits can represent the decimal integers from 0 to $2^{16} - 1$ (65,535). More complicated coding schemes are necessary to represent negative numbers, numbers with fractions, and numbers in scientific notation. Bit combinations also can represent characters. In one coding scheme, 01001101 represents *M* and 01101101 represents *m.*

The patterns of bits that represent data and instructions vary from one computer to another. Even on the same computer, different programming languages can use different binary representations for the same data. A single programming language may even use the same pattern of bits to represent different things in different contexts. (People do this too. The four letters that form the word *tack* have different meanings depending on whether you are talking about upholstery, sailing, sewing, paint, or horseback riding.) The point is that the patterns of bits by themselves are meaningless; it is the way the patterns are interpreted that gives them their meaning.

Fortunately we no longer have to remember binary coding schemes. Today the process of coding is usually just a matter of writing down the data in letters, numbers, and symbols. The computer automatically converts these numbers, letters, and symbols into binary form. Still, as you work with computers, you will continually run into numbers that are related to powers of 2—numbers like 256 and 65,536—reminders that the binary number system is fundamental to the representation of data.

What Is a Programming Language?

A characteristic of humans is that we use tools to help solve our problems. The tools we have developed equip us to deal with a wide variety of situations that we encounter daily. Some of these tools, such as scissors and hammers, are tangible objects. Others, such as paragraphs and mathematical equations, are more abstract.

Because problems come in many forms, they usually require different tools. For example, writing a note to your roommate and writing a term paper for your history class are both problems in written communication. Although you might use a single run-on sentence for the note, this writing tool is inadequate for the term paper. Without such tools as sections and paragraphs, your ability to communicate ideas to your history professor is limited (as is the grade you will receive). The larger a problem, the more it requires organizational tools. To build a bookshelf, you may need only some hand tools such as a hammer and screwdriver. To build a house, however, the architect organizes the walls and open space with blueprints. The planner who designs a housing development uses maps and scale models to organize groups of houses, streets, and utilities.

A programming language provides a set of tools. These tools range from those needed to control the individual electrical circuits in the computer to organizational tools that help a large group of programmers work together on a major project. As we have used computers to solve larger and larger problems, programming languages have evolved to include more of these organizational tools.

In the computer, all data, whatever its form, is stored and used in binary codes—strings of 0s and 1s. When computers were first developed, the only programming language available was the primitive instruction set built into each machine—the **machine language** or *machine code*.

Even though most computers perform the same kinds of operations, their designers choose different sets of binary codes for each instruction. So the machine code for one computer is not the same as for another.

When programmers used machine language for programming, they had to enter the binary codes for the various instructions, a tedious process that was prone to error. Moreover, their programs were difficult to read and modify. In time, **assembly languages** were developed to make the programmer's job easier.

Machine language The language, made up of binary-coded instructions, that is used directly by the computer.

Assembly language A low-level programming language in which a mnemonic is used to represent each of the machine language instructions for a particular computer.

Instructions in assembly language are in an easy-to-remember form called a *mnemonic* (pronounced "ni-'mä-nik"). Typical instructions for addition and subtraction might look like this:

Assembly Language	**Machine Language**
ADD	100101
SUB	010011

The only problem with assembly languages was that computers could not directly execute instructions written in them. So special programs called **assemblers** were developed to translate the instructions written in assembly language into machine code.

The assembler was a step in the right direction, but programmers still were forced to think in terms of individual machine instructions. Eventually, high-level programming languages were developed. These languages are easier to use than assembly languages or machine code because they are closer to the domain of the problem and do not require us to understand the details of the computer (see Figure 1-8).

A program called a **compiler** translates programs in high-level languages (Ada, C, C++, Java, Pascal, COBOL, or FORTRAN, for example) into machine language. If you write a program in a high-level language, you can usually run it on any computer that has the appropriate compiler. This is because most high-level languages are *standardized,* which means that an official description of the language exists.

Assembler A program that translates an assembly language program into machine code.

Compiler A program that translates a high-level language into machine code.

A program in a high-level language is called a **source program.** To the compiler program, a source program is just input data. The compiler translates the source program into a machine language program called an **object program** (see Figure 1-9). Optionally, a compiler can also produce a compilation listing—a copy of the source program with line numbers, error and warning messages, and statistics on the compilation process.

FIGURE 1-8 Levels of Abstraction

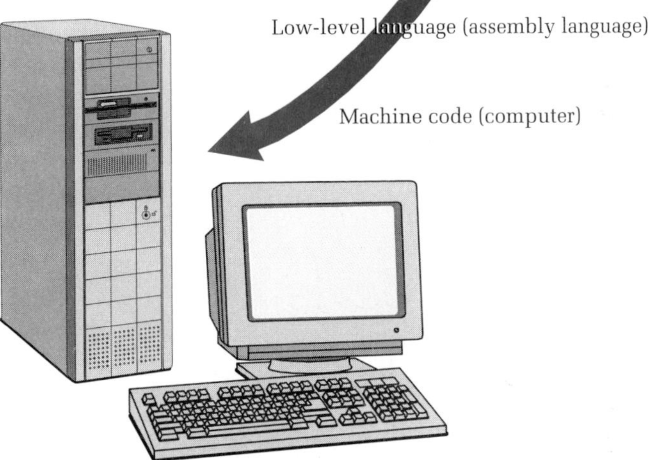

Source program A program written in a high-level programming language.

Object program The machine language version of a source program.

Notice in Figure 1-10 that compilation and execution are two distinct processes. During *compilation*, the computer runs the compiler program. During *execution*, the object program replaces the compiler program in the computer's memory. The computer then runs the object program, doing whatever the program instructs it to do.

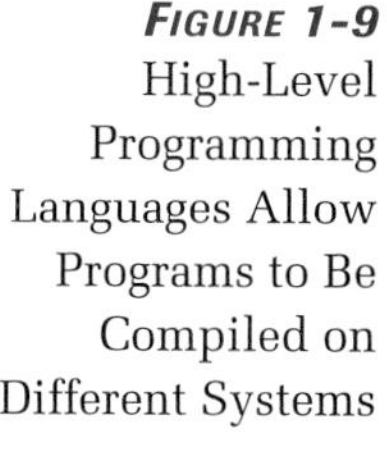

Figure 1-9 High-Level Programming Languages Allow Programs to Be Compiled on Different Systems

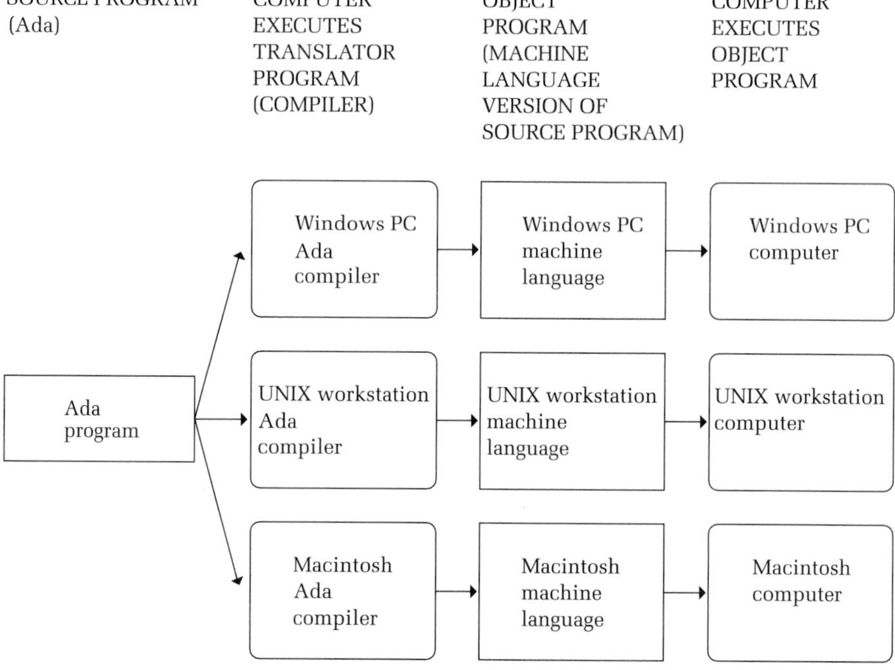

Figure 1-10 Compilation/ Execution

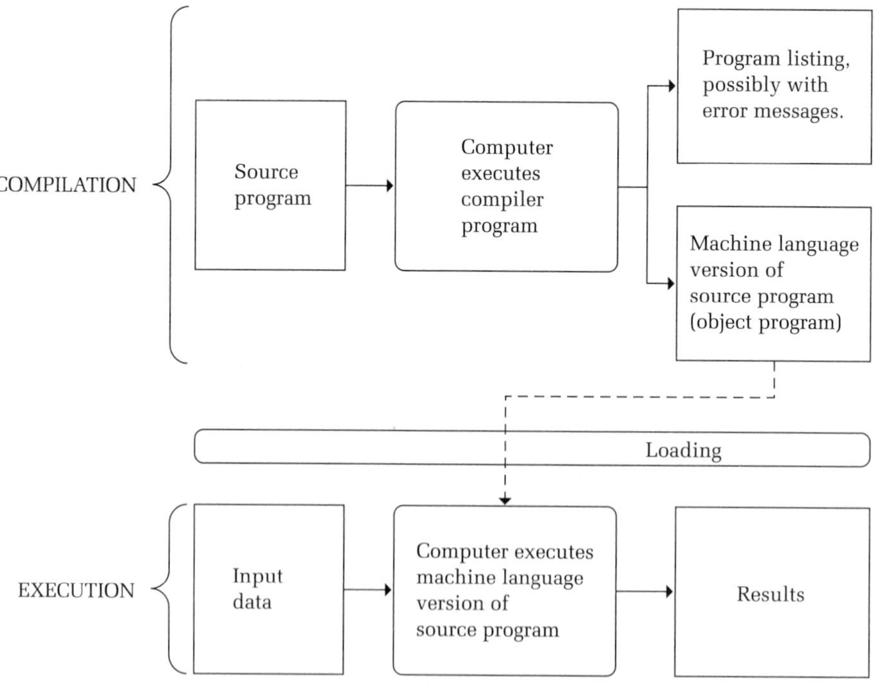

The basic instructions in a programming language reflect the functions a computer can perform.

- A computer can transfer data from one place to another.
- A computer can input data from an input device (a keyboard, for example) and output data to an output device (a screen, for example).
- A computer can store data in and retrieve data from its memory and its secondary storage.
- A computer can compare two data values for equality or inequality.
- A computer can perform arithmetic operations (addition and subtraction, for example) very quickly.

Programming languages require that we use certain structures to express algorithms as programs. There are four basic ways of structuring statements (instructions) in Ada and in other languages: sequentially, conditionally, repetitively, and procedurally (see Figure 1-11). A *sequence* is a series of statements that are executed one after another. *Selection*, the conditional structure, executes different statements depending on certain conditions. The repetitive structure, the *loop*, repeats statements until certain conditions are met. And the *procedure* enables us to structure a program by breaking it into smaller subprograms.

Assume you're driving a car. Going down a straight stretch of road is like following a *sequence* of instructions. When you come to a fork in the road, you must decide which way to go and then take one or the other branch of the fork. This is what the computer does when it encounters a *selection* (sometimes called a *branch* or *decision*) in a program. Sometimes you have to go around the block several times to find a place to park. The computer does the same sort of thing when it encounters a *loop* in a program.

A *procedure* is a process that consists of multiple steps. Every day, for example, you follow a procedure to get from home to work. It makes sense, then, for someone to give you directions to a meeting by saying, "Go to the office, and then go four blocks west," without repeating all the steps you have to take to get to the office. Procedures allow us to write parts of our programs separately and then assemble them into final form. They can greatly simplify the task of writing a program.

Problem-Solving Techniques

You solve problems every day, often unaware of the process you are going through. In a learning environment you usually are given most of the information you need: a clear statement of the problem, the necessary input, and the required output. In real life, the process is not always so simple. You often have to define the problem yourself and then decide what you have to work with and what the results should be.

FIGURE 1-11
Basic Structures of Programming Languages

SEQUENCE

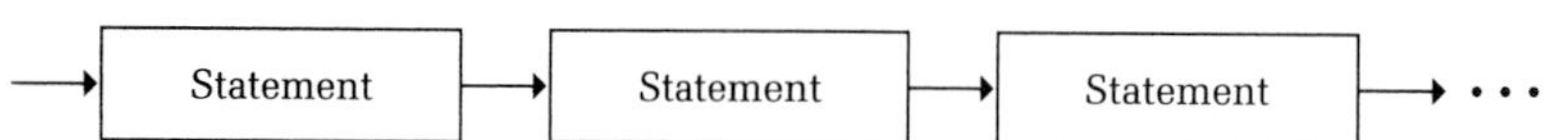

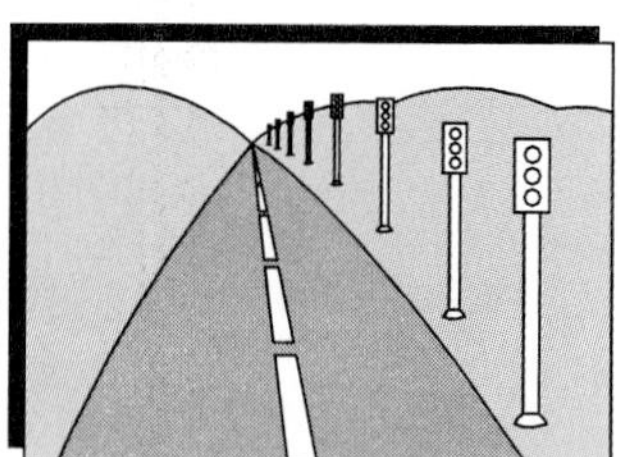

SELECTION (also called *branch* or *decision*)

If condition Then statement1 Else statement2

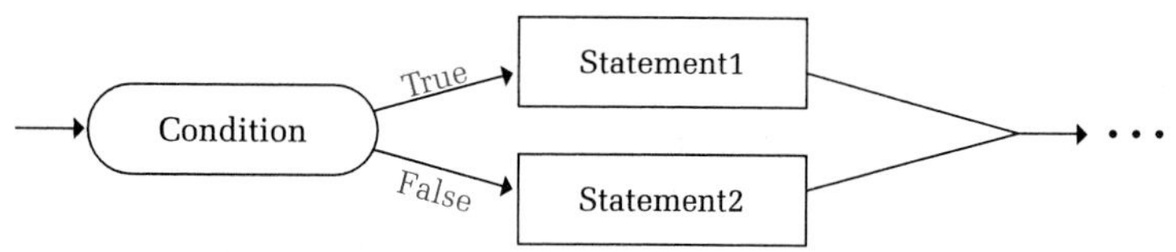

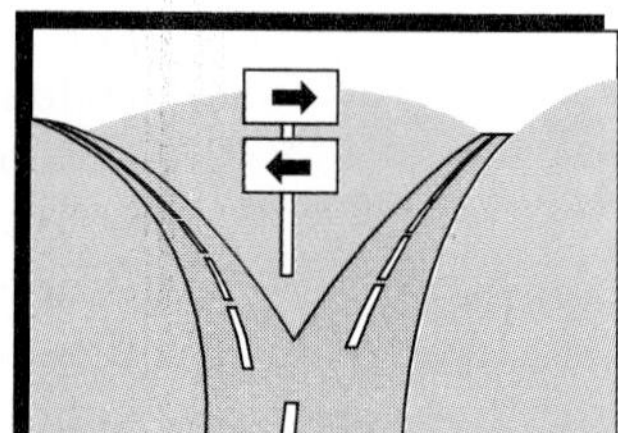

LOOP (also called *repetition* or *iteration*)

Loop Exit When condition

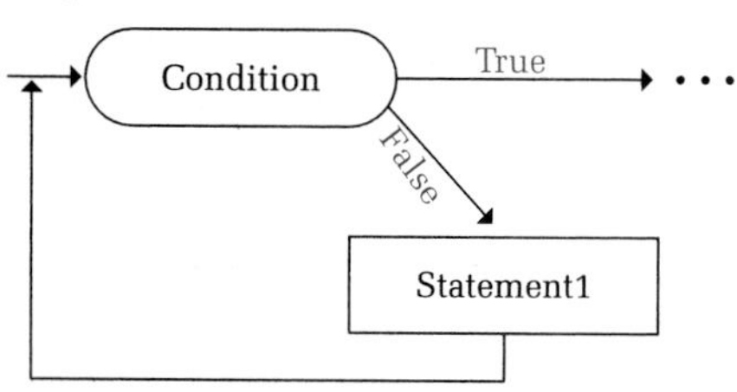

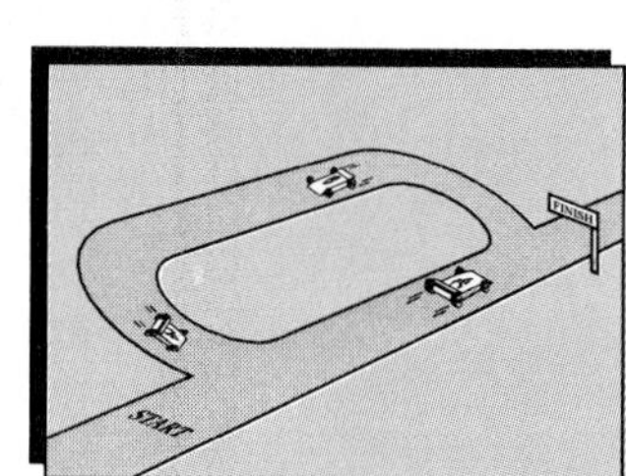

SUBPROGRAM (also called *procedure, function, method,* or *subroutine*)

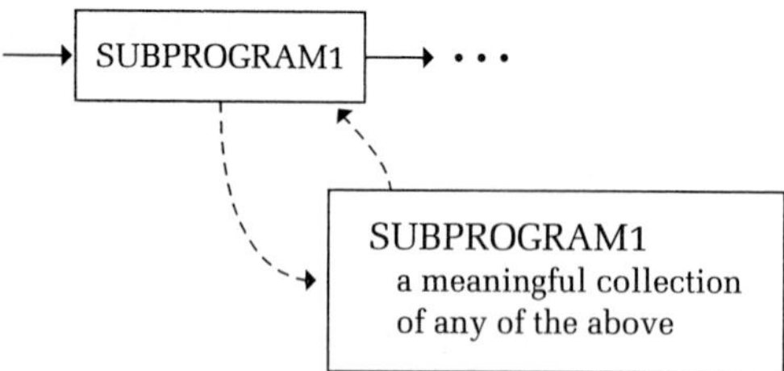

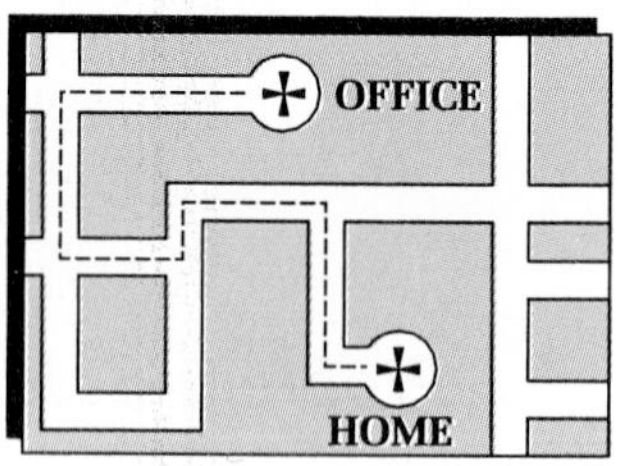

After you understand and analyze a problem, you must come up with a model that describes the essence of your problem and its solution. Such models include one or more algorithms. Earlier, we defined an algorithm as a step-by-step procedure for solving a problem in a finite amount of time. Although you work with algorithms all the time, most of your experience with them is in the context of *following* them. You follow a recipe, play a game, assemble a toy, take medicine. In the problem-solving phase of computer programming, you will be *designing* algorithms, not following them. This means you will have to be conscious of the strategies you use to solve problems in order to apply them to programming problems.

Ask Questions

If you are given a task orally, you ask questions—when? why? where?—until you understand exactly what you have to do. If your instructions are written, you might put question marks in the margin; underline a word or sentence; or in some other way indicate that the task is not clear. Your questions may be answered by a later paragraph, or you might have to discuss them with the person who gave you the task.

These are some of the questions you will be asking in the context of programming.

- What do I have to work with; that is, what is my data?
- What does the data look like?
- How much data is there?
- How will I know when I have processed all the data?
- What should my output look like?
- How many times is the process going to be repeated?
- What error conditions might come up?

Look for Things That Are Familiar

Never reinvent the wheel. If a solution exists, use it. If you've solved the same or a similar problem before, just repeat your solution. People are good at recognizing similar situations. We don't have to learn how to go to the store to buy milk, then to buy eggs, and then to buy candy. We know that going to the store is the same; only what we buy is different.

In programming you will see certain problems again and again in different guises. A good programmer immediately recognizes a subtask he or she has solved before and plugs in the solution. For example, finding the daily high and low temperature is really the same problem as finding the highest and lowest grades on a test. You want the largest and smallest values of a set of numbers (see Figure 1-12).

Classification is a common mechanism for using the familiar to understand the new. You are probably familiar with the classification of such

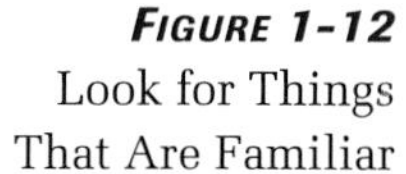

FIGURE 1-12
Look for Things That Are Familiar

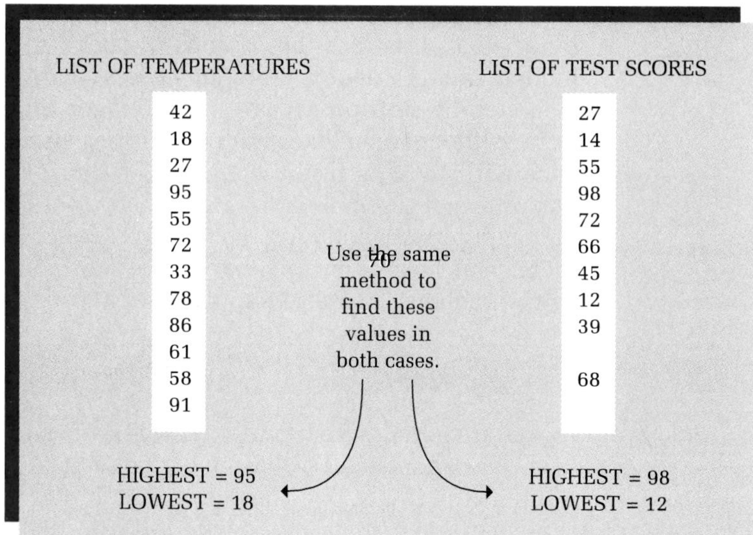

things as plants, animals, or minerals. In such classifications, we move from general descriptions to more specific descriptions. For example, *silicate* is a name geologists use to describe a large group of minerals made up predominantly of the elements silicon and oxygen bonded together to form tetrahedra. *Tectosilicates* are a subgroup of silicates characterized by the organization of their tetrahedra into a three-dimensional framework. *Feldspars* are a subgroup of tectosilicates characterized by low-symmetry crystal structures. *Microcline* is a kind of feldspar with the chemical composition $KAlSi_3O_8$. Notice how this classification scheme begins with a very generalized description for a large group of minerals and progresses to more specific subclasses describing smaller groups of minerals. Finally, we reach the most specific thing in the classification: an individual mineral.

Solve by Analogy

Often a problem will remind you of a problem that you have seen before. You may find the problem at hand easier to solve if you remember how you solved the other problem. In other words, draw an analogy between the two problems. For example, a solution to a perspective projection problem from an art class might help you figure out how to compute the distance to a landmark when you are on a cross-country hike. As you work your way through the new problem, you will come across things that are different than they were in the old problem, but usually these are just details that you can deal with one at a time.

Analogy is really just a broader application of the strategy of looking for things that are familiar. When you are trying to find an algorithm for solving a problem, don't limit yourself to computer-oriented solutions. Step back and try to get a larger view of the problem. Don't worry if your analogy doesn't match perfectly—the only reason for starting with an analogy is that it gives you a place to start (see Figure 1-13). The best programmers are people who have broad experience in solving all kinds of problems.

Means-Ends Analysis

Often the beginning state and the ending state are given; the problem is to define a set of actions that can be used to get from one to the other. Suppose you want to go from Boston, Massachusetts, to Austin, Texas. You know the beginning state (Boston) and the ending state (Austin). The problem is how to get from one to the other.

In this example, you have lots of choices. You can fly, walk, hitchhike, ride a bike, or whatever. The method you choose depends on your circumstances. If you're in a hurry, you'll probably decide to fly.

Once you have narrowed down the set of actions, you have to work out the details. It can help to establish intermediate goals that are easier to meet than the overall goal. Let's say there is a really cheap, direct flight to Austin from Newark, New Jersey. You might decide to divide the trip into legs—Boston to Newark and then Newark to Austin. Your intermediate goal is to get from Boston to Newark. Now you have to examine only the means of meeting that intermediate goal (see Figure 1-14).

The overall strategy of means-ends analysis is to define the ends and then to analyze your means of getting between them. The process translates easily to computer programming. You begin by writing down what the input is and what the output should be. Then you consider the actions a computer can perform and choose a sequence of actions that can transform the data into results.

Divide and Conquer

We often break large problems into smaller units that we can handle more easily. Cleaning the whole house may seem overwhelming; cleaning the

Figure 1-13 Analogy

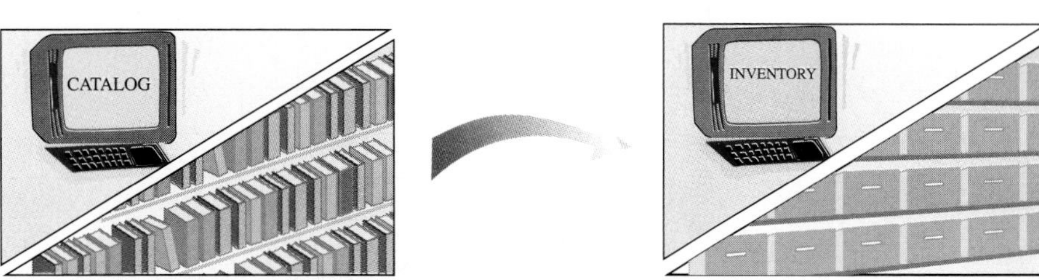

A library catalog system can give insight into how to organize a parts inventory.

Figure 1-14 Means-Ends Analysis

Start: Boston **Goal:** Austin	**Means:** *Fly,* walk, hitchhike, bike, drive, sail, bus
Start: Boston **Goal:** Austin	**Revised Means:** Fly to Chicago and then Austin; *fly to Newark and then Austin:* fly to Atlanta and then Austin
Start: Boston **Intermediate Goal:** Newark **Goal:** Austin	**Means to Intermediate Goal:** *Commuter flight,* walk, hitchhike, bike, drive, sail, bus
Solution: Take commuter flight to Newark and then catch cheap flight to Austin	

rooms one at a time seems much more manageable. The same principle applies to programming. We break a large problem into smaller pieces that we can solve individually (see Figure 1-15). The top-down methodology we describe in Chapter 3 is based on the principle of divide and conquer.

The Building-Block Approach

Another way of attacking large problems is to see whether there are any existing solutions for smaller pieces of the problem. It may be possible to put some of these solutions together end to end to solve most of the big problem. This strategy is really just a combination of the look-for-familiar-things and divide-and-conquer approaches. You look at the big problem and see that it can be divided into smaller problems for which solutions already exist. Solving the big problem is just a matter of putting the existing solutions together, like mortaring together blocks to form a wall (see Figure 1-16).

Figure 1-15 Divide and Conquer

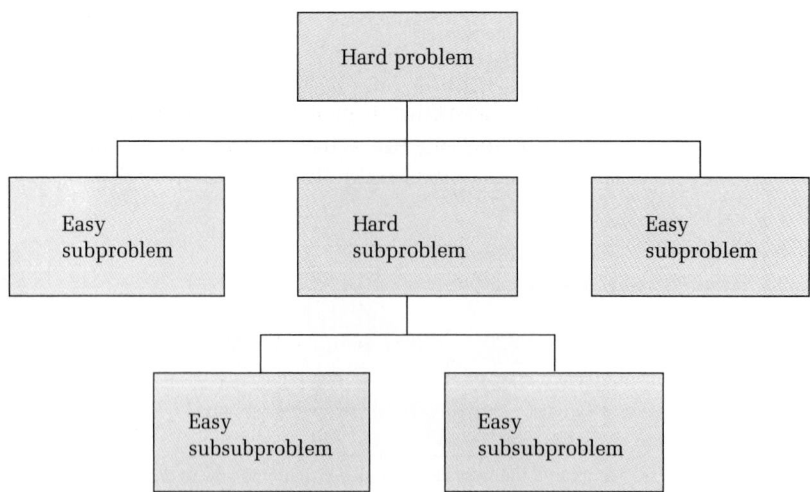

FIGURE 1-16
Building-Block Approach

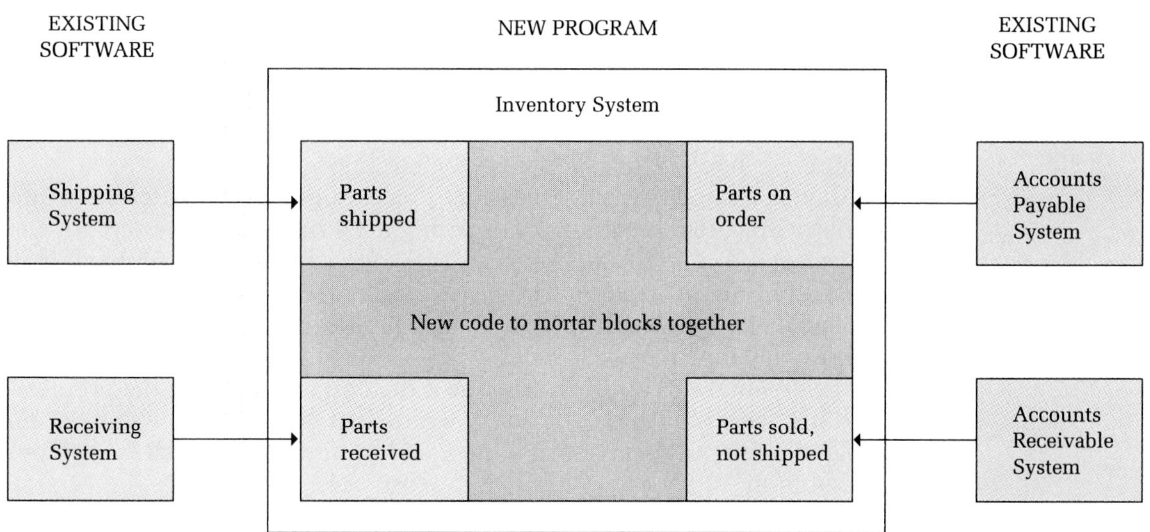

Merging Solutions

Another way to combine existing solutions is to merge them on a step-by-step basis. For example, to compute the average of a list of values, we must both sum and count the values. If we already have separate solutions for summing values and for counting values, we can combine them. But if we first do the summing and then do the counting, we have to read the list twice. We can save steps if we merge these two solutions: read a value and then both add it to the running total and increase our count by one before going on to the next value. Whenever the solutions to subproblems duplicate steps, you should think about merging them instead of joining them end to end.

How to Start

Writers are all too familiar with the experience of staring at a blank page, not knowing how to begin. Programmers have the same difficulty when they first tackle a big problem. They look at the problem and it seems overwhelming.

Remember that you always have a place to begin solving any problem: Write the problem down on paper in your own words so that you understand it. Once you begin to try to paraphrase the problem, you can focus on each of the subparts individually instead of trying to tackle the entire problem at once. This process gives you a clearer picture of the overall problem. It helps you see pieces of the problem that look familiar or that are analogous to other problems you have solved. It also pinpoints areas where something is unclear, where you need more information.

As you write down a problem, you tend to group things together into small understandable chunks. These might be natural places to split the problem up—to divide and conquer. Your description of the problem may collect all of the information about data and results into one place for easy reference. Then you will be able to see the beginning and ending states necessary for a means-ends analysis.

Most mental blocks are created by a misunderstanding of the problem. Rewriting the problem in your own words is a good way to focus on the subparts of the problem, one at a time, and to understand what is required for a solution.

Algorithmic Problem Solving

Coming up with a step-by-step procedure for solving a particular problem is not always cut-and-dried. In fact, it is usually a trial-and-error process requiring several attempts and refinements. We test each attempt to see if it really solves the problem. If it does, fine. If it doesn't, we try again. Typically, you will use a combination of all of the techniques we've described to solve any nontrivial problem.

Remember that the computer can only do certain things, as we discussed earlier. Your primary concern, then, is how to make the computer transform, manipulate, calculate, or process the input data to produce the wanted output. If you keep in mind the allowable instructions in your programming language, you won't design an algorithm that is difficult or impossible to code.

In the case study at the end of this chapter we develop a program for calculating employees' weekly wages. It gives you an idea of the thought processes involved in writing an algorithm and coding it as a program and shows you what a complete Ada program looks like.

Software Engineering

Throughout this book we emphasize a disciplined software engineering approach to developing programs. In the next sections we'll explain why such a disciplined approach to programming is needed.

Programming at Many Scales

In order to provide some context for the topics of this book, it's helpful to have an understanding of the range of programming problems that exist in the real world. Obviously we can't cover every possibility, but we'll try to give you a flavor of what is out there.

Programming projects range in size from the student or computer hobbyist writing a short program to try out something new to multi-company programming projects involving hundreds of people. Between these extremes are many other sizes of efforts. There are people who use programming in their professions, although it isn't their primary job. For example, a scientist might sit down at the computer and write a highly specialized program to analyze some data from an experiment.

There are also many specialized professional programming jobs: business data processing, tool making (compiler writers, word processor developers, and so on), research and development support, graphical display development, entertainment software writing, and so on. An individual can develop an expertise and specialize in one of these areas. However, one person can only produce fairly small programs (a few tens of thousands of lines of code at best). Work of this kind is called *programming in the small.*

Larger applications, such as developing a new air traffic control system, may involve hundreds of thousands or even millions of lines of code. These require teams of programmers, many of whom are specialists. But those specialists must be organized in some manner or they will waste most of their time just trying to communicate with each other.

Usually a hierarchical organization is set up along the lines of the chain of command of a large corporation. One person, the *chief architect* or *project director*, determines the basic structure of the program, and then delegates the responsibility to implement the major modules. In the case of a smaller project, the modules might go directly to programmers. For a larger project, the project director might give the modules to team leaders who further decompose them and delegate the submodules to individual programmers or groups of programmers. At each stage, the person in charge must have the knowledge and experience necessary to define the next lower level of the hierarchy and to estimate the resources necessary to implement the program. This sort of organization is called *programming in the large.*

In the history of programming, there is a classic example of what happens when a large program develops without careful organization and proper language support. In the 1960s, IBM developed a major new operating system called OS/360, which was one of the first true examples of programming in the large. After the operating system was written, over a thousand significant errors were found. In spite of years of effort to fix these errors, it was never possible to get the number of errors below a thousand, and sometimes the fixes produced far more errors than they eliminated.

The reason for these problems was that the code was badly organized, and different pieces were so interrelated that nobody could keep it all straight; a seemingly simple change in one part of the code would cause several other parts of the system to fail. Eventually, at great expense, IBM created an entirely new system using better organization and tools.

In his book, *The Mythical Man-Month*, Frederick Brooks documented his experiences as project manager for OS/360. He showed that the methods they used for developing software were inadequate for large projects. Techniques used to write small programs simply did not work on large programs. Major programming projects were frequently years behind schedule, did not work well, and cost much more than predicted.

The term *software crisis* was coined in the late 1960s to describe the inability to keep up with the demand for new computer programs and to manage the rising costs of software development. The discipline of **software engineering** emerged to solve this crisis. Although there are many definitions of software engineering, all emphasize the use of sound engineering principles in the development of programs. The software life cycle described earlier in this chapter is an example of a software engineering method. We'll discuss the steps in this method in more detail and introduce other software engineering methods throughout this text.

Software engineering A disciplined approach to the design, production, and maintenance of computer software that is developed on time and within cost estimates, requiring tools that help manage the size and complexity of the resulting software products.

Software engineering does not deal just with technical issues. As large projects require a team approach, a software engineer must possess management skills and interpersonal sensitivity. Report writing and public speaking are also part of the software engineer's job. Good communication among team members is essential for the success of any large team project.

Modern programming languages can help a great deal in supporting software engineering principles. The Ada language was designed specifically for the development of large programs. It permits programmers to develop and compile separate parts of a program and to test them independently before putting them together. This makes it much easier for many people to work together on a program. The Ada system notes when a programmer changes a piece of code and makes sure that the most recent version is used whenever the program is put together. We'll look at some of these features briefly in the next section and in more detail in later chapters.

Of course, all of these software engineering methods and language features are hard to appreciate when you are writing a small program for a class assignment. But rest assured that the experience you gain with them here will be valuable as you begin to develop larger programs.

In those early days of computing, everyone expected an occasional error to occur, and it was still possible to get useful work done with a faulty system. Today, however, computers are used more and more in life-critical applications such as medical equipment and aircraft control systems. Many of these applications involve large-scale programming. If you were stepping onto a modern jetliner just now, you might well pause and wonder, "Just what sort of methods did they use when they wrote the programs for this thing?"

The Ada Programming Language

Ada is a programming language for large-scale projects. Programming to solve large problems requires both simple tools and elaborate organizational tools. Ada has instructions for the basic functions that a computer can actually perform (transfer data, input and output data, store and retrieve data, compare values, and perform arithmetic) and for the four ways that a computer can structure statements (sequence, selection, loop, and procedure). Unlike many commonly used high-level languages, Ada also has organizational tools to help a programming team develop large software systems.

Through Ada's organizational tools, programmers can follow the problem-solving strategies discussed earlier. The primary method for solving large problems is to divide them into a number of smaller components (the principle of divide and conquer). Experience from developing large software systems has shown that the greatest efficiency and best quality are obtained when each of these smaller problems can be solved and programmed individually. Then, the solutions do not become interdependent—a result that greatly simplifies the system and reduces potential sources of errors. Let's look at an analogy from house construction. The plumbing and electrical wiring in a house are kept separate. Different people install them. If the two weren't independent, you might receive a shock whenever you took a shower because of an unexpected interdependency between the wiring and plumbing.

Packages Ada has an organizational tool, called the **package,** that helps us keep our solutions to subproblems apart. You can think of a package as a protective covering around a complicated apparatus. The package acts as an interface that enables us to use the contents without knowing the details of their construction. Again using the example of the house, you don't have to know how the house is wired to use the interface to the wiring (electrical outlets).

Package An Ada tool that allows programmers to implement a solution to a subproblem separately from the solutions to other subproblems.

You employ this packaging concept every day when you use a car. A car is a very complicated device consisting of multiple subsystems (engine, brakes, suspension, and so on). Yet you do not have to know how all of these components work and interact in order to drive a car. The engineers who designed the car supply us with a simple set of operations (an interface) that allows us to drive the car easily. We learn that in order to stop, we simply press down on the brake pedal. We do not need to think about or understand how the braking system operates. It would be disastrous if, every time we wanted to stop, we had to think, "The brake pedal is a lever with a mechanical advantage of 10.6 coupled to a hydraulic system with a mechanical advantage of 7.3 that presses a semimetallic shoe against a steel disk. The coefficient of friction of the shoe/disk contact is..."

In the construction of a complicated mechanism, the interface design should receive as much attention as the details of the actual device. Automotive engineers spend considerable time designing the layout of a new car's controls. Imagine how difficult it would be to drive a car if you had to operate it by typing commands on a keyboard. For those with poor typing or spelling skills, such an interface could result in frequent accidents. Ada's packages allow us to develop good interfaces by separating the design of the interface from the internal details of the package. In the next chapter, you will learn to use packages that come with the Ada compiler. Later, you will learn to design and write your own packages that you can share with other programmers.

Generic Units Creating a library of packages is a common way to support the problem-solving techniques of the look-for-familiar-things and building-block approaches. If we had a package that could find the daily highest and lowest temperature, it would not take much work for us to write a nearly identical package that could find the highest and lowest grades in a set of test scores. To make things even easier for the programmer, Ada has other tools, called **generic units,** that will actually do this work for us. We need only describe what changes need to be made, and the Ada compiler will construct a new solution for us.

Inheritance Turning a general solution into a more specific one is a common use of the look-for-familiar-things approach to problem solving. To make this task easier, Ada has a feature called **inheritance.** Using inheritance, a programmer can easily extend a previously developed general solution by adding only the information that distinguishes the specific from the general solution. Inheritance plays a major role in the problem-solving method called object-oriented programming.

Tasks As the use of parallel-processing computers increases, it is important that high-level languages have a mechanism for the programmer to define what operations may be done in parallel. Ada programmers use **tasks,** program units that execute concurrently, to accomplish this. Very few other languages have such a capability. None has such a standardized safe mechanism as Ada has for this form of programming.

Ada is a very rich programming language. Because we cannot cover all of its features in this text, we concentrate on those that are most useful for beginning the study of algorithmic problem solving. You may learn the more advanced features of Ada in future courses or more advanced books.*

Generic unit An Ada tool that allows programmers to easily reuse solutions to similar subproblems.

Inheritance A mechanism that allows Ada programmers to extend a general solution to a more specific one.

Task A program unit that executes concurrently with other program units.

BACKGROUND INFORMATION

The Origins of Ada

The U.S. Department of Defense (DOD) is a major developer and user of computer software. In 1974, the DOD and its contractors were using hundreds of languages and dialects. This confusing state of affairs made it very difficult to reuse existing software in new projects. Also, because most programmers knew only a few languages well, it was hard for them to move from one project to another. As a result, it was estimated that the future cost of software development would exceed more than $3 billion per year. Clearly, a single standard programming language was needed.

The DOD assigned Lieutenant Colonel William Whitaker to lead a group to define the requirements for a programming language that could meet the needs of all the DOD's embedded-systems applications. While Whitaker handled the administrative and political aspects of the project, a technical team under Dr. David Fisher produced a description of these requirements. The document they developed was known as Strawman, and this was sent to experts in both the civilian and military communities whose comments were used to produce a revised version of the document, called Woodenman. More than 100 expert teams in 15 countries then reviewed the Woodenman requirements. Tinman, the next version, took these teams' comments into account. In 1976, 23 existing programming languages were compared to the Tinman requirements. Although none was appropriate, three languages (Algol 68, Pascal, and PL/I) were sufficiently compatible that they could

*Such as J.G.P. Barnes, *Programming in Ada 95,* 2nd edition, Addison-Wesley, 1998.

be modified to be acceptable. In the next version of the requirements, called Ironman, the group took the broad discussions of Tinman and produced a concise language description that was organized as a manual.

The DOD then held a competition to design the language. Fifteen companies submitted proposals, nearly all based on Pascal. Four of these firms (Cii Honeywell Bull, Intermetrics, SofTech, and SRI International) received contracts to begin their designs. In 1978, the DOD chose Cii Honeywell Bull and Intermetrics to do further design work based on another revision of the requirements, called Steelman. More than 900 review teams evaluated the two finalists. Cii Honeywell Bull of France, led by Dr. Jean Ichbiah, won this final competition. For his accomplishments, Dr. Ichbiah was awarded the Legion d'Honneur by the president of France.

A member of Whitaker's group, navy commander John Cooper, named the language Ada in 1979. The name honored the world's first computer programmer, Lady Ada Augusta, Countess of Lovelace (1815–1852), daughter of the poet Lord Byron. Ada Lovelace was a talented mathematician who worked with Charles Babbage. Babbage had designed the first programmable (mechanical) computer, called the "analytical engine." Although the analytical engine was never completed (the parts were beyond the capabilities of technicians to produce), Ada wrote several programs for it and thus is credited by many as the world's first computer programmer.

The American National Standards Institute (ANSI) approved an official description of the Ada programming language in 1983. This description is titled *Reference Manual for the Ada Programming Language ANSI/MIL-STD-1815A-1983,* but is usually called the ARM (Ada Reference Manual). The ANSI/MIL standard specification number (1815) was chosen for the year of Ada Lovelace's birth. The International Standards Organization (ISO) approved Ada as an international standard in 1987.

The Ada language designers saw that the compilers for nearly all other standardized languages did not adhere strictly to their standards, giving rise to different dialects of the language. As a result, programs written in one dialect often did not run on a computer with a compiler of a different dialect. For example, programs written in Microsoft Visual C++ ® might not work with Borland C++ ®. The Ada Joint Program Office (AJPO), a descendant of Whitaker's group, took steps to prevent the spread of different Ada dialects. They developed a suite of nearly 2,000 test programs. In 1998, the Ada Resource Association (ARA) took over the certification test suite from the AJPO, as part of transitioning Ada support from government to private industry. Compilers that compile and execute all of these test programs successfully are certified as conforming. Ada is the only language to enforce standards in this manner. Throughout this book, we adhere to the Ada standard. We used a certified Ada compiler to compile all of the example programs.

The strict standards enforced by the compiler validation process are an important reason for the success of the Ada language. Ada programs written for one computer system almost always compile and run on other computers. Few other programming languages can make such a claim. This rigid standardization has some drawbacks. It does not allow the language to take immediate advantage of advances in computer science or the knowledge gained from years of using Ada. The original designers understood this dilemma and, following the requirements of the ANSI and ISO procedures, suggested a regular revision process for the language. In 1988, the AJPO established the Ada 9X Project for conducting the revision of the Ada standard. Christine Anderson managed this ambitious project. The first step was to prepare a technical requirements specification. Over 750 revision requests submitted by the Ada community were analyzed by the requirements specification team led by John Goodenough. Under the watchful eye of an international team of distinguished reviewers, S. Tucker Taft revised the language. In 1995 the International Standards Organization approved the new Ada standard (ISO/IEC 8652:1995). The new language, frequently called Ada 95 to distinguish it from the original, increased the flexibility of Ada while retaining the inherent reliability for which Ada has become noted. As stated in the Preface to the *Ada 95 Rationale,* "Ada 95 is a coherent and reliable foundation vehicle for developing the major applications of the next decade". *

Ada has taken its place as one of today's important high-level languages. Although it was developed by the DOD, its use is not limited to defense applications. In fact, the first significant use of Ada was by a commercial trucking company. Ada's strengths for developing large systems are exploited in a wide range of applications including avionics software for nearly every aircraft in the world, air traffic control systems, global positioning systems, steel rolling mills, medical diagnostic tools, cellular telephones, high-speed trains, online investment services, and many more. As indicated by material published in the professional journals, it is playing a significant role in research and development as well.

PROBLEM-SOLVING CASE STUDY

A Company Payroll

Specification

Problem A small company needs an interactive program (the payroll clerk will input the data) to figure its weekly payroll. The input data and each employee's wages should be saved on a secondary storage file. The screen should display the total wages for the week so that the payroll clerk can transfer the appropriate amount into the payroll account.

Discussion At first glance, this seems to be a simple problem. But if you think about how you would do it by hand, you see that you need to ask questions about the specifics of the process: What employee data is input? How are wages computed? In what file are the results to be stored? How does the clerk indicate that all of the data has been entered?

*John Barnes (Editor), *Ada 95 Rationale : The Language, the Standard Libraries* (Lecture Notes in Computer Science, 1247), Springer Verlag, 1997.

PROBLEM-SOLVING CASE STUDY *cont'd.*

- The data for each employee will include an employee identification number, the employee's hourly pay rate, and the hours worked that week.
- Wages equal the employee's pay rate times the number of hours worked, up to 40 hours. If an employee worked more than 40 hours, wages equal the employee's pay rate times 40 hours, plus one and one-half times the employee's regular pay rate times the number of hours worked above 40.
- The results should be stored in a file called *Payfile.dat.*
- There is no employee number 0, so the clerk can indicate the end of the data by entering 0 when asked for an employee number.

Let's apply the *divide-and-conquer* approach to this problem. There are three obvious steps in almost any problem of this type:

1. Get the data.
2. Compute the results.
3. Output the results.

First we need to get the data. We require three pieces of data for each employee: employee identification number, hourly pay rate, and number of hours worked. So that the clerk will know when to enter each value, we must have the computer output a message that indicates when it is ready to accept each of the values (this is called a *prompting message*, or a *prompt*). Then, we take these steps to input the data:

```
Prompt the user for the employee number.
Get the employee number.
Prompt the user for the employee's hourly pay rate.
Get the pay rate.
Prompt the user for the number of hours worked.
Get the number of hours worked.
```

The next step is to compute the wages. Let's apply *means-ends analysis.* Our starting point is the set of data values that was input; our desired ending, the payroll for the week. We know that if there is no overtime, wages are simply the pay rate times the number of hours worked. If the number of hours worked is greater than 40, however, wages are 40 times the pay rate plus the number of overtime hours times one and one-half the pay rate. The number of overtime hours is computed by subtracting 40 from the total number of hours worked. To figure the wages, take the following steps:

```
If hours worked is greater than 40.0, then
    wages = (40.0 × pay rate) + (hours worked − 40.0) × 1.5 × pay rate
otherwise
    wages = hours worked × pay rate
```

PROBLEM-SOLVING CASE STUDY cont'd.

The last step, outputting the results, is simply a matter of having the computer put the employee number, the pay rate, the number of hours worked, and the wages earned into the file *Payfile.dat:*

Put the employee number on the list.
Put the pay rate on the list.
Put the hours worked on the list.
Put the wages earned on the list.

There are two things we've overlooked. First, we must repeat this process for each employee, and second, we must compute total wages for the week. Let's use the *building-block approach* to combine our three main steps (getting the data, computing the wages, outputting the results) with a structure that repeats the steps for each employee as long as the employee number is not 0. When the employee number is 0, this structure will skip to the end of the algorithm. We'll also insert a step just after the wages are computed that adds them to a running total.

Finally, we must take care of a couple of housekeeping chores. Before we start processing, we create the output file that receives the results, and we set the running total to zero. At the end of the algorithm, we must tell the computer to close the output file (similar to closing a ledger book when you finish making entries) and then stop processing.

The complete algorithm follows. Calculating the wages is written as a separate procedure that is defined after the main algorithm. Notice that the algorithm is simply a very precise description of the same steps you would follow to do this process by hand.

Main Algorithm

```
Prepare to write a list of the employees' wages (open File Payfile.dat)
Set the total payroll to 0
Repeat the following steps
    Prompt the user for the employee number (put message on the screen)
    Get the employee number
    Exit this loop structure if the employee number is 0
    Prompt the user for the employee's hourly pay rate
    Get the pay rate
    Prompt the user for the number of hours worked
    Get the hours worked
    Perform the procedure for calculating pay (below)
    Add the employee's wages to the total payroll
    Put the employee number on the list (file Payfile.dat)
    Put the pay rate on the list (file Payfile.dat)
    Put the hours worked on the list (file Payfile.dat)
    Put the wages on the list (file Payfile.dat)
When an employee number equal to 0 is read, continue with the following steps:
Put the total company payroll on the screen
Close the File Payfile.dat
Stop
```

PROBLEM-SOLVING CASE STUDY *cont'd.*

Procedure for Calculating Pay

If hours worked is greater than 40.0, then

wages = (40.0 × pay rate) + (hours worked − 40.0) × 1.5 × pay rate

otherwise

wages = hours worked × pay rate

Before we implement this algorithm, we need to test it. Programming Warm-up Exercise 3 asks you to carry out this test.

The Ada program for this algorithm follows. We include it to give you an idea of what you'll be learning. If you've had no previous exposure to programming, you probably won't understand most of the program. Don't worry; you will soon. In fact, throughout this book as we introduce a new construct, we often refer you back to Program Payroll. One more thing: The words on a line after the symbol -- are called comments and are used to document the program. They are here to help you understand the program; the Ada compiler ignores them.

```
with Ada.Text_IO;
with Ada.Float_Text_IO;
with Ada.Integer_Text_IO;

procedure Payroll is

-- This program computes the wages for each employee and the total payroll
-- for the company

   Max_Regular_Hours : constant Float  := 40.0;  -- Maximum normal work hours
   Overtime_Factor   : constant Float  :=  1.5;  -- Overtime pay rate factor
   Minimum_Wage      : constant Float  :=  5.75; -- Minimum hourly pay rate
   Maximum_Wage      : constant Float  := 99.99; -- Maximum hourly pay rate
   Payroll_File_Name : constant String := "Payfile.dat";

   ----------------------------------------------------------------------
   procedure Calc_Pay (Rate  : in  Float;       -- Hourly pay
                       Hours : in  Float;       -- Hours this week
                       Pay   : out Float) is    -- Wages earned

   -- Calc_Pay computes an employee's pay from their pay rate and the hours
   -- worked this week, taking overtime into account

   begin    -- Procedure Calc_Pay
      if Hours > Max_Regular_Hours then
         Pay := Max_Regular_Hours * Rate
                + (Hours - Max_Regular_Hours) * Overtime_Factor * Rate;
      else
         Pay := Hours * Rate;
      end if;
   end Calc_Pay;
```

PROBLEM-SOLVING CASE STUDY cont'd.

```
------------
   Pay_Rate     : Float   range Minimum_Wage .. Maximum_Wage; -- Hourly pay rate
   Hours        : Float   range 0.0 .. 80.0;               -- Hours worked
   Wages        : Float   range 0.0 .. 8_000.00;           -- Wages earned
   Total        : Float   range 0.0 .. Float'Last;         -- Total payroll
   Employee_ID  : Integer range   0 .. 999;                -- Employee ID number
   Payroll_File : Ada.Text_IO.File_Type;                   -- Company payroll file

begin     -- Program Payroll

   -- Create the output file
   Ada.Text_IO.Create (File => Payroll_File,
                       Name => Payroll_File_Name);

   -- Initialize company total wages
   Total := 0.0;

   Employee_Loop:        -- Repeat for each employee
   loop
      -- Prompt for and get an employee's number
      Ada.Text_IO.Put (Item => "Enter employee number: ");
      Ada.Integer_Text_IO.Get (Item => Employee_ID);
                                                -- An employee number of zero
      exit Employee_Loop when Employee_ID = 0;  -- indicates we are finished and
                                                -- can exit the loop
      -- Prompt for and get the employee's pay rate
      Ada.Text_IO.Put        (Item => "Enter pay rate: ");
      Ada.Float_Text_IO.Get (Item => Pay_Rate);

      -- Prompt for and get the number of hours the employee worked this week
      Ada.Text_IO.Put        (Item => "Enter hours worked: ");
      Ada.Float_Text_IO.Get (Item => Hours);

      -- Determine the employee's wages
      Calc_Pay (Rate  => Pay_Rate,
                Hours => Hours,
                Pay   => Wages);

      -- Add this employee's wages to the company total
      Total := Total + Wages;

      -- Put results in the pay file
      Ada.Integer_Text_IO.Put (File => Payroll_File,  Item => Employee_ID);
      Ada.Float_Text_IO.Put (File => Payroll_File,
                             Item => Pay_Rate,
                             Fore => 6,
                             Aft  => 2,
                             Exp  => 0);
```

PROBLEM-SOLVING CASE STUDY cont'd.

```
      Ada.Float_Text_IO.Put (File => Payroll_File,
                             Item => Hours,
                             Fore => 6,
                             Aft  => 1,
                             Exp  => 0);
      Ada.Float_Text_IO.Put (File => Payroll_File,
                             Item => Wages,
                             Fore => 6,
                             Aft  => 2,
                             Exp  => 0);
      Ada.Text_IO.New_Line (File => Payroll_File);

   end loop Employee_Loop;

   -- Display the total payroll on the screen
   Ada.Text_IO.New_Line (Spacing => 2);
   Ada.Text_IO.Put  (Item => "Total payroll is $");
   Ada.Float_Text_IO.Put (Item => Total,
                          Fore => 1,
                          Aft  => 2,
                          Exp  => 0);
   Ada.Text_IO.New_Line;

   -- Close the pay file
   Ada.Text_IO.Close (File => Payroll_File);

end Payroll;
```

Summary

We think nothing of turning on a television and sitting down to watch it. It's a communication tool we use to enhance our lives. Computers are becoming as common as televisions, just a normal part of our lives. And like television sets, computers are based on complex principles but are designed for use by people without degrees in electrical engineering.

Computers are dumb; we must tell them what to do. A true computer error is extremely rare (usually due to a component malfunction or an electrical fault). Because we instruct the computer what to do, most errors in computer-generated output are really human errors.

Computers are composed of five basic parts: the memory unit, the arithmetic/logic unit, the control unit, and input and output devices. The arithmetic/logic unit and control unit together are called the central processing unit. The physical parts of the computer are called hardware. The programs that are executed by the computer are called software.

System software is a set of programs designed to simplify the user/computer interface. It includes the compiler, the operating system, and the editor.

Computer programming is a process of planning a sequence of steps for a computer to follow. It involves a problem-solving phase and an implementation phase. After analyzing a problem, we develop and test a general solution model (data objects and algorithms). This model becomes a specific solution—our program—when we write it in a high-level programming language. The sequence of instructions that makes up our program is then compiled into machine code, the language the computer uses. After correcting any errors or "bugs" that show up during testing, we are ready to use our program.

Data and instructions are represented as binary numbers (numbers consisting of just 1s and 0s) in electronic computers. The process of converting data and instructions into a form usable by the computer is called coding.

A programming language reflects the range of operations a computer can perform. The basic control structures in a programming language—sequence, selection, loop, and procedure—are based on these fundamental operations. In this text, you will learn to write programs in the high-level programming language called Ada.

We've said that problem solving is an integral part of the programming process. Although you might have little experience programming computers, you have lots of experience solving problems. The key is to stop and think about the strategies you use to solve problems and then to employ those strategies to devise workable algorithms. Among those strategies are asking questions, looking for things that are familiar, solving by analogy, applying means-ends analysis, dividing the problem into subproblems, using existing solutions to small problems to solve a larger problem, merging solutions, and paraphrasing the problem in order to overcome a mental block.

Today, the computer plays an important role in science, engineering, business, government, and the arts. Learning to program in Ada, a language suitable for implementing the solutions to large and small problems, can help you use this powerful tool effectively.

Quick Check

The Quick Check will help you decide if you've met the goals set forth at the beginning of each chapter. If you understood the material in the chapter, the answer to each question should be fairly obvious. After reading a question, check your response against the answers listed at the end of the Quick Check. If you don't know an answer or don't understand the answer that is provided, turn to the page(s) listed at the end of the question to review the material.

1. What is a computer program? (p. 3)
2. What are the five basic components of a computer? (p. 3)
3. What is the difference between hardware and software? (p. 8)
4. What are the two phases in writing a program? (p. 13)
5. Is an algorithm the same as a program? (p. 14–15)
6. What are the advantages of using a standardized high-level programming language? (p. 20–22)
7. What does the compiler do? (p. 20)
8. What part does the object program play in the compilation and execution process? (p. 20–21)
9. What is the divide-and-conquer approach? (p. 27)
10. What is the major difference between "programming in the small" and "programming in the large"? (p. 31)
11. Describe two features of the Ada programming language that are useful for developing large software systems. (p. 33–34)

Answers

1. A computer program is a sequence of instructions performed by a computer. **2.** The basic components of a computer are the memory unit, arithmetic/logic unit, control unit, and input and output devices. **3.** Hardware comprises the physical components of the computer; software is the collection of programs that run on the computer. **4.** The two phases of the programming process are problem solving and implementation. **5.** No. All programs are algorithms, but not all algorithms are programs. **6.** A high-level programming language can be run on many different computers. **7.** The compiler translates a program written in a high-level language into machine language. **8.** The object program is the machine-language version of a program. It is created by the compiler. The object program is what is loaded into the computer's memory and executed. **9.** The divide-and-conquer approach is a problem-solving technique that breaks a large problem into smaller, simpler subproblems. **10.** Programming in the large involves an organized group of programmers while programming in the small can be done by a single programmer. **11.** Through packages, programmers can employ a simple interface to make use of a complicated solution to a subproblem without needing to know the details of that solution. Generic units allow programmers to reuse previous solutions to subproblems easily.

Exam Preparation Exercises

1. Put a check next to each item that is a peripheral device.
   _____ a. Disk drive
   _____ b. Arithmetic/logic unit
   _____ c. Tape drive
   _____ d. Printer
   _____ e. Card reader
   _____ f. Memory
   _____ g. Auxiliary storage
   _____ h. Control unit
   _____ i. Terminal

2. Next to each item, indicate whether it is hardware (H) or software (S).
   _____ a. Disk drive
   _____ b. Memory
   _____ c. Compiler
   _____ d. Arithmetic/logic unit
   _____ e. Editor
   _____ f. Operating system
   _____ g. Object program
   _____ h. Terminal
   _____ i. Central processing unit
3. Explain why the following series of steps is not a good algorithm, and then rewrite the series so it is.
   Shampooing
   1. Rinse
   2. Lather
   3. Repeat
4. The compiler program takes one file as input and outputs another file.
   a. What are the two files?
   b. Which one is the input file?
   c. Some compilers output a second file. What does this other file contain? (*Hint:* See Figure 1-10.)
5. In the following recipe for chocolate pound cake, identify steps that are branches (selection) and loops. Also identify references to procedures outside of the algorithm.

Preheat oven to 350 degrees
Line the bottom of a 9-inch tube pan with wax paper
Sift $2\frac{3}{4}$c flour, $\frac{3}{4}$t cream of tartar, $\frac{1}{2}$ t soda, $1\frac{1}{2}$ t salt,
    and $1\frac{3}{4}$c sugar into a large bowl
Add 1 c shortening to bowl
If using butter, margarine, or lard,
    then add $\frac{2}{3}$ c milk to bowl,
    else (for other shortenings) add 1 c minus 2 T of milk to bowl
Add 1 t vanilla to mixture in bowl
If mixing with a spoon,
    then see the instructions in the introduction to the chapter on cakes,
    else (for electric mixers) beat the contents of bowl for 2 minutes at
        medium speed, scraping the bowl and beaters as needed
Add 3 eggs plus 1 extra egg yolk to bowl
Melt 3 squares of unsweetened chocolate and add to the mixture in bowl
Beat the mixture for 1 minute at medium speed
Pour the batter into the tube pan
Put the pan into the oven and bake for 1 hour and 10 minutes
Perform the test for doneness described in the introduction to the chapter on cakes
Repeat the test once each minute until the cake is done
Remove the pan from oven and allow cake to cool for 2 hours
Follow the instructions for removing the cake from the pan, given in the
    introduction to the chapter on cakes
Sprinkle powdered sugar over the cracks in top of cake just prior to serving

6. a. What features of Ada discussed in this chapter support programming in the large?
   b. What features of Ada (and most other programming languages) support programming in the small?
7. Means-ends analysis is a problem-solving technique.
   a. What are three things you must know in order to apply means-ends analysis to a problem?
   b. What is one way of combining this technique with the divide-and-conquer strategy?
8. Show how you would use the divide-and-conquer approach to solve the problem of finding a job.

Programming Warm-up Exercises

1. Write an algorithm for driving from where you live to the nearest airport that has regularly scheduled flights.
2. Write an algorithm for making a peanut butter and jam sandwich. The instructions must be very simple and exact because the person making the sandwich has no knowledge of food preparation and takes every word literally.
3. Use the following data set to test the payroll algorithm presented on page **40**. Follow each step of the algorithm just as it is written, as if you were a computer. Then check your results by hand to be sure that the algorithm is correct.

ID Number	Pay Rate	Hours Worked
327	8.30	48.5
201	6.60	40.0
29	12.50	40.0
166	9.25	51.5
254	7.00	32.0

CHAPTER 2

Ada Syntax, Semantics, and the Program Development Process

GOALS

After reading this chapter, you should be able to

- read syntax definitions in order to understand the formal rules governing Ada programs
- create and recognize Ada identifiers
- understand what a data type is
- declare constants and variables
- assign values to variables
- construct and evaluate simple arithmetic expressions
- write simple output statements
- understand how procedures and parameters are used
- write simple Ada programs
- know the steps involved in entering a program and getting it to run correctly
- format the layout of output

The Elements of Ada Programs

Programmers develop solutions to problems using a programming language. In this chapter, we start looking at the rules and symbols that make up the Ada programming language. We also review the steps required to create a program and make it work on a computer.

Syntax and Semantics

A programming language is a set of rules, symbols, and special words used to construct a program. There are rules for both **syntax** (grammar) and **semantics** (meaning).

Syntax The formal rules governing how valid instructions (constructs) are written in a programming language.

Semantics The set of rules that determines the meaning of instructions (constructs) written in a programming language.

Syntax is a formal set of rules that defines exactly what combinations of letters, numbers, and symbols can be used in a programming language. These rules are the blueprints we use to "build" programs. They allow us to take the elements of a programming language—the basic building blocks of the language—and assemble them into *constructs* (syntactically correct structures). The syntax of Ada is specified in the *Ada 95 Reference Manual.** Throughout this text we use the acronym ARM to refer to this language reference manual. There is no room for ambiguity in the syntax rules of a programming language because the computer can't think; it doesn't "know what we mean." To avoid ambiguity, syntax rules themselves must be written in a very simple, precise, formal language called a **metalanguage.**

Metalanguage A language used to describe another language.

Metalanguage is the word *language* with the prefix *meta*, which means "beyond" or "more comprehensive." A metalanguage is a language that goes beyond a normal language by allowing us to speak precisely about that language. It is a language used to talk about languages.

Learning to read a metalanguage is like learning to read the rules for a sport—once you understand the notations, you can read the rule book. It's true that many people learn a sport simply by watching others play, but

*Tucker Taft and Robert A. Duff (Editors), *Ada 95 Reference Manual: Language and Standard Libraries : International Standard ISO/IEC 8652:1995(E)* (Lecture Notes in Computer Science, 1246), Springer Verlag, 1997.

what they learn is usually just enough to allow them to take part in casual games. You could learn Ada by following the examples in this book, but a serious programmer, like a serious athlete, must take the time to read and understand the rules.

One of the oldest computer-oriented metalanguages is the *Backus-Naur Form (BNF)*, which is named for John Backus and Peter Naur, who developed it in 1960. The ARM uses a simple variant of BNF (called Extended Backus-Naur Form—EBNF) to define the syntax of Ada. These syntax definitions use the following special symbols.

::=	Stands for "is defined as"
[ ]	Used to enclose an optional item
{ }	Used to enclose an item that may be repeated zero or more times
|	Stands for "or" (used to separate alternative items)

In this book, boldface items denote literals, that is, symbols or words that should be written exactly as shown. Punctuation marks in EBNF rules are also literals. Lowercase words, called *nonterminal symbols*, are those further defined in a separate EBNF rule.

Let's look at an example. An integer number in Ada must be at least one digit long. It may or may not have more than one digit. It may or may not contain underline characters. However, it may not begin or end with an underline character, and there may not be two underline characters in a row. No + or − signs are allowed in an integer number.

The last paragraph is quite a lengthy description for such a simple concept. To avoid ambiguity, the English-language definition of an integer number had to be quite lengthy. Contrast it with the two-line EBNF definition of an integer number:

```
integer  ::=  digit{[ _ ]digit }
digit    ::=  0 | 1 | 2 | 3 | 4 | 5 | 6 | 7 | 8 | 9
```

Of course, you need to understand how to read the EBNF definition to use it. Let's go through it one line at a time. The first line is read, "An integer is defined as a digit followed by an item that can be repeated zero or more times. This item contains an optional underline character followed by a digit." The first line contains the nonterminal symbol *digit* whose definition must be examined (something we left out of the English-language description) in order to complete the definition of integer. The definition of digit, given in the second line, is simply any one of the actual digits 0 through 9. With some practice, you will be able to understand an EBNF definition faster and more precisely than the equivalent English-language definition.

Here are some examples of valid and invalid Ada representations of the integer number 4157.

`4157`	Valid	
`4_157`	Valid	
`4_1_57`	Valid	
`_4157`	Invalid	An integer must begin with a digit
`4157_`	Invalid	Underline must be followed by a digit
`41__57`	Invalid	The first underline is *not* followed by a digit
`+4_157`	Invalid	No + signs allowed

One final note: metalanguages only show how to write instructions that the compiler can translate. They do not define what those instructions do (their semantics). Formal languages for defining the semantics of a programming language exist, but they are beyond the scope of this text. Throughout this book we describe the semantics of Ada in English.

EBNF is used throughout this book. There are times when the conciseness of this metalanguage, combined with the richness of the Ada language, make it difficult to comprehend fully all of the implications of a particular rule. The definition of an Ada program (called a compilation) is such a case. Because an Ada program may be built from many different parts, its EBNF definition goes on for several pages before all of the nonterminal symbols are defined. Rather than go into all of this detail, we often will introduce syntax using a *simplified EBNF definition*, one that does not include all of the available alternatives. Appendix B contains the full EBNF definition for Ada. Here is a simplified EBNF definition of an Ada program.

ada_program ::= [context_clause]
procedure *program*_name **is**
  [declarative_part]
begin
  sequence_of_statements
end *program*_name;

Use this EBNF definition to determine the context clause, declarative part, and sequence of statements in the following valid Ada program.

```
with Ada.Text_IO;
procedure Hello is

   Greeting : constant String := "Hello Mildred!";

begin
   Ada.Text_IO.Put (Item => Greeting);
   Ada.Text_IO.New_Line;
end Hello;
```

An Ada program begins with an optional context clause in which we list any library units (packages) the program requires. These packages contain information and operations that can be used by the program. In our example, the context clause consists of a single line: "`with Ada.Text_IO;`". After the context clause is a line that begins with the word `procedure` and the name of the program. Following the specification of our program name is an optional declarative part in which we write declarations that define the terms used in the program. The term "Greeting" is defined in our example. The word `begin` signals the start of the actual instructions, or *sequence of statements*, that are translated into machine language. When we run our program, these instructions are executed. Our example contains a sequence of two statements. The end of the program is indicated by the word `end` followed by the program name and a semicolon.

When you finish this chapter, you will know enough about the syntax and semantics of declarations and statements in Ada to allow you to write programs that perform calculations and print the results. But before we can write declarations and statements, we must first look at how names are written in Ada and at some of the basic elements of a program.

Identifiers

Ada uses **identifiers** to name things. Some identifiers are defined in the language and are reserved for specific uses (see Appendix A for a list of these). All others are defined by the programmer. Identifiers are made up of letters (A–Z, a–z) and digits (0–9), but must begin with a letter. Identifiers can also contain underline characters (_) to make them easier to read. Here are some examples of valid identifiers:

```
Hello      J9      Box_22      Get_Data      Bin3      Count
```

Identifier A name associated with a process or object and used to refer to that process or object.

Now that you have seen the English-language definition of an identifier, let's look at a simplified EBNF definition.*

*Ada 95 letters include all the accented letters as well as the 26 letters shown in this simplified EBNF definition. These extended sets of letters are called identifier letters.

identifier	::=	letter{[_]letter_or_digit}
letter_or_digit	::=	letter | digit
letter	::=	upper_case_letter | lower_case_letter
upper_case_letter	::=	**A | B | C | D | E | F | G | H | I | J | K | L | M | N | O | P | Q | R | S | T | U | V | W | X | Y | Z**
lower_case_letter	::=	**a | b | c | d | e | f | g | h | i | j | k | l | m | n | o | p | q | r | s | t | u | v | w | x | y | z**
digit	::=	**0 | 1 | 2 | 3 | 4 | 5 | 6 | 7 | 8 | 9**

Use this EBNF definition and the list of reserved words in Appendix A to confirm that the following examples of user-defined identifiers are invalid:

Invalid Identifier	**Explanation**
`Get Data`	Blanks are not allowed in identifiers
`40Hours`	Identifiers must begin with a letter
`Box-22-`	-character not allowed in an identifier
`AmountIn$`	$ character not allowed in an identifier
`Procedure`	Reserved words cannot be identifiers
`Box22_`	Underline must precede a letter or digit
`_Box22`	Identifiers must begin with a letter
`Box__22`	The first of the two underlines does not precede a letter or digit

Program Payroll in Chapter 1 contains the user-defined identifiers in the following list. Notice that the names chosen convey indications of their use. (The other identifiers in the program are predefined in Ada.)

Identifier	**How It Is Used**
`Payroll`	The name of the program
`Max_Regular_Hours`	Maximum normal work hours
`Overtime_Factor`	Overtime pay rate factor
`Pay_Rate`	An employee's hourly pay rate
`Rate`	Also used for an employee's pay rate
`Hours`	The number of hours an employee worked
`Wages`	Weekly wages for an employee
`Pay`	Also used for the weekly wages of an employee
`Total`	Sum of weekly wages for all employees (total company payroll)
`Employee_ID`	Employee identification number
`Payroll_File`	The output file (where the employee number, pay rate, hours, and wages for each employee are written)

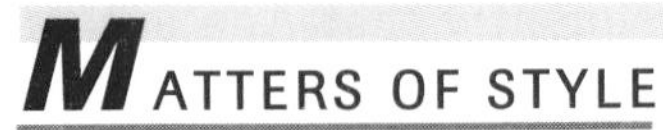

Using Meaningful, Readable Identifiers

The names we use to refer to things in our programs are totally meaningless to the computer. The computer functions the same whether we call the value 3.14159265, Pi, or Cake, as long as we always call it the same thing. However, it is much easier for a person to figure out how a program works if the names we choose for elements actually tell something about them. Whenever you have to make up a name for something in a program, try to pick one that will be meaningful to a person reading the program. Names of objects should be nouns or noun phrases. Use verbs or verb phrases to name actions.

With Ada you can write names with uppercase and lowercase letters because Ada treats them the same. Some languages are *case-sensitive:* uppercase and lowercase letters are different. Ada is not case-sensitive and thus the identifiers

```
PART_NUMBER    part_number    PaRt_NuMbEr    Part_Number
```

are considered to be the same name. As you can see, the last of these forms is the easiest to read. In addition, underline characters are *not* ignored by Ada. The identifier *PartNumber* is different from those listed. In this book we use both uppercase and lowercase letters in identifiers; and, to make multiple-word identifiers easier to read, we use underlines to separate the words and capitalize each word. We urge you to follow this style.

Whatever you use, be consistent throughout a program. Even though it makes no difference to the computer, a person reading the program will find inconsistent capitalization to be very confusing.

Now that we've seen how to write identifiers, we'll look at some of the program elements that Ada allows us to name.

Data Types

A computer program operates on data (stored internally in memory; stored externally on disk or tape; or input from a keyboard, text scanner, or electrical sensor) and produces output. In Ada, each piece of data must be of a specific type. The **data type** determines how the data is represented in the computer and the kinds of processing the computer can perform on it. Selecting appropriate data types is an important task we carry out during the problem-solving phase of software development.

Data type A collection of values and the operations that can be performed on those values.

Some types of data are used so frequently that Ada automatically defines them for us. Programmers define other data types specifically for their problems. We use the standard (predefined) data types until Chapter 4, where we will show you how to define your own.

Ada defines four simple types of data. You are already familiar with three of them: integer numbers, real (floating-point) numbers, and strings. You'll soon be equally familiar with the fourth type—Boolean.

BACKGROUND INFORMATION

Data Storage

Where does a program get the data it needs to operate? The computer's memory stores data. Remember that memory is divided into a large number of separate locations or cells, each of which can hold a piece of data. Each memory location has an address we refer to when we store or retrieve data. We can visualize memory as a set of post office boxes with the box numbers as the addresses used to designate particular locations.

Of course the actual "address" of each location in memory is a binary number in a machine language code. In Ada we use identifiers to name memory locations, and then the compiler assigns a machine address and keeps track of it for us. This is one of the advantages of a high-level language: It frees us from having to keep track of the actual memory locations in which our data and instructions are stored.

Integer Integers are whole numbers; they have no fractional part. Underlines are used in long integer literals in place of commas, to make them easier to read. Here are some examples of integer literals:

1_257   72_567_852   447_130

An underline does not affect the value of the literal. You can write twelve as 1_2 or 12. If you choose to use underlines in your literal integers, it is good programming style to use them only where you would customarily use commas.

Theoretically, integers can have any number of digits; practically, the computer limits their size. Because this limit varies among machines, Ada has two predefined attributes that we can use to determine the range of integers that a particular computer can support. *Integer'Last* (pronounced "integer tick last") and *Integer'First* are the largest (most positive) and the smallest (most negative) integer numbers that can be represented in the particular computer being used. On many popular PCs, Integer'Last and Integer'First have the values 2,147,483,647 ($2^{31} - 1$) and −2,147,483,648 (-2^{31}). By the end of this chapter, you'll be able to write an Ada program to determine the values for your computer.

Employee_ID, the identifier for the employee identification number in Program Payroll in Chapter 1, is an example of an identifier of the integer data type.

Floating-Point Floating-point numbers are one of the two ways Ada represents what mathematicians call *real numbers*. These numbers have an integer part and a fractional part, with a decimal point in between. They also may have an exponent, as in scientific notation. In scientific notation a number is written as a decimal value multiplied by a power of 10 to indicate the actual position of the decimal point. Instead of writing 3.504×10^{12}, however, we write 3.504E+12 to indicate the same exponent in Ada. Here are some examples of floating-point numbers:

127.54   −0.57   193_145.8523   1.74536E−12   3.652E2   3.652E+2

Whichever style we choose to use, floating-point numbers are stored in a manner similar to scientific notation. Because the decimal point always "floats" to the front of the number, they are all called floating-point numbers.

In Program Payroll, the identifiers Max_Regular_Hours, Overtime_Factor, Minimum_Wage, Maximum_Wage, Rate, Hours, Pay, Pay_Rate, Wages, and Total are all floating-point identifiers because they identify data items that may have integer and fractional parts.

String Data type String describes data consisting of one or more characters—letters, digits, or special symbols. Here are some examples:

```
"Hello Mildred"
"Four score and twenty years ago"
"4,592"
"$$$$***///"
```

Ada's primary character set is the international character set standard called ISO 8859-1. This character set contains 256 different characters. Of these, 191 are printable and may be used to form strings. Appendix C lists the characters in the ISO 8859-1 character set. Ada also supports the international character set called ISO 10646 BMP that contains 65,536 different characters.

Notice that each string is enclosed in quotation marks. Programmers commonly refer to these quotation marks as double quotes. The Ada compiler needs the quotation marks to differentiate string data from identifiers and other data types. "Amount" (in quotes) is the string made up of the letters *A*, *m*, *o*, *u*, *n*, and *t* in that order. Amount (without the quotes) is an identifier, the name of a place in memory. The quotation marks around the string data "841" and " + " likewise differentiate them from the integer 841 and the addition sign. Notice also that the blank (space) is a character that may be used in a string.

If you include a quotation mark in a string, you must type two of them with no space in between. For example, a string formed from the sentence

Mildred said "Hi there!" to the clerk.

would look like

```
"Mildred said ""Hi there!"" to the clerk."
```

You can't add "841" and "37", but you can compare data values of type String. Ada's character set is ordered in what is known as its collating sequence. From the order of the characters in Appendix C, you can see that the letters and digits are ordered as we would expect; that is, "A" < "B" < "C" . . . and "0" < "1" < "2" . . . . Numbers come before letters ("7" < "A") and lowercase letters come after uppercase letters ("A"< "a"). The space character comes before any other printable character. Extending this concept to strings containing more than one character is just like alphabetizing words, using this collating sequence as an extended alphabet. "Chip" is less than "John", which is less than "Nell". In strings, uppercase and lowercase letters are not the same: "Anne" and "Mildred" are both less than "anne". In Program Payroll, the identifier Payroll_File_Name is a String identifier.

Boolean Boolean is a type with just two values: True and False.* It is used to choose alternative courses of action in a program (selection), which is an important part of all programming languages, as you will see in Chapter 4.

Declarations

Identifiers are used to name *objects* and *processes* (and other things that we will introduce later). An object is a value stored at some location in memory, and a process is a group of instructions stored at some location in memory. For now, we are concerned only with objects. Constants and variables are fundamental objects. A constant contains a value that cannot be changed, and a variable contains a value that can be changed. Thus, an identifier can be the name of a memory location whose contents never change or the name of a memory location whose contents can change.

How do we tell the computer what an identifier represents? With a **declaration.** A declaration associates a name (an identifier) with a description of an object or process in an Ada program (just as a dictionary definition associates a name with a description of the thing being named). In a declaration we name an identifier and what it represents. The compiler may then pick a location in memory and associate it with the identifier. We don't have to know the actual address of the memory location because the computer keeps track of it for us.

Declaration The association of an identifier with a process or object so that the user can refer to that process or object by name.

We make declarations in the declarative part of our program. Here, for example, are two sections taken from the declarative part of Program Payroll where the constants and variables are declared:

```
Max_Regular_Hours : constant Float  := 40.0;  -- Maximum normal work hours
Overtime_Factor   : constant Float  :=  1.5;  -- Overtime pay rate factor
Minimum_Wage      : constant Float  :=  5.75; -- Minimum hourly pay rate
Maximum_Wage      : constant Float  := 99.99; -- Maximum hourly pay rate
Payroll_File_Name : constant String := "Payfile.dat";

Pay_Rate      : Float   range Minimum_Wage .. Maximum_Wage; -- Hourly pay rate
Hours         : Float   range 0.0 .. 80.0;                 -- Hours worked
Wages         : Float   range 0.0 .. 8_000.00;             -- Wages earned
Total         : Float   range 0.0 .. Float'Last;           -- Total payroll
Employee_ID   : Integer range   0 .. 999;                  -- Employee ID number
Payroll_File  : Ada.Text_IO.File_Type;                     -- Company payroll file
```

*Data type Boolean is named for George Boole (1815–1864), an English mathematician who described a system of logic using variables with just two values, True and False. (See the Background Information box on page 176.)

Remember that the words on a line after the symbol (--) are called comments. They are ignored by the compiler. These comments help us understand the purpose of each declaration.

There is a different form of declaration for each kind of object or process in Ada. The forms of declaration for constants and variables are introduced here; we'll cover others in later chapters. As a general rule, you must declare or define all identifiers in Ada before they are used. This is why all the declarations are grouped together at the beginning of a program unit, in the *declarative part.*

Constants A **literal** (or literal value) is a value written directly in a program. All numbers—integer and floating-point—are called numeric literals. String literals are a series of characters enclosed in quotation marks (strings). Here are some examples of these three types of literals:

```
16        32.3        "Howdy boys"
```

All of the examples of integer numbers, floating-point numbers, and strings given in the previous sections are literals. We can use numeric literals as part of arithmetic expressions (as you will see later in this chapter). For example, we can write a statement that adds the literals 5 and 6 and places the result in the variable Sum.

Literal Any value written directly in a program.

Although string literals are put in quotation marks, integer literals and floating-point literals are not, because there is no chance that they will be confused with identifiers. Why? Because identifiers must start with a letter, and numbers must start with a digit.

An alternative to the literal is the **constant,** which is defined in the declarative part of a program. A constant is one way of naming a value. Instead of using the literal value in a statement, we give it a name in the declarative part of the program, then use that name in the statement. For example, we can write a statement that divides the literal value 4,571.12 by 3.14159. Or we can define a constant in the declarative part for each of those values, and then use the constant names in the statement. We can use either

```
4_571.12 / 3.14159        or        Assigned_Frequency / Pi
```

but the latter is more readable.

Constant A name for a data value that cannot be changed.

It may seem easier to use a literal than to use a constant. But in fact, constants make a program easier to read because they make the meaning of literal values clearer. As we shall see, constants also make it easier to change a program later on. Five constants are declared in Program Payroll in Chapter 1.

Now let's see how to declare constants. Here is a *simplified* EBNF definition of a constant object declaration:

constant_object_declaration ::= identifier : **constant** subtype := literal_value;
subtype ::= **Integer | Float | String | Boolean**

And here are some valid constant declarations:

```
Stars          : constant String  := "********";
Pi             : constant Float   :=  3.14159;
Interest_Rate  : constant Float   :=  0.07;
Tax_Rate       : constant Float   :=  0.07;
Max_Points     : constant Integer :=  20;
Message        : constant String  := "Error condition";
Pay_Taxes      : constant Boolean :=  True;
```

The reserved word `constant` appears after the colon in each constant declaration, and the declaration is terminated with a semicolon. **Reserved words** are words that have special meaning in Ada; they cannot be used as programmer-defined identifiers. (Appendix A lists the 69 reserved words in Ada.) Following the word `constant` is the name of a type (Integer, Float, String, Boolean, or one of the other types we'll introduce later) that defines the kind of value associated with this constant. Finally, there is an assignment operator (a colon and an equal sign) and the value we want to assign to this constant.

Reserved word A word that has special meaning in Ada; it cannot be used as a programmer-defined identifier.

In Program Payroll, the constants Max_Regular_Hours, Overtime_ Factor, Minimum_Wage, Maximum_Wage and Payroll_File_ Name are defined. If the company changes its overtime rate from time and a half to double time, we need to change only the value of the constant Overtime_Factor from 1.5 to 2.0 for our program to work with the new rate.

Make sure that you assign the constant the correct type of value. The Ada compiler will give you an error message if the type of the value does not agree with the type you declared for the constant. For example, suppose we increase our overtime factor in Program Payroll from time and a half to double time as follows:

```
Overtime_Factor : constant Float := 2;    -- Contains an error
```

This is an error because we are attempting to assign an integer literal to a float constant. Changing the literal to 2.0 solves this problem.

SOFTWARE ENGINEERING TIP

Using Constants

It's a good idea to use constants instead of literals. In addition to making your program more readable, it can make it easier to modify. Suppose you wrote a program to compute taxes. In several places you used the literal 0.05, which at the time was the sales tax rate. Now the rate has gone up to 0.06. To change your program, you have to locate every literal 0.05 and change it to 0.06. And if 0.05 was used for other reasons—to compute deductions, for example—you would have to look at each place where it is used, figure out what it is used for, and then decide whether it needs to be changed.

This process is much simpler if you use a constant. Instead of using a literal in your program, suppose you had defined a constant, Tax_Rate, with a value of 0.05. and a second constant, Deduction_Rate, also with a value of 0.05. To change the tax rate in your program, you would simply change the definition to make Tax_Rate equal to 0.06. This one modification changes all of the tax-rate computations without affecting other places, such as when computing deductions, where 0.05 was used.

Constants also are reliable; they protect us from mistakes. If you mistype a name, the Ada compiler will tell you that the name has not been defined. On the other hand, even though we recognize that the number 3.14149 is a mistyped version of pi (3.14159), the number is perfectly acceptable to the compiler. It won't warn us that anything is wrong.

Variables Now we turn to variables, which are also defined in the declarative part of the program.

A program operates on data. Data is stored in memory. While a program is executing, different values may be stored in the same memory location at different times. This kind of memory location is called a **variable** and its content is the *variable value.* The symbolic name that we assign to a variable memory location is the *variable name* or *variable identifier* (see Figure 2-1). In practice, we simply refer to the variable name as the *variable.*

Variable A location in memory, referenced by an identifier, in which a data value that can be changed is stored.

FIGURE 2-1
Variable

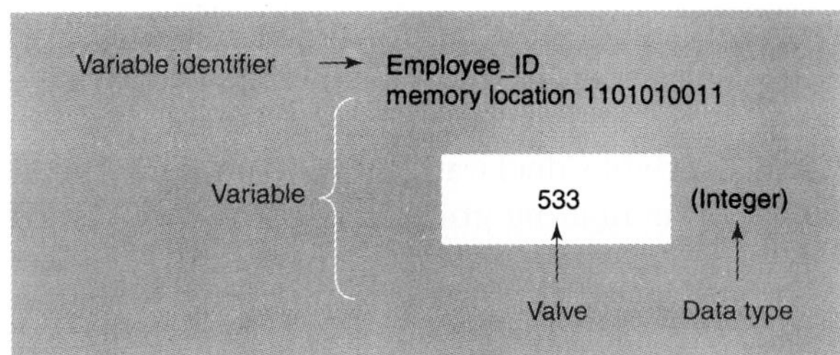

Declaring a variable means specifying both its name and its data type. This tells the compiler to associate a name with a memory location whose content will be of a specific type (integer, float, string, Boolean, or one of the other types we'll introduce later).

Ada is a strongly typed language. This means that a variable can contain data values only of the type specified in its declaration. If the Ada compiler comes across instructions that try to store a value of the wrong data type, it gives an error message, usually something like "RESULT TYPE NOT THE SAME AS VARIABLE TYPE."

Here is a simplified EBNF definition of a variable declaration:

variable_object_declaration ::= identifier : subtype [**range** simple_expression .. simple_expression];

Notice that there is a colon between the identifier and the subtype and that the declaration is terminated with a semicolon. The optional range constraint specifies the legal range of values that a numeric variable* may hold. The lower and upper bounds of this range are given by two simple arithmetic expressions separated by the two periods. Usually these arithmetic expressions are simply literals or constants. These are valid variable declarations:

```
Pay_Rate    : Float range Minimum_Wage .. Maximum_Wage;
Hours       : Float range 0.0 .. 80.0;
Sum         : Float;
Employee_ID : Integer range 0 .. 999;
Count       : Integer;
Found       : Boolean;
Name        : String (1..10);
```

Notice the two numbers separated by two periods and enclosed in parentheses after the type mark String. We must include these numbers so that the Ada compiler will know how many characters the string variable contains. The string variable Name contains 10 characters (numbered 1

*In Chapter 4 we show how to specify legal ranges for nonnumeric variables.

through 10). Later you will learn how these numbers may be used to process individual characters in a string variable.

Look at the variables declared in Program Payroll in Chapter 1. These variable declarations tell the compiler to set up locations in memory for four floating-point variables—Pay_Rate, Hours, Wages, and Total—and to set up one location for an integer variable called Employee_ID. (We explain type Ada.Text_IO.File_Type in Chapter 3.) The comments after each variable declaration in the program help explain to the reader what each variable represents.

Executable Statements

To this point we've looked only at ways of defining objects in a program. Now we turn our attention to ways of manipulating or performing operations on those objects.

Assignment The value of a variable is changed through an **assignment statement.** For example,

```
Num := 10;
```

assigns the value 10 to the variable Num (puts the value 10 into the memory location called Num). As with all Ada statements, the assignment statement is terminated with a semicolon. The semantics (meaning) of the assignment operator (:=) is "becomes"; the value of the variable *becomes* the value written after the assignment operator. Any previous value that the variable had is replaced by this value. Figure 2-2 illustrates this assignment.

Assignment statement A statement that stores the value of an expression in a memory location corresponding to the named variable.

Here's the EBNF definition of an assignment statement:

assignment_statement ::= *variable*_name := expression;

Notice the use of italics in this EBNF definition. Names that begin with an italicized part are equivalent to the name without the italicized part. The italicized part simply conveys additional meaning within the context of the definition. Think of the italicized part as a comment, not actually part of the definition. If we wanted to look up the definition of *variable*_name in Appendix B, we would look under name not *variable*_name.

FIGURE 2-2
Assignment

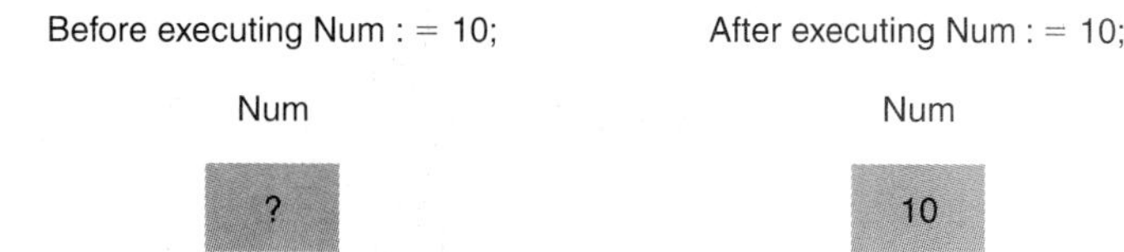

Only one variable can be on the left-hand side of an assignment statement. An assignment statement is *not* like a math equation ($x + y = z + 4$); the expression (what is on the right-hand side of the assignment operator) is evaluated, and that value is stored in the single variable on the left of the assignment operator.

The value assigned to a variable must be of the same type as the variable and within the legal range of values for that variable. Given the declarations

```
Num  : Integer;
ID   : Integer range 0..5_000;
Next : Integer;
Rate : Float range 0.0 .. 1.0;
Test : Boolean;
Name : String (1..7);
```

the following are valid assignments:

Assignment Statement	Explanation
`Rate :=  0.36;`	Rate becomes 0.36
`Test :=  True;`	Test becomes True
`ID   :=  2_856;`	ID becomes 2,856
`Name := "Mildred";`	Name becomes Mildred
`Next :=  ID;`	Next becomes the same as ID (2,856)

The last assignment statement is a little different than the ones above it. The expression in this assignment is not a literal, it is the variable ID. Remember that assignment is a right-to-left operation. In this assignment statement, Next becomes the value of ID. So, after this statement, Next and ID have the same value. Variables used on the right side of an assignment statement do not change. Thus, while Next is assigned a new value, ID remains the same (see Figure 2-3).

These are not valid assignments:

FIGURE 2-3
Assignment of ID to Next

Assignment Statement	**Explanation**
`ID   := 2.5;`	ID is integer; 2.5 is a floating-point literal
`ID   := 9_000;`	9,000 is not in the legal range for ID
`Rate := 5;`	Rate is float; 5 is an integer literal
`Name := 3;`	Name is string; 3 is an integer literal
`Test := "A";`	Test is Boolean; "A" is a string literal
`Name := "Hello";`	Name must contain 7 characters
`Test := "True";`	Test is Boolean; "True" is a string literal
`Num  := Rate;`	Num is integer; Rate is float
`Rate := 36.1`	36.1 is not in the legal range for Rate
`ID + Num := 4;`	Multiple variables on the left side

Variables keep their assigned values until they are changed by another statement.

Simple Expressions Simple expressions are made up of constants, variables, and operators. These are all valid simple expressions:

```
ID + 2          Rate - 6.0
4 - ID          Rate
ID - Num        "Mildred " & "Smedley"
```

One of the consequences of Ada's strong typing is that the types in an arithmetic expression must be the same. The Ada compiler gives an error if, for example, you attempt to add an integer and a floating-point number together. Although this trait may seem inconvenient at first, you will learn later how it helps prevent hard-to-find errors in your programs.

The operators allowed in an expression depend on the data type of the constants and variables in the expression. The most commonly used operators are

`+`	addition
`-`	subtraction
`*`	multiplication
`/`	division
`rem`	remainder from integer division
`abs`	absolute value
`**`	exponentiation
`&`	concatenation

Integer addition, subtraction, multiplication, and absolute value operate as you would expect. You are probably familiar with integer division, although you may not have used it since elementary school. When you divide one integer by another integer, you get an integer quotient and an integer remainder. Programming languages use two separate operators to carry out this integer division. The / operator gives the integer quotient; rem gives the remainder.

```
  3 ← 6/2          3 ← 7/2
2)6              2)7
  6                6
  0 ← 6 rem 2      1 ← 7 rem 2
```

Integer exponentiation (raising an integer to a power) is only allowed for nonnegative powers. Here are some examples of integer arithmetic:

Integer Expression	Value
`3 + 6`	9
`3 - 6`	-3
`2 * 3`	6
`8 / 2`	4
`8 / 8`	1
`8 / 9`	0
`8 / 7`	1
`5 / -2`	-2
`7 / 0`	error (cannot divide by zero)
`8 rem 8`	0
`8 rem 9`	8
`8 rem 7`	1
`0 rem 7`	0
`7 rem 0`	error (cannot divide by zero)
`12 rem 5`	2
`-12 rem 5`	-2
`-12 rem -5`	-2
`12 rem -5`	2
`5 ** 2`	25
`5 ** -2`	error (negative exponent)
`abs 17`	17
`abs -4`	4

The sign of the result of a remainder operation is always the same as the sign of the dividend, as illustrated by the last four rem examples. Although it is obvious to you that the expression 7/0 is an error, it is less obvious that 7 rem 0 results in the same error; the computer cannot divide by zero in either case.

Because variables are allowed in expressions, the following are valid assignment statements:

```
ID  := Num + 6;
ID  := Num / 2;
Num := ID * 2;
Num := 6 rem ID;
ID  := ID + 1;
Num := Num + ID;
```

Notice that the same variable can appear on both sides of the assignment operator. In the case of

```
Num := Num + ID
```

the value in Num and the value in ID are added together; then the sum of the two values is stored in Num, replacing the previous value stored there (see Figure 2-4). This example shows the difference between mathematical equality and assignment. The mathematical equality

$$Num = Num + ID$$

is true only if ID is equal to zero. The assignment statement

```
Num := Num + ID;
```

is valid for *any* value of ID.

Floating-point values are added, subtracted, and multiplied just as integer values are. Absolute values of floating-point operands also behave in the same way. Division with floating-point numbers gives the results that you are used to with your hand-held calculator (7.0 / 2.0 is 3.5). Because division with floating-point numbers has no remainder, rem can *not* be used with them.

The exception to the rule of not mixing types in an expression is the exponentiation operator. Whether the number you wish to raise to a power is an integer or a floating-point number, the power must always be an integer. Unlike integer exponentiation, floating-point numbers may be raised to a negative power. Some examples of floating-point arithmetic:

FIGURE 2-4 Assignment Is Different Than Equality

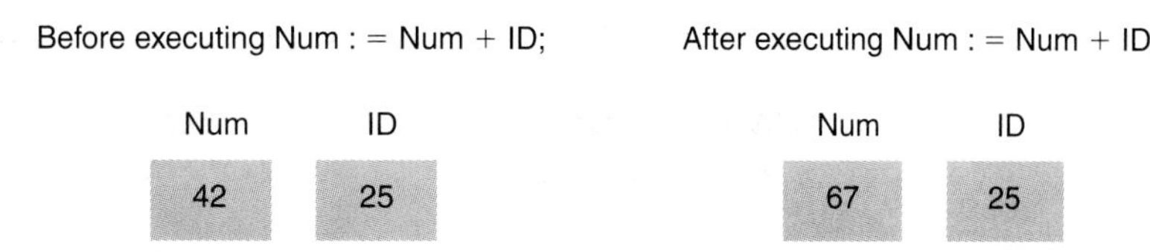

Floating-Point Expression	Value
`5.34 - 3.22`	`2.12`
`4.82E+2 + 7.3`	`489.3`
`3.54E-5 * 1.5E+12`	`5.31E+7`
`5.55E+2 / 5.0E+5`	`1.11E-3`
`4.1 ** 3.0`	error (exponent must be integer)
`4.1 ** 3`	`68.921`
`abs 3.54E-5`	`3.54E-5`
`abs -47.8`	`47.8`

The concatenation operator, &, is used to combine two strings into a single string. Here are two examples:

String Expression	Value
`"Hello " & "Mildred"`	`"Hello Mildred"`
`"Good" & "bye"`	`"Goodbye"`

String literals must fit on a single line. Programmers commonly use the concatenation operator to obtain longer strings by combining shorter strings typed on separate lines as illustrated in the following example:

```
Message : constant String := "The computer system will be down between " &
                             "2:00 AM and 5:00 AM this Thursday";
```

This example also illustrates that you may write an Ada statement (a declaration in this case) over more than one line. In general, you may type any statement over several lines. Just break it at any point where you can use a space character, *except*, of course, at space characters in string literals. Ada uses the semicolon to determine the end of every statement in a program.

Output: Packages and Procedures

Have you ever asked someone, "Do you know what time it is?" only to have the person smile smugly and say, "Yes, I do"? This is similar to the situation that currently exists between you and the computer. You now know enough Ada syntax to tell the computer to perform simple calculations, but the computer won't give you the answers until you tell it to display them.

Ada does not have any special statements to display answers. Why doesn't a language as powerful as Ada have output statements built into it? Remember that Ada was designed by the DOD. The DOD wished to use a single language to program all of its equipment. Much of its equipment involves *embedded computer systems*—computer systems that are only one part of a larger piece of equipment. You probably have used many different embedded computers without even realizing it. Every modern automobile, microwave oven, VCR, and compact disc player has a computer built into it. Computers embedded within a device like a microwave oven do not use an ordinary keyboard and screen for input and output. They have special I/O devices (buttons and LED displays) that require special instructions.

To allow for a wide range of I/O devices, Ada keeps instructions for input and output in packages that are stored in a library. Some of these packages are predefined by the Ada language, and others are written by Ada programmers and put in a library for others to use.

In Chapter 1 we said that a package acts as a protective covering around a complicated apparatus. Each package provides an interface that enables us to use the contents without knowing the details of their construction. Output to a device like a video display screen involves the management of many complicated details. By encapsulating these details in a package, Ada allows us to display answers without needing to worry about how it is actually accomplished.

Output of String Data The interface for Ada's predefined library package Ada.Text_IO contains procedures for doing input and output with common I/O devices (keyboards, video display screens, printers, disks, and tapes). Remember what a procedure is? In Chapter 1 we discussed the four basic programming structures: sequence, selection, loop, and procedure. There we said that a **procedure** is a process that consists of multiple steps. We *call* a procedure (use its steps) by writing its name, often followed by a *list of parameters*.

Procedure A programming structure that allows replacement of a group of statements with a single statement.

The **parameter list** is a way for your program to communicate with a procedure. Each parameter in the list has a name and a value. Parameter values can be literals, constants, variables, or expressions. Here's an example call of procedure Put that displays a string:

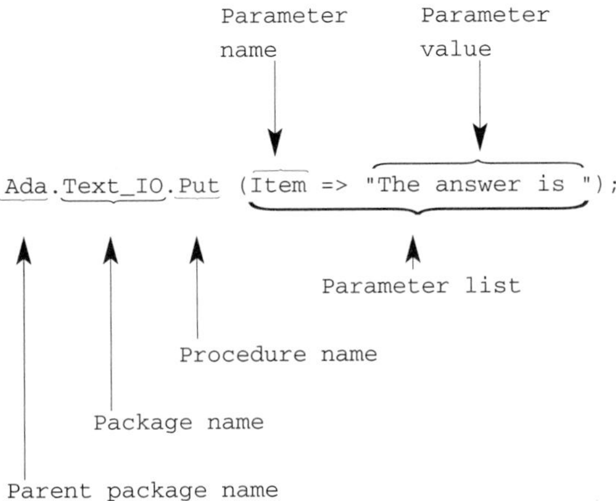

The parameter list in this example contains a single parameter whose name is Item. This is the item we wish to display. The arrow symbol (=>) after the parameter name points to the value we want to give it: the string literal `"The answer is "`.

Parameter list A mechanism for communicating with a procedure.

Procedure Put contains many statements. However, we do not need to know anything about these statements to use it. Any time we need to display a string, we just pass that string as a parameter in a call to procedure Put. The procedure will do all the work necessary to display our string.

Because there are many different procedures called Put, we need to specify which one we want to use. We use **prefixing** to designate exactly which procedure we want to call. By using the parent package name, the package name, and the procedure name (separated by a periods), we tell the Ada compiler that we wish to call a Put procedure that is in the package Text_IO, which is a child of the package Ada.

Prefixing Designating an identifier with the hierarchy of names of packages in which it is declared.

Ada.Text_IO is a standard package that is supplied with every validated Ada compiler. All standard resources are organized under three parent packages: Ada, Interfaces, and System. The package named Ada serves as the parent of most other standard library packages. Resources for combining Ada statements with statements written in other programming languages in the same program are found in the package Interfaces and its children. Finally, package System and its children provide the definitions of characteristics of the particular environment in which the program runs. While this text discusses some of the resources in the parent package Ada, we cannot describe them all. After you are comfortable with the EBNF notation and become more familiar with Ada, you should have little difficulty in reading the ARM to learn about the many other standard resources available.

Most packages used by Ada programmers do not come with the Ada compiler. They are written by programmers for specific applications. For example, if we were writing a program to control a microwave oven, we might use a Put procedure in a package called Microwave_IO like this:

```
Microwave_IO.Put (Item => "Low");
```

This package may have been written by one of your team members or supplied by the manufacturer of the display unit used in the oven.

When you use a procedure like Put, the computer temporarily suspends operation of your program, starts the Put subprogram running, and gives it the data from the parameter list. When Put has finished displaying the data, the computer goes back to your program and picks up where it left off.

The parameter list makes it possible for the same subprogram to work on many different sets of data. Here we use the same Put procedure twice to display two different values:

```
Ada.Text_IO.Put (Item => "Mildred ");
Ada.Text_IO.Put (Item => "Smedley");
```

The output from these two calls to Put is the single line:

```
Mildred Smedley
```

To display the first and last name on separate lines, we use the procedure New_Line in package Text_IO. This procedure terminates (ends) a line. Here is an example of its use:

```
Ada.Text_IO.Put (Item => "Mildred");
Ada.Text_IO.New_Line;                    -- terminate the line after Mildred
Ada.Text_IO.Put (Item => "Smedley");
Ada.Text_IO.New_Line;                    -- terminate the line after Smedley
```

It produces the output:

```
Mildred
Smedley
```

Output of Numeric Data Put procedures for the output of integer and floating-point data are found in the child packages Integer_Text_IO and Float_Text_IO. As in the case of Text_IO.Put, these Put procedures use a parameter named Item to specify the value to output. Here is an example of their use:

```
Ada.Integer_Text_IO.Put (Item => 42);
Ada.Float_Text_IO.Put   (Item => 17.76);
```

These two lines produce the following output:

```
        42 1.77600E+01
```

Notice that the floating-point number is displayed in scientific notation. Later in this chapter we show how to format numeric output to produce more readable results. To output each number on a separate line we can include a call to procedure New_Line after we display the integer value.

```
Ada.Integer_Text_IO.Put (Item => 42);
Ada.Text_IO.New_Line;
Ada.Float_Text_IO.Put   (Item => 17.76);
```

Commenting a Program

All that you need to create a working program is the correct combination of declarations and executable statements. The compiler ignores comments, but they are of enormous help to anyone who must read the program. A comment starts with two adjacent hyphens (--) and extends to the end of the line. A comment can appear on any line of a program. The compiler ignores anything on the line after the hyphens. They are there for the benefit of human readers of the program. Here is how comments might be used at the beginning of a program to describe what it does:

```
-- This program computes the weight and balance of a Beechcraft
-- Starship-1 airplane, given the amount of fuel, number of
-- passengers, and weight of luggage in fore and aft storage.
-- It assumes that there are two pilots, a standard complement
-- of equipment, and that passengers weigh 170 lbs. each.
```

Here are comments used to describe the purpose of a variable:

```
Fuel_Load : Float range 0.0 .. Fuel_Capacity;     -- Pounds of fuel. Jet-A
                                                  -- fuel weighs 6.7 pounds
                                                  -- per gallon.
```

It is good programming style to write fully commented programs. A comment should appear at the beginning of a program to explain what the program does. Each constant definition and variable declaration should have a comment that explains the role of the identifier, that is, how the identifier is used. In addition, comments should introduce each major step in a long program and should explain anything that is unusual or difficult to read (for example, a lengthy formula). When writing comments, try to put yourself in the place of someone reading the program for the first time.

It is important to make your comments concise and to arrange them in the program so that they are easy to see and it is clear what they refer to. If comments are too long or crowd the statements of the program, they make the program difficult to read—just the opposite of what you intended!

Experienced programmers write most of their comments during the problem-solving phase of the programming process. They realize the advantages that writing down explanations has on their own understanding of the problem and its solution. If they cannot express their solution as a comment, it is unlikely that it can be written in Ada. Commenting is an important part of the programming methodology we introduce in Chapter 3.

BACKGROUND INFORMATION

Ada Lovelace

On December 10, 1815, Anna Isabella (Annabella) Byron, whose husband was Lord Byron, gave birth to a daughter, Augusta Ada. Ada's father was a romantic poet whose fame derived not only from his works but also from his wild and scandalous behavior. His marriage to Annabella was strained from the beginning and Annabella left Byron just a little more than a month after Ada was born. By April of that year, Annabella and Byron signed separation papers and Byron left England, never to return.

Byron's writings show that he greatly regretted that he was unable to see his daughter. In one poem, for example, he wrote of Ada,

I see thee not. I hear thee not.
But none can be so wrapt in thee.

Byron died in Greece at the age of 36, and one of the last things he said was,

Oh my poor dear child! My dear Ada! My God, could I but have seen her!

Meanwhile, Annabella, who was eventually to become a baroness in her own right, and who was herself educated as both a mathematician and a poet, carried on with Ada's upbringing and education. Annabella gave Ada her first instruction in mathematics, but it soon became clear that Ada's gift for the subject was such that it required more extensive tutoring. Ada received further training in mathematics from Augustus DeMorgan, who is today famous for one of the basic theorems of Boolean algebra, which forms the basis for modern computers. By the age of eight, Ada also had demonstrated an interest in mechanical devices and was building detailed model boats.

When she was 18, Ada visited the Mechanics Institute to hear Dr. Dionysius Lardner's lectures on the "difference engine," a mechanical calculating machine being built by Charles Babbage. She became so interested in the device that she arranged to be introduced to Babbage. It was said that, upon seeing Babbage's machine, Ada was the only person in the room to understand immediately how it worked and to appreciate its significance.

Ada and Babbage became good friends and she worked with him for the rest of her life, helping to document his designs, translating writings about his work, and developing programs to be used on his machines. Unfortunately, Babbage never completed construction of any of his designs. Even so, today Ada is recognized as being the first computer programmer in history. That title, however, does not do full justice to her genius.

Around the time that Babbage met Ada, he began the design for an even more ambitious machine called the "analytical engine," which we now recognize was the first programmable computer. Ada instantly grasped the implications of the device and foresaw its application in ways that even Babbage did not imagine. Ada believed that mathematics eventually would develop into a system of symbols that could be used to represent anything in the universe. From her notes, it is clear that Ada saw that the analytical engine could go beyond arithmetic computations and become a general manipulator of symbols, and thus it would be capable of almost anything. She even suggested that such a device could eventually be programmed with rules of harmony and composition so that it could produce "scientific" music. In effect, Ada foresaw the field of artificial intelligence over 150 years ago.

In 1842, Babbage went to Turin, Italy, and gave a series of lectures on his analytical engine. One of the attendees was Luigi Menabrea, who was so impressed that he wrote an account of Babbage's lectures. At age 27, Ada decided to translate the account into English with the intent to add a few of her own notes about the machine. In the end, her notes were twice as long as the original material, and the document, "The Sketch of the Analytical Engine," became the definitive work on the subject.

It is obvious from Ada's letters that her "notes" were entirely her own and that Babbage was acting as a sometimes unappreciated editor. At one point, Ada wrote to him,

I am much annoyed at your having altered my Note. You know I am always willing to make any required alterations myself, but that I cannot endure another person to meddle with my sentences.

Ada gained the title Countess of Lovelace when she married Lord William Lovelace. The couple had three children, but Ada was so consumed by her love of mathematics that she left their upbringing to her mother. For a woman of that day, such behavior was considered almost as scandalous as some of her father's exploits, but her husband was actually quite supportive of her work.

In 1852, Ada died from cancer. Sadly, if she had lived just one year longer, she would have witnessed the unveiling of a working difference engine built from one of Babbage's designs by George and Edward Scheutz in Sweden. Like her father, Ada lived only until she was 36, and, even though they led much different lives, she undoubtedly admired Byron and took inspiration from his unconventional and rebellious nature. At the end, Ada asked to be buried beside him at the family's estate.

Program Construction

Now we can collect the statements we've been discussing into a program. As you saw earlier, Ada programs are made up of a context clause, a procedure name for the program, a declarative part, and a sequence of statements. Here we repeat the template for a program given earlier:

ada_program ::= [context_clause]
procedure *program*_name **is**
[declarative_part]
begin
sequence_of_statements
end *program*_name;

Here's an example of a program:

```
with Ada.Text_IO;
with Ada.Float_Text_IO;

procedure Temperature is

-- This program computes the midpoint between
-- the freezing and boiling points of water

-- Declarative part begins here

   -- Constants
   Freeze : constant Float := 32.0;       -- Freezing point of water
   Boil   : constant Float := 212.0;      -- Boiling point of water
```

```
   -- Variables
   Avg_Temp : Float;                    -- The result of averaging
                                        -- Freeze and Boil

begin      -- The executable statements begin here.

   -- Display the constants
   Ada.Text_IO.Put        (Item => "Water freezes at ");
   Ada.Float_Text_IO.Put  (Item => Freeze);
   Ada.Text_IO.New_Line;
   Ada.Text_IO.Put        (Item => "and boils at ");
   Ada.Float_Text_IO.Put  (Item => Boil);
   Ada.Text_IO.Put        (Item => " degrees.");
   Ada.Text_IO.New_Line;
   Ada.Text_IO.New_Line;

   -- Calculate the average
   Avg_Temp := Freeze + Boil;
   Avg_Temp := Avg_Temp / 2.0;

   -- Display the average
   Ada.Text_IO.Put        (Item => "Halfway between is ");
   Ada.Float_Text_IO.Put  (Item => Avg_Temp);
   Ada.Text_IO.Put        (Item => " degrees.");
   Ada.Text_IO.New_Line;

end Temperature;
```

The first two lines of the program are the context clause telling the compiler that this program uses the library packages Ada.Text_IO and Ada.Float_Text_IO. The next line names the program. It is composed of the reserved word `procedure`, the name for the program, and the reserved word `is`. Following the line with the program's name is a comment that explains what the program does.

The declarative part defines the constants Freeze and Boil and declares the variable Avg_Temp. Comments explain how each identifier is used. The order of the declarations in this example is not important. We could have declared the variable first or mixed the constant and variable declarations. Just be sure to declare every identifier *before* it is used. The order used here is a matter of programming style.

The sequence of statements following the reserved word `begin` is the executable part of the program. The line with the reserved word `end` and the name of the program marks the end of the program. The statement section is the portion of the program that is translated into machine language instructions. During the execution phase, these instructions get executed.

This program was written for Fahrenheit temperatures. Because it uses constants, you can easily modify it for Celsius temperatures by changing the values of constants Freeze and Boil.

Program Entry, Correction, and Execution

Once we have the program written on paper, how do we get it into the machine? The most common way is to enter it on the keyboard of a computer. In this section, we examine the program entry process in general. You will need to consult manuals, course handouts, or the built-in help functions for your specific environment to learn the details.

Entering a Program

The first step in entering a program is to get the computer's attention. With a personal computer, this sometimes means turning it on. With computers that are left on constantly, moving or clicking the mouse, or pressing the Enter key will usually get the computer's attention. Many computers in university laboratories require you to go through a logon sequence where you enter a user name and a password. The password system protects information that you store in the computer from being tampered with or destroyed by someone else.

Once the computer is ready to accept your commands, you tell it that you want to enter a program by typing a command or clicking on an icon that tells it to run the editor. As we discussed in Chapter 1, the editor allows you to create and modify programs by entering information into an area of the computer's secondary memory called a **file.**

File A named area in secondary storage that is used to hold a collection of data; the collection of data itself.

A file in the computer's memory is like a file folder in a filing cabinet. It is a collection of information that has a name associated with it. You usually choose the name for the file when you create it or save it. From that point on, you refer to the file by the name you've given it.

There are so many different types of editors, each with different features, that we can't begin to describe them all here. But we can describe some of their general characteristics. The basic unit of information in an editor is a display screen full of characters. The editor will let you change anything that you see on the screen. Most computer keyboards have a special group of keys called *cursor keys.* (The *cursor* is the mark on the screen that indicates the point where you are typing.) The cursor keys are a set of arrows that point up, down, right, and left (see Figure 2-5). Each time you press one of them, the cursor moves one line up or down, or one character

Figure 2-5
Computer Keyboard

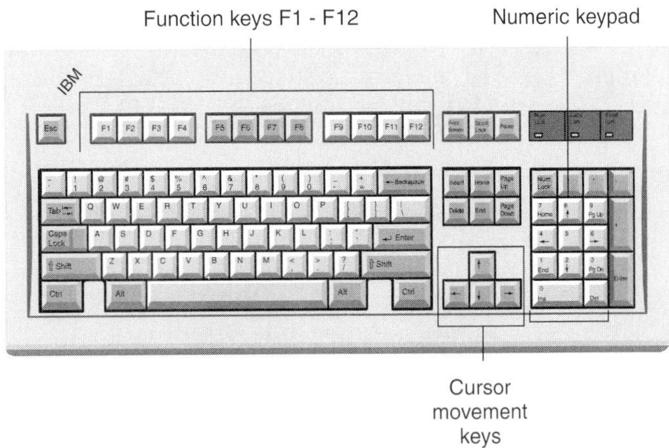

right or left. You can use these keys to move the cursor to any point on the screen. The keyboard also may contain other command keys that let you look at other parts of the file, delete characters or lines, insert new lines, and so on. Personal computer editors let you use a mouse to position the cursor and perform other editing functions.

When you create a new file, the editor clears the screen to show you that the file is empty. Then you enter your program, using the keyboard and mouse to go back and make corrections as necessary. Figure 2-6 shows what a display screen looks like for a typical editor.

Compiling and Running a Program

Once your program is stored in a file, you compile it by issuing a command to run the Ada compiler. Editors often have a button on their toolbar that you may click on with the mouse to compile the program displayed on your screen. The compiler translates the program and then stores the machine language version in a file. On some systems, the compiler also creates and stores a listing in another file called a listing. A *listing* is a copy of the program with line numbers and messages from the compiler inserted into it. Usually the messages indicate errors in the program that are preventing the compiler from completing the translation. Other systems just display the first error in the program and automatically position the cursor at that point. If there are errors, you have to determine their cause, go back to the editor and fix them, and then run the compiler again.

After a program has compiled successfully, most systems require a step called *linking* or *binding*. The linking process combines your program's machine language instructions with the machine instructions contained in the library packages your program uses. The result of linking and binding is a file of machine language instructions that can be executed. We'll discuss more about the details of compilation and linking in Chapter 12.

FIGURE 2-6
Display Screen for Screen Editor

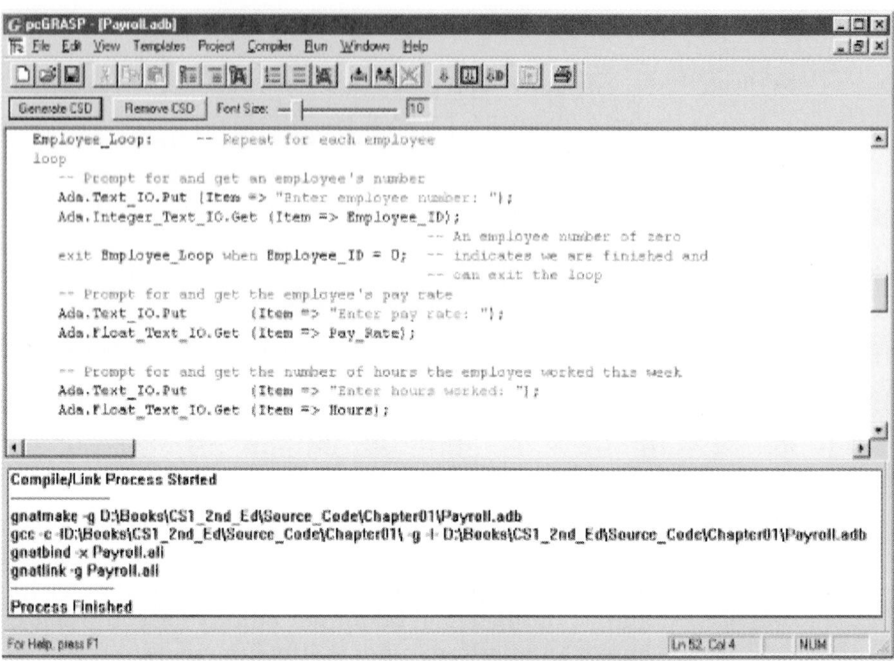

Once a program has been linked, you use a separate command or icon click to run it. Whatever series of commands your system uses, the result is the same: Your program is loaded into memory and executed by the computer.

Debugging

Several kinds of errors can arise during the programming process. The Ada compiler detects *compile-time errors* during the translation of the source program into machine language. Because compile-time errors usually result from violations of the Ada syntax, they often are called *syntax errors.* The Ada compiler also can detect some statements that will result in an error during the running of the program. One of the Programming Warm-up Exercises at the end of this chapter gives you the opportunity to encounter the compiler error messages displayed by your Ada compiler for some common errors.

Execution errors occur during the running of a program. There are two kinds of execution errors: exceptions and logical errors. *Exceptions* are errors detected by the computer and include mistakes such as dividing by zero or calculating an integer that is too large for the computer. When an exception occurs, the computer halts your program and displays an error message. Exceptions also are called run-time errors.

Even though your program runs, it still can contain errors. The computer will do exactly what you tell it to do, even if that's not what you wanted it to do. If your program doesn't do what it should, it has a *logical error*. The computer will *not* display an error message for this kind of error. Instead, the answers you receive will be wrong.

Execution errors often result from a faulty design. You must go back to the algorithm and fix it, and then go to the editor and change the program. Finally, you compile, link, and run the program again. You must repeat the debugging process until the program does what it is supposed to do (see Figure 2-7).

SOFTWARE ENGINEERING TIP

Understanding Before Changing

When you are in the middle of getting a program to run and you come across an error, it's tempting to start changing parts of the program to see if it will work. *Don't!* You'll nearly always makes things worse. It's essential that you understand what is causing the error and that you carefully think through the solution. The only thing you should try is running the program with different input data to determine the pattern of the unexpected behavior.

There is no magic trick—changing an identifier name, for example—that automatically can fix a program. If the compiler tells you that an identifier is unexpected or an end is missing, you have to examine the program in light of the syntax rules and determine precisely what the problem is. Perhaps you accidentally left out the semicolon required at the end of every statement. Or maybe you mistyped a variable declaration.

A good rule of thumb is that, if the source of a problem isn't immediately obvious, leave the computer and go somewhere where you can quietly look over a printed copy of the program. Studies show that people who do all of their debugging away from the computer actually get their programs to work in less time and, *in the end, produce better programs* than those who continue to work on the machine—more proof that there is still no mechanical substitute for human thought.*

More About Expressions

The expressions we've used so far have contained at most a single operator. Now let's look at more complicated expressions.

*Basili, V. R., Selby, R. W., "Comparing the Effectiveness of Software Testing Strategies," *IEEE Trans. on Software Engineering*. SE-13, no. 12, pp. 1278–1296.

FIGURE 2-7 Debugging Procedure

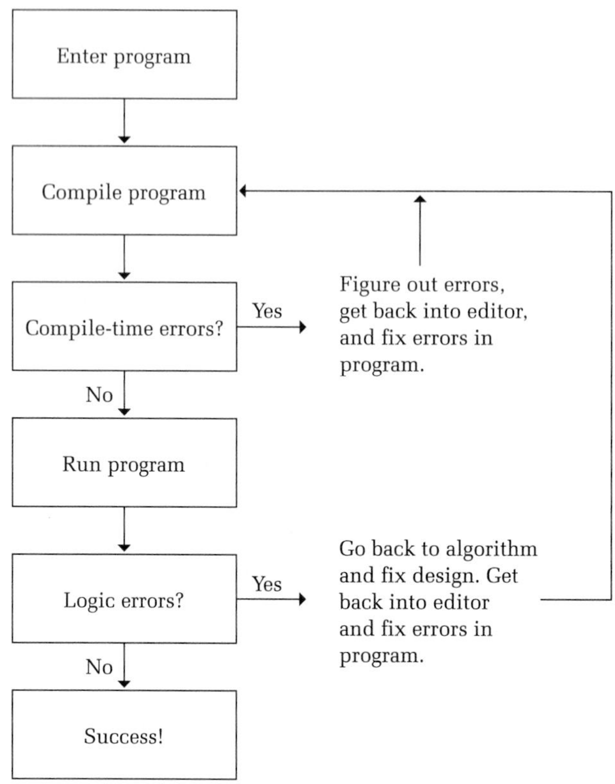

Precedence Rules

Expressions can be made up of many constants, variables, and operators. In what order are the operations performed? For example, in the assignment statement

```
Avg_Temp := Freeze + Boil / 2.0;
```

is Freeze + Boil calculated first or is Boil / 2.0 calculated first? Ada operators are ordered the same way mathematical operators are—left to right according to *precedence rules*. The Ada operators introduced earlier are divided into four precedence classes:

Highest Precedence Operators	**	abs	
Multiplying Operators	*	/	rem
Unary Adding Operators	+	-	
Binary Adding Operators	+	-	&

As the class name indicates, the operators in the class at the top of this list have the highest precedence. The last class, the binary adding operators, have the lowest precedence. Therefore the assignment statement divides Boil by 2.0 first and then adds Freeze to the result. You can change the order of evaluation by using parentheses. In the statement

```
Avg_Temp := (Freeze + Boil) / 2.0;
```

Freeze and Boil are added first, and then their sum is divided by 2.0. We evaluate expressions, called subexpressions, in parentheses first, and then follow the precedence of the operators.

When there are multiple operators with the same precedence, we evaluate them from left to right. If we have the statement

```
A := (A + B) / A * 2.0;
```

where A and B are float variables, we evaluate the expression in the parentheses first, then divide the sum of A and B by A, and multiply the result by 2.0. The result is assigned to the memory location corresponding to variable A.

Consecutive exponentiation operators are an exception to the left-to-right evaluation rule. Ada does not allow consecutive exponentiation operators. This means that the expression

```
4 ** 3 ** 2        -- Illegal expression
```

must be written as either

```
(4 ** 3) ** 2    or    4 ** (3 ** 2)
```

Expressions with multiple *nonconsecutive* exponentiation operators do not require parentheses. Here are some examples:

```
5 ** 4 * 3 ** 2
8 ** 2 - 5 ** 2
```

It is a good idea to use extra parentheses in a complex expression if they make it easier to understand. The following three expressions perform the same computation, but the second is the easiest to read. It groups together logically related terms so that the reader doesn't need to know Ada's precedence rules. The third expression shows that too many parentheses can make an expression even more awkward to read.

```
Distance := Head_Start + Speed * Time - Handicap ;
Distance := Head_Start + (Speed * Time) - Handicap ;
Distance := ((Head_Start + (Speed * Time)) - Handicap) ;
```

Here are some more examples of expressions:

Expression	Result
`10 / 2 * 3`	15
`10 rem 3 - 4 / 2`	-1
`5 * 2 / 4 * 2`	4
`5 * 2 / (4 * 2)`	1
`5 + 2 / (4 * 2)`	5
`8 ** 2 - 5 ** 2`	39

The unary adding operators work with a single operand. The unary − operator is used to change the sign of its operand (negation). The unary + operator does not change its operand. It is called the identity operator. Here are some examples:

```
Distance     := - Distance;                    -- Negate the Distance
Displacement := - (Force_Constant * Force);    -- Negate the
                                               -- multiplication

Velocity     := + Velocity                     -- Leave Velocity
                                               -- unchanged
```

The parentheses in the second example are included only for clarity; Ada's precedence rules specify that multiplication is done before negation. Ada's order of precedence is not the same as that in other programming languages. By getting in the habit of using additional parentheses for clarity, you will find it easy to translate your expressions into another language when the need should arise.

It is important to keep in mind the precedence of the unary adding operators to avoid syntax errors. For example, at first glance, the Ada expression

```
2.0 ** -N
```

appears to be the proper way to write the mathematical expression 2^{-n}. But precedence requires that exponentiation is carried out before negation is done. There is, however, no value to the right of the exponentiation operator—instead, Ada finds the negation operator. The Ada compiler will give an error message like MISSING OPERAND. You must use parentheses to form a subexpression to do the negation *before* the exponentiation as follows:

```
2.0 ** (-N)
```

Static Expressions

A static expression is an expression that the Ada compiler can evaluate. It is made of literals, constants, and operators. Because it is evaluated before program execution, a static expression cannot contain variables. We use static expressions when defining constants in order to improve program clarity, ease of modification, and reliability. For example, the constant definitions

```
Tax_Rate           : constant Float :=  0.07;
Percent_Tax        : constant Float :=  7.0;

Pi                 : constant Float :=  3.14159;
Degrees_Per_Radian : constant Float := 57.29578;
```

are easier to understand and easier to change if you write them as

```
Tax_Rate           : constant Float := 0.07;
Percent_Tax        : constant Float := 100.0 * Tax Rate;

Pi                 : constant Float := 3.14159;
Degrees_Per_Radian : constant Float := 360.0 / (2.0 * Pi);
```

Static expressions also help to prevent typographical errors. An error made in typing the value of 57.29578 is not as easily noticed as an error in typing 360.0 / (2.0 * Pi).

Type Conversions

Earlier we discussed that, except for the exponentiation operator, the types in arithmetic expressions must be the same. Sometimes it is necessary to perform calculations with data of different types. Ada allows us to convert one numeric type to another through *explicit type conversions.* Converting integer values to float values is straightforward. However, when converting a float value to integer, something must be done with the fractional portion of the floating-point value. Ada rounds float values to the nearest integer. If the float value is exactly halfway between two integers, rounding is to the integer farthest from zero. So 3.5 rounds to 4 and −2.5 rounds to −3.

To convert a value to another type, you enclose it in parentheses and precede it with the name of the type you want, as shown in these examples:

Expression	Value
`Float(67)`	`67.0`
`Integer(47.4)`	`47`
`Integer(-456.8)`	`-457`
`Float(14 rem 4)`	`2.0`
`Integer(4.4 + 5.3)`	`10`
`Integer(4.4) + Integer(5.3)`	`9`

You can use expressions involving explicit type conversions in assignment statements. If Avg_Weight and Sum are float variables and Num is an integer variable, the following statements are valid:

```
Avg_Weight := Sum / Float(Num);
Num        := (Num + 2) * Integer(Sum);
```

Frequent use of explicit type conversions in a program is an indication that you may have selected an inappropriate type for your data. The different data types help prevent us from combining values that should not be combined. Explicit type conversions defeat this protection. It is therefore good programming style to avoid the use of explicit type conversions. We look at this subject in greater detail in Chapter 7.

BACKGROUND INFORMATION

Strongly Typed Languages

As we have seen, Ada supports many different data types. It also provides ways of creating new data types. We take for granted that Ada checks our programs to ensure that we are not using incompatible types—for example, that we are not dividing an integer by a string. This aspect of Ada, however, is not found in every programming language. In the language C, it is possible to mix the use of data types freely; integers and characters are just patterns of bits, and the arithmetic operators can operate on both.

Languages such as Ada, for which it is possible to enforce type compatibility strictly, are said to be strongly typed. Ada is one of only a few languages that truly is strongly typed. Pascal, for example, often is said to be strongly typed, but it actually has an obscure loophole in its typing system that permits incompatible types to be mixed. Other languages, such as C, tout their lack of type checking as a feature.

Why would anyone want a language that doesn't have type checking? In writing software such as compilers and operating systems, it sometimes is convenient to be able to ignore the data type of a value. Thus some programmers may prefer languages that allow them easily to forego compatibility checking. Of course, doing so requires that they be especially careful when writing programs that use different types. It is a bit like performing a high-wire act without the benefit of a safety net!

The advantage of a strongly typed language is that it helps us to catch some of our programming mistakes—it ensures a certain amount of safety. In building large and complex software systems, the correct functioning of the programs may be more important than making certain operations more convenient for a programmer to code. For example, the program for a jetliner's autopilot must operate correctly even if the programmer has to make the effort to be explicit about type conversions. Strong typing is one of the aspects of Ada that supports the development of correct software. It has the side effect of making programmers think more carefully about their use of data types, and there is no substitute for extra thought in creating a correct program.

Formatting Output

Line Spaces and Blanks

There are two basic procedures in package Ada.Text_IO for formatting (organizing) output: New_Line and Put. To insert blank lines you should use the New_Line procedure, and to insert blank space within lines, use spaces enclosed in quotes as the Item parameter of the Put procedure. For example, if we wanted to produce the following pattern of output:

```
 *    *    *    *    *    *    *    *    *

*    *    *    *    *    *    *    *    *    *

 *    *    *    *    *    *    *    *    *
```

we would write the following Ada statements:

```
Ada.Text_IO.Put (Item => "  *    *    *    *    *    *    *    *    *");
Ada.Text_IO.New_Line;
Ada.Text_IO.New_Line;
Ada.Text_IO.Put (Item => "*    *    *    *    *    *    *    *    *    *");
Ada.Text_IO.New_Line (Spacing => 2);
Ada.Text_IO.Put (Item => "  *    *    *    *    *    *    *    *    *");
Ada.Text_IO.New_Line;
```

All of the blanks and asterisks are enclosed in quotes so that they will be printed just as they are written in the program. Notice the pair of calls to New_Line after the first call to procedure Put. The first call of the pair ends the line of asterisks and the second provides a blank line. A simpler method to accomplish the same results is illustrated in the call to New_Line after the second call to procedure Put. Here we used a parameter named Spacing to let the New_Line procedure know that we wanted two new lines.

Integer Numbers

Unless you specify otherwise, integer items are formatted automatically when they are printed. This automatic formatting varies from compiler to compiler. In this book we use the convention that integers are aligned automatically at the right in a field that is 10 character positions wide.

Ada does not confine us to automatic formatting. You can control the format of each integer you wish to display through an additional parameter, Width, in the call to procedure Put. The value given to Width specifies the number of columns the integer should occupy when it is output. The value of Item is printed right-justified; blanks are automatically inserted to the left to fill up the field. Let's look at some examples:

Put Statement	Output (❑ means blank)
`Ada.Integer_Text_IO.Put (Item => 7_132);`	❑❑❑❑❑❑7132
`Ada.Integer_Text_IO.Put (Item => 7_132, Width => 7);`	❑❑❑7132
`Ada.Integer_Text_IO.Put (Item => 7_132, Width => 5);`	❑7132
`Ada.Integer_Text_IO.Put (Item => 7_132, Width => 3);`	7132

These examples show that a comma is required to separate parameters in the parameter list. The last example shows that, if Width is not large enough for the Item value, Width is extended automatically to make room for all of the digits. This automatic extension is useful when you want a variable to print in as few columns as possible. If Width is given the value 1, the field always extends to just the number of places required to print the value. For example, if the variable Total has the value 149,573

```
Ada.Text_IO.Put (Item => "Total inventory is ");
Ada.Integer_Text_IO.Put (Item => Total, Width => 1);
Ada.Text_IO.Put (Item => " widgets. ");
Ada.Text_IO.New_Line;
```

will print

```
Total inventory is 149573 widgets.
```

If the value of Total is 6, the output is

```
Total inventory is 6 widgets.
```

If the value of Total is −1, the output is

```
Total inventory is -1 widgets.
```

Float Numbers

Float values are printed automatically in scientific (E) notation with one digit before the decimal point and the system's default (assumed) value for the number of digits after the decimal point. You can control the number of columns before the decimal point, the number of digits after the decimal point, and the number of digits in the exponent. Ada calls these three parts of the Float output value the Fore, Aft, and Exp fields as shown here (❑ means blank).

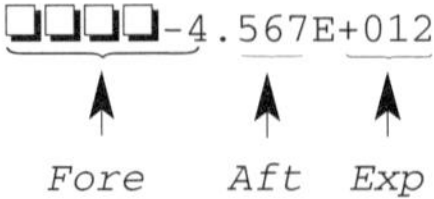

These field names are also the names of additional parameters that you may supply in your call to the Put procedure. The value of each of these parameters determines the width of the corresponding field.

The value of Exp determines the number of columns that the exponent will occupy. This width includes the required plus or minus sign. It does not include the letter E that comes before the exponent field. If you give Exp a value smaller than is necessary to display the sign and exponent, Exp is extended automatically. When you give Exp the value zero, however, no exponent is printed, and instead the float value is displayed in common decimal form.

Aft sets the number of digits displayed after the decimal point. The output is *rounded* to this number of decimal places. A decimal point is always printed. Even if you give Aft the value zero, one digit still displays to the right of the decimal point.

The Fore field can contain leading blanks, a minus sign (for negative numbers), and digits. The value of Fore determines the number of *columns* in this field. The number of *digits* printed in the Fore field depends on whether the number is being displayed in scientific notation or in common decimal form. If the number is being displayed in scientific notation (Exp is greater than zero), the Fore field will contain exactly one digit. On the other hand, if the number is being displayed in common decimal form (Exp is zero), the Fore field will have as many digits as are needed to represent the whole part of the number. No matter whether you choose scientific or common decimal notation, if you give Fore a value smaller than is necessary to display the digits and sign (for negative numbers), Fore will extend automatically.

Unless Exp or Fore is extended automatically, the total number of columns used to display a float value in scientific notation form is equal to *Fore + Aft + Exp + 2*. The 2 accounts for the decimal point and the letter E. A number displayed in common decimal form uses *Fore + Aft + 1* columns.

Let's look at some examples. First an example of a call to procedure Put showing the formatting parameters:

```
Ada.Float_Text_IO.Put (Item => 1_493.6,
                       Fore => 3,
                       Aft  => 5,
                       Exp  => 4);
```

You can write procedure calls on a single line or, like this example, spread over several lines. We believe that Ada programs are easier to read when procedure calls with more than two parameters are written with each name and value on a separate line. Whatever layout form you choose to use, the commas between parameters are always required. The order of the parameters is not important; the same results are obtained with the following statement:

```
Ada.Float_Text_IO.Put (Aft  => 5,
                       Item => 1_493.6,
                       Exp  => 4,
                       Fore => 3);
```

Now we'll look at some examples showing the effect of formatting parameters on output.

Item	Fore	Aft	Exp	Output (❏ means blank)
1_493.6	3	5	4	❏❏1.49360E+003
1_493.6	3	5	3	❏❏1.49360E+03
1_493.6	3	5	2	❏❏1.49360E+3
1_493.6	3	5	1	❏❏1.49360E+3
1_493.6	3	5	0	1493.60000
1_493.6	3	3	0	1493.600
1_493.6	4	3	0	1493.600
1_493.6	5	3	0	❏1493.600
1_493.6	6	3	0	❏❏1493.600

```
1_493.6   3     5     3     ❑❑1.49360E+03
1_493.6   3     4     3     ❑❑1.4936E+03
1_493.6   3     3     3     ❑❑1.494E+03
1_493.6   3     2     3     ❑❑1.49E+03
1_493.6   3     1     3     ❑❑1.5E+03
1_493.6   3     0     3     ❑❑1.5E+03

1_493.6   3     3     3     ❑❑1.494E+03
1_493.6   2     3     3     ❑1.494E+03
1_493.6   1     3     3     1.494E+03
```

MATTERS OF STYLE

Program Layout

As far as the compiler is concerned, Ada statements are free format: They can appear anywhere on a line, and more than one can appear on a line. One statement can extend over many lines as long as you do not break it in the middle of identifiers, reserved words, literals, or compound symbols (such as :=). It is extremely important that your programs be readable, both for your own sake and for the sake of anyone else who has to use them.

When you write an outline for an English paper, you follow certain rules of indentation to make it readable. These same kinds of rules can make your programs easier to read.

Take a look at the following program for computing the cost per square foot of a house. Although it compiles and runs correctly, it does not conform to any formatting standards.

```
with Ada.Text_IO; with Ada.Float_Text_IO;
procedure House_Cost is -- This program computes the cost per square foot of
-- living space for a house, given the dimensions of
-- the house, the number of stories, the size of the
-- nonliving space, and the total cost less land.
Width:constant Float:=30.0;        -- Width of the house
       Length:constant Float:=40.0;        -- Length of the house
Stories:constant Float:=2.5;         -- Number of full stories
   Price:constant Float:=150_000.0;      -- Selling price less land
Non_Living_Space:constant Float:=825.0;  -- Garage, closets, etc
Gross_Footage:Float;      -- Total square footage
Living_Footage:Float;      -- Living area
Cost_Per_Foot:Float;      -- Cost/foot of living area
begin  -- House Cost
Gross_Footage:=Length*Width*Stories;Living_Footage:=Gross_Footage
-Non_Living_Space;Cost_Per_Foot:=Price/Living_Footage;
Ada.Float_Text_IO.Put(Item=>Cost_Per_Foot,Fore=>4,Aft=>2,Exp=>0);
Ada.Text_IO.New_Line;end House_Cost;
```

Now look at the same program with proper formatting:

```
with Ada.Text_IO;
with Ada.Float_Text_IO;

procedure House_Cost is

-- This program computes the cost per square foot of
-- living space for a house, given the dimensions of
-- the house, the number of stories, the size of the
-- nonliving space, and the total cost less land.

   Width   : constant Float := 30.0;         -- Width of the house
   Length  : constant Float := 40.0;         -- Length of the house
   Stories : constant Float := 2.5;          -- Number of full stories
   Price   : constant Float := 150_000.0;    -- Selling price less land
   Non_Living_Space : constant Float := 825.0;  -- Garage, closets, etc

   Gross_Footage  : Float;     -- Total square footage
   Living_Footage : Float;     -- Living area
   Cost_Per_Foot  : Float;     -- Cost/foot of living area

begin  -- House Cost
   Gross_Footage  := Length * Width * Stories;
   Living_Footage := Gross_Footage - Non_Living_Space;
   Cost_Per_Foot  := Price / Living_Footage;
   Ada.Float_Text_IO.Put (Item => Cost_Per_Foot,
                          Fore => 4,
                          Aft  => 2,
                          Exp  => 0);
   Ada.Text_IO.New_Line;
end House_Cost;
```

Need we say more?

Appendix I talks about programming style. Use it as a guide when you are writing your programs.

The Use Package Clause

Throughout this book, we always prefix our use of an identifier from a package. This is done by preceding the identifier with the appropriate package names. For example, we use the statement

```
Ada.Text_IO.New_Line;
```

to call the procedure New_Line contained in package Text_IO, which is a child of package Ada.

Ada's `use` clause permits us to utilize package identifiers such as New_Line without prefixing. You put `use` clauses after the `with` clauses in a program's context clause. Here, for example, is Program Payroll from Chapter 1 rewritten using three `use` clauses.

```
with Ada.Text_IO;
use  Ada.Text_IO;
with Ada.Float_Text_IO;
use  Ada.Float_Text_IO;
with Ada.Integer_Text_IO;
use  Ada.Integer_Text_IO;

procedure Payroll is

-- This program computes the wages for each employee and the total payroll
-- for the company

   Max_Regular_Hours : constant Float  := 40.0;  -- Maximum normal work hours
   Overtime_Factor   : constant Float  :=  1.5;  -- Overtime pay rate factor
   Minimum_Wage      : constant Float  :=  5.75; -- Minimum hourly pay rate
   Maximum_Wage      : constant Float  := 99.99; -- Maximum hourly pay rate
   Payroll_File_Name : constant String := "Payfile.dat";

   ----------------------------------------------------------------------------
   procedure Calc_Pay (Rate  : in  Float;       -- Hourly pay
                       Hours : in  Float;       -- Hours this week
                       Pay   : out Float) is    -- Wages earned

   -- Calc_Pay computes an employee's pay from their pay rate and the hours
   -- worked this week, taking overtime into account

   begin    -- Procedure Calc_Pay
      if Hours > Max_Regular_Hours then
         Pay := Max_Regular_Hours * Rate
                + (Hours - Max_Regular_Hours) * Overtime_Factor * Rate;
      else
         Pay := Hours * Rate;
      end if;
   end Calc_Pay;

   ----------------------------------------------------------------------------
   Pay_Rate      : Float   range Minimum_Wage .. Maximum_Wage; -- Hourly pay rate
   Hours         : Float   range 0.0 .. 80.0;               -- Hours worked
   Wages         : Float   range 0.0 .. 8_000.00;           -- Wages earned
   Total         : Float   range 0.0 .. Float'Last;         -- Total payroll
```

```
   Employee_ID  : Integer range   0 .. 999;          -- Employee ID number
   Payroll_File : Ada.Text_IO.File_Type;             -- Company payroll file

begin     -- Program Payroll

   -- Create the output file
   Create (File => Payroll_File,
           Name => Payroll_File_Name);

   -- Initialize company total wages
   Total := 0.0;

   Employee_Loop:       -- Repeat for each employee
   loop
      -- Prompt for and get an employee's number
      Put (Item => "Enter employee number: ");
      Get (Item => Employee_ID);
                                                -- An employee number of zero
      exit Employee_Loop when Employee_ID = 0;  -- indicates we are finished and
                                                -- can exit the loop
      -- Prompt for and get the employee's pay rate
      Put (Item => "Enter pay rate: ");
      Get (Item => Pay_Rate);

      -- Prompt for and get the number of hours the employee worked this week
      Put (Item => "Enter hours worked: ");
      Get (Item => Hours);

      -- Determine the employee's wages
      Calc_Pay (Rate  => Pay_Rate,
                Hours => Hours,
                Pay   => Wages);

      -- Add this employee's wages to the company total
      Total := Total + Wages;

      -- Put results in the pay file
      Put (File => Payroll_File,  Item => Employee_ID);
      Put (File => Payroll_File,
           Item => Pay_Rate,
           Fore => 6,
           Aft  => 2,
           Exp  => 0);
      Put (File => Payroll_File,
           Item => Hours,
           Fore => 6,
           Aft  => 1,
           Exp  => 0);
```

```
      Put (File => Payroll_File,
           Item => Wages,
           Fore => 6,
           Aft  => 2,
           Exp  => 0);
      New_Line (File => Payroll_File);

   end loop Employee_Loop;

   -- Display the total payroll on the screen
   New_Line (Spacing => 2);
   Put (Item => "Total payroll is $");
   Put (Item => Total,
        Fore => 1,
        Aft  => 2,
        Exp  => 0);
   New_Line;

   -- Close the pay file
   Close (File => Payroll_File);

end Payroll;
```

Notice that none of the I/O procedure calls in this version of Program Payroll are prefixed.

When the Ada compiler comes across a call to a procedure without a prefix, it looks at all the packages named in `use` clauses and determines which procedure to call. The compiler examines the procedure name, the number of parameters, and the type of parameters in the procedure call to determine which package is appropriate. If the compiler is unable to make this determination, it will display an error message. The programmer must prefix each ambiguous procedure call with a package name.

The advantage to using a `use` clause is that you don't have to type so many characters when entering your Ada program. As Ada programs are often longer than BASIC, C, C++, and Java programs, this is attractive to programmers familiar with these languages.

The advantage of avoiding `use` clauses and prefixing all references to package identifiers is the additional documentation provided. For example, it is impossible to determine whether the identifier Part is of type Integer, Float, or String from this non-prefixed call to procedure Put:

```
Put (Item => Part);
```

To determine the type of Part, the reader of the program must search the declarative part of the program. In a large program such a search may take a significant amount of time. By prefixing the procedure call like this

```
Ada.Integer_Text_IO.Put (Item => Part);
```

it is immediately clear that Part is of type Integer. Ada was designed for writing large programs. In a program that contains hundreds of thousands of statements and hundreds of packages, the information supplied by prefixing is invaluable.

It is clear that the benefits of comments and meaningful variable names far outweigh the effort required to type the additional characters. We believe that the effort required to prefix all package identifiers is just as worthwhile. Therefore, nearly all of the examples in this text use prefixing rather than the `use` clause.

PROBLEM-SOLVING CASE STUDY

Mileage

Specification

Problem Write a program to calculate the miles per gallon a car gets on a trip, given the amounts in gallons of the fill-ups and the starting and ending mileage. The starting mileage was 67,308.0; the ending mileage, 68,750.7. During the trip, the car was filled up four times. The four amounts were 11.7, 14.3, 12.2, and 8.5 gallons. Assume that the tank is full initially and that the last fill-up was at the end of the trip.

Output The quantities on which the calculations are based and the computed miles per gallon rounded off to the nearest whole number, all appropriately labeled.

Discussion If you calculated this by hand, you would add up the gallon amounts, then divide the sum into the mileage traveled, and round the result off to the nearest whole number. The mileage traveled is, of course, just the ending mileage minus the starting mileage. This is essentially the algorithm we use in the program. Let's make all of the quantities constants so that it will be easier to change the program later. Here is the algorithmic solution.

```
Amt1 := 11.7
Amt2 := 14.3
Amt3 := 12.2
Amt4 := 8.5

Start_Miles := 67,308.0
End_Miles := 68,750.7

MPG := Integer ( (End_Miles - Start_Miles) / (Amt1+Amt2+Amt3+Amt4) )
```

PROBLEM-SOLVING CASE STUDY cont'd.

Write the fill-up amounts
Write a blank line
Write the starting mileage
Write the ending mileage
Write a blank line
Write the mileage per gallon

Object Modeling From the algorithm we can create tables of constants and variables that will help us write the declarative part of the program.

Constants

Name	Value	Role
Amt1	11.7	Number of gallons for fill-up 1
Amt2	14.3	Number of gallons for fill-up 2
Amt3	12.2	Number of gallons for fill-up 3
Amt4	8.5	Number of gallons for fill-up 4
Start Miles	67,308.0	Starting mileage
End Miles	68,750.7	Ending mileage

Variables

Name	Data Type and Range	Role
MPG	Integer, 4 to 100	Computed miles per gallon

Now we're ready to write the program. Let's call it Mileage. We can take the declarations from the table and create the program statements from the algorithm. Program comments are also taken from the table and algorithm. We must also label the output and format it neatly.

Program

```
with Ada.Text_IO;
with Ada.Float_Text_IO;
with Ada.Integer_Text_IO;

procedure Mileage is

-- This program computes miles per gallon given four amounts
-- for gallons used, and starting and ending mileages

   Amt1 : constant Float := 11.7;       -- Number of gallons for fill-up 1
   Amt2 : constant Float := 14.3;       -- Number of gallons for fill-up 2
   Amt3 : constant Float := 12.2;       -- Number of gallons for fill-up 3
   Amt4 : constant Float :=  8.5;       -- Number of gallons for fill-up 4
```

PROBLEM-SOLVING CASE STUDY cont'd.

```
   Start_Miles : constant Float := 67_308.0;   -- Starting mileage
   End_Miles   : constant Float := 68_750.7;   -- Ending mileage

   MPG : Integer range 4 .. 100;               -- Computed miles per gallon

begin      -- Mileage
   MPG := Integer( (End_Miles - Start_Miles) / (Amt1 + Amt2 + Amt3 + Amt4) );
   Ada.Text_IO.Put (Item => "For the gallon amounts: ");
   Ada.Text_IO.New_Line (Spacing => 1);
   Ada.Float_Text_IO.Put (Item => Amt1,
                          Fore => 4,
                          Aft  => 1,
                          Exp  => 0);
   Ada.Text_IO.Put (Item => ',');
   Ada.Float_Text_IO.Put (Item => Amt2,
                          Fore => 4,
                          Aft  => 1,
                          Exp  => 0);
   Ada.Text_IO.Put (Item => ',');
   Ada.Float_Text_IO.Put (Item => Amt3,
                          Fore => 4,
                          Aft  => 1,
                          Exp  => 0);
   Ada.Text_IO.Put (Item => ',');
   Ada.Float_Text_IO.Put (Item => Amt4,
                          Fore => 4,
                          Aft  => 1,
                          Exp  => 0);
   Ada.Text_IO.New_Line (Spacing => 2);
   Ada.Text_IO.Put  (Item => "a starting mileage of ");
   Ada.Float_Text_IO.Put (Item => Start_Miles,
                          Fore => 6,
                          Aft  => 1,
                          Exp  => 0);
   Ada.Text_IO.New_Line (Spacing => 1);
   Ada.Text_IO.Put (Item => "and an ending mileage of ");
   Ada.Float_Text_IO.Put (Item => End_Miles,
                          Fore => 6,
                          Aft  => 1,
                          Exp  => 0);
   Ada.Text_IO.New_Line (Spacing => 2);
   Ada.Text_IO.Put (Item => "the mileage per gallon is ");
   Ada.Integer_Text_IO.Put (Item  => MPG,
                            Width => 3);
   Ada.Text_IO.New_Line (Spacing => 1);

end Mileage;
```

PROBLEM-SOLVING CASE STUDY *cont'd.*

The output from this program is

```
For the gallon amounts:
  11.7,  14.3,  12.2,   8.5

a starting mileage of  67308.0
and an ending mileage of  68750.7

the mileage per gallon is  31
```

PROBLEM-SOLVING CASE STUDY

Filling Down Comforters

Specification

Problem The Champlain Quilt company manufactures a line of goose down-filled comforters and is preparing to bid on a project that will require it to fill its quilts with different grades of down. The weight of down required to fill a quilt depends on the down's density and the volume of quilt to be filled. The company has hired you to write a program that will compute the volume of down required and the weight and the cost of filling the quilt.

Output The filling volume of the quilt, in cubic inches. The weight of down and cost to fill the quilt with the three different grades of down.

Discussion From interviewing the company's engineers, you learn that their quilts are built by sewing cotton fabric to form a dozen $6\frac{1}{4}$-inch-diameter tubes that are filled with down. Each quilt is 104 inches long. One ounce of premium-grade goose down fills up 1000 cubic inches; one ounce of ordinary-grade down fills up 700 cubic inches; and one ounce of low-grade down fills up 500 cubic inches. The three grades of down cost $0.97, $0.54, and $0.32 per ounce. In a math text, you find that the volume of a cylinder can be calculated from the formula

$$\pi r^2 h$$

where r is the radius of the cylinder and h is its height. The height of the quilt's cylinders is the length of the quilt.

Our first job is to divide the diameter of a quilt cylinder in half to get the radius. Then we can apply the formula to get the volume of each cylinder. We calculate the total volume needed to fill the quilt by multiplying

PROBLEM-SOLVING CASE STUDY *cont'd.*

the volume per cylinder by the number of cylinders making up the quilt. To determine the weight of down to fill a quilt, we must divide the total volume by the loft of each of the three grades of down. Finally, we determine the total cost by multiplying the weight by the cost per ounce of down. Here's the algorithm:

```
Radius := Diameter / 2
Tube volume := π * Radius ** 2 * Length
Fill Volume := 12 * Tube Volume
Premium Weight := Fill Volume / Premium Loft
Ordinary Weight := Fill Volume / Ordinary Loft
Economy Weight := Fill Volume / Economy Loft
Premium Cost := Premium Weight * Premium Price
Ordinary Cost := Ordinary Weight * Ordinary Price
Economy Cost := Economy Weight * Economy Price
Display Fill Volume
Display Premium Weight
Display Premium Cost
Display Ordinary Weight
Display Ordinary Cost
Display Economy Weight
Display Economy Cost
```

Object Modeling From the algorithm we can create a table of quantities and variables to help us write the declarative part of the program.

Constants

Name	Value	Role
Diameter	6.25	Diameter of a quilt cylinder
Length	104.0	Length of a quilt
Num Cylinders	12	Number of cylinders in a quilt
Premium Loft	1,000.0	Cubic inches for 1 oz premium down
Ordinary Loft	700.0	Cubic inches for 1 oz ordinary down
Economy Loft	500.0	Cubic inches for 1 oz economy down
Premium Price	0.97	Dollars per oz of premium down
Ordinary Price	0.54	Dollars per oz of ordinary down
Economy Price	0.32	Dollars per oz of economy down
Pi	3.14159265	Ratio of circumference to diameter

Variables

Name	Value	Radius
Radius	Float, positive	Radius of a quilt cylinder
Tube Volume	Float, positive	Volume of a quilt cylinder

PROBLEM-SOLVING CASE STUDY cont'd.

`Fill Volume`	`Float, positive`	Total volume to fill a quilt
`Premium Weight`	`Float, positive`	Oz of premium down to fill a quilt
`Ordinary Weight`	`Float, positive`	Oz of ordinary down to fill a quilt
`Economy Weight`	`Float, positive`	Oz of economy down to fill a quilt
`Premium Cost`	`Float, positive`	Cost to fill a quilt with premium down
`Ordinary Cost`	`Float, positive`	Cost to fill a quilt with ordinary down
`Economy Cost`	`Float, positive`	Cost to fill a quilt with economy down

Now we're ready to write the program, which we'll call Quilt. We can take the declarations from the tables and the program statements from the algorithm. We have labeled the output with explanatory messages and formatted it with appropriate field widths. We've also added comments where needed.

Program

```
with Ada.Text_IO;
with Ada.Float_Text_IO;

procedure Quilt is

-- This program computes the weight of down required and the cost of
-- filling quilts with each of three different grades of goose down
-- given the lofts and costs of each grade

   -- Dimensions of tubes to be filled with down (inches)
   Diameter : constant Float := 6.25;
   Length   : constant Float := 104.0;

   Num_Tubes : constant Integer := 12;     -- Tubes per quilt

   -- Lofts of different down grades (cubic inches per ounce)
   Premium_Loft  : constant Float := 1_000.0;
   Ordinary_Loft : constant Float :=   700.0;
   Economy_Loft  : constant Float :=   500.0;

   -- Price (in dollars) per ounce of different down grades
   Premium_Price  : constant Float := 0.97;
   Ordinary_Price : constant Float := 0.54;
   Economy_Price  : constant Float := 0.32;

   Pi : constant Float := 3.14159265;  -- Ratio of circumference to diameter
```

PROBLEM-SOLVING CASE STUDY cont'd.

```
Radius       : Float range 0.0..Float'Last; -- Radius of a tube (inches)
Tube_Volume  : Float range 0.0..Float'Last; -- Volume of a tube (cubic inches)
Total_Volume : Float range 0.0..Float'Last; -- Volume of quilt (cubic inches)

-- Weights of different down grades to fill a quilt (ounces)
Premium_Weight  : Float range 0.0..Float'Last;
Ordinary_Weight : Float range 0.0..Float'Last;
Economy_Weight  : Float range 0.0..Float'Last;

-- Cost to fill a quilt with different down grades (dollars)
Premium_Cost  : Float range 0.0..Float'Last;
Ordinary_Cost : Float range 0.0..Float'Last;
Economy_Cost  : Float range 0.0..Float'Last;

begin
-- Compute volume of down needed to fill a quilt
Radius := Diameter / 2.0;
Tube_Volume := Pi * Radius ** 2 * Length;
Total_Volume := Float(Num_Tubes) * Tube_Volume;

-- Compute weights and costs of different grade downs to fill a quilt
Premium_Weight  := Total_Volume / Premium_Loft;
Premium_Cost    := Premium_Weight * Premium_Price;
Ordinary_Weight := Total_Volume / Ordinary_Loft;
Ordinary_Cost   := Ordinary_Weight * Ordinary_Price;
Economy_Weight  := Total_Volume / Economy_Loft;
Economy_Cost    := Economy_Weight * Economy_Price;

-- Display the results
Ada.Text_IO.Put  (Item => "It requires ");
Ada.Float_Text_IO.Put (Item => Total_Volume,
                       Fore => 1,
                       Aft  => 2,
                       Exp  => 0);
Ada.Text_IO.Put  (Item => " cubic inches of down to fill a quilt.");
Ada.Text_IO.New_Line (Spacing => 2);
Ada.Text_IO.Put (Item => "The weight and cost for");
Ada.Text_IO.New_Line;
Ada.Text_IO.Put  (Item => "   Premium down is ");
Ada.Float_Text_IO.Put (Item => Premium_Weight,
                       Fore => 6,
                       Aft  => 2,
                       Exp  => 0);
Ada.Text_IO.Put  (Item => " ounces    $");
Ada.Float_Text_IO.Put (Item => Premium_Cost,
                       Fore => 1,
                       Aft  => 2,
                       Exp  => 0);
```

PROBLEM-SOLVING CASE STUDY cont'd.

```
   Ada.Text_IO.New_Line;
   Ada.Text_IO.Put  (Item => "    Ordinary down is");
   Ada.Float_Text_IO.Put (Item => Ordinary_Weight,
                          Fore => 6,
                          Aft  => 2,
                          Exp  => 0);
   Ada.Text_IO.Put  (Item => " ounces     $");
   Ada.Float_Text_IO.Put (Item => Ordinary_Cost,
                          Fore => 1,
                          Aft  => 2,
                          Exp  => 0);
   Ada.Text_IO.New_Line;
   Ada.Text_IO.Put  (Item => "    Economy down is ");
   Ada.Float_Text_IO.Put (Item => Economy_Weight,
                          Fore => 6,
                          Aft  => 2,
                          Exp  => 0);
   Ada.Text_IO.Put  (Item => " ounces     $");
   Ada.Float_Text_IO.Put (Item => Economy_Cost,
                          Fore => 1,
                          Aft  => 2,
                          Exp  => 0);
   Ada.Text_IO.New_Line;
end Quilt;
```

Notice how most of the comments in this program are taken directly from our algorithm or tables of quantities and variables. The output from this program is

```
It requires 38288.16 cubic inches of down to fill a quilt.

The weight and cost for
   Premium down is     38.29 ounces     $37.14
   Ordinary down is    54.70 ounces     $29.54
   Economy down is     76.58 ounces     $24.50
```

Testing and Debugging

Beginning Ada programmers are sometimes frustrated by the large number of compile-time errors generated during the initial compilation of their programs. These errors are usually the result of violations of Ada syntax. Learning to understand EBNF definitions and making use of Appendix B will help you learn Ada's syntax. Study the examples given in the text and compare them to your code. While we encourage you to work on your own, don't spend hours trying to decipher a syntax error. Seek help from someone more experienced with Ada programming who has probably seen that error message dozens of times.

One syntax error in a program can cause the compiler to report many errors. For example, misspelling the word "Float" in a variable declaration will probably result in an error message for the declaration and an error message for *every* line of the program that contains that variable. Only the first of the reported errors is real. The other reported errors, called secondary errors or cascaded errors, are a direct consequence of the first error. To avoid laboring on secondary error messages, correct the errors in the order given by the compiler.

The locations of errors and the messages given by a compiler when it detects an error are not always accurate. If you can't find anything wrong with the line that the compiler indicates is incorrect, look at the lines preceding it. Understanding the meaning of the various error messages given by your compiler takes practice. Programming Warm-up Exercise 7 will help you learn the meaning of some of the more common error messages you will encounter.

Testing and Debugging Hints

1. Every Ada statement and declaration ends with a semicolon.
2. Remember that a program ends with `end` followed by the program name and a semicolon.
3. You must declare every identifier that isn't predefined by Ada. If you use a name that you haven't declared, you will get an error message.
4. Double-check every expression according to the precedence rules to be sure that the operations are performed in the necessary order.
5. When possible, avoid using explicit type conversions.
6. For each assignment statement, check that the expression result has the same data type as the variable to the left of the :=.
7. If the cause of an error in a program is not obvious, leave the computer and study a printed listing. Change your program only after you understand the source of the error.
8. Check output generated against your hand-calculated results. Just because your program produces output does not necessarily mean that it is correct output. Remember logical errors.

Summary

The syntax (grammar) of the Ada language is defined by a metalanguage. In this text we use a form of metalanguage called Extended Backus-Naur Form (EBNF). We describe the semantics (meaning) of Ada statements in English.

Identifiers are used in Ada to name things. Some identifiers are predefined; others are defined by the programmer. Ada includes 69 predefined identifiers called *reserved words*. The identifiers you can use are restricted to those not reserved by the Ada language. Ada's reserved words are listed in Appendix A.

Identifiers are associated with memory locations by declarations. A declaration may give a name to a location whose value does not change (a constant) or to one whose value does change (a variable). Every constant or variable has an associated data type. The basic predefined data types in Ada are Integer, Float, Boolean, and String.

You can use the assignment operator to change the value of a variable by assigning it the value of an expression. Expressions can contain more than one operator. The order in which the operations are performed is determined by precedence rules. Absolute value and exponentiation are performed first; then multiplication and division; then unary addition (identity) and subtraction (negation); and finally binary addition and subtraction. Multiple operations of the same class are performed from left to right. You can use parentheses to override the precedence rules.

A procedure is a subprogram called (used) by writing its name, often followed by a list of parameters. Your program communicates with a subprogram using the parameters. Each parameter in the list has a name and a value.

The package Text_IO contains a Put procedure that you can use to display string data and a New_Line procedure to terminate output lines and control the spacing between lines. Package Float_Text_IO contains a Put procedure to display floating-point numbers, and package Integer_Text_IO contains a Put procedure to display integer numbers.

You can control the format of numeric output by supplying the Put procedure with additional parameters.

Quick Check

1. Use the following EBNF definition to decide whether your last name is a valid Ada identifier. (pp. 48–50)

```
identifier          ::=  letter{[ _ ]letter_or_digit}
letter_or_digit     ::=  letter | digit
letter              ::=  upper_case_letter | lower_case_letter
upper_case_letter   ::=  A | B | C | D | E | F | G | H | I | J |
                         K | L | M | N | O | P | Q | R | S | T |
                         U | V | W | X | Y | Z
lower_case_letter   ::=  a | b | c | d | e | f | g | h | i | j |
                         k | l | m | n | o | p | q | r | s | t |
                         u | v | w | x | y | z
digit               ::=  0 | 1 | 2 | 3 | 4 | 5 | 6 | 7 | 8 | 9
```

2. Define an Ada constant that gives the name Pi to the value 3.14159. (p. 59)
3. Which of the following words are Ada reserved words? (*Hint:* Look in Appendix A.)

```
begin   pi   procedure   integer   Max_Int
```

4. Declare an integer variable called Count, a float variable called Sum, and a string variable called Description. (pp. 60–61)
5. Assign the value 10 to the integer variable Toes. (pp. 62–64)
6. You want to divide 9 by 5.
   a. How would you write the expression if you want the quotient to be a floating-point number?
   b. How would you write it if you want the quotient to be an integer number? (pp. 64–66)
7. What is the value of the following Ada expression? (p. 65)

```
5 / 2
```

8. Write a Put statement to print out the title of this book (*Programming and Problem Solving with Ada 95*). (pp. 68–70)
9. What will the following statements print out? (p. 71)

```
Ada.Text_IO.Put (Item => "The answer is ");
Ada.Integer_Text_IO.Put (Item => 2 + 2);
Ada.Text_IO.New_Line;
```

10. Fill in the blanks in the following Ada program.

```
with ____________________;
with ____________________;
__________________ Circle is

   -- Constants

Pi : ______________ ______________ := 3.14159;   -- Ratio of circumference
                                                  -- to diameter

   -- Variables

   Circumference : __________________ __   -- The computed circumference
                                           -- of the circle

______________    -- Circle
```

```
Circumference ___ 2.0  *  Pi  *  7.0 __
   Ada.Text_IO.Put  (___________ => "The circumference of a circle of ");
   Ada.Text_IO.Put  (___________ => "radius 7 is ");
   Ada.Float_Text_IO.Put (___________=> Circumference);
   _________.New_Line;

____________ Circle __
```

(pp. 74–75)

11. What does an explicit type conversion from a float value to an integer value do with the fractional part of the float value? (p. 83)
12. What should you do if a program fails to run correctly and the reason for the error is not immediately obvious? (p. 79)
13. How would you write the following formula as an Ada expression that produces a float value as a result?

$$\frac{9}{5}C + 32$$

(pp. 79–82)

14. What is the result of evaluating the following expression?

$$(1 + 2 \times 2) / 1 + 1$$

(pp. 79–82)

15. Assume a float variable called Pay contains the amount 327.66101. Write a Put statement to print it in dollars and cents with three leading blanks. (pp. 87–88)

Answers

1. Unless your last name is hyphenated, it is probably a valid Ada identifier. **2.** `Pi : constant float := 3.14159;` **3.** `begin` and `procedure` are the only reserved words in the list.

4.
```
Count       : Integer;
Sum         : Float ;
Description : String (1..10);
```

5. `Toes := 10;` **6.** 9.0 / 5.0 gives a float result; 9 / 5 gives an integer result. **7.** 2

8. `Ada.Text_IO.Put (Item => "Programming and Problem Solving with Ada 95");`

9. `The answer is          4`

10.
```
with Ada.Text_IO;
with Ada.Float_Text_IO;
procedure Circle is

   -- Constants

Pi : constant Float := 3.14159;      -- Ratio of circumference
                                     -- to diameter

   -- Variables

   Circumference : Float ;       -- The computed circumference
                                 -- of the circle

begin    -- Circle

   Circumference := 2.0 * Pi * 7.0 ;
   Ada.Text_IO.Put (Item => "The circumference of a circle of ");
   Ada.Text_IO.Put (Item => "radius 7 is ");
   Ada.Float_Text_IO.Put (Item => Circumference);
   Ada.Text_IO.New_Line;

end Circle ;
```

11. Rounded to the nearest whole number. **12.** Get a fresh printout of the program, leave the computer, and study the program until you understand the cause of the problem. Then correct the algorithm and the program as necessary before going back to the computer and making any changes to the program file. **13.** `9.0 / 5.0 * C + 32.0` **14.** The result is 6. **15.**

```
Ada.Float_Text_IO.Put (Item => Pay,
                       Fore => 6,
                       Aft  => 2
                       Exp  => 0);
```

Exam Preparation Exercises

1. Mark the following as valid or invalid identifiers:

		Valid	Invalid
a.	Item#1	______	______
b.	Data	______	______
c.	Y	______	______
d.	1Set	______	______
e.	Investment	______	______
f.	Bin-2	______	______
g.	Num5	______	______
h.	Sq Ft	______	______
i.	Big_Foot	______	______

2. Given the EBNF definitions:

```
dwit     ::=  twitnit{twitnit}
twitnit  ::=  twit{twit}nit{nit}
twit     ::=  X | Y | Z
nit      ::=  1 | 2 | 3
```

mark the following "dwits" as either valid or invalid:

	Valid	**Invalid**
a. XYZ	________	________
b. 123	________	________
c. X1	________	________
d. 23Y	________	________
e. XY12	________	________
f. Y2Y	________	________
g. XY2	________	________
h. XY23X1	________	________

3. Using the EBNF definitions given for *Label* in Appendix B, mark each of the following labels as valid or invalid:

Label	**Valid**	**Invalid**
a. Hello	________	________
b. Good Bye	________	________
c. <Hello>	________	________
d. <<Hello>>	________	________
e. <<Good_Bye>>	________	________

4. Using the EBNF definition for *mode* given in Appendix B, mark each of the following modes as valid or invalid:

Mode	**Valid**	**Invalid**
a. in	________	________
b. out	________	________
c. in out	________	________
d.	________	________
e. inout	________	________

5. Using the EBNF definition for *relational_operator* given in Appendix B, mark each of the following relational operators as valid or invalid:

Relational Operator	**Valid**	**Invalid**
a. =	________	________
b. :=	________	________
c. not	________	________
d. <>	________	________
e. <=	________	________
f. < =	________	________
g. not =	________	________
h. /=	________	________
i. |	________	________
j. =<	________	________
k. ;	________	________

6. Using the EBNF definition for *enumeration_literal* given in Appendix B, mark each of the following enumeration literals as valid or invalid. Note that graphic_character is not defined in the Ada syntax summary in Appendix B. You may assume that a graphic character is any character present on your keyboard:

Enumeration Literal	**Valid**	**Invalid**
a. Hello	______	______
b. Good Bye	______	______
c. 'A'	______	______
d. '$'	______	______
e. "H"	______	______
f. constant	______	______

7. Formatting a program incorrectly causes an error. (True or False?)
8. Mark the following constructs as either valid or invalid. Assume all variables are of type Integer.

Construct	**Valid**	**Invalid**
a. `X * Y := c`	______	______
b. `Y := Con;`	______	______
c. `X : constant Integer;`	______	______
d. `X : integer;`	______	______
e. `A := B rem C;`	______	______

9. Match each of the following terms to the correct definition. There is only one correct definition for each term.

____ a. program
____ b. algorithm
____ c. compiler
____ d. identifier
____ e. translation phase
____ f. execution phase
____ g. variable
____ h. constant
____ i. memory
____ j. syntax
____ k. semantics

(1) A symbolic name made up of letters, digits, and underline characters but beginning with a letter
(2) A place in memory where a data value that cannot be changed is stored
(3) A program that takes a program written in a high-level language and translates it into machine code
(4) An input device
(5) The time spent planning a program
(6) Grammar rules
(7) Meaning
(8) A program that translates assembly language instructions into machine code
(9) When the machine code version of a program is being run
(10) A place in memory where a data value that can be changed is stored
(11) When a program in a high-level language is translated into machine code
(12) The part of the computer that holds both program and data
(13) A step-by-step outline for solving a problem
(14) A sequence of instructions to a computer to perform a particular task

10. Compute the value of each expression if it is a legal expression. If the expression is not legal, indicate why.
    a. `10.0 / 3.0 + 5.0 * 2.0`
    b. `10 rem 3 + 5 rem 2`
    c. `10 / 3 + 5 / 2`
    d. `12.5 + (2.5 / (6.2 / 3))`
    e. `-4 * (-5 + 6)`
    f. `13 rem 5 / 3`
    g. `(10 / 3 rem 2) / 3`
    h. `5.0 rem 3.0`
11. What is the value of Result in each of the following statements (assume Result is Integer)?
    a. `Result := 15 rem 4;`
    b. `Result := 7 / 3 + 2;`
    c. `Result := 2 + 7 * 5;`
    d. `Result := 45 / 8 * 4 + 2;`
    e. `Result := 17+(21 rem 6) * 2;`
    f. `Result := (4 * 2 + 2) ** 2;`
12. Which of the following are reserved words and which are user-defined identifiers?

	Reserved	User-Defined
a. end	________	________
b. sort	________	________
c. put	________	________
d. rem	________	________
e. The_End	________	________

13. Reserved words can be used as variable names. (True or False?)
14. If A = 5 and B = 2, show what each of the following statements produces:

```
Ada.Text_IO.Put            (Item => "A = ");
Ada.Integer_Text_IO.Put (Item =>  A);
Ada.Text_IO.Put            (Item => " B = ");
Ada.Integer_Text_IO.Put (Item => B);
Ada.Text_IO.New_Line;

Ada.Text_IO.Put            (Item => "Sum = ");
Ada.Integer_Text_IO.Put (Item =>  A + B);
Ada.Text_IO.New_Line;

Ada.Text_IO.Put            (Item => "Sum = ");
Ada.Integer_Text_IO.Put (Item =>  A / B);
Ada.Text_IO.New_Line;

Ada.Text_IO.Put            (Item => "Sum = ");
Ada.Integer_Text_IO.Put (Item =>  B - A);
Ada.Text_IO.New_Line;
```

15. Name two things that contribute to the readability of programs.
16. What is the purpose of the context clause in an Ada program? Of the declarative part?
17. What does the following program print?

```
with Ada.Text_IO;
with Ada.Integer_Text_IO;

procedure Exercise_17 is

   Pounds : constant := 10;

   Price  : Integer;
   Cost   : Integer;
   Ch     : String (1..1);
begin   -- Exercise_17
   Price := 30;
   Cost  := Price * Pounds;
   Ch := "A";
   Ada.Text_IO.Put (Item => "Cost is ");
   Ada.Text_IO.New_Line;
   Ada.Integer_Text_IO.Put (Item => Cost);
   Ada.Text_IO.New_Line;
   Ada.Text_IO.Put (Item => "Price is ");
   Ada.Integer_Text_IO.Put (Item => Price);
   Ada.Text_IO.Put (Item => "Cost is ");
   Ada.Integer_Text_IO.Put (Item => Cost);
   Ada.Text_IO.New_Line;
   Ada.Text_IO.Put (Item => "Grade ");
   Ada.Text_IO.Put (Item => Ch);
   Ada.Text_IO.Put (Item => " costs ");
   Ada.Text_IO.New_Line;
   Ada.Integer_Text_IO.Put (Item => Cost);
   Ada.Text_IO.New_Line;
end Exercise_17;
```

18. Translate the following Ada code into algebraic notation.

```
R1 := (-B + B ** 2 - (4 * A * C)) / (2 * A);
```

19. Given the following variable declarations, write the value determined by each of the following expressions. If the result is Float, include the decimal point in your answer.

```
X : Integer;
Y : Integer;
Z : Float;
```

For X = 4,
Y = 17, and
Z = 2.6

(a) `X / Y`
(b) `1.0 / Float(X) + 2.0`
(c) `Z * Float(Y)`
(d) `X + Y rem X`
(e) `14 / 15 * 2`
(f) `2 * X + Y - X`
(g) `X / 2`
(h) `2 * 3 - 1 rem 3`
(i) `X rem Y / X`

20. What is the output of the following Ada program? Assume a default Width of 10 if no Width parameter is specified. Be sure to use a ❑ to indicate each blank.

```
with Ada.Text_IO;
with Ada.Float_Text_IO;
With Ada.Integer_Text_IO;

procedure Assignment is

   Ch : String (1..1);
   X  : Integer;
   Y  : Float;

begin   -- Assignment
   Ch := "A";
   Ada.Text_IO.Put (Item => Ch);
   Ch := "B";
   Ada.Text_IO.Put (Item => Ch);
   Ada.Text_IO.New_Line;
   X := 413;
   Y := 21.8;
   Ada.Integer_Text_IO.Put (Item => X);
   Ada.Text_IO.Put (Item => " is the value of X");
   Ada.Text_IO.New_Line;
   Ada.Float_Text_IO.Put (Item => Y);
   Ada.Text_IO.Put (Item => " is the value of Y");
   Ada.Text_IO.New_Line;
end Assignment;
```

21. Write a short (300 word) essay on the value of sensible identifiers and comments in a program.

Programming Warm-up Exercises

1. Change the program in Exam Preparation Exercise 17 so that it prints the cost for 15 pounds.

2. Write the Ada expression for the following algebraic formula. Assume that *e* and π are float values and *n* is an integer value. The result should be a float value.

$$2 \pi e^{-n} n^n$$

3. Use an editor to create the following program. Fill in the information in comment lines within parentheses. Compile and run it.

```
with Ada.Text_IO;
with Ada.Float_Text_IO;

procedure Exercise_3 is

-- Programming Assignment One
-- (your name)
-- (date copied and run)
-- (description of the problem)

   -- Constants
   Debt          : constant Float := 300.00;    -- Original value owed
   Payment       : constant Float :=  22.40;    -- Payment
   Interest_Rate : constant Float :=   0.02;    -- Interest rate

   -- Variables
   Charge    : Float;       -- Interest times debt
   Reduction : Float;       -- Amount debt is reduced
   Remaining : Float;       -- Remaining balance

begin  -- Exercise 3
   Charge    := Interest_Rate * Debt;
   Reduction := Payment - Charge;
   Remaining := Debt - Reduction ;
   Ada.Text_IO.Put  (Item => "Payment ");
   Ada.Float_Text_IO.Put (Item => Payment,
                          Fore => 1,
                          Aft  => 2,
                          Exp  => 0);
   Ada.Text_IO.New_Line;
   Ada.Text_IO.Put  (Item => "Charge ");
   Ada.Float_Text_IO.Put (Item => Charge,
                          Fore => 1,
                          Aft  => 2,
                          Exp  => 0);
   Ada.Text_IO.New_Line;
   Ada.Text_IO.Put  (Item => "Balance owed ");
   Ada.Float_Text_IO.Put (Item => Remaining,
```

```
                              Fore => 1,
                              Aft  => 2,
                              Exp  => 0);
   Ada.Text_IO.New_Line;

end Exercise_3;
```

4. Copy and run the following program. Fill in the comments by using the pattern shown in Exercise 3. Such information is entered for the benefit of someone reading the program.

```
with Ada.Text_IO;
with Ada.Float_Text_IO;

procedure Exercise_4 is

   Total_Cost : constant Float   := 600.0;
   Pounds     : constant Integer :=  10;
   Ounces     : constant Integer :=  11;

   Total_Oz   : Integer;
   Unit_Cost  : Float;

begin  -- Exercise 4
   Total_Oz  := 16 * Pounds;
   Total_Oz  := Total_Oz + Ounces;
   Unit_Cost := Total_Cost / Float(Total_Oz);
   Ada.Text_IO.Put   (Item => "Cost per unit ");
   Ada.Float_Text_IO.Put (Item => Unit_Cost,
                          Fore => 1,
                          Aft  => 3,
                          Exp  => 0);
   Ada.Text_IO.New_Line;
end Exercise_4;
```

(Notice how hard it is to tell what the program does without the comments already in the code.)

5. Complete the following Ada program. The program should find and output the perimeter and area of a rectangle given the length and the width. Be sure to label the output. And don't forget to use comments.

```
with Ada.Text_IO;
With Ada.Float_Text_IO;

procedure Rectangle is

   -- This program finds the perimeter and the area of a rectangle
   -- given the length and width.
```

```
   -- Variables
   Length    : Float;     -- The length of the rectangle
   Width     : Float;     -- The width of the rectangle
   Perimeter : Float;     -- The perimeter of the rectangle
   Area      : Float;     -- The area of the rectangle

begin  -- Rectangle

   Length := 10.0;       -- Assigns a value to Length
   Width  :=  5.0;       -- Assigns a value to Width

   -- Fill in the rest of this program
   -- Don't forget to use comments

end Rectangle;
```

6. Write an assignment statement to calculate the sum of the numbers from 1 to N using Gauss's formula:

$$Sum = [\, N(N + 1) \,] / 2$$

   Store the result in the integer variable Sum.

7. The syntax error messages displayed by a compiler are sometimes confusing. In this exercise you will become more familiar with some of the common syntax error messages produced by your Ada compiler. Enter, compile, and run the program given in Programming Warm-up Exercise 3. Then make each of the following changes and compile the program and observe the syntax error message your compiler produces. *Be sure to have only one of these errors in your program at a time.* That is, undo each change before making the next one.
   (a) Leave out the context clause "with Ada.Text_IO;"
   (b) Substitute "procedre" for "procedure"
   (c) In the first assignment statement of the program, replace the underscore character in the variable Interest_Rate with a blank
   (d) Leave out the declaration of the variable Charge
   (e) Leave off the semicolon in the declaration of the variable Charge
   (f) Leave off the semicolon in the first executable statement
   (g) Use a value of 2.5 instead of 2 for an Aft parameter in one of the Put statements
   (h) Leave off "Ada.Text_IO." in one of the New_Line statements
   (i) Misspell the parameter name Aft in one of the Put statements

Programming Problems

1. Write an Ada program that will print your initials in large block letters, with each letter made up of the same character it represents. The letters should be a minimum of seven printed lines high and should appear in a row. For example, if your initials are DOW, your program should print out

```
DDDDDDD          OOOOO          W           W
D       D       O     O         W           W
D        D     O       O        W           W
D        D     O       O        W     W     W
D        D     O       O        W   W   W   W
D       D       O     O         W W       W W
DDDDDDD          OOOOO          WW         WW
```

Be sure to include appropriate comments in your program, choose meaningful identifiers, and use indentation as we do in the programs in this chapter.

2. Write a program that will print out the values of the smallest (most negative) and largest Integer values available on your computer with your Ada compiler. The output should identify these values. Be sure to include appropriate comments in your program and use indentation.
3. Write an Ada program that converts a Celsius temperature to its Fahrenheit equivalent. The formula is

$$\text{Fahrenheit} = \frac{9}{5}\,\text{Celsius} + 32$$

Make the centigrade temperature a constant so that its value can be changed easily. The program should print both the value of the centigrade temperature and its Fahrenheit equivalent, with appropriate identifying messages. Use comments, with meaningful identifiers, and indentation.

4. Write a program to calculate the diameter, the circumference, and the area of a circle given a radius of 6.75. Assign the radius to a float variable, and then output the radius with an appropriate message. Define a constant Pi with the value 3.14159. The program should output the diameter, the circumference, and the area, each on a separate line, with identifying labels. Use an Exp value of zero and the values of Fore and Aft so that the decimal part will contain 5 digits and the total number of columns used for a number is 10.
5. Write a program that outputs the results of the following expressions. Be sure to print appropriate messages to identify each result.

```
7 / 1     7 rem 1
7 / 2     7 rem 2
7 / 3     7 rem 3
7 / 4     7 rem 4
7 / 5     7 rem 5
7 / 6     7 rem 6
7 / 7     7 rem 7
7 / 8     7 rem 8
7 / 9     7 rem 9
```

CHAPTER 3

Input and Design Methodology

GOALS

After reading this chapter, you should be able to

- use Get procedures to read numeric data into a program
- use Get and Get_Line procedures to read string data into a program
- use the Skip_Line procedure to skip over data
- write appropriate prompting messages for interactive programs
- know when file input/output is appropriate and how it differs from interactive input/output
- write programs that use files instead of the keyboard and screen
- apply top-down design methodology to solve a simple problem and code it in Ada, using self-documenting code

Getting Data into Programs

One of the biggest advantages of computers is that they enable a program to be used with many different sets of data. To do this, we must keep the data separate from the program until we execute it. Then instructions in the program copy values from the data set into variables in the program. After storing these values in the variables, the program can perform calculations with them (see Figure 3-1).

The process of placing values from an outside data set into variables in a program is called *input*. The data for the program can come from an input device or from a file on an auxiliary storage device. We look at file input later in this chapter; here we consider the standard input device—the keyboard.

Input of Numeric Data

To input numeric data, we use a procedure called Get. The packages Integer_Text_IO and Float_Text_IO that we used in Chapter 2 contain Get procedures for the input of integer and float values. Let's look at some examples that use these procedures. Given the following variable declarations

```
Employee_ID : Integer range 0..999;
Pay_Rate    : Float   range Minimum_Wage..Maximum_Wage;
```

FIGURE 3-1 Separating the Data from the Program

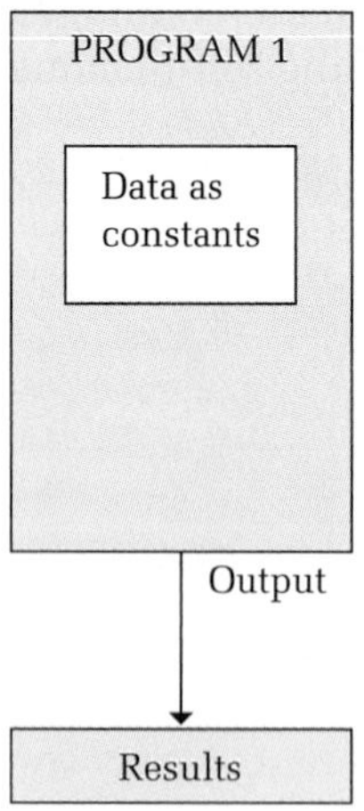

This program must be changed to work with different data values.

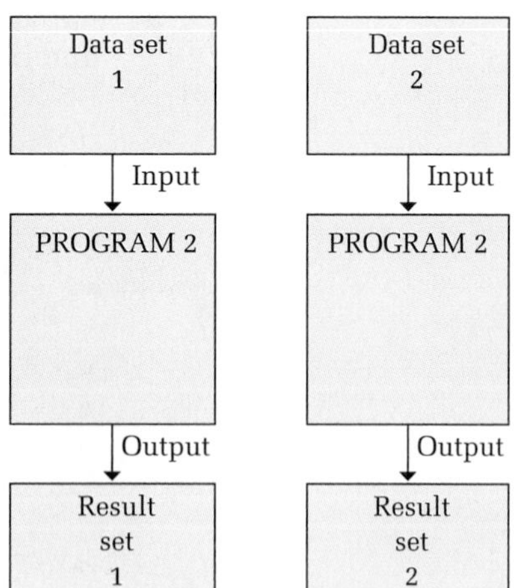

This program inputs its data from outside, so it can work with different data sets without being changed.

we can use Get procedures to accept numbers typed on the keyboard while our program is running.

```
Ada.Integer_Text_IO.Get (Item => Employee_ID);   -- Get an employee number
                                                 -- from the keyboard
Ada.Float_Text_IO.Get   (Item => Pay_Rate);      -- Get the employee's hourly
                                                 -- wage from the keyboard
```

Each of these calls has a parameter list with a single parameter named Item. The first statement gets a number from the keyboard and places it into the integer variable Employee_ID. The second statement gets a number from the keyboard and places it into the float variable Pay_Rate. Unlike the parameter Item for a Put procedure, which can be given a value that is a literal, expression, constant, or variable, the parameter Item for a Get procedure must be a variable. Why? Because the Get parameter Item specifies where the input value is to be placed, and only variables can have their values changed while a program is running.

The data typed on the keyboard must agree with the type of data expected by the Get procedure and any range restrictions of the variable given for parameter Item. If the word *Hello* is entered for an employee number (wrong type of data), the exception DATA_ERROR will occur and the program will stop with an error message. If the negative number −42 is entered for an employee number (outside of the range of Employee_ID), the exception CONSTRAINT_ERROR will occur and the program will stop with a different error message. In Chapter 9 we will show you how to give users a "second chance" when they mistype numeric data. For now, just be very careful when typing data for your programs.

Remember that in Chapter 1 we defined an interactive program as one in which the user communicates directly with the computer. There is a certain "etiquette" involved in writing interactive programs that has to do with instructions for the user. To get data into an interactive program, we use *input prompts*—printed messages that explain what the user should enter. Without these messages, the user has no idea what to type into a program. Here is a sample of a program segment showing the proper use of prompts:

```
Ada.Text_IO.Put         (Item => "Enter an employee number: ");
Ada.Integer_Text_IO.Get (Item => Employee_ID);
Ada.Text_IO.Put         (Item => "Enter the employee's hourly wage: ");
Ada.Float_Text_IO.Get   (Item => Pay_Rate);
```

Here's the dialog with the program segment with the input typed by the user shown in color:

```
Enter an employee number: 671
Enter the employee's hourly wage: 9.65
```

The amount of information you put into your prompts depends on who is going to be using the program. If you are writing a program for people who are not familiar with computers, you should make your messages more detailed. For example, "Type a three-digit Employee Identification Number, then press Enter." If the program is going to be used frequently by the same people, you could shorten the prompts: "Enter ID." and "Enter Wage." If the program is for very experienced users, you can prompt for several values at once and have them type all of the values on one input line. A call to the New_Line procedure can be used so that the data is entered on the line after the prompt as shown in this program segment,

```
Ada.Text_IO.Put (Item => "Enter an employee number and hourly wage.");
Ada.Text_IO.New_Line;
Ada.Integer_Text_IO.Get (Item => Employee_ID);
Ada.Float_Text_IO.Get   (Item => Pay_Rate);
```

which gives the following output (input typed by the user shown in color):

```
Enter an employee number and hourly wage.
671 9.65
```

In this example the user typed a space to separate the two numbers. They may also separate the numbers by typing them on different lines like this:

```
Enter an employee number and hourly wage.
671
9.65
```

Another nice feature you can add to your interactive programs is called *echo printing*. By displaying the data values just entered, the user can verify that they were entered correctly. Here's a sample program segment showing the proper use of prompts and echo printing:

```
-- Prompt for and get the data from the user
Ada.Text_IO.Put         (Item => "Enter an employee number: ");
Ada.Integer_Text_IO.Get (Item => Employee_Num);
Ada.Text_IO.Put         (Item => "Enter the employee's hourly wage: ");
Ada.Float_Text_IO.Get   (Item => Pay_Rate);
Ada.Text_IO.New_Line    (Spacing => 2);

-- Echo print the data entered by the user
Ada.Text_IO.Put         (Item => "Employee number: ");
Ada.Integer_Text_IO.Put (Item => Employee_ID, Width => 1);
Ada.Text_IO.Put         (Item => ", Hourly wage: $");
Ada.Float_Text_IO.Put   (Item => Pay_Rate,
```

```
                             Fore => 1,
                             Aft => 2,
                             Exp => 0);
Ada.Text_IO.New_Line;
```

which gives the following output (input typed by the user shown in color):

```
Enter an employee number: 671
Enter the employee's hourly wage: 9.65

Employee number: 671, Hourly wage: $9.65
```

Input of String Data

Strings are sequences of graphic characters (see Appendix C). We must treat string data differently from numeric data. For example, although blanks are used to separate numeric data values, the blank is an important part of a string data value. (Imagine trying to read this book with all the blanks removed!) The package Text_IO contains two different procedures for reading string data: Get and Get_Line.

Get Procedure Get reads characters from the keyboard until the string variable is filled. In the following declaration, Message is declared to be a string that holds 10 characters:

```
Message : String (1..10);
```

The following program segment prompts users to enter a message, gets what they type and stores it in the variable Message, and echo prints their input.

```
Ada.Text_IO.Put (Item => "Enter a 10 character message.");
Ada.Text_IO.New_Line;
Ada.Text_IO.Get (Item => Message);
Ada.Text_IO.Put (Item => Message);
```

After the prompt has been displayed, Text_IO's Get procedure will wait for the user to type 10 characters. These 10 characters may be on a single line or could span several lines as illustrated in these four different possibilities (the input is again shown in color).

```
Enter a 10 character message          ← The prompt
Hello Mary                            ← 10-character input
Hello Mary                            ← Echo print

--------------------------------
```

```
Enter a 10 character message.          ← The prompt
1234567890                             ← 10-character input
1234567890                             ← Echo print

--------------------------------

Enter a 10 character message.          ← The prompt
Hello                                  ← First 5 characters of input
 Mary                                  ← Remaining 5 characters
Hello Mary                             ← Echo print

--------------------------------

Enter a 10 character message.          ← The prompt
Hel                                    ← First 3 characters of input
lo M                                   ← Next 4 characters
ary                                    ← Remaining 3 characters
Hello Mary                             ← Echo print
```

Notice that you do not have to use quotation marks around string data values when you input them. When you write string literals in programs, you have to put quotes around them to distinguish them from identifiers. But when a data value is read in, the particular Get procedure used determines whether the characters the user types are interpreted as an integer, float, or string value. Integer_Text_IO.Get gets integer data, Float_Text_IO.Get gets float data, and Text_IO.Get gets string data.

Get_Line Procedure Before we learn the specifics of the Get_Line procedure, we must look more at how a set of data is organized. A data set is a sequence of lines. Each line is a sequence of characters defined in the ISO 8859-1 character set (shown in Appendix C). A *line terminator* marks the end of each line of data. When you use the Get procedure to read a string, it ignores line terminators. We have used both blanks and line terminators to separate numeric input values. When reading a number, the Get procedure skips over any line terminators or blanks that come before it. Because leading spaces and line terminators are skipped, we can hit the space bar or Enter key as many times as we like between numbers.

Where does the line terminator come from? What is it? The first question is easy. When you are working at a keyboard, you generate a line terminator yourself each time you hit the Return or Enter key. You also can generate a line terminator with a call to the New_Line procedure. New_Line outputs a line terminator when it tells the screen or printer to go to the next line.

The answer to the second question varies from computer system to computer system. The Ada language does not define the line terminator. It is either a nonprintable control character or a sequence of nonprintable control characters that the system recognizes. Because the procedures in

Text_IO handle the line terminator automatically, you do not need to know exactly what it is.

The Get_Line procedure in package Text_IO reads characters into a string variable until one of the following conditions is met:

1. the string is filled *or*
2. the line terminator is found.

Because it may encounter the line terminator before the string is filled, Get_Line has an additional parameter that is assigned the position of the last character put into the string by Get_Line. For the string variables we've declared so far, this also happens to be the number of characters read. Using the declarations

```
Message            : String (1..10);
Position_Last_Char : Integer range 0 .. 10;
```

and the statements

```
Message := "**********";                    -- Fill message with asterisks
Ada.Text_IO.Put (Item => "Enter a message.");
Ada.Text_IO.New_Line;
Ada.Text_IO.Get_Line (Item => Message,
                      Last => Position_Last_Char);
Ada.Text_IO.Put (Item => Message);
Ada.Text_IO.New_Line;
Ada.Text_IO.Put (Item => "Entered ");
Ada.Integer_IO.Put (Item => Position_Last_Char, Width => 1);
Ada.Text_IO.Put (Item => " characters");
Ada.Text_IO.New Line;
```

we could obtain any of the following sets of output (user input is shown in color).

```
Enter a message.            ← Prompt
Hello Mary                  ← 10-character input
Hello Mary                  ← Echo print
Entered 10 characters       ← Position in the string of the
                              last character read
```

```
Enter a message.            ← Prompt
Hello                       ← 5-character input
Hello*****                  ← Echo print
Entered 5 characters        ← Position in the string of the
                              last character read
```

```
----------------------------------

Enter a message.                    ← Prompt
H                                   ← 1-character input
H*********                          ← Echo print
Entered 1 character                 ← Position in the string of the
                                      last character read

----------------------------------

Enter a message.                    ← Prompt
                                    ← No characters input (just Return)
**********                          ← Echo print
Entered 0 characters                ← Position in the string of the
                                      last character read

----------------------------------

Enter a message.                    ← Prompt
Hello Mildred                       ← 13-character input
Hello Mild                          ← Echo print
Entered 10 characters               ← Position in the string of the
                                      last character read
```

The string variable Message is declared to hold 10 characters. Observe its contents when the user enters fewer than 10 characters on the line. The characters entered are placed in the string starting at the beginning (position 1). If the user enters fewer than 10 characters, the original characters (asterisks in this example) remain in the unfilled portion of the string. If the user enters more than 10 characters, the first 10 characters are placed in the string and the remaining characters on the input line are ignored.

THEORETICAL FOUNDATIONS

More About Procedures and Parameters

We've defined a procedure as a type of subprogram. When your program tells the computer to follow the instructions in a subprogram, the program is *calling* the subprogram. When the program calls the subprogram, the parameters in the parameter list are *passed* to the subprogram. When the subprogram finishes, the computer *returns* to the statement following the call statement that invoked the subprogram.

The parameters to the different Put procedures are used to transfer information in to the procedures. This information includes the item we want displayed and the values that specify the layout (format) in which we want them displayed. So *in parameters* are given values that can be literals, constants, variables, or expressions. With the Get procedures, the parameter Item is used to transfer information out of the procedure to our program. And *out parameters* must be variables. The variables store the information passed out of the procedure while the subprogram is running. The point to remember is that you can use parameters both to transfer data into a procedure and to transfer results back out.

String Slices

In some cases we may want to just print a portion of a string variable. Ada allows us to work with part of a string, which is called a *slice*. A slice of a string is indicated by following the string variable with a **range** of character positions in parentheses. The range is given as beginning and ending character positions separated by two periods.

You can use string slices anywhere you can use a string. Let's look at some string expressions that use slices. Assume that the string variable Message contains the string `"ABCDEFGHIJ"`.

String Expression	Value
`Message (1..5)`	"ABCDE"
`Message (3..7)`	"CDEFG"
`Message (6..10)`	"FGHIJ"
`Message (3..3)`	"C"
`Message (5..4)`	""
`Message (0..5)`	error
`Message (2..12)`	error
`Message (12..0)`	""
`Message (4..6) & Message (1..3)`	"DEFABC"

Any range with a first position greater than the last position is called a **null range.** A null range contains no values. String slices with a null range are called **null strings** because they contain no characters. In our examples, Message (5..4) is a null string. The two errors in this table are a result of using a range of positions that are not within the declared range (1..10) of string variable Message. Why then is Message (12..0) not an error? Because 12..0 is a null range and contains no values; Ada does not need to check to see whether it is within the range declared for the string variable.

Range The set of values between a specified first and last value, including those values.

Null range A range with a first value greater than its last value. A null range contains no values.

Null string A string containing no characters.

There is one more detail you need to know before you can use string slices. The bounds in a range do not have to be literals; they can be constants, variables, or even expressions. Let's modify our last program segment to echo only the characters that the user entered.

```
Message := "**********";                                   -- Fill message with stars
Ada.Text_IO.Put (Item => "Enter a message.");
Ada.Text_IO.New_Line;
Ada.Text_IO.Get_Line (Item => Message,
                      Last => Position_Last_Char);
Ada.Text_IO.Put (Item => Message (1..Position_Last_Char)); -- Display slice
Ada.Text_IO.New_Line;
```

The major change in this code is that we display a slice of the string variable Message instead of displaying its entire contents. Also, we no longer display the value of Position_Last_Char. Here are some example sets of output that we could obtain from this section of code.

```
Enter a message.          ← Prompt
Hello Mary                ← 10-character input
Hello Mary                ← Echo print

-----------------------------

Enter a message.          ← Prompt
Hello                     ← 5-character input
Hello                     ← Echo print

-----------------------------

Enter a message.          ← Prompt
H                         ← 1-character input
H                         ← Echo print

-----------------------------

Enter a message.          ← Prompt
                          ← No characters input (just Return)
                          ← Echo print (null string)
```

Let's use our knowledge of input to modify the mileage program developed in Chapter 2 so that, instead of defining the data in the program, it is accepted from the keyboard. We also have added a string variable for the make of car, in case the user owns more than one car.

```
with Ada.Text_IO;
with Ada.Float_Text_IO;
with Ada.Integer_Text_IO;

procedure Mileage is

-- This program computes miles per gallon given four amounts
-- for gallons used, and starting and ending mileages

   Capacity  : constant Float := 25.0;   -- Maximum gas tank size

   Car_Make : String (1..20);           -- Make of car
   Last     : Integer range 0..20;      -- Number of letters in
                                        -- Car_Make

   Amt1 : Float range 0.0 .. Capacity;  -- Gallons for fill-up 1
   Amt2 : Float range 0.0 .. Capacity;  -- Gallons for fill-up 2
   Amt3 : Float range 0.0 .. Capacity;  -- Gallons for fill-up 3
   Amt4 : Float range 0.0 .. Capacity;  -- Gallons for fill-up 4

   Start_Miles : Float range 0.0 .. Float'Last;  -- Starting mileage
   End_Miles   : Float range 0.0 .. Float'Last;  -- Ending mileage

   MPG : Integer range 4 .. 100;                -- Computed miles per gallon

begin     -- Mileage
   -- Get the data
   Ada.Text_IO.Put (Item => "Enter the make of your car");
   Ada.Text_IO.New_Line (Spacing => 1);
   Ada.Text_IO.Get_Line (Item => Car_Make, Last => Last);

   Ada.Text_IO.Put (Item => "Enter the number of gallons for 4 fill-ups.");
   Ada.Text_IO.New_Line  (Spacing => 1);
   Ada.Float_Text_IO.Get (Item => Amt1);
   Ada.Float_Text_IO.Get (Item => Amt2);
   Ada.Float_Text_IO.Get (Item => Amt3);
   Ada.Float_Text_IO.Get (Item => Amt4);

   Ada.Text_IO.Put (Item => "Enter the starting and ending mileages.");
   Ada.Text_IO.New_Line  (Spacing => 1);
   Ada.Float_Text_IO.Get (Item => Start_Miles);
   Ada.Float_Text_IO.Get (Item => End_Miles);
```

```
   -- Calculate the miles per gallon
   MPG := Integer( (End_Miles - Start_Miles) / (Amt1 + Amt2 + Amt3 + Amt4) );

   -- Echo print input data
   Ada.Text_IO.New_Line (Spacing => 2);
   Ada.Text_IO.Put (Item => "Car Make: " & Car_Make (1..Last) );
   Ada.Text_IO.New_Line (Spacing => 2);
   Ada.Text_IO.Put (Item => "For the gallon amounts: ");
   Ada.Text_IO.New_Line (Spacing => 1);
   Ada.Float_Text_IO.Put (Item => Amt1,
                          Fore => 4,
                          Aft  => 1,
                          Exp  => 0);
   Ada.Text_IO.Put (Item => ',');
   Ada.Float_Text_IO.Put (Item => Amt2,
                          Fore => 4,
                          Aft  => 1,
                          Exp  => 0);
   Ada.Text_IO.Put (Item => ',');
   Ada.Float_Text_IO.Put (Item => Amt3,
                          Fore => 4,
                          Aft  => 1,
                          Exp  => 0);
   Ada.Text_IO.Put (Item => ',');
   Ada.Float_Text_IO.Put (Item => Amt4,
                          Fore => 4,
                          Aft  => 1,
                          Exp  => 0);
   Ada.Text_IO.New_Line (Spacing => 2);
   Ada.Text_IO.Put  (Item => "a starting mileage of ");
   Ada.Float_Text_IO.Put (Item => Start_Miles,
                          Fore => 6,
                          Aft  => 1,
                          Exp  => 0);
   Ada.Text_IO.New_Line (Spacing => 1);
   Ada.Text_IO.Put (Item => "and an ending mileage of ");
   Ada.Float_Text_IO.Put (Item => End_Miles,
                          Fore => 6,
                          Aft  => 1,
                          Exp  => 0);
   Ada.Text_IO.New_Line (Spacing => 2);

   -- Display the results
   Ada.Text_IO.Put (Item => "the mileage per gallon is ");
   Ada.Integer_Text_IO.Put (Item  => MPG,
                            Width => 3);
   Ada.Text_IO.New_Line (Spacing => 1);

end Mileage;
```

Here is a sample run of this program with our input shown in color:

```
Enter the make of your car
Subaru
Enter the number of gallons for 4 fill-ups.
11.7 14.3
12.2 8.5
Enter the starting and ending mileages.
67308.0 68750.7


Car Make: Subaru

For the gallon amounts:
  11.7,  14.3,  12.2,   8.5

a starting mileage of  67308.0
and an ending mileage of  68750.7

the mileage per gallon is  31
```

Input of Mixed Data Types

All of our examples to this point have involved getting data of a single type. In this section we examine the details necessary for us to write programs that get values of a variety of data types.

The Reading Marker Before we explore the effects of mixing calls to Get for numeric values and Get and Get_Line for string values, we introduce the concept of the **reading marker.** The reading marker works like a bookmark, but, instead of marking a place in a book, it keeps track of the point in the input data where the computer should continue reading. The reading marker indicates the next character to be read.

Reading marker An indicator that keeps track of the point in the input data where the computer should continue reading.

Numeric Data As we saw earlier, each input line has a *line terminator* that tells the computer where one line ends and the next begins. Each input line contains zero or more characters. Float_Text_IO.Get and Integer_Text_IO.Get read and process these characters. These Get procedures turn groups of characters into numbers.

Let's look at the behavior of the reading marker when we get integer data values. Each of the following three lines of input data contain eleven characters (nine digit characters and two blanks).

```
123 456 789¶
987 654 321¶
888 777 666¶
```

We use the ¶ symbol to represent line terminators. The reading marker, which indicates the next character to be read, is shown as a shaded gray mark. Before we have called any Get procedures, the next character to read is the character 1 (first character on the first line).

The following table shows the details of four sequential calls to Integer_Text_IO.Get. The left column shows the procedure call, the middle column shows the effect of the procedure call on the variable, and the right column shows the effect of the call on the reading marker. A, B, C, and D are integer variables. We use a gray box to indicate the position of the reading marker after the procedure call and we draw use color to show all the characters that have been processed at this point.

Statements	*Variables*	*Marker Position After Get*
`Ada.Integer_Text_IO.Get (Item => A);`	A 123	123 456 789¶ 987 654 321¶ 888 777 666¶
`Ada.Integer_Text_IO.Get (Item => B);`	B 456	123 456 789¶ 987 654 321¶ 888 777 666¶
`Ada.Integer_Text_IO.Get (Item => C);`	C 789	123 456 789¶ 987 654 321¶ 888 777 666¶
`Ada.Integer_Text_IO.Get (Item => D);`	D 987	123 456 789¶ 987 654 321¶ 888 777 666¶

The four calls to Integer_Text_IO.Get get the numbers 123, 456, 789, and 987, just as we would expect. After each procedure call, the reading marker is left on the item that signaled the end of the characters comprising the number—in these examples, a blank or a line terminator.

The input of float numbers works the same way. The following table illustrates the effect of three sequential calls to procedure Float_Text_IO.Get. P, Q, and R are float variables. Again we use a gray box to indicate the position of the reading marker after the procedure call and we use color to show all the characters that have been processed at this point.

Statements	*Variables*	*Marker Position After Get*
`Ada.Float_Text_IO.Get (Item => P);`	P 123.0	123 64.7¶ 98.4 324¶ 128 84.1¶
`Ada.Float_Text_IO.Get (Item => Q);`	Q 64.7	123 64.7¶ 98.4 324¶ 128 84.1¶
`Ada.Float_Text_IO.Get (Item => R);`	R 98.4	123 64.7¶ 98.4 324¶ 128 84.1¶

As with getting integer values, the reading marker is left on the item that signaled the end of the characters comprising the number—a blank or a line terminator.

String Data String data is treated differently from numeric data. Because leading blank characters are ignored when reading numeric data, we often use them to separate numbers. Blank characters in string data are *not* ignored.

Do you remember the difference between Get and Get_Line? Get reads enough characters to fill the string item, *skipping over line terminators if necessary*. Get_Line reads characters until the item is filled *or* a line terminator is encountered. If Get_Line finds the line terminator before the string is filled, it advances the reading marker to the beginning of the next line.

Let's look at some examples that use these three lines of data:

```
ABC DEF G3R¶
HIJK LMNOP¶
Lovelace¶
```

Initially, the reading marker is on the *A* character. The following table shows the details of five sequential calls to Text_IO.Get using these three lines of data. As before, the left column shows the procedure call, the middle column shows the effect of the call on the variable, and the right column shows the effect of the call on the reading marker. U, V, W, X, and Y are String (1..5) variables.

Statements	*Variables*	*Marker Position After Get or Get_Line*
`Ada.Text_IO.Get (Item => U);`	U "ABC D"	ABC DEF G3R¶ HIJK LMNOP¶ Lovelace¶
`Ada.Text_IO.Get (Item => V);`	V "EF G3"	ABC DEF G3R¶ HIJK LMNOP¶ Lovelace¶
`Ada.Text_IO.Get (Item => W);`	W "RHIJK"	ABC DEF G3R¶ HIJK LMNOP¶ Lovelace¶
`Ada.Text_IO.Get (Item => X);`	X " LMNO"	ABC DEF G3R¶ HIJK LMNOP¶ Lovelace¶
`Ada.Text_IO.Get (Item => Y);`	Y "PLove"	ABC DEF G3R¶ HIJK LMNOP¶ Lovelace¶

Each of the calls to Text_IO.Get in the above table reads exactly five characters—enough to fill the string variable. Before each call, the reading marker indicates the first character that the Text_IO.Get procedure will read. Notice that blanks are not ignored—they are placed into the variable as any other character. The third and fifth calls to Text_IO.Get in the table demonstrate how the Text_IO.Get procedure ignores line terminators. It continues to take characters from the input stream until the string variable is filled.

Now let's look at how the procedure Text_IO.Get_Line affects the reading marker. When there are enough characters on the line to fill the string variable, Get_Line moves the reading marker exactly as Get does. When there are not enough characters on the line to fill the string variable, the characters are placed into the variable and the reading marker is advanced to the next line. The next table shows the details of six sequential procedure calls. Again, the left column shows the procedure call, the middle column shows the effect of the call on the variables, and the right column shows the effect of the call on the reading marker. U, V, W, X, and Y, and Z are String (1..5) variables. Initially all six of these string variables contain "*****". L and M are integer variables.

Statements	*Variables*	*Marker Position After Get or Get_Line*
`Ada.Text_IO.Get (Item => U);`	U "ABC D"	ABC DEF G3R¶ HIJK LMNOP¶ Lovelace¶
`Ada.Text_IO.Get (Item => V);`	V "EF G3"	ABC DEF G3R¶ HIJK LMNOP¶ Lovelace¶
`Ada.Text_IO.Get_Line (Item => W` `Last => L);`	W "R****" L 1	**ABC DEF G3R¶** HIJK LMNOP¶ Lovelace¶
`Ada.Text_IO.Get (Item => X);`	X "HIJK "	ABC DEF G3R¶ HIJK LMNOP¶ Lovelace¶
`Ada.Text_IO.Get (Item => Y);`	Y "LMNOP"	ABC DEF G3R¶ HIJK LMNOP¶ Lovelace¶
`Ada.Text_IO.Get_Line (Item => Z` `Last => M);`	Z "*****" M 0	**ABC DEF G3R¶** **HIJK LMNOP¶** Lovelace

Pay particular attention to the effects of the calls to procedure Text_IO.Get_Line. Before the first call to the Get_Line procedure, the reading marker is on the last character of the first line, *R*. The Get_Line procedure reads only one character before it finds the line terminator. Only the letter *R* is placed into the variable W. The other four characters in variable W are unchanged. Variable L is given a value of *1*, the position of the last character placed into W. Since the line terminator was encountered *before* the string variable was filled, the reading marker is advanced to the next line.

Before the last call to procedure Text_IO.Get_Line, the reading marker is on a line terminator. Remember that the reading marker indicates where reading is to begin. In this case, Get_Line immediately finds a line terminator. *No* characters are placed into variable W; its original five characters remain. Get_Line sets variable M to *0* to indicate that no characters were placed into W. Since the line terminator was encountered *before* the string variable was filled, the reading marker is advanced to the next line.

Skip_Line Procedure As we showed in the previous sections, the Get procedures for numeric and string input skip over line terminators: Get_Line is stopped by them. This can cause some problems when Get and Get_Line are used together. The following program segment illustrates these problems:

```
-- Prompt for Data
Ada.Text_IO.Put (Item => "Enter two integers and two strings");
Ada.Text_IO.New_Line;

-- Num1 and Num2 are Integer, Str1 and Str2 are String(1..8)
Ada.Integer_Text_IO.Get (Item => Num1);
Ada.Integer_Text_IO.Get (Item => Num2);
Ada.Text_IO.Get_Line (Item => Str1, Last => Last1);
Ada.Text_IO.Get_Line (Item => Str2, Last => Last2);

-- Echo print
Ada.Text_IO.Put (Item => "The integers: ");
Ada.Integer_Text_IO.Put (Item => Num1);
Ada.Integer_Text_IO.Put (Item => Num2);
Ada.Text_IO.New_Line;

Ada.Text_IO.Put (Item => "The 1st string: ");
Ada.Text_IO.Put (Item => Str1 (1..Last1) );
Ada.Text_IO.New_Line;

Ada.Text_IO.Put (Item => "The 2nd string: ");
Ada.Text_IO.Put (Item => Str2 (1..Last2) );
Ada.Text_IO.New_Line;
```

Here is the dialog obtained from running the program segment (input is shown in color). We pressed the Enter key twice before the number 67 was entered and typed five spaces before the number 51.

```
Enter two integers and two strings



67
     51
Hello
The integers:          67          51
The 1st string:
The 2nd string: Hello
```

The program seems to have echo-printed the data before a second string could be entered. The value printed for the first string suggests that it is a null string (contains no characters) or a blank string (contains only blank characters). The value printed for the second string is what was entered for the first string.

What went wrong? To see what happened, we need to consider exactly what these input procedures do. Remember that Get procedures for numeric values skip over any blanks or line terminators that come *before* the number. That's why it is possible to press the Enter key several times before entering 67 and type spaces before entering 51. However, these numeric Get procedures do not skip over any blanks or line terminators that come *after* the number. The reading marker is set to the next character to be read. Let's use the reading marker to see exactly what happens with each input procedure call.

Statements	*Variables*	*Marker Position After Get or Get_Line*
`Ada.Integer_Text_IO.Get (Item => Num1);`	Num1 67	¶ ¶ 67¶ 51¶ Hello¶
`Ada.Integer_Text_IO.Get (Item => Num2);`	Num2 51	¶ ¶ 67¶ 51¶ Hello¶
`Ada.Text_IO.Get_Line (Item => Str1;` `                      Last => Last1);`	Str1 "????????" Last1 0	¶ ¶ 67¶ 51¶ Hello¶
`Ada.Text_IO.Get_Line (Item => Str2;` `                      Last => Last2);`	Str2 "Hello???" Last2 5	¶ ¶ 67¶ 51¶ Hello¶

Follow the reading marker carefully through these four procedure calls. The question marks in the string variables indicate unknown characters. The second call to Integer_Text_IO.Get leaves the reading marker on the line terminator *after* 51. When we call Get_Line to get the first string, it finds the line terminator following 51. Because Get_Line stops reading when it encounters a line terminator, it stops and sets Last1 to zero to indicate a null string. Now the line terminator has been processed, and the second call to Get_Line gets Hello.

One way to solve this problem is to type the first message on the same line as the second integer, like this:

```
67
   51Hello
Mildred
```

Now the first call to Get_Line will find the five characters `H e l l o` before it encounters the line terminator. The details are shown in the next table.

Statements	*Variables*	*Marker Position After Get or Get_Line*
`Ada.Integer_Text_IO.Get (Item => Num1);`	Num1 [67]	67¶ 51Hello¶ Mildred¶
`Ada.Integer_Text_IO.Get (Item => Num2);`	Num2 [51]	67¶ 51Hello¶ Mildred¶
`Ada.Text_IO.Get_Line (Item => Str1;` `Last => Last1);`	Str1 ["Hello???"] Last1 [5]	67¶ 51Hello¶ Mildred¶
`Ada.Text_IO.Get_Line (Item => Str2;` `Last => Last2);`	Str2 ["Mildred?"] Last2 [7]	67¶ 51Hello¶ Mildred¶

This solution illustrates another feature of numeric input. The Get procedures for numeric data values stop reading when a non-numeric character is encountered. The non-numeric character (the letter "H" in this example) is not read; it is still available to be read by the next call to an input procedure.

This, however, is not a very attractive answer to our problem. It is difficult to read the data without a space between the integer data 51 and the string data Hello. If we enter a space between the integer and the string, the space is read into the string variable before the actual message. A better solution is to use procedure Skip_Line in package Text_IO. When this procedure is called, it moves the reading marker to the beginning of the next line. Here's what our program segment looks like with the addition of a call to Skip_Line:

```
-- Prompt for Data
Ada.Text_IO.Put (Item => "Enter two integers and two strings");
Ada.Text_IO.New_Line;

-- Num1 and Num2 are Integer, Str1 and Str2 are String(1..8)
Ada.Integer_Text_IO.Get (Item => Num1);
Ada.Integer_Text_IO.Get (Item => Num2);
Ada.Text_IO.Skip_Line;                        -- This line added to previous example

Ada.Text_IO.Get_Line (Item => Str1, Last => Last1);
Ada.Text_IO.Get_Line (Item => Str2, Last => Last2);

-- Echo print
Ada.Text_IO.New_Line;
Ada.Text_IO.Put (Item => "The integers: ");
Ada.Integer_Text_IO.Put (Item => Num1);
Ada.Integer_Text_IO.Put (Item => Num2);
Ada.Text_IO.New_Line;

Ada.Text_IO.Put (Item => "The 1st string: ");
Ada.Text_IO.Put (Item => Str1 (1..Last1) );
Ada.Text_IO.New_Line;

Ada.Text_IO.Put (Item => "The 2nd string: ");
Ada.Text_IO.Put (Item => Str2 (1..Last2) );
Ada.Text_IO.New_Line;
```

And here's a sample dialog with the program segment followed by a trace of the input/output calls:

```
Enter two integers and two strings
67
     51
Hello
Mildred

The integers:          67          51
The 1st string: Hello
The 2nd string: Mildred
```

Statements	Variables	Marker Position After Get or Get_Line
`Ada.Integer_Text_IO.Get (Item => Num1);`	Num1 [67]	67¶ 51¶ Hello¶ Mildred¶
`Ada.Integer_Text_IO.Get (Item => Num2);`	Num2 [51]	67¶ 51¶ Hello¶ Mildred¶
`Ada.Text_IO.Skip_Line;`		67¶ 51¶ Hello¶ Mildred¶
`Ada.Text_IO.Get_Line (Item => Str1;` `Last => Last1);`	Str1 ["Hello???"] Last1 [5]	67¶ 51¶ Hello¶ Mildred¶
`Ada.Text_IO.Get_Line (Item => Str2;` `Last => Last2);`	Str2 ["Mildred?"] Last2 [7]	67¶ 51¶ Hello¶ Mildred¶

The Skip_Line procedure is most useful when using the Get_Line procedure *after* getting a numeric value, as illustrated in our last example. You can also use it to skip over entire lines of input data.

File Input/Output

Although we tend to use examples of interactive I/O in this book, many programs are written using file I/O. Remember that in batch processing, the user and the computer do not interact during the actual processing. Data for such processing comes from files, and the output is placed into files. Often, interactive programs need to store data such as user preferences in files between runs.

File I/O is not restricted to batch processing. When an interactive program must read in many data values, the usual practice is to prepare them ahead of time, storing them in a file. This allows the user to go back and make changes or corrections to the data as necessary before running the program. When an interactive program is designed to display a lot of data, the output can be sent directly to a high-speed printer or another file. This allows the user to examine the data at leisure after the program has been run. In the next section we discuss input and output with files.

Programs that are designed for file I/O do not need to print prompting messages for input. It is often a good idea, however, to echo-print each data value that is read. Echo printing allows the person reading the output to verify that the input values were prepared correctly. Because file-oriented programs tend to print large amounts of data, their output often is in the form of a table—columns with descriptive headings.

Files In everything we've done so far, we've assumed that the input to our programs comes from the keyboard and that the output from our programs goes to the screen. Ada refers to the keyboard and screen as the *standard input file* and *standard output file*.

Strictly speaking, the keyboard and screen aren't files—at least not in the same sense as the files in which we enter our programs. A true *file* is a named area in secondary memory that holds a collection of information (for example, the program code we have entered). The information in a file usually is stored on an auxiliary storage device, such as a disk (see Figure 3-2).

The reason we sometimes call the keyboard and screen *files* is because we treat them the same way we treat other files. Our programs read data from the keyboard in the same way they read data from a file. And they write output to the screen in the same way they write output onto a file.

Why would we want a program to read data from a file instead of the keyboard? If a program is going to read a large quantity of data, it is easier to enter the data into a file with an editor than to enter it while the program is running. With the editor, we can go back and correct mistakes. Also we do not have to enter the data all at once; we can take a break and

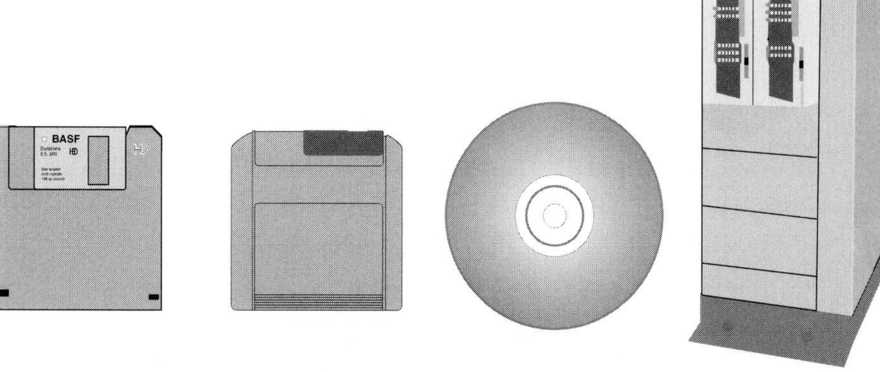

FIGURE 3-2
Auxiliary Storage

come back later. And if we want to rerun the program, having the data stored on a file allows us to do so without reentering the data.

Why would we want the output from a program to be written on a file? The contents of a file can be displayed on a screen or printed. This gives us the option of looking at the output over and over again without having to rerun the program. Also, the output stored on a file can be read into another program as input. For example, Program Payroll given in Chapter 1 writes its output to file *Payfile.dat*. We could take *Payfile.dat* and read it into another program that prints out paychecks. Finally, it also gives your instructor a chance to look at your answers!

How to Use Files If we want a program to use files, we have to do four things:

1. Declare a variable for each file.
2. Prepare each file for reading or writing with a call to Text_IO's Open or Create procedures.
3. Include the file variable as an additional parameter in each call to Get, Get_Line, Put, New_Line, or Skip_Line.
4. Sever the connection to each file with a call to Text_IO's Close procedure.

Declaring file variables Every file you wish to use must have a variable associated with it. We declare file variables the same way that we declare any variable: We specify the name, followed by a colon and the data type of the name. Standard library package Text_IO has a data type called File_Type that we use to declare file variables. Suppose we want Program Mileage (page 95) to read data from a file and to write its output to a second file. We would declare file variables as

```
In_MPG  : Ada.Text_IO.File_Type;     -- Holds gallon amounts and mileages
Out_MPG : Ada.Text_IO.File_Type;     -- Holds miles per gallon output
```

Preparing files with Open or Create We must prepare the declared files for either reading or writing. We use Text_IO's procedure Open to prepare a file for reading and procedure Create to create a new file for writing. Whether a file is prepared through the Open or Create procedure, the call puts it in an *open state*. Here is an example call to each of these procedures:

```
Ada.Text_IO.Open (File => In_MPG,
                  Mode => Ada.Text_IO.In_File,
                  Name => "MPG.DAT");
```

```
Ada.Text_IO.Create (File => Out_MPG,
                    Name => "RESULTS");
```

In both of these calls, the parameter *File* is given a file variable, and the parameter *Name* is given a string whose value is the name used by the computer's operating system for the file. In Chapter 2 you learned Ada's rules for creating identifier names. Your computer's operating system has its own rules for creating file names, which are probably different from Ada's rules. For example, in many systems it is okay to use a period in naming a file, but the period is not permitted in an Ada identifier. One purpose of Open and Create is to match an Ada identifier (a file variable) to the file name employed by the operating system. Then, when you want access to a particular file, you use the Ada file variable rather than the system's name for the file (see Figure 3-3).

The Open procedure prepares a file that already exists. The exception NAME_ERROR occurs and your program halts and displays an error message if there is no file with the name you supplied. You use the *Mode* parameter to specify whether you will use this existing file for input or output. The Mode parameter is assigned one of three values that are predefined in package Text_IO:

Mode	**Meaning**
In_File	The file is used for input. The reading marker is set to the first character in the file.
Out_File	The file is used for output. The original contents of the file are destroyed.
Append_File	The file is used for output with new data added after the original contents.

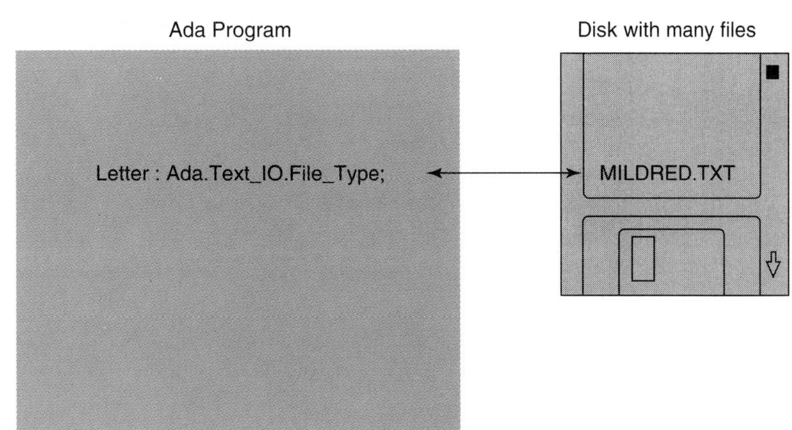

FIGURE 3-3 Preparing a File Associates an Ada Identifier (Letter) with a Disk File Name (MILDRED.TXT)

You cannot write to a file that is in mode In_File—that is, you can use it only to input data. If you try to use a file in mode In_File with a call to Put or New_Line, the exception MODE_ERROR occurs. MODE_ERROR will also occur if you attempt to read from a file that is in mode Out_File or Append_File.

As its name suggests, the Create procedure creates a new file with the given name. This new file is put into mode Out_File. An attempt to use Get, Get_Line, or Skip_Line with a file in mode Out_File results in the exception MODE_ERROR. Writing starts at the beginning of the newly created file.

Because these two procedures *prepare* files for reading or writing, you must call them before you make any calls to Put, New_Line, Get, Get_Line, or Skip_Line that refer to the files. It's a good idea to put these calls at the very beginning of your program so that the files are prepared before the program does anything else.

Specifying files in Text_IO procedures Each call that you make to procedure Get, Get_Line, Skip_Line, Put, and New_Line that uses a particular file must include the parameter *File*. We give this parameter the file variable we wish to use. In our mileage example the statements used to read the input data would look like this:

```
Ada.Float_Text_IO.Get (File => In_MPG, Item => Amt1);
Ada.Float_Text_IO.Get (File => In_MPG, Item => Amt2);
Ada.Float_Text_IO.Get (File => In_MPG, Item => Amt3);
Ada.Float_Text_IO.Get (File => In_MPG, Item => Amt4);
Ada.Float_Text_IO.Get (File => In_MPG, Item => Start_Miles);
Ada.Float_Text_IO.Get (File => In_MPG, Item => End_Miles);
```

You must also add a File parameter to all of the calls to output procedures. Here are some of them for Program Mileage:

```
Ada.Text_IO.Put (File => Out_MPG,
                 Item => "Car Make: " & Car_Make(1..Last) );

Ada.Text_IO.New_Line (File => Out_MPG, Spacing => 2);

Ada.Text_IO.Put (File => Out_MPG, Item => "For the gallon amounts: ");

Ada.Float_Text_IO.Put (File => Out_MPG,
                       Item => Amt1,
                       Fore => 4,
                       Aft  => 1,
                       Exp  => 0);

Ada.Integer_Text_IO.Put (File => Out_MPG,
                         Item  => MPG,
                         Width => 3);
```

Although this program did not call the Skip_Line procedure, here is an example of Skip_Line with a File parameter:

```
Ada.Text_IO.Skip_Line (File => In_MPG);
```

What happens if you forget to specify the File parameter in a particular I/O procedure call? Calls to output procedures will write to the screen. Calls to input procedures will try to obtain data from the keyboard. Because no prompt is displayed on the screen, the user is unaware that the program is waiting for data from the keyboard, and it may appear that the program has stopped executing. If your program appears to have stopped running, you may have left a File parameter out of an input procedure call. Leaving the File parameter out of a call to procedure Skip_Line is a particularly common error made by both beginning and experienced Ada programmers.

Finishing up When you have finished with a file, you must sever the connection between the file variable and the file. This is accomplished with a call to the Close procedure. This procedure has a single parameter: the file to be closed.

```
Ada.Text_IO.Close (File => In_MPG);
Ada.Text IO.Close (File => Out_MPG);
```

The system may alter or delete files that are not closed when a program terminates. Many systems automatically close all open files when the program finishes. However, because this is not defined by the Ada language, it is best to close all files through calls to the Close procedure. These calls can be the last statements in the program.

BACKGROUND INFORMATION

Charles Babbage

The British mathematician Charles Babbage (1791–1871) is generally credited with designing the world's first computer. Unlike the electronic computers of today, however, Babbage's machine was mechanical. It was made of gears and levers—the predominant technology of the 1820s and 1830s.

Babbage actually designed two different machines. The first, called the "Difference Engine," was for use in computing mathematical tables. For example, the difference engine could produce a table of squares:

x	x^2
1	1
2	4
3	9
4	16
.	.
.	.
.	.

It was essentially a very complex calculator and could not be programmed. The reason that Babbage designed the difference engine was not to speed up the computation of tables but to improve their accuracy. At that time, all tables were produced by hand, a tedious and error-prone job. Because much of science and engineering depended on the use of accurate tables, an error could have serious consequences. Even though the difference engine could perform the calculations only a little faster than a human, it could do so without error. In fact, one of its most important features was that it would stamp its output directly onto copper plates that could be placed into a printing press, thereby avoiding even typographical errors.

By 1833 the project to build the difference engine had run into financial trouble. The engineer whom Babbage had hired to do the construction was dishonest and had drawn the project out as long as possible so as to extract more money from Babbage's sponsors in the British government. Eventually they became tired of waiting for the machine and withdrew their support. Babbage lost interest in it at about the same time because he had developed the idea for a much more powerful machine, which he called the "Analytical Engine"—a truly programmable computer.

Babbage's idea for the analytical engine originated with his preparations to build the difference engine. Before starting its construction, he set off on a tour of Europe to survey the best technology of the time so that he could use it in his own project. One of the technologies he saw was the Jacquard automatic loom, in which a series of paper cards with punched holes was fed through the machine to produce a woven cloth pattern. The pattern of holes constituted a program for the loom and made it possible to weave patterns of arbitrary complexity automatically. In fact, its inventor even had a detailed portrait of himself woven by one of his machines.

Babbage realized that this sort of device could be used to control the operation of a computing machine. Instead of calculating just one type of formula, such a machine could be programmed to perform arbitrarily complex computations, including the manipulation of algebraic symbols. As Ada Lovelace elegantly put it, "We may say most aptly that the Analytical Engine weaves algebraic patterns, just as the Jacquard loom weaves flowers and leaves." It is clear that Babbage and Lovelace fully understood the power of a programmable computer and even contemplated the notion that someday such machines could achieve artificial thought.

Unfortunately, Babbage never completed construction of either of his machines. Some historians believe that he never finished them because the technology of the period could not support such complex machinery. But most feel that Babbage's failure was his own doing. He was both brilliant and somewhat eccentric (it is known that he was afraid of Italian organ grinders, for example). As a consequence, he tended to abandon projects midway through so that he could concentrate on newer and better ideas. He always believed that his new approaches would let him complete a machine in less time than if he continued with his old ideas.

Thus when he died, Babbage had numerous pieces of computing machines and partial drawings of designs, but none of the plans was sufficiently complete to produce a single working computer. After his death, his inventions were mostly dismissed and ignored until modern computers were developed. Only then did historians recognize the true importance of his contributions. Babbage stumbled upon the idea of the computer a full century before it was developed. Today we can only imagine how different the world would be had he succeeded.

Programming Methodology

The programming process consists of a problem-solving phase and an implementation phase. In Chapter 1 we discussed some strategies for solving problems, and in Chapter 2 we saw how some simple programs are implemented. Here we describe a methodology for developing data models and algorithmic solutions for more complex problems. This methodology will help you write algorithms that are easy to implement as Ada programs and, consequently, programs that are readable, understandable, and easy to debug and modify.

Top-Down Design

The technique we use is known as **top-down design** (it's also called *stepwise refinement* and *modular programming*). It allows us to use the divide-and-conquer approach that we talked about in Chapter 1.

Top-down design A technique for developing a program in which the problem is divided into more easily handled subproblems, the solutions of which create a solution to the overall problem.

In top-down design, we work from the abstract (a list of the major parts of a solution) to the particular (data types and algorithmic steps that can be translated directly into Ada code). You also can think of this as working from a high-level solution that leaves the details of implementation unspecified down to a fully detailed solution.

The easiest way to solve a problem is to give it to someone else and say, "Solve this problem." This is the most abstract level of a problem solution—a single-statement solution that encompasses the entire problem without specifying any of the details of implementation. It's at this point that programmers are called in. Our job is to turn this abstract solution into a concrete solution—a program.

We start by breaking the solution into a series of major steps. In the process, we move to a lower level of abstraction—some of the implementation details are now specified. Each of the major steps becomes an independent subproblem that we can work on separately. In a very large project, one person (the *chief architect* or *team leader*) would formulate the subproblems and then give them to other members of the programming team, saying "Solve this problem." In the case of a small project, we just give the subproblems to ourselves. Then we choose one subproblem at a time and break it into another series of smaller subproblems. The process continues until each subproblem can be solved directly.

Why do we work this way? Why not simply write out all of the details? Because it is much easier to focus on one problem at a time. For example, suppose you are working on a program to print out certain values and discover that you need a complex formula to calculate an appropriate width parameter for one of them. Calculating widths is not the purpose of the program. If you shift your focus to the calculation, you are more likely to forget some detail of the printing process. What you do is write down an abstract step—"Calculate the width required"—and go on with the problem at hand. Once you've completed the general solution, you can go back to solving the step that does the calculation.

By subdividing the problem, you create a hierarchical structure called a *tree structure*. Each level of the tree is a complete solution to the problem that is less abstract than the level above it. Figure 3-4 shows a solution tree for a problem. Steps that are shaded have enough implementation details specified to be translated directly into Ada statements. These are **concrete steps.** Those that are not shaded are **abstract steps;** they reappear as subproblems in the next level down. Each box represents a **module.** Modules are the basic building blocks of top-down solutions. The diagram in Figure 3-4 is also called a *module structure chart.*

Concrete step A step for which the implementation details are fully specified.

Abstract step A step in which some implementation details remain unspecified.

Module A self-contained collection of steps that solves a problem or subproblem; can contain both concrete and abstract steps.

FIGURE 3-4
Hierarchical Solution Tree

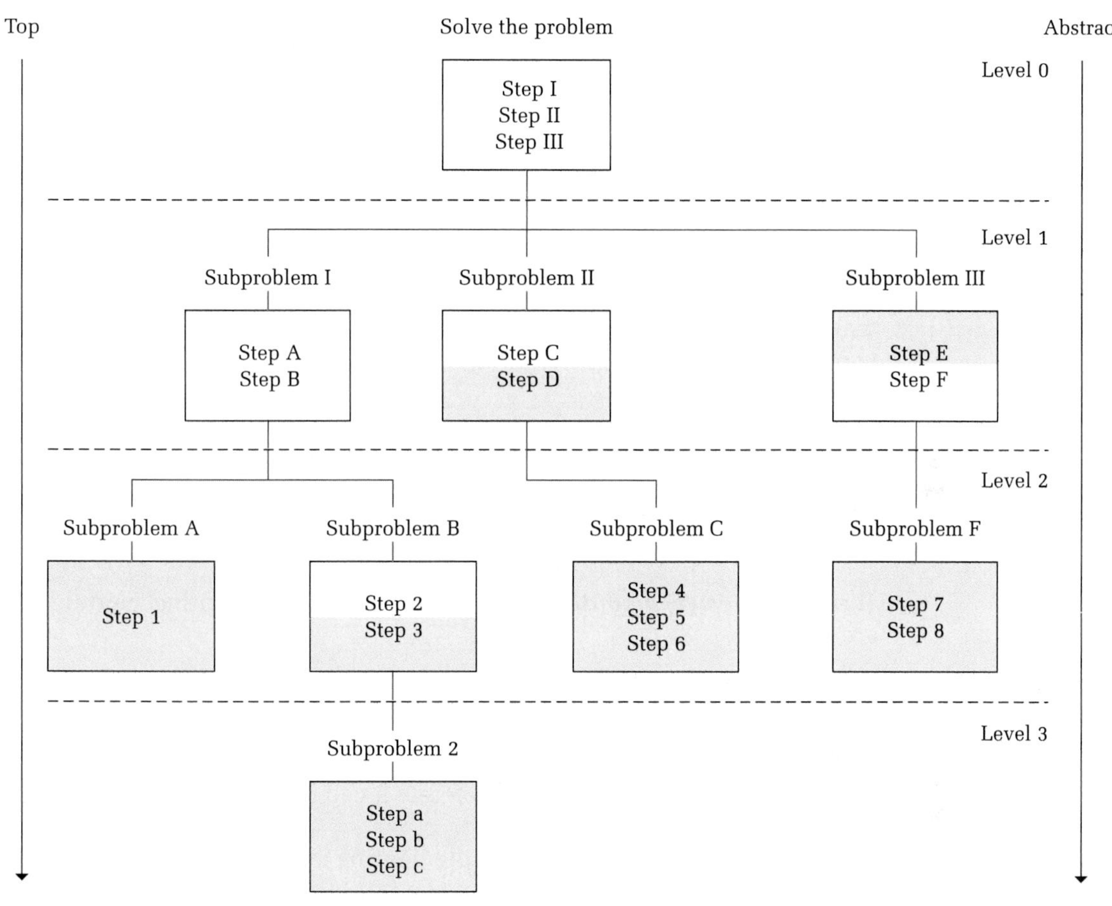

Modules A module begins life as an abstract step in the next higher level of the solution tree. It is completed when it solves a given subproblem: when it specifies a series of steps that does the same thing as the higher-level abstract step. At this stage a module is **functionally equivalent** to the abstract step.

Functional equivalence A property of a module—it performs exactly the same operation as the abstract step it defines. A pair of modules are functionally equivalent to each other if they each accomplish the same abstract operation.

A properly designed module contains only concrete steps that directly address the given subproblem and abstract steps for significant new subproblems. This is called **functional cohesion.** The idea behind functional cohesion is that each module should do just one thing and do it well. Functional cohesion is not a well-defined property; there is no quantitative measure of cohesion. It is a product of the human need to organize things into neat chunks that are easy to understand and remember. Knowing which details to make concrete and which details to leave abstract is a matter of experience, circumstance, and personal style. For example, you might decide to include a field width calculation in a printing module, if there isn't too much detail in the rest of the module so that it becomes confusing. On the other hand, if the calculation is performed several times, it makes sense to write it as a separate module and just refer to it each time you need it.

Functional cohesion A property of a module in which all concrete steps are directed toward solving just one problem, and any significant subproblems are written as abstract steps.

Writing cohesive modules Here's one approach to writing modules that are cohesive.

1. Think about how you would solve the subproblem by hand.
2. Begin writing down the major steps.
3. If a step is simple enough so that you can see how to implement it directly in Ada, it is at the concrete level; it doesn't need any further refinement.
4. If you have to think about implementing a step as a series of smaller steps or as several Ada statements, it is still at an abstract level.
5. If you are trying to write a series of steps and start to feel overwhelmed by details, you are probably bypassing one or more levels of abstraction. Stand back and look for pieces that you can write as more abstract steps.

We could call this the "procrastinator's technique." If a step is cumbersome or difficult, put it off to a lower level; don't think about it today, think about it tomorrow. Of course tomorrow does come, but the whole process then can be applied to the subproblem. A trouble spot often seems much simpler when you can focus on it. And eventually the whole problem is broken down into manageable units.

As you work your way down the solution tree, you make a series of design decisions. If a decision proves awkward or wrong (and many times it will!), it's easy to backtrack (go back up the tree to a higher-level mod-

Figure 3-5
Design Tree for Program Quilt

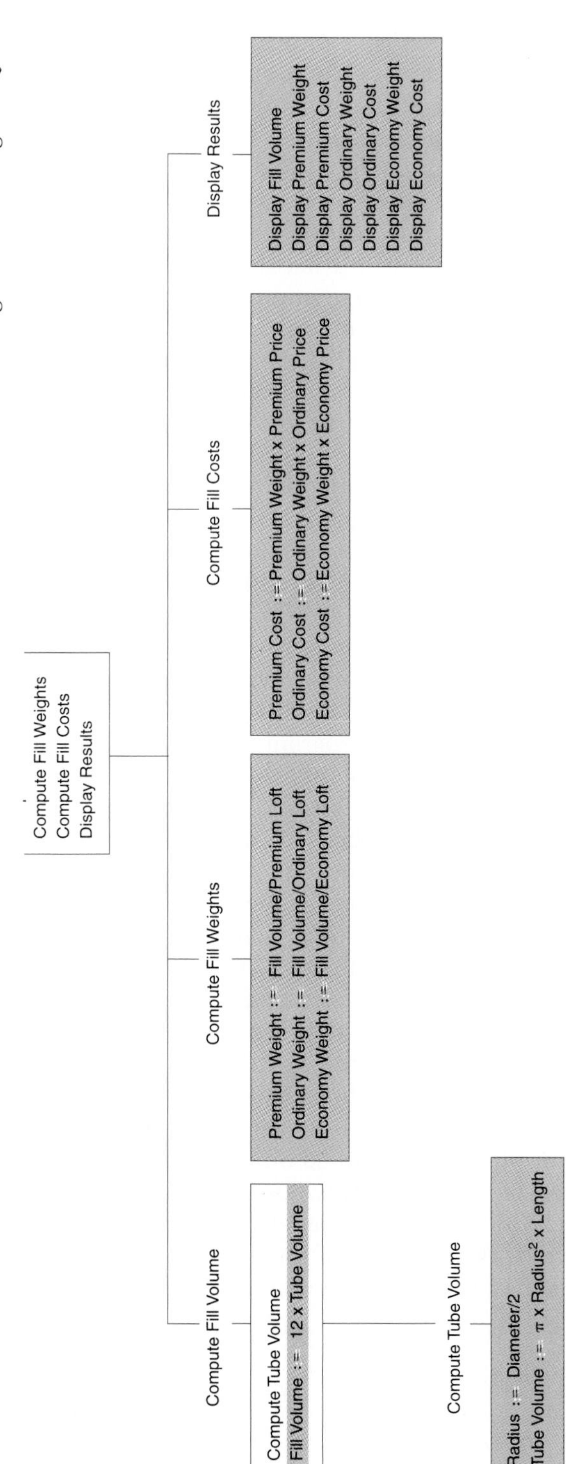

ule) and try something else. You don't have to scrap your whole design—only the small part you are working on. There may be many intermediate steps and trial solutions before you reach a final design.

The modules developed for the case studies throughout this book are presented as though we wrote them down that way the first time. Nothing could be further from the truth! The designs shown are the final product of a long process of trying and discarding many different ones. To show all of the intermediate attempts we made would easily double the size of this text. So don't hesitate to throw out a design and begin again. And don't be discouraged if it takes you a number of attempts to achieve a design. The problem-solving phase of the programming process takes time. If you spend the bulk of your time analyzing and designing a solution, coding and implementing the program will take very little time.

You'll find it easier to implement a design if you write the steps in pseudocode. *Pseudocode* is a mixture of English statements and Ada-like control structures that can easily be translated into Ada. (We've been using pseudocode in the algorithms in the Problem-Solving Case Studies.) When a concrete step is written in pseudocode, it should be possible to rewrite it directly as a statement in a program.

Implementing a Design The product of top-down design is a hierarchical solution to a problem with multiple levels of abstraction. Figure 3-5 shows the top-down design we developed for program Quilt. This kind of solution forms the basis for the implementation phase of programming.

How do we translate a top-down design into an Ada program? If you look closely at Figure 3-5, you can see that we can assemble the concrete steps (those that are shaded) into a complete algorithm for solving the problem. Their position in the tree determines the order in which they are assembled. We start at the top of the tree, at level 0, with the first step "Compute Fill Volume." Because it is abstract, we must go to the next level, level 1. There we find a series of steps that correspond (are functionally equivalent) to this step. The first of these steps, "Compute Tube Volume," is abstract, so we must go to the next level, level 2. There we find a corresponding series of concrete steps; this series of steps becomes the first part of our algorithm. Because the conversion process is now concrete, we can go back a level to level 1 and go on to the next step, calculating the Fill Volume. This step is concrete; we can copy it directly into the algorithm. Now we are ready to return to level 0. The last three steps at level 0 are abstract, so we work with each of them in order at level 1, making them concrete. Here's the resulting nonhierarchical algorithm.

Radius := Diameter / 2
Tube volume := π × Radius ^{2} × Length
Fill Volume := 12 × Tube Volume.
Premium Weight := Fill Volume / Premium Loft
Ordinary Weight := Fill Volume / Ordinary Loft
Economy Weight := Fill Volume / Economy Loft
Premium Cost := Premium Weight × Premium Price
Ordinary Cost := Ordinary Weight × Ordinary Price
Economy Cost := Economy Weight × Economy Price
Display Fill Volume
Display Premium Weight
Display Premium Cost
Display Ordinary Weight
Display Ordinary Cost
Display Economy Weight
Display Economy Cost

From this algorithm we can construct a table of the constants and variables required, and then we can write the declarative part and sequence of statements for the program.

In practice, you will not write your design as a tree diagram but as a series of modules grouped by levels of abstraction, as we've done here:

Quilt Level 0
Compute Fill Volume
Compute Fill Weights
Compute Fill Costs
Display results

Compute Fill Volume Level 1
Compute Tube Volume
Fill Volume := 12 × Tube Volume

Compute Fill Weights
Premium Weight := Fill Volume / Premium Loft
Ordinary Weight := Fill Volume / Ordinary Loft
Economy Weight := Fill Volume / Economy Loft

Compute Fill Costs
Premium Cost := Premium Weight × Premium Price
Ordinary Cost := Ordinary Weight × Ordinary Price
Economy Cost := Economy Weight × Economy Price

Display Results
Display Fill Volume
Display Premium Weight
Display Premium Cost
Display Ordinary Weight
Display Ordinary Cost
Display Economy Weight
Display Economy Cost

Compute Tube Volume **Level 2**
Radius := Diameter / 2
Tube volume := $\pi \times$ Radius $^2 \times$ Length

The type of implementation that we've introduced here is called *flat* or *inline* implementation. We are flattening the hierarchical structure of the solution by writing all of the steps as one long sequence. This kind of solution is adequate when a solution is short and has only a few levels of abstraction, and the programs it produces are clear and easy to understand, assuming appropriate comments and good style.

Longer programs with more levels of abstraction are difficult to work with as flat implementations. In Chapter 6 you'll see that it is possible to translate a hierarchical design directly into a hierarchical implementation. Each module is implemented as a separate subprogram, and the abstract steps in the design are replaced with calls to those subprograms.

Another advantage of implementing modules as subprograms is that you can pick them up and use them in other programs. Over time you will build up a library of your own subprograms to complement those in Ada's standard library.

We postpone a detailed discussion of hierarchical implementations until Chapter 6 because our programs remain short enough for flat implementations to suffice. In the meantime, we examine flow of control, preconditions and postconditions, interface design, and other important concepts you'll need to develop hierarchical implementations.

Object-Oriented Design

Up to now we have discussed one specific design methodology—top-down structured design, which also is called stepwise refinement. Another methodology, object-oriented design, has become popular in recent years.

As you might expect, the basis of the object-oriented methodology is something called an *object.* An object is simply an entity or some *thing* that makes sense in the context of the problem being solved. Groups of objects with similar properties and behaviors are described by an *object class* (often shortened to *class*). For example, the Ada textbook that you are currently reading is an object. It is a member of a class of similar objects that we call books. An object class is similar to an Ada type. Like types, object classes have attributes and operations associated with them. For example, books have an attribute specifying whether they are fiction or nonfiction and operations to check them out of and return them to the library.

More advanced object-oriented design involves much more than defining objects and classes; it is concerned with mechanisms for creating new types of objects and for structuring the relationships between them (the terms *encapsulation*, *inheritance*, and *polymorphism* often are used to describe these mechanisms).

An object-oriented design begins with an examination of a problem to determine the obvious object classes that make up its solution. Usually this is done by considering all of the nouns in the problem description. Complicated classes are decomposed into simpler classes. For example, we might decompose a book class into hardcover and paperback classes. We also can combine classes with common attributes and common operations into more general classes. For example, we might combine borrowers and librarians to form a class called people.

Both top-down design and object-oriented design are based on hierarchies. A top-down design is a tree structure composed of modules—collections of concrete and abstract steps. Because top-down design is based on actions or functions, it is known as a *functional design method.* An object-oriented design is a tree structure of objects (things) rather than of functions (actions). In this text we make use of both hierarchies. We use subprograms to implement functional hierarchies and subtypes to implement class hierarchies. We work with relatively simple problems to help you develop your design skill. In later courses you will add more sophisticated techniques necessary to solve even larger problems.

We use this outline for the hierarchical designs in our case studies:

Problem statement
Input description
Output description
Assumptions (if any)
Discussion
Algorithms
Object Modeling
Program

SOFTWARE ENGINEERING TIP

Documentation

As you create your top-down design, you are developing documentation for your program. *Documentation* is the written problem specifications, design, development history, and actual code of a program.

Good documentation helps users read and understand a program and is invaluable when software is being modified (maintained). If you haven't looked at your program for six months and need to change it, you'll be happy that you documented it well. Of course, if someone else has to use and modify your program, documentation is indispensable.

Documentation is both external and internal to the program. External documentation includes specifications, the development history, and the top-down design. Internal documentation includes the program format and

self-documenting code—meaningful identifiers and comments. You can use the pseudocode from your top-down designs as comments in your programs.

This kind of documentation may be sufficient for someone reading or maintaining your programs. However, if a program is to be used by people who are not programmers, you must provide a user's manual as well.

Be sure to keep documentation up to date. Indicate any changes you make in a program in all pertinent documentation. Use self-documenting code to make your program more readable.

Self-documenting code A program containing meaningful identifiers as well as judiciously used clarifying comments.

PROBLEM-SOLVING CASE STUDY

Mixing Proportions

Specification

Problem Determine the amount of oil and vinegar to mix together given the proportions of each and the total amount of salad dressing required.

Input Two whole number values for the proportions of oil and vinegar, the first for the parts of oil and the second for the parts of vinegar.
A real number value for the total amount of salad dressing required.
A string value for the units of measurement.

Output The input data with a message that identifies each number (echo printing).
The amount of each of the two components required to make the total amount of mixture.

Assumptions We assume that all data entered by the user of our program is correct. Further, we assume that the unit of measurement the user enters contains no more than 20 characters.

Discussion Mixing ingredients from proportional amounts is a common problem. For example, Grandma Smedley's recipe for salad dressing combines oil and vinegar in the proportions of 9 to 4. Because proportions have no units, we can choose whatever units are most convenient for us. One batch of her dressing can be made by combining 9 ounces of oil and 4 ounces of vinegar. A much larger batch can be produced by combining 9 gallons of oil and 4 gallons of vinegar. We have defined *batch* here to mean

PROBLEM-SOLVING CASE STUDY cont'd.

the total number of units obtained by adding the two proportion values together. For our salad dressing, one batch is 13 parts (9 parts of oil plus 4 parts of vinegar). If our units are ounces, then one batch is 13 ounces. If our units are gallons, then one batch is 13 gallons.

We can calculate the amount of oil and vinegar required to double the batch (make 26 parts) by multiplying the parts of each ingredient by 2 like this:

$9 \times 2 = 18$ parts of oil
$4 \times 2 = 8$ parts of vinegar

Using this approach, we can make any number of batches by multiplying the parts by the number of batches we want to make. To fix four and one-half batches, we perform the following calculations.

$9 \times 4.5 = 40.5$ parts of oil
$4 \times 4.5 = 18.0$ parts of vinegar

It takes a little algebra to determine the amount of each ingredient needed to prepare a specific volume of salad dressing. We can set up the following equation to determine how much oil and vinegar it takes to make up 16 ounces of Grandma Smedley's salad dressing:

$$9n + 4n = 16$$

where n is the *number of batches* required to produce the desired amount (16 ounces in this example). Solving for n, we have

$$n = 16/13 = 1.23$$

showing that we must make 1.23 batches in order to have 16 ounces of dressing.

Now that we know the number of batches needed and the proportions of each ingredient, we can determine the amount of each ingredient.

Amount of salad oil $= 9 \times 1.23 = 11.08$ ounces

Amount of vinegar $= 4 \times 1.23 = 4.92$ ounces

We generalize this example in our algorithmic solution.

Proportions **Level 0**
Get Data
Print Data
Determine Amount of Each Ingredient
Print Amount of Each Ingredient

PROBLEM-SOLVING CASE STUDY cont'd.

Get Data — **Level 1**
Get Parts of Oil
Get Parts of Vinegar
Get Total Amount
Get Units

Print Data
Put Parts of Oil
Put Parts of Vinegar
Put Total Amount
Put Units

Determine Amount of Each Ingredient
Determine Number of Batches Required
Amount of Oil := Parts of Oil × Number of Batches
Amount of Vinegar := Parts of Vinegar × Number of Batches

Print Amount of Each Ingredient
Put Amount of Oil
Put Units
Put Amount of Vinegar
Put Units

Determine Number of Batches Required — **Level 2**
Number of Batches := Amount Desired / (Parts of Oil + Parts of Vinegar)

Object Modeling Most of the data objects in our algorithm are positive integer and real numbers that can be modeled using the predefined types Integer and Float with appropriate ranges. The units of measurement entered by the user can be any sequence of characters. We use type String for this data. Consistent with our assumptions we arbitrarily selected a maximum string size of 20 characters.

Module Structure Chart

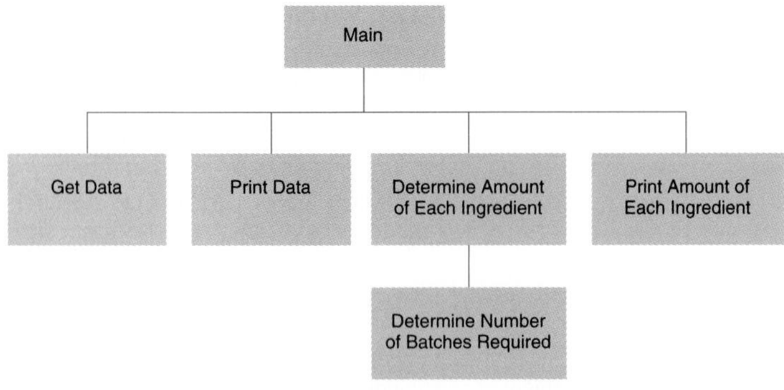

Variables

Name	*Data Type and Range*	*Role*
Parts Of Oil	Integer, positive	Proportion of salad oil
Parts Of Vinegar	Integer, positive	Proportion of vinegar
Total Amount	Float, positive	Amount of mixture needed
Units	String, 20 characters	Measurement units used
Num Batches	Float, positive	Number of batches needed
Amount Oil	Float, positive	Amount of salad oil
Amount Vinegar	Float, positive	Amount of vinegar

Here is the complete program. It includes the prompt messages, output labels, and output formatting required in an interactive program. Notice how we've used the module names as comments to help distinguish the modules from one another in our flat implementation.

Program

```
with Ada.Text_IO;
with Ada.Float_Text_IO;
with Ada.Integer_Text_IO;

procedure Proportions is

-- This program determines the amount of oil and vinegar necessary
-- to make a desired amount of salad dressing using the proportions
-- supplied by the user.

   -- Constants
   Max_Length : constant Integer := 20;      -- Maximum number of characters

   -- Variables

   Parts_Of_Oil     : Integer range 1..Integer'Last; -- Proportion of salad oil
   Parts_Of_Vinegar : Integer range 1..Integer'Last; -- Proportion of vinegar

   Units     : String (1..Max_Length);               -- Measurement units used
   Last_Char : Integer range 0..Max_Length;          -- For string slice range

   Total_Amount   : Float range 0.0..Float'Last;     -- Amount of dressing needed
   Num_Recipes    : Float range 0.0..Float'Last;     -- Number of recipes needed
   Amount_Oil     : Float range 0.0..Float'Last;     -- Amount of oil
   Amount_Vinegar : Float range 0.0..Float'Last;     -- Amount of vinegar
```

```
begin
   -- Get the data
   Ada.Text_IO.Put (Item => "Enter the proportions of oil and vinegar.");
   Ada.Text_IO.New_Line;
   Ada.Integer_Text_IO.Get (Item => Parts_Of_Oil);
   Ada.Integer_Text_IO.Get (Item => Parts_Of_Vinegar);
   Ada.Text_IO.Put (Item => "Enter the amount of salad dressing desired.");
   Ada.Text_IO.New_Line;
   Ada.Float_Text_IO.Get (Item => Total_Amount);
   Ada.Text_IO.Skip_Line;
   Ada.Text_IO.Put (Item => "Enter the units of measurement you're using.");
   Ada.Text_IO.New_Line;
   Ada.Text_IO.Get_Line (Item => Units, Last => Last_Char);
   Ada.Text_IO.New_Line;

   -- Print the data
   Ada.Text_IO.Put (Item => "The ingredients are mixed in the proportion of ");
   Ada.Text_IO.New_Line;
   Ada.Integer_Text_IO.Put (Item => Parts_Of_Oil, Width => 1);
   Ada.Text_IO.Put (Item => " parts of oil to ");
   Ada.Integer_Text_IO.Put (Item => Parts_Of_Vinegar, Width => 1);
   Ada.Text_IO.Put (Item => " parts of vinegar.");
   Ada.Text_IO.New_Line;
   Ada.Text_IO.New_Line;
   Ada.Text_IO.Put (Item => "To prepare ");
   Ada.Float_Text_IO.Put (Item => Total_Amount,
                          Fore => 1,
                          Aft  => 1,
                          Exp  => 0);
   Ada.Text_IO.Put (Item => " " & Units (1..Last_Char) );
   Ada.Text_IO.Put (Item => " of salad dressing,");
   Ada.Text_IO.New_Line;

   -- Determine Number of Recipes Required
   Num_Recipes := Total_Amount / Float (Parts_Of_Oil + Parts_Of_Vinegar);

   -- Determine Amount of Each Ingredient
   Amount_Oil     := Float (Parts_Of_Oil) * Num_Recipes;
   Amount_Vinegar := Float (Parts_Of_Vinegar) * Num_Recipes;

   -- Print Amount of Each Ingredient
   Ada.Text_IO.Put (Item => "combine ");
   Ada.Float_Text_IO.Put (Item => Amount_Oil,
                          Fore => 1,
                          Aft  => 1,
                          Exp  => 0);
   Ada.Text_IO.Put (Item => " " & Units (1..Last_Char) );
   Ada.Text_IO.Put (Item => " of salad oil with ");
   Ada.Float_Text_IO.Put (Item => Amount_Vinegar,
```

```
                         Fore => 1,
                         Aft  => 1,
                         Exp  => 0);
   Ada.Text_IO.Put (Item => " " & Units (1..Last_Char) );
   Ada.Text_IO.Put (Item => " of vinegar.");
   Ada.Text_IO.New_Line;

end Proportions;
```

Here is a sample dialog obtained from running this program:

```
Enter the proportions of oil and vinegar.
9 4
Enter the amount of salad dressing desired.
16.0
Enter the units of measurement you're using.
ounces

The ingredients are mixed in the proportion of
9 parts of oil to 4 parts of vinegar.

To prepare 16.0 ounces of salad dressing,
combine 11.1 ounces of salad oil with 4.9 ounces of vinegar.
```

Testing and Debugging

An important part of implementing a program is testing it (checking the results). By now you should realize that there is nothing magical about the computer. It is no more infallible than whoever is writing the instructions and entering the data. Don't trust it to give you the correct answers until you've verified enough of them by hand to convince yourself that the program is working.

In these Testing and Debugging sections, we offer tips on how to test your programs and what to do if a program doesn't work the way you expect. But don't wait until you've found a bug to read the Testing and Debugging sections. It's much easier to prevent bugs than it is to fix them.

The two most common error messages in testing programs that input data values are DATA_ERROR and CONSTRAINT_ERROR. The DATA_ERROR message tells you that the data you entered is not of the correct data type. Inadvertently typing a character which is not valid in a number is the most common reason to see the DATA_ERROR message. For example, typing 16.O (where we typed the letter O rather than the digit 0) for the desired amount of salad dressing gives us a DATA_ERROR in Program Proportions. If you have entered the data correctly, check your program for the correct type, number, and order of Get procedure calls. Leaving out or inserting one can cause your prompts and data entry to "march out of step." Check your use of the Skip_Line procedure. It may be skipping over data you thought the program was reading.

CONSTRAINT_ERROR commonly means that one of the numbers entered was out of the legal range for the value. For example, entering a proportion of −3 gives us a CONSTRAINT_ERROR in Program Proportions. If you have entered the data correctly, follow the same suggestions we made for DATA_ERROR. In addition, you should check to see that all of the ranges you supplied in your variable declarations are reasonable.

The NAME_ERROR, MODE_ERROR, and END_ERROR exceptions can occur when you are using files. NAME_ERROR occurs when you try to open a file that does not exist. Check the files on your disk and the spelling of the name in your program. For some systems, the file name has to include the disk name or letter as well as the name of the file. MODE_ERROR occurs when the program tries to input from a file that is set for output (the mode of the file is Out_File or Append_File) or output to a file that is set for input (the mode of the file is In_File). Check to make sure you are using the correct files in your I/O calls. END_ERROR occurs when the program tries to get a value from a file after it already has read all of the data available in it. This simply may mean that the data file was not prepared properly. Alternatively, you may have extra Get calls or have used Skip_Line to skip over *needed* data.

When you are using files, remember to include a File parameter in all your Get, Get_Line, Skip_Line, Put, and New_Line procedure calls. If you forget to include the input file, the program stops and waits for input from the keyboard. If you forget to include the output file, you get unexpected output on the screen. Finally, avoid the potential corruption of files by closing them before your program terminates.

By giving you a framework that can help you organize and keep track of all of the details in designing and implementing a program, top-down design should help you avoid these errors in the first place.

In later chapters, you'll see that you can test modules separately. If you make sure that each module works by itself, your program should work when you put all the modules together. Testing modules separately is less work than trying to test an entire program. In a smaller section of code it's less likely that multiple errors will combine to produce behavior that's difficult to analyze.

Testing and Debugging Hints

1. Use the top-down design methodology to avoid making mistakes.
2. If your data is mixed (string and numeric values), be sure to deal with intervening blanks and line terminators.
3. Echo-print input data to verify that each value is where it belongs and in the proper format.

4. Be sure that a file is in the proper mode (In_File, Out_File, or Append_File) before you try to perform I/O operations on it.
5. When a program inputs from or outputs to a file, be sure each file I/O statement from or to a file includes a File parameter.

Summary

Programs operate on data. If data and programs are kept separate, the data is available to use with other programs, and the same program can be run with other sets of input data. Get procedures are used to copy values from an input device into variables in the program.

The end of every data line is marked by a line terminator. You create a line terminator every time you press the Return key. Your program generates a line terminator each time the New_Line procedure is called.

The standard library packages, Float_Text_IO and Integer_Text_IO, contain Get procedures for the input of floating-point and integer values. These procedures skip over any blanks or line terminators that come before the numeric data.

Package Text_IO contains Get and Get_Line procedures for reading string values. The Get procedure *ignores* line terminators and reads characters until the string is filled. Get_Line reads characters until the string is filled *or* a line terminator is found.

Interactive programs prompt the user for each data entry and directly inform the user of errors. Designing an interactive dialog is an exercise in the art of communication.

File I/O allows data to be prepared before a program is run and allows the program to run again with the same data in the event a problem crops up during processing.

When a program requires a large amount of data, it should come from a file rather than the keyboard. Similarly, a program that produces a large amount of output should write it to a file rather than to the screen. By writing the results to a file, the output from one program can be used as input to another program. There are four things you have to do to utilize files: (1) declare file variables; (2) prepare the files for reading or writing with Open or Create; (3) include a File parameter in each Get, Get_Line, Skip_Line, Put, and New_Line procedure that does not read from the keyboard or write to the screen; and (4) sever the connection to the file with a call to the Close procedure.

Top-down design is a method for tackling large programming problems. It begins with an abstract solution that is then divided into major steps. Each step becomes a subproblem that is analyzed and subdivided further. A concrete step is one that can be translated directly into Ada; those that need more refinement are abstract steps. A module is a collection of concrete and abstract steps that solves a subproblem.

Careful attention to top-down design, program formatting, and documentation produces highly structured and readable programs.

Quick Check

1. Write two Ada procedure calls to input values into two integer variables, X and Y. (p. 118–119)
2. Input prompts should acknowledge the user's experience.
   a. What sort of message would you have a program print to prompt a novice user to input a social security number?
   b. How would you change the wording of the prompting message for an experienced user? (pp. 119–120)
3. When is the Skip_Line procedure most useful? (p. 138)
4. If a program is going to input 1000 numbers, is interactive input appropriate? (pp. 138–139)
5. What are the four things that you have to remember to do in order to use files? (pp. 140)
6. How many levels of abstraction are there in a top-down design before you reach the point at which you can begin coding a program? (pp. 146–150)

Answers

1.
```
Ada.Integer_Text_IO.Get (Item => X);
Ada.Integer_Text_IO.Get (Item => Y);
```
2. a. Please type a nine-digit social security number, then press Enter. b. Enter SSN. **3.** The Skip_Line procedure is most useful when using the Get_Line procedure *after* getting a numeric value. **4.** No. File input is more appropriate for programs that input large amounts of data. **5.** (1) Declare file variables. (2) Use Open or Create to prepare each file for reading or writing. (3) Make sure that each I/O procedure call that uses a file has a File parameter. (4) Close the file when done. **6.** There is no fixed number of levels of abstraction. You keep refining the solution through as many levels as necessary until the steps are all concrete.

Exam Preparation Exercises

1. What is the main advantage of having a program input its data rather than writing all the data values as constants in the program?
2. Given this line of data:

```
17 13 7 3
```

and these procedure calls:

```
Ada.Integer_Text_IO.Get (Item => E);
Ada.Integer_Text_IO.Get (Item => F);
Ada.Text_IO.Skip_Line;
```

   a. What is the value of each variable after the Gets are completed?
   b. What happens to any leftover data values in the input?
   c. Where is the reading marker after these three calls?
3. The line terminator signals the end of a line.
   a. How do you generate a line terminator from the keyboard?
   b. How do you generate a line terminator in a program's output?
4. Float values can be read into Integer variables. True or false?
5. a. Spaces may be used to separate numeric data values being entered into an Ada program. True or false?
   b. Line terminators may be used to separate numeric data values being entered into an Ada program. True or false?
6. Given this data

```
14 21 64
19 67 91
73 89 27
23 96 47
```

   what are the values of integer variables A, B, C, and D after the following program segment is executed?

```
Ada.Integer_Text_IO.Get (Item => A);
Ada.Text_IO.Skip_Line;
Ada.Integer_Text_IO.Get (Item => B);
Ada.Integer_Text_IO.Get (Item => C);
Ada.Text_IO.Skip_Line;
Ada.Text_IO.Skip_Line;
Ada.Integer_Text_IO.Get (Item => D);
Ada.Text_IO.Skip_Line;
```

7. Define the following terms as they apply to interactive I/O.
   a. Input prompt
   b. Echo printing
8. List three benefits of using top-down design in programming.
9. Put a check next to each data line that would cause a DATA_ERROR if entered for the following code segment:

```
A : Float;
B : Integer;
C : Integer;

Ada.Float_Text_IO.Get   (Item => A);
Ada.Integer_Text_IO.Get (Item => B);
Ada,Integer_Text_IO.Get (Item => C);
Ada.Text_IO.Skip_Line
```

```
____     5  8  9
____     5.0  8  9.0
____     5  8.0  9
____     5.0  Hello
```

10. The following exceptions occur during input or output with files. Describe the cause of each.
    a. NAME_ERROR
    b. MODE_ERROR
    c. END_ERROR
11. A NAME_ERROR exception can be raised with improper use of the Create procedure. True or false?
12. Every file should be closed before a program terminates.
    a. What does the Close procedure do?
    b. What could happen if you forget to close a file before your program terminates?

Programming Warm-up Exercises

1. Write the necessary Get calls that input the following data values into the Float variables Length, Height, and Width.

```
10.25  7.625  4.5
```

2. Write the necessary Get and Skip_Line calls that input the first two data values on each of the following lines into the Float variables Length1, Height1, Length2, and Height2.

```
10.25  7.625  4.5
8.5   1.0   0.0
```

3. Write a set of variable declarations and a series of Get and Skip_Line procedure calls to read the following lines of data into variables of the appropriate type. You can make up the variable names. Notice that the two numeric values on the second line are separated from one another by a single blank and that there are no blanks to the left of the first character on each line.

```
765Mildred
47.5 45
Horace
```

4. Write a program segment (declarations and statements) that reads three names from the keyboard and then writes them to the screen one by one. The names may be of different length (but less than 30 characters) and are entered one name to a line.

5. Write a program segment for an interactive program to input values for a person's age, height, weight, and first name. Assume that the person using the program is a novice user. How would you rewrite the code for an experienced user?
6. Enter (or obtain a copy through the publisher's Web site at www.jbpub.com/) and compile Program Mileage given on page 95. Run the program with correct data of your choice. Note what exception occurs if you try running the program with this same correct data except
   a. enter integer values instead of floating-point values.
   b. enter floating-point values with no digits after the decimal point.
   c. enter floating-point values with no digits before the decimal point.
   d. enter strings instead of a floating-point values.
   e. enter a floating-point value for a make of car.
7. Modify Program Mileage you used in the previous exercise so it reads its data from a file but still writes its results to the screen. You will need to consult the manual for your specific computer to learn the rules for naming files.
   a. Run the program *before* you create the input data file. What exception occurs?
   b. Create a data file with correct data and try running the program again.
   c. Remove one of the values for gallons from the data file and try running the program again. What exception occurs?
8. Enter (or obtain a copy through the publisher's Web site at www.jbpub.com/) and compile Program Proportions given on page 154. Run the program with correct data of your choice. Note what exception occurs if you try running the program with this same correct data except
   a. enter an integer value instead of a floating-point value for the amount of dressing desired.
   b. enter floating-point values for the proportions.
9. Use top-down design to write an algorithm for starting an automobile with a manual transmission.
10. Use top-down design to write an algorithm for logging on to your computer system, and entering and running a program. The algorithm should be simple enough for a novice user to follow.
11. Fill in the blanks in the following program, which should read two integer values from file `Numbers.Dat` and output them to file `Results`. Each number in the output file should be on a separate line.

```
with ____________________;
with ____________________;
procedure Copy is

   A        : Integer;
   In_Data  : Ada.Text_IO.____________________;
   Out_Data : Ada.Text_IO.____________________;
```

```
begin
   Ada.Text_IO.Open    (____________ => In_Data,
                        ____________ => ____________,
                        ____________ => "Numbers.Dat");

   Ada.Text_IO.Create  (____________ => Out_Data,
                        ____________ => "RESULTS");
   Ada.Integer_Text_IO.Get (______________________, Item => A);
   Ada.Integer_Text_IO.Put (______________________, Item => A);
   Ada.______________________________________________________;
   Ada.Integer_Text_IO.Get (______________________, Item => A);
   Ada.Integer_Text_IO.Put (______________________, Item => A);
   Ada.______________________________________________________;
   Ada.Text_IO.______________________________;
   Ada.Text_IO.______________________________;
end Copy;
```

12. An interactive program takes some of its input from a disk file and some from the keyboard. When the program is first tested, the computer seems to "hang." Nothing is displayed on the screen and the program never terminates. What did the programmer probably leave out?

Programming Problems

1. Write a top-down design and interactive Ada program to read an invoice number, quantity ordered, and unit price (all integers), and compute the total price. The program should write out the invoice number, quantity, unit price, and total price with identifying phrases. Format with indentation, and use appropriate comments and meaningful identifiers. Make sure you give informative prompts for each data value.
2. Modify your design and Ada program in the previous exercise to read a 10-character description of the item instead of an invoice number.
3. Write a top-down design and Ada program to read an amount of money invested (float), the interest rate in percent (float), the number of years (integer), and the number of times per year interest is compounded (integer). The program should echo print the input. It should also print the amount of money in the account after the given number of years. You can calculate this amount with the following formula:

$A = P(1 + i / q)^{nq}$ where

q is the number of times per year interest is compounded
n is the number of years
I is the interest rate (as a fraction, not percent)
P is the original investment
A is the amount

As always, format with indentation, and use appropriate comments and meaningful identifiers. Write the program to be run interactively with informative prompts for each data value.

4. Write a top-down design and Ada program to read the lengths (float) and widths (float) of three rooms and display the total square feet rounded to the nearest tenth of a square foot and the average area rounded to the nearest hundredth of a square foot. As always, format with indentation, and use appropriate comments and meaningful identifiers. Give informative prompts for each data value.
5. Modify the proportions case study so that calculations are made for a recipe with three ingredients rather than two.
6. Write a top-down design and Ada program to read five words from the keyboard (one word per line). Echo print each word and display the number of characters it contains. After the last word has been processed display the average number of letters per word rounded to the nearest tenth of a letter. You may assume that all words will contain less than 25 letters.

CHAPTER

Boolean and Enumeration Types, Conditions, and Selection Control Structures

GOALS

After reading this chapter, you should be able to

- construct a Boolean expression to evaluate a given condition
- construct an if-then-else statement to perform a specific task
- construct an if-then statement to perform a specific task
- construct a set of nested if statements to perform a specific task
- construct an if-elsif statement to perform a specific task
- declare and use an enumeration type
- determine the preconditions and postconditions for a module, and use them to perform an algorithm trace
- trace the execution of an Ada program
- test and debug an Ada program

So far, the computer has executed the statements in our programs in their physical order. It has executed the first statement, then the second, and so on until it has executed all of the statements. But what if we want the computer to execute the statements in some other order? Suppose we want to check the validity of input data and then either perform a calculation or print an error message, not both. To do this we must be able to ask a question and then, based on the answer, choose one or another course of action. The order in which we want the statements to be executed is called the *logical order*. The if statement allows us to execute statements in a logical order—an order that is different from their physical order. With it we can ask a question and do one thing if the answer is yes (True) or another if the answer is no (False). In the first part of this chapter, we deal with asking questions; then we deal with the if statement itself.

In Chapter 2 we defined a data type as a collection of values and the operations that can be performed on those values. Frequently the predefined data types—Integer, Float, String, and Boolean—are inadequate to represent all of the data in a program. Ada has a mechanism for creating new data types; that is, we can define new data types ourselves—types that better model the data in our problem. In the last part of this chapter, we will examine how to define and use one kind of programmer-defined type: the enumeration data type.

Conditions and Boolean Expressions

To ask a question in Ada, we make an assertion. If the assertion we make is true, the answer to the question is yes. If the statement is not true, the answer to the question is no. For example, if we want to ask, "Are we having spinach for dinner tonight?" we would say, "We are having spinach for dinner tonight." If the assertion is true, the answer to the question is yes. If not, the answer is no.

So asking a question in Ada means making an assertion that is either True or False. The computer *evaluates* the assertion, checking it against some internal condition (the values stored in certain variables, for instance) and seeing whether it is True or False.

Boolean Expressions

In Ada, assertions take the form of conditions called Boolean expressions. Just as an arithmetic expression is made up of numeric values and operations, a **Boolean expression** is made up of Boolean values and operations.

Boolean expression An expression that evaluates to either True or False, the only values of the Boolean data type.

A Boolean expression can be as simple as a single value or a complex combination of values (constants and variables), relational operators, and logical operators. Let's look at each of these in detail.

Boolean Variables and Constants The data type Boolean has just two literals: True and False. A Boolean variable is a variable declared to be of type Boolean, which means that its contents can be either True or False. For example, if Data_OK is a Boolean variable, then

```
Data_OK := True;
```

is a valid assignment statement.

Relational Operators We can also assign values to Boolean variables by setting them equal to the result of comparing two expressions with a relational operator. Relational operators test a relationship between two values.

Let's look at an example. In this program fragment, Test is a Boolean variable, and A and B are integer variables.

```
Ada.Integer_Text_IO.Get (Item => A);      -- Compares A and B using the "less
Ada.Integer_Text_IO.Get (Item => B);      -- than" relational operator and
Test := A < B;                            -- assigns the Boolean result to Test
```

By comparing two values, we assert that a relationship (like "less than") exists between them. If the relationship does exist, the assertion is True; if not, it is False. These are the relationships that we can test for in Ada:

=	Equal to
/=	Not equal to
>	Greater than
<	Less than
>=	Greater than or equal to
<=	Less than or equal to

For example, if X is 5 and Y is 10, the following expressions are all True.

```
X /= Y
Y >  X
X <  Y
Y >= X
X <= Y
```

If X is "Mildred" and Y is "Rick", the expressions are still True because when the relational operator < is used with strings it means "comes before alphabetically" or more properly "comes before according to the collating sequence of the character set."

In the Latin-1 character set (Appendix C), all of the uppercase letters are in alphabetical order, as are the lowercase letters, but all of the uppercase letters come before the lowercase letters. Numbers come before all letters. The space character comes before any other printable character. Here are some examples that illustrate these relations.

Expression	Value
`"Mary" < "Pam"`	`True`
`"mary" < "pam"`	`True`
`"mary" < "Pam"`	`False`
`"MacDonald" = "Macdonald"`	`False`
`"MacDonald" < "Macdonald"`	`True`
`"  Hello" < "Hello"`	`True`

Of course we have to be careful to compare things that are of the same type—that is, integer numbers with integer numbers, float numbers with float numbers, and strings with strings. Comparing a value of type String to a value of type Integer, for instance, makes no sense and produces a syntax error message (even if the string value contains only digits as characters). For example, the comparisons

```
"50" < "97"
```

and

```
50 < 97
```

are valid, but

```
"50" < 97
```

generates a syntax error message.

We can use relational operators not only to compare variables or constants but also to compare the results of arithmetic expressions. In the following table we compare the results of adding 3 to X and multiplying Y by 10 for different values of X and Y:

Value of X	Value of Y	Expression	Result
12	2	`X + 3 <= Y * 10`	`True`
20	2	`X + 3 <= Y * 10`	`False`
17	2	`X + 3 =  Y * 10`	`True`
100	5	`X + 3 >  Y * 10`	`True`
7	1	`X + 3 /= Y * 10`	`False`

In the last example, the value of X + 3 and the value of Y * 10 are both 10. The expression *10 not equal to 10* is False.

Relational operators with float values Do not compare float numbers for equality (=) or inequality (/=)! Float numbers are not stored with perfect accuracy. Also, small errors are likely to arise when you perform calculations on float numbers. As a result, two float values that should be equal rarely are *exactly* equal. The = and /= operators test for exact equality. To handle this problem we always test float numbers for *near equality*. To do a near equality test, we compute the difference between the two numbers and see whether this difference is less than some maximum allowable difference.

For example, suppose we would like to know if the gas capacities of two large dirigibles (over 50 million cubic feet) are the same. These capacities are stored in the float variables Hindenburg_Volume and Graf_Zeppelin_Volume. How close must these two volumes be for us to consider them equal? With some subjectivity, we pick a value of 1000 cubic feet. This value is about 0.002% of the total volumes of these large airships. If their gas capacities are within 1000 cubic feet of each other, we will consider them to have equal volumes. The following Boolean expression evaluates to True if the two dirigibles have nearly equal gas capacities:

```
abs (Hindenburg_Volume - Graf_Zeppelin_Volume)  <  1000.0
```

Notice the use of absolute value in this Boolean expression. Because we do not know which of the two values is larger, we use the absolute value to calculate the *positive* difference between them.

In our example, if the difference is less than 1000 cubic feet, we say that the two gas volumes are close enough to call them equal. You must choose this acceptable difference with an understanding of your problem and solution needs. Testing the weights of two planets for near equality is much different than testing the weights of two sand grains.

Relational operators with Boolean values Only rarely do we apply the relational operators to Boolean values. However, there are some situations in which it is handy to be able to test whether two Boolean variables are equal (or different). Ada defines False to be less than True (truth is always greater than falsehood).

Logical Operators Logical operators are the reserved words `and`, `or`, and `not`. We can make more complex assertions by combining relational expressions with logical operators. For example, suppose we want to determine whether a final score is greater than 90 and a midterm score is greater than 70. In Ada, we would write the expression

```
(Final_Score > 90)  and  (Midterm_Score > 70)
```

The `and` operator requires both relationships to be True in order for the overall result to be True. If either or both of the relationships are False, `and` makes the entire result False.

Look at the example again. The computer first evaluates each of the relational operations (because they are enclosed in parentheses), producing two temporary Boolean results. They are then combined by the `and` operation to produce the final result.

The `or` operation also takes two Boolean values and combines them. If either or both are True, the result is True. Both values must be False for the result to be False. Now we can determine whether the midterm grade is an A or the final grade is an A. If either the midterm grade or the final grade equals A, the assertion is True. In Ada, we write the expression

```
(Midterm_Grade = "A")  or  (Final_Grade = "A")
```

The `and` and `or` operators always appear between two expressions; they are binary operators. The `not` operation precedes an expression; it is a unary operator. `Not` takes one Boolean value and gives its opposite as the result. If `(Grade = "A")` is False, then `not(Grade = "A")` is True. `Not` gives us a convenient way of reversing the meaning of an assertion. For example,

```
not (Hours > 40)
```

is the equivalent of

```
Hours <= 40
```

In some contexts the first form is clearer; in others, the second makes more sense.

The following pairs of expressions are equivalent:

```
not (A = B)                  A /= B

not ((A = B) or (A = C))     (A /= B) and (A /= C)

not ((A = B) and (C > D))    (A /= B) or (C <= D)
```

Take a close look at these expressions to be sure you understand why they are equivalent. It may help to try evaluating them with some values for A, B, C, and D. Notice the pattern here: The expression on the left is just the one to its right with `not` added and the relational and logical operators reversed (for example, = instead of /= and `or` instead of `and`). Remember this pattern. It allows you to rewrite expressions in the simplest form.*

You can apply logical operators to the results of comparisons; you can also apply them directly to variables of type Boolean. For example, instead of writing

```
Elector := (Age >= 18) and (District = 23);
```

to assign a value to Boolean variable Elector, we could use two intermediate Boolean variables, Voter and Constituent.

```
Voter       :=  Age >= 18;
Constituent :=  District = 23;
Elector     :=  Voter and Constituent;
```

The following tables summarize the results of applying `and` and `or` to a pair of Boolean values (represented here by Boolean variables X and Y).

Value of X	Value of Y	Value of X `and` Y
True	True	True
True	False	False
False	True	False
False	False	False

Value of X	Value of Y	Value of X `or` Y
True	True	True
True	False	True
False	True	True
False	False	False

And this table summarizes the results of applying the `not` operator to a Boolean value (represented by Boolean variable X).

Value of X	Value of `not` X
True	False
False	True

*In Boolean algebra, the pattern is formalized by a theorem called DeMorgan's law.

One final note about the and and or operators. When you use both of these operators in the same expression, you must use parentheses to indicate the order in which you want to evaluate them. More on this requirement when we look at precedence levels in the next section.

BACKGROUND INFORMATION

George Boole

Boolean algebra is named for its inventor, English mathematician George Boole. Boole was born in 1815. His father, a tradesman, began teaching him mathematics at an early age. But Boole initially was more interested in classical literature, languages, and religion—interests he maintained throughout his life. By the time he was 20, he had taught himself French, German, and Italian. He was well versed in the writings of Aristotle, Spinoza, Cicero, and Dante; and he wrote several philosophical papers.

At 16, to help support his family, Boole took a position as a teaching assistant in a private school. His work there and a second teaching job left him little time to study. A few years later, he opened a school and began to learn higher mathematics on his own. In spite of his lack of formal training, his first scholarly paper was published in the *Cambridge Mathematical Journal* when he was just 24. Boole went on to publish over 50 papers and several major works before he died in 1864, at the peak of his career.

Boole's *The Mathematical Analysis of Logic* was published in 1847. It would eventually form the basis for the development of digital computers. In the book, Boole set forth the formal axioms of logic (much like the axioms of geometry) on which the field of symbolic logic is built.

Boole drew on the symbols and operations of algebra in creating his system of logic. He associated the value 1 with the universal set (the set representing everything in the universe) and the value 0 with the empty set and restricted his system to these two quantities. He then defined operations that are analogous to subtraction, addition, and multiplication. Variables in the system have symbolic values. For example, if a Boolean variable P represents the set of all plants, then the expression $1-P$ refers to the set of all things that are not plants. We can simplify the expression, using $-P$ to mean "*not* plants." ($0-P$ is simply 0 because we can't remove elements from the empty set.) The subtraction operator in Boole's system corresponds to the not operator in Ada. In an Ada program, we might set the value of the Boolean variable Plant to True when the name of a plant is entered, and not Plant is True when the name of anything else is input.

The expression $0+P$ is the same as P. However, $0 + P + F$, where F is the set of all foods, is the set of all things that are either plants *or* foods. So the addition operator in Boole's algebra is the same as the Ada or operator.

```
   Ada.Text_IO.Put (Item => "Attempted division by zero.");
   Ada.Text_IO.New_Line;
   Ada.Text_IO.Put (Item => "Result set to largest possible integer.");
   Ada.Text_IO.New_Line;
   Result := Integer'Last;
end if;
```

The if-then Form

You occasionally will run into a situation where you want to say, "If a certain condition exists, then perform some action; otherwise, don't do anything." In other words, you want the computer to skip a sequence of instructions if a certain condition isn't met. This can be done with the form of the if statement called an if-then statement. This is its EBNF definition:

if_then_statement ::= **if** condition **then**
    sequence_of_statements
  end if;

Here's an example of an if-then statement. Notice the indentation and the placement of the statements that follow the if-then.

```
Ada.Text_IO.Put ("You are ");
if Age < 18 then
   Ada.Text_IO.Put(Item => "not ");
end if;
Ada.Text_IO.Put (Item => "an eligible voter");
Ada.Text_IO.New_Line;
```

If Age is less than 18, this code fragment displays "You are not an eligible voter". If Age is greater than or equal to 18, the printing of "not" is skipped and "You are an eligible voter" is displayed. Figure 4-5 shows the flow of control for an if-then statement.

As another example, let's say you are writing a program to compute income taxes. One of the lines on the tax form says, "Subtract line 23 from line 17 and enter result on line 24; if result is less than zero, enter zero and check box 24A." You can use an if-then statement to do this in Ada:

```
Result := Line_17 - Line_23;
if Result < 0.0 then
   Ada.Text_IO.Put (Item => "Check box 24A");
   Ada.Text_IO.New_Line;
   Result := 0.0;
end if;
Line_24 := Result;
```

This code does exactly what the tax form says it should. It computes the result of subtracting line 23 from line 17. Then it looks to see if Result

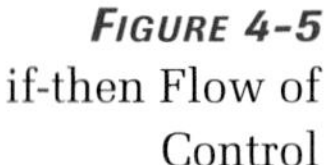

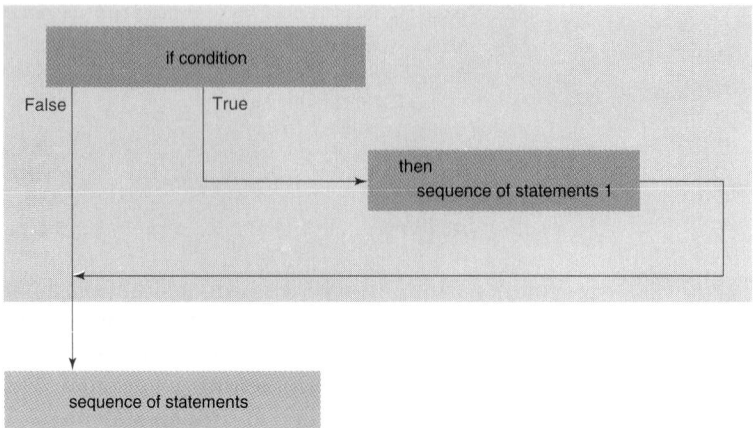

FIGURE 4-5
if-then Flow of Control

is less than zero. If it is, the fragment prints a message telling the user to check box 24A and then sets Result to zero. Finally, the calculated result (or zero, if the result is less than zero) is stored in a variable called Line_24.

Nested if Statements

There are no restrictions on what the statements can be in an if statement's sequence of statements. Therefore an if within an if is okay. In fact an if within an if within an if is legal. The only limitation here is the fact that people cannot follow a structure that is too involved. And readability is one of the marks of a good program.

When we place an `if` within an `if`, we are creating a *nested control structure*. Control structures nest, as mixing bowls do—smaller ones tucked inside larger ones. Here's an example:

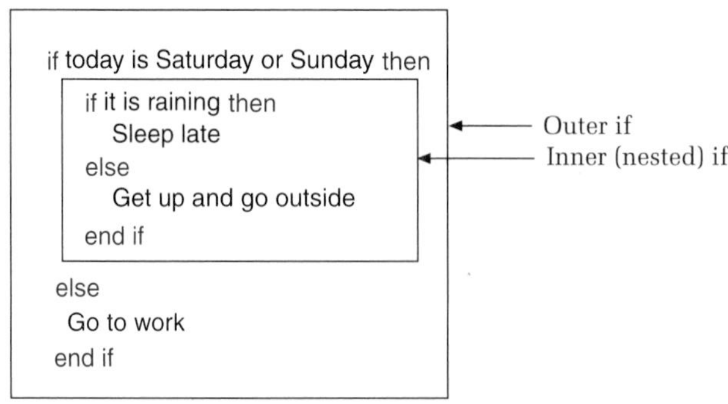

FIGURE 4-6
Flow of Control for a Nested if Statement

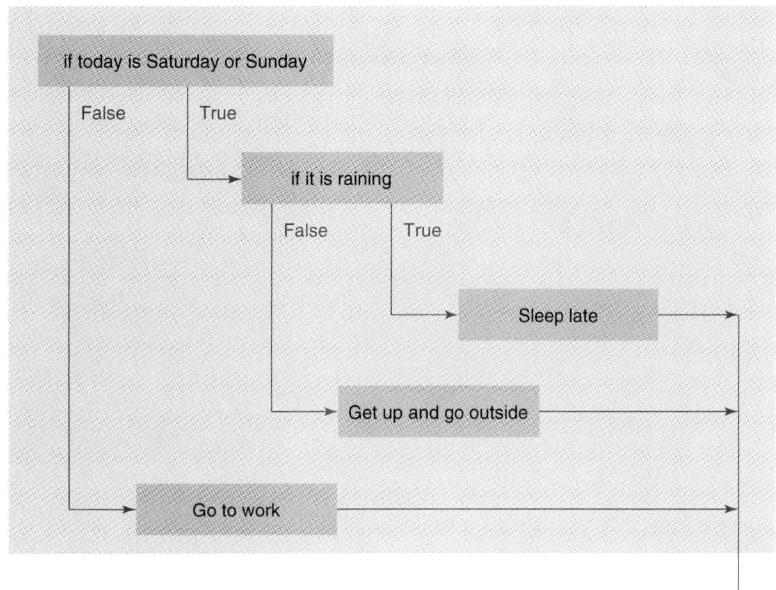

Figure 4-6 shows the flow of control for this particular nested control structure.

When one condition is dependent on another condition, it is particularly helpful to use the nested if. For example, suppose we want to print "Failing" if a student's average exam score is below 50. The average exam score is calculated by dividing the student's total exam points by the number of exams taken. However, some students are auditing the class and not taking exams, so we also must check that students do have exam scores. We could write the test

```
if (Num_Exams > 0)  and  (Total_Exam_Points / Num_Exams < 50) then
   Ada.Text_IO.Put (Item => "Failing");
   Ada.Text_IO.New_Line;
end if;
```

But this code causes the program to crash on the data for the first auditing student because the computer can't divide Total_Exam_Points by zero. We have to test for a nonzero number of exams *before* we test the second condition.

```
if Num_Exams > 0 then
   if Total_Exam_Points / Num_Exams < 50 then        -- Nested if
      Ada.Text_IO.Put (Item => "Failing");
      Ada.Text_IO.New_Line;
   end if;
end if;
```

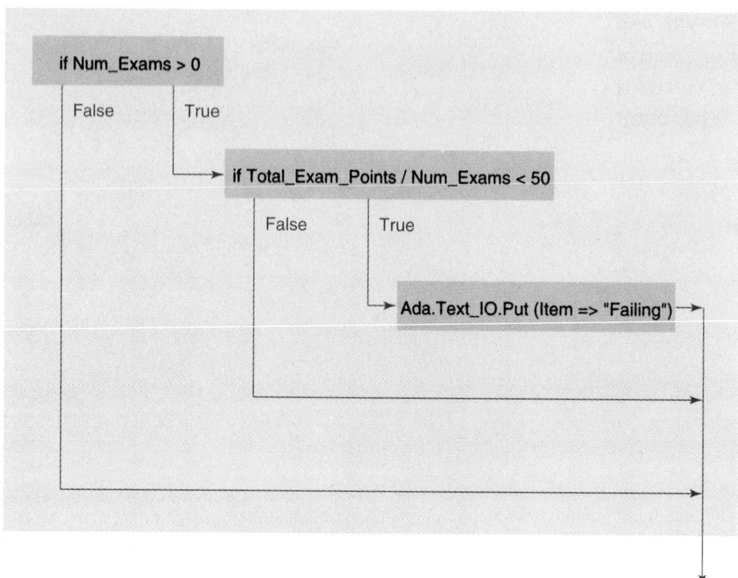

Figure 4-7
if-and-then-if Flow of Control

This code fragment implements what is called a *sequential and*, or an *if-and-then-if* control structure. Figure 4-7 shows the flow of control for this code fragment.

Whenever you come across a problem in which some condition must be tested before another condition is tested, a nested if structure is appropriate. In Chapter 12 we show another way to accomplish this.

The if-elsif Form

In general, you can code any problem that involves more than two alternative courses of action more efficiently with nested if statements. For example, to print out a month's number given its three-letter abbreviation, we could use a sequence of 12 if statements.

```
if Month = "Jan" then
   Month_Num := 1;
end if;
if Month = "Feb" then
   Month_Num := 2;
end if;
if Month = "Mar" then
   Month_Num := 3;
end if;
   .
   .
   .
if Month = "Dec" then
```

```
   Month_Num := 12;
end if;

Ada.Integer_Text_IO.Put (Item => Month_Num);
```

But the equivalent nested if structure

```
if Month = "Jan" then
   Month_Num := 1;
else
   if Month = "Feb" then
      Month_Num := 2;
   else
      if Month = "Mar" then
         Month_Num := 3;
      else
            .
            .
            .
               else
                  if Month = "Dec" then
                     Month_Num := 12;
                  end if;
               end if;
            .
            .
            .
      end if;
   end if;
end if;

Ada.Integer_Text_IO.Put (Item => Month_Num);
```

is more efficient because it makes fewer comparisons (in the sequential program fragment, you must test all 12 assertions even if the month is January.) The nested structure, however, is harder to read, and it is easy to make an error in indentation or leave out one of the "end ifs". Ada provides a mechanism to avoid these problems. We can use the reserved word `elsif` for choosing one of many alternatives (such as choosing one month out of 12). Here is the EBNF definition of the if statement with this option added:

if_statement ::= **if** condition **then**
  sequence_of_statements
{**elsif** condition **then**
  sequence_of_statements}
[**else**
  sequence_of_statements]
end if;

The elsif portion can be repeated zero or more times, and the else part is optional. The two previous forms of the if statement we gave are just simplified versions of this definition. A solution using `elsif` to print a month's number appears in the following program fragment.

```
if Month = "Jan" then
   Month_Num := 1;
elsif Month = "Feb" then
   Month_Num := 2;
elsif Month = "Mar" then
   Month_Num := 3;
   .
   .
   .
elsif Month = "Nov" then
   Month_Num := 11;
else                              -- Reaching here means that Month must be Dec
   Month_Num := 12;
end if;

Ada.Integer_Text_IO.Put (Item => Month_Num);
```

Notice that we did not test an assertion that Month is equal to "Dec". At this point, because we already have tested for the 11 other months, we assume that the month must be December. Be careful—this assumption may not be correct! If a user entered "Jnu" instead of "Jun" for the month, this segment would print an incorrect month number (12). It would be better to change the last part of this program fragment.

```
   .
   .
   .
elsif Month = "Dec" then
   Month_Num := 12;
else
   Ada.Text_IO.Put (Item => "Invalid month abbreviation.");
   Month_Num = 0;     -- Use zero for invalid month abbreviation
end if;

Ada.Integer_Text_IO.Put (Item => Month_Num);
```

The use of nested if statements to solve this problem is a correct solution and is often the best solution in programming languages that do not have the if-elsif form. Because Ada has the if-elsif form, using nested if statements for problems like this is considered bad style. Also note that the if-elsif has only one `end if` whereas the nested if statements have many.

It's important to note one difference between the series of if statements and the if-elsif: More than one alternative can be taken by the series of ifs, but the if-elsif can select only one. To see why this is important, consider the analogy of filling out a questionnaire. Some questions are like a series of if statements, asking you to circle all the items in a list that apply to you (such as all your hobbies). Other questions ask you to circle only one item in a list (your age group, for example) and are thus like an if-elsif structure. Both kinds of questions occur in programming problems. Being able to recognize which type of question is being asked will permit you to immediately select the appropriate control structure.

The if-elsif is also effective when you want to compare a series of consecutive ranges of values. For example, the Ski Wax Selection Case Study at the end of this chapter involves printing different messages for different ranges of temperatures. We present two solutions for one of the modules—one using a sequence of if statements, and the other using an if-elsif structure. As you'll see, the if-elsif version uses fewer comparisons, so it's more efficient.

As fast as modern computers are, many applications require so much computation that inefficient algorithms can waste hours of computer time. Always be on the lookout for ways to make your programs more efficient, as long as doing so doesn't make them difficult to understand. It's usually better to sacrifice a little efficiency for the sake of readability.

Enumeration Data Types

The built-in data types—Boolean, Integer, Float, and String—are not adequate to describe some classes of data. For example, in the previous section we used both integers and strings to represent months of the year. Although we often use numbers for months of the year, it is difficult to recognize an isolated integer literal as a month (is 4 the month of April or a third of a carton of eggs?). Also, because integers can take on values less than 1 and greater than 12, using them to represent months can lead to unexpected errors. Although using strings to represent months may eliminate the ambiguity of literals, they still allow the possibility of invalid data values ("Jnu" instead of "Jun").

Accurate Modeling

A major principle of object-oriented design is accurate modeling of the things (data) in our problems. We introduced ranges with numeric variables as one way of improving the modeling of numeric objects. While such a range would allow us to restrict a number representing a month to twelve possible values, it does not help us identify isolated data (again, is 4 the month of April or a third of a carton of eggs?). Numbers are not good models of months!

Ada allows us to define new data types that are more appropriate for representing this sort of data by listing (enumerating) all the values that make up the type. The values used in this listing must be legal Ada identifiers. The identifiers in the list are separated by commas and the list is enclosed in parentheses. Data types defined in this way are called **enumeration data types.**

Enumeration data type An ordered set of literal values (identifiers) defined as a data type.

The simplified EBNF definition for an enumeration type declaration is:

enumeration_type ::= **type** identifier **is** enumeration_type_definition;
enumeration_type_definintion ::= (identifier {, identifier})

Let's look at some examples. Here are declarations for an enumeration type used to represent the months of the year and two enumeration types used to represent the different chess game pieces.

```
   Type identifier          List of identifiers (literal values)
          |                              |
          v                              v
type Month_Type is          (Jan, Feb, Mar, Apr, May, Jun,
                             Jul, Aug, Sep, Oct, Nov, Dec);

type Chess_Piece_Type  is  (Pawn, Rook, Knight, Bishop, Queen, King);

type Player_Color_Type is  (Black, White);
```

As a matter of style, we usually add the suffix "_Type" to make it clear that the type identifier represents a type rather than a variable or constant. We write the definition of new types in the declarative part of the program where we also define constants and variables. The order of declarations in this part is not important to the Ada compiler as long as you declare an identifier before you use it. You must declare a type before you declare a constant or variable of that type.

We could use any valid identifiers to represent the months. For example, using the full month names (January) rather than three-letter abbreviations might make the enumeration literals even clearer to someone reading our program.

Without knowing it, you have already used an enumeration type: Boolean. In package Standard (where all the predefined types are defined), type Boolean is declared as

```
type Boolean is (False, True);
```

Some programming languages use the integers 0 and 1 to represent False and True. With such a representation, it is possible to use arithmetic operators with Boolean values and obtain results that are neither 0 nor 1. By using an enumeration type for type Boolean, Ada ensures that a Boolean value may only be False or True. And, since arithmetic operators are not defined for enumeration types, Ada prevents us from using them with Boolean values.

After declaring a new type, we can declare constants and variables of that type, such as

```
IRS_Tax_Month : constant Month_Type := Apr;

Month_Of_Birth          : Month_Type;
Inspection_Expiration : Month_Type range Jul .. Dec;

My_Piece : Chess_Piece_Type;
Opponent : Player_Color_Type;
```

We have included a range in the declaration of variable Inspection_Expiration to restrict the values it can take to the months from the second half of the year. We did not include any range in the declaration of variable Month_Of_Birth; its value may be any of the twelve months. Here are some assignment statements that give values to these enumeration variables:

```
Month_Of_Birth          :=  Feb;
Inspection_Expiration :=  Nov;

My_Piece := Bishop;
Opponent := White;
```

Nov is not a variable name or a string. Nov is a *literal* of the data type Month_Type in the same way that 12 is a literal of the data type Integer. Nov is one of the values that the variables Month_Of_Birth and Inspection_Expiration can contain. Similarly, Bishop is a literal of the data type Chess_Piece_Type, and White is a literal of the data type Player_Color_Type. Remember that Ada treats uppercase and lowercase letters in identifiers the same. Feb, feb, and FEB are three different ways we can type the second literal in our list of months.

In our definition of an enumeration type, we said that the literal values making up the type are ordered. They are ordered according to the way they are listed in the type declaration. Because the values are ordered, we can apply relational operators to them. The relational operators are interpreted as "comes before" and "comes after" in the ordering of the data type. So Dec > Jun and Feb <= Jun are both True expressions. Here is a program fragment that makes use of the ordering of our enumeration data type:

```
if  Month_Of_Birth <= Inspection_Expiration then
   Ada.Text_IO.Put (Item => "Renew driver's license.");
else
   Ada.Text_IO.Put (Item => "Get car inspected.");
end if;
Ada.Text_IO.New_Line;
```

The Ski Wax Selection Case Study at the end of this chapter further illustrates the use of relational operators with enumeration types.

Input and Output of Enumeration Types

Enumeration types present a problem for the designers of programming languages. Because individual programmers design their own enumeration types to accurately model objects in their specific problems, language designers cannot supply the specific procedures for doing input and output with enumeration values. Many languages, such as Pascal and C++, circumvent this problem by not supporting direct input and output of enumeration values. In this section we examine the elegant way the Ada language designers provided for the input and output of enumeration values.

Generic Units Because the Float, Integer, and String data types are predefined in the Ada language, procedures for the input and output of values of these types are also available. We use the procedures in packages Float_Text_IO, Integer_Text_IO, and Text_IO to get and put values of these three types. In order to do input and output with our own enumeration types, we must create new packages with the necessary procedures. To make this task easy, Ada provides **generic units.** Generic units are like the recipes we use in cooking. Like recipes, generic units are not *directly* useful. You do not eat the recipe for chocolate chip cookies; you eat the cookies produced by following the recipe. Similarly we do not use the procedures of a generic unit; we use the procedures in the package obtained by instantiating the generic unit. **Instantiation** is the construction of a useable package from a generic template. It is analogous to following a recipe.

Generic unit A template for constructing packages and subprograms.
Instantiation The creation of a useable package from a generic template.

We often make substitutions in recipes. For example, substituting *M & M's®* for chocolate chips gives us one variation of the basic chocolate chip recipe while substituting *Reeses Pieces®* gives us another variation. When we instantiate a generic package, we supply information through parameters that the Ada compiler uses to tailor the template to our needs. As you will see in the next section, instantiation is easy; it can be done in a single line.

Package Enumeration_IO Within package Text_IO is a generic package, called Enumeration_IO, that contains the necessary procedures for the input and output of enumeration types. We instantiate a new package from this template for each different enumeration type for which we need Get and Put procedures. We use a parameter to specify a particular enumeration type. Here are some example instantiations.

```
-- Instantiate package for Month_Type input and output
package Month_IO is new Ada.Text_IO.Enumeration_IO (Enum => Month_Type);

-- Instantiate package for Chess_Piece_Type input and output
package Chess_Piece_IO is new Ada.Text_IO.Enumeration_IO
                              (Enum => Chess_Piece_Type);

-- Instantiate package for Player_Color_Type input and output
package Player_Color_IO is new Ada.Text_IO.Enumeration_IO
                               (Enum => Player_Color_Type);

-- Instantiate package for Boolean input and output
package Boolean_IO is new Ada.Text_IO.Enumeration_IO (Enum => Boolean);
```

The package names Month_IO, Chess_Piece_IO, Player_Color_IO, and Boolean_IO are identifiers that we have chosen. We use the parameter *Enum* to tell the Ada compiler what type we want this new package to handle. Newly created packages Month_IO, Chess_Piece_IO, Player_Color_IO, and Boolean_IO each contain Put and Get procedures for their specific types. Here are some examples of their use.

```
Month_IO.Put        (Item  => Month_Of_Birth);
Chess_Piece_IO.Put  (Item  => My_Piece);
Boolean_IO.Put      (Item  => Data_OK);
Month_IO.Put        (Item  => Inspection_Expiration,
                     Width => 4,
                     Set   => Ada.Text_IO.Lower_Case);

Month_IO.Get         (Item => Month_Of_Birth);
Player_Color_IO.Get  (Item => Opponent);
```

Put displays an enumeration literal. The optional *Width* parameter functions like the one used with the output of integer values. Use Width to obtain trailing blanks and to make neat columns. With the optional *Set* parameter, you can choose to have the enumeration literal displayed in all uppercase or all lowercase letters (the default is uppercase). The identifiers Upper_Case and Lower_Case are themselves enumeration literals defined and used by package Text_IO (see Appendix D). The following table illustrates the effect of these parameters on the printing of the enumeration value Dec.

Width	**Set**	**Output (❑ means blank)**
1	Upper_Case	DEC
2	Lower_Case	dec
3	Upper_Case	DEC
4	Lower_Case	dec❑
5	Lower_Case	dec❑❑
6	Lower_Case	dec❑❑❑
7	Upper_Case	DEC❑❑❑❑

Get reads an enumeration literal. As with reading integer values, any leading blanks and line terminators are skipped. Because we are reading an enumeration literal, the case of the data entered does not matter. A DATA_ERROR exception is raised if the data value obtained is not a valid enumeration literal for the enumeration type being read. For example, a DATA_ERROR occurs if we enter the value Jnu for a month. While having the program terminate with a DATA_ERROR may be frustrating, it is far better than having the program continue running, using the bad data, and displaying incorrect results. In Chapter 9 we will show you how to allow users to reenter their data after a DATA_ERROR occurs.

PROBLEM-SOLVING CASE STUDY

The Lumberyard

Specification

Problem You've been hired by a local lumberyard to help computerize its operations. Your first assignment is to write a program that computes the total amount of a customer order in standard units. We are given the product type, the number of pieces, and the dimensions of the lumber. The yard sells two products: lumber of specific dimensions and plywood panels. The standard unit used depends on the type of product.

Dimensioned lumber is sold by the *board foot*, which is equivalent to 1 square foot of lumber that is 1 inch thick, or 144 cubic inches. For example, if a customer orders 14 boards that are 2 inches thick, 4 inches wide and 8 feet long, the number of board feet is calculated as

14 pieces × (2 in. × 4 in. × (8 ft × 12 in./ft)) / 144 cubic in. per board foot

The minimum and maximum sizes for dimensioned lumber at this yard are $\frac{1}{2}$ in. and 4 in. for thickness, 1 in. and 16 in. for width, and 1 ft and 16 ft for length.

At this lumberyard, plywood panels are sold by the *full sheet.* A full sheet is 48 inches wide, 96 inches long, and 1 inch thick, or 4608 cubic inches. All plywood is sold in 48-inch widths. If a customer orders 6 sheets of 8-feet long, $\frac{3}{4}$-inch-thick plywood, the number of full sheets is calculated as

6 sheets × ($\frac{3}{4}$ in. × (8 ft. × 12 in./ft.) × 48 in.) / 4608 cubic in. per full sheet

The minimum sheet length is 1 ft and the maximum is 12 ft. Thicknesses available are $\frac{1}{4}$, $\frac{3}{8}$, $\frac{1}{2}$, $\frac{5}{8}$, $\frac{3}{4}$, $\frac{4}{4}$, and $\frac{5}{4}$ in.

Input The input for each order consists of three entries: the type of product (dimensioned lumber or plywood), quantity ordered, and three whole numbers to specify the product size. For dimensioned lumber, these three numbers are the thickness (inches), width (inches), and length (feet). For plywood, the first number is the length (feet) and the other two numbers are the numerator and denominator of a fraction of an inch specifying the panel's thickness. For example, a numerator of 3 and a denominator of 4 indicates a panel thickness of $\frac{3}{4}$ in.

Output The program should display appropriate prompts, a neatly formatted version of the input (echo print), the number of standard units rounded to one decimal place, and the name of the unit (board feet or full sheets).

Assumptions We assume that all data entered by the user of our program is correct.

Discussion To do this by hand, you would first get the type of product and quantity. For dimensioned lumber, you would get the thickness, width, and length. After converting the length to inches you would multiply the four numbers together to get the total volume. Then you would divide the result by 144 cubic inches to obtain the number of board feet. For plywood, you would get the length and the numerator and denominator of the thickness fraction. To calculate the number of full sheets, you would divide the numerator by the denominator to get the thickness, convert the length from feet to inches, and then multiply the dimensions (don't forget the width) by the number of pieces to get the volume in cubic inches. You would divide this quantity by the volume of one full sheet (4608 cubic inches) to get the number of sheets. This process can be translated directly into the following algorithm.

Lumberyard **Level 0**
Prompt for product type
Get Product
if Product is Lumber then
  Process Lumber
else
  Process Plywood

Process Lumber **Level 1**
Get Lumber Data
Board Feet := Quantity * (Thickness * Width * (Length *12)) / 144
Put Quantity, Thickness, Width, and Length
Put Board Feet

Process Plywood
Get Plywood Data
Full Sheets := Quantity * (Numerator / Denominator * (Length *12) * 48) / 4608
Put Quantity, thickness fraction, and Length
Put Full Sheets

Get Lumber Data **Level 2**
Prompt for number of boards
Get Quantity
Prompt for thickness, width, and length of boards
Get Thickness, Width, and Length of boards

Get Plywood Data
Prompt for number of sheets
Get Quantity
Prompt for length and thickness fraction of sheets
Get Length, Numerator, and Denominator

Module Structure Chart

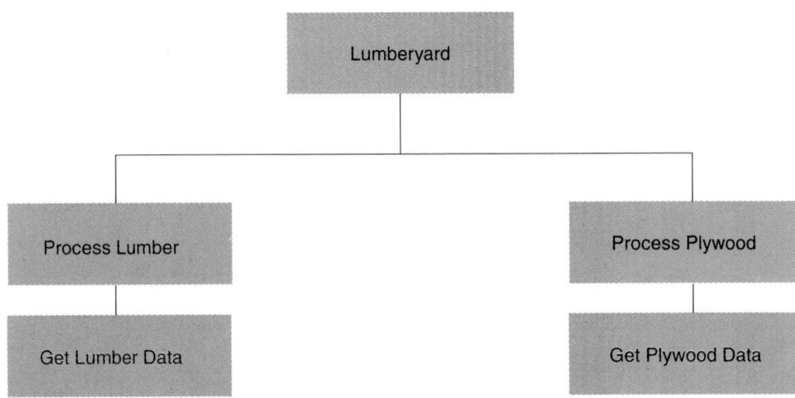

Object Modeling Before we can translate our algorithm into Ada code, we need to determine the most appropriate types for the variables and constants (the objects) we used in it. Most of the objects are numeric values. The addition of appropriate ranges to the predefined types Integer and Float provides more accurate modeling of these quantities. Any attempts to use values outside of these ranges will result in a CONSTRAINT_ERROR. We use the limits supplied in the problem definition for many of these numbers. Other numbers may be limited to positive values.

The remaining data to model is the product. The product has two possible values: Dimensioned Lumber and Plywood. At first glance we might think of implementing the product as a String. While String is a better choice than a numeric type (as exemplified by the prompt "Enter 1 for Lumber and 2 for Plywood"), there is a better choice: an enumeration type. We can define an enumeration type with just the two possible products. There are several advantages of using an enumeration type rather than a String. Any typographical errors the user may make will automatically raise DATA_ERROR; we are guaranteed that the user has entered a valid value. Because the Get procedures for enumeration values skip over leading blanks and leading line terminators, it is easier to input enumeration values than string values. Finally, unlike string values, enumeration values are not case sensitive; the user can enter the product using any combination of uppercase and lowercase letters.

Types

Name	**List of Values**
Product_Type	(Lumber, Plywood)

Constants

Name	**Value**	**Role**
Board_Foot_Inches	144.0	Cubic inches in 1 board foot
Full_Sheet_Inches	4608.0	Cubic inches in 1 full sheet
Plywood_Width	48.0	Width of all plywood pieces

Variables

Name	**Data Type and Range**	**Role**
Product	Product_Type	Indicates Lumber or Plywood
Quantity	Integer, positive	Number of boards or sheets
Lumber_Thickness	Float, 0.5 to 4	Thickness of lumber (inches)
Lumber_Width	Float, 1 to 16	Width of lumber (inches)
Lumber_Length	Float, 1 to 16	Length of lumber (feet)
Board_Feet	Float, nonnegative	Total number of board feet

Name	Data Type and Range	Role
Plywood_Length	Float, 1 to 12	Length of plywood sheet (feet)
Numerator	Integer, 1 to 5	Numerator for plywood thickness fraction
Denominator	Integer, 2 to 8	Denominator for plywood thickness fraction
Full_Sheets	Float, nonnegative	Total number of full sheets

Program

```
with Ada.Text_IO;
with Ada.Float_Text_IO;
with Ada.Integer_Text_IO;

procedure Lumberyard is

-- This program computes the total amount of a customer order in standard
-- units, given the type of product, quantity of product, and dimensions.

-- Assumptions: All input data entered by the user is valid

   -- Types
   type Product_Type is (Lumber, Plywood);

   -- Instantiate package for product input and output
   package Product_IO is new Ada.Text_IO.Enumeration_IO (Enum => Product_Type);

   -- Constants
   Board_Foot_Inches : constant Float := 144.0;    -- Cubic inches per board foot
   Full_Sheet_Inches : constant Float := 4608.0;   -- Cubic inches per full sheet
   Plywood_Width     : constant Float := 48.0;     -- Width of plywood (inches)

   -- Variables

   Product  : Product_Type;                        -- Indicates Lumber or Plywood
   Quantity : Integer range 1..Integer'Last;       -- Number of boards or sheets

   Lumber_Thickness : Float range 0.5..4.0;        -- Thickness of lumber (inches)
   Lumber_Width     : Float range 1.0..16.0;       -- Width of lumber (inches)
   Lumber_Length    : Float range 1.0..16.0;       -- Length of lumber (feet)
   Board_Feet       : Float range 0.0..Float'Last; -- Total number of board feet

   Plywood_Length : Float   range 1.0..12.0;       -- Length of plywood (feet)
   Numerator      : Integer range 1..5;            -- Thickness fraction numerator
   Denominator    : Integer range 2..8;            -- and denominator
   Full_Sheets    : Float   range 0.0..Float'Last; -- Total number of full sheets
```

```
begin
   -- Prompt for and get product type
   Ada.Text_IO.Put (Item => "Enter product (Lumber or Plywood)");
   Ada.Text_IO.New_Line;
   Product_IO.Get (Item => Product);
   Ada.Text_IO.New_Line;

   if Product = Lumber then  -- Process an order for lumber
      -- Get Lumber Data
      -- Prompt for and get the quantity
      Ada.Text_IO.Put (Item => "Enter the number of boards: ");
      Ada.Integer_Text_IO.Get (Item => Quantity);
      Ada.Text_IO.New_Line;

      -- Prompt for and get the board dimensions
      Ada.Text_IO.Put (Item => "Enter thickness, width, and length");
      Ada.Text_IO.New_Line;
      Ada.Float_Text_IO.Get (Item => Lumber_Thickness);
      Ada.Float_Text_IO.Get (Item => Lumber_Width);
      Ada.Float_Text_IO.Get (Item => Lumber_Length);
      Ada.Text_IO.New_Line (Spacing => 2);

      -- Calculate total number of board feet
      Board_Feet := Float(Quantity) * Lumber_Thickness * Lumber_Width *
                    (Lumber_Length * 12.0) / Board_Foot_Inches;

      -- Display results
      Ada.Text_IO.Put (Item => "Quantity   :  ");
      Ada.Integer_Text_IO.Put (Item => Quantity, Width => 1);
      Ada.Text_IO.New_Line;
      Ada.Text_IO.Put (Item => "Dimensions :  ");
      Ada.Float_Text_IO.Put (Item => Lumber_Thickness,
                             Fore => 1,
                             Aft  => 1,
                             Exp  => 0);
      Ada.Float_Text_IO.Put (Item => Lumber_Width,
                             Fore => 6,
                             Aft  => 1,
                             Exp  => 0);
      Ada.Float_Text_IO.Put (Item => Lumber_Length,
                             Fore => 6,
                             Aft  => 1,
                             Exp  => 0);
      Ada.Text_IO.New_Line;
      Ada.Text_IO.Put (Item => "Board feet :  ");
      Ada.Float_Text_IO.Put (Item => Board_Feet,
                             Fore => 1,
                             Aft  => 1,
                             Exp  => 0);
```

```
   else   -- The order must be for plywood
      -- Get plywood data
      -- Prompt for and get quantity
      Ada.Text_IO.Put (Item => "Enter the number of sheets: ");
      Ada.Integer_Text_IO.Get (Item => Quantity);
      Ada.Text_IO.New_Line;

      -- Prompt for and get the sheet dimensions
      Ada.Text_IO.Put (Item => "Enter length and 2 thickness numbers");
      Ada.Text_IO.New_Line;
      Ada.Float_Text_IO.Get   (Item => Plywood_Length);
      Ada.Integer_Text_IO.Get (Item => Numerator);
      Ada.Integer_Text_IO.Get (Item => Denominator);
      Ada.Text_IO.New_Line (Spacing => 2);

      -- Calculate total number of full sheets
      Full_Sheets := Float(Quantity) * (Float(Numerator) / Float(Denominator) *
                     (Plywood_Length * 12.0) * Plywood_Width) / Full_Sheet_Inches;

      -- Display results
      Ada.Text_IO.Put (Item => "Quantity    :  ");
      Ada.Integer_Text_IO.Put (Item => Quantity, Width => 1);
      Ada.Text_IO.New_Line;
      Ada.Text_IO.Put (Item => "Dimensions  :  ");
      Ada.Integer_Text_IO.Put (Item => Numerator, Width => 1);
      Ada.Text_IO.Put (Item => "/");
      Ada.Integer_Text_IO.Put (Item => Denominator, Width => 1);
      Ada.Float_Text_IO.Put (Item => Plywood_Width,
                             Fore => 6,
                             Aft  => 1,
                             Exp  => 0);
      Ada.Float_Text_IO.Put (Item => Plywood_Length,
                             Fore => 6,
                             Aft  => 1,
                             Exp  => 0);
      Ada.Text_IO.New_Line;
      Ada.Text_IO.Put (Item => "Full sheets : ");
      Ada.Float_Text_IO.Put (Item => Full_Sheets,
                             Fore => 1,
                             Aft  => 1,
                             Exp  => 0);
   end if;
   Ada.Text_IO.New_Line;
end Lumberyard;
```

This is a sample run of the program:

```
Enter product (Lumber or Plywood)
Lumber

Enter the number of boards: 45

Enter thickness, width, and length
2 6 10


Quantity   :  45
Dimensions :  2.0     6.0    10.0
Board feet :  450.0
```

This sample shows what happens when the product is plywood:

```
Enter product (Lumber or Plywood)
Plywood

Enter the number of sheets: 7

Enter length and 2 thickness numbers
9 1 2


Quantity    :  7
Dimensions  :  1/2    48.0     9.0
Full sheets : 3.9
```

We examine this program in more detail in the testing and debugging section of this chapter.

PROBLEM-SOLVING CASE STUDY

Ski Wax Selection

Specification

Problem The Wicks Corporation manufactures a line of 14 different waxes for cross-country skiing. Because many of their customers have a difficult time selecting the proper wax to use, the company has decided to sell a hand-held computer to aid in the selection. You've contracted to write the program for this computer. Wax choice depends on temperature and snow conditions. The waxes come in various degrees of hardness that are divided into six color groups. A skier selects a wax color on the basis of temperature. All of the color groups except Yellow and White have three varieties (Special, Standard, and Extra) to account for variations in snow conditions (Powder, Packed, and Crusty). The two waxes for the highest and lowest temperature extremes (Yellow and White) come only in Standard. Your program should read the current temperature and snow condition and print out the most appropriate wax using the following guidelines.

Temperature Guidelines (used to select a wax group)

Wax Group	Temperature (degrees Fahrenheit)
Yellow	38° < Temperature
Red	31° < Temperature <= 38°
Violet	26° < Temperature <= 31°
Blue	18° < Temperature <= 26°
Green	5° < Temperature <= 18°
White	Temperature <= 5°

Snow condition is used to select a variety of waxes other than the extreme-temperature waxes (Yellow and White).

Wax Variety	Snow Condition
Special	Powder
Standard	Packed
Extra	Crusty

Input

Air temperature, an integer value between –40 and 50
Snow condition (Powder, Packed, or Crusty)

Output

Input prompt message
Temperature (echo print)
Snow condition (echo print)
Appropriate wax (variety and color)

Assumptions We assume that all data entered by the user of our program is correct.

Discussion After obtaining the input data, our first task is to compare the temperature with the limits of each wax group. Once we find the correct range, we select the corresponding color. Next we need to test whether the color selected is one of the extreme colors (White or Yellow). If it isn't, we can check the snow condition to determine the best variety to use. We can make all of these comparisons and tests using if statements.

Ski Wax **Level 0**
Obtain Temperature
Obtain Snow Condition
Determine Best Wax
Print Wax Selection Report

Obtain Temperature **Level 1**
Prompt for temperature value input
Get Temperature

Obtain Snow Condition
Prompt for Snow Condition value input
Get Snow Condition

Determine Best Wax
Determine Wax Color
Determine Wax Variety

Print Wax Selection Report
Put Temperature
Put Snow Condition
Put Wax Variety
Put Wax Color

Determine Wax Color **Level 2**
```
if Temperature > 38 then
   Wax Color := Yellow
if Temperature <= 38 and > 31 then
   Wax Color := Red
if Temperature <= 31 and > 26 then
   Wax Color := Violet
if Temperature <= 26 and > 18 then
   Wax Color := Blue
if Temperature <= 18 and > 5 then
   Wax Color := Green
if Temperature <= 5 then
   Wax Color := White
```

```
Determine Wax Variety
If Wax Color is not one of the two extreme values then
   If Snow Condition is Powder then
      Wax Variety := Special
   If Snow Condition is Packed then
      Wax Variety := Standard
   If Snow Condition is Crusty then
      Wax Variety := Extra
else
   Wax Variety := Standard
```

Module Determine Wax Color has 6 if statements and a total of 10 comparisons. Because we are choosing one color from a number of alternatives, we can code this module more efficiently with `elsifs`. The middle ifs seem to require compound Boolean conditions; however, the if-elsif structure makes this unnecessary because we wouldn't be executing the branch unless one of the conditions was satisfied already. Here's the rewritten module:

```
Determine Wax Color                                        Level 2
if Temperature > 38 then
   Wax Color := Yellow
elsif Temperature > 31 then
   Wax Color := Red
elsif Temperature > 26 then
   Wax Color := Violet
elsif Temperature > 18 then
   Wax Color := Blue
elsif Temperature > 5 then
   Wax Color := Green
else
   Wax Color := White
```

In this version we have five relational operators; our first solution had 10. Because it uses fewer operations to accomplish the same function, the `elsif` version is more efficient. We can make similar improvements to the module Determine Wax Variety.

```
Determine Wax Variety
If Wax Color is not one of the two extreme values then
   if Snow Condition is Powder then
      Wax Variety := Special
   elsif Snow Condition is Packed then
      Wax Variety := Standard
   else
      Wax Variety := Extra
else
   Wax Variety := Standard
```

Figure 4-8 shows how the flow of control works in our improved version of module Determine Wax Color.

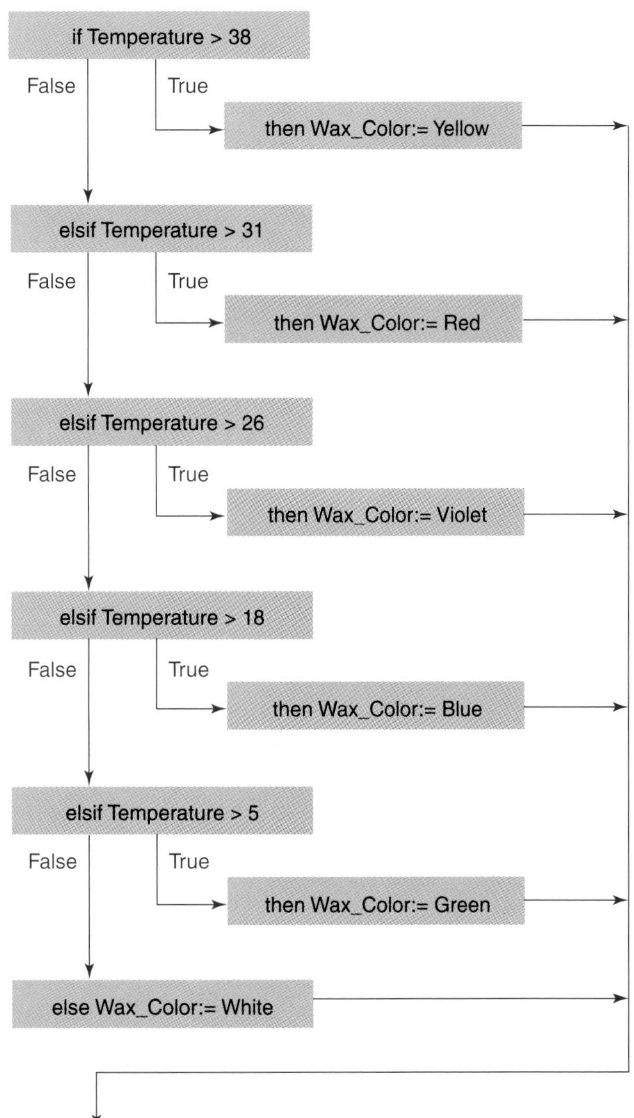

Figure 4-8
Flow of Control for Module Determine Wax Color

Module Structure Chart

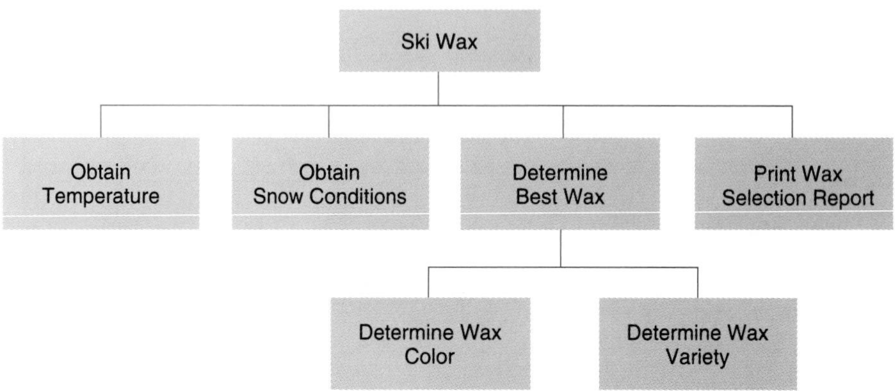

Object Modeling We could use string types for snow condition, wax color, and wax variety values. However, because we can easily list all of the possible values, it is better to define enumeration types. We can order the color values according to their temperature ranges to make testing for the extreme values easier.

Types

Name	**List of Values**
Snow_Type	(Powder, Packed, Crusty)
Color_Type	(White, Green, Blue, Violet, Red, Yellow)
Variety_Type	(Special, Standard, Extra)

Variables

Name	**Data Type and Range**	**Role**
Temperature	Integer, –40 to 50	The air temperature
Snow_Condition	Snow_Type	The condition of the snow
Wax_Color	Color_Type	The wax group selected
Wax_Variety	Variety_Type	The wax variety selected

Program

```
with Ada.Text_IO;
with Ada.Integer_Text_IO;

procedure Ski_Wax is

-- This program outputs the best Wicks ski wax to use on your
-- cross country skis given the temperature and snow conditions

-- Assumptions: All input data entered by the user is valid

   -- Types
      -- for snow conditions
   type Snow_Type is (Powdered, Packed, Crusty);
      -- for waxes
   type Color_Type is   (White, Green, Blue, Violet, Red, Yellow);
   type Variety_Type is (Special, Standard, Extra);

   -- Instantiate new packages for enumerated I/O
   package Snow_IO    is new Ada.Text_IO.Enumeration_IO (Enum => Snow_Type);
   package Color_IO   is new Ada.Text_IO.Enumeration_IO (Enum => Color_Type);
   package Variety_IO is new Ada.Text_IO.Enumeration_IO (Enum => Variety_Type);

   -- Variables

   Temperature    : Integer range -40..50;  -- The air temperature
   Snow_Condition : Snow_Type;              -- The condition of the snow
   Wax_Color      : Color_Type;             -- The wax group selected
   Wax_Variety    : Variety_Type;           -- The wax variety selected

begin  -- Ski_Wax

   -- Obtain Temperature
   Ada.Text_IO.Put (Item => "Enter the air temperature: ");
   Ada.Integer_Text_IO.Get (Item => Temperature);

   -- Obtain Snow Condition
   Ada.Text_IO.Put (Item => "Enter snow condition (Powdered, Packed, Crusty): ");
   Snow_IO.Get (Item => Snow_Condition);

   -- Determine the best wax to use

   -- Determine Wax Color
   if Temperature > 38 then
      Wax_Color := Yellow;
   elsif Temperature > 31 then
      Wax_Color := Red;
   elsif Temperature > 26 then
      Wax_Color := Violet;
   elsif Temperature > 18 then
      Wax_Color := Blue;
```

```
   elsif Temperature > 5 then
      Wax_Color := Green;
   else
      Wax_Color := White;
   end if;

   -- Determine Wax Variety (The first and last colors come only in Standard)
   if (Wax_Color > White)  and  (Wax_Color < Yellow) then
      if Snow_Condition = Powdered then
         Wax_Variety := Special;
      elsif Snow_Condition = Packed then
         Wax_Variety := Standard;
      else
         Wax_Variety := Extra;
      end if;
   else
      Wax_Variety := Standard;
   end if;

   -- Print wax selection report
   Ada.Text_IO.New_Line;
   Ada.Text_IO.Put (Item => "For an air temperature of ");
   Ada.Integer_Text_IO.Put (Item => Temperature, Width => 1);
   Ada.Text_IO.Put (Item => " degrees and ");
   Snow_IO.Put (Item => Snow_Condition, Set => Ada.Text_IO.Lower_Case);
   Ada.Text_IO.Put (Item => " snow conditions,");
   Ada.Text_IO.New_Line;
   Ada.Text_IO.Put (Item => "the recommended Wicks ski wax is ");
   Variety_IO.Put (Item => Wax_Variety, Set => Ada.Text_IO.Upper_Case);
   Ada.Text_IO.Put (Item => " ");
   Color_IO.Put (Item => Wax_Color, Set => Ada.Text_IO.Upper_Case);
   Ada.Text_IO.New_Line;
end Ski_Wax;
```

Here are two sample runs of Program Ski_Wax. As usual, we show the user's input in color.

```
Enter the air temperature: 20
Enter snow condition (Powdered, Packed, Crusty): crusty

For an air temperature of 20 degrees and crusty snow conditions,
the recommended Wicks ski wax is EXTRA BLUE
```

```
Enter the air temperature: 42
Enter snow condition (Powdered, Packed, Crusty): Powdered

For an air temperature of 42 degrees and powdered snow conditions,
the recommended Wicks ski wax is STANDARD YELLOW
```

Testing and Debugging

In Chapter 1 we discussed the problem-solving and implementation phases of computer programming. Testing is an integral part of both phases. Here we test both phases of the process used to develop Program Lumberyard. Testing in the problem-solving phase is done after the solution is developed. In the implementation phase we test the algorithm after it is translated into a program, and again after the program has compiled successfully. The compilation itself constitutes another stage of testing that is performed automatically.

The Problem-Solving Phase: The Algorithm Trace

To test at the problem-solving phase, we do a *trace* of the algorithm. For each module in the top-down design, we establish two sets of assertions called preconditions and postconditions. **Preconditions** are assertions that should be true before a module is executed. A precondition is an assumption made by the module. **Postconditions** are assertions that should be true after the module executes. True postconditions show that a module has done its job correctly. Every module should be written to guarantee that its postconditions (results) are met *if* its preconditions (assumptions) are met. Algorithm traces are done to check these guarantees. In a trace, we follow through the algorithm to confirm that, given the preconditions, the steps fulfill the postconditions.

Preconditions Assertions that should be true before a module begins executing.

Postconditions Assertions that should be true after a module is executed.

The preconditions for the main module are usually the problem assumptions. The postconditions for the main module are usually that it outputs the correct values for the given input. The preconditions and postconditions for lower-level modules are the implicit assumptions we made and the behavior we expected when we wrote down the abstract step. Writing explicit assumptions and expected behavior for each abstract step requires an unambiguous understanding of the step. Such understanding is crucial to the successful application of the divide-and-conquer approach to problem solving. Do not be discouraged if you cannot immediately articulate preconditions and postconditions for the modules you write. The skill will come with reading examples, practice, and experience.

Once we have established a set of preconditions and a set of postconditions for every module in our design, we examine each module in turn, working from the top to the bottom of our module structure chart. To examine a module, we trace through its steps by hand. At each step, we determine the current conditions. Conditions include such things as the values of variables, position of the reading marker, and output. If the step is an abstract step (it references another lower-level module), we verify that the preconditions of that module are met by the current conditions. If the preconditions of the lower-level module are met, we assume—for the time being—that the lower-level module works (it meets its postconditions). When we finish the steps in the module, the current conditions should agree with the postconditions of the module. If they do, we have shown that the module has met its precondition and postcondition guarantee.

Let's look at an example in detail. The following table gives specific preconditions and postconditions for all of the modules in our Lumberyard algorithm.

Module	**Preconditions**	**Postconditions**
Main	Input data entered by the user is valid.	Quantity and dimensions of the desired product are displayed. Either the number of board feet ordered is displayed or the number of full sheets of plywood ordered is displayed.
Process Lumber	Product is Lumber.	The quantity and dimensions of the lumber ordered are displayed. The number of board feet ordered is displayed.
Process Plywood	Product is Plywood.	The quantity and dimensions of the plywood ordered are displayed. The number of full sheets ordered is displayed.
Get Lumber Data	Input data entered by the user is valid	Quantity, Thickness, Width, and Length are valid. Get Plywood Data Input data entered by the user is valid. Quantity, Numerator, Denominator, and Length are valid.

Now that we've established the preconditions and postconditions, we are ready to begin our algorithm trace. Lumberyard's main module references two lower-level modules: Process Lumber and Process Plywood. Our first task is to verify that the conditions in the main module satisfy the preconditions of each of these referenced modules. The precondition for module Process Lumber is that the Product is Lumber. The Boolean expression in the if statement of the main module directly tests this assertion. We will only call module Process Lumber if Product is Lumber. Because the preconditions for Process Lumber are met, we can assume—for the time being—that Process Lumber works; it meets its two postconditions.

What about the precondition for module Process Plywood? It states that the Product is Plywood. There is no Boolean expression in the main module that tests this condition. Because it is in the else part of the if statement, we call module Process Plywood if Product is *anything other than* Lumber. For example, if Product were Pizza, we would call module

Process Plywood without satisfying its precondition. Have we discovered a flaw in this algorithm? The answer to this question is in the object model we developed for Product. We used an enumeration type with only two possible values. Our enumeration type ensures that if Product is not Lumber than it must be Plywood. If we modeled Product as a string type rather than an enumeration type, we would have no guarantee that Product is Plywood when Process Plywood is called—our algorithm would require another if statement to confirm that Product was Plywood.

Our second task is to confirm that the steps in the main module ensure that its two postconditions are met. Having confirmed the validity of the preconditions of all the lower-level modules referenced by the main module, we are assuming that they will meet their postconditions. Because the main module calls exactly one of these two modules and the postconditions of each of these lower-level modules are equivalent to the main module's postconditions, we conclude that the postconditions of the main module are satisfied.

We are now ready to trace the lower-level modules and confirm that the assumptions we made about their correct behavior are indeed true. Let's start with Process Lumber. It has a single abstract step—Get Lumber Data. The precondition for this module is that the input data entered by the user is valid. This is an assumption made in our problem. Our use of ranges in the object models we developed for the input data help to fulfill this assumption, but do not guarantee it. In an exercise at the end of this chapter we ask you to add some additional checks to guarantee this assumption. In the next chapter we discuss validation of user input in more detail. For now, we assume that the users of our programs enter only valid data. Because its precondition is met, we assume that the postconditions of Get Lumber Data are also met. Now, does Process Lumber satisfy its postconditions? The third step in this module satisfies the first postcondition. We double-check the formula used in the calculation of board feet. This calculation and the output of the result satisfy the module's second postcondition.

We have completed the trace of two of the five modules in the Lumberyard algorithm. Try your hand at completing the algorithm trace by examining the remaining three modules in detail. Once we've completed the algorithm trace, we have to correct any discrepancies and repeat the process. When we know that the modules do what they are supposed to do, we start translating the top-down design into our programming language.

The Implementation Phase

Now that we've talked about testing in the problem-solving phase, we can turn to testing in the implementation phase. In this phase, you need to test at several points.

Code Check After the code is written, you should go over it line by line, to be sure that you've faithfully reproduced the top-down design—this process is known as code checking. In a team programming situation, you ask other team members to *walk through* the algorithm and read the code with you to double-check the design and code.

Execution Trace You also should take some actual values and hand-calculate what the output should be by doing an execution trace. When you execute the program, you can use these same values as input and check the results.

The computer is a very literal device—it does exactly what we tell it to do, which may or may not be what we want it to do. We try to make sure that a program does what we want by tracing the execution of the statements.

We use the following nonsense program to demonstrate the technique. We keep track of the values of the program variables on the right-hand side, indicating variables with undefined values with a dash. When a variable is assigned a value, we list that value in the appropriate column.

Statement	**Value of** A	B	C
`with Ada.Integer_Ada.Text_IO;`			
`procedure Trace is`			
`   X : constant Integer := 5;`			
`   A : Integer;`			
`   B : Integer;`			
`   C : Integer;`			
`begin`			
`   B := 1;`	—	1	—
`   C := X + B;`	—	1	6
`   A := X + 4;`	9	1	6
`   A := C;`	6	1	6
`   B := C;`	6	6	6
`   A := A + B + C;`	18	6	6
`   C := C rem X;`	18	6	1
`   C := C * A;`	18	6	18
`   A := A rem B;`	0	6	18
`   Ada.Integer_Text_IO.Put (Item => A);`	0	6	18
`   Ada.Integer_Text_IO.Put (Item => B);`	0	6	18
`   Ada.Integer_Text_IO.Put (Item => C);`	0	6	18
`end Trace;`			

Testing Selection Control Structures To test a program with branches, we have to execute each branch at least once and verify the results. Here, for example, is a code fragment containing three if-then-else statements (see Figure 4-9) that displays a message about a student's status based on an average of several test scores.

```
-- Display Student Status
Ada.Float_Text_IO.Get    (Item => Exam_Score_Sum);
Ada.Integer_Text_IO.Get (Item => Number_Of_Exams);
if Number_Of_Exams > 0 then
   Average := Exam_Score_Sum / Float (Number_Of_Exams);
   if Average >= 60.0 then
      Ada.Text_IO.Put (Item => "Passing");
      if Average < 70.0 then
         Ada.Text_IO.Put (Item => ", but marginal.");
      else
         Ada.Text_IO.Put (Item => ".");
      end if;
   else
      Ada.Text_IO.Put (Item => "Failing!");
   end if;
else
   Ada.Text_IO.Put (Item => "No exams taken.");
end if;
```

We need a series of data sets to test the different branches. For example, we could use the following sets of values for the input values of Exam_Score_Sum and Number_Of_Exams.

	Exam_Score_Sum	**Number_Of_Exams**
Set 1	0	0
Set 2	159	3
Set 3	328	4
Set 4	204	3

Figure 4-10 shows the flow of control through the branching structure of this code fragment for each of these data sets. We cannot calculate an average with Set 1 as this student took no exams. Set 2 is valid and gives an average of 53, which is failing. Set 3 is valid and gives an average of 82, well above passing. Set 4 gives an average of 68, which is marginally passing.

Every branch in the program is executed at least once through this series of test runs; eliminating any of the test data sets would leave at least one branch untested. This series of data sets provides **minimum complete coverage** of the program's branching structure. Whenever you test a program with branches in it, you should design a series of tests that covers all of the branches. It may help to draw diagrams like those in Figure 4-10 so that you can see which branches are being executed.

FIGURE 4-9
Flow of Control for Display Student Status

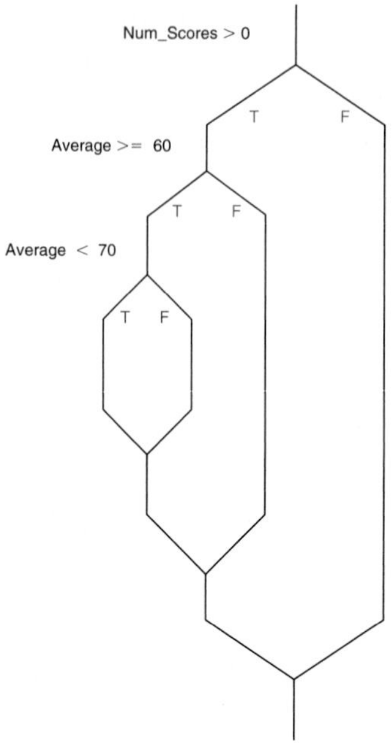

FIGURE 4-10
Flow of Control for Each of Four Data Sets

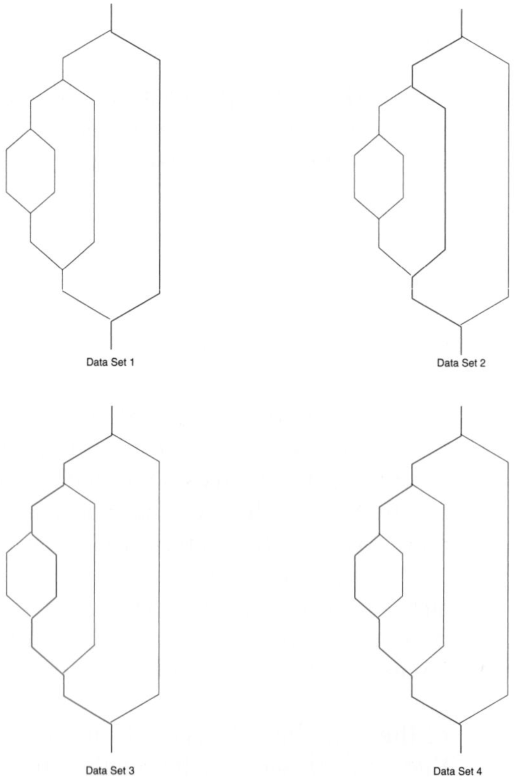

Minimum complete coverage A testing strategy in which the minimum number of data sets are used to execute every branch in the program at least once.

Because an action in one branch of a program often affects processing in a later branch, it is crucial to test as many *combinations of branches,* or **paths,** through a program as possible. This way we can be sure that there are no interdependencies that could cause problems. Figure 4-11 shows the flow of control in a program with an additional branch prior to that of the one shown in Figure 4-9. Shouldn't we try all possible paths? Yes, in theory we should; however, the number of paths in even a small program is large. There are eight possible paths in Figure 4-11, requiring eight different data sets to test. Only four sets of data are needed for minimum complete coverage of the branching structure shown in this figure.

Path The sequence of statements executed in one run of a program.

Path coverage A testing strategy in which data sets are chosen to test as many paths as possible in the program.

The approach to testing that we've used here is called **code coverage** because the test data is designed by looking at the code of the program. Another approach to testing, **data coverage,** attempts to test as many allowable data values as possible without regard to the program code. Complete data coverage is as impractical as complete code coverage for most programs. Even if the number of exams taken in our program fragment is limited to range from 0 to 4, the number of data sets needed to try every possible combination of number of exams and sum of exam scores is astounding.

Code coverage Any testing strategy based on inspecting the code of the program.

Data coverage Any testing strategy based on the possible ranges of input data.

Often, testing is a combination of these two strategies. Instead of trying every possible data value (data coverage), we examine the code (code coverage) and look for ranges of values for which processing is identical. Then we test the values at the boundaries and, sometimes, at a value in the middle of each range. For example, a simple condition, such as

```
Test < 0
```

divides the integers into two ranges:

```
Integer'First to -1
0 to Integer'Last
```

Thus, we should test the four values Integer'First, −1, 0, and Integer'Last. A compound condition, such as

```
(Test >= 0) and (Test <= 100)
```

divides the integers into three ranges:

```
Integer'First to -1
0 to 100
101 to Integer'Last
```

Thus, we have six values to test. In addition, to verify that the compound relational operators are correct, we should test for values of 1 (> 0) and 99 (< 100).

Conditional branches are only one factor in developing a testing strategy. We'll consider other factors in later chapters.

Tests Performed Automatically During Compilation and Execution Once you have coded a program and prepared test data, the program is ready for compiling. The compiler produces two distinct outputs: a report of any errors, which may be in the form of a program listing, and the translated version of the program.

FIGURE 4-11 Paths and Branches

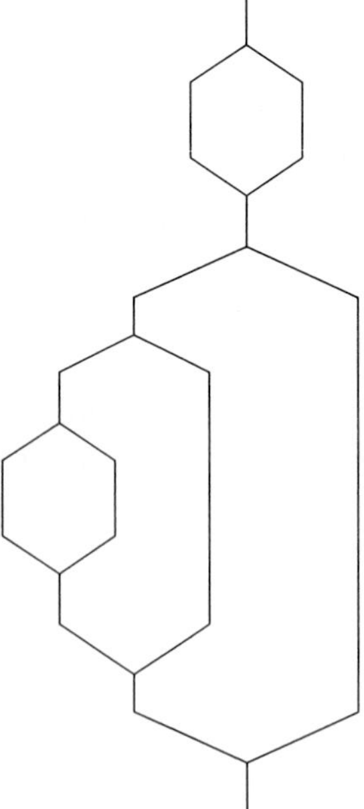

Errors can be syntactic or semantic. The compiler finds syntactic errors. For example, the compiler warns you when reserved words are misspelled, identifiers are undefined, semicolons are missing, and operand types are mismatched. But it won't find all of your typing errors. If you type > instead of <, you won't get an error message. It is up to you to design test data and carefully check the code to detect semantic errors.

Semantic errors are mistakes that give you the wrong answer. They are more difficult to locate than syntactic errors and usually surface when a program is executing. Ada detects only the most obvious semantic errors—those that result in an invalid operation (dividing by zero, for instance) or a value outside the specified range of a variable. By using more appropriate types (enumeration rather than string) and by including appropriate ranges in our declarations we can give Ada more information that it can use to find semantic errors. Although semantic errors sometimes are caused by typing errors, they more often are a product of a faulty design (algorithm or data model).

By walking through the algorithm checking preconditions and postconditions, inspecting the code, tracing the execution of the program, and developing a thorough test strategy, you should be able to avoid—or at least quickly locate—semantic errors in your programs.

Figure 4-12 illustrates the testing process we've been discussing. The figure shows where syntax and semantic errors occur and in which phase they can be corrected.

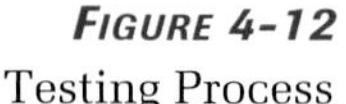

FIGURE 4-12
Testing Process

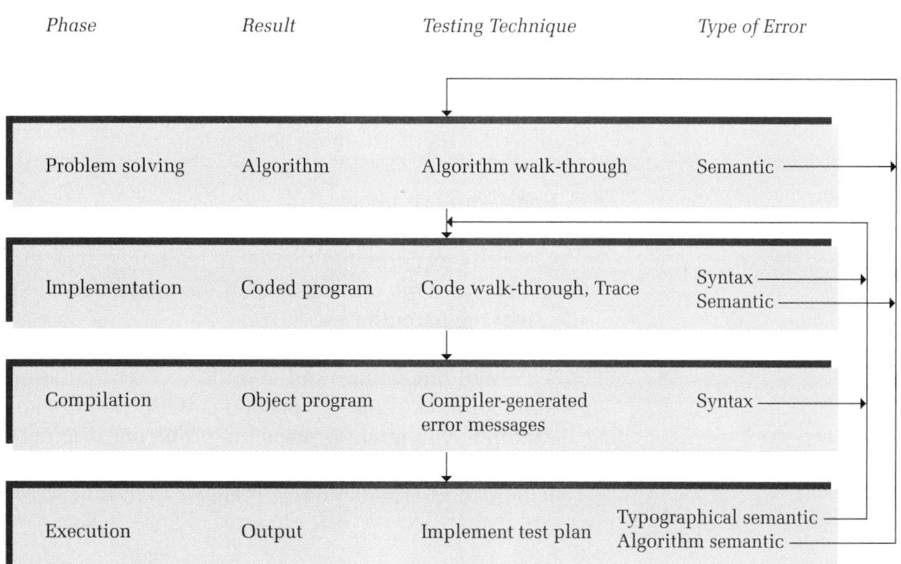

Testing and Debugging Hints

1. Echo print all input data. This way you know your input data is what it is supposed to be.
2. Expect bad data. If a data value must be positive, include a range on the variable declaration. Alternatively, omit the range and use an if statement to test the value and display your own error message. For example, instead of using a range in the declaration of Temperature in Program Ski_Wax, we could insert the following statement after getting the temperature from the user:

```
if (Temperature > 50)  or  (Temperature < -40) then
   Ada.Text_IO.Put (Item => "Temperature data is out of range.");
else
    .
    .
    .
```

   This if statement tests the limits of reasonable skiing temperatures and executes the rest of the program only if the data is reasonable.
3. Use parentheses to make your Boolean expressions clear and correct.
4. Be sure that the opening and closing parentheses match up. To verify that parentheses are properly paired, start with the innermost pair and draw a line connecting them. Do the same for the others, working your way out to the outermost pair.

((Total / Scores) > 50) and ((Total / (Scores – 1)) < 100)

5. Take some sample values and try them by hand.
6. If your program produces an answer that does not agree with a value you've calculated by hand, try these suggestions:

   - Redo your arithmetic.
   - Recheck your input data.
   - Carefully examine the section of code that does the calculation. If you're in doubt about the order in which the operations are performed, insert clarifying parentheses.
   - Check for integer overflow. The value of an integer variable may have exceeded Integer'Last in the middle of a calculation. Reorganize the expression to eliminate problems with intermediate calculations. For example, you might replace the problematic expression 3 * Integer'Last / 4 with 3 * (Integer'Last / 4). Make similar checks for integer underflow, in which an intermediate result is less than Integer'First.

- Check that you did not compare float values for equality with = or /=.
- Check the conditions in branching statements to be sure that the correct branch is taken under all circumstances.

7. Define and use enumeration data types rather than strings when possible. Restricting the valid values a variable can hold allows Ada to find invalid data at run time.

Summary

Using Boolean expressions is a way of asking questions while a program is running. The program evaluates each Boolean expression, assigning it the value True if the expression is true or False if the expression is not true.

The if statement allows you to take different paths through a program based on the value of a Boolean expression. The if-then-else gives you the ability to choose between two courses of action; the if-then allows you to choose whether or not to take a particular course of action. The branches of an if-then or if-then-else can include any statements, even other if statements. With elsif you can choose one of multiple courses of action.

Enumeration types are defined to better represent certain classes of data than is possible with the built-in types. You can create an enumeration type by listing the identifiers that make up the possible values of the type. The identifiers are ordered according to the way they are listed in the declaration. Once we define the enumeration type, we can use it to declare constants, declare variables, and instantiate packages for input and output of enumeration values.

The algorithm trace requires us to define preconditions and postconditions for each module in an algorithm. Then we have to verify that those assertions exist at the beginning and end of each module. By testing a design in the problem-solving phase, we can eliminate errors that can be more difficult to detect in the implementation phase.

An execution trace is a way of finding program errors once you've entered the implementation phase. It's a good idea to trace a program before you run it so that you have some sample results against which you can check the program's output.

Quick Check

1. Write an Ada expression that compares the string variable Name to the literal "Horace" and evaluates to True if Name is less than "Horace". (p. 172)
2. Write an Ada expression that evaluates to True if Name is between "Alice" and "Nick" inclusive. (pp. 174–175)
3. What kind of statement would you use to make an Ada program print out "Middle of roster." if the value in Name is between "Horace" and "Oliver"

inclusive, and print out "Not middle of roster." if the value in Name is outside that range? (pp. 181–182)

4. What kind of statement would you use to make an Ada program print out "Middle of roster." only if the value in Name is between "Horace" and "Oliver" inclusive? (pp. 183–184)
5. On a telephone, each of the digits 2 through 9 has a segment of the alphabet associated with it. What kind of control structure would you use to decide which segment a given letter falls into and to print out the corresponding digit? (pp. 186–189)
6. The following Boolean expression contains a syntax error. What is the error? Correct the expression. (pp. 177–178)

```
(A < B) and (A < C) or (B = C)
```

7. When should you use an enumeration type instead of a built-in type? (pp. 189–190)
8. In what phase of the program development process should you carry out an execution trace? (p. 212)
9. You've written a program that prints out the corresponding digit on a phone given a letter of the alphabet. Everything seems to work right except that you can't get the digit "5" to display; you keep getting the digit "6". What steps would you take to find and fix this bug? (pp. 218–219)

Answers

1. Name < "Horace" **2.** (Name >= "Alice") and (Name <= "Nick") **3.** An if-then-else statement **4.** An if-then statement **5.** An if-elsif statement **6.** We must use parentheses to indicate the order of evaluation in an expression that contains both `and` and `or` operators. The correct expression is

```
((A < B) and (A < C)) or (B = C)
```

7. When the built-in type's range of values does not adequately represent the desired values. **8.** The implementation phase **9.** Carefully review the section of code that should display "5". Check the branching condition and output statement there. Use some sample values and perform an execution trace.

Exam Preparation Exercises

1. Given these values for Boolean variables X, Y, and Z:

X = True, Y = False, Z = True

evaluate the following Boolean expressions. In the blank next to each expression, write a T if the result is True or an F if the result is False.

____ a. `(X and Y) or (X and Z)`
____ b. `(X or not Y) and (not X or Z)`
____ c. `(X or Y) and Z`
____ d. `not (X or Y) and Z`
____ e. `X or (Y and Z)`

2. Write an equivalent expression, without using any parentheses, for each of the following expressions. You may change any of the relational or logical operators.
   a. `not (Change < 1.00)`
   b. `not (Change > 0.0 and Change < 1.00)`
   c. `not (First_Name = "Mildred" or Last_Name = "Smedley")`
   d. `not (not (Change < 1.00);`
3. Write an expression that evaluates to True if the values of the float variables Weight_1 and Weight_2 are close enough to be considered equal.
   a. The weights are of two people (in pounds).
   b. The weights are of two canaries (in pounds). Assume that the typical canary weighs around 0.07 pounds.
   c. The weights are of two bulldozers (in pounds). Assume that a typical bulldozer weighs around 20,000 pounds.
4. Given these values for integer variables I, J, K, and L:

I = 6, J = 7, K = 11, L = 11

what is the output of the following code?

```
Ada.Text_IO.Put (Item => "Madam");
if I < J then
   if K /= L  then
      Ada.Text_IO.Put (Item => How");
   else
      Ada.Text_IO.Put (Item => "Now ");
      Ada.Text_IO.Put (Item => "I'm");
   end if;
end if;
if I >= J  then
   Ada.Text_IO.Put (Item => "Brown ");
   Ada.Text_IO.Put (Item => "Cow");
else
   Ada.Text_IO.Put (Item => "Adam");
end if;
```

5. Given the integer variables X, Y, and Z, where X is 3, Y is 7, and Z is 6, what is the output from each of the following code fragments?

a.
```
if  X <= 3 then
   Ada.Integer_Text_IO.Put (Item => X + Y);
   Ada.Text_IO.New Line;
end if;
Ada.Integer_Text_IO.Put (Item => X + Y);
```

b.
```
if  X /= -1  then
   Ada.Integer_Text_IO.Put (Item => X);
   Ada.Text_IO.New Line;
else
   Ada.Integer_Text_IO.Put (Item => Y);
   Ada.Text_IO.New Line;
end if;
```

c.
```
if  X /= -1  then
   Ada.Integer_Text_IO.Put (Item => X);
   Ada.Text_IO.New Line;
   Ada.Integer_Text_IO.Put (Item => Y);
   Ada.Text_IO.New Line;
   Ada.Integer_Text_IO.Put (Item => Z);
   Ada.Text_IO.New Line;
else
   Ada.Text_IO.Put (Item => "Y");
   Ada.Text_IO.New Line;
   Ada.Text_IO.Put (Item => "Z");
   Ada.Text_IO.New Line;
end if;
```

6. Given this code fragment

```
if  Height >= Min Height  then
   if Weight >= Min Weight  then
      Ada.Text_IO.Put (Item => "Eligible to serve.");
      Ada.Text_IO.New Line;
   else
      Ada.Text_IO.Put (Item => "Too light to serve.");
      Ada.Text_IO.New Line;
   end if;
else
   if  Weight >= Min Weight  then
      Ada.Text_IO.Put (Item => "Too short to serve.");
      Ada.Text_IO.New Line;
   else
      Ada.Text_IO.Put (Item => "Too short and too light to serve.");
      Ada.Text_IO.New Line;
   end if;
end if;
```

a. What is the output when Height exceeds Min_Height and Weight exceeds Min_Weight?

b. What is the output when Height is less than Min_Height and Weight is less than Min_Weight?

7. Match each Boolean expression in the left column with the Boolean expression in the right column that tests for the same condition.

___ a. (X < Y) and (Y < Z)	(1) not (X /= Y) and (Y = Z)
___ b. (X > Y) and (Y >= Z)	(2) not ((X <= Y) or (Y < Z)
___ c. (X /= Y) or (Y = Z)	(3) (Y < Z) or (Y = Z) or (X = Y)
___ d. (X = Y) or (Y <= Z)	(4) not (X >= Y) and not (Y >= Z)
___ e. (X = Y) and (Y = Z)	(5) not ((X = Y) and (Y /= Z))

8. The following expressions make sense but are invalid according to Ada's rules of syntax. Rewrite them so that they are valid Boolean expressions.

a. X < Y <= Z

b. X, Y, and Z are greater than 0

c. X is equal to neither Y nor Z

d. X = Y and Z

9. Given these values for Boolean variables X, Y, and Z

X = True, Y = True, Z = False

indicate whether each expression is True (T) or False (F).

____ a. not (Y or Z) or X

____ b. Z and X and Y

____ c. not Y or (Z or not X)

____ d. Z or (X and (Y or Z))

____ e. X or (X and Z)

10. For each of the following problems, decide which of the branching statements (if-then-else, if-then, or if-elsif) is more appropriate. Explain your answers.

a. Students who are candidates for admission to a college submit their SAT scores. If a student's score is equal to or above a certain value, print a letter of acceptance for the student. Otherwise print a rejection notice.

b. A business is charged one of five different rates depending on the amount of electricity consumed.

c. For employees who work more than 40 hours a week, calculate overtime pay and add it to their regular pay.

d. In solving a quadratic equation, whenever the value of the discriminant (the quantity under the square root sign) is negative, print out a message noting that the roots are imaginary.

e. In a computer-controlled sawmill, if a cross section of a log is greater than certain dimensions, adjust the saw to cut 4-inch by 8-inch beams; otherwise, adjust the saw to cut 2-inch by 4-inch studs.

11. The following nested if structure has five possible branches depending on the values read into Integer variables A, B, and C. Minimum complete coverage of this structure requires five different data sets. Create five appropriate data sets to test this structure.

```
Ada.Integer_Text_IO.Get (Item => A);
Ada.Integer_Text_IO.Get (Item => B);
Ada.Integer_Text_IO.Get (Item => C);
if  A = B  then
   if  B = C  then
      Ada.Text_IO.Put (Item => "All numbers are the same.");
      Ada.Text_IO.New Line;
   else
      Ada.Text_IO.Put (Item => "First two are the same.");
      Ada.Text_IO.New Line;
   end if;
elsif  B = C  then
      Ada.Text_IO.Put (Item => "Last two are the same.");
      Ada.Text_IO.New Line
elsif  A = C  then
      Ada.Text_IO.Put (Item => "First and last are the same.");
      Ada.Text_IO.New Line;
else
      Ada.Text_IO.Put (Item => "All numbers are different.");
      Ada.Text_IO.New Line;
end if;
```

a. Test data set 1: A = ________ B = ________ C = ________
b. Test data set 2: A = ________ B = ________ C = ________
c. Test data set 3: A = ________ B = ________ C = ________
d. Test data set 4: A = ________ B = ________ C = ________
e. Test data set 5: A = ________ B = ________ C = ________

12. If X and Y are Boolean variables, do the following two expressions test the same condition?

    X /= Y (X or Y) and not (X and Y)

13. What is the output of the following code fragment?

```
type Suit Type is (Spades, Clubs, Hearts, Diamonds);

Card_1 : Suit_Type;
Card_2 : Suit_Type;
Card_3 : Suit_Type;
   .
   .
   .
   Card_1 := Hearts;
   Card_2 := Spades;
   Card_3 := Diamonds;

   if  (Card_1 < Card_2) and (Card_2 < Card_3)  then
      Ada.Text_IO.Put (Item => "Horace wins ");
   elsif  (Card_1 > Card_2)  and  (Card_2 > Card_3)  then
      Ada.Text_IO.Put (Item => "Mildred wins ");
   else
```

```
   Ada.Text_IO.Put (Item => "No one wins ");
end if;
Ada.Text_IO.Put (Item => "the game.");
Ada.Text_IO.New Line;
```

14. Using the code fragment of the previous exercise, state whether each of the following is True, False, or an invalid comparison.
    a. Card_1 < Card_3
    b. Card_3 = Clubs
    c. Spades <= Diamonds
    d. Card_2 = Suit_Type
    e. Card_1 and Card_2 < Diamonds
15. a. Write an Ada statement to instantiate a package that contains Get and Put procedures for values of type Suit_Type defined in Exercise 13.
    b. Using the package you instantiated in part *a*, write an Ada statement to display the value of Card_1.
    c. Using the package you instantiated in part *a*, write an Ada statement to read a suit value from the keyboard and put it in Card_2.
    d. What exception is raised if a user misspells Diamonds when entering data for the input statement you wrote for part *c*?
16. Using the EBNF definition of the if statement given on page 187, determine which of the following if statements are syntactically correct and which are not.

a.
```
if Value < 100 then
   Ada.Text_IO.Put (Item => "low");
elsif Value < 200 then
   Ada.Text_IO.Put (Item => "medium");
elsif
   Ada.Text_IO.Put (Item => "high");
end if;
```

b.
```
if Value < 100 then
   Ada.Text_IO.Put (Item => "low");
else
   Ada.Text_IO.Put (Item => "medium");
elsif Value < 200 then
   Ada.Text_IO.Put (Item => "high");
end if;
```

c.
```
if Value < 100 then
   Ada.Text_IO.Put (Item => "low");
elsif Value < 200 then
   Ada.Text_IO.Put (Item => "medium");
else
   Ada.Text_IO.Put (Item => "high");
end if;
```

17. What are the disadvantages of using a string data type for the product type in the Lumberyard case study?

Programming Warm-up Exercises

1. Write an *assignment* statement that assigns True to the Boolean variable Available if Number_Ordered is less than or equal to Number_On_Hand minus Number_Reserved.
2. Declare Eligible to be a Boolean variable, and use an assignment statement to set its value to True.
3. Write an assignment statement that assigns True to the Boolean variable Candidate if SAT_Score (Integer) is greater than or equal to 1100, GPA (Float) is not less than 2.5, and Age (Integer) is greater than 15. Otherwise Candidate should be False.
4. Given the declarations

```
Left_Page    : Boolean;
Page_Number  : Integer;
```

   write an assignment statement that sets Left_Page to True if Page_Number is even. (*Hint:* An integer is even if the remainder, after dividing it by 2, is 0.)
5. Write a nested if statement that assigns to the variable Biggest the greatest value contained in variables I, J, and K. Assume the three values are distinct.
6. Rewrite the following if-then-else statement using two if-then statements.

```
if  Year rem 4 = 0  then
   Ada.Integer_Text_IO.Put (Item => Year, Width => 4);
   Ada.Text_IO.Put         (Item => " is a leap year.");
   Ada.Text_IO.New Line;
else
   Year := Year + 4 - Year rem 4;
   Ada.Integer_Text_IO.Put (Item => Year, Width => 4);
   Ada.Text_IO.Put         (Item => " is the next leap year.");
   Ada.Text_IO.New Line;
end if;
```

7. Write the preconditions and postconditions for the modules in the algorithm for Program Ski_Wax (the second case study of this chapter).
8. Simplify the following program segment, taking out unnecessary comparisons.

```
if Age > 64  then
   Ada.Text_IO.Put (Item => "Senior voter");
end if;
if Age < 18  then
   Ada.Text_IO.Put (Item => "Under age");
end if;
if (Age >= 18)  and  (Age < 65)  then
   Ada.Text_IO.Put (Item => "Regular voter");
end if;
```

9. Given the float variables X1, X2, Y1, Y2, and M, write a program segment to find the slope (M) of a line through points X1 and Y1, and X2 and Y2. Use the formula

$$M = \frac{(Y1 - Y2)}{(X1 - X2)}$$

to determine the slope of the line. If X1 equals X2, the line is vertical and the slope is undefined. Your program segment should print the slope with an appropriate label. If the slope is undefined, it should print the message "Slope undefined".

10. Using the declaration of type Suit_Type from Exam Preparation Exercise 13,
    a. write the Ada statement necessary to create a package for input and output of this type.
    b. write the Ada statements to print the values of the variables Card_1, Card_2, and Card_3 on separate lines using lowercase letters.

11. While the ranges we used for the dimension variables in the Lumberyard case study help catch invalid input, they do not handle all possible errors. Add the code to check for invalid plywood thicknesses. Valid thicknesses are $\frac{1}{4}$, $\frac{3}{8}$, $\frac{1}{2}$, $\frac{5}{8}$, $\frac{3}{4}$, $\frac{7}{8}$, $\frac{4}{4}$, and $\frac{5}{4}$ inches.

12. The experienced users of the Lumberyard program have requested a change. Instead of typing out the entire words Lumber and Plywood, they would like to enter simply L for dimensioned lumber and P for plywood.
    a. One way to make this change is to replace the enumeration type used with a string of one character. What is the major disadvantage in using a string instead of an enumeration type?
    b. Change the enumeration type so that the values are L and P rather than Lumber and Plywood.
    c. Some users of the program still prefer to enter the words rather than the letters. Change the enumeration type so it contains all four possible values. What other changes must we make to the program so that users may enter any of the four values when prompted for the product type?

Programming Problems

1. Using a top-down design, write an Ada program that inputs a single uppercase letter and prints out the corresponding digit on the telephone. The letters and digits on a telephone are grouped this way:

2 = ABC	4 = GHI	6 = MNO	8 = TUV
3 = DEF	5 = JKL	7 = PRS	9 = WXY

No digit corresponds to either Q or Z. For these letters your program should print a message indicating that they are not used on a telephone. The program might operate like this.

```
Enter a single letter, and I will tell you what
the corresponding digit is on the telephone.
R
The digit 7 corresponds to the letter R on the telephone.
```

Here's another example:

```
Enter a single letter, and I will tell you what
the corresponding digit is on the telephone.
Q
There is no digit on the telephone that corresponds to Q.
```

Your program should print a message indicating that there is no matching digit for any nonalphabetic character the user enters (see Appendix C). Include the lowercase letters with the invalid characters. The program should echo print the input letter as part of the output. Use proper indentation, appropriate comments, and meaningful identifiers throughout the program.

2. People who deal with historical dates use a number called the Julian day in calculating the number of days between two events. The Julian day is the number of days that have elapsed since January 1, 4713 BC. For example, the Julian day for October 16, 1956, is 2,435,763. There are formulas for computing the Julian day from a given date and vice versa. One very simple formula computes the day of the week from a given Julian day.

   Day of the week = (Julian day + 1) rem 7

   This formula gives a result of 0 for Sunday, 1 for Monday, and so on up to 6 for Saturday. For Julian day 2,435,763, the result is 2 (a Tuesday). Your job is to write an Ada program that inputs a Julian day, computes the day of the week using the formula, and then prints out the name of the day that corresponds to that number. Be sure to echo print the input data and to use proper indentation and comments.

   A sample run of your program might show

```
Enter a Julian day number:
2451545
Julian day number 2451545 is a SATURDAY.
```

3. You can compute the date for any Easter Sunday from 1982 to 2048 as follows (all variables are of type Integer):

```
A is Year rem 19
B is Year rem 4
C is Year rem 7
D is (19 * A + 24) rem 30
E is (2 * B + 4 * C + 6 * D + 5) rem 7
Easter Sunday is March (22 + D + E) *
```

   Write a program that inputs the year and outputs the date (month and day) of Easter Sunday for that year. Echo print the input as part of the output. For example:

*Notice this formula can give a date in April.

```
Enter the year (for example, 1994):
1985
Easter is Sunday, April 7, in 1985.
```

4. The algorithm for computing the date of Easter described in the previous problem can be extended easily to work with any year from 1900 to 2099. There are four years, 1954, 1981, 2049, and 2076, for which the algorithm gives a date that is 7 days later than it should be. Modify the program for Problem 3 to check for these years and subtract 7 from the day of the month. This correction does not cause the month to change. Be sure to change the documentation for the program to reflect its broadened capabilities.
5. Write an Ada program that calculates and prints the diameter, the circumference, or the area of a circle, given the radius. The program should prompt for what type of calculation is requested, read an appropriate enumeration literal, prompt for a radius, read a float number, and, finally, display the result of the desired circle calculation. The program should echo print the input data. The output should be appropriately labeled and formatted to two decimal places. Your output might look like this:

```
What circle calculation do you wish to do?
Area
What is the radius of the circle?
6.75
The area for a circle with a radius of 6.75 is 143.14
```

   Here are the formulas you'll need:

   Diameter $= 2\ r$

   Circumference $=2\ \pi\ r$

   Area of a circle $= \pi\ r^2$

   Use 3.14159 for π. r is the radius.
6. Write an Ada program that determines the winner in a game of "rock, paper, scissors." In this game, two players choose simultaneously either rock, paper, or scissors. Whether a player wins or loses depends not only on that player's choice but also on the opponent's. The rules are:

   Rock breaks scissors: rock wins.

   Paper covers rock: paper wins.

   Scissors cuts paper: scissors wins.

   All matching combinations are ties.

   Your program should prompt for and read the two players' choices and print out the winner. Your output might look something like this:

```
Enter the choices made by the two players
scissors rock
The second player's choice of rock beats scissors
```

Here's another example:

```
Enter the choices made by the two players
paper paper
The game is a tie
```

Define and use an appropriate enumeration type for a player's choice. Use the minimum number of comparisons to determine the winner.

CHAPTER 5

Looping

GOALS

After reading this chapter, you should be able to

- construct syntactically correct loop and exit statements
- construct count-controlled loops with loop and exit statements
- construct event-controlled loops with loop and exit statements
- construct counting loops with loop and exit statements
- construct summing loops with loop and exit statements
- construct a nested loop
- choose data sets that test a looping program comprehensively

In Chapter 4 we said that the flow of control in a program can differ from the physical order of the statements. The physical order is the order in which the statements appear in a program; the order in which we want the statements to be executed is called the *logical order*.

The if statement is one way of making the logical order different from the physical order. Looping control structures are another. A **loop** executes the same statements over and over again.

In this chapter we discuss different types of loops and how they are constructed using the loop and exit statements. We also discuss nested loops, loops that contain other loops, and introduce a notation for comparing the amount of work done by different algorithms.

Loop A control structure that causes a sequence of statements to be repeated a number of times.

Loop and Exit Statements

The loop statement repeats the execution of a sequence of statements. Here is its simplified EBNF definition:

```
loop_statement ::=  [loop_simple_name: ]
                    loop
                       sequence_of_statements
                    end loop [loop_simple_name];
```

The computer executes the sequence_of_statements over and over, without stopping. This is called an *infinite loop*. We can stop it only by shutting off the computer or issuing an operating-system command to terminate the program. Why would we ever want an infinite loop? There are many cases where it is important that the program repeat the same sequence of statements as long as the computer is operating. For example, here is the pseudocode for a heart-monitoring machine used with intensive-care patients.

```
Heart_Monitor:
loop
   Get the patient's heart rate
   if the heart rate is not within a safe range then
      Turn on nursing station alarm
      Display a warning message
   else
      Display heart rate
   end if
end loop Heart_Monitor
```

In most cases, however, it is desirable to stop further repeated execution of the sequence of statements when some particular condition has been met. We use the exit statement to end execution of the statements in the loop and pass control to the statement following the loop statement. Here's an example of a loop with an exit statement that might be used in a vending-machine program.

```
Coin_Input_Loop:
loop
   Get Coin
   Add value of Coin to Total
   exit Coin_Input_Loop when Total >= Price
end loop Coin_Input_Loop
```

The EBNF definition of the exit statement is

exit_statement ::= **exit** [loop_name] [**when** condition];

The optional names in the loop and exit statements make it easier to read the program, particularly if there are many loops. Notice that you need to use a colon where the name of the loop is first defined. If the loop statement uses an optional loop name, it is good style to use it in the exit statement as well.

Usually, the exit statement, like the if statement, tests a condition. If the Boolean expression making up the condition is True, control transfers to the first statement following the end of the loop. If the condition is False, control continues in the normal sequential manner.

You may place the exit statement anywhere in the sequence of statements within the loop statement. A loop in which the exit statement is the first statement is called a *pretest loop*. A *posttest loop* is one in which the exit statement is the last statement in the loop. A *midtest loop* is one in which the exit statement is not the first or last statement in the loop. Figure 5-1 shows the flow of control for these three types of loops.

Generally, pretest loops are considered easier to read because you need not look any further for the loop termination condition; it is right at the beginning of the loop. Also, in most cases, we want to design our loops for the possibility that the sequence of statements in the loop is not executed at all. Because testing in posttest and midtest loops is done after some other statements in the loop have been executed, at least some of the sequence of statements always execute at least one time. Most of the loops we use in this book are pretest loops.

While it is legal to have two or more exit statements in a loop, it is usually easier to understand loops with a single exit statement. Try to avoid writing loops with multiple exit statements.

Although *if* and *exit* (with its optional condition) are alike, there are fundamental differences between them (compare Figure 5-1 to Figure 4-5).

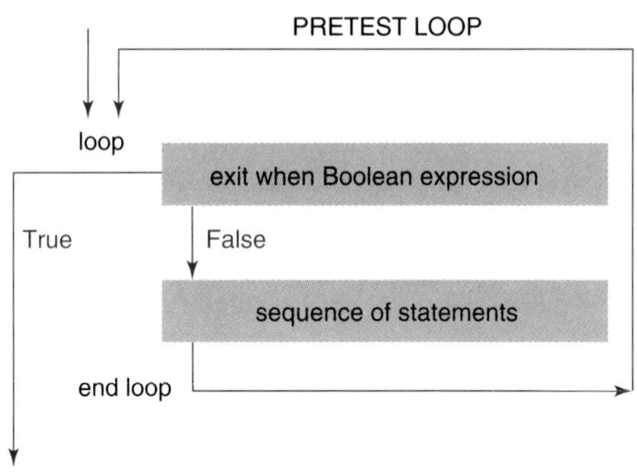

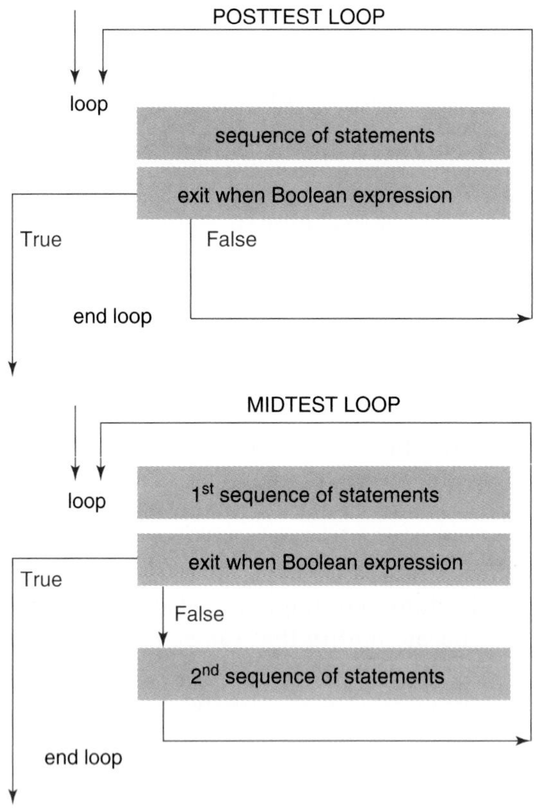

Figure 5-1
Flow of Control: Pretest, Posttest, and Midtest

In the if structure, a sequence of statements is either skipped or executed exactly once. In the loop statement, the sequence of statements may be executed zero, one, or more times.

Phases of Loop Execution

The sequence of statements (including the exit statement) in a loop is called the *body* of the loop. The loop body is executed in several phases:

- The place where the flow of control first passes to a statement inside the loop is the **loop entry.**
- Each time the body of a loop is executed, a pass is made through the loop. This pass is called an **iteration.**
- The exit statement makes a **conditional test.**
- When the last iteration is complete and the flow of the control has passed to the first statement following the loop, the program has **exited the loop.** The condition that causes a loop to be exited is the **termination condition.**

Loop entry The point at which the flow of control first passes to a statement inside a loop.

Iteration An individual pass through, or repetition of, the body of a loop.

Conditional test The point at which the Boolean expression is evaluated and the decision is made to either continue the loop or skip to the first statement following the loop.

Loop exit That point when the repetition of the loop body ends and control passes to the first statement following the loop.

The concept of looping is fundamental to programming. In the next section we look at patterns for the most common applications of loops and ways to implement them with the loop and exit statements. These looping situations come up again and again when you are analyzing problems and doing top-down design.

Loop Design Patterns

In solving problems, you will come across two major types of loops: A **count-controlled loop** repeats a specified number of times; an **event-controlled loop** repeats until something happens within the loop.

Count-controlled loop A loop that executes a specified number of times.

Event-controlled loop A loop that terminates when something happens inside the loop body to signal that the loop should be exited.

If you are making an angel food cake and the recipe reads "Beat the mixture 300 strokes," you are executing a count-controlled loop. If you are making a pie crust and the recipe reads "Cut with a pastry blender until the mixture resembles coarse meal," you are executing an event-controlled loop.

Count-Controlled Loops

We use a count-controlled loop when the number of iterations to perform is known (or can be calculated) *before* we start the loop. Count-controlled loops are pretest loops. They use a variable, which we call the **loop control variable,** in the exit statement's conditional test. Before entering a count-controlled loop, we must initialize (give a value to) the loop control variable. Then, as part of each iteration of the loop, we must increment the loop control variable. Here's an example:

```
Count := 1;                                            -- Initialization
Example_One:
loop
   exit Example_One when Count > Number_Of_Times;     -- Test
      :
   Ada.Text_IO.Put (Item => "Hello Mildred");          -- Repeated actions
      :
   Count := Count + 1;                                 -- Incrementation
end loop Example_One;
```

In this example, Count is the loop control variable. It is set to 1 before loop entry. The exit statement tests the expression

```
Count > Number_Of_Times
```

Look at the statement in which we increment the loop control variable. Notice its form:

```
variable := variable + 1;
```

This statement adds 1 to the value of the variable and the result replaces the old value. Variables that are used this way are called *counters.* In our example, Count is incremented with each iteration of the loop—we use it to count the iterations. The loop control variable of a count-controlled loop is always a counter.

Loop control variable A variable that is tested in an exit statement. Its value determines whether or not we exit the loop.

The number of iterations for this loop is determined by the value of Number_Of_Times. If its value is 3, the statements in the loop body will be executed 3 times. Perform an execution trace of the code to convince yourself that the number of iterations is equal to Number_Of_Times. Try it using a value of 0 for Number_Of_Times. You will see that we do not execute the statements in the loop body if Number_Of_Times is 0. Perhaps now you can see why count-controlled loops are pretest loops. If we used a posttest loop, we would always execute one iteration, even when Number_Of_Times was 0.

Our example illustrates the most common pattern for count-controlled loops:

- Just before the loop statement, initialize the loop control variable to 1.
- The exit statement is the first statement in the loop body. It tests whether the value of the loop control variable is greater than the number of iterations desired.
- Following the exit statement is the sequence of statements we want to repeat.
- The last statement in the loop body increments the loop control variable.

There are other patterns that we could use for our count-controlled loops. We could initialize the loop control variable to 0 instead of 1 and change the condition in the exit statement to test for equality rather than greater than. However, we feel that sticking to a single pattern reduces the chances that we make an error when writing loops.

Since count-controlled loops are so common in algorithms, Ada has a specialized loop statement, the **for statement,** that provides a more convenient syntax for this pattern. So you will not be confused by an additional set of loop statement rules, we have chosen to delay introduction of the for loop statement until Chapter 8. Read pages **445–451** if you would like to learn the details of the for statement now.

For statement A loop statement specifically for writing count-controlled loops. See Chapter 8 for details.

Event-Controlled Loops

We use an event-controlled loop when we do *not* know the number of iterations to perform ahead of time. We exit an event-controlled loop after some event occurs inside the loop. There are several common patterns for event-controlled loops. In this section we look at sentinel-controlled, calculation-controlled, and data-validation loops. In all of these loops, the termination condition depends on some event occurring while the loop body is executing.

Sentinel-Controlled Loops Loops are often used to read in and process long lists of data. Each time the loop body executes, a new piece of data is read and processed. We can use a special data value, called a *sentinel*, to signal the program that there is no more data to be processed. Looping continues as long as the data value read is not the sentinel; it stops when the program recognizes the sentinel. In other words, reading the sentinel value is the *event* that stops the looping process.

Often our biggest problem in designing a program with a sentinel-controlled loop is determining what to use as a sentinel value. We must find some value that cannot be confused with real data. A sentinel value must be something that never shows up in the normal input to a program. For example, if a program reads test scores, we could use a negative score as a sentinel value.

```
Score_Loop:
loop
   Ada.Integer_Text_IO.Get (Item => Test_Score);     -- Get a test score
   exit Score_Loop when Test_Score < 0;
      .
      .                                               -- Process the test score
      .
end loop Score_Loop;
```

Each score is read in; if it is not the sentinel, it gets processed. When the sentinel value is read, the exit condition becomes True, and the loop exits *without* processing the sentinel value. The sentinel-controlled loop is a midtest loop.

Our score example illustrates the pattern for sentinel-controlled loops. The first thing we do is get some data. Next comes the exit statement with a check for the sentinel value. Finally it reaches the sequence of statements to process the data.

What happens if you forget to enter the correct sentinel value? In an interactive program, the loop continues prompting for input data. At that point you can enter a random data value, but you will probably get incorrect results. If the input to the program is from a file, once all the values have been read from the file, the exception END_ERROR occurs as soon as the program attempts to get a data value. There isn't any data left because the computer has reached the end of the file.

Calculation-Controlled Loops In this kind of event-controlled loop, the event is a result of a calculation made in the loop body. As an example we look at Newton's method for finding the square root of a number (X). This method uses successive approximations, each using the preceding approximation ($A_{preceding}$) as a starting point to obtain a more accurate approximation (A) from the following equation:

$$A = \frac{1}{2}(A_{preceding} + X / A_{preceding})$$

To determine the square root of 3, we arbitrarily choose 1.5 (half of 3) as our first approximation. Any choice will do, but the closer our initial guess, the faster we will find a good approximation to the square root. Using the formula with X equal to 3 and $A_{preceding}$ equal to 1.5, we calculate a better approximation as

$$A = \frac{1}{2}(1.5 + 3 / 1.5) = 1.75$$

This second approximation is then used to calculate a third and better approximation, which is used to calculate a fourth and better approximation.

$$A = \frac{1}{2}(1.75 + 3 / 1.75) = 1.7321428$$
$$A = \frac{1}{2}(1.7321428 + 3 / 1.7321428) = 1.7320508$$

Notice we are repeating the same calculation over and over. It is an iterative method for approximating a square root, which is ideal for using a loop structure in a program.

Before writing the loop we have one more problem to solve. How do we know when our approximation is good enough to stop repeating the calculation and exit the loop? Our approximation is exact when its square equals X. This leads to the exit statement:

```
exit when  Approx ** 2 = X;
```

There is a problem with this solution. Because Newton's formula yields only an approximation, it may never calculate the exact answer. Instead, as discussed in Chapter 4, we check for near equality

```
exit when  abs(Approx ** 2 - X)  <  Tolerance;
```

where Tolerance is a constant or variable whose value is the error we are willing to tolerate in our result. Here's the code to determine and display the square root of X.

```
Approx := X / 2.0;                                   -- Choose an initial approximation
Calculate_Square_Root:   -- Calculate a square root
loop                     -- Each iteration, calculate a better approximation
   exit Calculate_Square_Root when  abs(Approx ** 2 - X)  <  Tolerance;
   Approx := 0.5 * (Approx + X / Approx);
end loop Calculate_Square_Root;
Ada.Float_Text_IO.Put (Item => X);                   -- Display value and
Ada.Float_Text_IO.Put (Item => Approx);              -- its square root
```

In this pretest loop, we first check to see whether the approximation is within our chosen tolerance. If it isn't, we use it to calculate a more accurate approximation.

Data-Validation Loops In all of our program examples we have made the assumption that all of the data entered by the user is valid. What happens if they enter data that is not valid? If the invalid data is the wrong type (for example, entering the word *Hello* when a number is required), the program halts with a DATA_ERROR exception. If the invalid data is outside the range we specified for a variable, the program halts with a CONSTRAINT_ERROR. If the invalid data is the correct type and within the range of the variable, the program will not halt. However, it is very likely that it will display incorrect results. While halting a program is an extreme action, it is usually better than producing incorrect results.

Let's look at an example. The Lumberyard problem in Chapter 4 included minimum and maximum values for the lumber dimensions (thickness, width, and length). We used these limits to specify ranges on the variables in our program. If the user of our program enters a dimension outside of these limits, it halts with a CONSTRAINT_ERROR. We also included ranges for plywood dimensions (thickness numerator, thickness denominator, and length). The ranges we used for the thickness fraction are not adequate to catch all invalid input data. We gave a range of 1..5 for the thickness numerator and 2..8 for the denominator. While these ranges would catch invalid thickness such as $\frac{11}{16}$ and $-\frac{1}{4}$, they do not catch $\frac{1}{3}$ and $\frac{5}{2}$ whose numerator and denominators are within the ranges we used. We must explicitly test the thickness data to determine if it is valid. We can perform a test for the seven valid plywood thickness in an if statement like this

```
if (Numerator = 1 and (Denominator = 4 or Denominator = 2))
      or
   (Numerator = 3 and (Denominator = 8 or Denominator = 4))
      or
   (Numerator = 4 and Denominator = 4)
      or
   (Numerator = 5 and (Denominator = 8 or Denominator = 4))      then
```

```
    -- Thickness data is valid. Continue to process the plywood order.

else

    -- Thickness data is invalid. Do no processing.

end if;
```

There is an advantage to performing the same test in an exit statement of a loop. We give the user the opportunity to try again. In a data-validation loop we continue iterating until the user enters valid data. Here's how we might write a data-validation loop for plywood thickness.

```
Thickness_Validation_Loop:    -- Validate plywood thickness
loop                          -- Each iteration, check one set of values
   Ada.Text_IO.Put (Item => "Enter thickness numerator and denominator");
   Ada.Text_IO.New_Line;
   Ada.Integer_Text_IO.Get (Item => Numerator);
   Ada.Integer_Text_IO.Get (Item => Denominator);

   exit Thickness_Validation_Loop    -- when the thickness is valid
        when (Numerator = 1 and (Denominator = 4 or Denominator = 2))
               or
             (Numerator = 3 and (Denominator = 8 or Denominator = 4))
               or
             (Numerator = 4 and Denominator = 4)
               or
             (Numerator = 5 and (Denominator = 8 or Denominator = 4))

   Ada.Text_IO.Put (Item => "Invalid thickness entered.  Please try again.");
   Ada.Text_IO.New_Line;
end loop Thickness_Validation_Loop;

-- Thickness data is valid. Continue to process the plywood order.
```

This example illustrates the pattern of a data-validation loop. First we get the data we wish to validate. We write the Boolean expression in the exit statement so that we exit the loop when the data is valid. The statements after the exit statement are executed only if the data is invalid. Here we usually display an appropriate message before returning to the first statement in the loop body.

Data-validation loops are midtest, event-controlled loops. We do not know before starting the loop how many iterations will be performed. The acquisition of valid data from the user is the event that signals the end of looping.

Looping Subtasks

We have been looking at ways to use loops to affect the flow of control in programs. But looping by itself does nothing. The loop body must perform a task in order for the loop to function. In this section we look at the patterns for three common tasks—event counting, summing, and keeping track of a previous value—that often are done in loops. We add these new patterns to the count-controlled-loop and event-controlled loop patterns we discussed in the previous sections.

Counting Counting things is a common task in a loop. For example, the following program fragment counts the number of characters in a sentence. We assume that the sentence ends with a period (which we do not want to include in our count of characters). Char is of type String(1..1)* and Char_Count is of type Integer.

```
Char_Count : = 0;                           -- Initialize counter
Char_Loop:                                  -- Count the number of characters
loop                                        -- Each iteration, process one character
   Ada.Text_IO.Get (Item => Char);          -- Get one character
   exit Char_Loop when Char = ".";
   Char_Count := Char_Count + 1;            -- Increment counter
end loop Char_Loop;
```

Do you recognize the loop pattern in this example? It is a sentinel-controlled loop. The loop continues until a period is read. The loop has a counter variable, but the loop is not a count-controlled loop. When the loop terminates, Char_Count contains the number of characters in the sentence. Notice that if a period is the first character, Count contains a 0, as it should. The counter variable in this example is called an **iteration counter** because its value equals the number of *complete* iterations through the loop.

Iteration counter A variable that is incremented with each complete iteration of a loop.

The pattern for counting consists of two parts. First, before the loop begins we initialize the counter variable to zero—nothing has been counted at this point. Then in the loop body we increment the counter.

Counting is not limited to iterations. For example, the following program fragment reads 100 numbers and counts how many of them are positive.

*In Chapter 7 we introduce type Character, a more appropriate type than String(1..1).

```
Count        := 1;      -- Loop control variable
Num_Positive := 0;      -- Count of positive numbers

Count_Positives         -- Count the number of positive numbers
loop                    -- Each iteration, process one number
   exit Count_Positives when Count > 100;
   Ada.Float_Text_IO.Get (Item => Number);
   if Number > 0.0 then
      Num_Positive := Num_Positive + 1; -- Increment count of positive numbers
   end if;
   Count := Count + 1;                  -- Increment loop control variable
end loop; Count positives
```

A count-controlled loop is appropriate in this example since we know ahead of time how many iterations the loop must make (100). The loop control variable, Count, is initialized to 1, tested in the exit statement, and incremented at the end of the loop. The variable Num_Positive keeps count of the number of positive numbers read. Again the pattern for counting consists of initializing the counter to zero before the loop and incrementing it within the loop.

The assignment statement that increments Num_Positive is not executed each time through the loop. Num_Positive is an **event counter.** An if statement is used to determine if the desired event—the acquisition of a positive number—has occurred.

Event counter A variable that is incremented each time a particular event occurs.

Summing Another common looping task is to sum a set of data values. Notice in the following count-controlled loop example that the summing operation is independent of how the loop is controlled. Summing can just as easily be used in a sentinel-controlled loop or in any other form of loop.

```
Sum   := 0.0;                       -- Initialize the sum
Count := 1;                         -- Initialize the loop control variable
Calc_Sum:                           -- Sum 50 numbers
loop                                -- Each iteration, add one number to the sum
   exit Calc_Sum  when  Count > 50;
   Ada.Float_Text_IO.Get (Item => Number);     -- Input a value
   Sum := Sum + Number;                        -- Add the value to sum
   Count := Count + 1;              -- Increment loop control variable
end loop Calc_Sum;
```

When this fragment has been executed, Sum contains the total of the 50 values read, Count contains 51, and Number contains the last value read. Like the pattern we use for counting, summing involves initializing the summing variable to zero before the loop. In the loop we add the new value to the sum.

Let's look at another example. We want to count and sum the first 10 odd numbers in a set of data. We need to test each number to see whether it is even or odd. If it is even, we do nothing. If it is odd, we increment the counter and add the value to our sum. We use an event-controlled loop because we do not know ahead of time how many numbers we must read to find 10 odd ones. Our event counter, Odd_Count, is used as a loop control variable. The event that ends the loop is the acquisition of the tenth odd number.

```
Odd_Count := 0;                                     -- Initialize the event counter
Sum       := 0;                                     -- Initialize the sum
Odd_Sum:              -- Sum the first 10 odd numbers
loop                  -- Each iteration, process one number
   exit Odd_Sum  when  Odd_Count = 10;
   Ada.Integer_Text_IO.Get (Item => Number);        -- Get the next value
   if (Number rem 2)  =  1  then                    -- Is the number odd?
      Odd_Count := Odd_Count + 1;                   -- Increment counter
      Sum       := Sum + Number;                    -- Add odd value to sum
   end if;
end loop Odd_Sum;
```

Keeping Track of a Previous Value Sometimes we want to remember the previous value of a variable. Suppose a thermocouple measures the temperature of an industrial furnace every minute. The thermocouple used sometimes gives inconsistent readings. A temperature reading is considered inconsistent if it differs by more than 2.5 degrees from the average of the two previous readings. We want to write a program that counts the number of inconsistent readings in a data set. To do this we need to keep track of three values—the current value being examined and the two previous values. All of the values in the data set are positive. We use a negative integer as a sentinel to indicate the end of the data set.

```
Event_Count := 0;                -- Initialize event counter
Value_Test:                      -- Count the number of inconsistent readings
loop                             -- Each iteration, check one reading
   Ada.Float_Text_IO.Get (Item => Current_Value);
   exit Value_Test when Current_Value < 0.0;
   Average := (Last_Value_1 + Last_Value_2) / 2.0;
   if abs (Current_Value - Average) > 2.5  then
      Event_Count := Event_Count + 1;
   end if;
```

```
   -- Save the two most recent values
   Last_Value_2 := Last_Value_1
   Last_Value_1 := Current_Value;
end loop Value_Test;
```

At the end of this loop, the current value and the most recent last value are saved for the next iteration. There is a problem in this example. The values of Last_Value_1 and Last_Value_2 are not defined before the *first* pass through the loop. Somehow we have to initialize these variables before they are used in the loop. We could assign them arbitrary values, but then we have the problem of those values being processed as actual data.

We can solve this problem by getting the first two values before entering the loop. Getting a data value before entering the loop is called a *priming read*. (The idea is similar to priming a pump by pouring a bucket of water into the mechanism before starting it.) Let's add two priming reads to the code.

```
Event_Count := 0;                                    -- Initialize event counter
Ada.Float_Text_IO.Get (Item => Last_Value_2);        -- Get the first two values in
Ada.Float_Text_IO.Get (Item => Last_Value_1);        -- the data set (priming reads)
Value_Test:                         -- Count the number of inconsistent readings
loop                                -- Each iteration, check one reading
   Ada.Float_Text_IO.Get (Item => Current_Value);
   exit Value_Test when Current_Value < 0.0;
   Average := (Last_Value_1 + Last_Value_2) / 2.0;
   if abs (Current_Value - Average) > 2.5  then
      Event_Count := Event_Count + 1;
   end if;
   -- Save the two most recent values
   Last_Value_2 := Last_Value_1
   Last_Value_1 := Current_Value;
end loop Value_Test;
```

Study this loop carefully by performing an execution trace. It's going to come in handy. There will be many times when you must keep track of previous input values in addition to the current value. The pattern here is to declare a variable for each previous value you need to keep track of and use priming reads to obtain the initial previous values. At the end of the loop, transfer values from current to previous for the next iteration.

How to Design Loops

It's one thing to understand how a loop works when you look at it, but it is something else again to select a pattern and design a loop that solves a problem. In this section we look at how to design loops. We can divide the design process into two tasks: designing the control flow and designing the processing that takes place in the loop. And we can break each task into three phases: the task itself, initialization, and update. It's also important to specify the state of the program when it exits the loop: A loop that leaves variables and files in a mess is not well designed.

So there are seven different points to consider in designing a loop:

1. What is the condition that ends the loop?
2. How should the condition be initialized?
3. How should the condition be updated?
4. What is the process being repeated?
5. How should the process be initialized?
6. How should the process be updated?
7. What is the state of the program on exiting the loop?

We use these questions as a checklist. Together with our knowledge of common loop patterns, the first three questions help us design the parts of the loop that control its execution. The next three help us design the processing within the loop. The last question reminds us to make sure that the loop exits in an appropriate manner.

Designing the Flow of Control

The most important step in loop design is deciding what should make the loop stop. If the termination condition isn't well thought out there's the potential for an infinite loop and other mistakes. So here is our first question:

- What is the condition that ends the loop?

This question usually can be answered through a close examination of the problem statement looking for phrases that match the loop patterns described earlier. For example:

Key Phrase in Problem Statement	**Termination Condition**
"Sum 365 temperatures"	The loop ends when a counter exceeds 365 (count-controlled loop).
"Process until 10 odd integers have been read"	The loop ends when the 10th odd number has been input (event-controlled loop).
"The end of the data is indicated by a negative test score"	The loop ends when a negative input value is encountered (sentinel-controlled loop).

Now we need statements that make sure the loop gets started correctly and statements that allow the loop to reach the termination condition. So we have to ask the next two questions:

- How should the condition be initialized?
- How should the condition be updated?

Initialization of the condition occurs outside of the loop, while updating the conditions occurs in the loop body. The specific answers to these two questions depend on the type of termination condition.

Count-Controlled Loops If the loop is count-controlled, we initialize the condition by giving the loop control variable an initial value. In our preferred pattern for a count-controlled loop we use an initial value of 1. However, if the processing statements inside the loop require the counter to run through a specific range of values, the initial value should be the lowest value in that range.

The condition is updated by increasing the value of the counter by 1 for each iteration. (Occasionally you will come across a problem that requires a counter to count from some value down to a lower value. In this case the initial value is the greater value, and the counter is decremented by 1 for each iteration.) So for count-controlled loops, these are the answers to the questions:

- Initialize the iteration counter to 1.
- Increment the iteration counter at the end of each iteration.

Event-Controlled Loops If the loop is controlled by a variable that is counting an event within the loop, the control variable usually is initialized to 0 (before we start, no events have occurred) and is incremented each time the event occurs. For such loops that use an event counter, these are the answers to the questions:

- Initialize the event counter to 0.
- Increment the event counter each time the event occurs.

Sentinel-controlled and data-validation loops With both loops there is no initialization necessary. To update the condition, a value is read at the beginning of each iteration. So, for sentinel-controlled and data-validation loops, we answer our questions this way:

- No initialization is necessary.
- Input a new value for processing at the beginning of each iteration.

Calculation-controlled loops Depending on the calculation involved, there may or may not be any initialization required. Many numerical calculations require an initial estimate. To update the condition, a calculation is made that brings us closer to the termination condition. Such a calculation is said to be *convergent.*

- Initialize any values required for the calculation.
- The calculation used brings us closer to the exit condition.

Designing the Process Within the Loop

Once we've determined the looping structure itself, we can fill in the details of the process. In designing the process, we first must decide what we want a single iteration to do. Assume for a moment that the process is going to execute only once.

- What jobs must the process perform?
- What is the process being repeated?

To answer these question, we have to take another look at the problem statement. The definition of the problem may require the process to sum up data values or to keep a count of data values that satisfy some test. For example:

Count the number of negative integers in a set of 100 values.

This statement tells us that the process to be repeated is a counting operation. Here's another example:

Read a stock price for each business day in a week and compute the average price.

In this case, part of the process involves reading a data value. We have to conclude from our knowledge of how an average is computed that the process also involves summing the data values.

In addition to counting and summing, another common loop process is reading data, performing a calculation, and writing out a result. There are many other operations that can appear in looping processes. (We've mentioned only the simplest here; we'll look at some other processes later on.)

After we've determined the operations to be performed if the process is executed only once, we design the parts of the process that are necessary for it to be repeated correctly. We often have to add some steps to take into account the fact that the loop executes more than once. This part of the design typically involves initializing certain variables before the loop and then reinitializing or updating them before each subsequent iteration.

- How should the process be initialized?
- How should the process be updated?

If the process within a loop requires that several different counts and sums be performed, each must have its own statements to initialize variables, increment counting variables, or add values to sums. Just deal with each counting or summing operation by itself: First write the initialization statement, and then write the incrementing or summing statement. After you've done this for one operation, go on to the next.

The Loop Exit

When the termination condition occurs and the flow of control passes to the statement following the loop, the variables used in the loop still contain values. If input files are used, there still may be data left; and if output files are used, they may have new content. If these variables or files are used elsewhere in the program, the loop must leave them in a ready to be used state. So, the final step in designing a loop is answering this question:

- What is the state of the program on exiting the loop?

Now we have to consider the consequences of our design and to double-check its validity. Suppose we've used an event counter and that later processing depends on the number of events. It's important to be sure (with an algorithm trace) that the value left in the counter is exactly the number of events—that it is not off by 1. Look at this code segment:

```
Iteration_Count := 1;
Zero_Count      := 1;
Count_The_Zeros:
loop
   exit Count_The_Zeros when Iteration_Count > 10;
   Ada.Integer_Text_IO.Get (Item => Number);
   if Number = 0 then
      Zero_Count := Zero_Count + 1;
   end if;
   Iteration_Count := Iteration_Count + 1;
end loop Count_The_Zeros;
Ada.Integer_Text_IO.Put (Item => Zero_Count, Width => 4);
```

This loop reads 10 integers and counts the number that are 0. However, when the loop terminates, Zero_Count equals the actual number of 0s plus 1 because the loop initializes the event counter to 1 before any events take place. By determining the state of Zero_Count at loop exit, we've detected a flaw in the initialization. Zero_Count should be initialized to 0.

Commenting Loops

The comments we write for our loops can be a great help to both the loop designer and the maintenance programmer who must quickly develop an understanding of the logic. The answers to our seven design questions provide complete documentation of our design decisions. However, most programmers balk at including such lengthy comments in their programs. So we recommend that you include two comments with each loop that you design.

- What is accomplished when we exit this loop? (Design question 7)
- What is accomplished in each iteration of this loop? (Design questions 3 and 6)

Now let's look at a complete example of loop design. The problem is to determine how many times the letter *W* appears in a sentence such as "How now brown cow." For simplicity we assume that the end of a sentence is marked by a period, question mark, or exclamation point.

- What is the condition that ends the loop?

This loop is a sentinel-controlled loop. It is terminated whenever a period, question mark, or exclamation point is read.

- How should the condition be initialized?

Our pattern for sentinel loops requires no initialization.

- How should the condition be updated?

Our pattern for sentinel loops is that we must read a new value (a character in this problem) each time through the loop.

Now that we have answered all three questions for the flow of control, we can write a skeleton for our loop with the logic that controls the loop action, along with our comments.

```
Letter : String (1..1);
    .
    .
    .
W_Loop:   -- Count all the Ws in a sentence
loop      -- Each iteration, check one letter in the sentence
```

```
   Ada.Text_IO.Get (Item => Letter);
   exit W_Loop when  Letter = "."  or  Letter = "?"  or  Letter = "!";

   -- processing goes here

end loop W_Loop;
```

- What is the process being repeated?

We are counting the number of *W*s in a sentence. The problem did not specify anything about the case of the letter. We will count both uppercase and lowercase occurrences. An if statement can be used to test the current letter.

```
if Letter = "W"  or  Letter = "w"  then
   W_Count := W_Count + 1;
end if;
```

- How should the process be initialized?

The process uses an event counter, W_Count, to count the number of *W*s. This counter must be initialized to 0.

- How should the process be updated?

The counter is incremented every time a *W* is encountered.

- What is the state of the program on exiting the loop?

The counter W_Count contains the number of *W*s in a sentence.

We can now use the answers to our seven design questions to complete the loop.

```
Letter   : String (1..1);
W_Count : Integer range 0..Integer'Last;
   .
   .
   .
W_Count := 0;
W_Loop: :   -- Count all the Ws in a sentence
loop        -- Each iteration, check one letter in the sentence
   Ada.Text_IO.Get (Item => Letter);
   exit W_Loop when  Letter = "."  or  Letter = "?"  or  Letter = "!";
   if Letter = "W"  or  Letter = "w"  then
      W_Count := W_Count + 1;
   end if;
end loop W_Loop;
```

Designing correct loops depends as much on experience as it does on the application of design methodology. At this point you may want to read through the first problem-solving case study at the end of the chapter to see how the loop design process is applied to some real problems.

Nested Logic

In Chapter 4 we described nested if statements. Loop statements also can be nested. Both loop and if statements contain a sequence of statements and are themselves statements. So the body of a loop statement or the branch of an if statement can contain other loop and if statements. By nesting, we can create complex control structures.

Suppose we want to extend our code for calculating square roots, repeating it for all the float values in a data set. Because we can't take the square root of a negative value, we have a good sentinel to mark the end of our data. Here is the resulting sentinel-controlled loop.

```
Read_Data:   -- Calculate the square root of all the given numbers
loop         -- Each iteration, one square root is calculated and displayed
   Ada.Float_Text_IO.Get (Item => X);
   exit Read_Data when X < 0.0;

   -- Calculate and display the square root of X

end loop Read_Data;
```

We can insert the calculation-controlled loop that approximates the square root of a number that we showed on page 240 in place of the comment.

```
Read_Data:   -- Calculate the square root of all the given numbers
loop         -- Each iteration, one square root is calculated and displayed
   Ada.Float_Text_IO.Get (Item => X);
   exit Read_Data when X < 0.0;

   Approx := X / 2.0;          -- Choose an initial approximation
   Calculate_Square_Root:      -- Calculate a square root
   loop                        -- Each iteration, calculate a better approximation
      exit Calculate_Square_Root when  abs(Approx ** 2 - X)  <  Tolerance;
      Approx := 0.5 * (Approx + X / Approx);
   end loop Calculate_Square_Root;
   Ada.Float_Text_IO.Put (Item => X);          -- Display value and
   Ada.Float_Text_IO.Put (Item => Approx);     -- its square root

end loop Read_Data;
```

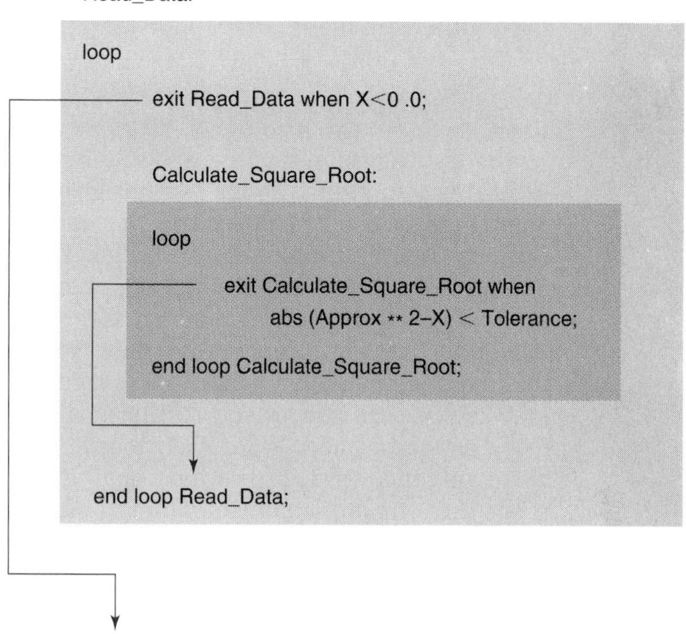

Figure 5-2 Flow of Control with Nested Loops

Notice how we indented the inner loop (the one that calculates the square root) within the outer loop (the data loop). The flow of control in this nested loop structure is illustrated in Figure 5-2.

Let's examine the general pattern of a simple nested loop.

```
-- Initialize outer loop
Outer:
loop
   .
   .
   .
   -- Initialize inner loop
   Inner:
   loop
      -- Inner loop test, processing, and update
   end loop Inner;
   .
   .
   .
end loop Outer;
```

Each loop has its own initialization, and each loop body must have an exit statement (test) and update. The dots represent places where testing, processing, and updating may take place in the outer loop. It's possible for an outer loop to do no processing other than repeatedly executing the inner loop. On the other hand, the inner loop might be just a small part of the processing done by the outer loop; there could be many statements preceding or following the inner loop.

Designing Nested Loops

As the last example illustrated, designing nested loops is no different than designing two simple loops. To design a nested loop, we begin with the outer loop. We select the most appropriate loop pattern and answer the seven questions to complete its design. The process being repeated (design question 6) includes the nested loop as one of its steps. Because that step is more complex than a single statement, our top-down design methodology tells us to make it a separate module. We use the same process to design that loop independent of the module containing the outer loop.

We used this approach in the design of the last program fragment. Once we had a module for each loop, combining them into one program was straightforward. In the next chapter we will learn to write our own procedures to implement modules. Using our own procedures, we need never have physically nested loop statements; each loop is contained in a separate procedure.

THEORETICAL FOUNDATIONS

The Magnitude of Work

There is usually more than one way to solve a problem. This may leave the programmer trying to choose the most efficient algorithm by deciding how much **work** is necessary to execute it.

How do we measure the amount of work required to execute an algorithm? We use the total number of steps executed as a measure of work. One statement, such as an assignment, may require only one step; another, such as a loop, may require many steps. We define a step as any operation roughly equivalent in complexity to a comparison, an I/O operation, or an assignment.

Work A measure of the effort expended by the computer in performing a computation.

Given an algorithm with just a sequence of statements (no branches or loops), the number of steps performed relates directly to the number of statements. When we introduce branches, however, we make it possible to skip some statements in the algorithm. Branches allow us to subtract steps without physically removing them from the algorithm because only one branch executes at a time. But because we always want to express work in terms of the worst case scenario (the maximum number of steps), we use the number of steps in the longest branch.

Now consider the effect of a loop. If a loop repeats a sequence of 15 statements 10 times, it performs 150 steps. With loops a short program can have many steps.

Now that we have a measure for the work done in an algorithm, we can compare algorithms. For example, if Algorithm A always executes 3124 steps and Algorithm B always does the same task in 1321 steps, then we can say that Algorithm B is more efficient—it takes fewer steps to accomplish the same task.

If an algorithm always takes the same number of steps, we say that it executes in *constant time*. Be careful: constant time doesn't mean small; it means that the amount of work done is bounded (limited) by a constant that does not change from one run to another. This bounding constant may be very large.

If a loop executes a fixed number of times, the work done is greater than the number of statements but still is constant. But what happens if the number of loop iterations can change from one run to the next? Suppose we have N data values to be processed in a loop. If the loop reads and processes one value during each iteration, then the loop executes N iterations. The amount of work done thus depends on a variable—the number of data values. Algorithms that perform work directly proportional to the number of data values are said to execute in linear time. If we have a loop that executes N times, the number of steps to be executed is linearly dependent on N.

Specifically, the work done by an algorithm with a data-dependent loop is

$$\overbrace{(S_1 \times N)}^{\text{Steps performed by the loop}} + \underbrace{S_0}_{\text{Steps performed outside the loop}}$$

where S_1 is the number of steps in the loop body (a constant for a given loop), N is the number of iterations (a variable), and S_0 is the number of steps outside the loop. Notice that, if N grows very large, the first term dominates the execution time—that is, S_0 becomes an insignificant part of the total execution time.

What about a data-dependent loop that contains a nested loop? The number of steps in the inner loop, S_2, and the number of iterations performed by the inner loop, N_2, must be multiplied by the number of iterations in the outer loop N_1:

$$\overbrace{(S_2 \times N_2 \times N_1)}^{\text{Steps performed by the nested loop}} + \overbrace{(S_1 \times N_1)}^{\text{Steps performed by the outer loop}} + \overbrace{S_0}^{\text{Steps performed outside the outer loop}}$$

By itself, the inner loop performs $S_2 \times N_2$ steps, but, because it is repeated N times by the outer loop, it accounts for a total of $S_2 \times N_2 \times N_1$ steps. If N_2 is a constant, then the algorithm still executes in linear time.

Now, suppose that, for each of the N outer loop iterations, the inner loop performs N steps ($N_2 = N_1 = N$). Here the formula for the total steps is

$$(S_2 \times N \times N) + (S_1 \times N) + S_0$$

or

$$(S_2 \times N^2) + (S_1 \times N) + S_0$$

Because N^2 grows much faster than N (for large values of N), the inner loop term (N^2) accounts for the majority of steps executed and the work done. So the corresponding execution time is essentially proportional to N^2. If we have a doubly nested loop, where each loop depends on N, then the expression is

$$(S_3 \times N^3) + (S_2 \times N^2) + (S_1 \times N) + S_0$$

and the work and time are proportional to N^3 whenever N is reasonably large.

Table 5-1 shows the number of steps required for each increase in the exponent of N. As you can see, each time the exponent increases by 1, the number of steps is multiplied by an additional order of magnitude (factor of 10). That is, if N is made 10 times greater, the work involved in an N^2 algorithm increases by a factor of 100, and the work involved in an N^3 algorithm increases by a factor of 1000. To put this in more concrete terms, an algorithm with a triply nested loop, in which each loop depends on the number of data values, takes 1000 steps for 10 input values and 1 trillion steps for 10,000 values. On a computer that executes 1 million instructions per second, the latter case would take over 11 days to run.

The table also shows that the steps outside of the innermost loop account for an insignificant portion of the total number of steps as N gets bigger. Because the innermost loop dominates the total time, we classify an algorithm according to the highest order of N that appears in its work expression, called the *order of magnitude,* or simply the *order* of that expression. So we talk about algorithms being "order N squared" (or cubed or so on), or we describe them with what is called "Big-O notation." We express this order by putting the highest-order term in parentheses with an uppercase O in front. For example $O(1)$ is constant time; $O(N)$ is linear time; $O(N^2)$ is quadratic time; and $O(N^3)$ is cubic time.

Determining the orders of different algorithms allows us to compare the work they require without having to program and execute them. For example, if you have a quadratic algorithm and a linear algorithm that perform the same task, you probably would choose the linear algorithm. We say "probably" because an $O(N^2)$ algorithm actually may execute fewer steps than an $O(N)$ algorithm for small values of N. Remember that, if N is small, you must consider the constants and lower-order terms in the work expression.

Although we generally ignore the lower-order terms, they do exist, giving us a polynomial expression when all the terms are written out. Such algorithms are thus said to execute in *polynomial time* and form a broad class of algorithms that encompasses everything we've discussed so far.

TABLE 5-1
Steps in Nested Loops

N	N^0 (Constant)	N^1 (Linear)	N^2 (Quadratic)	N^3 (Cubic)
1	1	1	1	1
10	1	10	100	1,000
100	1	100	10,000	1,000,000
1,000	1	1,000	1,000,000	1,000,000,000
10,000	1	10,000	100,000,000	1,000,000,000,000

In addition to polynomial-time algorithms, we encounter a logarithmic-time algorithm in Chapter 12. There are also factorial ($O(N!)$) and exponential ($O(2^N)$) class algorithms, which can require vast amounts of time to execute and are beyond the scope of this course. For now, the important point to remember is that the looping control structure allows an algorithm to perform more work than the number of statements it contains.

PROBLEM-SOLVING CASE STUDY

Average Income by Gender

Specification

Problem You've been hired by a law firm that is working on a sex discrimination case. Your firm has obtained a data set that contains the salaries for every employee in the company. There is one line in the file for each employee in the company that contains a salary amount followed by the word Female or Male followed by a position title. As a first pass in the analysis of this data, you've been asked to compute the average income for females and the average income for males.

Input
From the keyboard
 The name of the file containing the salary information.
From the file
 One line per employee containing their salary, gender (Male or Female), and 50-character position title.

Output The number of females and their average income, and the number of males and their average income.

Assumptions We assume that the file name entered by the user is valid as is all the data in that file. So that we won't divide by zero, we also assume that there is data for at least one female and one male in the file.

Discussion The problem breaks down into four main steps. First we have to obtain the name of and prepare the data file. Then we can process the data, counting and summing the salary amounts for each sex. Next we compute the averages. Finally, we have to print the results.

The second step is the most difficult. It involves a loop with several subtasks. We'll use our checklist of questions to develop these subtasks in detail.

1. *What is the condition that ends the loop?* Because salaries are never negative, we can use a negative salary to terminate the loop. We will have to add a negative sentinel to the end of the data file.
2. *How should the condition be initialized?* No initialization is necessary in our pattern for a sentinel-controlled loop.
3. *How should the condition be updated?* We must read a new salary at the beginning of each iteration.
4. *What is the process being repeated?* From our knowledge of how to compute an average, we know that we have to count the number of amounts and divide this number into the sum of the amounts. Because we have to do this separately for females and males, the process consists of four parts: counting the females and summing their incomes, and then counting the males and summing their incomes. We develop each of these in turn.
5. *How should the process be initialized?* Female_Count and Female_Sum should be set to zero. Male_Count and Male_Sum also should be set to zero.
6. *How should the process be updated?* When a female income is input, Female_Count is incremented, and the income is added to Female_Sum. Otherwise an income is assumed to be for a male, so Male_Count is incremented, and the amount is added to Male_Sum.
7. *What is the state of the program on exiting the loop?* Female_Count contains the number of input values followed by the word Female, and Female_Sum contains the sum of the values followed by the word Female; Male_Count contains the number of input values followed by the word Male, and Male_Sum holds the sum of those values.

From the description of how the process is updated, we can see that the loop must contain an if-then-else statement, with one branch for female incomes and the other for male incomes. Each branch must increment the correct event counter and add the income amount to the correct total. After the loop has exited, we have enough information to compute and print the averages, dividing each total by the corresponding count.

Now we're ready to write the complete algorithm:

Incomes **Level 0**

Get the name of the data file
Prepare the data file
Count and sum incomes
Compute average incomes
Output results

Count and Sum Incomes **Level 1**

Initialize counts and sums
loop
    Get Salary
    exit when Salary < 0
    Get Sex
    Process employee

Compute Average Incomes

Female_Average := Female_Sum / Female_Count
Male_Average := Male_Sum / Male_Count

Output Results

Put Female_Count
Put Female_Average
Put Male_Count
Put Male_Average

Initialize Counts and Sums **Level 2**

Female_Average := 0
Female_Sum := 0
Male_Average := 0
Male_Sum := 0

Process Employee

If Sex is Female then
    Increment Female_Count
    Add Salary_Amount to Female_Sum
Else
    Increment Male_Count
    Add Salary_Amount to Male_Sum

Module Structure Chart

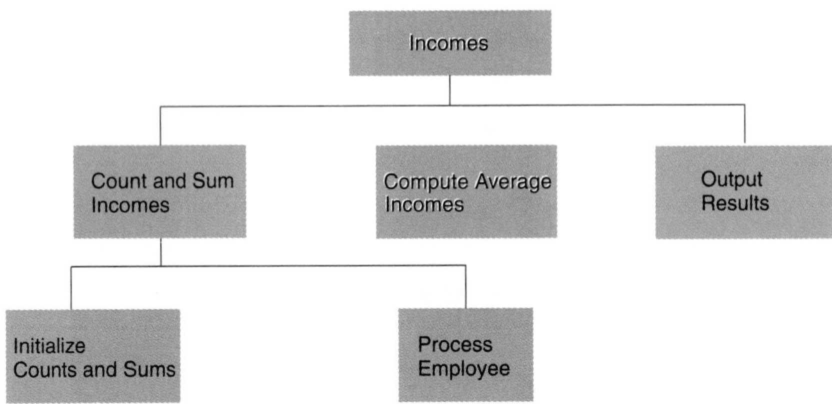

Object Modeling As there are exactly two different genders, this data is best modeled with an enumeration type. While at first it seems appropriate to limit salary ranges to positive values, this range prevents us from using a negative value as a sentinel to signal the end of our data.

Types

Name	**List of Values**
Gender_Type	(Female, Male)

Variables

Name	**Data Type and Range**	**Role**
File_Name	String (1..40)	Name of data file
Name_Length	Integer, 1 to 40	Number of characters in File_Name
Data_File	File_Type	The data file
Salary_Amount	Float	Employee's salary
Sex	Gender_Type	Employee's gender
Female_Count	Integer, nonnegative	Number of female employees

Male_Count	Integer, nonnegative	Number of male employees
Female_Sum	Float, nonnegative	Sum of female salaries
Male_Sum	Float, nonnegative	Sum of male salaries
Female_Average	Float, nonnegative	Average female salary
Male_Average	Float, nonnegative	Average male salary

Program

```
with Ada.Text_IO;
with Ada.Integer_Text_IO;
with Ada.Float_Text_IO;

procedure Incomes is

-- This program reads income amounts that are classified by
-- gender and computes the average income for each gender

    -- Enumerated type for gender
   type Gender_Type is (Female, Male);

   -- Instantiate packages for Gender I/O
   package Gender_IO  is new Ada.Text_IO.Enumeration_IO (Enum => Gender_Type);

   -- Variables

   File_Name      : String (1..40);          -- Name of data file
   Name_Length    : Integer range 1..40;     -- Number of characters in File_Name
   Data_File      : Ada.Text_IO.File_Type;   -- The data file

   Salary_Amount  : Float;                   -- Amount of income for a person
   Sex            : Gender_Type;             -- The gender of that person

   Female_Count    : Integer range 0..Integer'Last;  -- Number of female employees
   Male_Count      : Integer range 0..Integer'Last;  -- Number of male employees

   Female_Sum      : Float range 0.0..Float'Last;    -- Sum of female salaries
   Male_Sum        : Float range 0.0..Float'Last;    -- Sum of male salaries

   Female_Average : Float range 0.0..Float'Last;     -- Average female salary
   Male_Average   : Float range 0.0..Float'Last;     -- Average male salary

begin
   -- Get the name of the data file
   Ada.Text_IO.Put (Item => "Enter the name of the salary data file.");
   Ada.Text_IO.New_Line;
   Ada.Text_IO.Get_Line (Item => File_Name,
                         Last => Name_Length);
```

```
-- Prepare the data file
Ada.Text_IO.Open (File => Data_File,
                  Mode => Ada.Text_IO.In_File,
                  Name => File_Name (1..Name_Length));

-- Count and sum the incomes

-- Initialize counts and sums
Female_Count := 0;          -- Initialize female count
Female_Sum   := 0.0;        -- Initialize female sum
Male_Count   := 0;          -- Initialize male count
Male_Sum     := 0.0;        -- Initialize male sum

Input_Loop: -- Sum and count all employees
loop        -- Each iteration, one employee's salary data is processed
   Ada.Float_Text_IO.Get (File => Data_File,      -- Get a person's salary
                          Item => Salary_Amount);
   exit Input_Loop when Salary_Amount < 0.0;      -- Check for sentinel
   Gender_IO.Get (File => Data_File,              -- Get the employee's gender
                  Item => Sex);
   Ada.Text_IO.Skip_Line (File => Data_File);     -- Skip over job title

   -- Process the employee's data
   if Sex = Female then
      Female_Count := Female_Count + 1;             -- Increment Female_Count
      Female_Sum   := Female_Sum + Salary_Amount;   -- Sum female salary
   else
      Male_Count := Male_Count + 1;                 -- Increment Male_Count
      Male_Sum   := Male_Sum + Salary_Amount;       -- Sum male salary
   end if;
end loop Input_Loop;

-- Compute average incomes
Female_Average := Female_Sum / Float (Female_Count);
Male_Average   := Male_Sum   / Float (Male_Count);

   -- Output results
Ada.Text_IO.Put (Item => "For ");
Ada.Integer_Text_IO.Put (Item => Female_Count, Width => 1);
Ada.Text_IO.Put (Item => " females, the average income is $");
Ada.Float_Text_IO.Put (Item => Female_Average,
                       Fore => 1,
                       Aft  => 2,
                       Exp  => 0);
```

```
   Ada.Text_IO.New_Line;
   Ada.Text_IO.Put (Item => "For ");
   Ada.Integer_Text_IO.Put (Item => Male_Count, Width => 1);
   Ada.Text_IO.Put (Item => " males, the average income is $");
   Ada.Float_Text_IO.Put (Item => Male_Average,
                          Fore => 1,
                          Aft  => 2,
                          Exp  => 0);
   Ada.Text_IO.New_Line;
end Incomes;
```

Testing With a sentinel-controlled loop, the obvious test cases are normal values (nonnegative) and sentinel values (negative).

Then we should test input values of both Female and Male for the gender and try some typical data (so we can compare the results with our hand-calculated values) and some atypical data (to see how the process behaves). An atypical data set for testing a counting operation is no data (first salary entered is a sentinel), which should result in a count of zero. Any other result for the count indicates an error. For a summing operation, atypical data might include zero values.

Program Incomes was not designed to handle empty data sets or negative income values. An empty data set will cause both Female_Count and Male_Count to equal zero at the end of the loop. Although this is correct, the statements that compute average income will cause the program to crash because they will be dividing by zero. Negative income would simply be treated as a sentinel value.

To correct the empty-data-set problem, we should insert an if-then-else statement to test for the error condition before the average is calculated. When an error is detected, the program should print an error message instead of carrying out the usual computation. This prevents a crash and allows the program to keep running. We call a program that can recover from erroneous input and keep running a *robust* program.

After entering the data file name during our first run of this program, it halted with a DATA_ERROR exception. No answers were displayed. This exception indicates that the type of our data does not match the type of our variable. We could not find any bad values in the data file. Keeping track of the position of the reading marker while performing an execution trace showed us the problem—the job title present after the gender. We added a call to Skip_Line to move the reading marker over this unused data.

PROBLEM-SOLVING CASE STUDY

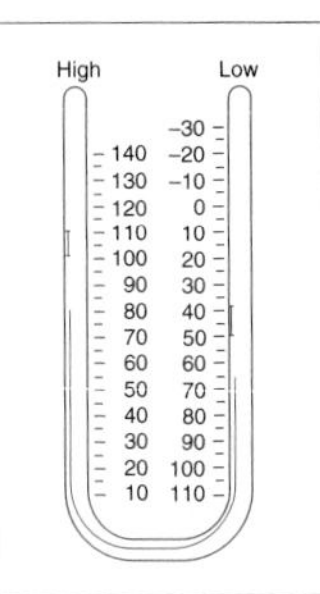

High and Low Temperatures

Specification Here's another problem in loop design. In this case we design a count-controlled loop that finds the minimum and maximum values in a data set. Finding the smallest or largest value is a common problem. Use the solution developed here as a pattern for future similar problems.

Problem A heating-oil company uses the temperature range for each day to determine its customers' typical oil use and to schedule deliveries. The firm has hired you to take hourly outdoor temperature readings for each 24-hour period and find the day's high and low temperatures from this data. Because you won't be getting much sleep on this job, you decide that it would be a good idea to have the computer find the maximum and minimum values.

Input Twenty-four numbers representing hourly temperatures.

Output
The day's high temperature.
The day's low temperature.

Assumptions The temperatures are whole numbers ranging from –50 to 70 degrees Fahrenheit.

Discussion This is easy to do by hand. We simply scan the list, looking for the highest and lowest values. How do we simulate this process in an algorithm? Well, let's look carefully at what we actually are doing to find the largest value in a list of numbers.

```
45
39
51
47
36
```

Looking only at the first number in our list, we can say that 45 is the largest number we have seen so far. We compare the largest we have seen with the second number and find that 45 is still the largest number we have seen. Comparing 45 to the third value shows a new highest value. 51 becomes the largest number we have seen. We repeat the process until we run out of numbers. The process we repeat is the comparison of the current number with the largest we have seen so far. Notice that when we started we did not compare the first number to another one. At the *start* of our scan down the list, it is the largest value. Here is our solution in pseudocode.

```
Largest So Far := first number of list
loop from the 2nd to the last number in the list
  if Current Number > Largest So Far then
    Largest So Far := Current Number
  end if
end loop
```

We use the same process to find the smallest number, only we remember the smaller number instead of the larger one. Now that we have a rough solution, let's refine the loop by answering our seven loop design questions. While the following answers may seem obvious as you read them, it took us several attempts to write them in this form. We frequently modify our first answers when we work on the later questions.

1. *What is the condition that ends the loop?* We know that there will be exactly 24 values on the list so we can use a count-controlled loop. We exit after processing the 24th value. We exit the loop when the loop control variable exceeds 24.
2. *How should the condition be initialized?* Our pattern for count-controlled loops initializes the counter to 1. But in this case we process the 1st value in the list before the loop—there is no greatest value with which to compare it. So in this solution we initialize our loop control variable to 2, indicating that the 1st value was processed before the loop.
3. *How should the condition be updated?* Consistent with our count-controlled loop pattern, the counter should be incremented at the end of each iteration.
4. *What is the process being repeated?* The process reads a value, echo prints it, and checks to see whether it should replace the current high or low value.
5. *How should the process be initialized?* Our process is checking a current temperature against the highest and lowest seen. What values do we use to initialize these two extremes? As we discussed previously, we use the first temperature read. The first temperature is both the highest and the lowest we have seen before we start the loop with the 2nd temperature.
6. *How should the process be updated?* In each iteration, a new temperature is input and compared with High and Low. If it exceeds High, it replaces the old value of High. If it is less than Low, it replaces the old value of Low. Otherwise High and Low are unchanged. This tells us that the loop contains two if-then statements, one each for comparing the input value against High and Low.

7. *What is the state of the program on exiting the loop?* Twenty-four temperature values have been input and echo printed. The loop control variable equals 25. High contains the largest of the input values, and Low contains the smallest.

```
Temperature Extremes                                    Level 0
Initialize extremes
Reading Number := 2
loop
   exit when Reading Number > Last Reading
   Get Temperature
   Update Extremes
Display High
Display Low

Initialize Extremes                                     Level 1
Get first temperature reading
Low  := first temperature reading
High := first temperature reading

Update Extremes
if Temperature < Low then
   Low  := Temperature
if Temperature > High then
   High := Temperature
```

Module Structure Chart

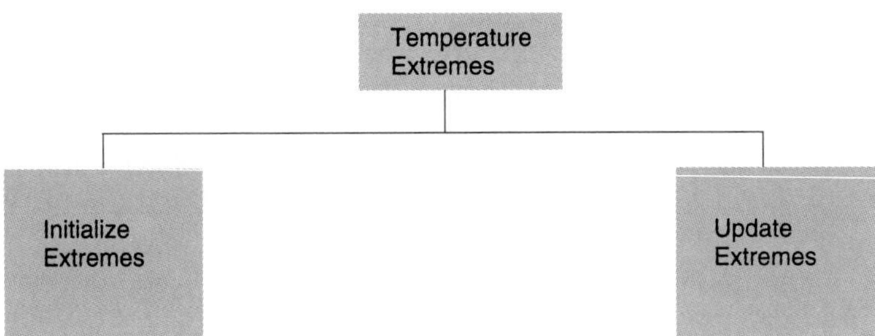

Object Modeling

Constants

Name	Value	Role
Last_Reading	24	The number of temperature readings

Variables

Name	Data Type and Range	Role
Temperature	Integer, –50 to 70	An hourly temperature reading
High	Integer, –50 to 70	Highest temperature so far
Low	Integer, –50 to 70	Lowest temperature so far
Reading_Number	Integer, 1 to 25	Loop control variable

Program

```
with Ada.Text_IO;
with Ada.Integer_Text_IO;

procedure Temperature_Extremes is

-- This program calculates the high and low temperatures
-- from 24 hourly temperature readings

   Last_Reading   : constant Integer := 24;    -- Number of temperatures

   Temperature    : Integer range -50..70;     -- A temperature reading
   High           : Integer range -50..70;     -- Highest temperature so far
   Low            : Integer range -50..70;     -- Lowest temperature so far
   Reading_Number : Integer range   1..25;     -- Loop control variable

begin
   Ada.Text_IO.Put (Item => "Enter 24 temperatures");
   Ada.Text_IO.New_Line (Spacing => 2);

   -- Initialize the extremes to the first value
   Ada.Integer_Text_IO.Get (Item => High);
   Low := High;

   -- Initialize loop control variable
   Reading_Number := 2;   -- We have already processed the first temperature
```

```
   Input_Loop: -- Process all the temperatures
   loop        -- Each iteration, one temperature is compared to the extremes
      exit Input_Loop when Reading_Number > Last_Reading;
      Ada.Integer_Text_IO.Get (Item => Temperature);
      if Temperature < Low then                  -- Lowest temperature so far?
         Low := Temperature;
      end if;
      if Temperature > High then                 -- Highest temperature so far?
         High := Temperature;
      end if;
   -- Update loop ending condition
   Reading_Number := Reading_Number + 1;
   end loop Input_Loop;

   -- Print high and low temperatures
   Ada.Text_IO.New_Line;
   Ada.Text_IO.Put (Item => "High temperature is ");
   Ada.Integer_Text_IO.Put (Item => High, Width => 1);
   Ada.Text_IO.New_Line;
   Ada.Text_IO.Put (Item => "Low temperature is ");
   Ada.Integer_Text_IO.Put (Item => Low, Width => 1);
   Ada.Text_IO.New_Line;
end Temperature_Extremes;
```

Testing Program Temperature_Extremes reads 24 integer values. We can test the loop-exit statements by entering data values until the program outputs the high and low temperatures. If the program doesn't input exactly 24 numbers, there must be an error in the control of the loop.

We should try data sets that present the high and low temperatures in different orders. For example, we should try one set with the highest temperature as the first value and another set with it as the last. We should do the same for the lowest temperature. We also should try a data set in which the temperature goes up and down several times and another in which the temperatures are all the same. Finally, we should test the program on some typical sets of data and check the output with results we've determined by hand. For example, given this data:

```
25  27  27  27  30  30  35  40  50  50  52  55
55  55  55  54  54  53  50  50  49  47  41  39
```

the output would look like this.

```
High temperature is 55
Low temperature is 25
```

Testing and Debugging

Loop Testing Strategy

Even if a loop has been properly designed and verified, it is still important to test it rigorously because there is always the chance of an error creeping in during the implementation phase. Because loops allow us to input many data sets in one run, and because there is the potential for each iteration to be affected by preceding ones, the test data for a looping program is usually more extensive than for a program with just sequential or branching statements. In order to test a loop thoroughly, we have to check for the proper execution of both a single iteration and multiple iterations.

Remember that a loop has seven parts (corresponding to the seven questions in our checklist). A test strategy must test each part. Although all seven parts aren't implemented separately in every loop, the checklist reminds us that some loop operations may serve multiple purposes, each of which should be tested. For example, the incrementing statement in a count-controlled loop may be updating both the process and the ending condition. So it's important to verify that it performs both actions properly with respect to the rest of the loop.

It's good practice to test a loop for three cases: (1) when the loop is skipped entirely, (2) when the loop body is executed just once, and (3) when the loop executes some normal number of times.

Statements following a loop often depend on its processing. If a loop can be skipped, those statements may not execute correctly. If it's possible to execute a single iteration of a loop, the results can show whether the body performs correctly in the absence of the effects of previous iterations, which can be very helpful when you're trying to isolate the source of an error. Obviously it's important to test a loop under normal conditions with a wide variety of inputs. If possible, you should test the loop with real data in addition to mock data sets. Count-controlled loops should be tested so that you are sure they execute exactly the right number of times. And finally, if there is any chance that a loop might never exit, your test data should try to make that happen.

Testing a program can be as challenging as writing it. To test a program, you have to step back, take a fresh look at what you've written, and then attack it in every way possible to make it fail. This isn't always easy to do, but it's necessary in order to have robust programs.

Testing and Debugging Hints

1. Plan your test data carefully to test all sections of a program.
2. Beware of infinite loops, where the expression in the exit statement never becomes True. The symptom: The program doesn't stop.

   If you have created an infinite loop, check your logic and the syntax of your loops. In a count-controlled loop, make sure the loop control variable is incremented within the loop. In a calculation-controlled loop, ensure that the results of the calculation converge.
3. Check the loop termination conditions carefully and confirm that something in the loop causes them to be met. Watch closely for values that go one iteration too long or too short.
4. Trace the execution of the loop by hand. Simulate the first few passes and the last few passes very carefully to see how the loop really behaves.
5. If all else fails, use debug Put statements—calls to Put procedures inserted in a program to help debug it.* They output a message that indicates the flow of execution in the program or reports the values of variables at certain points in the program.

   If you want to know the value of variable Sum at a certain point in a program, you could insert this code:

```
Ada.Text_IO.Put (Item => "Sum = ");
Ada.Integer_Text_IO.Put (Item => Sum);
Ada.Text_IO.New_Line;
```

   If this code is in a loop, you will get as many values of Sum as there are iterations of the body of the loop.

   After you have debugged your program, you can remove the debug statements, or just precede them with (--) so that they'll be treated as comments. This way you can just remove the comment delimiters if you need to use the statements again.
6. An ounce of prevention is worth a pound of debugging. Use the checklist questions and design your loop correctly to begin with. It may seem like extra work, but it really pays off in the long run.

Summary

The loop statement is a looping construct that allows the program to repeat a sequence of statements over and over again. The exit statement stops the repeated execution of the statements. When the condition in the exit statement becomes True, any remaining statements in the loop are skipped and execution continues with the first statement following the loop.

*An alternative to debug Put statements is a debugger—a program that allows you to observe the values of the variables while your program is running.

Pretest loops have the exit statement as the first statement in the loop body, posttest loops have the exit statement as the last statement in the loop body, and midtest loops have the exit statement in some place other than the first or last statement.

With the loop and exit statements, you can construct several types of loops that you will use again and again. These types of loops fall into two major patterns: count-controlled loops and event-controlled loops.

In a count-controlled loop, the loop body repeats a specified number of times. We use count-controlled loops when the number of iterations is known (or can be calculated) before execution reaches the loop statement. You initialize a counter variable right before the loop statement. This variable is the loop control variable. The control variable is tested against the limit in the condition of the exit statement. The last statement in the loop body increments the control variable. The for loop statement (Chapter 8) provides another way to write count-controlled loops.

Event-controlled loops continue executing until something inside the body signals that the looping process should stop. We use event-controlled loops when we do not know ahead of time the number of iterations needed. Sentinel-controlled loops and calculation-controlled loops are two common forms of the event-controlled loop pattern.

Sentinel-controlled loops are midtest loops that use a special data value as a signal to stop reading. The first statements in a sentinel-controlled loop body get some data. The exit statement immediately follows and tests the input value(s) to see if it is actual data or a signal to end the loop. The statements that process the data follow the exit statement. This processing may include reading additional data.

Counting is a looping operation that keeps track of how many times a loop is repeated or how many times some event occurs. This count can be used in computations or to control the loop. A counter is a variable that is used for counting. It may be the loop control variable in a count-controlled loop, an iteration counter in a counting loop, or an event counter that counts the number of times a particular condition occurs in a loop.

Summing is a looping operation that keeps a running total of certain values. It is similar to counting in that the variable that holds the sum is initialized outside the loop. The summing operation, however, adds up unknown values; the counting operation adds a constant (usually 1) to the counter each time.

When you design a loop, there are seven points to consider: how the termination condition is initialized, tested, and updated; how the process in the loop is initialized, performed, and updated; and the state of the program upon loop exit. By answering the checklist questions, you can bring each of these points into focus.

Commenting loops helps both the designer and maintainer understand the purpose and logic of each loop.

To design a nested loop structure, simply begin with the outermost loop. When you get to where the inner loop must appear, make it a separate module and come back later to its design.

Looping programs often produce a large amount of output that can be easier to read in table form, with a heading for each column. Tables are easy to print using Width or Fore and Aft specifications.

The process of testing a loop is based on the answers to the checklist questions and execution patterns that might occur (for example, executing a single iteration, multiple iterations, an infinite number of iterations, or no iterations at all).

Quick Check

1. What are the four parts of a count-controlled loop? (p. 236)
2. Give two reasons why pretest loops are more commonly used than posttest loops. (p. 233)
3. Write the loop-exit code that loops until the value of integer variable Event_Count equals 25. (p. 238)
4. Write the code for a sentinel-controlled loop that loops until a negative value of the integer variable Course_Number is read. (p. 238).
5. What is the difference between a counting operation in a loop and a summing operation in a loop? (p. 242–244)
6. What is the difference between a loop control variable and an event counter? (pp. 242–243)
7. What is meant by a convergent iterative calculation? (p. 248)
8. What kind of loop would you use in a program that reads the closing price of a stock for each day of the week? (p. 236)
9. How would you extend the loop in question 7 to make it read 52 weeks' worth of prices? (pp. 252–253)
10. How would you test a program that is supposed to count the number of females and the number of males in a data set? (Assume that females are coded with the word Female in the data; males, with the word Male.) (pp. 269–270)

Answers

1. The process being repeated, plus initializing, testing, and incrementing the loop control variable. **2.** They are easier to read and they allow for the possibility that the loop body will be executed zero times.

3.
```
Count_Loop:
loop
   exit Count_Loop when Event_Count = 25;
   .
   .
   .
end loop Count_Loop;
```

4.
```
Sentinel_Loop:
   loop
      Ada.Integer_Text_IO.Get (Item => Course_Number);
      exit Sentinel_Loop when Course_Number < 0;
      .
      .
      .
   end loop Sentinel_Loop;
```
5. A counting operation increments with each iteration of the loop by a fixed value; a summing operation adds unknown values to the total. **6.** A loop control variable controls the loop; an event counter simply counts certain events within the loop. **7.** The calculation used brings us closer to the exit condition. **8.** Because there are 5 days in a business week, you would use a count-controlled loop that runs from 1 to 5. **9.** Nest the original loop inside a count-controlled loop that runs from 1 to 52. **10.** Run the program with data sets that have a different number of females and males, only females, only males, illegal values (other words), and an empty data set.

Exam Preparation Exercises

1. In one or two sentences, explain the difference between loops and branches.
2. What does the following loop print out? (Number is of type Integer.)

```
Number := 1;
Exercise_Loop:
loop
   exit Exercise_Loop when Number > 10;
   Number := Number + 1;
   Ada.Integer_Text_IO.Put (Item => Number);
   Ada.Text_IO.New_Line;
end loop Exercise_Loop;
```

3. By rearranging the order of the statements (don't change the way they are written) to that of our count-controlled loop pattern, make the loop in exercise 2 print the numbers from 1 to 10.
4. When the following code is executed, how many iterations of the loop will be performed?

```
Number := 2;
Done := False;
Exercise_Loop:
loop
   exit Exercise_Loop when Done;
   Number := Number * 2;
   if Number > 64 then
      Done := True;
   end if;
end loop Exercise_Loop;
```

5. What is the output of this nested loop?

```
K := 3;
Outer_Loop:
loop
   exit Outer_Loop when K < 1;
   J := K;
   Inner_Loop:
   loop
      exit Inner_Loop when J < 1;
      Ada.Integer_Text_IO.Put (Item => J)
      J := J - 1;
   end loop Inner_Loop;
   Ada.Integer_Text_IO.Put (Item => K);
   Ada.Text_IO.New_Line;
   K := K - 1
end loop Outer_Loop;
```

6. The following code segment is designed to write out the even numbers between 1 and 15. It has two flaws in it.

```
X := 2;
Even_Loop:
loop
   exit Even_Loop when X = 15;
   X := X + 2;
   Ada.Integer_Text_IO.Put (Item => X);
end loop Even_Loop;
```

   a. What is the output of the code as written?
   b. Correct the code so that it works as intended.

7. The following code segment is supposed to echo print positive integers. A negative integer is used as a sentinel value.

```
Number := Integer'Last;
Echo_Positive:
loop
   exit Echo_Positive when Number < 0;
   Ada.Integer_Text_IO.Get (Item => Number);
   Ada.Integer_Text_IO.Put (Item => Number);
end loop Echo_Positive;
```

   a. What is the output if the input is 45 37 92 −4?
   b. Rewrite the code so that it works properly.

8. What sentinel value would you choose for a program that reads telephone numbers as integers?

9. Given this code fragment:

```
N : constant Integer := 8;

Sum    : Integer;
K      : Integer;
Number : Integer;
Flag   : Boolean;
   .
   .
   .
Sum  := 0;
K    := 1;
Flag := False;
Exercise_Loop:
loop
   exit Exercise_Loop when  (K > N)  or  Flag;
   Ada.Integer_Text_IO.Get (Item => Number);
   if Number > 0 then
      Sum := Sum + Number;
   elsif Number = 0 then
      Flag := True;
   end if;
   K := K + 1;
end loop Exercise_Loop;
Ada.Text_IO.Put (Item => "End of test. ");
Ada.Integer_Text_IO.Put (Item => Sum, Width => 1);
Ada.Text_IO.New_Line;
```

and these data values:

```
5  6  -3  7  -4  0  5  8  9
```

a. What is printed out by this code?
b. Does the data fully test the program? Explain your answer.

10. Here is a simple count-controlled loop.

```
Count := 1;
Count_Loop:
loop
   exit Count_Loop when Count >= 20;
   Ada.Integer_Text_IO.Put (Item => Count);
   Count := Count + 1;
end loop Count_Loop;
```

a. What is the output of this loop?
b. Change the exit statement in this loop to match that in our count-controlled loop pattern. Now what output does the loop produce?

11. Given the code fragment (all variables are type Integer):

```
Outer_Loop:
loop
   Ada.Integer_Text_IO.Get(Item => X);
   exit Outer_Loop when X < 0;
   Y := X;
   Z := 1;
   Inner_Loop:
   loop
      exit Inner_Loop when Y = 0;
      Z := Y * Z;
      Y := Y - 1;
   end loop Inner_Loop;
   Ada.Integer_Text_IO.Put (Item => X);
   Ada.Integer_Text_IO.Put (Item => Z);
   Ada.Text_IO.New_Line;
end loop Outer_Loop;
```

and these data values:

```
4  7  -5  12  0  6  19 -22
```

what is printed?

12. Using the EBNF definitions for the loop and exit statements given in this chapter, determine whether each of the following loops uses correct syntax. Do not be concerned with what the loop does (all are infinite loops), just the syntax.

a.
```
First_Loop:
loop
   exit First_Loop when Broccoli    > 2  or
                   when Cauliflower = 7;
end loop First_Loop;
```

b.
```
Second_Loop:
loop
   exit Second_Loop when Broccoli    > 2 or
                         Cauliflower = 7;
end loop Second_Loop;
```

c.
```
Third_Loop:
loop
   exit Third_Loop when Broccoli    > 2;
   exit Third_Loop when Cauliflower = 7;
end loop Third_Loop;
```

Programming Warm-up Exercises

1. Write a program segment that sets a Boolean variable Danger to True and stops reading in data if Pressure (a Float variable being read in) exceeds 510.0.
2. Write a program segment that counts the number of times the integer 28 occurs in a file of 100 integers.
3. Write a nested loop code segment that produces this output

```
1
1 2
1 2 3
1 2 3 4
```

4. Write a program segment that reads grades for a class (any size) and finds the class average. Grades range from 0 to 100 inclusive.
5. Write a program segment that reads in 100 integers and then counts and prints out the number of positive integers and the number of negative integers. If a value is 0, it should not be counted.
6. Write a program segment that adds up the even integers from 16 to 26 inclusive.
7. Program Temperature_Extremes uses two if statements to check for the extreme temperatures. Rewrite these tests using a single if statement.
8. Write a program segment that prints out the sequence of all the hour and minute combinations in a day, starting with 1:00 a.m. and ending with 12:59 a.m.
9. Rewrite the code segment for exercise 8 so that it prints the times in 10-minute intervals, arranged as a table of 6 columns with 24 rows.
10. Change Program Incomes so that it does not crash if there are no females in the data set or if there are no males in the data set.
11. Review the Chapter 3 program on mixing proportions given on page 157. Making the assumption that the amount of vinegar in a salad dressing should never exceed the amount of oil, add a data validation loop to ensure the user's data meets this criterion.

12. The logic for calculating square root on page 240 fails for very large values of *X*. The result of squaring one-half of such a large number (the initial guess) in the exit statement may exceed Float'Last and halt the program with a CONSTRAINT_ERROR. Modify this code fragment so it works for all possible values of *X*. (*Hint:* Use a different calculation for determining an initial guess.)

Programming Problems

1. Write a top-down design and an Ada program that inputs an integer and a one-character string. The output should be a diamond composed of the character and extending the width specified by the integer. For example, if the integer is 11 and the character is an asterisk (*), the diamond would look like this:

```
     *
    ***
   *****
  *******
 *********
***********
 *********
  *******
   *****
    ***
     *
```

   If the integer entered is an even number, round it to the next highest odd number. Use meaningful variable names, proper indentation, appropriate loop comments, and good prompting messages.
2. Write a top-down design and an Ada program that inputs integers larger than 1 and calculates the sum of the squares from 1 to those integers. For example, if the integer equals 4, the sum of the squares is 30 (1+4+9+16). The output should be the value of the integer and the sum, properly labeled. A negative input value signals the end of the data.
3. You are putting together some music tapes for a party. You've arranged a list of songs in the order in which you want to play them. However, you would like to minimize the empty tape left at the end of each side of a cassette (a cassette plays for 45 minutes on a side). So you want to figure out the total time for a group of songs and see how well they fit. Write a top-down design and an Ada program to help you do this. The program should input a reference number and a time for each song until it encounters a reference number of 0. Each time should be entered in the form of minutes and seconds (two integer values). For example, if song number 4 takes 7 minutes and 42 seconds to play, the data entered for that song would be

```
4  7  42
```

   The program should echo print the data for each song and the current running-time total. The last data (reference number 0) should not be added to the total time. After all of the data has been read, the program should print a message indicating the time remaining on the tape.

If you are writing this program to read data from a file, the output should be in the form of a table with columns and headings. For example:

```
Song       Song Time            Total Time
Number   Minutes   Seconds   Minutes   Seconds
----      ----      ----      ----      ----
  1         5        10         5        10
  2         7        42        12        52
  5         4        19        17        11
  3         4        33        21        44
  4        10        27        32        11
  6         8        55        41         6
  0         0         1        41         6

There are 3 minutes and 54 seconds of tape left.
```

If you are using interactive input, your output should have prompting messages interspersed with the results. For example:

```
Enter the song number:
1
Enter the number of minutes:
5
Enter the number of seconds:
10
Song number 1, 5 minutes and 10 seconds
Total time is 5 minutes and 10 seconds.
For the next song,
Enter the song number:
.
.
.
```

Use meaningful variable names, proper indentation, and appropriate comments. If you're writing an interactive program, use good prompting messages. The program should discard any invalid data sets (negative numbers, for example) and print an error message indicating that the data set has been discarded and what was wrong with it.

4. Write a top-down design and an Ada program to calculate the two roots of a quadratic equation of the form:

$$ax^2 + bx + c = 0$$

using the quadratic formula:

$$\text{Root}_1 = \frac{-b + \sqrt{b^2 - 4ac}}{2a}$$

$$\text{Root}_2 = \frac{-b - \sqrt{b^2 - 4ac}}{2a}$$

Your program should prompt for, read, and echo print the values of a, b, and c (all float values). If the quantity $b^2 - 4ac$ is negative, display a message indicating that the roots are imaginary. Otherwise calculate and display (with appropriate labels) the two roots. Use Newton's method with a tolerance of 0.00001 to calculate an approximation of the square root.

5. Extend programming problem 4 to work with a data set of many quadratic equations. Determine the best method for the user to indicate the end of the data set.

CHAPTER

6

Subprograms

GOALS

After reading this chapter, you should be able to

- write a program that uses procedures to reflect the structure of your top-down design
- write a module of your own design as a procedure
- define and use parameters and local variables correctly
- determine the scope of each identifier in a program
- design, code, and invoke a function properly
- know when to use a function rather than a procedure

You have been using procedures since the Put procedure was introduced in Chapter 2. By now you should be quite comfortable with the idea of calling these subprograms to perform a task. So far, we have not considered how subprograms are created. That is the topic of this chapter.

You might wonder why we waited until now to look at programmer-defined subprograms. The reason lies in the major purpose for using subprograms: We write our own subprograms to help organize and simplify large and complex programs. Until now our programs have been relatively small and simple so that we didn't need to write subprograms. Now that we've covered the basic control structures, we are ready to introduce subprograms so that we can begin writing larger and more complex programs.

Ada has two forms of subprograms: the procedure and the function. The main difference between them is the way they are called. A procedure call is a statement in a program; a function call is part of an expression.

Program Design with Procedures

From the beginning you have been designing your programs as collections of modules. Many of these modules are naturally implemented as programmer-defined procedures. Now you will learn how to turn the modules in your design into procedures.

When to Use Procedures

In general, you can code any module as a procedure or function, although some are so simple that it really is unnecessary. Thus, in designing a program, we frequently need to decide which modules we should implement as procedures. We should base our decision on whether the overall program will be easier to understand as a result. (There are other factors that can affect this decision, but for now this is the simplest heuristic [strategy] to use.)

If a module is only a single line, it is probably best to write it directly into the program. Turning it into a procedure would only complicate the overall program, which defeats the purpose of using subprograms. On the other hand, if a module is many lines long, it will be easier to understand the program if you turn the module into a procedure.

Keep in mind that whether you choose to code a module as a procedure or not will merely affect the readability of the program and may make it more or less convenient to change the program later. However, your choice will not affect the correct functioning of the program.

Writing Modules as Procedures

Turning a module into a procedure is quite simple to do in Ada. Let's look at a program using procedures. As our example, we use Program Lumberyard from Chapter 4. Here is its design.

Lumberyard **Level 0**

Prompt for product type
Get Product
if Product is Lumber then
  Process Lumber
else
  Process Plywood

Process Lumber **Level 1**

Get Lumber Data
Board Feet := Quantity × (Thickness × Width × (Length × 12)) / 144
Put Quantity, Thickness, Width, and Length
Put Board Feet

Process Plywood

Get Plywood Data
Full Sheets := Quantity × (Numerator / Denominator × (Length × 12) × 48) / 4608
Put Quantity, thickness fraction, and Length
Put Full Sheets

Get Lumber Data **Level 2**

Prompt for number of boards
Get Quantity
Prompt for thickness, width, and length of boards
Get Thickness, Width, and Length of boards

Get Plywood Data

Prompt for number of sheets
Get Quantity
Prompt for length and thickness fraction of sheets
Get Length, Numerator, and Denominator

We write the level 0 module as the *main subprogram* (what we called *the program* in previous chapters) and the level 1 and 2 modules as procedures. Our main subprogram for Lumberyard is:

```
begin   -- Program Lumberyard

   -- Prompt for and get product type
   Ada.Text_IO.Put (Item => "Enter product (Lumber or Plywood)");
   Ada.Text_IO.New_Line;
   Product_IO.Get (Item => Product);
   Ada.Text_IO.New_Line;
```

```
   if Product = Lumber then    -- Process an order for lumber
      Process_Lumber;
   else                        -- The order must be for plywood
      Process_Plywood;
   end if;
   Ada.Text_IO.New_Line;       -- Next statement executed after calls
                               -- to Process_Lumber or Process_Plywood
end Lumberyard;
```

This main subprogram is nearly identical to the level 0 module of our top-down design. It contains seven **procedure calls** to five different procedures: one call to Ada.Text_IO.Put, two calls to Ada.Text_IO.New_Line, one call to Product_IO.Get, one call to Process_Lumber, and one call to Process_Plywood.

When procedure Ada.Text_IO.Put is called, control transfers to the procedure. The procedure does everything needed to display the string "Enter product (Lumber or Plywood)." Then control returns to the statement that follows the call statement—the call statement to procedure Ada.Text_IO.New_Line.

When procedure Ada.Text_IO.New_Line is called, control transfers to the procedure. The procedure does everything needed to advance the writing marker to the next line. Then control returns to the statement that follows the call statement—the call statement to procedure Product_IO.Get.

When procedure Process_Lumber is called, control transfers to the procedure. The procedure does everything needed to process an order for dimensioned lumber. Then control returns to the statement that follows the call statement—the call to procedure Ada.Text_IO.New_Line. When procedure Process_Plywood is called, control transfers to the procedure. The procedure does everything needed to process an order for sheets of plywood. Then control returns to the statement that follows the call statement—the call to procedure Ada.Text_IO.New_Line

---

Procedure call A statement that transfers control to a procedure. When the procedure finishes, control is returned to the statement following the call statement. In Ada, a procedure call statement is the name of the procedure followed by an optional parameter list.

Procedure Construction

Now that we've seen an example of how a program is written with procedures, we need to look at some of the important points of procedure construction and use. Let's start by examining the code for procedure Process_Lumber.

```
procedure Process_Lumber is
-- This procedure processes an order for dimensioned lumber

   -- Local Variables
   Quantity         : Integer range 1..Integer'Last; -- Number of boards
   Lumber_Thickness : Float   range 0.5..4.0;        -- Thickness (inches)
   Lumber_Width     : Float   range 1.0..16.0;       -- Width (inches)
   Lumber_Length    : Float   range 1.0..16.0;       -- Length (feet)
   Board_Feet       : Float   range 0.0..Float'Last; -- Total board feet

begin -- Process Lumber
   Get_Lumber_Data (Quantity  => Quantity,
                    Thickness => Lumber_Thickness,
                    Width     => Lumber_Width,
                    Length    => Lumber_Length);
   -- Calculate total number of board feet
   Board_Feet := Float(Quantity) * Lumber_Thickness * Lumber_Width *
                 (Lumber_Length * 12.0) / Board_Foot_Inches;
   -- Display results
   Ada.Text_IO.Put (Item => "Quantity   :  ");
   Ada.Integer_Text_IO.Put (Item => Quantity, Width => 1);
   Ada.Text_IO.New_Line;
   Ada.Text_IO.Put (Item => "Dimensions :  ");
   Ada.Float_Text_IO.Put (Item => Lumber_Thickness,
                          Fore => 1,
                          Aft  => 1,
                          Exp  => 0);
   Ada.Float_Text_IO.Put (Item => Lumber_Width,
                          Fore => 6,
                          Aft  => 1,
                          Exp  => 0);
   Ada.Float_Text_IO.Put (Item => Lumber_Length,
                          Fore => 6,
                          Aft  => 1,
                          Exp  => 0);
   Ada.Text_IO.New_Line;
   Ada.Text_IO.Put (Item => "Board feet :  ");
   Ada.Float_Text_IO.Put (Item => Board_Feet,
                          Fore => 1,
                          Aft  => 1,
                          Exp  => 0);
end Process_Lumber;
```

Just as with any other identifier in Ada, the name of a procedure is not allowed to include blanks. After the procedure name and a brief comment describing the procedure is a list of variable declarations. These variables may only be used by the statements in the procedure. We call these **local variables.** Following the declarations of local variables is the reserved word `begin`, a sequence of executable statements, and an `end` statement.

Most all of the statements in this procedure are calls to other procedures. In fact, the assignment statement that calculates the total board feet of the order is the only statement that is *not* a procedure call statement.

Local variable A variable declared within a procedure that is not accessible outside of that procedure.

Procedure Syntax

We define a procedure in two parts: a procedure declaration that specifies how the procedure is used and a procedure body that specifies how the procedure works. Here is a simplified EBNF definition of the procedure declaration:

```
procedure_declaration      ::=  procedure_specification ;
procedure_specification    ::=  procedure identifier [parameter_list]
parameter_list             ::=  (parameter_specification {; parameter_specification})
parameter_specification    ::=  identifier : mode subtype_mark
mode                       ::=  in | out | in out
```

Notice that a procedure declaration is simply a procedure specification followed by a semicolon.

Here is the simplified EBNF definition of the procedure body. Since an Ada program is a procedure, this definition looks just like the definition we gave for an Ada program in Chapter 2.

```
procedure body  ::=  procedure_specification is
                        [declarative_part]
                     begin
                        sequence_of_statements
                     end procedure_identifier;
```

Both the procedure declaration and the procedure body contain the *specification* of the procedure. For now we don't need to be concerned with the declaration of a procedure; the specification included with the body is all that we need. But we will see its use in Chapter 12 when we discuss writing our own packages.

Parameters

The definition of procedure specification includes an optional parameter list. As you know from your experience with procedures Get and Put, parameters are used to transfer information to and from a procedure. For example, in the following call

```
Ada.Integer_Text_IO.Get (Item => Quantity);
```

a value is transferred from the procedure to the variable Quantity. Like variables, parameters are names for memory locations used to store values. Item names a different memory location than Quantity. When procedure Get has finished its job, the value in Item is copied into Quantity.

Now let's look at an example of a parameter list. Here is the procedure that implements the module Get Lumber Data in our Lumberyard design.

```
procedure Get_Lumber_Data (Quantity  : out Integer;     -- Number of pieces
                           Thickness : out Float;       -- The dimensions
                           Width     : out Float;       -- of the
                           Length    : out Float) is    -- pieces
-- This procedure prompts for and obtains the data for an order of
-- dimensioned lumber

begin -- Get Lumber Data
   -- Prompt for and get the quantity
   Ada.Text_IO.Put (Item => "Enter the number of boards: ");
   Ada.Integer_Text_IO.Get (Item => Quantity);
   Ada.Text_IO.New_Line;

   -- Prompt for and get the board dimensions
   Ada.Text_IO.Put (Item => "Enter thickness, width, and length");
   Ada.Text_IO.New_Line;
   Ada.Float_Text_IO.Get (Item => Thickness);
   Ada.Float_Text_IO.Get (Item => Width);
   Ada.Float_Text_IO.Get (Item => Length);
   Ada.Text_IO.New_Line (Spacing => 2);
end Get_Lumber_Data;
```

The parameter list is in parentheses after the procedure name. There are four parameters declared in the parameter list of procedure Get_Lumber_Data. Here is a call to procedure Get_Lumber_Data taken from the procedure for processing a lumber order that we gave on page 285:

```
Get_Lumber_Data (Quantity  => Quantity,
                 Thickness => Lumber_Thickness,
                 Width     => Lumber_Width,
                 Length    => Lumber_Length);
```

Notice that the names used to the left of the => symbol match the names in the procedure's parameter list.

The parameters in the procedure specification are called the **formal parameters.** These are what we called *parameter names* in Chapter 2. What we called *parameter values* are the **actual parameters.** The formal parameter and actual parameter names may be different (like Width and

Lumber_Width) or, coincidentally, the same (like Quantity). Even when they are the same, each is associated with a different memory location. Actual parameters can be expressions rather than names, as in

```
Ada.Integer_Text_IO.Put (Item => 5 + 2 * Count);.
```

Formal parameter A variable declared in a procedure specification.

Actual parameter A variable or expression associated with a formal parameter name in a call to a procedure.

Parameter Types Like a variable declaration, a formal parameter specification must include an identifier and its data type. The data type of an actual parameter must *match* the type of the corresponding formal parameter. For now, match means that the type of the corresponding actual and formal parameters must be identical. In Chapter 7 we'll give you detailed rules for less strict parameter type matching. If the actual and formal parameters are not of the same type, the compiler will display an error message. The error message issued by most compilers for a parameter type mismatch is not very informative to beginning Ada programmers. Expect a message similar to INVALID PARAMETER LIST IN CALL OR INCONSISTENCY DETECTED DURING OVERLOAD RESOLUTION.

The data type of a formal parameter may be any type. String types, however, present a problem that we will not discuss until Chapter 7. Also, you cannot use a range in the declaration of a formal parameter. For now we restrict parameter types to Integer, Float, Boolean, enumeration types, and File_Type.

Parameter Modes Every formal parameter specification includes a mode to indicate the direction of data transfer between the caller and the procedure. The mode for each parameter is specified after the colon following the parameter name. There are three different modes available:

in	The value of the actual parameter is copied into the formal parameter when the procedure is called. The value is transferred into the procedure.
out	The value of the formal parameter is copied into the actual parameter after the last statement in the procedure has been executed. The value is transferred out of the procedure.
in out	The value of the actual parameter is copied into the formal parameter when the procedure is called. After the last statement in the procedure has been executed, the value of the formal parameter is copied back into the actual parameter. So two different data transfers are executed with an *in out* parameter. A value is transferred into the procedure and a modified value is transferred out.

We choose a mode based on the direction of data transfer required for the parameters. Select mode *in* when the caller needs to transfer a value into a procedure. Use mode *out* to transfer a result from the procedure back to the caller. Use mode *in out* when the caller needs to pass a value that the procedure uses, changes, and transfers back.

The formal parameters of procedure Get_Lumber_Data are all *out* parameters. When control returns from this procedure to procedure Process_Lumber, the values of formal parameters Quantity, Thickness, Width, and Length are copied into the actual parameters Quantity, Lumber_Thickness, Lumber_Width, and Lumber_Length.

Although the parameters in Get_Lumber_Data are all the same mode, they do not have to be. We can give each parameter in the list a different mode. Typically a procedure is passed a number of values and returns a result determined from those values. Here, for example, is a procedure that is given two Float values and returns the average of them.

```
procedure Calculate_Average (Value_1 : in  Float;
                             Value_2 : in  Float;
                             Average : out Float) is
begin
   Average := (Value_1 + Value_2) / 2.0;
end Calculate_Average;
```

The mode you choose for a formal parameter affects how you may use it. A formal *in* parameter is effectively a constant; the procedure cannot change it. The Ada compiler will issue an error message if your procedure attempts to change a formal *in* parameter. The actual parameter for an *in* mode formal parameter may be an expression. Before control transfers to the procedure, the expression is evaluated and the result is copied into the formal parameter. We could use the following call to procedure Calculate_Average.

```
Calculate_Average (Value_1 => 0.7 * Exam_Grade,
                   Value_2 => 0.3 * Quiz_Grade,
                   Average => Final_Grade);
```

The actual parameter for *out* or *in out* modes cannot be an expression. Each of these modes requires a variable to copy a value into when the procedure is finished. Thus, the following call to Calculate_Average is illegal.

```
Calculate_Average (Value_1 => 0.7 * Exam_Grade,
                   Value_2 => 0.3 * Quiz_Grade,
                   Average => Final_Grade + Midterm_Grade);  -- Illegal call
```

We cannot put the answer calculated by this procedure in the expression Final_Grade + Midterm_Grade.

An *out* parameter is a variable that should be assigned a value by the procedure. This may be accomplished with an assignment statement or a call to another procedure (such as Get). Some Ada compilers will issue an error or warning message if you neglect to assign a value to an *out* formal parameter.

There are no restrictions on the use of *in out* formal parameters. You should not, however, use this mode just to get around the limitations established for the other modes. These constraints were designed to help programmers avoid difficult-to-find semantic errors. To take advantage of this help, choose the mode of your parameters solely on the direction of data transfer required. Select *in out* only if the procedure uses a value that is passed to it and then changes the value before returning it.

Because the data is transferred between the actual and formal parameters, we can call a procedure with different actual parameters. We have made use of this ability frequently in our calls to the Get and Put procedures. We can use the same Put procedure to display a different value each time we call it. This brings up a second major reason for using procedures. (The first is the ease with which we can translate our top-down design into our programming language.) Once we have declared a subprogram, we can call it from many places in the program. Use of multiple calls can save a great deal of effort in coding many problem solutions. If there is a task that must be performed in more than one place in a program, we can avoid repetitive coding by writing it as a procedure and then calling it wherever we need it.

Procedure Placement

Where are procedures physically located? Ada gives us several choices. These include placing them in files separate from our main subprogram, in packages, or nested within our main subprogram. In this chapter we use the last option and place procedures within our main subprogram.

When a procedure is written within our main subprogram, we do not need a separate declaration; the procedure specification in the body serves as the declaration of the procedure. The procedure body goes in the declarative portion of the program. We have already seen that declarations of types, constants, and variables as well as instantiations of packages from Enumeration_IO also go in this portion of the program. The only rule that Ada imposes on the order of declarations is that an identifier must be defined before it is used. For example, we must define the enumeration type before we instantiate a package for its input and output.

While Ada does not restrict the order, for now we recommend the following order. In particular, the declaration of variables for the main subprogram should follow all procedure bodies.

1. declaration of user defined types
2. declaration of constants
3. instantiations of generic packages
4. procedure bodies
5. declaration of variables for the main subprogram

Your instructor may prefer that you use some other order for programs you write.

Our simplified EBNF definition indicates that a procedure body may contain its own declarative part. This means that we can declare programmer-defined types, constants, and variables locally within a procedure. Because procedure bodies are written in declarative parts, we can also declare a procedure within a procedure. This nesting of procedures allows us to code even complicated top-down designs without losing the structure of the problem. We'll return to the topics of local declarations and nested procedures later in this chapter.

Let's look at an example to illustrate the placement of procedures within a program. Here is the Program Lumberyard written using four procedures to implement the two level 1 and two level 2 modules of our design. Look at the order in which types, constants, package instantiations, procedures, and variables are declared.

```
with Ada.Text_IO;
with Ada.Float_Text_IO;
with Ada.Integer_Text_IO;

procedure Lumberyard is

-- This program computes the total amount of a customer order in standard
-- units, given the type of product, quantity of product, and dimensions.

-- Assumptions: All input data entered by the user is valid

   -- Types
   type Product_Type is (Lumber, Plywood);

   -- Instantiate package for product input and output
   package Product_IO is new Ada.Text_IO.Enumeration_IO (Enum => Product_Type);

   -- Constants
   Board_Foot_Inches : constant Float := 144.0;     -- Cubic inches per board foot
   Full_Sheet_Inches : constant Float := 4608.0;    -- Cubic inches per full sheet
   Plywood_Width     : constant Float := 48.0;      -- Width of plywood (inches)

   ---------------------------------------------------------------------------
   procedure Get_Lumber_Data (Quantity  : out Integer;     -- Number of pieces
                              Thickness : out Float;       -- The dimensions
```

```
                              Width       : out Float;        -- of the
                              Length      : out Float) is     -- pieces
-- This procedure prompts for and obtains the data for an order of
-- dimensioned lumber

begin -- Get Lumber Data
   -- Prompt for and get the quantity
   Ada.Text_IO.Put (Item => "Enter the number of boards: ");
   Ada.Integer_Text_IO.Get (Item => Quantity);
   Ada.Text_IO.New_Line;

   -- Prompt for and get the board dimensions
   Ada.Text_IO.Put (Item => "Enter thickness, width, and length");
   Ada.Text_IO.New_Line;
   Ada.Float_Text_IO.Get (Item => Thickness);
   Ada.Float_Text_IO.Get (Item => Width);
   Ada.Float_Text_IO.Get (Item => Length);
   Ada.Text_IO.New_Line (Spacing => 2);
end Get_Lumber_Data;

----------------------------------------------------------------------------
procedure Get_Plywood_Data (Quantity    : out Integer;     -- Number of pieces
                            Numerator   : out Integer;     -- Thickness
                            Denominator : out Integer;     -- fraction
                            Length      : out Float) is    -- Sheet length
-- This procedure prompts for and obtains the data for an order of plywood


begin -- Get Plywood Data
   -- Prompt for and get quantity
   Ada.Text_IO.Put (Item => "Enter the number of sheets: ");
   Ada.Integer_Text_IO.Get (Item => Quantity);
   Ada.Text_IO.New_Line;

   -- Prompt for and get the sheet dimensions
   Ada.Text_IO.Put (Item => "Enter length and 2 thickness numbers");
   Ada.Text_IO.New_Line;
   Ada.Float_Text_IO.Get   (Item => Length);
   Ada.Integer_Text_IO.Get (Item => Numerator);
   Ada.Integer_Text_IO.Get (Item => Denominator);
   Ada.Text_IO.New_Line (Spacing => 2);
end Get_Plywood_Data;


----------------------------------------------------------------------------
procedure Process_Lumber is
-- This procedure processes an order for dimensioned lumber
```

```
   -- Local Variables
   Quantity          : Integer range 1..Integer'Last; -- Number of boards
   Lumber_Thickness  : Float   range 0.5..4.0;        -- Thickness (inches)
   Lumber_Width      : Float   range 1.0..16.0;       -- Width (inches)
   Lumber_Length     : Float   range 1.0..16.0;       -- Length (feet)
   Board_Feet        : Float   range 0.0..Float'Last; -- Total board feet

begin -- Process Lumber
   Get_Lumber_Data (Quantity  => Quantity,
                    Thickness => Lumber_Thickness,
                    Width     => Lumber_Width,
                    Length    => Lumber_Length);
   -- Calculate total number of board feet
   Board_Feet := Float(Quantity) * Lumber_Thickness * Lumber_Width *
                 (Lumber_Length * 12.0) / Board_Foot_Inches;

   -- Display results
   Ada.Text_IO.Put (Item => "Quantity    :  ");
   Ada.Integer_Text_IO.Put (Item => Quantity, Width => 1);
   Ada.Text_IO.New_Line;
   Ada.Text_IO.Put (Item => "Dimensions :  ");
   Ada.Float_Text_IO.Put (Item => Lumber_Thickness,
                          Fore => 1,
                          Aft  => 1,
                          Exp  => 0);
   Ada.Float_Text_IO.Put (Item => Lumber_Width,
                          Fore => 6,
                          Aft  => 1,
                          Exp  => 0);
   Ada.Float_Text_IO.Put (Item => Lumber_Length,
                          Fore => 6,
                          Aft  => 1,
                          Exp  => 0);
   Ada.Text_IO.New_Line;
   Ada.Text_IO.Put (Item => "Board feet :  ");
   Ada.Float_Text_IO.Put (Item => Board_Feet,
                          Fore => 1,
                          Aft  => 1,
                          Exp  => 0);
end Process_Lumber;

----------------------------------------------------------------------------
procedure Process_Plywood is
-- This procedure processes an order for plywood

   -- Local Variables
   Quantity       : Integer range 1..Integer'Last; -- Number of sheets
   Plywood_Length : Float   range 1.0..12.0;       -- Length (feet)
   Numerator      : Integer range 1..5;            -- Thickness
```

```
      Denominator    : Integer range 2..8;            -- fraction
      Full_Sheets    : Float   range 0.0..Float'Last; -- Number of full sheets

   begin -- Process Plywood
      Get_Plywood_Data (Quantity    => Quantity,
                        Length      => Plywood_Length,
                        Numerator   => Numerator,
                        Denominator => Denominator);
      -- Calculate total number of full sheets
      Full_Sheets := Float(Quantity) * (Float(Numerator) / Float(Denominator) *
                     (Plywood_Length * 12.0) * Plywood_Width) / Full_Sheet_Inches;

      -- Display results
      Ada.Text_IO.Put (Item => "Quantity    :  ");
      Ada.Integer_Text_IO.Put (Item => Quantity, Width => 1);
      Ada.Text_IO.New_Line;
      Ada.Text_IO.Put (Item => "Dimensions  :  ");
      Ada.Integer_Text_IO.Put (Item => Numerator, Width => 1);
      Ada.Text_IO.Put (Item => "/");
      Ada.Integer_Text_IO.Put (Item => Denominator, Width => 1);
      Ada.Float_Text_IO.Put (Item => Plywood_Width,
                             Fore => 6,
                             Aft  => 1,
                             Exp  => 0);
      Ada.Float_Text_IO.Put (Item => Plywood_Length,
                             Fore => 6,
                             Aft  => 1,
                             Exp  => 0);
      Ada.Text_IO.New_Line;
      Ada.Text_IO.Put (Item => "Full sheets : ");
      Ada.Float_Text_IO.Put (Item => Full_Sheets,
                             Fore => 1,
                             Aft  => 1,
                             Exp  => 0);
   end Process_Plywood;

----------------------------------------------------------------------------
   -- Variables for main subprogram
   Product  : Product_Type;         -- Indicates Lumber or Plywood

begin -- Program Lumberyard
   -- Prompt for and get product type
   Ada.Text_IO.Put (Item => "Enter product (Lumber or Plywood)");
   Ada.Text_IO.New_Line;
   Product_IO.Get (Item => Product);
   Ada.Text_IO.New_Line;

   if Product = Lumber then  -- Process an order for lumber
      Process_Lumber;
```

```
   else   -- The order must be for plywood
      Process_Plywood;
   end if;
   Ada.Text_IO.New_Line;
end Lumberyard;
```

We could declare the three constants in this program in any order. There is no requirement forcing us to declare Board_Feet_Inches before Full_Sheet_Inches. However, there is a restriction on the order we placed the four procedures. Because procedure Process_Lumber calls procedure Get_Lumber_Data, the latter procedure must come before the former. Similarly, procedure Get_Plywood_Data must come before procedure Process_Plywood.

Notice that the main subprogram for Lumberyard uses only a single variable—Product. This variable is the only variable in this version of Program Lumberyard. The other variables are now local to the procedures. These variables are not needed outside of the procedures in which they are declared. The main subprogram has no need to know the dimensions of the lumber in a customer's order.

Because Program Lumberyard is a simple program, it may seem more complicated with its modules written as procedures. However, it is clear that the revised program resembles our top-down design much more closely than the original version. If you handed this code to some friends, they would start at the bottom, look at the main subprogram and immediately tell you what it does—it gets product type and processes an order for that type. If you asked them to be more specific, they could then move upward in the program and study the body of each procedure. They would begin with a high-level view of the problem and then analyze the lower-level modules as necessary without having to read the entire program or look at a module structure chart. As our programs grow to include many modules nested several levels deep, the ability to read a program in the same manner as a top-down design will greatly aid in the development and debugging process.

Flow of Control in Procedure Calls

Notice that we have declared our procedures in the declarative part of the main subprogram, before the executable statements of the main subprogram. During compilation, the procedures and the program are translated in the order in which they physically appear. When the program is executed, however, control begins at the first statement in the main subprogram, and the program proceeds in logical sequence. When the name of a procedure is encountered as a statement, logical control passes to the first statement in the procedure body. The statements in the procedure execute in logical order. After the last one executes, control returns to the point

FIGURE 6-1
Physical Versus Logical Ordering of Procedures

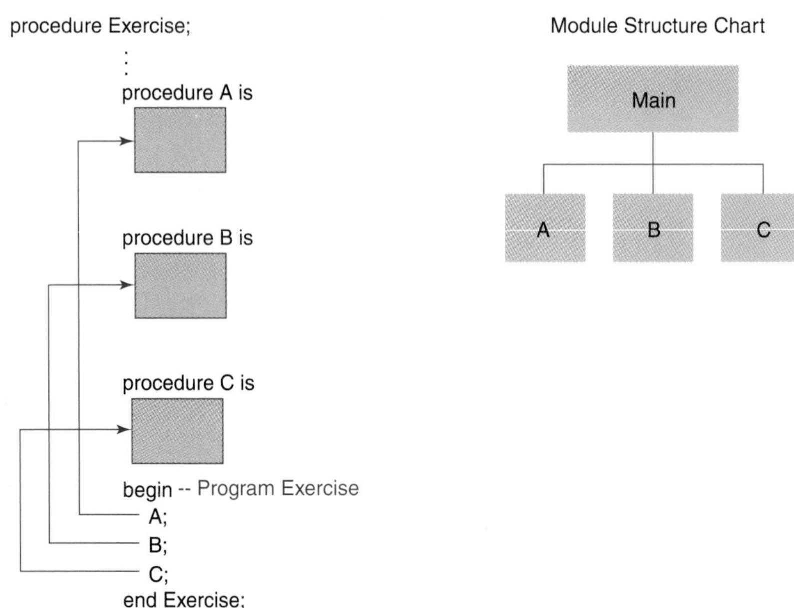

immediately following the call. Because procedure calls alter the logical order of execution, procedures are considered to be control structures. Figure 6-1 illustrates this physical versus logical ordering of procedures.

Although the statements in the procedures appear first in the Lumberyard program, execution begins with the first statement in the main subprogram (the call to Ada.Text_IO.Put that displays the prompt for the user to enter a product type). When Process_Lumber is called, control passes to its first statement and subsequent statements in the procedure. After the last statement in Process_Lumber is executed, control returns to the main subprogram at the point following the call (the call to Ada.Text_IO.New_Line).

The logical order of the Lumberyard program with procedures is identical to the logical order of our original version developed in Chapter 4, but the structure of the top-down design is maintained in the coding of the second version.

MATTERS OF STYLE

Naming and Formatting Procedures

When you choose a name for a procedure, keep in mind how calls to it will look. A call is written as a statement; therefore, it should sound as if it is doing something. For this reason, it is a good idea to choose a name that is a verb or has a verb as part of it. For example, the statement

```
Best_Ski_Wax (Temperature => Outside_Temperature);
```

has no verb to explain its use. Adding the verb "Display" makes the name sound like an action.

```
Display_Best_Ski_Wax (Temperature => Outside_Temperature);
```

When you are choosing a name for a procedure, write down sample calls with different names until you come up with one that tells someone reading the program exactly what the procedure does.

Formatting our procedures, like formatting our programs, helps us to understand them better. In the following example heading, we observe a specific formatting style. A comment appears next to each formal parameter to explain it.

```
procedure Get_Shift_Total (Workers    :  in  Integer;    -- Number of workers
                           Production :  out Float) is   -- Pounds produced
```

Each procedure should also have its own block of introductory comments, just like those at the start of a program.

You should also use comments in the form of rows of dashes before a procedure to make the procedure stand out from the surrounding code. Notice how these lines make it easy to find the four procedures in our Lumberyard example.

It's important to put as much care into documenting each procedure as you would put into documenting a program.

Procedure Options

Local Variables

Because a procedure contains a declarative part, it can include variable declarations within the procedure itself. As we said earlier, these variables are called local variables because they are accessible only from within the procedure in which they are declared. As far as the rest of the program is concerned, they don't exist. If you tried to access the contents of a local variable from the main subprogram, the Ada compiler would issue an error such as IDENTIFIER IS NOT DEFINED.

We use local variables when the procedure needs to store a value that is not needed in the main subprogram or in any other procedure. This is consistent with the principles of top-down design. To prevent confusion, we intentionally hide the details of lower-level modules when working on a higher-level module. This hiding of detail applies to data as well as instructions. For example, when designing the main module for Program Lumberyard, we did not worry about how to calculate and print the equivalent board feet for a lumber order. We leave that task for module Process_Lumber. However, when designing this Level 1 module, we find that we need a variable to store the results of the calculation. We declare local variable Board_Feet in procedure Process_Lumber to store this result, which is not needed by the main subprogram.

Local variables are destroyed when the procedure returns; therefore, every time the procedure is called, its local variables start out with their values undefined. Because every call to a procedure is independent of every other call to that same procedure, the local variables must be initialized within the procedure itself.

Because the values of local variables are destroyed when the procedure returns, we cannot use them to store values between calls to a procedure. If a procedure calculates a value that we want to employ in a later call to the same procedure, the value must be passed back to the calling program through a parameter. The next time the procedure is called, the main subprogram can pass that value back to the procedure.

Named and Positional Parameter Association

When we call a procedure, an association or match is made between the actual and formal parameters in our call. This association can be made in two ways. We have been using a method called **named association.** With this method, we specify the name of the formal parameter as well as the actual parameter that we wish to associate with that formal parameter. We use the arrow symbol (=>) to associate the formal and actual parameters. The order of the parameters in a call statement using named association does not have to be the same as the order of the formal parameters in the procedure specification.

Named association Association of actual and formal parameters by explicitly naming the formal parameter in the call to the subprogram.

Before we discuss the second method of associating actual and formal parameters, let's look at an analogy from daily life. You're at the local discount catalog showroom to buy a Father's Day present. To place your order, you fill out an order form. The form has places to write in the quantity of an item and its catalog number and places where the order clerk will fill in the availability and price. You write down what you want and hand the form to the clerk. You wait for the clerk to check whether the items are available and to look up the price. She returns the form, and you see that the items are in stock and that the price is $48.50. You pay the clerk and go on about your business. (See illustration below.)

Acme Catalog Showroom
Nobody Beats Acme's Prices!

Instructions:

1. Fill in catalog number and quantity.
2. Give this form to a sales clerk.
3. Wait for the clerk to return the form with the current price and availability of your item.

Catalog Number A-734-5

Quantity 1

In Stock *Yes*

Acme's Price *$ 48.50*

This illustrates how procedure calls work. The clerk is like a procedure. You, acting as the main subprogram, have her do some work for you. You give her some information: the catalog number and quantity. These are her *in* parameters. You wait until she returns some information to you: the availability of the item and its price. These are the clerk's *out* parameters. The clerk does this task all day long with different *in* values. Each order activates the same process. The shopper waits until the clerk returns information based on the shopper-supplied values.

Your order form is analogous to the actual parameters of a procedure call. The names on the form represent variables in the main subprogram. When you hand the form to the clerk, some of the places contain information and some are empty. The clerk enters your information into her computer terminal. Her terminal entries may use different names like "Code," "Units," "In Warehouse," and "Price" to describe the data. These are her terms (formal parameters) for what your order form calls "Catalog Number," "Quantity," "In Stock," and "Acme's Price" (the actual parameters). When she is finished, she copies the output on her screen onto your order form.

An experienced clerk may not even bother reading the names on your order form every time; she knows that the first item is the code (Catalog Number), the second is the Units (Quantity), and so on. In other words, she looks only at the position of each space on the form. This is how she associates actual parameters and formal parameters: by their relative positions in the two parameter lists.

Ada also permits parameter association by position. Using **positional association,** you could replace the call to procedure Get_Lumber_Data in Program Lumberyard with

```
Get_Lumber_Data (Quantity, Lumber_Thickness, Lumber_Width, Lumber_Length);
```

The first actual parameter, Quantity, is associated with the first formal parameter, Quantity. The second actual parameter, Lumber_Thickness, is associated with the second formal parameter, Thickness; and so on for the two remaining parameters.

Positional association Association of actual and formal parameters by their positions in the actual and formal parameter lists.

There are two disadvantages to using positional association in your procedure calls. First, it is very easy to write the actual parameters in the wrong order. Many a programmer has spent hours tracking down an error in a program only to find that it was the result of swapping two names in a positional association procedure call. Second, the lack of formal parameter names makes it more difficult to read the program without constantly flipping between the procedure call statement and the procedure declaration.

Sometimes the extra information provided by named association is not especially helpful. For example, when there is only one parameter, there is no possibility of mixing up the order. In this case, we recommend positional association. We can write

```
Ada.Text_IO.Put ("Mildred went to the beach today.");
```

instead of

```
Ada.Text_IO.Put (Item => "Mildred went to the beach today.");
```

with no loss of information to the person reading our program.

Designing Procedures

We've looked at some examples of procedures and covered the formal definition of a procedure. But how do we design procedures? First, we need to be more specific about what procedures do. We've said that they allow us to organize our programs more like our top-down designs, but what is the real advantage of doing that?

The body of a procedure is like any other segment of code, except that it is contained in a declarative part. Isolating a segment of code in a separate area means that its implementation details can be "hidden" from view. As long as you know how to call a procedure and what its function is, you can use it without knowing how it works. For instance, you don't know how the code for procedure Put is written (its implementation is hidden from view), yet you still can use it effectively.

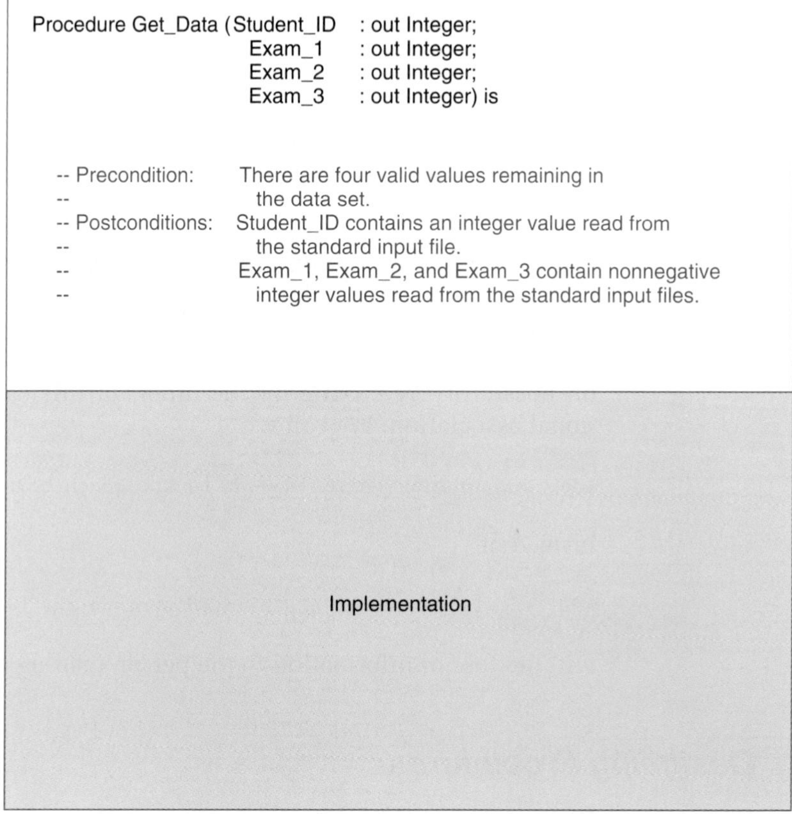

Procedure Get_Data (Student_ID : out Integer;
Exam_1 : out Integer;
Exam_2 : out Integer;
Exam_3 : out Integer) is
-- Precondition: There are four valid values remaining in
-- the data set.
-- Postconditions: Student_ID contains an integer value read from
-- the standard input file.
-- Exam_1, Exam_2, and Exam_3 contain nonnegative
-- integer values read from the standard input files.
Implementation

FIGURE 6-2 Procedure Interface (Visible) and Implementation (Hidden)

The specification of what a procedure does and how it is called defines its **interface** (see Figure 6-2). By concealing a module implementation, or encapsulating the module—**information hiding**—we can make changes to it without changing the body of the main subprogram as long as the interface remains the same. For example, you might rewrite the body of a procedure using a more efficient algorithm.

Interface A connecting link at a shared boundary that permits independent systems to meet and act on or communicate with each other. The formal definition of the purpose of a subprogram and the mechanism for communicating with it.

Information hiding Hiding the implementation details of a module.

Information hiding is what we do in the top-down design process when we postpone the solution of a difficult subproblem. We write down its function, what information it takes and what it returns, and then write the rest of our design as if we already had solved the subproblem. We could hand this interface specification to someone else, who could develop a procedure for us that solves the subproblem. We need not be concerned about how it works as long as it conforms to the interface specification. Interfaces and information hiding are the basis for team programming in which programmers work together to solve a large problem.

Thus, designing a procedure can (and should) be divided into two tasks: designing the interface and designing the implementation. We already know how to design an implementation—it is merely a segment of code that corresponds to one module in an algorithm. To design the interface, we must define the function of the subprogram and the mechanism for communicating with it.

You already know how to specify the function of a subprogram. Because a procedure corresponds to a module, its function is defined by the preconditions and postconditions of the module. All that remains is to define the mechanism for communicating with the procedure. To do this, make a list of the following items.

1. Values that the procedure *receives* from the caller.
2. Values the procedure produces and *returns* to the caller.
3. Values the caller has that the procedure changes (*receives* and *returns*).

Decide which identifiers inside the module fit each of the descriptions in this list. These identifiers become the variables defined in the formal parameter list for the procedure. The formal parameters are then declared in the procedure heading with the appropriate modes (*in*, *out*, or *in out*). All other variables that the procedure needs are local and must be declared as local variables in the declarative part of the procedure itself. This process may be repeated for all the modules at each level.

Nesting

Whenever our top-down design has more than two levels of modules, there is the potential for nesting procedures within other procedures. Ada permits statements inside a procedure to access identifiers declared outside the procedure. In this section we examine the rules that control how external access takes place, both in simple cases and in cases where procedures are nested.

FIGURE 6-3
Declarative Region of Procedure Process_Lumber

```
procedure Process _ Lumber is

   Quantity          : Integer  range  1..Integer'Last;  --  Number of boards
   Lumber_Thickness  : Float    range  0.5..4.0;         --  Thickness (inches)
   Lumber_Width      : Float    range  1.0..16.0;        --  Width (inches)
   Lumber_Length     : Float    range  1.0..16.0;        --  Length (feet)
   Board_Feet        : Float    range  0.0..Float'Last;  --  Total board feet

begin -- Process Lumber
   .
   .
   .
end Process_Lumber
```

Declarative Regions

If we list all the places from where an identifier could be accessed, we would describe that identifier's *scope of access*, often just called its *scope*. Ada's rules for determining the scope of an identifier are based on the notion of **declarative regions.** Each subprogram has its own declarative region. The declarative region of a subprogram begins immediately after the subprogram name and goes to the end of its body. Figure 6-3 illustrates the declarative region of procedure Get_Lumber_Data from Program Lumberyard given on page 291.

Declarative region A subprogram declaration together with the corresponding body.

Identifiers declared immediately within a declarative region are said to be **local** to the region. The variables Quantity, Lumber_Thickness, Lumber_Width, Lumber_Length, and Board_Feet declared in procedure Process_Lumber are local to the declarative region of this procedure.

FIGURE 6-4
Declarative Region of Procedure Get_Lumber_Data

```
procedure Get_Lumber_Data   (Quantity  : out Integer;  --  Number of pieces
                             Thickness : out Float;    --  The dimensions
                             Width     : out Float;    --   of the
                             Length    : out Float) is --   pieces
begin -- Get Lumber Data
   .
   .
   .
end Get_Lumber_Date;
```

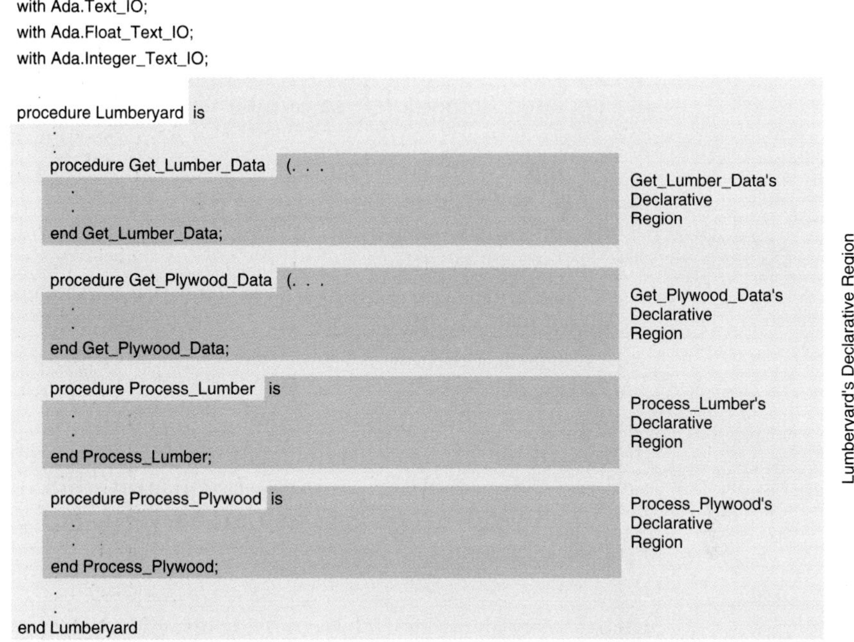
with Ada.Text_IO;
with Ada.Float_Text_IO;
with Ada.Integer_Text_IO;
procedure Lumberyard is
procedure Get_Lumber_Data (. . .
end Get_Lumber_Data;
Get_Lumber_Data's Declarative Region
procedure Get_Plywood_Data (. . .
end Get_Plywood_Data;
Get_Plywood_Data's Declarative Region
procedure Process_Lumber is
end Process_Lumber;
Process_Lumber's Declarative Region
procedure Process_Plywood is
end Process_Plywood;
Process_Plywood's Declarative Region
end Lumberyard
Lumberyard's Declarative Region

FIGURE 6-5 Declarative Regions for Program Lumberyard

Local Any identifier declared immediately inside of a given declarative region.

Figure 6-4 shows the declarative region of procedure Get_Lumber_Data. Notice that its four parameters are within the declarative region. Parameters are local to the declarative region of the procedure in which they are declared.

When procedures are nested, so are their declarative regions. Figure 6-5 shows the declarative regions for Program Lumberyard, which is made up of a main subprogram and its four procedures.

Declarations in outer (enclosing) declarative regions are said to be **global** with respect to an inner declarative region. Using Figure 6-5 as a guide, review Program Lumberyard on page 291. The following identifiers are declared *immediately* in Lumberyard's declarative region.

- Enumeration type Product_Type
- Package Product_IO
- Constants Board_Foot_Inches, Full_Sheet_Inches, and Plywood_Width
- Procedures Get_Lumber_Data, Get_Plywood_Data, Process_Lumber, and Process_Plywood
- Variable Product

Lumberyard's declarative region encloses the regions of its four procedures. All ten of these declarations are therefore global to each of the procedure's declarative regions. Local and global are relative terms. Plywood_Width is local to Lumberyard and global to procedure Process_Plywood.

Global Any identifier declared outside of a given declarative region.

We can use the same name for an identifier as long as the names are declared in different declarative regions. The identifier Quantity is used twice in Program Lumberyard—once in procedure Process_Lumber and once in procedure Process_Lumber. Identifiers with the same name are called **homographs.** While the names are the same, each is associated with a different storage location in the computer's memory.

Homograph Each of multiple declarations with identical names.

Scope Rules

With an understanding of declarative regions we are ready to look at the details for determining an identifier's *scope*. The rules for determining where in the program an identifier may be used are called **scope rules**. Here are the two rules that govern where in the program an identifier may be accessed (its scope).

1. The scope of an identifier includes all the statements following its definition, within the declarative region containing the definition. This includes all nested declarative regions, except as noted in rule 2.
2. The scope of an identifier does not extend to any nested declarative region that contains a locally defined homograph.

The second rule is sometimes called **name precedence.** When homographs exist, the local identifier takes precedence within the procedure.

Scope rules The rules that determine where in the program an identifier may be accessed.

Name precedence When a homograph exists, the local identifier in a procedure takes precedence over any global identifier in any references that the procedure makes to that identifier.

Here's a simple program to illustrate the scope rules:

```
with Ada.Text_IO;
with Ada.Integer_Text_IO;
with Ada.Float_Text_IO;

procedure Scope_Example_1 is

      -- The following type is local for the main subprogram (Scope_Example_1)
      -- and global for procedures Dog and Cat
   type Bird_Type is (Canary, Robin, Dove, Goldfinch, Cardinal);

      -- The following new package is also local for the
      -- main subprogram and global for procedures Dog and Cat
   package Bird_IO is new Ada.Text_IO.Enumeration_IO (Enum => Bird_Type);

   A : constant Integer   := 17;        -- These four identifiers
   B : constant Integer   := 18;        -- are local for the main
   C : constant Float     := 19.0;      -- program and global for
   D : constant Bird_Type := Dove;      -- procedures Dog and Cat

   -------------------------------------------------------------------
```

```
   procedure Dog (C : in Float) is     -- The formal parameter C prevents
                                       --    access to global C from
                                       --    procedure Dog (it is a homograph)

      B : Float;       -- This homograph of constant B declared above prevents
                       -- access to that Integer constant from this procedure
   begin    -- Dog
      B := 2.3;                                     -- Assignment to local B
      Ada.Integer_Text_IO.Put (Item  => A,          -- Output global A (= 17)
                               Width => 4);
      Ada.Float_Text_IO.Put   (Item => B,           -- Output local B (= 2.3)
                               Fore => 3,
                               Aft  => 1,
                               Exp  => 0);
      Ada.Float_Text_IO.Put   (Item => C,           -- Output local C (= 7.5)
                               Fore => 3,
                               Aft  => 1,
                               Exp  => 0);
   end Dog;

   -----------------------------------------------------------------------
   procedure Cat (A : in Integer) is   -- The formal parameter A prevents
                                       -- access to global A from
                                       -- procedure Cat (it is a homograph)

      E : Float;                       -- Local to procedure Cat

   begin   -- Cat
      Bird_IO.Put (Item => D);         -- Output global D (= Dove)
      E := 0.5 * Float (A);            -- Assignment to local E
      Dog (C => E);                    -- Pass copy of local E to procedure Dog
   end Cat;

-------------------------------------------------------------------------
   F : Integer;                        -- Local for the main subprogram

begin   -- Scope Example 1
   F := 15;                            -- Assignment to local F
   Cat (A => F);                       -- Pass copy of local F to procedure Cat
end Scope_Example_1;
```

Try doing an execution trace of this program. The output is

```
DOVE  17  2.3  7.5
```

There are two approaches to studying the scopes in a program such as this. One way is to select an identifier and determine which procedures may use (access) that identifier. Another way is to select a procedure and determine all the identifiers it may access.

Let's look at the scope of five identifiers: A, B, Cat, E, and F.

The Integer constant A is declared immediately within the declarative region of Program Scope_Example_1. It is accessible from the main subprogram and from within procedure Dog. It is not accessible from within procedure Cat because that procedure has a parameter with the same name. Our second scope rule states that local identifiers have name precedence.

The Integer constant B is also declared immediately within the declarative region of Program Scope_Example_1. It is accessible from the main subprogram and from within procedure Cat. It is not accessible from within procedure Dog because that procedure has a local variable with the same name.

Procedure Cat is declared immediately within the declarative region of Program Scope_Example_1. It may be called (is accessible) from the main subprogram. Procedure Cat is not accessible from procedure Dog. Our first scope rule states that an identifier's accessibility begins at its declaration. Since procedure Cat is declared after procedure Dog, it cannot be called from procedure Dog.

The Float variable E is declared immediately within the declarative region of procedure Cat. It is accessible only from within procedure Cat. Our first scope rule states that accessibility cannot go outside of the declarative region in which it is defined.

Finally, the Integer variable F is declared immediately within the declarative region of Program Scope_Example_1. It may only be used in the main subprogram. Variable F is not accessible to procedures Dog or Cat because it is declared after these two procedures.

Now let's look at the scopes in this program from the perspective of one procedure and what identifiers we can access from it. Procedure Dog can access Bird_Type, Bird_IO, constants A and D, parameter C, and local variable B. Procedure Dog cannot access constants B or C, procedure Cat, or variables E or F. Use the scope rules to determine why procedure Dog cannot access these five identifiers.

We can summarize all of the scope information for this program in a scope table that lists all of the identifiers in the program on the left and all of the procedures on the right. Table 6-1 is a scope table for Program Scope_Example_1. You can follow across a row to see which of the three procedures can access a given identifier. Or you can follow down a column to see which of the 13 identifiers are accessible from a given procedure.

TABLE 6-1

IDENTIFIER		**CAN BE ACCESSED FROM PROCEDURE**		
Declarative Region	*Name*	*Dog*	*Cat*	*Scope_Example_1*
Scope_Example_1				
	Bird_Type	Yes	Yes	Yes
	Bird_IO	Yes	Yes	Yes
	A	Yes	No	Yes
	B	No	Yes	Yes
	C	No	Yes	Yes
	D	Yes	Yes	Yes
	Dog	Yes	Yes	Yes
	Cat	No	Yes	Yes
	F	No	No	Yes
Dog				
	C	Yes	No	No
	B	Yes	No	No
Cat				
	A	No	Yes	No
	E	No	Yes	No

On the next page there is a more complicated example of procedure nesting. To simplify the example, we show only the declarations. Note how procedure Two is declared within procedure One.

```
procedure Scope_Example_2 is

   A1 : constant Integer := 15;      -- These two constants are local for
   A2 : constant Boolean := True;    -- the main subprogram and global for all
                                     -- other procedures

   ------------------------------------------------------------------------
   procedure Three (A1 :  in Integer;      -- Prevents access to main A1
                    B2 : out Boolean) is

      C1 : Integer;     -- These two variables are
      D2 : Integer;     -- local to Three
   begin  -- Three
     .
     .
     .
   end Three;

   ------------------------------------------------------------------------
   procedure One is

      A1 : constant Integer := 4; -- Prevents access to main A1
      B1 : constant Integer := 7; -- Local to One

      ---------------------------------------------------------------------
      procedure Two is

         A1 : Integer;   -- Homograph prevents access to A1 in One
         C1 : Integer;   -- Local to Two, no conflict with C1 in Three
      begin  -- Two
        .
        .
        .
      end Two;

      B2 : Integer;     -- Local to One, no conflict with B2 in Three
   begin  -- One
     .
     .
     .
   end One;

---------------------------------------------------------------------------
   M1 : Float;                -- Local for the main subprogram.  Global for but
                              -- not accessible to procedures One, Two, or Three
begin  -- Scope_Example_2
  .
  .
  .
end Scope_Example_2;
```

Let's look at Program Scope_Example_2 in terms of the declaration regions it defines. Figure 6-6 shows the headings and declarations in Program Scope_Example_2 with the declarative regions shown as boxes. Notice that the formal parameters for a procedure are inside the procedure's box, but the procedure name itself is outside. If the name of the procedure were inside the box, the program couldn't call the procedure. This demonstrates that the procedure name is just an identifier declared in the declarative region surrounding the procedure, and that it has the same scope as any other identifier declared in that declarative region.

From our scope rules, we know that anything inside a box can refer to anything above it in a larger surrounding box, but outside-in references aren't allowed. Thus, a statement in procedure Two could access any identifier declared above it in either procedure One or in the main subprogram. A statement in Two could not access identifiers declared in Three because it would have to enter the Three box from outside. Also note that the main subprogram can call Three and One, but it cannot call Two.

Name precedence is implemented by the compiler as follows: When a statement refers to an identifier, the compiler first checks the local declarations. If the identifier isn't local, the compiler works its way outward through each level of nesting until it finds an identifier with the same spelling. If there is an identifier with the same name declared at a level even further out, it is never reached. If the compiler reaches the declarations of the main subprogram and still can't find the identifier, an error message such as IDENTIFIER IS UNDEFINED will result. Such a message

FIGURE 6-6 Declarative Regions for Program Scope_Example_2

```
procedure Scope_Example_2  is

   A1  :  constant Integer  : = 15;
   A2  :  constant Boolean : = True;

   procedure Three  (A1  :    in Integer;
                     B2  :  out Boolean) is
      C1  :  Integer;
      D2  :  Integer;

   procedure One  is

      A1  :  constant Integer  : =  4;
      B1  :  constant Integer  : =  5;

      procedure Two  is

         A1  :  Integer;
         C1  :  Integer;

      B2  :  Integer;

M1  :  Float;
```

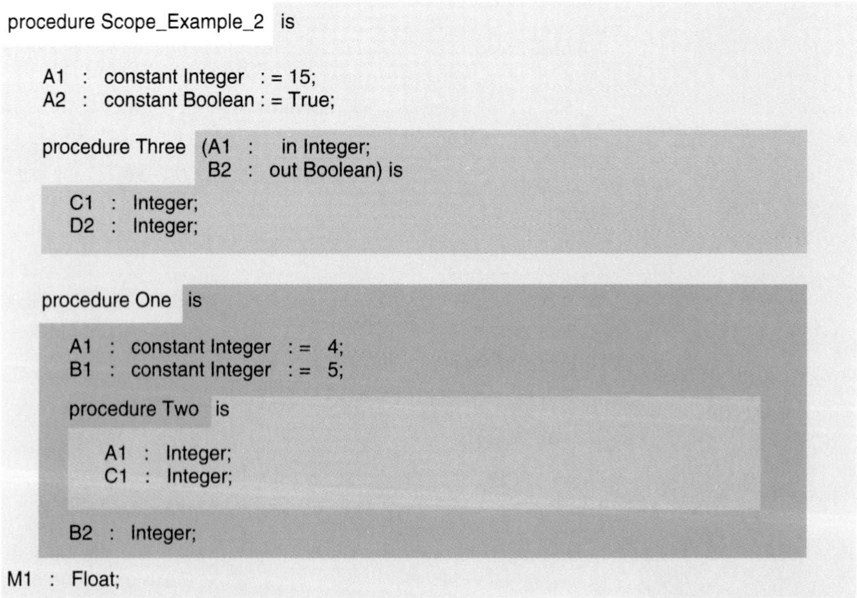

most likely indicates that there is a misspelling, or that the identifier was not declared before the reference to it, or that it was not declared at all. It also may indicate, however, that the procedures are nested so that the identifier's scope doesn't include the reference.

Table 6-2 is a scope table for Program Scope_Example_2. You can follow across a row to see which of the four procedures can access a given identifier. Or you can follow down a column to see which of the 15 identifiers are accessible from a given procedure. Make sure you can understand all of its entries by looking at the program and applying the scope rules.

TABLE 6-2

IDENTIFIER		CAN BE ACCESSED FROM PROCEDURE			
Declarative Region	*Name*	*One*	*Two*	*Three*	*Scope_Example_2*
Scope_Example_2					
	A1	No	No	No	Yes
	A2	Yes	Yes	Yes	Yes
	Three	Yes	Yes	Yes	Yes
	One	Yes	Yes	No	Yes
	M1	No	No	No	Yes
One					
	A1	Yes	No	No	No
	B1	Yes	Yes	No	No
	Two	Yes	Yes	No	No
	B2	Yes	No	No	No
Two					
	A1	No	Yes	No	No
	C1	No	Yes	No	No
Three					
	A1	No	No	Yes	No
	B2	No	No	Yes	No
	C1	No	No	Yes	No
	D2	No	No	Yes	No

You may notice from our scope rules that a statement in a procedure can call *that* procedure. For example, we see that we can access (call) procedure Three from within procedure Three. This process, called *recursion*, is the topic of Chapter 13.

Avoiding Use of Global Variables Through Declaration Order

The only restriction that Ada imposes on the order of declarations within a declarative part of a program arises from the first scope rule: a resource must be declared before it can be used. Our recommended order of declarations given on page 291 puts variable declarations after the procedures. Program Scope_Example_2 on page 311 illustrates this order. The declaration of the main subprogram variable M1 is placed after the declaration of the two procedures in Scope_Example_2's declarative part. The local variable B2 is declared after the local procedure Two in the declarative part of procedure One. Table 6-2 shows that the access to these two variables is restricted to local use; they may not be accessed *globally* by any procedure in the program. The use of global variable references is a poor programming practice that can lead to program bugs. These bugs are extremely hard to locate and usually take the form of unwanted side effects.

Side Effects Suppose you included the following statement in an Ada program.

```
Ada.Float_Text_IO.Put (Item => Exam_Average);
```

You would expect that the call to Float_Text_IO.Put would display the value of Exam_Average. You would be surprised if this Put procedure also changed the value of variable Sum used in the calculation of the average. This would be an example of an unexpected and unwanted **side effect.**

Side effect Any effect of one module on another module that is not a part of the explicitly defined interface between them. (A module is a procedure, a function, or the main subprogram.)

Side effects can occur easily when a procedure accesses a global variable. An error in the procedure might change the value of a global variable in an unexpected way, causing an error in the main subprogram.

The symptoms of a side-effect error are misleading because the trouble appears in one part of the program when it really is caused by something in another part. To avoid such errors, the only external effect that a procedure should have is to transfer information through the well-structured interface of the parameters. If procedures only modify their local variables and parameters, there won't be any side effects. By declaring variables after procedures, we ensure that global access to these variables is impossible.

Global Constants and Data Types Contrary to what you might think, it is acceptable to reference constants, programmer-defined data types, and package instantiations globally. Because the values of global constants cannot be changed while the program is running, no side effects can occur.

There are two advantages to referencing constants globally: ease of change and consistency. If we have to change the value of a constant, it's easier to change just one global definition than to change a local definition in every procedure. By defining a constant in only one place, we also ensure that all parts of the program will use exactly the same value.

A data type has no value to be changed. It is a pattern for a class of data used to limit the particular values a variable may hold. Because nothing about the type can be changed, no side effects can occur when using global types. In fact, the type must be global in order to use parameters to pass values of a programmer-defined type.

This is not to say that you should define all constants and programmer-defined types globally. If a type or constant is needed in only one procedure, then you should define it locally within that procedure. A problem with using global constants is the extra work in reusing the procedure in another program. We must copy both the procedure and the constant.

Here is the best rule for knowing where to define types and constants: You should declare a constant or type in the lowest-level declarative region that contains all the references to it. Quite often this is the declarative region of the main subprogram.

Designing Programs with Nesting

The advantage of nesting procedures is that the structure of the resulting program matches the hierarchical design. Each procedure encapsulates all of the details of a module (including all the modules that implement its abstract steps). If we ever want to reuse a procedure in another program, we simply copy it; everything it needs is in the procedure.

While nesting makes reusing a procedure in another program easier, it makes reusing it in the same program more difficult. Suppose we wanted, in Program Scope_Example_2 on page 311, to call procedure Two from both procedure One and procedure Three. As the program is currently organized (procedure Two is nested in procedure One), only procedure One can call procedure Two. To keep the nesting consistent with the design, we need to nest a copy of procedure Two in procedure Three. This solution presents a severe maintenance problem. If we find later that we must modify procedure Two, we must be sure to modify both copies.

Nesting procedures can make a program difficult to read. A procedure containing several nested procedures has many lines of code between its parameter list and its begin statement. We find ourselves flipping back and forth between the executable statements at the bottom and the parameter list and comments at the top. Excessive indentation is another problem with nesting procedures. We indent each nested procedure to show its depth of nesting. As the nesting becomes deeper, the indentation increases and forces us to use shorter lines.

Whether or not you nest procedures is a matter of style and the constraints of your top-down design. It is acceptable to list the procedures sequentially without nesting as long as you declare each one before you call it. We tend to restrict our use of nesting to very small procedures that are called by only one procedure. For reuse of procedures in other programs, we make use of programmer-defined packages (Chapter 12) to organize related procedures into a single unit.

Overloading Subprogram Names

In Chapter 2 we said that, except in special circumstances, each identifier could represent just one thing. In this chapter we have seen how the same identifier name in different declarative regions can represent different locations in memory. The visibility of homographs is determined by name precedence.

Ada provides a way to use the same identifier name for different subprograms even if they are declared in the same region. This is known as *overloading* of subprograms. We have been using overloaded procedure names since Chapter 2. Standard library package Text_IO contains many different Get and Put procedures (see Appendix D). Without overloading, a different name would be necessary for each of these procedures.

You can overload a subprogram name only if Ada can use the formal parameter list to tell them apart. This is similar to using the other words in a sentence to determine which definition of a word with several definitions is intended. If someone says, "I hammered the *tack* into the wall," we understand the word *tack* to be a short sharp-pointed nail. On the other hand, if someone says, "We were running a starboard *tack*," we understand the word *tack* refers to the direction of a ship with respect to the wind.

Both the number of parameters and the types of the parameters help to distinguish between overloaded procedures. Here, for example, is a program that has three procedures called Calc_Average.

```
procedure Overload is

-- This program illustrates the overloading of subprogram names.
-- It includes three procedures called Calc_Average.

   -----------------------------------------------------------------
   procedure Calc_Average (Value_1 :  in Integer;     -- First Calc_Average
                           Value_2 :  in Integer;
                           Result  : out Float) is

   -- This procedure calculates the float average of two integers.
```

```
      begin  -- Calc Average
         Result := Float(Value_1 + Value_2)  /  2.0;
      end Calc_Average;

      ---------------------------------------------------------------------
      procedure Calc_Average (Value_1 :  in Integer;  -- Second Calc_Average
                              Value_2 :  in Integer;
                              Result  : out Integer) is

      -- This procedure calculates the integer average of two integers.

      begin  -- Calc Average
         Result := (Value_1 + Value_2) / 2;
      end Calc_Average;

      ---------------------------------------------------------------------
      procedure Calc_Average (Value_1 :  in Integer;   -- Third Calc_Average
                              Value_2 :  in Integer;
                              Value_3 :  in Integer;
                              Result  : out Float) is

      -- This procedure calculates the float average of three integers.

      begin  -- Calc Average
         Result := Float(Value_1 + Value_2 + Value_3)  /  3.0;
      end Calc_Average;

   ------------------------------------------------------------------------
      Integer_Result : Integer;
      Float_Result   : Float;

   begin  -- program Overload
      Calc_Average (Value_1 => 33,              -- Call to second Calc_Average
                    Value_2 => 86,
                    Result  => Integer_Result);
      Calc_Average (Value_1 => 33,              -- Call to first Calc_Average
                    Value_2 => 86,
                    Result  => Float_Result);
      Calc_Average (Value_1 => 15,              -- Call to third Calc_Average
                    Value_2 => 54,
                    Value_3 => 63,
                    Result  => Float_Result);
   end Overload;
```

The first call to procedure Calc_Average has three actual parameters: the first two are Integer literals and the third is an Integer variable. This actual parameter list matches only the formal parameter list of the second Calc_Average procedure we declared. It does not match the third Calc_Average procedure because that procedure has four formal parameters. It does not match the first Calc_Average procedure because the third actual parameter of the call is of type Integer and the first Calc_Average requires an actual parameter of type Float.

The second call has three actual parameters that match the first Calc_Average procedure, and the third call's actual parameters match the third declared procedure.

Why would we want to use the same name for three different procedures? We always try to choose an identifier name to reflect its purpose. Although each of these three procedures are different, they all perform the same function—calculate an average. Programming languages that do not allow overloading of subprogram names require programmers to make up meaningful names for different procedures that perform the same function. Can you think of three different *meaningful* names for the three Calc_Average procedures?

Because overloading must work for positional parameter association as well as named parameter association, Ada does not distinguish between overloaded subprograms whose formal parameter lists differ only in the names used for the formal parameters. We would get an error message if we tried to declare a fourth Calc_Average procedure in Program Overload as follows:

```
procedure Calc_Average (One_Value     : in  Integer;
                        Another_Value : in  Integer;
                        Average       : out Float) is
   .
   .
   .
```

Only the number of parameters and their types are used to resolve overloaded subprogram names. Ada sees no difference between this procedure and the first one we declared.

Do you remember the syntax error messages you received when you tried to call a procedure with an actual parameter whose type did not match the type of the formal parameter? Many compilers issue messages like ERROR IN OVERLOAD RESOLUTION. The Ada compiler was trying to find a procedure whose name and formal parameters matched the ones in your call statement. When it could not find one, it displayed the error message. If you have never made this mistake, try Programming Warm-up Exercise 7 in Chapter 2.

Function Subprograms

In the first part of this chapter we discussed procedures. In this section we look at the second type of subprogram—the *function.* The main difference between procedures and functions is the way that they are called. A procedure call is a statement in a program; a function call is part of an expression. Often we can simplify the coding of complex expressions by defining our own functions, which is especially helpful when the expression is used repeatedly in a program.

A function returns a single result value that is used directly in the expression containing the call to the function. Calling functions is very similar to using the explicit type conversions we introduced in Chapter 2. For example, suppose we need to calculate the difference in the radii of two circles given their areas. A formula to calculate this difference is:

$$\sqrt{A_1/\pi} - \sqrt{A_2/\pi}$$

We could code our square root algorithm from Chapter 5 as a procedure and calculate the difference in radii with the following code segment.

```
Calculate_Square_Root (Value  => Area_1 / Pi,
                       Result => Radius_1);
Calculate_Square_Root (Value  => Area_2 / Pi,
                       Result => Radius_2);
Difference := Radius_1 - Radius_2;
```

The formal parameter Value is an *in* parameter, and the formal parameter Result is an *out* parameter. Because Calculate_Square_Root returns only one value, we can write it as a function instead of a procedure. Here's an example of using a function called Sqrt that returns the square root of its single parameter.

```
Result := Sqrt (37.2);
```

You call a function by using it in an expression. In this example the expression consists of only the function call. The square root of 37.2 is calculated, returned to the expression, and then assigned to result.

Here's how the code for determining the difference in radii would be written using function Sqrt instead of procedure Calculate_Square_Root.

```
Difference := Sqrt (Area_1 / Pi)  -  Sqrt (Area_2 / Pi);
```

This version of the code segment is much more intuitive—it looks just like our algebraic expression. Because Sqrt is a function, you know immediately that all its parameters receive values and that it returns just one value (the square root of the given value). Because there is only one parameter, we have used positional parameter association rather than named parameter association. Even with multiple parameters, positional parameter association is used frequently with function subprograms to keep the expression as short as possible.

Let's look at the function body for Sqrt. The code should be familiar to you from Chapter 5.

```
function Sqrt (X : in Float) return Float is

   -- This function calculates an approximation of the square root
   -- of the given value. It works only for nonnegative values.

   Tolerance : constant Float := 0.00001;
   Approx    : Float;

begin
   Approx := X / 2.0;
   Calculate_Square_Root:
   loop
      exit Calculate_Square_Root when abs(Approx ** 2 - X) < Tolerance;
      Approx := 0.5 * (Approx + X / Approx);
   end loop Calculate_Square_Root;
   return Approx;
end Sqrt;
```

The function definition looks very much like a procedure definition. The first difference is that it begins with the word *function* rather than *procedure*. Another difference is seen after the listing of the function's formal parameters. Here we see the reserved word `return` followed by a data type (Float in this example). A function returns one value, not through a parameter but through the name of the function. The data type at the end of the function specification defines the type of value that the function will return.

The last statement in the function body is a return statement. This statement consists of the reserved word `return` followed by an expression whose value is the result of the function. The return statement transfers control back to the expression that called the function. The value returned is then used in that expression (see Figure 6-7). Every function body must contain at least one return statement. Although we can have multiple return statements in a function, in most cases, it is good programming style to use only one return statement per function.

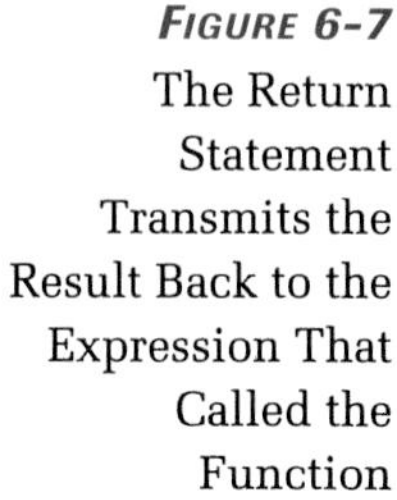

Figure 6-7
The Return Statement Transmits the Result Back to the Expression That Called the Function

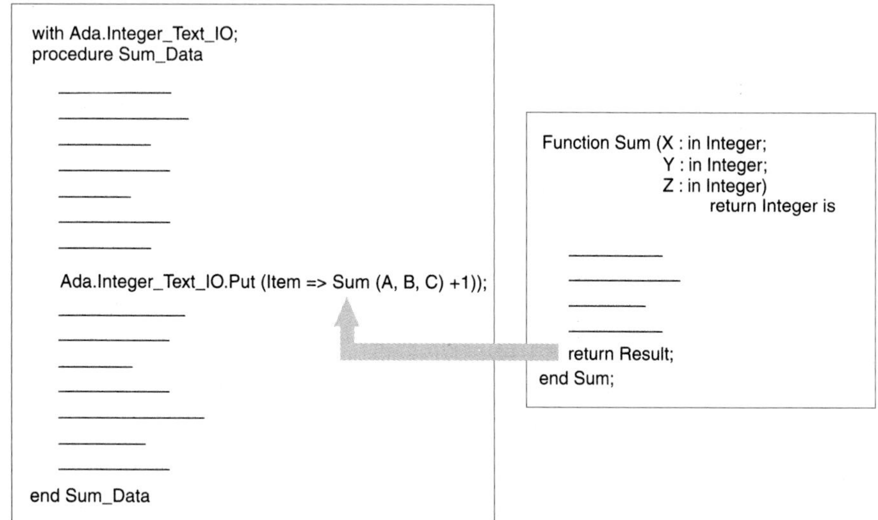

Ada requires that *in* mode be used for all formal parameters defined in a function specification. It will issue an error message if you attempt to use *out* or *in out* parameters with a function.

Now that we have seen function subprograms, we give a simplified EBNF definition of a function declaration and body. The definition of parameter_list is the same as it was for procedures. As with procedures, if you write the function in the declarative region of the main subprogram, the declaration may be omitted.

function_declaration	::=	function_specification;
function_specification	::=	**function** designator [parameter_list] **return** subtype_mark
designator	::=	*function*_identifier | operator_symbol

function_body	::=	function_specification **is**
		  [declarative_part]
		begin
		  sequence_of_statements
		end designator;

Let's look at another example of a function. One operation that is frequently used in calculating probabilities is the factorial. For example, 5 factorial (written 5! in mathematical notation) is $5 \times 4 \times 3 \times 2 \times 1$. Zero factorial is, by definition, equal to 1. A function to calculate a factorial has one integer parameter. We use repeated multiplication, decrementing the multiplier on each iteration, to compute the factorial of this parameter.

```
function Factorial (X : in Integer) return Integer is

   -- This function computes X!
```

```
   Result     : Integer;   -- Holds partial product
   Multiplier : Integer;   -- Used to form partial product and to end loop

begin  -- Factorial
   Multiplier := X;      -- Initialize multiplier to value
                         -- whose factorial is desired
   Result     := 1;      -- Initialize result
   Multiply_Loop:
   loop
      exit Multiply_Loop when Multiplier <= 1;
      Result     := Result * Multiplier;
      Multiplier := Multiplier - 1;
   end loop Multiply_Loop;
   return Result;
end Factorial;
```

Functions, like procedures, have their own declarative regions. Identifiers declared within these regions are local to the functions. Just as with procedures, we can overload function names. In addition to their formal parameter lists, the compiler can use the type of the result returned to distinguish between overloaded function names.

Boolean Functions

Functions are not restricted to returning numerical results; they can return a value of any data type. Boolean functions can be particularly useful when a branch or loop condition depends on some complex condition. Rather than code the condition directly into the if or exit statement, we can call a Boolean function to form the controlling expression. Using a well-chosen function name often makes programs easier to read. The if statement

```
exit Thickness_Validation_Loop    -- when the thickness is valid
     when (Numerator = 1 and (Denominator = 4 or Denominator = 2))
            or
          (Numerator = 3 and (Denominator = 8 or Denominator = 4))
            or
          (Numerator = 4 and Denominator = 4)
            or
          (Numerator = 5 and (Denominator = 8 or Denominator = 4))
```

is far less clear than

```
exit Thickness_Validation_Loop when Valid_Thickness(Numerator, Denominator);
```

The function Valid_Thickness looks like this:

```
function Valid_Thickness (Numerator   : in Integer;
                          Denominator : in Integer) return Boolean is
-- Return True if the fraction formed from the Numerator and
-- Denominator represent a valid plywood thickness

   Result : Boolean;
begin
   Result := (Numerator = 1 and (Denominator = 4 or Denominator = 2))
               or
             (Numerator = 3 and (Denominator = 8 or Denominator = 4))
               or
             (Numerator = 4 and Denominator = 4)
               or
             (Numerator = 5 and (Denominator = 8 or Denominator = 4));
   return Result;
end Valid_Thickness;
```

Operator Functions

The EBNF definition of a function given on page 321 uses the term *designator* for the name of the function. A designator can be either an identifier or an operator symbol. So far, we have used identifiers for all of our example function names. The following function body illustrates the use of the operator symbol + for a function name. Notice that the operator symbol is enclosed in quotation marks.

```
function "+" (Left  : in Integer;
              Right : in Float   ) return Float is

-- This function adds an Integer value and Float value

begin
   return  Float(Left) + Right;   -- Convert the integer to a float and add
end "+";
```

We can call this function like any other function, as shown in the following code fragment.

```
Total         : Float;
Length        : Float;
Circumference : Integer;
    .
    .
    .
Total := "+" (Circumference, Length);
```

When a function designator is an operator symbol, Ada permits us to use it just like any binary operator. We can write the assignment statement calling the function "+" to calculate the sum of Circumference and Length more conveniently as

```
Total := Circumference + Length;        -- Call to our function "+"
```

When called in this manner, the function designator is not enclosed in quotation marks. Because the operands in this expression are really actual parameters for the function "+," the order of the operands is important. The following assignment statement contains an illegal call to our function "+" because the first parameter is type Float and the second parameter is type Integer.

```
Total := Length + Circumference;        -- Illegal call to function "+"
```

You should employ operator symbols as function designators only when the objective of the function is compatible with the meaning of the operator. It is poor programming style, for example, to use "-" as a designator for a function that returns the smaller of two values.

As with procedures, we can overload function names only if the Ada compiler can tell them apart through their formal parameter list. In addition, the compiler can use the type of the result returned to distinguish between overloaded function designators.

When to Use Functions

There aren't any formal rules for determining when to use a procedure and when to use a function, but here are some guidelines.

1. If the module must return more than one value or modify any actual parameters, do not use a function.
2. If the module must perform I/O, do not use a function.
3. If there is only one value returned from the module and it is a Boolean value, a function is appropriate.
4. If there is only one value returned and that value is to be used immediately in an expression, a function is appropriate.
5. When in doubt, use a procedure. You can recode any function as a procedure, with the function name becoming an *out* parameter of the procedure.
6. If both a procedure and a function are acceptable, use the form you feel more comfortable using.

Standard Mathematical Functions

The package Ada.Numerics.Elementary_Functions contains many commonly used mathematical operations written as functions. These include square root, logarithms, exponentiation, and trigonometric functions. The functions in this package are listed in Appendix H. Here is a program that demonstrates their use.

```
with Ada.Text_IO;
with Ada.Float_Text_IO;
with Ada.Integer_Text_IO;
with Ada.Numerics;                        -- For the value of Pi
with Ada.Numerics.Elementary_Functions;   -- For the math functions
use  Ada.Numerics.Elementary_Functions;

procedure Trig_Table is

-- This program displays a table of Sines and Cosines
-- of values from 0 to 359 degrees

   Radians_Per_Degree : constant Float := 2.0 * Ada.Numerics.Pi / 360.0;

   Degrees  : Integer range 0..360;      -- Loop control variable

begin -- Trig Table
   -- Display table headings
   Ada.Text_IO.Put ("Degrees");
   Ada.Text_IO.Set_Col (To => 12);  -- Move writing marker to column 12
   Ada.Text_IO.Put ("Sine");
   Ada.Text_IO.Set_Col (To => 22);  -- Move writing marker to column 22
   Ada.Text_IO.Put ("Cosine");
   Ada.Text_IO.New_Line (2);

   -- Display the values
   Degrees := 0;
   Table_Loop:     -- This loop displays a trig table
   loop            -- Each iteration, one row of the table is displayed
      exit Table_Loop when Degrees > 359;
      -- Display degrees
      Ada.Integer_Text_IO.Put (Item => Degrees, Width => 5);
      -- Display the sin
      Ada.Text_IO.Set_Col (To => 10);
      Ada.Float_Text_IO.Put (Item => Sin( Radians_Per_Degree * Float(Degrees)),
                             Fore => 2,
                             Aft  => 4,
                             Exp  => 0);
```

```
      -- Display the cosine
      Ada.Text_IO.Set_Col (To => 21);
      Ada.Float_Text_IO.Put (Item => Cos( Radians_Per_Degree * Float(Degrees)),
                             Fore => 2,
                             Aft  => 4,
                             Exp  => 0);
      Ada.Text_IO.New_Line;
      Degrees := Degrees + 1;
   end loop Table_Loop;
end Trig_Table;
```

This program uses the resources of many packages in the standard library. The package Ada.Numerics contains a value of π accurate to 50 digits, and Ada.Numerics.Elementary_Functions contains the Sin and Cos functions. Notice our use of the use clause in Program Trig_Table. While we normally avoid using a use clause in our programs, we make an exception for the standard numeric libraries. In this case, we believe that prefixing makes the code more difficult to read.

We have also used a new procedure, Set_Col, from package Text_IO to help us set up the columns in the table. This procedure moves the writing marker (the cursor when displaying to a screen) to the given column.

The calls to functions Sin and Cos are made as actual parameters to the Put procedure. The results returned by these functions are passed directly to the display procedure.

PROBLEM-SOLVING CASE STUDY

Running Records

Specification

Problem The Roadrunner Track Club is attempting to set a new record for the number of kilometers run by the club in a week. The club has asked you to write a program that will calculate and display the number of kilometers run by each club member, the number of members reporting their distances, the total number of kilometers run by all members in the club, and the club member who ran the greatest distance.

Input
From the keyboard

- The name of the file containing running distance information.

PROBLEM-SOLVING CASE STUDY *cont'd.*

From the file

- One line per member containing the member's club identification number (a whole number between 1 and 1,000) and the seven distances (one for each day of the week). To mark the end of the data, the last line of the file contains only a zero.

Output A table with one line for each member of the club. Each line in this table contains the club member's ID number and the total number of kilometers run (to 2 decimal places).

A summary report containing the total number of members participating this week, the total number of kilometers run, and the ID and distance run by the member who ran the greatest distance.

Assumptions

- The data file exists and all its data is valid.
- The file name entered is valid and contains no more than 80 characters.
- There is at least one data set in the file before the sentinel value.
- There are no ties for the greatest distance run.

Design In most all of our case studies we give our final design with only a few words on the alternatives that we considered. As this is our first hierarchical design intended for implementation with procedures rather than a single flat program, we present more of the details of our design process, including first attempts that we later modify.

Basically the solution to this problem involves processing all of the club member data sets in the file and then displaying a summary report. We can use a sentinel-controlled loop to process all the members. Our first design of the main module is

Running (version 1) **Level 0**

```
Prepare Data File
loop
  Get Member ID from Data File
  exit when Member ID = 0
  Process One Member
Display Summary Statistics
Close Data File
```

PROBLEM-SOLVING CASE STUDY cont'd.

Because the abstract steps in this module will be implemented as separate procedures we must now add communications between modules to our algorithms and data models. We start with modeling the data in our main module. The objects explicitly given in the main module are a data file and a member identification number.

Name	Data Type and Range	Role
Data_File	File_Type	The data file
Member_ID	Integer, 0 to 1,000	ID for one club member

Which, if any, of these objects does the module Process One Member require to do its job? To answer this question we must decide exactly *what* Process One Member does. We do not have to know *how* this level 1 module accomplishes its task. Process One Member must display one line with the member's ID number and the total distance he or she ran. We obtained the member's ID in the main subprogram. We can pass it to Process One Member as an *in* parameter. Our main module does not have the total distance this member ran. We must calculate that value from the seven distances in the data file. Now we have two choices. We could have our main subprogram read the seven distances for the member and pass them or their sum to Process One Member. Or, we could pass the file to Process One Member and have it read and sum the data. Of course we must also pass the member ID that the main subprogram has already obtained from the file. We select the second method because it keeps all of the details of processing the data for one member in the module Process One Member.

Now that we know *what* Process One Member is to do, let's decide *how* it will do it. Here is an algorithm for this module that includes the data transferred *in* from the main subprogram:

Process One Member (version 1) **Level 1**

```
  in    ID, Data File
Distance := 0.0
Day Number := 1
loop
  exit when Day Number > 7
  Get Day Distance from Data File
  Add Day Distance to Distance
  Increment Day Number
Put ID
Put Distance
```

Here are the objects in module Process One Member.

PROBLEM-SOLVING CASE STUDY cont'd.

Name	Data Type and Range	Role
Distance	Float, 0 to 350	Kilometers run by this club member
Day_Number	Integer, 1 to 8	Loop control variable
Day_Distance	Float, 0 to 50	Running distance for one day
Data_File	File_Type	The data file
ID	Integer, 0 to 1,000	ID for current club member

Our next abstract step in the main module is Display Summary Statistics. The statistics we must display are the total number of members, the total kilometers run by all members, and the member who ran the most kilometers this week. Neither of the two modules we wrote calculate these values. Where should they be calculated? To calculate them in module Display Summary Statistics would require it to read the data in the file a second time. But we do not yet know how to reset the reading marker to the start of the file. Also, because input and output are such slow processes, we would prefer not to read the data a second time. So instead we decide to calculate the three values before calling module Display Summary Statistics.

We need to change the designs we worked on earlier. The main subprogram looks like a good place to determine the number of members running this week. Each iteration of the main subprogram loop processes one club member. We can include a counter that we increment each time through the loop. We can also add the distance that member ran to the club total. But where do we get that member's total? It was calculated in the module Process One Member. We simply need to pass that total *out* of Process One Member to the main subprogram.

In Chapter 5 we showed you a pattern for finding the largest or smallest value. We can modify that pattern to suit this problem. We are looking for the largest member total. Member weekly distances are available in module Process One Member and the main module so we can check in either place to see if the current member's weekly distance is greater than the greatest total seen so far. We decided to do this checking in the main subprogram (our reasoning is described in the background section on page 336 where we discuss functional cohesion). Our method for initializing the greatest value here is different than what we used in Chapter 5; we initialize the greatest distance to zero rather than to the first member processed.

Here then is our final design. We include a separate object model for each module. For every module that communicates information through parameters, we include a list of parameter names for each possible mode (*in*, *out*, and *in out*).

PROBLEM-SOLVING CASE STUDY cont'd.

Running (final design) **Level 0**

```
Prepare Data File
Member Count := 0
Club Distance := 0.0
Greatest := 0.0
Put Headings
loop
   Get Member ID from Data File
   exit when Member ID = 0
   Process One Member
   Increment Member Count
   Add Member Distance to Club Distance
   If Member Distance > Greatest then
      Greatest := Member Distance
      ID of Greatest := Member ID
Display Summary Statistics
Close Data File
```

Name	Data Type and Range	Role
Data_File	File_Type	The data file
Member_Count	Integer, nonnegative	Number of club members
Club_Distance	Float, nonnegative	Total kilometers run by club members
Greatest	Float, 0 to 350	Greatest distance run by a member
ID_Of_Greatest	Integer, 0 to 1,000	ID of member who ran greatest distance
Member_Distance	Float, 0 to 350	Kilometers run by one member this week
Member_ID	Integer, 0 to 1,000	ID for one club member

Prepare Data File **Level 1**

```
   out    File
Prompt user
Get File Name
Open File
```

Name	Data Type and Range	Role
File	File_Type	The data file
File_Name	String (1..80)	The name of the data file
Name_Length	Integer, 1 to 80	Number of characters in File_Name (used for slicing)

PROBLEM-SOLVING CASE STUDY cont'd.

```
Process One Member (final design)
  in       ID
  in out   Data File
  out      Distance
Distance := 0.0
Day Number := 1
loop
  exit when Day Number > 7
  Get Day Distance
  Add Day Distance to Distance
  Increment Day Number
Put ID
Put Distance
```

Name	Data Type and Range	Role
ID	Integer, 0 to 1,000	Club member number
Distance	Float, 0 to 350	Kilometers run by this club member
Day_Number	Integer, 1 to 8	Loop control variable
Day_Distance	Float, 0 to 50	Running distance for one day

```
Display Summary Statistics
  in    Total Distance, Member Count, Greatest Distance, ID of Greatest
Put Member Count
Put Total Distance
Put Greatest Distance
Put ID of Greatest
```

Name	Data Type and Range	Role
Total_Distance	Float, nonnegative	Total kilometers run by club members
Member_Count	Integer, nonnegative	Number of club members
Greatest_Distance	Float, 0 to 350	Greatest distance run by a member
ID_Of_Greatest	Integer, 0 to 1,000	Member who ran greatest distance

Module Structure Chart The structure chart for our design includes a new feature. The data passed between modules is shown along with arrows indicating the direction of data transfer.

PROBLEM-SOLVING CASE STUDY cont'd.

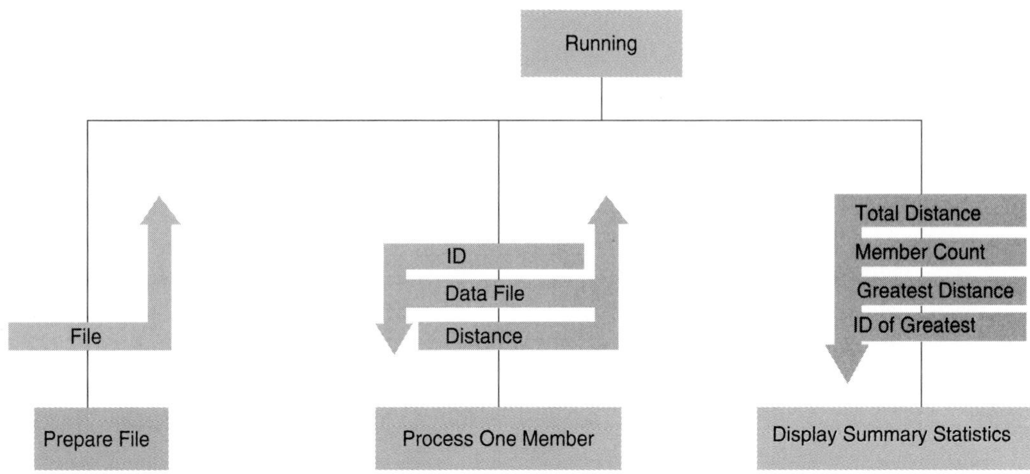

Implementation

```
with Ada.Text_IO;
with Ada.Integer_Text_IO;
with Ada.Float_Text_IO;

procedure Running is

-- This program calculates the weekly running totals for individuals
-- and the total distance for all runners

-- Assumptions
-- The file name entered is valid and contains no more than 80 characters.
-- The data file exists and all its data is valid.
-- There is at least one data set in the file before the sentinel value.
-- There are no ties for the greatest distance run.

   Running_Days_Per_Week : constant Integer := 7;

   ----------------------------------------------------------------------------
   procedure Prepare_File (File : out Ada.Text_IO.File_Type) is
   -- This procedure prompts for the name and opens File for input
   --
   -- Preconditions  : File name entered by user is valid
   --
   -- Postconditions : File is opened for input

      File_Name   : String (1..80);          -- Name of the data file
      Name_Length : Integer range 1..80;     -- Number of characters in File_Name
```

PROBLEM-SOLVING CASE STUDY cont'd.

```
begin -- Prepare File
   Ada.Text_IO.Put ("Please enter the name of the file containing" &
                    " this week's running data");
   Ada.Text_IO.New_Line;
   Ada.Text_IO.Get_Line (Item => File_Name,
                         Last => Name_Length);
   Ada.Text_IO.Open (File => File,
                     Mode => Ada.Text_IO.In_File,
                     Name => File_Name (1..Name_Length));
   Ada.Text_IO.New_Line (2);
end Prepare_File;

----------------------------------------------------------------------------
procedure Process_One_Member (ID        : in     Integer;
                              Data_File : in out Ada.Text_IO.File_Type;
                              Distance  :    out Float) is
-- This procedure processes the running data for a single club member
--
-- Preconditions  : Data_File is open for input
--                  There are seven values available in Data_File
--                  Values in Data_File are valid
--
-- Postconditions : Distance is total distance run by ID this week
--                  ID and Distance are displayed on a single line

   Day_Number   : Integer range 1..8;         -- Loop control variable
   Day_Distance : Float   range 0.0..50.0;    -- Distance run in one day

begin -- Process One Member
   Distance   := 0.0;    -- Initialize sums and
   Day_Number := 1;      -- counters

   Day_Loop:  -- Sum the running distances for the week
   loop       -- Each iteration, one day of running is processed
      exit Day_Loop when Day_Number > Running_Days_Per_Week;
      Ada.Float_Text_IO.Get (File => Data_File, Item => Day_Distance);
      Distance   := Distance + Day_Distance;    -- Update sum
      Day_Number := Day_Number + 1;             -- Update counter
   end loop Day_Loop;

   -- Display member data
   Ada.Integer_Text_IO.Put (Item => ID,  Width => 6);
   Ada.Float_Text_IO.Put   (Item => Distance,
                            Fore => 13,
                            Aft  => 1,
                            Exp  => 0);
   Ada.Text_IO.New_Line;
end Process_One_Member;
```

PROBLEM-SOLVING CASE STUDY *cont'd.*

```
---------------------------------------------------------------------------
procedure Display_Summary_Statistics (Total_Distance    : in Float;
                                      Member_Count      : in Integer;
                                      Greatest_Distance : in Float;
                                      ID_of_Greatest    : in Integer) is
-- This procedure displays the club's weekly summary statistics
--
-- Preconditions  : none
--
-- Postconditions : The four parameters are displayed

begin -- Display Summary Statistics
   Ada.Text_IO.New_Line (2);
   Ada.Integer_Text_IO.Put (Item => Member_Count, Width => 1);
   Ada.Text_IO.Put (" club members ran ");
   Ada.Float_Text_IO.Put (Item => Total_Distance,
                          Fore => 1,
                          Aft  => 1,
                          Exp  => 0);
   Ada.Text_IO.Put (" kilometers this week.");
   Ada.Text_IO.New_Line;
   Ada.Text_IO.Put ("Member number ");
   Ada.Integer_Text_IO.Put (Item => ID_of_Greatest, Width => 1);
   Ada.Text_IO.Put (" ran the greatest distance: ");
   Ada.Float_Text_IO.Put (Item => Greatest_Distance,
                          Fore => 1,
                          Aft  => 1,
                          Exp  => 0);
   Ada.Text_IO.Put (" kilometers.");
end Display_Summary_Statistics;


------------------------------------------------------------------------------

   Data_File       : Ada.Text_IO.File_Type;          -- The data file
   Member_Count    : Integer range 0..Integer'Last;  -- Number of club members
   Club_Distance   : Float   range 0.0..Float'Last;  -- Kilometers run by club
   Greatest        : Float   range 0.0..350.0;       -- Greatest distance run
   ID_Of_Greatest  : Integer range 1..1000;          -- Greatest distance runner
   Member_Distance : Float   range 0.0..350.0;       -- Kilometers for one member
   Member_ID       : Integer range 0..1000;          -- ID for one club member

begin -- Running
   Prepare_File (Data_File);

   Club_Distance  := 0.0;    -- Initialize sums,
   Greatest       := 0.0;    -- extremes, and
```

PROBLEM-SOLVING CASE STUDY cont'd.

```
   Member_Count    := 0;      -- counters

   Ada.Text_IO.Put ("Member ID     Kilometers"); -- Heading
   Ada.Text_IO.New_Line (2);

   Member_Loop:  -- Process the running totals of all club members
   loop          -- Each iteration, one member is processed
      Ada.Integer_Text_IO.Get (File => Data_File, Item => Member_ID);
      exit Member_Loop when Member_ID = 0;   -- exit on sentinel

      Process_One_Member (ID        => Member_ID,
                          Data_File => Data_File,
                          Distance  => Member_Distance);

      -- Update club statistics
      Member_Count  := Member_Count  + 1;
      Club_Distance := Club_Distance + Member_Distance;
      if Member_Distance > Greatest then
         Greatest        := Member_Distance;
         ID_Of_Greatest  := Member_ID;
      end if;
   end loop Member_Loop;

   Display_Summary_Statistics (Total_Distance    => Club_Distance,
                               Member_Count      => Member_Count,
                               Greatest_Distance => Greatest,
                               ID_of_Greatest    => ID_Of_Greatest);
   Ada.Text_IO.Close (Data_File);
end Running;
```

Here is the output from a sample run of this program. User input is shown in color.

```
Please enter the name of the file containing this weeks running data
RunningData.txt

Member ID     Kilometers

    15           28.0
    73            7.1
    92           89.0
    32           14.0
    14           29.2
    11           56.0

6 club members ran 223.3 kilometers this week.
Member number 92 ran the greatest distance: 89.0 kilometers.
```

PROBLEM-SOLVING CASE STUDY *cont'd.*

Beginning programmers often select the wrong mode for their parameters. So be sure that you study the parameter modes used for each parameter in this program. Because *in out* mode is meant for values that are copied in, modified, and copied back out you may wonder why we chose this mode for parameter File in procedure Process_One_Member. While this procedure does not change the file by writing to it, it does change the file's reading marker. So we copy in the file,* modify its reading marker, and copy it back out.

Testing We have included preconditions and postconditions in each of our procedures that we can use to perform an algorithm trace. After we are convinced that our algorithm meets these assertions, we are ready to compose test data sets for execution tests.

What shall we use for input in our test runs? Don't just use a single data file to test this program. Try data files with data for just one club member, two members, and many members. Try data files with the member who ran the most kilometers in the first line, the last line, and a middle line.

The output from this program, given valid test data, is a report consisting of two sections. The first section is the individual member weekly running distance totals. There should be one line in this section for each line of input. Check that the first and last lines of data processed correctly—it's in these lines that errors in loop control most often appear. Compare the individual members' weekly totals in this section with your hand-calculated results. The second section is the member count, the total distance run by the entire club, and the ID and distance run by the member with the greatest weekly total. Again compare these values with your hand-calculated result. These tests are based on our knowledge of the loops used in this program and thus are a form of code coverage.

SOFTWARE ENGINEERING TIP

Control Abstraction, Functional Cohesion, and Communication Complexity

Our design for Program Running contains two loops: one in the main module that processes members and one in module Process One Member that processes one day's running distance. If we had implemented our design without procedures, these two loops would be nested. Our implementation with procedures preserves the single loop

*Ada does not copy the entire file when it copies a file parameter. Only a reference to the file is copied.

PROBLEM-SOLVING CASE STUDY cont'd.

per module of our design. A good design hides the complexity of the program by reducing each of the major control structures to an abstract action performed by a procedure call. In other words, one major control structure per module. This aspect of a design is called **control abstraction.**

Control abstraction The separation of the logical properties of an action from its implementation. Also called procedural abstraction.

Control abstraction can serve as a guideline for deciding which modules to code as subprograms and which to code directly. If a module contains a control structure more complex than a simple branch, it should almost certainly be a subprogram. For example, procedure Display_Summary_Statistics lacks control abstraction. In fact, we could substitute calls to the I/O procedures for the call to Display_Summary_Statistics. If a module does not contain a control structure, you must consider other factors. Is it lengthy or is it called from more than one place? Is it something that might be changed in the future?

Somewhat related to control abstraction is the concept of **functional cohesion:** a module should perform exactly one abstract action. If you can state the function that a module performs in one sentence with no conjunctions, then it is highly cohesive. A module that has more than one primary purpose is lacking in cohesion.

Functional cohesion A property of a module that indicates how closely all its steps are directed toward solving just one problem. Higher is better.

A module that only partially fulfills a purpose also lacks cohesion. You should combine such a module with whatever other modules are directly related to it. For example, it would make no sense to have a separate procedure for displaying the running club totals and another for displaying the information on the member who ran the greatest distance. Displaying the summary statistics is one abstract action.

A third and related aspect of a module's design is its **communication complexity**–the amount of information that passes through a module's interface. A module's communication complexity is often an indicator of its cohesiveness. Usually, if a module requires a large number of parameters, it is either trying to accomplish too much or it is only partially fulfilling a purpose. You should step back and see whether there is an alternative way to divide the problem so that a minimal amount of information is communicated between modules.

Communication complexity The amount of information that passes through a module's interface. Lower is better.

PROBLEM-SOLVING CASE STUDY

Starship Weight and Balance

Specification

Problem The company you work for has just upgraded its fleet of corporate aircraft by adding the ultramodern Beechcraft Starship-1.* As with any airplane, it is essential that the pilot know the total weight of the loaded plane at takeoff and its center of gravity. If the plane weighs too much, it won't be able to lift off. If its center of gravity is outside the limits established for the plane, it might be impossible to control. Either situation can lead to a crash. You have been asked to write a program that will determine the weight and center of gravity of this new plane.

Input Number of crew members, number of passengers, weight of closet contents, baggage weight, fuel in gallons.

Output Total weight, center of gravity.

Assumptions

- The average passenger weighs 170 pounds.
- Fuel weighs 6.7 pounds per gallon.
- Passengers fill the seat rows in the following order: row 2, row 1, row 3, and row 4.

Design As with most real-world problems, the basic solution is simple, but it is complicated by special cases. We use functions to hide the complexity so that the main subprogram remains simple.

The total weight is basically the sum of the empty weight of the airplane plus the weight of each of the following: crew members, passengers, baggage, contents of the storage closet, and fuel. We use the standard average weight of a person, 170 pounds, to compute the total weight of the people. The weight of the baggage and the contents of the closet are obtained from the user. Fuel weighs 6.7 pounds per gallon. Thus, total weight is equal to

```
Total Weight = Empty Weight
               + (Crew + Passengers) × 170
               + Baggage Weight + Closet Contents Weight + Fuel × 6.7
```

*The avionics software (software that controls the operation of the aircraft during flight) of nearly every aircraft in the world, including the Beechcraft Starship, is written in Ada.

PROBLEM-SOLVING CASE STUDY cont'd.

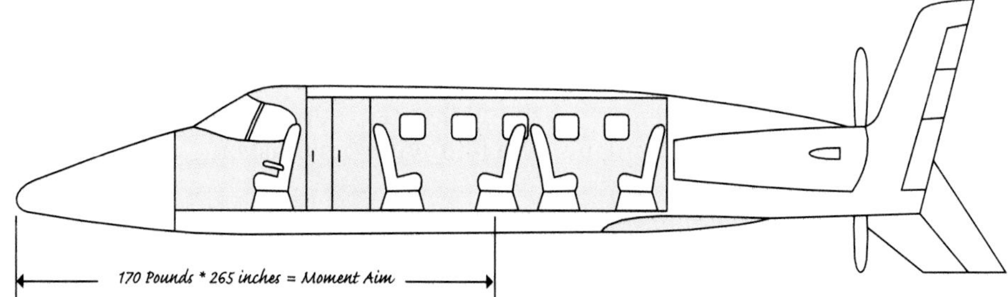

FIGURE 6-8 Moment Arm for Passengers Sitting in Row 2

To compute the center of gravity, we first multiply each weight by its distance from the front of the airplane. We then sum the products of the multiplications, called moment arms or simply moments, and divide that sum by the total weight (see Figure 6-8). The formula is:

```
Center Of Gravity =   ( Empty Moment
                      + Crew Moment
                      + Passenger Moment
                      + Cargo Moment
                      + Fuel Moment ) / Total Weight
```

The Starship-1 manual gives the distance from the front of the plane to the crew's seats, closet, baggage compartment, and fuel tanks. There are four rows of passenger seats, so the calculation for center of gravity depends on where the individual passengers sit. We have to make some assumptions about how passengers will arrange themselves. Each row has two seats. The most popular seats are in row 2 because they are near the entrance and face forward. Once row 2 is filled, passengers usually take seats in row 1, facing their traveling companions. Row 3 is usually the next to fill up, even though it faces backward because row 4 is a fold-down bench seat that is less comfortable than the armchairs in the forward rows. The following table gives the distance from the nose of the plane to each of the "loading stations."

Loading Station	Distance from Nose (inches)
Crew seats	143
Row 1 seats	219
Row 2 seats	265
Row 3 seats	295
Row 4 seats	341
Closet	182
Baggage	386

PROBLEM-SOLVING CASE STUDY cont'd.

The distance for the fuel varies because there are several tanks and the tanks are in different places. As fuel is added to the plane, it automatically flows into the different tanks so that the center of gravity changes as they are filled. There are four formulas for computing the distance from the nose to the "center" of the fuel tanks, depending on how much fuel is being loaded into the plane. The following table lists these distance formulas.

Gallons of Fuel (G)	*Distance (D) Formula*
0–59	$D = 314.6$
60–360	$D = 305.8 + (-0.01233 \times (G - 60))$
361–520	$D = 303.0 + (-0.12500 \times (G - 361))$
521–565	$D = 323.0 + (-0.04444 \times (G - 521))$

We can define one function for each of the different moments, and we'll call these functions Crew_Moment, Passenger_Moment, Cargo_Moment, and Fuel_Moment. We then compute the center of gravity with the formula we gave earlier and the following parameters:

```
Center_Of_Gravity = ( Crew_Moment (Crew)
                    + Passenger_Moment (Passengers)
                    + Cargo_Moment (Closet, Baggage)
                    + Fuel_Moment (Fuel) + Empty_Moment) / Total_Weight
```

The empty weight of the Starship is 9,887 pounds, and its empty center of gravity is 319 inches from the front of the airplane. Thus the empty moment is 3,153,953 inch-pounds. These values are included along with others from the Starship manual in the following table of constants.

Name	**Value**	**Role**
Average_Weight	170	Average weight of a person
Lbs_Per_Gal	6.7	Jet-A fuel weighs 6.7 lbs per gal.
Empty_Weight	9,887	Standard empty weight
Empty_Center	319	Standard empty center or gravity
Empty_Moment	Empty_Center * Empty_Weight	Standard empty moment
Max_Closet	160	Maximum weight (lbs) of closet contents
Max_Baggage	525	Maximum weight (lbs) of baggage contents

PROBLEM-SOLVING CASE STUDY cont'd.

Min_Weight	Empty_Weight +	Minimum flying weight
	1 * Average_Weight +	one crew
	10 * Lbs_Per_Gal	ten gallons of fuel
Max_Weight	Empty_Weight +	Maximum flying weight
	10 * Average_Weight +	two crew, eight passengers
	565 * Lbs_Per_Gal +	565 gallons of fuel
	Max_Closet + Max_Baggage	all the luggage

We now have enough information to write the algorithm to solve this problem. In addition to printing the results, we'll also print a warning message that states the assumptions of the program and tells the pilot to double-check the results by hand if the weight or center of gravity is near the allowable limits.

Starship **Level 0**

Get Data
Total Weight := Empty Weight + (Passengers + Crew) * Average_Weight + Baggage +
    Closet + Fuel * Lbs_Per_Gal
Center Of Gravity := (Crew Moment(Crew) + Passenger Moment (Passengers) +
    Cargo Moment(Closet, Baggage) + Fuel Moment(Fuel) +
    Empty Moment) / Total Weight
Print Total Weight and Center of Gravity
Print Warning

Name	Data Type and Range	Role
Crew	Integer, 1 to 2	Number of crew members
Passengers	Integer, 0 to 8	Number of passengers
Closet	Float, 0 to Max_Closet	Weight (lbs) of closet contents
Baggage	Float, 0 to Max_Baggage	Weight (lbs) of baggage compartment contents
Fuel	Float, 10 to 565	Gallons of fuel
Total_Weight	Float, Min_Weight to Max_Weight	Weight of the loaded plane
Center_Of_Gravity	Float	Center of gravity of loaded Starship

Get Data **Level 1**

out Crew, Passengers, Closet, Baggage, Fuel
Prompt for input data
Get Crew, Passengers, Closet, Baggage, and Fuel

PROBLEM-SOLVING CASE STUDY cont'd.

Name	Data Type and Range	Role
Crew	Integer, 1 to 2	Number of crew members
Passengers	Integer, 0 to 8	Number of passengers
Closet	Float, 0 to Max_Closet	Weight (lbs) of closet contents
Baggage	Float, 0 to Max_Baggage	Weight (lbs) of baggage compartment contents
Fuel	Integer, 10 to 565	Gallons of fuel

Crew Moment **Level 1**

```
   in      Crew
Return Crew * Average_Weight * Crew_Distance
```

Variable Name	Data Type and Range	Role
Crew	Integer, 1 to 2	Number of crew members

Constant Name	Value	Role
Crew_Distance	143	Distance from front of plane to crew seats
Average_Weight	170	Average weight of a person

Passenger Moment **Level 1**

```
   in      Passengers
Moment := 0.0
Passengers Left := Passengers
if Passengers Left > 6 then
   Moment := Moment + (Passengers_Left - 6) * Average_Weight * Row4
   Passengers Left := 6
if Passengers Left > 4 then
   Moment := Moment+(Passengers_Left -4) * Average_Weight * Row3
   Passengers Left := 4
if Passengers Left >2 then
   Moment := Moment+(Passengers_Left -2) * Average_Weight * Row2
   Passengers := 2
if Passengers Left > 0 then
   Moment := Moment+Passengers_Left * Average_Weight * Row1
Return Moment
```

PROBLEM-SOLVING CASE STUDY cont'd.

Variable Name	Data Type and Range	Role
Passengers	Integer, 0 to 8	Number of passengers on the plane
Passengers_Left	Integer, 0 to 8	Number of passengers whose moments have not yet been calculated
Moment	Float	The passenger moment arm (inch-pounds)

Constant Name	Value	Role
Row1	219	Distance of row 1 seats from front of plane
Row2	265	Distance of row 2 seats from front of plane
Row3	295	Distance of row 3 seats from front of plane
Row4	341	Distance of row 4 seats from front of plane
Average_Weight	170	Average weight of a person

Cargo Moment **Level 1**

```
    in    Closet, Baggage
Return Closet * Closet_Distance + Baggage * Baggage_Distance
```

Variable Name	Data Type and Range	Role
Closet	Float, 0 to Max_Closet	Weight (lbs) of closet contents
Baggage	Float, 0 to Max_Baggage	Weight (lbs) of baggage compartment contents

Constant Name	Value	Role
Closet_Distance	182	Distance from front of plane to closet
Baggage_Distance	386	Distance from front of plane to baggage compartment

PROBLEM-SOLVING CASE STUDY cont'd.

Fuel Moment **Level 1**

```
   in      Fuel
Fuel Weight := Fuel * Lbs_Per_Gal
if Fuel < 60 then
   Fuel Distance := Fuel * 314.6
elsif Fuel < 361 then
   Fuel Distance := 305.8 + (-0.01233 * Fuel - 60)
elsif Fuel < 521 then
   Fuel Distance := 303.0 + (-0.125 * Fuel - 361)
else
   Fuel Distance := 323.0 + (-0.04444 * Fuel - 521)
Return Fuel Distance * Fuel Weight
```

Name	Data Type and Range	Role
Fuel	Float, 10 to 565	Gallons of fuel
Fuel_Weight	Float	Pounds of fuel
Fuel_Distance	Float	Distance from front of plane to fuel center of gravity

Module Structure Chart

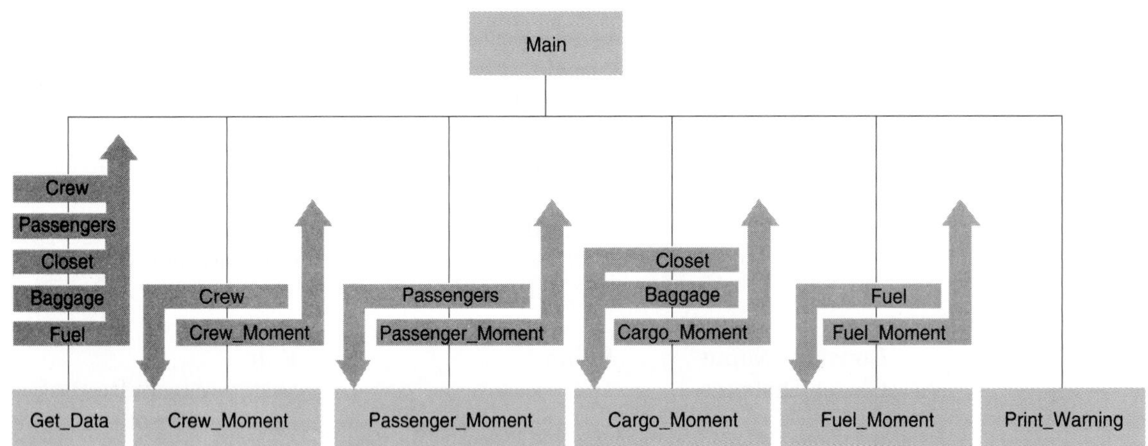

Implementation

```
with Ada.Text_IO;
with Ada.Integer_Text_IO;
with Ada.Float_Text_IO;

procedure Starship is
```

PROBLEM-SOLVING CASE STUDY *cont'd.*

```
-- This program computes the total weight and center of gravity of a Beechcraft
-- Starship-1, given the number of crew members and passengers, weight of closet
-- and baggage compartment cargo, and gallons of fuel loaded.

-- Assumptions
   -- The average passenger weighs 170 pounds.
   -- Passengers fill the seat rows in the order: row 2, row 1, row 3 and row 4.

-- The output is approximate and should be hand checked
-- if the Starship-1 is loaded near its operational limits.

   -- Constants

   Average_Weight : constant Float := 170.0;  -- Average person weighs 170 lbs.
   Lbs_Per_Gal    : constant Float := 6.7;    -- Jet-A weighs 6.7 lbs per gal.
   Empty_Weight   : constant Float := 9887.0; -- In pounds
   Empty_Center   : constant Float := 319.0;  -- Center of gravity in inches
   Empty_Moment   : constant Float :=         -- In inch-pounds
                     Empty_Center * Empty_Weight;
   Max_Closet     : constant Float := 160.0;  -- Max lbs in closet
   Max_Baggage    : constant Float := 525.0;  -- Max lbs in baggage compartment
   Min_Weight     : constant Float :=         -- Minimum flying weight
                      Empty_Weight +          -- empty plane
                      Average_Weight +        -- one crew member
                      10.0 * Lbs_Per_Gal;     -- ten gallons of fuel
   Max_Weight     : constant Float :=         -- Maximum flying weight
                      Empty_Weight +          -- empty plane
                      10.0 * Average_Weight + -- two crew, eight passengers
                      565.0 * Lbs_Per_Gal +   -- 565 gallons of fuel
                      Max_Closet + Max_Baggage; -- all the luggage

   ----------------------------------------------------------------------------
   procedure Get_Data (Crew       : out Integer;  -- Number of crew
                       Passengers : out Integer;  -- Number of passengers
                       Closet     : out Float;    -- Pounds in closet
                       Baggage    : out Float;    -- Pounds in baggage
                       Fuel       : out Float) is -- Gallons of fuel

   -- This procedure prompts for input of Crew, Passengers, Closet,
   -- Baggage, and Fuel values and returns the five values entered.

   -- Preconditions  : None
   --
   -- Postconditions : The five parameters are given the values entered
```

PROBLEM-SOLVING CASE STUDY cont'd.

```
begin    -- Get Data
   Ada.Text_IO.Put ("Enter the number of crew.");
   Ada.Text_IO.New_Line;
   Ada.Integer_Text_IO.Get (Crew);
   Ada.Text_IO.New_Line;

   Ada.Text_IO.Put ("Enter the number of passengers.");
   Ada.Text_IO.New_Line;
   Ada.Integer_Text_IO.Get (Passengers);
   Ada.Text_IO.New_Line;

   Ada.Text_IO.Put ("Enter the pounds of cargo in the closet");
   Ada.Text_IO.New_Line;
   Ada.Float_Text_IO.Get (Closet);
   Ada.Text_IO.New_Line;

   Ada.Text_IO.Put ("Enter the pounds of baggage in the aft compartment");
   Ada.Text_IO.New_Line;
   Ada.Float_Text_IO.Get (Baggage);
   Ada.Text_IO.New_Line;

   Ada.Text_IO.Put ("Enter the number of U.S. gallons of fuel loaded");
   Ada.Text_IO.New_Line;
   Ada.Float_Text_IO.Get (Fuel);

end Get_Data;

----------------------------------------------------------------------------
function Crew_Moment (Crew : in Integer)  return Float is

-- Given the number of crew members, this function computes the
-- crew moment arm in inch-pounds

-- Preconditions  : Crew is 1 or 2

-- Postconditions : The crew moment arm is returned

   Crew_Distance : constant Float := 143.0;   -- Distance of crew seats to front

begin  -- Crew Moment
   return  Float(Crew) * Average_Weight * Crew_Distance;
end Crew_Moment;

----------------------------------------------------------------------------
function Passenger_Moment (Passengers : in Integer)  return Float is
```

PROBLEM-SOLVING CASE STUDY cont'd.

```
-- Given the number of passengers, this function computes the
-- passenger moment arm in inch-pounds
--
-- This function assumes that the first two passengers sit in row 2, the second
-- two in row 1, the next two in row 3, and remaining passenges in row 4

-- Preconditions  : Passengers is between 0 and 8

-- Postconditions : The passenger moment arm in inch-pounds is returned

   Row1 : constant Float := 219.0;   -- Distance of row 1 seats from front
   Row2 : constant Float := 265.0;   -- Distance of row 2 seats from front
   Row3 : constant Float := 295.0;   -- Distance of row 3 seats from front
   Row4 : constant Float := 341.0;   -- Distance of row 4 seats from front

   Moment          : Float;               -- Sum of passenger moments
   Passengers_Left : Integer range 0..8;  -- Number of passengers whose moments
                                          -- have not yet been calculated
begin  -- Passenger Moment
   Passengers_Left := Passengers;   -- At this point, no passenger moments have
   Moment          := 0.0;          -- been calculated

   if Passengers_Left > 6  then          -- Calculate for passengers 7 and 8
      Moment := Moment + Float(Passengers_Left - 6) * Average_Weight * Row4;
      Passengers_Left := 6;              -- 6 passengers remain
   end if;
   if Passengers_Left > 4  then          -- Calculate for passengers 5 and 6
      Moment := Moment + Float(Passengers_Left - 4) * Average_Weight * Row3;
      Passengers_Left := 4;              -- 4 passengers remain
   end if;
   if Passengers_Left > 2  then          -- Calculate for passengers 3 and 4
      Moment := Moment + Float(Passengers_Left - 2) * Average_Weight * Row1;
      Passengers_Left := 2;              -- Two passengers remain
   end if;
   if Passengers_Left > 0  then          -- Calculate for passengers 1 and 2
      Moment := Moment + Float(Passengers_Left) * Average_Weight * Row2;
   end if;
   return Moment;
end Passenger_Moment;

-----------------------------------------------------------------------------
function Cargo_Moment (Closet  : in Float;   -- Pounds in closet
                       Baggage : in Float)   -- Pounds in baggage compartment
                       return Float is
```

PROBLEM-SOLVING CASE STUDY cont'd.

```
-- This function computes the total moment arm in inch-pounds for
-- cargo loaded into the front closet and aft baggage compartment

-- Preconditions  : Closet  is between 0 and Max_Closet
--                  Baggage is between 0 and Max_Baggage
--
-- Postconditions : The total moment for cargo is returned

   Closet_Distance  : constant Float := 182.0; -- Distance from front to closet
   Baggage_Distance : constant Float := 386.0; -- Distance from front to aft
                                               -- baggage compartment
begin  -- Cargo Moment
   return Closet * Closet_Distance  +  Baggage * Baggage_Distance;
end Cargo_Moment;

-------------------------------------------------------------------------------
function Fuel_Moment (Fuel : in Float)  return Float is

-- Given the gallons of fuel on board, this function computes the
-- moment arm in inch-pounds for this fuel
--
-- Due to fuel tank layout, there are four different formulas to calculate
-- the fuel moment.  The formula used is selected on the basis of the
-- amount of fuel on board.

-- Preconditions  : Fuel is between 10 and 565 gallons
--
-- Postconditions : The moment arm for the fuel is returned

   Fuel_Weight   : Float;       -- Weight of fuel in pounds
   Fuel_Distance : Float;       -- Distance from front of plane

begin  -- Fuel Moment
   Fuel_Weight := Fuel * Lbs_Per_Gal;

   -- Based on the amount of fuel, select one of four formulas to
   -- calculate the center of gravity of the fuel.
   if Fuel < 60.0  then
      Fuel_Distance := Fuel * 314.6;
   elsif Fuel < 361.0  then
      Fuel_Distance := 305.8 + (-0.01233 * (Fuel - 60.0));
   elsif Fuel < 521.0  then
      Fuel_Distance := 303.0 + ( 0.12500 * (Fuel - 361.0));
   elsif Fuel < 565.0  then
      Fuel_Distance := 323.0 + (-0.04444 * (Fuel - 521.0));
   end if;
```

PROBLEM-SOLVING CASE STUDY *cont'd.*

```
   return  Fuel_Distance * Fuel_Weight;
end Fuel_Moment;

-----------------------------------------------------------------------------
procedure Print_Warning is

-- This procedure warns the user of assumptions made by the
-- program and when to double-check the program's results

-- Preconditions  : None
--
-- Postconditions : The warning message is printed

begin
   Ada.Text_IO.Put ("Notice:  This program assumes that passengers fill");
   Ada.Text_IO.New_Line;
   Ada.Text_IO.Put ("  the seat rows in order 2, 1, 3, 4, and that each");
   Ada.Text_IO.New_Line;
   Ada.Text_IO.Put ("  passenger and crew weighs 170 pounds.");
   Ada.Text_IO.New_Line;
   Ada.Text_IO.Put ("  The center of gravity calculations for fuel are");
   Ada.Text_IO.New_Line;
   Ada.Text_IO.Put ("  approximate.  If the aircraft is loaded near its");
   Ada.Text_IO.New_Line;
   Ada.Text_IO.Put ("  limits, the pilot's operating handbook should be");
   Ada.Text_IO.New_Line;
   Ada.Text_IO.Put ("  used to compute weight and center of gravity ");
   Ada.Text_IO.New_Line;
   Ada.Text_IO.Put ("  with more accuracy.");
   Ada.Text_IO.New_Line;
end Print_Warning;


-------------------------------------------------------------------------------
   Crew          : Integer range 1..2;          -- Number of crew on board
   Passengers    : Integer range 0..8;          -- Number of passengers
   Closet        : Float range 0.0..Max_Closet;  -- Weight in closet
   Baggage       : Float range 0.0..Max_Baggage; -- Weight in baggage compartment
   Fuel          : Float range 10.0..565.0;     -- Gallons of fuel
   Total_Weight  : Float range                  -- Total weight of loaded plane
                       Min_Weight..Max_Weight;
   Center_Of_Gravity : Float;              -- Center of gravity of loaded Starship
```

PROBLEM-SOLVING CASE STUDY cont'd.

```
begin  -- Starship Weight
   Get_Data (Crew       => Crew,
             Passengers => Passengers,
             Closet     => Closet,
             Baggage    => Baggage,
             Fuel       => Fuel);
   Ada.Text_IO.New_Line (2);

   Total_Weight := Empty_Weight +
                   Float(Passengers + Crew) * Average_Weight +
                   Baggage + Closet +
                   Fuel * Lbs_Per_Gal;

   Center_Of_Gravity := (Empty_Moment +
                         Crew_Moment(Crew) +
                         Passenger_Moment(Passengers) +
                         Cargo_Moment(Closet, Baggage) +
                         Fuel_Moment(Fuel) )  /  Total_Weight;

   Ada.Text_IO.Put ("Total weight of the Starship is ");
   Ada.Integer_Text_IO.Put (Item => Integer(Total_Weight), Width => 1);
   Ada.Text_IO.Put (" pounds.");
   Ada.Text_IO.New_Line (2);
   Ada.Text_IO.Put ("Center of gravity of the Starship is ");
   Ada.Integer_Text_IO.Put (Item => Integer(Center_Of_Gravity), Width => 1);
   Ada.Text_IO.Put (" inches from the front of the plane.");
   Ada.Text_IO.New_Line(2);

   Print_Warning;

end Starship;
```

Testing Because the output of this program can be used to make decisions that could result in property damage, injury, or death, it is essential that the program be tested thoroughly. Start by using the subprogram preconditions and postconditions to do an algorithm trace. Several of the preconditions mention specific ranges on parameters. As we cannot specify a range with the type given for a parameter, we specified the valid values in our preconditions. As the local variables and main subprogram variables include ranges, it is easy to show that all the preconditions concerning parameter ranges are satisfied. The program will halt with a CONSTRAINT_ERROR exception if the user enters any values outside of the given ranges. We prefer to halt the program than to allow it to continue and produce incorrect output.

If possible, check the program's output against sample calculations done by experienced pilots for actual flights. Otherwise, compare the output to what you calculate by hand. Test the program by trying maximum and minimum input values in different combinations. In addition to this data coverage approach, you should design test data sets to check each of the different formulas used in calculating moments. If pilots were really going to use this program, we should include data validation loops in procedure Get_Data. While the ranges we used in our variable declarations ensure the program will not output results calculated from out-of-range data, giving a pilot multiple opportunities to enter valid data makes the program easier to use.

Testing and Debugging

The combination of the formal parameters defined in a subprogram, along with the actual parameters that are passed to it, constitutes the interface between the subprogram and the caller. Errors that occur with the use of subprograms usually are due to an incorrect interface between the calling subprogram and the called subprogram.

Mismatched actual and formal parameter lists can be one source of errors. The Ada compiler will ensure that the lists have the same number of parameters and that they match in type. It's the programmer's responsibility, however, to verify that each actual parameter list contains the correct variables. This is a matter of comparing the formal parameter definition to the actual parameter list in every call to the procedure. This job is much easier if you

1. give each formal parameter a distinct name
2. describe its function in a comment
3. use named association

You can avoid mistakes in writing an actual parameter list by using descriptive variable names in the main subprogram because they clearly state exactly what information you are passing to a procedure.

Another source of error is the failure to ensure that the preconditions for a module are met before it is called. For example, if a procedure assumes that a parameter value is positive when it is called, then the program must ensure that this is true before making the call to the procedure. If a procedure behaves incorrectly, review its preconditions, then trace the program execution up to the point of the call to verify them. You can waste a lot of time trying to locate a bug in a correct procedure when the error is really in the part of the program prior to the call.

If the parameters match and you have established the preconditions correctly, then the source of the error is most likely in the procedure itself.

Trace the procedure to verify that it transforms the preconditions into the proper postconditions. Check that all local variables are initialized properly.

One helpful technique to use while debugging a procedure is to insert debug calls to Put procedures to print the values of the parameters immediately before and after calls to the procedure. Sometimes it is also helpful to print the values of all local variables at the end of the procedure. This information provides a "snapshot" of the procedure (a picture of its status at a particular moment in time) at its two most critical points, and it is useful in verifying traces.

To test a procedure thoroughly, you must arrange the input data so that each precondition is pushed to its limits, and then you must verify the postconditions. For example, if a procedure requires a parameter to be within a certain range, try calling the procedure with values within that range and at its extremes.

Because functions are simply another form of subprogram, you can apply the same testing and debugging techniques that you use for procedures to functions. The only difference is that you must use an expression, rather than a procedure call, in a driver to call the function.

Stubs and Drivers

One of the advantages of a modular design is that you can test the design long before the code has been written for all of the modules. If we test each module individually, then we can assemble the modules into a complete program with much greater confidence that the program is correct. In this section we will introduce a technique for testing a module separately.

Suppose you are given the code for a module and your job is to test it. How would you test a single module by itself? First of all, it must be called by something (unless it is the main subprogram). Second, it may have calls to other modules that aren't available to you. To test the module, you must fill in these missing links.

When a module contains calls to other modules, we can write dummy procedures called **stubs** to satisfy those calls. A stub usually consists of a call to a Put procedure that prints a message like "Procedure such-and-such just got called." Even though the stub is a dummy, it allows us to determine whether the procedure is called at the right time by the program or calling procedure.

Stub A dummy procedure or function that assists in testing part of a program. A stub has the same name and interface as a procedure or function that would be called by the part of the program being tested, but it is usually much simpler.

You can also use a stub to print the set of values that are passed to it; this tells us whether or not the module under test is supplying the proper information. The stub must assign values to its *out* mode parameters and should change *in out* mode parameters to simulate data being read or results being computed to give the module something to keep working on. Because we can choose the values that are returned by the stub, we have better control over the conditions of the test run.

Here is a stub that simulates procedure Process_One_Member in Program Running.

```
procedure Process_One_Member (ID        : in     Integer;
                              Data_File : in out Ada.Text_IO.File_Type;
                              Distance  :    out Float) is

-- Stub for procedure Process_One_Member in program Running

begin -- Process One Member
   Ada.Text_IO.Put ("Process One Member called with ID of ");
   Ada.Integer_Text_IO.Put (ID);
   Ada.Text_IO.New_Line;
   Distance := 10.0;                        -- return dummy value
end Process_One_Member;
```

This stub is simpler than the procedure it simulates, which is typical because the object of using stubs is to provide a simple, predictable environment for testing a module.

In addition to supplying a stub for each call in the module, you must provide a dummy main subprogram—a **driver**—to call the module you are testing. A driver contains the bare minimum of definitions required to call the module being tested.

Driver A simple main subprogram that is used to call a procedure or function being tested. The use of a driver permits direct control of the testing process.

By surrounding a module with a driver and stubs, you gain complete control of the conditions under which it executes. This allows you to test different situations and combinations that may reveal errors. The following program is a driver for function Passenger_Moment in Program Starship.

```
with Ada.Text_IO;
with Ada.Float_Text_IO;
with Ada.Integer_Text_IO;

procedure Test_Driver is

   Average_Weight : constant Float := 170.0;
```

```
----------------------------------------------------------------------------
function Passenger_Moment (Passengers : in Integer)  return Float is

-- Given the number of passengers, this function computes the
-- passenger moment arm in inch-pounds
--
-- This function assumes that the first two passengers sit in row 2, the second
-- two in row 1, the next two in row 3, and remaining passenges in row 4

-- Preconditions  : Passengers is between 0 and 8

-- Postconditions : The passenger moment arm in inch-pounds is returned

   Row1 : constant Float := 219.0;    -- Distance of row 1 seats from front
   Row2 : constant Float := 265.0;    -- Distance of row 2 seats from front
   Row3 : constant Float := 295.0;    -- Distance of row 3 seats from front
   Row4 : constant Float := 341.0;    -- Distance of row 4 seats from front

   Moment          : Float;                -- Sum of passenger moments
   Passengers_Left : Integer range 0..8;   -- Number of passengers whose moments
                                           -- have not yet been calculated
begin  -- Passenger Moment
   Passengers_Left := Passengers;    -- At this point, no passenger moments have
   Moment          := 0.0;           -- been calculated

   if Passengers_Left > 6  then             -- Calculate for passengers 7 and 8
      Moment := Moment + Float(Passengers_Left - 6) * Average_Weight * Row4;
      Passengers_Left := 6;                 -- 6 passengers remain
   end if;
   if Passengers_Left > 4  then             -- Calculate for passengers 5 and 6
      Moment := Moment + Float(Passengers_Left - 4) * Average_Weight * Row3;
      Passengers_Left := 4;               -- 4 passengers remain
   end if;
   if Passengers_Left > 2  then             -- Calculate for passengers 3 and 4
      Moment := Moment + Float(Passengers_Left - 2) * Average_Weight * Row1;
    Passengers_Left := 2;                 -- Two passengers remain
   end if;
   if Passengers_Left > 0  then             -- Calculate for passengers 1 and 2
      Moment := Moment + Float(Passengers_Left) * Average_Weight * Row2;
   end if;
   return Moment;
end Passenger_Moment;

----------------------------------------------------------------------------
   Passengers : Integer;

begin  -- Test Driver
   loop
      Ada.Integer_Text_IO.Get (Passengers);
```

```
      exit when Passengers < 0;
      Ada.Float_Text_IO.Put (Item => Passenger_Moment (Passengers));
      Ada.Text_IO.New_Line;
   end loop;
end Test_Driver;
```

This driver is missing many of the niceties of a normal program. There are no ranges on its variables, no prompts, and the output is not neatly formatted. In addition to copying the function Passenger_Moment that we wish to test, we also had to copy the global constant Average_Weight into our driver.

Stubs and drivers are very useful in team programming. The programmers develop the overall design and the interfaces between the modules. Each programmer then designs and codes one or more of the modules and uses drivers and stubs to test the code. When the programmers have coded and tested all of the modules, they assemble them into what should be a working program. The testing done with assembled modules that were individually tested is called *integration testing.*

For team programming to succeed, it is essential that all of the module interfaces be explicitly defined and that the coded modules adhere strictly to the specifications for those interfaces. Obviously, team programmers must carefully avoid global variable references because it is impossible for each programmer to know how the rest of the team is using every variable. By placing variable declarations at the end of the declarative region, we ensure that no procedure can access a variable outside of it.

Testing and Debugging Hints

Follow the documentation guidelines carefully when writing subprograms (see Appendix I). As your programs become more complex, it becomes increasingly important to adhere to documentation and formatting standards. Label the begin statement of each procedure with the procedure name. Even if the procedure name seems to define the process being done, describe that process in comments. Use comments to explain the purposes of all the formal parameters and local constants and variables in a procedure.

1. Carefully define the preconditions and postconditions of each module and include them as comments in the subprogram.
2. Use *in* mode parameters to pass values to procedures and functions, *out* mode parameters to return results from procedures, and *in out* mode parameters to pass values to procedures that are modified and returned.

3. Formal *out* mode and *in out* mode parameters require variables as actual parameters while *in* mode parameters can have any expression as an actual parameter.
4. Choose the best type for every formal parameter and locally declared variable. Use appropriate ranges on local variables.
5. Use named parameter association rather than positional parameter association when calling procedures with more than one parameter.
6. Place variable declarations after procedures so you cannot accidently reference global variables directly from inside a procedure.
7. Be cautious with overloading subprogram names. Use overloading only for subprograms that have the similar objectives.

Summary

Ada's functions and procedures allow us to write programs in modules. Therefore the structure of a program can parallel its top-down design even when the program is complicated. To make your main subprogram look exactly like level 0 of your top-down design, simply write each module as a subprogram. The main subprogram then executes the subprograms in logical sequence.

Ada provides two kinds of subprograms—procedures and functions—for us to use. We call a procedure by writing the procedure's name with an optional parameter list as a statement. A function is called from within an expression and returns a single result value that is used in the evaluation of the expression.

Communication between the calling subprogram and the called subprogram is handled through the use of two lists of identifiers: the formal parameter list (which includes the mode and type of each parameter) in the procedure specification and the actual parameter list in the calling statement. The identifiers in these lists are matched by name (named parameter association) or by their position (positional parameter association).

Part of the top-down design process involves determining a) what data must be received by the lower-level module; b) what information must be returned from it; and c) what data must be received by it, modified, and returned from it. This list of values, together with the preconditions and postconditions of a module, defines its interface. The list of values becomes the formal parameter list. The mode of each parameter in this list is based on the directions of data transfer.

You may call subprograms from more than one place in a program. The parameter-matching mechanism allows the use of different variables as actual parameters to the same subprogram. You can use multiple calls to a subprogram, from different places and with different actual parameters, to simplify greatly the coding of many complex programs.

In addition to having variables defined in its formal parameter list, a subprogram may have local variables declared within it. These variables are accessible only within the declarative region in which they are declared. Local variables must be initialized each time the subprogram containing them is called because their values are destroyed when the subprogram returns.

Anything that is declared outside a subprogram is called global with respect to that subprogram. Avoid references to global variables. If you place all variable declarations at the end of the declarative part, Ada's scope rules will prohibit access to global variables.

All communications between the modules of a program should be through the formal and actual parameter lists. The use of global constants, programmer-defined types, and package instantiations are acceptable programming practices because they add consistency and make a program easier to change while avoiding the pitfalls of side effects.

The scope of a declaration refers to the parts of the program from which it is visible. According to the scope rules, an identifier is visible to all statements between its definition and the end of its declarative region, except those in nested blocks that declare an identifier with the same name. The formal parameters of a subprogram have the same scope as local variables declared in the subprogram.

If you want to call a subprogram from more than one place, don't nest it. If one subprogram is an integral part of another and has no functional meaning in any other context, nest it.

Well-designed and well-documented subprograms that are free of side effects often can be reused in other programs. Many programmers keep a collection of subprograms that they use repeatedly.

Overloading allows us to use the same name for subprograms that perform the same function with minor variations. You may overload subprogram names as long as they can be distinguished by the number of parameters or the types of parameters.

You can use stubs and drivers to test subprograms in isolation from the rest of a program. They are particularly useful in the context of team programming projects.

Quick Check

1. If a design has one level 0 module and three level 1 modules, how many procedures is it likely to have? (pp. 282–283)
2. Where in a program are procedures declared? (pp. 290-291)
3. What would a call to a procedure with the specification

```
procedure Quick_Check (Size   : in  Integer;
                       Circle : in  Boolean;
                       Area   : out Float);
```

look like if the actual parameters were the variables Radius (an Integer), the literal True, and Result (a Float)?
   a. Using named parameter association. (pp. 286–288)
   b. Using positional parameter association. (pp. 298–300)
4. a. Where in a procedure are local variables defined, and what are their initial values equal to? (pp. 297–298)
   b. How can you tell whether an identifier reference inside a procedure is local or global? (pp. 303–306)
   c. When does the scope of an identifier exclude a nested region? (p. 307)
5. Name one way that a procedure can be used to simplify the coding of an algorithm. (p. 290)
6. The actual parameter for *out* mode can be an expression. (True or False) (pp. 288–289)
7. For each of the following, decide whether a function or a procedure is the most appropriate implementation. (p. 324)
   a. Selecting the larger of two values for further processing in an expression.
   b. Printing a paycheck.
   c. Computing the area of a hexagon.
   d. Testing whether an input value is valid and returning True if it is.
   e. Computing the two roots of a quadratic equation.
8. What would the function specification for a function called Minimum look like if it has two Integer parameters called Num_1 and Num_2 and returns an Integer result? (pp. 319–322)
9. What would a call to Minimum look like if the actual parameters are a variable called Deductions and the literal 2000? (pp. 319–322)
10. Distinguish between an *in* mode parameter and input; between an *out* mode parameter and output. (pp. 288–290)

Answers

1. Three. **2.** In the declarative portion. Our style is to declare them after programmer-defined types, constants, and package instantiations but before variable declarations.

3. a.
```
Quick_Check (Size   => Radius,
             Circle => True,
             Area   => Result);
```
b.
```
Quick_Check (Radius, True, Result);
```
4. a. In the declarative part of the procedure after any local types, local constants and local subprograms. They are initially undefined. b. If the variable is not defined in the formal parameter list or in the procedure's declarative part, then that reference is global. c. When the nested region declares an identifier with the same name. **5.** The coding may be simplified if it's possible to call the procedure from more than one place in the program.
6. False. **7.** a. function b. procedure c. function d. function e. procedure
8.
```
function Minimum (Num_1 : in Integer;
                  Num_2 : in Integer) return Integer
```
9.
```
Result := Minimum (Deductions, 2000);
```
10. Input and output refer to the movement of data between our program and the outside world through I/O devices such as keyboards, magnetic disks, and display screens. Parameters are used to transfer data from one part of a program to another part of the program. An *in* parameter is used to transfer data from one part of a program (the caller) into a subprogram. An *out* parameter is used to transfer data from a subprogram to the part of a program that called it.

Exam Preparation Exercises

1. Define the following:

procedure call	actual parameter
parameter list	*in* parameter
formal parameter	*out* parameter
procedure specification	*in out* parameter
procedure body	local variable
homograph	overloading

2. List four advantages of using procedures and top-down design.
3. Show what is printed by the following program.

```
with Ada.Text_IO;
with Ada.Integer_Text_IO;

procedure Pre_Exam is

   procedure Test (Z : out Integer;
                   X : out Integer;
                   A : out Integer) is
   begin  -- Test
      Ada.Integer_Text_IO.Get (Z);
      Ada.Integer_Text_IO.Get (X);
      Ada.Integer_Text_IO.Get (A);
   end Test;

   A : Integer;
   B : Integer;
   C : Integer;

begin  -- Pre_Exam
   Test (Z => A,
         X => B,
         A => C);
   Ada.Integer_Text_IO.Put (A);
   Ada.Integer_Text_IO.Put (B);
   Ada.Integer_Text_IO.Put (C);
end Pre_Exam;
```

Use these data items: 3 2 4

4. Show the output of the following program.

```
with Ada.Text_IO;
with Ada.Integer_Text_IO;

procedure Example is
```

```
   procedure Test (S : in out Integer;
                   T : in out Integer) is
   begin  -- Test
      S := S + 2;
      T := 4 * S;
      Ada.Text_IO.Put ("In procedure Test, the variables equal ");
      Ada.Integer_Text_IO.Put (S);
      Ada.Integer_Text_IO.Put (T);
      Ada.Text_IO.New_Line;
   end Test;

   D : Integer;
   E : Integer;

begin  -- Example
   D := 12;
   E := 14;
   Ada.Text_IO.Put ("In main subprogram before the call, "  &
                    "the variables equal ");
   Ada.Integer_Text_IO.Put (D);
   Ada.Integer_Text_IO.Put (E);
   Ada.Text_IO.New_Line;
   Test (S => D,  T => E);
   Ada.Text_IO.Put ("In main subprogram after the call, "  &
                    "the variables equal ");
   Ada.Integer_Text_IO.Put (D);
   Ada.Integer_Text_IO.Put (E);
   Ada.Text_IO.New_Line;
end Example;
```

5. Number the marked statements in the following program to show the order in which they will be executed (the logical order of execution).

```
      with Ada.Text_IO;
      with Ada.Integer_Text_IO;

      procedure Execute is

         procedure Logical (Value_1 :  in Integer;
                            Value_2 : out Integer) is
            Value_3 : Integer;

         begin  -- Logical
_____       Ada.Integer_Text_IO.Get (Value_3);
_____       Value_2 := Value_1 * Value_3;
         end Logical;

         Number : Integer;
```

```
      begin   -- Execute
____     Text_IO.Put("Exercise");
____     Ada.Text_IO.New_Line;
____     Logical (Value_1 => 5, Value_2 => Number);
____     Ada.Integer_Text_IO.Put (Number);
____     Ada.Text_IO.New_Line;
      end Execute;
```

6. How many of the marked statements in the preceding program are *not* procedure calls?
7. What would be the result if the `Ada.Integer_Text_IO.Put(Number);` in Exercise 5 were changed to `Ada.Integer_Text_IO.Put(Value_1);`?
8. Based on how the parameters are used within each procedure, fill in the correct mode for each parameter in the following procedures.

a.
```
procedure One (Squirrel : ____ Integer;
               Rabbit   : ____ Integer) is
begin
   Squirrel := 5;
   Rabbit   := 15;
end One;
```

b.
```
procedure Two (Squirrel : ____ Integer;
               Rabbit   : ____ Integer) is
begin
   if Rabbit > 17 then
      Squirrel := 5;
   else
      Squirrel := 15;
   end if;
end Two;
```

c.
```
procedure Three (Squirrel : ____ Integer;
                 Rabbit   : ____ Integer) is
begin
   Ada.Integer_Text_IO.Put (Item => Squirrel, Width => 5);
   Ada.Integer_Text_IO.Put (Item => Rabbit,   Width => 5);
end Three;
```

d.
```
procedure Four (Squirrel : ____ Integer;
                Rabbit   : ____ Integer) is
begin
   Ada.Integer_Text_IO.Get (Item => Squirrel);
   Ada.Integer_Text_IO.Get (Item => Rabbit);
end Four;
```

e.
```
procedure Five (Squirrel : ____ Integer;
                Chipmunk : ____ Integer;
                Rabbit   : ____ Integer) is
begin
   Rabbit := (Squirrel + Chipmunk) / 2;
end Five;
```

f.
```
procedure Six (Squirrel : ____ Integer;
               Chipmunk : ____ Integer;
               Rabbit   : ____ Integer) is
begin
   Rabbit := (Rabbit + Squirrel + Chipmunk) / 3;
end Six;
```

g.
```
procedure Seven (Squirrel : ____ Integer;
                 Chipmunk : ____ Integer;
                 Rabbit   : ____ Integer) is
begin
   Rabbit   := (Rabbit + Squirrel + Chipmunk) / 3;
   Chipmunk := (Rabbit + Squirrel) / 2;
end Seven;
```

h.
```
procedure Eight (Squirrel : ____ Integer;
                 Chipmunk : ____ Integer;
                 Rabbit   : ____ Integer) is
begin
   Rabbit   := (Rabbit + Squirrel) / 2;
   Chipmunk := (Rabbit + 2 * Squirrel) / 4;
end Eight;
```

i.
```
procedure Nine (Squirrel : ____ Integer;
                Chipmunk : ____ Integer;
                Rabbit   : ____ Integer) is
   Count : Integer;
   Value : Integer;

begin
   Text_IO.Put (Item => "Enter ");
   Ada.Integer_Text_IO.Put (Item => Squirrel, Width => 1);
   Ada.Text_IO.Put (Item => " values.");
   Ada.Text_IO.New_Line;
   Chipmunk := 0;
   Count    := 1;
   Sum_Loop:
   loop
      exit Sum_Loop when Count > Squirrel;
      Ada.Integer_Text_IO.Get (Value);
      Chipmunk := Chipmunk + Value;
      Count := Count + 1;
   end loop Sum_Loop;
   Rabbit   := Sum / Squirrel;
 end Nine;
```

9. A particular procedure can be a nested region relative to the program that contains it and an enclosing region to any procedures declared within it. (True or False)

10. Identifiers declared within a declarative region are accessible to all statements that are part of that declarative region, including those in nested blocks (assuming the nested blocks don't have local identifiers with the same names). (True or False)
11. If a procedure contains a locally declared constant with the same name as a constant in an enclosing declarative region, no confusion will result because references to constants in procedures are first interpreted as references to local constants. (True or False)
12. Given the nested declarative regions

```
procedure Scope_Rules is
   A : Constant Integer := 17;
   B : Constant Integer := 27;

   procedure Region_1 is
      A1 : Constant Integer := 37;
      B1 : Constant Integer := 47;

      procedure Region_2 is
         A  : Constant Integer := 57;
         A2 : Constant Integer := 67;
         B2 : Constant Integer := 77;

      begin  -- Region_2
         .
         .
         .
      end Region_2;

   begin  -- Region_1
      .
      .
      .
   end Region_1;

   procedure Region_3 is
      A3 : Constant Integer := 87;
      B3 : Constant Integer := 97;

   begin  -- Region_3
      .
      .
      .
   end Region_3;

begin  -- Scope_Rules
   .
   .
   .
end Scope_Rules;
```

a. A and B declared immediately within Scope_Rules are global constants, accessible from all parts of Program Scope_Rules, *including* procedure Region_2. (True or False)
b. Because Scope_Rules is the outermost region, statements in its body can reference all constants declared in inner regions, including Region_2. (True or False)
c. Because procedure Region_2 is the innermost region, its local constants can be accessed by all other regions. (True or False)
d. Constant A1 is global with respect to procedure Region_2. (True or False)
e. Constant B2 is local to procedure Region_1. (True or False)
f. The procedure call statement `Ada.Integer_Text_IO.Put(A1);` would be legal in procedure Region_1. (True or False)
g. The procedure call statement `Ada.Integer_Text_IO.Put(A3 + A1);` would be legal in procedure Region_3. (True or False)
h. Constants A2 and B2 are not defined in any outer declarative region. (True or False)
i. The statement `Ada.Integer_Text_IO.Put(A);` in procedure Region_2 would display the local constant A rather than the global constant A. (True or False)
j. Constants A1 and B1 are global with respect to procedure Region_2, local to procedure Region_1, and not defined to the program outer region. (True or False)

13. a. Draw a scope diagram like Figure 6-6 for Program Scope_Rules in the previous exercise.
    b. Construct a scope table like Table 6-2 for Program Scope_Rules in the previous exercise.
14. The following program is an example of poor procedure interface design. The main subprogram variable X is declared before that program's three procedures.
    a. What is the output of this program?

```
with Ada.Text_IO;
with Ada.Integer_Text_IO;

procedure Params is

   X : Integer;

   procedure Out_Param (A : out Integer) is
   begin
      A := 3;
   end Out_Param;

   procedure Local is
      X : Integer;
   begin
      X := 5;
   end Local;
```

```
   procedure Global is
   begin
      X := 7;
   end Global;

begin   -- Params
   X := 15;
   Out_Param (A => X);
   Ada.Text_IO.Put ("X equals ");
   Ada.Integer_Text_IO.Put (Item => X, Width => 1);
   Ada.Text_IO.New_Line;
   Local;
   Ada.Text_IO.Put ("X equals ");
   Ada.Integer_Text_IO.Put (Item => X, Width => 1);
   Ada.Text_IO.New_Line;
   Global;
   Ada.Text_IO.Put ("X equals ");
   Ada.Integer_Text_IO.Put (Item => X, Width => 1);
   Ada.Text_IO.New_Line;
end Params;
```

  b. What would happen if the first declaration of main subprogram variable X were moved after the three procedures?

15. Prepare a scope table for Program Lumberyard on page 291.
16. a. Why should you avoid using global variables?
    b. How does the declaration order recommended in this chapter prevent us from using global variables?
17. What output is produced by the execution of the following program? The program is not intended to make any sense, only to test your knowledge of scope rules and side effects.

```
with Ada.Integer_Text_IO;
procedure Scope_Out is

   A : Integer;         -- These main subprogram variables
   B : Integer;         -- are not declared in the
   C : Integer;         -- recommended place.

   procedure One (X : in  Integer;
                  Y : in  Integer;
                  Z : out Integer) is

      A : Integer;

   begin  -- One
      A := 1;
      B := 7;
      Z := X + Y;
   end One;
```

```
begin  -- Scope_Out
   A :=  4;
   B :=  5;
   C := 12;
   One (X => A, Y => B, Z => C);
   Ada.Integer_Text_IO.Put (A);
   Ada.Integer_Text_IO.Put (B);
   Ada.Integer_Text_IO.Put (C):
end Scope_Out;
```

18. A function call is always a component of an expression, but a procedure call is always a statement in itself. (True or False)
19. Given the following function specification

```
function High_Bracket (Income     : in Integer;
                       Deductions : in Integer) return Boolean is
```

is the following statement a legal call to the function if Gross_Income and Total_Deductions are of type Integer?

```
if High_Bracket (Gross_Income, Total_Deductions) then
   Ada.Text_IO.Put("Upper Class");
end if;
```

20. You are given the following function Test:

```
function Test (X : in Float;
               Y : in Float;
               Z : in Float) return Float is
begin
   if (X > Y) or (Y > Z) then
      return 0.5;
   else
      return -0.5;
   end if;
end Test;
```

and an Ada program in which the variables A, B, C, D, and Result are declared to be of type Float. In the calling program, A := –5.0, B := –6.2, C := 0.1, and D := 16.2. What is the value of Result when each of the following calls return?

a. `Result := Test (5.2, 5.3, 5.6);`
b. `Result := Test (abs(A), C, D);`

21. Given the following module structure chart:

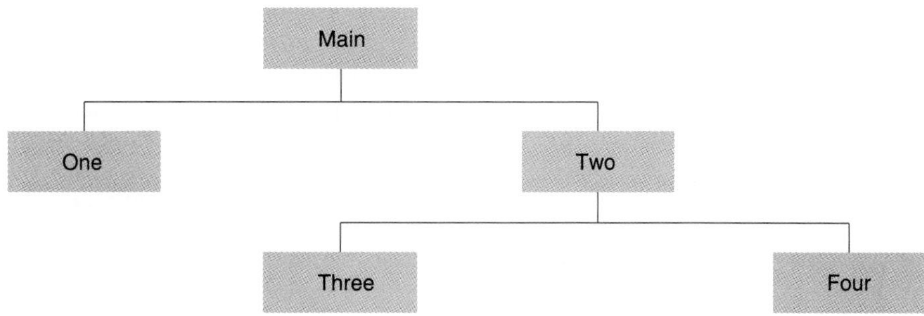

draw two scope diagrams like Figure 6-6 to indicate how these modules could be nested

a. using as little procedure nesting as possible and
b. as much nesting as possible.

22. Given the following scope diagram:

procedure Red (X : in out Integer) is

procedure Blue is

procedure Green (Y : in Float) is

a. Procedure Blue can call procedure Red. (True or False)
b. Procedure Blue can call procedure Green. (True or False)
c. Procedure Green can call procedure Red. (True or False)
d. Procedure Green can call procedure Blue. (True or False)
e. Procedure Red can call procedure Blue. (True or False)
f. Procedure Red can call procedure Green. (True or False)

23. Given the following four procedure specifications:

i.
```
procedure Match (Oak   : in     Float;
                 Maple :    out Integer;
                 Birch : in out Integer) is
```
ii.
```
procedure Match (Oak   : in     Integer;
                 Maple :    out Integer;
                 Birch : in out Integer) is
```
iii.
```
procedure Match (Oak   : in     Integer;
                 Maple :    out Integer;
                 Birch : in out Integer;
                 Pine  :    out Float) is
```
iv.
```
procedure Match (Oak   : in     Float;
                 Maple :    out Integer;
                 Birch : in out Integer;
                 Pine  :    out Float) is
```

and the following variable declarations:

```
Tree : Integer;
Leaf : Integer;
Nut  : Integer;
Root : Float;
Bark : Float;
```

tell which of the above procedures is called by each of the following procedure calls. Answer *none* if the procedure call does not match any of the previous procedure specifications.

a. `Match (Maple => Tree, Oak => 17.0, Pine => Root, Birch => Leaf);`
b. `Match (Tree, 17.0, Root, Leaf);`
c. `Match (Oak => 13.2, Maple => Tree, Birch => Leaf);`
d. `Match (12, Tree, Leaf, Bark);`
e. `Match (Oak => Nut, Maple => Leaf, Birch => Tree);`
f. `Match (Oak => Nut, Maple => Leaf, Birch => Tree, Pine => Root);`

24. Why can we *not* overload the procedure name No_Overload with the following two procedures?

```
procedure No_Overload (A : in Integer;  B : out Float) is

procedure No_Overload (Apple : in Integer;  Banana : out Float) is
```

25. Procedure Passenger_Moment (page 346–347) in Program Starship contains a precondition stating that the *in* parameter Passengers must have a value between 0 and 8.
    a. How does Program Starship guarantee that this assertion is met when it calls function Passenger_Moment?
    b. Why is it *not* necessary to have a precondition in function Passenger_Moment stating that the *in* parameter Passengers must be a whole number?

Programming Warm-up Exercises

1. Write the *procedure specification* for a procedure called Maximum that accepts a pair of integers and returns the greater of the two.
2. Complete the following procedure so that, when it returns, the original values in First_Number and Second_Number are halved.

```
procedure Halve (First_Number  : in out Integer;
                 Second_Number : in out Integer) is
```

3. Write a procedure named Increment, with one parameter of type Integer that adds 15 to the value received in the parameter and returns the new value to the calling program.
4. Complete the procedure Get_Fraction that gets a Float value from the keyboard and returns the fractional part of that value in a parameter called Fraction. For example, if the input is 16.753, Item should return the value 0.753.

```
procedure Get_Fraction (Item : out Float) is
```

5. a. What is wrong with the following procedure *body?* It is a subtle syntax error commonly made by Ada programmers. Look carefully at the EBNF definition for procedure body given in this chapter.

```
procedure Contains_Syntax_Error (Value : in Integer);
begin
   Ada.Text_IO.Put ("The value is ");
   Ada.Integer_Text_IO.Put (Value);
end Contains_Syntax_Error;
```

   b. Compile this procedure and record your error message(s).
6. Complete the following procedure that uses a data-validation loop to ensure that the value obtained from the user and returned through the parameter Passengers is between 0 and 8.

```
procedure Get (Passengers : out Integer) is
```

7. a. Write a procedure called Find_Circumference that finds the circumference of a circle given its radius. The formula for calculating the circumference of a circle is π multiplied by 2 times the radius. As we did in program Trig_Table on page 325, use Pi in package Ada.Numerics for π.
   b. Rewrite the procedure as a function.
8. Write a procedure that is given three whole numbers and returns their sum and a Boolean variable equal to True if all three numbers are positive (or False otherwise).
9. Write a procedure that will get a specified number of Float values from the keyboard and return their average. A call to this procedure might look like

```
Get_Mean (Of => 5, Mean => X);
```

   where Of specifies the number of values to be read and Mean is the result.
10. a. Write a procedure called Max_Value that returns the largest of three integers it receives from the calling program. A call to this procedure might look like

```
Max_Value (First   => Num_1,
           Second  => Num_2,
           Third   => Num_3,
           Largest => Max);
```

   b. Rewrite Max_Value as a function.
11. Complete the specification of the following procedure. (*Hint:* Make a list of all the identifiers in the procedure and notice which ones aren't declared locally.)

```
procedure Get_Average (                                  ) is

         Sales_1 : Float;
         Sales_2 : Float;

      begin   -- Get_Average
         Ada.Text_IO.Put ("Department");
         Ada.Integer_Text_IO.Put (Item => Dept_Num, Width => 1);
         Ada.Text_IO.New_Line;
         Ada.Float_Text_IO.Get (Sales_1);
         Ada.Float_Text_IO.Get (Sales_2);
         Ada.Text_IO.Put ("has weekly sales of ");
         Ada.Float_Text_IO.Put (Item => Sales_1,
                                Fore => 1,
                                Aft  => 2,
                                Exp  => 0);
         Ada.Text_IO.Put (" and ");
         Ada.Float_Text_IO.Put (Item => Sales_2,
                                Fore => 1,
                                Aft  => 2,
                                Exp  => 0);
```

```
        Ada.Text_IO.New_Line;
        Avg := (Sales_1 + Sales_2) / 2.0;
        Ada.Text_IO.Put ("for an average of ");
        Ada.Float_Text_IO.Put (Item => Avg,
                               Fore => 1,
                               Aft  => 2,
                               Exp  => 0);
        Ada.Text_IO.New_Line;
end Get_Average;
```

12. Write a procedure that will have three parameters—Hours, Minutes, and Elapsed_Time—passed to it. Elapsed_Time is an integer number of minutes to be added to the starting time passed in through Hours and Minutes. The resulting new time will be returned through Hours and Minutes. You may assume that Elapsed_Time is not negative. For example:

Before Call to Add_Time	**After Call to Add_Time**
Hours = 12	Hours = 16
Minutes = 44	Minutes = 2
Elapsed_Time = 198	Elapsed_Time = 198

13. The following program was written with very poor style: Global variable references were used in place of parameters. Rewrite it without global references using good programming style.

```
with Ada.Text_IO;
with Ada.Integer_Text_IO;

procedure Side_Effects is

   A : Integer;
   B : Integer;
   C : Integer;

   procedure Mash_Globals is

      Temp : Integer;

   begin   -- Mash_Globals
      Temp := A + B;
      A := B + C;
      B := Temp;
   end Mash_Globals;
```

```
begin  -- Side_Effects
   Ada.Integer_Text_IO.Get (A);
   Ada.Integer_Text_IO.Get (B);
   Ada.Integer_Text_IO.Get (C);
   Mash_Globals;
   Ada.Integer_Text_IO.Put (A);
   Ada.Integer_Text_IO.Put (B);
   Ada.Integer_Text_IO.Put (C);
   Ada.Text_IO.New_Line;
end Side_Effects;
```

14. Given two Float parameters called High and Low, write the specification for a function called Epsilon that returns a Float result.
15. Given three Float parameters called Num_1, Num_2, and Difference, write the *specification* for a function called Equal that returns a Boolean result.
16. Write the body for the function you specified in the previous question. True should be returned if the absolute difference between Num_1 and Num_2 is less than the value in Difference. Otherwise return False.
17. Write a function called Compass_Heading that returns the average of its four Float parameters: True_Course, Wind_Corr_Angle, Variance, and Deviation.
18. Write a function called Minimum that returns the smallest of its three Integer parameters.
19. Using the square root function found in package Ada.Numerics.Elementary_Functions, solve Programming Problem 4 in Chapter 5.

Programming Problems

1. Develop a design and write an Ada program to print a calendar for one year, given the year and the day of the week that January 1 falls on. It may help to think of this task as printing 12 calendars, one for each month, given the day of the week that a month starts on and the number of days in the month. Each successive month starts on the day of the week that follows the last day of the preceding month. Years that are divisible by four are leap years. Here is a sample run for an interactive system.

```
What year do you want a calendar for?
1985

What day of the week does January 1 fall on?
Tuesday

   1985
```

```
         January
 S  M  T  W  T  F  S
--------------------
       1  2  3  4  5
 6  7  8  9 10 11 12
13 14 15 16 17 18 19
20 21 22 23 24 25 26
27 28 29 30 31

         February
 S  M  T  W  T  F  S
--------------------
                1  2
 3  4  5  6  7  8  9
10 11 12 13 14 15 16
17 18 19 20 21 22 23
24 25 26 27 28

           .
           .
           .

         December
 S  M  T  W  T  F  S
--------------------
 1  2  3  4  5  6  7
 8  9 10 11 12 13 14
15 16 17 18 19 20 21
22 23 24 25 26 27 28
29 30 31
```

Implement your hierarchical design with subprograms. Be sure to use appropriate types and ranges for the objects in your design. When writing your program, be sure to use proper indentation and style, meaningful identifiers, and plenty of comments.

2. Write an interactive Ada program to calculate the volume and surface area of a cylinder, given the radius (R) and the length (L). The program must instruct the user to input the radius and the length. Use one procedure to calculate the volume and another to calculate the surface area.

   The formula for calculating the volume of a cylinder is $\pi R^2 L$. The formula for calculating the surface area is $2\pi R^2 L$. As we did in program Trig_Table on page 325, use Pi in package Ada.Numerics for π.

3. Write a top-down design and an Ada program with procedures that will help you balance your checking account. The program should let you enter the initial balance for the month, followed by a series of transactions. For each transaction entered, the program should echo print the transaction data, the current balance for the account, and the total service charges. Service charges are $0.10 for a deposit and $0.15 for a check. If the balance drops below

$500.00 at any point during the month, a service charge of $5.00 will be assessed for the month. If the balance drops below $50.00, the program should print a warning message. If the balance becomes negative, an additional service charge of $10.00 should be assessed for each check until the balance becomes positive again.

A transaction will take the form of a letter, followed by a blank and a real number. There may be any number of spaces before and after the letter. If the letter is a *C* or a *c*, then the number is the amount of a check. If the letter is a *D* or a *d*, then the number is the amount of a deposit. The last transaction will consist of the letter *E* or an *e*. A sample run might look like this.

```
Enter the beginning balance:
879.46


Enter a transaction:
 c 400.00

Transaction:  Check in amount of $400.00
Current balance:  $479.46
Service charge:  Check - $0.15
Service charge:  Below $500 - $5.00
Total service charges:  $5.15


Enter a transaction:
D 100.0

Transaction:  Deposit in amount of $100.00
Current balance:  $579.46
Service charge:  Deposit - $0.10
Total service charges:  $5.25


Enter a transaction:
  e

Transaction:  End
Current balance:  $579.46
Total service charges:  $5.25
Final balance:  $574.21
```

As usual, your program should use proper style and indentation, meaningful identifiers, and appropriate comments.

4. Develop a top-down design and write an Ada program for a computer to be used as a cash register at Alan's Bake Shop. For each sale, the program should prompt for and get the product category, quantity purchased, and price. The total amount of purchase should be calculated and displayed. Then the program should prompt for and get the amount of money received from the customer. It should then display the amount of change (a float value) and the bills and coins needed to make up that change. For example, if the amount of change is $7.32, the customer would be given one five-dollar bill, two one-dollar bills, one quarter, one nickel, and two pennies.

   At the end of the day the clerk enters the category Done. The program should then display the total amount of sales in each of the five categories and terminate.

   Input

   Product Category (Cake, Pie, Bread, Roll, Cookie, or Done)

   Quantity

   Price

   Amount of money received from customer

   Output

   Total amount of purchase

   Change returned to customer; in addition to the amount of change, display the number of five-dollar bills, one-dollar bills, quarters, dimes, nickels, and pennies

   At the end of the day (when Done is entered) display the total dollars of sales for each of the five product categories.

5. Develop a design and write a program to produce a bar chart of gourmet popcorn production for a cooperative farm group on a farm-by-farm basis. The input to the program will be a series of data sets with each set representing the production for one farm. The output will be a bar chart that identifies each farm and displays its production in pints of corn per acre. Following the last data set is a null line (a line with no characters).

   Each data set will consist of two lines. On the first line is the name of a farm. On the second line is a real number representing acres planted, a space, and a whole number representing pint jars of popcorn produced.

   The output will be a single line for each farm, with the name of the farm starting in the first column on a line and the bar chart starting in column 30. Each mark in the bar chart will represent 250 jars of popcorn per acre. The production goal for the year is 5,000 jars per acre. A vertical bar should appear in the chart for farms with lower production, or a special mark should appear for farms with production greater than or equal to 5,000 jars per acre. For example, given the input file

```
Orville's Acres
114.8    43801
Hoffman's Hills
 77.2    36229
Jiffy Quick Farm
 89.4    24812
Jolly Good Plantation
183.2   104570
Organically Grown Inc.
 45.5    14683
```

the output would be

```
                  Pop Co-Op

Farm Name                   Production in
                            Thousands of
                            Pint Jars per Acre
                               1   2   3   4   5   6
                            --|--|--|--|--|--|
Orville's Acres             ***************    |
Hoffman's Hills             *******************|
Jiffy Quick Farm            ***********        |
Jolly Good Plantation       *******************#****
Organically Grown Inc.      *************      |
```

Use procedures to implement your hierarchical design. As usual, your program should use proper style and indentation, meaningful identifiers, and appropriate comments.

CHAPTER 7

Types and Subtypes

GOALS

After reading this chapter, you should be able to

- use the most common attributes with predefined and programmer-defined data types.
- use the predefined discrete type Character
- declare and use your own floating-point, integer, and decimal data types
- use type conversion functions
- declare and use subtypes
- do input and output with programmer-defined types and subtypes
- choose between declaring a subtype and declaring a type

Object modeling is a very important part of the software design process. Except for the use of programmer-defined enumeration types, our modeling has consisted of choosing a predefined type and optional range that best models each *individual* object in our design. In Chapter 3 we said that groups of objects with similar properties and behaviors are described by an object class (often shortened to class). In this chapter we continue our study of object classes through a detailed examination of types.

In Chapter 2 we defined a data type as the general form of a class of data items. In this chapter we give a fuller, more formal definition of data type. We will review the predefined simple data types (Float, Integer, and Boolean) and programmer-defined enumeration types in terms of the expanded definition. We also introduce the predefined simple data type, Character.

In Chapter 4 we showed that there are times when Ada's predefined data types cannot adequately represent all the data in a program. We introduced enumeration types as a mechanism for creating new data types. In this chapter we show how to create new numeric data types that model the objects in our problem more accurately than the predefined types Integer and Float.

Data Types

A **data type** is a formal description of a set of values (called the *domain*) and the basic operations that can be applied to these values. Let's begin by examining the familiar Integer, Float, and enumeration types in light of this definition. The formal description of Integer values and their allowable operations comes from mathematics: The integer numbers are the set of whole numbers from $-\infty$ to $+\infty$, and the operations include +, −, /, *, rem, abs, and the relational operators. As a computer cannot represent an infinite number of different values, Ada limits the set of integers. The constants Min_Int and Max_Int in the package System contain the values of the most negative and most positive integer we can use. The formal description of Float also comes from mathematics: Float numbers are the set of real numbers from $-\infty$ to $+\infty$, and the operations are the same as those for the Integers except that rem is excluded. Different computers place different limits on the range and precision of float numbers that the system can represent.

Data type A formal description of a set of values (called the *domain*) and the basic operations that can be applied to these values.

The values of enumeration types are defined in the declaration of the type, and the operations are the relational operators. The definitions for

Boolean variables come from Boolean algebra; a Boolean variable can have the value True or False, and the set of operations allowed on these values is `and`, `or`, and `not`. Because Ada's Boolean type is a predefined enumeration type, the relational operations are also available.

Integer types, floating types, and enumeration types have two properties in common. Each is made up of indivisible, or atomic, elements, and each is ordered. Data types with these properties are called **scalar data types.**

Scalar data type A data type in which the values are ordered and each value is atomic (indivisible).

When we say that a value is atomic, we mean that it has no component parts that can be accessed independently. For example, the string "Good Morning" is not atomic since it is composed of individual parts (characters) that can be accessed as slices. The integer 127 is an atomic type. This integer is stored in the computer's memory as a single value rather than as three independent digits.

When we say that the values are ordered, we mean that exactly one of the relations <, > , or = is true for any pair of values. For example:

```
1 < 2      3.562 < 106.22      False = False
```

Integer and enumeration data types have an additional property: Each value (except the first) has a unique predecessor, and each value (except the last) has a unique successor. Types with this property are called **discrete data types.** They also are known as *ordinal data types.*

Discrete data type A data type in which each value (except the first) has a unique predecessor and each value (except the last) has a unique successor. Also called ordinal data type.

Type Float is not discrete because a Float value has no *unique* predecessor or successor. If you add one more digit of precision, the predecessor and successor change; that is, 0.52 and 0.520 are the same, but the predecessor of 0.52 is 0.51, and the predecessor of 0.520 is 0.519.

Attributes

Ada has operators that are used with type identifiers. These operators are called attributes and are used to obtain characteristics of the type. In this section, we describe the eight most commonly used attributes. You can find descriptions of all attributes in the *Ada Reference Manual* (ARM).

There are four attributes commonly used with scalar types.

Attributes Commonly Used with Scalar Types

Attribute	Purpose
First	Returns the lower bound of the type.
Last	Returns the upper bound of the type.
Image	Returns a string equivalent to a given value.
Value	Returns a value equivalent to a given string.

As discrete types are also scalar types, we can also use these four attributes with any discrete type. The property of unique predecessors and successors provides four more commonly used attributes for discrete types.

Attribues Commonly Used with Discrete Types

Attribute	Purpose
Succ	Returns the successor of a given value.
Pred	Returns the predecessor of a given value.
Pos	Returns the position number of a given value in the type's set of values.
Val	Returns the value in a given position in the type's set of values.

We showed you in Chapter 2 how to use the attributes First and Last with the predefined types Integer and Float. We use the same syntax with other types and other attributes—the type name followed by an apostrophe followed by the attribute name. Let's look at some examples with the following programmer-defined enumeration type.

```
type Color_Type is (White, Green, Blue, Violet, Red, Yellow);
```

The expression

```
Color_Type'First
```

returns the lower bound (smallest) of the set of values constituting type Color_Type. It is read *color type tic first*. We use attributes much like we do function subprogram calls. For many attributes we need to supply a value as we provide parameter values for most functions. Here are some example attribute expressions with Color_Type and the results of evaluating them.

Expression	Result
`Color_Type'First`	`White`
`Color_Type'Last`	`Yellow`
`Color_Type'Succ(White)`	`Green`
`Color_Type'Succ(Blue)`	`Violet`
`Color_Type'Succ(Yellow)`	`CONSTRAINT_ERROR`
`Color_Type'Pred(Yellow)`	`Red`
`Color_Type'Pred(Red)`	`Violet`
`Color_Type'Pred(White)`	`CONSTRAINT_ERROR`
`Color_Type'Pos(White)`	`0`
`Color_Type'Pos(Green)`	`1`
`Color_Type'Pos(Yellow)`	`5`
`Color_Type'Val(0)`	`White`
`Color_Type'Val(1)`	`Green`
`Color_Type'Val(5)`	`Yellow`
`Color_Type'Val(6)`	`CONSTRAINT_ERROR`
`Color_Type'Image(Yellow)`	`"YELLOW"`
`Color_Type'Image(Red)`	`"RED"`
`Color_Type'Value("Yellow")`	`Yellow`
`Color_Type'Value("RED")`	`Red`
`Color_Type'Value(" GrEen ")`	`Green`
`Color_Type'Value("Purple")`	`CONSTRAINT_ERROR`

Note that the position number of the first value of an enumeration type is 0, not 1. The exception CONSTRAINT_ERROR occurs if we attempt to obtain the successor of the last value of the type or the predecessor of the first value of a type. The Image attribute for enumeration types returns a string consisting of all uppercase characters. The Value attribute is the inverse of Image. The Value attribute ignores leading and trailing blanks and considers uppercase and lowercase characters to be equivalent. CONSTRAINT_ERROR is raised if the given string does not represent any value of the type.

Here are some more examples using these attributes with the predefined types Boolean and Integer.

Expression	Result
`Boolean'First`	`False`
`Boolean'Last`	`True`
`Boolean'Succ(False)`	`True`
`Boolean'Succ(True)`	`CONSTRAINT_ERROR`
`Boolean'Pos(False)`	`0`
`Boolean'Pos(True)`	`1`
`Boolean'Val(0)`	`False`
`Boolean'Val(1)`	`True`
`Boolean'Image(True)`	`"TRUE"`

```
Boolean'Value(" False")        False
Integer'Succ(17)               18
Integer'Succ(0)                1
Integer'Succ(-14)              -13
Integer'Succ(Integer'Last)     CONSTRAINT_ERROR
Integer'Pred(17)               16
Integer'Pred(0)                -1
Integer'Pred(-14)              -15
Integer'Pos(17)                17
Integer'Pos(0)                 0
Integer'Pos(-14)               -14
Integer'Val(17)                17
Integer'Val(0)                 0
Integer'Val(-14)               -14
Integer'Image(17)              " 17"
Integer'Image(-14)             "-14"
Integer'Value(" 39")           39
Integer'Value("+93")           93
Integer'Value("-27")           -27
Integer'Value("Yellow")        CONSTRAINT_ERROR
```

The Pos and Val attributes are not very useful with integer types because an integer's value is its numeric position in the set of values. The first character of the string returned by Integer'Image is always a blank if the value is positive or a minus sign if the value is negative.

The value given to an attribute does not have to be a literal. It can be an expression with variables, as is illustrated in the following code fragment:

```
Wax_Color := Color_Type'First;   -- Initialize loop control variable to the
                                 -- first color in the domain of the type

Print_Loop:
loop
   Color_IO.Put (Item => Wax_Color);
   Ada.Text_IO.New_Line;
   exit Print_Loop when Wax_Color = Color_Type'Last;     -- Last color?
   Wax_Color := Color_Type'Succ(Wax_Color);              -- Go to the next color
end loop Print_Loop;
```

This loop is a count-controlled loop—one that executes a predetermined number of times. However, the loop control variable is an enumeration type rather than an Integer. Before the loop begins, the loop control variable, Wax_Color, is initialized to White, the first value in Color_Type. This color is displayed in the loop, and then the program checks to see whether we have printed the last color, Yellow. The last statement in the loop body is analogous to incrementing the loop counter. Wax_Color is set to the successor of the current value of Wax_Color.

You can use the Succ attribute to increment an integer loop control variable or counter. These two statements accomplish the same task:

```
Count := Count + 1;
Count := Integer'Succ(Count);
```

Character Data Type

Now let's look at how we can apply our new definition of a data type to character data. We have been using strings to represent characters since Chapter 2, where we said that string data consists of zero (the null string) or more characters. Ada strings are not atomic. Situations do arise when we need an atomic data type to represent characters. Ada fills this need by predefining another type—Character. Type Character is a predefined enumeration type that provides a set of 256 different atomic values and a basic set of operations that can be applied to them. These 256 characters are ordered in the collating sequence (see Appendix C).

A Character literal is a character enclosed in apostrophes. Here are some examples.

```
'a'   'A'   '*'   '2'   '$'   ' '
```

The apostrophes often are referred to as *single quotes*. Recall that we enclose strings in *double quotes* ("). The type of quote distinguishes whether a literal is a character or a string. In Ada, the one-character string literal "J" is not the same as the character literal 'J' even though they look very similar. We declare and assign values for constants and variables of type Character the same way we declare and assign values to other constants and variables. For example:

```
Average_Grade  : constant Character := 'C';

Middle_Initial : Character;
Letter_Grade   : Character;
     .
     .
     .
Middle_Initial := 'W';
Letter_Grade   := 'B';
```

Character literals exist for only 191 characters—the *graphic characters*. Most keyboards have keys for about 95 of the graphic characters. The remaining characters, called *control characters*, are defined as named Character constants in the predefined package Ada.Characters.Latin_1.

Here are some of the control character constants available from this package.

Control Character	Function
Ada.Characters.Latin_1.BEL	Bell
Ada.Characters.Latin_1.BS	Backspace
Ada.Characters.Latin_1.HT	Horizontal tab
Ada.Characters.Latin_1.ESC	Beginning of an escape sequence

We'll use one of these control characters in the next section and others in later chapters. Package Ada.Characters.Latin_1 is included in Appendix C.

Character Input/Output

Package Ada.Text_IO contains Put and Get procedures for characters. Put outputs a single character to the standard output file. Here's an example:

```
Ada.Text_IO.Put (Item => 'H');
Ada.Text_IO.Put (Item => 'e');
Ada.Text_IO.Put (Item => 'l');
Ada.Text_IO.Put (Item => 'l');
Ada.Text_IO.Put (Item => 'o');
Ada.Text_IO.Put (Item => Ada.Characters.Latin_1.BEL);
Ada.Text_IO.New_Line;
```

which displays the line

```
Hello
```

and then rings the bell on the output device. The control character defined by the constant Ada.Characters.Latin_1.BEL does not appear on the screen or paper. It, like all control characters, directs the output device to perform some function other than displaying text. In this case, it instructs the output device to sound a bell-like tone.

When Get is used to read data into Character variables, a single character is read. As with all the other Get procedures that we have seen, the Get procedure for characters skips over any leading line terminators. Leading blanks are *not* skipped; the blank is an important character. Given the data

```
A10
Quick
Fox
```

and given that Do, Re, Me, Fa, and So are Character variables, the calls to Get and Skip_Line produce the result shown in the table. As in such previous tables, the left column shows the procedure call, the middle column shows the effect of the call on the variable, and the right column shows the effect of the call on the reading marker. Recall that the reading marker, denoted by the shaded gray block, indicates the next character to be read. As before, we use color for all the characters that have been processed at this point and use the symbol ¶ to indicate a line terminator.

Statements	*Variables*	*Marker Position After Get*
`Ada.Text_IO.Get (Item => Do);`	Do A	A10¶ Quick¶ Fox¶
`Ada.Text_IO.Get (Item => Re);`	Re 1	A10¶ Quick¶ Fox
`Ada.Text_IO.Get (Item => Me);`	Me 0	A10¶ Quick¶ Fox
`Ada.Text_IO.Get (Item => Fa);`	Fa Q	A10¶ Quick¶ Fox
`Ada.Text_IO.Skip_Line;`		A10¶ Quick¶ Fox
`Ada.Text_IO.Get (Item => So);`	So F	A10¶ Quick¶ Fox

Working with Characters as a Discrete Type

Because type Character is an enumeration type, we can use all of the operations associated with enumeration types. These operations include the relational operators and all the discrete type attributes.

Expression	Result
`'a' < 'c'`	`True`
`'a' < 'C'`	`False`
`' ' < 'A'`	`True`
`'2' > 'A'`	`False`
`Character'Succ('A')`	`'B'`
`Character'Pred('A')`	`'@'`
`Character'Pos('A')`	`65`
`Character'Pos('a')`	`97`
`Character'Pos('1')`	`49`
`Character'Val(83)`	`'S'`

We can use the Pos attribute to convert a digit that is read in character form to its numeric equivalent. Because the characters '0' to '9' are consecutive in Ada's collating sequence, subtracting Character'Pos('0') from the Pos of any digit in character gives the digit in numeric form.

```
Character'Pos('0')  -  Character'Pos('0')  =  48  -  48  =  0
Character'Pos('1')  -  Character'Pos('0')  =  49  -  48  =  1
Character'Pos('2')  -  Character'Pos('0')  =  50  -  48  =  2
```

Why would we want to do this? In some circumstances the Get procedures in Float_Text_IO and Integer_Text_IO are inadequate for reading a particular data set. Using the Pos attribute allows us to read numerical data as characters and then convert them to numbers.

Another example using the Character attributes Pos and Val is shown in function To_Lower, which converts uppercase letters to lowercase.

```
function To_Lower (Ch : in Character) return Character is

-- Converts an uppercase letter to lowercase. Any other
-- character given is returned unchanged.

   -- Shift is the position difference between equivalent
   -- uppercase and lowercase letters.
   Shift : constant Integer := Character'Pos('a') - Character'Pos('A');

   Lower_Position : Integer;          -- The position of the lowercase
                                      -- equivalent of Ch

begin  -- To Lower

   if (Ch >= 'A')  and  (Ch <= 'Z') then    -- Is Ch an uppercase letter?
   -- Calculate the position of the equivalent lowercase letter
      Lower_Position := Character'Pos (Ch) + Shift;
      -- Return the value of the letter at the calculated position
      return Character'Val(Lower_Position);
```

```
   else  -- Not an uppercase letter, return Ch unchanged
      return Ch;
   end if;
end To_Lower;
```

You need not type in the previous function when you need to convert uppercase characters to lowercase. Package Ada.Characters.Handling contains this function and its counterpart that converts a character to uppercase. It also contains functions for testing whether a letter is a member of a particular category. Control characters, graphics characters, letters, lowercase letters, uppercase letters, and digits are just some of the categories for which package Ada.Characters.Handling has membership functions.

Wide Characters

While the 256 different characters making up the domain of type Character are adequate for most Roman-based languages, it lacks characters used in other languages. For example, it does not contain the Cyrillic letters used in the Russian alphabet. The predefined discrete type Wide_Character facilitates direct use of character literals from all languages. Wide_Character contains 65,536 different characters in its domain. The first 256 characters in Wide_Character are identical to Character's domain.

Qualified Expressions

Having the same 256 characters in the domain of type Character and type Wide_Character can lead to ambiguities. Is the literal 'G' a Character literal or a Wide_Character literal? If the Ada compiler cannot determine the answer to this question from the context of the expression in which we use the literal, it will issue a syntax error message. We can remove any ambiguity by supplying additional information so that the type of the literal is not ambiguous. We do this by qualifying the literal with the name of the type to form a *qualified expression*.

```
'G'                      'G' could be a Character literal or Wide_Character literal
Character'('G')          'G' is a Character literal
Wide_Character'('G')     'G' is a Wide_Character literal
```

We can qualify any expression whose type is ambiguous. Here is a simplified EBNF definition of a qualified expression.

qualified_expression ::= subtype_mark'(expression)

Qualified expressions are also useful for non-character types. The following declarations contain some identical enumeration literals.

```
type Wax_Color_Type      is (White, Green, Blue, Violet, Red, Yellow);
type Traffic_Light_Color is (Green, Yellow, Red);
```

Is the enumeration literal Red a ski wax color or a traffic light color? If the determination cannot be made from the context of the expression containing the enumeration literal, we must form a qualified expression. Here are two possible qualified expressions.

```
Wax_Color_Type'(Red)
Traffic_Light_Color'(Red)
```

The types of these qualified expressions are unambiguous.

Operations with String and Character Types

As we mentioned earlier, the Character literal 'J' is not the same as the one-character String literal "J". We have seen this sort of difference before: The integer literal 2 is not the same as the one-character string literal "2". In the same way, Character and String are two different types; they have different sets of values and different operations. While we can compare two characters and we can compare two strings, we can't compare a character to a string.

Expression	Result
`'J' < 'Z'`	True
`"J" < "Z"`	True
`'J' < "Z"`	Syntax error—comparing different types

Ada's strong typing does not allow us to easily combine different type values in the same expression even though they appear similar to us. Because strings are composed of characters, and because there will be times when we want to use both types in one program, Ada provides several mechanisms to make it easier for us to work with strings and characters.

String Components and String Slices We discussed the String slice in Chapter 3. Slices allow us to manipulate part of a string by specifying a range of character positions in the string. If Name is a String variable, the expression

```
Name (3..3)          -- A one-character string slice
```

yields a one-character string. However, a one-character string is not the same as a character, and in certain situations we may want to access one component of a string as a Character value. We can do this by specifying a single numeric value or expression in parentheses after the string variable name, instead of a range. The expression

```
Name (3)        -- The third character of the string
```

gives us the third character in the string, which is type Character. The following code fragment demonstrates the access of a string's character components.

```
Name     : String (1..15);
Position : Integer;
     .
     .
     .
Name := "Mildred Smedley";

-- Display the entire string
Ada.Text_IO.Put (Item => Name);              -- Displays "Mildred Smedley"
Ada.Text_IO.New_Line;

-- Display a slice of the string
Ada.Text_IO.Put (Item => Name (5..7));       -- Displays "red"
Ada.Text_IO.New_Line;

-- Loop to display the first name (one character at a time)
Position := 1;           -- Initialize to position of first character
First_Name_Loop:         -- Each time through the loop, display one character
loop                     -- of the first name.
   exit First_Name_Loop when Name(Position) = ' ';  -- A blank terminates
                                                    -- the loop
   Ada.Text_IO.Put (Item => Name(Position));      -- Display a single character
   Position := Position + 1;                      -- Go on to the next
                                                  -- character position
end loop First_Name_Loop;
Ada.Text_IO.New_Line;
```

We have used string slices and string components to extract portions of a string value. By placing them on the *left* side of an assignment statement, we also can use them to change a string value. Here are some examples.

Assignment Statement	Value of Name
`Name        := "Mildred Smedley";`	`Mildred Smedley`
`Name(10)    := 't';`	`Mildred Stedley`
`Name(10..10) := "h";`	`Mildred Shedley`
`Name(9..15) := "Griffin";`	`Mildred Griffin`

The following code segment uses this capability to read and echo print a single word from a data set. For this example, we define a word as a group of characters followed by a blank character.

```
Word : String (1..15);
Last : Integer;           -- The position of the last character in the word
Ch   : Character;
    .
    .
    .
Last := 0;
Word_Loop:     -- Each iteration, one character is read
loop
   Ada.Text_IO.Get (Item => Ch);
   exit Word_Loop when Ch = ' ';   -- Reading a blank terminates the loop
   Last       := Last + 1;
   Word(Last) := Ch;
end loop Word_Loop;

-- Echo print word
Ada.Text_IO.Put (Item => Word(1..Last));
```

Concatenation We discussed String concatenation in Chapter 2. Our primary use of the concatenation operator has been to write string literals that are too long to fit on one line. We can also use the concatenation operator with literals, constants, and variables of type Character. We can combine a String value and a Character value into a single String value, and we can combine two Character values into a String value. For example:

Expression	Result
`"Mode" & 'l'`	`"Model"`
`'M' & "ale"`	`"Male"`
`'A' & 'C'`	`"AC"`

We can also use concatenation to include control characters in a string. Here, for example, we use concatenation operators to insert horizontal tab characters into a string that is printed as a table heading.*

```
Ada.Text_IO.Put (Item => "Name" & Ada.Characters.Latin_1.HT & "Address" &
                         Ada.Characters.Latin_1.HT & "Phone");
```

Characters or Strings? Character and String types are closely related. Character is a predefined enumeration type. Because Character is a discrete type, we can use all of the attributes available for discrete types. A String is composed of a fixed number of characters. We use Character variables when we need to process textual material character by character. We employ String variables when we need to process groups of related characters.

*Here is a place where we would recommend a use clause to eliminate the long prefix Ada.Characters.Latin_1.

When designing a solution to a problem that involves textual data, carefully weigh the advantages of each of these types before committing yourself to one or the other. Often a combination of Character and String variables is the best solution.

Programmer-Defined Scalar Data Types

In Chapter 1 we discussed the evolution of programming languages. Machine language instructions are binary codes. Assembly language uses mnemonics in place of these binary codes. In high-level languages such as Ada, the instructions are much closer to English.

We use the computer to solve problems. In essence, our programs are models of the problems we solve. Each step in the evolution of programming languages has taken us further from the language of the computer hardware and closer to the language of the problems. By using the language of the problem rather than the language of the machine, Ada permits us to build more understandable models of our problems than is possible in lower-level languages.

It is not just the nature of the instructions that has changed in the evolution of programming languages. The mechanisms for describing data also have evolved. The concept of a data type, as defined at the start of this chapter, is fundamental to most high-level programming languages. Machine and assembly language programs work with binary data. Any special properties possessed by the data in a particular problem are ignored. It is possible, for example, to multiply a character and an integer together. The predefined types in high-level languages like Ada were a great step forward. However, Float and Integer are still too general to describe the numeric data of a given problem adequately. Temperatures, pressures, purchase prices, and interest rates all have different properties that are lost when we use Float to represent them. By representing both the pressure and the temperature of the gases in a rocket engine as Float quantities, a programming error in which we mistakenly add pounds of pressure to degrees Celsius could go unnoticed. We can write a better model of our problem, and thus a better program, if we use data types that accurately reflect the nature of the data in a particular problem. One research study on the nature of major software problems indicates that poor models of scalar quantities were responsible for over 80% of the errors in the cases studied.*

One of Ada's strengths is that it allows programmers to create new data types by means of a **type declaration.** In the type declaration the programmer describes the domain of a new data type and assigns it a name. We already have seen how to declare one form of programmer-defined data types—enumeration types. Here we look at declaring other scalar data

*"My Hairiest Bug War Stories," M. Eisenstadt, *Communications of the ACM,* vol 40, pp. 30–37, 1997. An analysis of the war stories made available by the author showed that 15 of the 17 programming errors were due to problems with scalar values.

types. We introduce additional kinds of programmer-defined data types in later chapters. In future courses you will study other powerful mechanisms for modeling object classes and the relationships between them.

Type declaration The association of a type identifier with the definition of a new data type.

We declare types in the declarative section of a program. Once we have declared a new data type, we can use its identifier anywhere we use the standard types, such as in constant declarations, generic package instantiations, variable declarations, and formal parameter lists.

It is important to understand the distinction between type declarations and variable declarations. A type declaration describes only the set of values in a data type. No variables of that type exist until they are declared. Think of a type declaration as creating a pattern, and a variable declaration as creating something from that pattern. The simplified EBNF definition for a type declaration is:

type_declaration	::=	**type** identifier **is** type_definition;
type_definition	::=	enumeration_type definition |
		integer_type_definition |
		float_type_definition, |
		decimal_type_definition
enumeration_type_definition	::=	(identifier {,identifier})
integer_type_definition	::=	**range** range
float_type_definition	::=	**digits** *static*_simple_expression [**range** range]
decimal_type_definition	::=	**delta** *static*_simple_expression float_type_definition
range	::=	simple_expression . . simple_expression

Here are some examples of type declarations to which we will refer in the following sections.

```
type Inches            is digits 4 range 0.00..100.00;
type Feet              is digits 6 range 0.00..1000.00;

type Test_Score_Type   is range 0..100;
type Quiz_Score_Type   is range 0..10;

type Pesos             is delta 0.1  digits 9 range 0.0 ..1_000_000.0;
type Dollars           is delta 0.01 digits 8 range 0.00..  100_000.00;

type Day_Type          is (Monday, Tuesday, Wednesday, Thursday,
                           Friday, Saturday, Sunday);
```

There are four distinct categories of types in these examples. Inches and Feet are floating-point types, Test_Score_Type and Quiz_Score_Type are integer types, Pesos and Dollars are decimal types, and Day_Type is an enumeration type. We discussed enumeration types in Chapter 4 and again earlier in this chapter. In the next sections we look at programmer-defined floating-point, integer, and decimal types.

Floating-Point Type Declarations

Floating-point is the most common method for representing real numbers in the computer's memory. Ada's predefined type Float is, as its name implies, a floating-point type. A **floating-point type** uses a fixed number of digits (the mantissa) and a base raised to a power (the exponent) to approximate a real number. Here is an example.

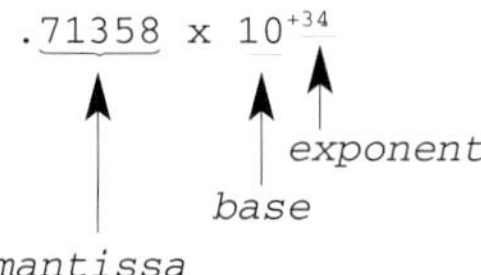

The base need not be 10. Here are some examples of floating-point numbers using other bases.

$.54722 \times 8^{-4}$ $.11011011 \times 2^{+1101}$ $.389 \times 16^{+6}$

Floating-point type A numeric type that uses a fixed number of digits and an exponent to approximate a real number.

Scientific notation, a decimal form of floating-point, illustrates the origin of the term floating. All of the following are representations of the same number.

$.0512 \times 10^{9}$ $.512 \times 10^{8}$ 5.12×10^{7} 51.2×10^{6} $512. \times 10^{5}$

The decimal point may float to any position. When the decimal point floats to the right we decrease the exponent to compensate. When it floats to the left, we increase the exponent.

To create our own floating-point type, we supply two pieces of information to specify its domain: the number of *digits of precision* and an optional *range*. In our examples

```
type Inches is digits 4 range 0.00..100.00;
type Feet   is digits 6 range 0.00..1000.00
```

we specified 4 digits of precision for type Inches and 6 digits of precision for type Feet.

The computer is limited to a finite number of digits. Thus floating-point values only approximate the real numbers we wish to store. For example, it requires an infinite number of digits to store the value of π exactly. If we need to use π in a problem, we must decide how many digits to use for our *approximation* of π.

Digits of Precision	Approximation of π
3	3.14
4	3.141
5	3.1416
6	3.14159

Determining the number of digits of precision to use in a floating-point type declaration can be a difficult task for beginning programmers. You will learn more about errors and precision of floating-point numbers in future courses. For now, just use some common sense when selecting the number of digits. Ask yourself, how precise is my data? For instance, suppose we need a type for length data. The length measurements are made with a high-quality ruler. Realistically, we can expect readings between 00.00 and 12.00 inches and four digits of precision. Why not five digits of precision (00.000 to 12.000 inches)? The human eye can't resolve one one-thousandth of an inch with an ordinary ruler. Using five digits of precision for this data misrepresents the true precision of the measurements; it gives the idea that the measurements are accurate to one one-thousandth of an inch.

Recall that a data type is a formal description of a set of values (called the domain) and the basic operations that can be applied to these values. The precision and range specified in a floating-point type declaration determine the domain of the type. The basic operations available for our own floating-point types are the same as those available for the predefined type Float.

Why would we want to declare our own floating-point type when Ada's predefined type Float is available? There are two big reasons for avoiding the predefined type Float. First, using our own floating-point types makes our programs easier to read. The variable declarations

```
Wall_Thickness  : Float range 0.5 .. 18.0;
Building_Length : Float;
Total_Length    : Float;
```

give less information about the variables than

```
Wall_Thickness  : Inches range 0.5 .. 18.0;
Building_Length : Feet;
Total_Length    : Feet;
```

In the second set of declarations, the valid ranges for Building_Length and Total_Length are those given in our declaration of type Feet. The range specification in the declaration of variable Wall_Thickness further limits the range of acceptable values for this variable from those in our declaration of type Inches. In all cases, these ranges allow us to take advantage of **automatic range checking** to help find errors when we are testing our program. When a value is assigned to a variable, the system checks that it is within the specified range. If it is not, a CONSTRAINT_ERROR exception occurs, the program is halted, and an error message is displayed.

Automatic range checking The automatic detection of the assignment of an out-of-range value to a variable.

The second reason for declaring our own floating-point types is to prevent inappropriate operations. For example, the assignment statement

```
Total_Length := Building_Length + Wall_Thickness;
```

is not appropriate because we are adding feet and inches together. If the Building_Length is 30 feet and the Wall_Thickness is 12 inches, this statement attempts to assign a value of 42 to Total_Length. This inappropriate assignment would succeed if all three variables were type Float. You have already experienced how Ada's strong typing prevents us from adding an Integer value and a Float value together. This strong typing also prevents us from adding a Feet value and an Inches value together. The compiler would issue an error message for the inappropriate assignment statement. To add the two quantities we must perform a conversion so that the values have the same units (either feet or inches). We discuss conversions later in this chapter (page 401).

Floating-Point Attributes Many different attributes are available to determine the characteristics of floating-point types. You can find descriptions of them all in the *Ada Reference Manual* (ARM). Here are five of the most useful.

Attribute	**Purpose**
First	Returns the lower bound of the type.
Last	Returns the upper bound of the type.
Image	Returns a string equivalent to a given value.
Value	Returns a value equivalent to a given string.
Digits	Returns the number of decimal digits of precision of the type.

We discussed First, Last, Image, and Value earlier in this chapter. These four attributes are available for all scalar types—types in which the values are ordered and each value is atomic. All floating-point types are scalar types. The following examples of all five attributes feature the two floating-point types we declared on page 392.

Expression	**Result**
`Inches'First`	0.00
`Inches'Last`	100.00
`Inches'Image(4.2)`	" 4.200E+00"
`Inches'Value ("   7.6    ")`	7.60
`Inches'Digits`	4
`Feet'First`	0.00
`Feet'Last`	1000.00
`Feet'Image(4.2)`	" 4.20000E+00"
`Feet'Value ("   7.6    ")`	7.60
`Feet'Digits`	6

Notice that the number of digits in the string resulting from evaluating 'Image attributes equals the digits of precision for the type.

Standard Mathematical Functions In Chapter 6, we introduced you to package Ada.Numerics.Elementary_Functions. This predefined package contains many commonly used mathematical functions. However, these functions only work with parameters of type Float. We cannot use them with our own floating-point types. We must create our own packages with the mathematical functions we need. As we did with the input and output of programmer-defined enumeration types in Chapter 4, we can make use of a standard generic package to create the packages we need. This generic package is called Ada.Numerics.Generic_Elementary_Functions. The following two statements create packages with elementary mathematical functions for Feet and Inches.

```
package Feet_Ops is new
          Ada.Numerics.Generic_Elementary_Functions (Float_Type => Feet);
package Inch_Ops is new
          Ada.Numerics.Generic_Elementary_Functions (Float_Type => Inches);
```

We need to include a with clause at the beginning of our program to access the generic package Ada.Numerics.Generic_Elementary_Functions.

Here is a demonstration of the square root function in the first package in a Pythagorean calculation.

```
A : Feet;
B : Feet;
C : Feet;
   .
   .
   .
C := Feet_Ops.Sqrt (A **2 + B **2);
```

Integer Type Declarations

As with floating-point types, the primary reasons we declare our own integer types rather than use the predefined type Integer is to improve readability and to prevent inappropriate operations. Here are the two examples of programmer-defined integer types given earlier in this chapter.

```
type Test_Score_Type is range 0..100;
type Quiz_Score_Type is range 0..10;
```

We can use the same operators with programmer-declared integer types as we used with the predefined type Integer. The range constraint in the type declaration limits the domain of our new type. The range we select may not include values less than SYSTEM.Min_Int or greater than SYSTEM.Max_Int. The operations available with programmer-declared integer types also include type attributes. We can use any of the attributes for discrete types with our own integer types. The following examples illustrate use of the First and Last attributes with our two new types.

Expression	Result
`Test_Score_Type'First`	0
`Test_Score_Type'Last`	100
`Quiz_Score_Type'First`	0
`Quiz_Score_Type'Last`	10

Decimal Type Declarations

The following program fragment sums three cents, one hundred thousand times. What do you think it displays?

```
Three_Pennies : constant Float := 0.03;
Total_Dollars : Float;
Count         : Integer;
. . .
```

```
Total_Dollars := 0.0;          -- Initialize the sum
Count         := 1;            -- and iteration counter
loop   -- Each iteration, add 3 cents to the total
   exit when Count > 100_000;
   Total_Dollars := Total_Dollars + Three_Pennies;
   Count := Count + 1;
end loop;

Ada.Float_Text_IO.Put (Item => Total_Dollars,
                       Fore => 10, Aft  => 2, Exp  => 0);
```

We would expect this program fragment to display a value of 3,000.00. Yet when compiled and run, this program displayed a value of 3,002.41. The result is off by 241 pennies! How could the computer be so wrong? To answer this question we must look at how the computer stores numbers. Floating-point and integer numbers are stored in binary form. Our decimal (base 10) numbers are converted to binary (base 2) numbers before being stored in memory. Here are some examples of equivalent decimal and binary integers.

43_{10}	101011_2
15_{10}	1111_2
98_{10}	1100010_2

All whole base 10 numbers can be written exactly in base 2. However, when a decimal number contains a fraction, it usually cannot be written *exactly* in binary. We cannot represent our three cents exactly in binary. Translating this decimal value yields a never-ending binary value.

0.03_{10} $\quad 0.000001111010111000010100011110101110000101\ldots_2$

Only a finite number of binary digits (bits) are used to store 0.03 as a binary floating-point number. While we can improve the accuracy of the representation by increasing the digits of precision, we can never store 0.03 exactly. There will always be some error. As demonstrated by the program fragment given, this representational error is magnified by repeated operations.

Many applications such as financial calculations cannot tolerate the errors resulting from the binary representation of data. For such applications Ada provides the means to store decimal numbers exactly. Here are two examples

```
type Pesos   is delta 0.1  digits 9 range 0.0 ..1_000_000.0;
type Dollars is delta 0.01 digits 8 range 0.00..  100_000.00;
```

The number after the reserved word `delta` specifies the precision of the decimal number. This precision must be a power of 10, such as 100.0, 10.0,

1.0, 0.1, 0.01, or 0.001. All values of the type are multiples of this number. So every Pesos value is a multiple of tenths of a peso and every Dollars value is a multiple of hundredths of a dollar. Another way of saying this is that Pesos are stored exactly to the nearest tenth and Dollars to the nearest hundredth. The number after the reserved word `digits` specifies the total number of decimal digits used to represent the number.

Together the precision and digits determine the *maximum* range for the type. With a precision of 0.1 and 9 digits, the maximum range of Pesos is −99,999,999.9 to +99,999,999.9. With a precision of 0.01 and 8 digits, the maximum range of Dollars is −999,999.99 to +999,999.99. The Ada compiler issues an error message if you attempt to specify a range that is greater than that allowed by the specified delta and digits. The optional range clauses included in our declarations further limit the ranges specified by the precision and digits.

Except for exponentiation, we can use the same operations and attributes with decimal numbers as we have with floating-point numbers. In addition, we can use the attribute Delta to query the precision of a decimal type. Here are the values of the Delta attributes for our two decimal types.

Expression	**Result**
`Pesos'Delta`	0.1
`Dollars'Delta`	0.01

After seeing the representational problems present in floating-point numbers, why would we choose to use floating-point numbers rather than decimal numbers when we need real numbers in our programs? Historically, floating-point representation has been the most common method for storing real numbers. Nearly every programming language uses floating-point to represent real numbers. The COBOL programming language, commonly used in financial applications, is a notable exception. Because of the widespread use of floating-point types, most of today's CPUs execute floating-point operations very quickly. In fact, a common measurement of CPU performance is Mega FLOPS (Millions of FLoating point OPerations per Second). We often find that decimal numbers require more memory to store and more time to carry out basic operations.

While using a decimal type would have eliminated the error in our penny summing program, there are still problems with decimal numbers. What should the answer be when we calculate the average of $5.71 and $6.30? Mathematically the result is $6.005. But using the decimal type Dollars, the result must be stored as either $6.00 or $6.01. The study of the errors in real number computer arithmetic is a major part of books and courses on numerical analysis and is beyond the scope of this book.

Input and Output

The predefined packages Ada.Float_Text_IO and Ada.Integer_Text_IO provide Get and Put operations for the predefined types Float and Integer. To do input and output with values of a programmer-defined type, we must create our own packages. But, as we did with programmer-defined enumeration types in Chapter 4, we can make use of generic packages to create the packages we need. All of the generic packages for programmer-defined scalar types are found inside of package Text_IO.

Ada.Text_IO.Enumeration_IO	Generic template for enumeration types
Ada.Text_IO.Float_IO	Generic template for floating-point types
Ada.Text_IO.Integer_IO	Generic template for integer types
Ada.Text_IO.Decimal_IO	Generic template for decimal types

Using the programmer-defined types declared on page 392, here are the statements to instantiate an I/O package for each different type.

```
package Day_IO  is new Ada.Text_IO.Enumeration_IO (Enum => Day_Type);

package Inch_IO is new Ada.Text_IO.Float_IO (Num => Inches);
package Feet_IO is new Ada.Text_IO.Float_IO (Num => Feet);

package Test_IO is new Ada.Text_IO.Integer_IO (Num => Test_Score_Type);
package Quiz_IO is new Ada.Text_IO.Integer_IO (Num => Quiz_Score_Type);

package Peso_IO   is new Ada.Text_IO.Decimal_IO (Num => Pesos);
package Dollar_IO is new Ada.Text_IO.Decimal_IO (Num => Dollars);
```

Each of the new packages we instantiate contains Get and Put procedures for the specified type. The specifications of all of these procedures are given in Appendix D. Here are some example calls.

```
Day        : Day_Type;
Thickness  : Inches;
Midterm    : Test_Score_Type;
Investment : Pesos;
   . . .
Day_IO.Put  (Item  => Day,
             Width => 12);
Inch_IO.Put (Item  => Thickness,
             Fore  => 4,
             Aft   => 2,
             Exp   => 0);
Test_IO.Put (Item  => Midterm,
             Width => 6);
```

```
Peso_IO.Put (Item  => Investment,
             Fore  => 8,
             Aft   => 1,
             Exp   => 0);
```

Notice that the formal parameters for the decimal type output procedure is identical to that for floating-point numbers.

Now that we can display decimal type values, we can rewrite the program fragment on page 397–398 that sums three pennies one hundred thousand times. In the following code fragment we use the decimal type Dollars and the package Dollar_IO declared previously.

```
Three_Pennies : constant Dollars := 0.03;
Total_Dollars : Dollars;
. . .
Total_Dollars := 0.0;        -- Initialize the sum
Count         := 1;          -- and iteration counter
loop   -- Each iteration, add 3 cents to the total
   exit when Count > 100_000;
   Total_Dollars := Total_Dollars + Three_Pennies;
   Count := Count + 1;
end loop;

Dollar_IO.Put (Item => Total_Dollars,
                       Fore => 10, Aft  => 2, Exp  => 0);
```

Recall that when we used type Float for Three_Pennies and Total_Dollars, the answer displayed was 3,002.41. This code displays the correct answer of 3,000.00 when executed on the same computer.

Combining Different Types

Ada's programmer-defined types enable us to define types that are more appropriate for the data with which we work. They make our programs easier to read and allow for automatic range checking. Another virtue of defining our own data types is that they prevent inappropriate operations.

In Chapter 2 we showed you how to employ explicit type conversions to convert Float type values to Integer type values, and vice versa. We can also use explicit type conversions with programmer-defined types. Use the type name of the type to which you want to convert in the same way you would use a function name. The program treats the value that you want to convert as an *in* parameter. Remember, the value itself, like any *in* parameter, does not change. We could, for example, add a test score and a quiz score by converting the quiz score to a test score. The following assignment statements, in which variables Point_Sum and Test_Score are Test_Score_Type, Quiz_Score is Quiz_Score_Type, and Int_Sum is Integer, illustrate explicit conversion.

```
Point_Sum  :=  Test_Score  +  Test_Score_Type(Quiz_Score);

Int_Sum    :=  Integer(Test_Score)  +  Integer(Quiz_Score);
```

In general, with explicit type conversions, the computer does not perform any numerical computations. Converting a Quiz_Score_Type of 8 to a Test_Score_Type yields the same numeric value—8. Computation is required only when converting from a predefined or programmer-defined float type to a predefined or programmer-defined integer type. In this conversion, a float value is rounded to the nearest whole value.

In many cases, however, it is necessary to perform some calculations to convert one type of value to another. In these situations explicit type conversions are inappropriate. Consider, for example, the float types Feet and Inches that we attempted to add together earlier. Although the explicit type conversion in the following statement is syntactically correct, the value assigned to Total_Length is not.

```
Total_Length := Building_Length + Feet(Wall_Thickness);    -- Logic error
```

If Building_Length is 50.0 feet and Wall_Thickness is 11.0 inches, this statement assigns a value of 61.0 feet to Total_Length. The correct result of adding 50 feet and 11 inches is 50.92 feet. To obtain the correct answer we must convert inches to feet by dividing by 12. Explicit type conversions do not perform these types of computations. It is up to us to ensure a correct conversion. A programmer-defined function such as the following will effect this kind of conversion.

```
function To_Feet (Value : in Inches) return Feet is
-- Converts a value in inches to a value in feet.
begin
   return  Feet(Value) / 12.0;
end To_Feet;
```

Then we can use this function to add the building length and wall thickness together like this:

```
Total_Length := Building_Length + To_Feet(Wall_Thickness);
```

where the total length is in feet. The return statement in the function could also be written as

```
return  Feet(Value / 12.0);
```

The division in this expression yields an answer with four digits of precision (that was declared for type Inches), but the division in the expression used in the function gives a result with six digits of precision. In some cases, the actual results may differ. Try to write these types of expressions so that operations are performed with the higher precision types.

Another approach for adding feet and inches values together is to write our own addition function that includes the necessary conversion

```
function "+" (Left : in Feet; Right : in Inches) return Feet is
-- A function that adds feet and inches
begin
   return Left + Feet(Right) / 12.0
end "+"
```

which we can call in an arithmetic expression like this:

```
Total_Length := Building_Length + Wall_Thickness; -- Call our own "+" function
```

Division and Multiplication of Decimal Types The rules for division and multiplication of decimal types are unique. We can multiply a decimal number by an Integer number or an Integer number by a decimal number. We can also divide a decimal number by an Integer number. But we can't divide an Integer number by a decimal number. The type of the result of these mixed Integer-decimal operations is the decimal type.

We can also multiply and divide *two different typed* decimal values. There is a set of rules that governs the type of the result of a multiplication or division of two different decimal types. Rather than learn and apply these rules, we recommend putting each mixed type operation in an explicit type conversion to set the type of the result. Given the declarations

```
type Dollars   is delta 0.01     digits 8 range 0.00 .. 100_000.00;
type Rate_Type is delta 0.000001 digits 8 range 0.00 .. 99.999999;

Rate  : Rate_Type;
Total : Dollars;
Num   : Integer;
```

the following table shows some operations and the types of the result.

Expression	**Type of Result**
`Num * Total`	Dollars
`Total * Num`	Dollars
`Num / Total`	illegal operation!
`Total / Num`	Dollars
`Dollars (Total * Rate)`	Dollars
`Dollars (Rate * Total)`	Dollars

`Dollars (Total / Rate)`	Dollars
`Rate_Type (Rate / Total)`	Rate_Type

We use this mixed type capability with explicit type conversion in the second case study of this chapter.

THEORETICAL FOUNDATIONS

Type Coercion and Conversion

Many languages allow the programmer to assign a value of any type to a variable of any other type. Needless to say, such a lack of restrictions has resulted in numerous errors and has cost a great amount of extra debugging time.

There are times, however, when it is useful to be able to assign a value of one type to a variable of another type. For example, we might want to assign a value in a type with a range of 1 . . 100 to an Integer variable. Such an assignment is called a *type coercion.* In a sense, we coerce a value of one type into being another type.

Ada strictly enforces strong typing by requiring the use of conversion functions (sometimes called *transfer functions* or *type casts*) to convert between any two numeric types. Conversion functions make the use of coercion explicit and thus add to the self-documenting quality of a program. They are an inconvenience, however, when they must be used in even the simplest cases. A language like Pascal tries to strike a balance by providing automatic coercion between similar types.

Ada provides the Pos attribute that converts any discrete type into an integer value. The Val attribute converts an integer value into a discrete type. These conversions are simple to perform because all discrete types are represented in the computer in a way that is similar to integers.

Coercion is inefficient when the binary representation of one type differs from another. For example, integer and float values are represented differently in the computer. The binary code for 67 is different than that for 67.0. Nonetheless, Ada allows us to use explicit type conversion to assign an integer value to a float variable. To do so, it coerces the integer representation into a float representation with a fraction and exponent. The coercion is done in the type conversion function by manipulating the bits of the integer value to form a float number—a time-consuming process.

Some people have criticized Ada for making it too difficult to mix integers and floats in computations. In response, Ada supporters answer that if programmers are required to perform each conversion explicitly, they will be more sparing in their use of *mixed mode arithmetic* and their programs will be more efficient.

We can write our own conversion functions or procedures as we did to convert values of type Inches to values of type Feet. A function that takes a character and returns a corresponding enumeration type value (as in converting 'M' to Mouse) is another example of a conversion function. As we use more data types in the chapters that follow, we will have an even greater need for converting between different data types.

Subtypes

By defining our own types, we make our programs easier to read and we get the benefits of automatic range checking. Most importantly, programmer-defined types prevent us from combining values of different types in an expression. This incompatibility of different types can eliminate the possibility of our incorrectly combining values (such as feet and inches) that should not be combined.

In some cases, two types are related so closely that using them together in expressions is common and desired. Although these types can be combined by employing explicit type conversions in expressions, Ada provides a better solution—the subtype.

Programmer-Defined Subtypes

Programmer-defined subtypes provide two advantages of programmer-defined types (readability and automatic range checking) but without the restrictions on combining values in an expression. As with types, we declare subtypes in the declarative part of the program. Here are some examples of subtype declarations.

```
subtype Negative      is Integer    range Integer'First..-1;
subtype Uppercase     is Character  range 'A'..'Z';
subtype Lowercase     is Character  range 'a'..'z';
subtype Non_Neg_Float is Float      range 0.00..Float'Last
subtype Name_String   is String (1..30);
```

And here is the simplified EBNF definition of a subtype declaration.

subtype_declaration	::=	**subtype** identifier **is** subtype_indication;
subtype_indication	::=	subtype_mark [constraint]
subtype_mark	::=	*type*_name | *subtype*_name
constraint	::=	float_constraint |
		range_constraint |
		index_constraint
float_constraint	::=	**digits** static_simple_expression [range_constraint]
range_constraint	::=	**range** range
index_constraint	::=	(range)
range	::=	simple_expression . . simple_expression

With subtypes we can name a subset of the values in a type. The *type* from which the subset is taken is called the **base type.** All of the operations of the subtype are defined by those of the base type.

Base type The type from which the operations and values for a subtype are taken.

The base type of the subtype Negative we declared earlier is Integer. All of the operations and attributes defined for type Integer are also available for subtype Negative. The operations defined for the subtypes Uppercase and Lowercase are the same as those for type Character, their base type. Similarly, the operations defined for the subtype Name_String are identical to those for type String.

We can declare subtypes as subsets of Ada's predefined types, programmer-defined types, or other subtypes. Here are some examples of subtypes declared as subsets of programmer-defined types and subtypes.

```
type     Pounds                is  Digits 6  range  0.0..1.0E+06;
subtype UPS_Weight_Type        is  Pounds    range  0.0..100.0;
subtype Freight_Weight_Type is  Pounds    range 50.0..10_000.0;

type     Day_Type              is (Monday, Tuesday, Wednesday, Thursday,
                                   Friday, Saturday, Sunday);
subtype Week_Day_Type          is  Day_Type  range Monday..Friday;
subtype Weekend_Day_Type       is  Day_Type  range Saturday..Sunday;

subtype Grade_Type             is  Uppercase range 'A'..'E';
subtype Pass_Grade_Type        is  Grade_Type range 'A'..'D';
```

Pounds is the base type for subtypes UPS_Weight_Type and Truck_Weight_Type. Day_Type is the base type for subtypes Week_Day_Type and Weekend_Day_Type. When a subtype is a subset of another subtype, it inherits the base type of that subtype. Grade_Type's base is Character because Grade_Type is a subset of the subtype Uppercase, whose base type is Character. Because Pass_Grade_Type is a subset of Grade_Type, its base type is also Character.

We can freely combine values of a subtype with any values in its base type or with any values of any other subtype that shares that base type. Take, for example, the following variable declarations:

```
Total_Weight   : Pounds;
Package_Weight : UPS_Weight_Type;
Crate_Weight   : Freight_Weight_Type;
```

Because all three of these variables have the same base type (Pounds), the statement

```
Total_Weight := 5.0 * Package_Weight + 2.0 * Crate_Weight;
```

is valid. This statement would not be valid if we had declared UPS_Weight_Type and Freight_Weight_Type as types instead of subtypes.

Earlier we used a type name in an expression explicitly to convert a value of one type to another type. We can use a subtype name in the same way. Here are some examples.

Expression	Value	Subtype of Value
UPS_Weight_Type(5)	5.0	UPS_Weight
Negative(-7.4)	−7	Negative
UPS_Weight_Type(150)	CONSTRAINT_ERROR	

In the first example, the integer literal 5 is explicitly converted to the UPS_Weight_Type value 5.0. In the second, the float literal −7.4 is converted to the Negative value −7. When converting a float type or subtype to an integer subtype, the value is rounded to the nearest whole value. If the resulting value is not in the domain of the subtype a CONSTRAINT_ERROR occurs, as the third example illustrates.

The EBNF definition for a subtype indicates that the constraint given after the subtype mark is optional. This allows us to use a subtype name to rename an existing type or subtype. For example, the following declarations

```
subtype Part_Num_Type is Integer;      -- Subtype declarations
subtype Velocity_Type is Float;        -- without constraints
```

declare subtypes Part_Num_Type and Velocity_Type, which are just new names for the predefined types Integer and Float. This allows us to improve the readability of our program without having to specify a range constraint on the type. And later, if we find that a constraint is appropriate, we simply add it to the subtype. Then all variables declared with it will have their new ranges checked automatically. If we had declared variables used to hold part numbers as type Integer rather than as Part_Num_Type, we would have to go through and change each variable declaration to reflect the added constraint.

Whenever you use the predefined types Integer or Float in a variable declaration, ask yourself whether a subtype could make your program easier to understand. Also consider whether there is a possibility that you may want to specify a range for that variable sometime in the future. Many experienced Ada programmers rarely use the predefined types Integer and Float in the declaration of variables. They use types Integer and Float as base types in the declaration of their own subtypes.

Predefined Subtypes

Ada has two predefined integer subtypes: Natural and Positive. They are declared within Ada as follows:

```
subtype Natural  is Integer range 0..Integer'Last;  -- These two subtypes are
subtype Positive is Integer range 1..Integer'Last;  -- predefined within Ada
```

As with subtypes that you define yourself, you may use Natural and Positive in the declarations of constants, variables, and additional subtypes. Here are some examples.

```
subtype Month_Num_Type is Positive range 1..12;

Seconds_Per_Minute : constant Natural := 60;

Elapsed_Time       : Natural;
```

Membership Operators

The limited range assigned to subtypes ensures that the value of a variable is reasonable. If we attempt to assign a value outside of the subtype's range to a variable, a CONSTRAINT_ERROR occurs, and the program halts. Subtype ranges also allow us to test a value ourselves to see whether it is in the domain of the subtype. Such tests are called **membership tests.** The result of a membership test is type Boolean. Ada uses the operators `in` and `not in` to perform these tests. Here are some expressions that use membership operators.

Expression	Result
`5 in Positive`	True
`Monday in Week_End_Type`	False
`102.3 not in UPS_Weight_Type`	True

Membership test An operation that determines whether or not a value belongs to the domain of a subtype.

The following function to convert an uppercase character to lowercase is identical to the one given on page 386 except that it uses one membership operator instead of two relational operators.

```
function To_Lower (Ch : in Character) return Character is

-- Converts an uppercase letter to lowercase. Any other
-- character given is returned unchanged.
```

```
   -- Shift is the position difference between equivalent
   -- uppercase and lowercase letters.
   Shift : constant Integer := Character'Pos('a') - Character'Pos('A');

   Lower_Position : Integer;          -- The position of the lowercase
                                      -- equivalent of Ch

begin  -- To Lower

   if Ch in Uppercase then     -- Is Ch an uppercase letter?
      -- Calculate the position of the equivalent lowercase letter
      Lower_Position := Character'Pos (Ch) + Shift;
      -- Return the value of the letter at the calculated position
      return Character'Val(Lower_Position);
   else  -- Not an uppercase letter, return Ch unchanged
      return Ch;
   end if;
end To_Lower;
```

Subtypes and Parameters

When a predefined or programmer-defined type is used for a formal parameter, the actual parameter must be of the same type or of a subtype with that type as its base type. This means that, if a procedure expects a parameter of a certain type and you have defined a subtype of that type, you can pass a variable of the subtype to the procedure. For example, given these variable declarations and procedure:

```
Total_Weight   : Pounds;
Package_Weight : UPS_Weight_Type;          -- A subtype of Pounds
Crate_Weight   : Freight_Weight_Type;      -- Another subtype of Pounds


procedure Print_Shipping_Cost (Weight : in Pounds) is
   .
   .
   .
```

the following are all valid calls to the procedure.

```
Print_Shipping_Weight (Weight => Total_Weight);
Print_Shipping_Weight (Weight => Package_Weight);
Print_Shipping_Weight (Weight => Crate_Weight);
```

If the formal parameter is an *out* or *in out* parameter, the returned value is checked automatically against the range of the actual parameter's subtype. A CONSTRAINT_ERROR exception occurs and the program halts if that value does not fall within the allowed range of the subtype. That is, a procedure is automatically prevented from returning an out-of-range value.

When you use a subtype for a formal parameter, the actual parameter must be of the base type or any subtype with the same base type. Thus the above procedure calls also are valid if we change the procedure Print_Shipping_Cost to

```
procedure Print_Shipping_Cost (Weight : in UPS_Weight_Type) is
   .
   .
   .
```

If the value of an actual parameter does not fall within the range of the formal *in* or *in out* parameter, a CONSTRAINT_ERROR occurs and the program is halted with an error. We are automatically prevented from passing an out-of-range value to a procedure.

Input and Output of Subtypes

As we saw earlier, Ada's strong typing requires that a new I/O package be instantiated for each new type. The generic packages Integer_IO, Float_IO, Decimal_IO, and Enumeration_IO found in Ada.Text_IO are used as the templates for instantiating new packages for integer types, float types, decimal types and enumeration types. The type for which we want the I/O package constructed is specified through a parameter—Num for integer, float, and decimal types and Enum for enumeration types. Generally, whenever you declare a new type, you also should declare a new I/O package to go with it. Of course, if you know that you'll never input or output a value of the new type, then there is no reason to do this.

Ada does not require a separate I/O package for every subtype we declare. We can instantiate an I/O package for the base type and use its Get and Put procedures for the subtype. For example, subtypes UPS_Weight_Type and Freight_Weight_Type share the same base type—Pounds. We can use the I/O package instantiated for pounds with both of these subtypes.

```
Pounds_IO.Get (Item => Package_Weight);
Pounds_IO.Put (Item => Crate_Weight,  Fore => 6,  Aft  => 1,  Exp  => 0);
```

While we can instantiate an I/O package for a subtype, there is usually no advantage in doing so. We discuss the details of such instantiations in Chapter 9 after we introduce exception handlers.

Named and Anonymous String Types

In a type or subtype declaration, we specify an identifier to use as a name for that type or subtype. Because these types and subtypes are given an identifier, they are called **named types.** Variables of these new types are declared using the type identifier. The predefined types and subtypes Integer, Float, Boolean, Natural, and Positive also are named types.

Named type A type or subtype defined with an identifying name.

The String type is different from all other types we have discussed. To define a string type completely, we must specify a range to indicate how many characters a variable of that type holds. We can give this range in a subtype declaration or in the declarations of individual variables. The following two examples are equivalent.

Example 1

```
-- Type declarations
subtype Name_String   is String(1..20);
subtype Street_String is String(1..30);
subtype City_String   is String(1..15);

-- Variable declarations
Name   : Name_String;
Street : Street_String;
City   : City_String;
```

Example 2

```
-- Variable declarations
Name   : String(1..20);
Street : String(1..30);
City   : String(1..15);
```

In the second example, the string subtype is fully declared in the variable declaration. As a result, these string types do not have an identifier associated with them. Such types are called **anonymous types.**

Anonymous type A type or subtype defined in the declaration of a variable. It has no identifying name.

The strings that we have used in previous chapters have been anonymous string types. Employing them is considered poor programming practice. Named types and subtypes, like constants, make a program more readable, more understandable, and easier to modify. Also, defining a type and declaring a variable are two distinct operations and should be kept separate.

In addition, only named types and subtypes are allowed in the formal parameter list of a function or procedure. This is why we did not use string parameters in previous chapters. For example:

```
procedure Example (Name : out String(1..20) ) is     -- illegal
```

is an illegal procedure declaration because explicit constraints are not permitted in the formal parameter list. The following procedure specification using the string subtype Name_String (as declared in the first example above) is legal.

```
procedure Example (Name : out Name_String) is
```

Types or Subtypes?

We have illustrated how programmer-defined types and subtypes make our programs easier to understand and debug. Because programmer-defined types and programmer-defined subtypes both limit the domain, how do we decide which to use in our Ada program?

To answer this question, we need to look at the major difference between types and subtypes. We can mix subtype values freely in an expression with values of its base type or with other subtypes that share this base type. In contrast, we may *not* mix type values in an expression with values of other types; using different types in the same expression requires the use of conversion functions (either explicit type conversions or ones that we write).

When to Use Subtypes

We recommend that, given a choice, you use subtypes. Doing so easily allows you to combine variables with different ranges in your expressions. Such expressions are usually easier to read than expressions containing conversion functions. Using subtypes also simplifies input and output. We need only instantiate packages for the base types used in our program. If we use types, we must instantiate a new package for each new type. As the previous section pointed out, you should always use a named string subtype rather than an anonymous type.

When to Use Types

Use types for those situations where you want to be sure to prevent the inadvertent mixing of particular variables. For example, weight and mass are two different physical quantities that are sometimes incorrectly thought to be different units for the same quantity. Weight, however, depends on gravitational attraction. This fact explains why you weigh different amounts on different planets even though your mass is constant. Combining a weight and a mass value without applying the correct conversion factor would be disastrous in a satellite navigation program. By declaring different types for these quantities, we help ensure that such a problem is avoided. Types are also more appropriate in team projects.

SOFTWARE ENGINEERING TIP

Program Portability

A program that we move from one computer to another without having to make any changes is a **portable program.** Although the Ada standard promotes portability, it can not guarantee it. Using the predefined types Integer and Float in a program may restrict its portability. Various computers may use different numbers or different arrangements of bits to store integer and float values. These computers may have different values for Integer'First, Integer'Last, Float'First, Float'Last, and Float'Digits. Thus one computer may be able to store integers as large as 2,147,483,647 and to store float values with 12 digits of precision whereas another may be restricted to integers no larger than 32,767 and float values with no more than 8 digits of precision.

By avoiding the predefined numeric types (Integer and Float) and subtypes (Natural and Positive) in the declaration of variables, and by specifying the range and precision in our own types and subtypes, we guarantee the range and precision of our variables. If another computer cannot accommodate our declarations, its Ada compiler will issue a syntax error to alert us to the limitations of that computer. This error, during the compilation of the Ada program on the new computer, is preferred to an error at run time that would not have occurred during our testing on the original computer.

Portable program A program that can be moved from one computer to another without having to make changes in the program.

Universal Types

What type is the literal 12.0? It appears that it could be type Float, Pounds, Feet, Inches, Dollars, or any other programmer-defined float or decimal type. In Ada, all numeric literals are one of two special types, called **uni-**

versal types. These two types are *universal_integer* and *universal_real*. The first is used for all literals without a decimal point (whole numbers), and the second for literals containing a decimal point. The range of the universal_integer is the largest range allowed by the computer on which the program is running. The range and number of digits of the universal_real are also the largest permitted by the computer.

Universal types The types of numeric literals. Integer literals are type universal_integer and float literals are type universal_real.

You may use universal integer values in an expression with any integer type or subtype. Universal real values may be used in an expression with any float or decimal type or subtype. When you use a universal type in an expression with another type or subtype, the universal value converts automatically to that type or subtype. Such a conversion is called an *implicit conversion* or *coercion* because it requires no explicit actions on our part. Here are some examples using several of the types declared earlier in this chapter.

```
Package_Weight : UPS_Weight_Type;
Page_Length    : Inches;
Word_Count     : Integer;
Total          : Float;
```

Expression	The Universal Value (Literal) Is Automatically Converted to
`2.0 * Package_Weight`	UPS_Weight_Type
`Page_Length - 2`	Inches
`Word_Count + 1`	Integer
`Total / 2.0`	Float

Named Numbers

Universal types are not restricted to numeric literals. We can also declare constants as universal_integer or universal_real types. Such constants are called **named numbers.** A named number is declared by not including a type in the declaration of a constant.

```
Pi    : constant :=  3.1415926;        -- Pi is universal_real
Shift : constant := 32;                -- Shift is universal_integer
```

We cannot mix constants that are declared with a type with other types in an expression without explicit type conversions. However, we can mix named numbers with other types where implicit type conversions can be made. This means that we can use Pi in an expression with any float type, and Shift in an expression with any integer type.

Named number A constant of type universal_integer or universal_real.

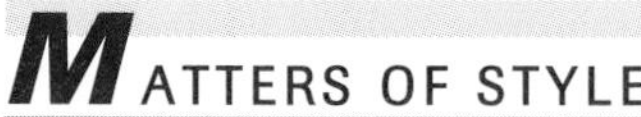

MATTERS OF STYLE

Declarative Part Style

We make declarations for named numbers, constants, variables, subprograms, types, and subtypes in the declarative part of our program or subprogram. We also do the instantiation of generic packages in this part of our program. Ada allows flexibility in the order of declarations. To maintain a consistent style, we generally will make our declarations in the following order.

1. Declaration of named numbers
2. Declaration of programmer-defined types and subtypes
3. Declaration of constants of programmer-defined types and subtypes
4. Instantiations of generic packages
5. Declaration of procedures and functions
6. Declaration of variables

However, because we must define any identifier before we can use it, there are situations in which we cannot group all similar declarations together in this order. In such cases, we will modify the order of declarations or mix different kinds of declarations. There is no particular advantage of this ordering over others. Consistency of ordering is what is important for readable programs.

PROBLEM-SOLVING CASE STUDY

The Rich Uncle

Specification

Problem Your rich uncle has just died, and in his desk you find two wills. One of them, dated several months ago, leaves you and your relatives a substantial part of his fortune; the other, dated last week, gives it all to his next-door neighbor. Being suspicious that the second will is a forgery, you decide to write a program to analyze writing style in order to

PROBLEM-SOLVING CASE STUDY cont'd.

compare the wills. The program will read the will from a text file. You have placed a '+' character in this file following the last character of the will. When the entire file has been read, the program will print a summary table showing the percentage of uppercase letters, lowercase letters, decimal digits, blanks, and end-of-sentence punctuation marks ('?', '!', '.') in the file.

Input

- The name of the file containing the text of the will (entered from keyboard).
- The text of the will (in a text file).

Output A table giving the name of each of the five character categories and what percentage of the total characters in the will that category represents.

Assumptions

- The name of the data file contains no more than 80 characters.
- The data file exists.
- There are no '+' characters in the will.
- A '+' character appears after the last character of text in the data file.

Design Doing this task by hand would be tedious but quite straightforward. You would set up five places to make marks, one for each of the categories of symbols to be counted. Then you would read the text character by character, determine which category to put each character in, and make a hash mark in the appropriate place. If the character doesn't fit in any category, you would make a hash mark in a left-over category. So we need six different counters that we must initialize to zero before we begin counting.

You can look at a character and immediately tell which category to mark. We will simulate this process using membership tests. We must declare subtypes to perform these membership tests. Looking at the collating sequence of Character given in Appendix C, we can see that the lowercase letters form a continuous block. Likewise, uppercase letters and digits are also all together. Here are the declarations for these three subtypes

```
subtype Lowercase is Character range 'a' .. 'z';
subtype Uppercase is Character range 'A' .. 'Z';
subtype Digit     is Character range '0' .. '9';
```

PROBLEM-SOLVING CASE STUDY *cont'd.*

Because the punctuation characters are not adjacent in the collating sequence, we cannot define a subtype for this category. We must test each punctuation character individually.

```
Category_Count                                        Level 0
Initialize all counters to zero
Get File_Name
Open the File
loop
   Get A_Character
   exit loop if A_Character is '+'
   Increment the appropriate counter
Close the File
Display percentages
```

We use six different counters in this module. The lowest value each can take is zero. We do not know ahead of time how high they can go. We use the predefined subtype Natural for all these counters. Here are the data modeling decisions for all objects in our level 0 algorithm.

Name	Data Type	Role
Lowercase_Count	Natural	Number of lowercase letters in the will
Uppercase_Count	Natural	Number of uppercase letters in the will
Digit_Count	Natural	Number of digits in the will
Blank_Count	Natural	Number of blanks in the will
Punctuation_Count	Natural	Number of punctuation characters in the will
Other_Count	Natural	Number of other characters in the will
File_Name	File_Name_String	The name of the file containing the will
File	File_Type	The data file
A_Character	Character	One character in the text of the will

What information do we need to exchange between this level 0 module and the level 1 module to increment the appropriate counter? We must pass it the character we just read so it can classify it and increment a counter. At level 0 we have not inspected the character and so we do not know into which category it falls. We pass all of the counters to our level 1 module and have it increment the appropriate counter. Because we are

PROBLEM-SOLVING CASE STUDY cont'd.

passing the counters in to the procedure, changing them, and passing them back out, we use the *in out* mode for these parameters. The character that the level 1 module classifies is not modified and so we pass it as an *in* mode parameter.

Increment Proper Counter **Level 1**

```
  in       A_Character
  in out   Uppercase_Count
  in out   Lowercase_Count
  in out   Digit_Count
  in out   Blank_Count
  in out   Punctuation_Count
  in out   Other_Count
if A_Character is uppercase then
  Increment Uppercase_Count
elsif A_Character is lowercase then
  Increment Lowercase_Count
elsif A_Character is a digit then
  Increment Digit_Count
elsif A_Character is a blank
  Increment Blank_Count
elsif A_Character is '?' or '!' or '.' then
  Increment Punctuation_Count
else
  Increment Other_Count
```

In order to display the percentages represented by each counter, we must pass all counters to the level 1 display procedure.

Display Percentages **Level 1**

```
  in   Uppercase_Count
  in   Lowercase_Count
  in   Digit_Count
  in   Blank_Count
  in   Punctuation_Count
  in   Other_Count
Set Total to sum of 6 counters
Display 100 × Uppercase_Count / Total
Display 100 × Lowercase_Count / Total
Display 100 × Digit_Counter / Total
Display 100 × Blank_Count / Total
Display 100 × Punctuation_Count / Total
```

PROBLEM-SOLVING CASE STUDY *cont'd.*

Module Structure Chart

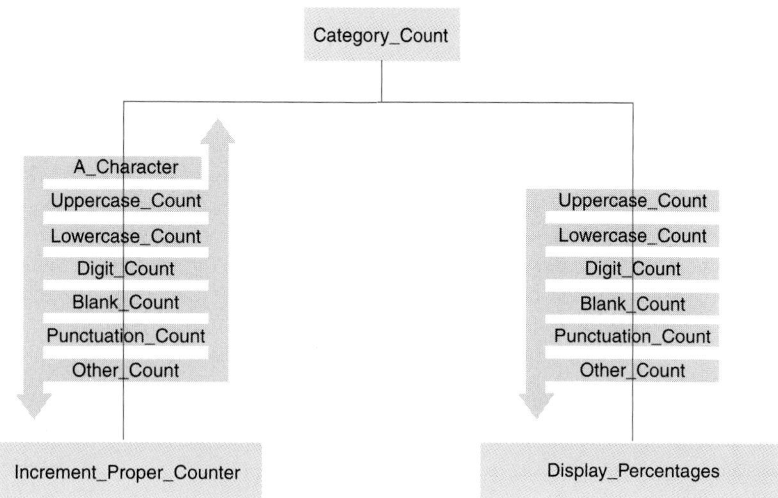

Implementation Here is the program produced from our design.

```
with Ada.Text_IO;
with Ada.Float_Text_IO;
procedure Category_Count is

-- This program analyzes the characters in a text file and displays a
-- table that shows the percentage of characters that belong to the
-- five categories: uppercase letters, lowercase letters, decimal
-- digits, blanks, and end-of-sentence punctuation marks.

-- Assumptions: The name of the data file contains no more than 80 characters.
--              The data file exists.
--              There are no '+' characters within the data.
--              A '+' character appears after the last character
--              of text in the data file as a sentinel.
```

PROBLEM-SOLVING CASE STUDY cont'd.

```
-- Subtypes for checking membership
subtype Uppercase is Character range 'A'..'Z';
subtype Lowercase is Character range 'a'..'z';
subtype Digit     is Character range '0'..'9';
-- Named type for file name
subtype File_String is String (1..80);

--------------------------------------
procedure Increment_Proper_Counter
          (A_Character       : in     Character;  -- Character to classify
           Uppercase_Count   : in out Natural;    --
           Lowercase_Count   : in out Natural;    -- The
           Digit_Count       : in out Natural;    -- six
           Blank_Count       : in out Natural;    -- classification
           Punctuation_Count : in out Natural;    -- counters
           Other_Count       : in out Natural) is --

-- The proper counter is incremented for A_Character
--
-- Preconditions  : None
--
-- Postconditions : The counter for the class in which A_Character fits is
--                  incremented. All other counters are unchanged.

begin  -- Increment Proper Counter
   if A_Character in Uppercase then
      Uppercase_Count := Uppercase_Count + 1;
   elsif A_Character in Lowercase then
      Lowercase_Count := Lowercase_Count + 1;
   elsif A_Character in Digit then
      Digit_Count := Digit_Count + 1;
   elsif A_Character = ' ' then
      Blank_Count := Blank_Count + 1;
   elsif A_Character = '?' or
         A_Character = '!' or
         A_Character = '.'    then
      Punctuation_Count := Punctuation_Count + 1;
   else
      Other_Count := Other_Count + 1;
   end if;

end Increment_Proper_Counter;

--------------------------------------
procedure Display_Percentages
             (Uppercase_Count   : in Natural;     --
              Lowercase_Count   : in Natural;     -- The
              Digit_Count       : in Natural;     -- six
```

PROBLEM-SOLVING CASE STUDY cont'd.

```
            Blank_Count       : in Natural;      -- classification
            Punctuation_Count : in Natural;      -- counters
            Other_Count       : in Natural) is   --

-- The total number of characters is calculated and the percentage
-- of each category of characters is printed.
--
-- Preconditions  : At least one counter is nonzero.
--
-- Postconditions : The percentage represented by each counter is displayed

   -- Local type
   subtype Non_Negative_Float is Float range 0.0 .. Float'Last;

   -- Local Variable
   Total : Non_Negative_Float;    -- Number of characters in the file

begin  -- Display_Percentages
   Total := Float (Uppercase_Count + Lowercase_Count   + Digit_Count +
                   Blank_Count     + Punctuation_Count + Other_Count);

   Ada.Text_IO.New_Line;
   Ada.Text_IO.Put (Item => "Percentage of uppercase letters           : ");
   Ada.Float_Text_IO.Put (Item => 100.0 * Float(Uppercase_Count) / Total,
                          Fore => 3,  Aft  => 2,  Exp  => 0);
   Ada.Text_IO.New_Line;
   Ada.Text_IO.Put (Item => "Percentage of lowercase letters           : ");
   Ada.Float_Text_IO.Put (Item => 100.0 * Float(Lowercase_Count) / Total,
                          Fore => 3,  Aft  => 2,  Exp  => 0);
   Ada.Text_IO.New_Line;
   Ada.Text_IO.Put (Item => "Percentage of decimal digits              : ");
   Ada.Float_Text_IO.Put (Item => 100.0 * Float(Digit_Count) / Total,
                          Fore => 3,  Aft  => 2,  Exp  => 0);
   Ada.Text_IO.New_Line;
   Ada.Text_IO.Put (Item => "Percentage of blank characters            : ");
   Ada.Float_Text_IO.Put (Item => 100.0 * Float(Blank_Count) / Total,
                          Fore => 3,  Aft  => 2,  Exp  => 0);
   Ada.Text_IO.New_Line;
   Ada.Text_IO.Put (Item => "Percentage of end-of-sentence punctuation : ");
   Ada.Float_Text_IO.Put (Item => 100.0 * Float(Punctuation_Count) / Total,
                          Fore => 3,  Aft  => 2,  Exp  => 0);
   Ada.Text_IO.New_Line;
end Display_Percentages;


-------------
```

PROBLEM-SOLVING CASE STUDY cont'd.

```
   -- The counters
   Uppercase_Count   : Natural;      -- Number of uppercase letters
   Lowercase_Count   : Natural;      -- Number of lowercase letters
   Digit_Count       : Natural;      -- Number of digits
   Blank_Count       : Natural;      -- Number of blanks
   Punctuation_Count : Natural;      -- Number of punctuation marks
   Other_Count       : Natural;      -- Number of other characters

   -- The data file
   File_Name : File_String;               -- File name
   Length    : Positive;                  -- Number of characters in File_Name
   File      : Ada.Text_IO.File_Type;     -- The file

   A_Character : Character;           -- One character from the file


begin  -- Category Count
   -- Prepare the input file
   Ada.Text_IO.Put ("Enter the name of the text file to analyze.");
   Ada.Text_IO.New_Line;
   Ada.Text_IO.Get_Line (Item => File_Name,
                         Last => Length);
   Ada.Text_IO.Open (File => File,
                     Name => File_Name (1..Length),
                     Mode => Ada.Text_IO.In_File);

   -- Initialize counters to zero
   Uppercase_Count   := 0;
   Lowercase_Count   := 0;
   Digit_Count       := 0;
   Blank_Count       := 0;
   Punctuation_Count := 0;
   Other_Count       := 0;

   Char_Loop:   -- Process all of the characters in the text file
   loop         -- Each iteration, process one character
      Ada.Text_IO.Get (File => File,  Item => A_Character);
      exit Char_Loop when A_Character = '+';    -- Check for sentinel value

      Increment_Proper_Counter (Uppercase_Count   => Uppercase_Count,
                                Lowercase_Count   => Lowercase_Count,
                                Digit_Count       => Digit_Count,
                                Blank_Count       => Blank_Count,
                                Punctuation_Count => Punctuation_Count,
                                Other_Count       => Other_Count,
                                A_Character       => A_Character);
   end loop Char_Loop;
   Ada.Text_IO.Close (File);     -- Done with data file, close it.
```

PROBLEM-SOLVING CASE STUDY cont'd.

```
   Display_Percentages (Uppercase_Count   => Uppercase_Count,
                        Lowercase_Count   => Lowercase_Count,
                        Digit_Count       => Digit_Count,
                        Blank_Count       => Blank_Count,
                        Punctuation_Count => Punctuation_Count,
                        Other_Count       => Other_Count);
end Category_Count;
```

Testing To be tested thoroughly, you must run Program Category_Count with all possible combinations of the categories of characters being counted. The following list is the minimum set of cases that you should test.

- All the categories of characters are present.
- Four of the categories are present; one is not. (Requires five test runs.)
- Only characters that fall into one of the five categories are present.
- Other characters are present.

The following percentages came from a sample run of the program on a large text file.

```
Percentage of uppercase letters           :  3.38
Percentage of lowercase letters           : 69.83
Percentage of decimal digits              :  0.42
Percentage of blank characters            : 19.20
Percentage of end-of-sentence punctuation :  1.05
```

PROBLEM-SOLVING CASE STUDY

Currency Conversions

Specification

Problem The money that your rich uncle left you is held in many banks in England, Japan, and the United States. At this point, it still is not clear how many different accounts he had in each of these three countries. You need a program to calculate the total amount of money (in dollars) in all of these accounts.

Input

From the file Rates.txt

- The number of U.S. dollars per English pound.
- The number of U.S. dollars per Japanese yen

From the keyboard, an unknown number of account balances. The accounts are entered in the following order:

- All of the U.S. accounts (balances in dollars).
- All of the English accounts (balances in pounds).
- All of the Japanese accounts (balances in yen).
- After the last account in each country is a sentinel value of zero.

Output

- Appropriate prompts.
- The total amount of money (in U.S. dollars) in all of these accounts.

Assumptions

- The exchange rates are 12 digit numbers with nine of these digits to the right of the decimal point.
- The file Rates.txt exists and contain the exchange rates for pounds and yen (in that order).
- All accounts have balances greater than zero.
- All account balances have no more than two digits to the right of the decimal point.
- The total value of the accounts in any country is less than one billion of that currency.
- The total value of all accounts is less than one billion U.S. dollars.

Design To do this calculation by hand, you would add up the account balances for each of the three currencies. Then for pounds and yen, you would use the exchange rates to determine the equivalent amount in dollars. Finally, you would add together the three balances to obtain the total.

We can use one loop to read and sum the English accounts, a second to read and sum the Japanese accounts, and a third for the U.S. accounts. Because an account has to have a balance greater than zero, we can use 0.00 as a sentinel.

We can declare a decimal type for each of the three different currencies and another decimal type for the two exchange rates. Each variable declaration will then make clear what currency that variable represents. We have decided to declare types rather than subtypes to prevent us from inadvertently combining different currencies in the same expression. We

PROBLEM-SOLVING CASE STUDY cont'd.

will need a function to convert pounds to dollars and another to convert yen to dollars.

```
Total_Assets                                                          Level 0
Open Rates_File
Get Dollars_Per_Pound from Rates_File
Get Dollars_Per_Yen from Rates_File
Close Rates_File
Get Total_Dollars in the United States accounts
Get Total_Pounds in the English accounts
Get Total_Yen in the Japanese accounts
Total_Dollars := Total_Dollars +
                 To_Dollars (Total_Pounds, Dollars_Per_Pound) +
                 To_Dollars (Total_Yen, Yen_Per_Pound
Display Total_Dollars
```

Object Name	Type	Role
Dollars_Per_Pound	Rate_Type	Conversion factor for pounds to dollars
Dollars_Per_Yen	Rate_Type	Conversion factor for yen to dollars
Total_Dollars	Dollars	Total of all U.S. bank accounts
Total_Pounds	Pounds	Total of all English bank accounts
Total_Yen	Yen	Total of all Japanese bank accounts

Type Name	Domain
Rate_Type	0.0 to 999.999999999
Dollars	0.0 to 999,999,999.99
Pounds	0.0 to 999,999,999.99
Yen	0.0 to 999,999,999.99

```
Get Total Dollars                                                     Level 1
  out    Total
Prompt user to enter Dollar account balances
Total := 0.00
loop
  Get an Account_Balance
  exit loop if Account_Balance is zero
  Add Account_Balance to Total
```

Object Name	Type	Role
Account_Balance	Dollars	Balance for one U.S. bank account
Total	Dollars	Total of all U.S. bank accounts

PROBLEM-SOLVING CASE STUDY cont'd.

Get Total Pounds **Level 1**

out Total

Prompt user to enter Pound account balances
Total := 0.00
loop
  Get an Account_Balance
  exit loop if Account_Balance is zero
  Add Account_Balance to Total

Object Name	Type	Role
Account_Balance	Pounds	Balance for one English bank account
Total	Pounds	Total of all English bank accounts

Get Total Yen **Level 1**

out Total

Prompt user to enter Yen account balances
Total := 0.00
loop
  Get an Account_Balance
  exit loop if Account_Balance is zero
  Add Account_Balance to Total

Object Name	Type	Role
Account_Balance	Yen	Balance for one Japanese bank account
Total	Yen	Total of all Japanese bank accounts

To_Dollars **Level 1**

in Amount
in Rate

Return Dollars (Rate × Amount)

Object Name	Type	Role
Amount	Pounds	Amount of pounds to convert to dollars
Rate	Rate_Type	Conversion rate

To_Dollars **Level 1**

in Amount
in Rate

Return Dollars (Rate × Amount)

Object Name	Type	Role
Amount	Yen	Amount of yen to convert to dollars
Rate	Rate_Type	Conversion rate

PROBLEM-SOLVING CASE STUDY cont'd.

Module Structure Chart

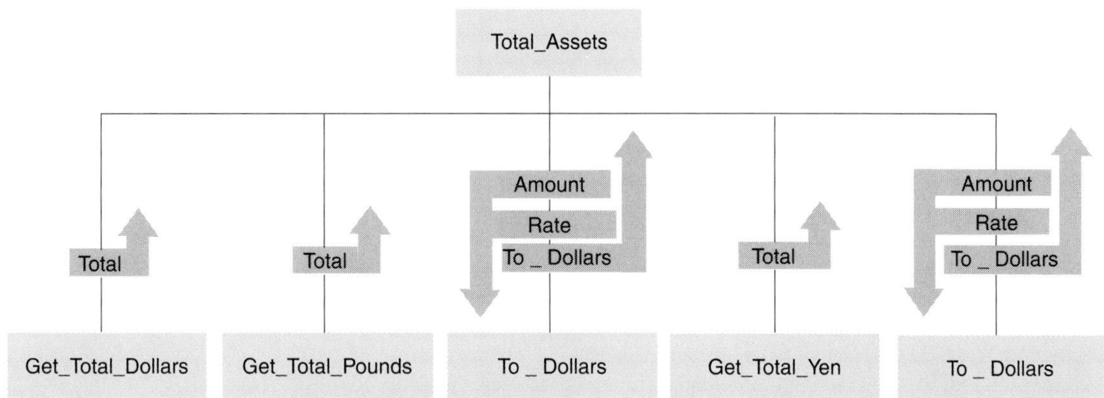

Implementation

```
with Ada.Text_IO;
procedure Total_Assets is

-- This program determines the total amount of dollars in accounts maintained
-- in England, Japan, and the United States.

-- Assumptions: The file Rates.txt exists and contains the exchange rates
--              for pounds and yen (in that order).
--              All accounts have balances greater than zero.
--              The total value of the accounts in any country is less
--              than 1 billion of that currency.
--              The total value of all accounts is less than 1 billion
--              U.S. dollars.

   -- Types for the various currencies and exchange rates
   type Dollars   is delta 0.01 digits 11 range 0.00..999_999_999.99;
   type Pounds    is delta 0.01 digits 11 range 0.00..999_999_999.99;
   type Yen       is delta 0.01 digits 11 range 0.00..999_999_999.99;
   type Rate_Type is delta 0.000000001 digits 12 range 0.00..999.999999999;

   -- Packages for currency I/O
   package Dollar_IO is new Ada.Text_IO.Decimal_IO (Num => Dollars);
   package Pound_IO  is new Ada.Text_IO.Decimal_IO (Num => Pounds);
   package Yen_IO    is new Ada.Text_IO.Decimal_IO (Num => Yen);
   package Rate_IO   is new Ada.Text_IO.Decimal_IO (Num => Rate_Type);
```

```
-----------------------------------------------
procedure Get_Total_Dollars (Total : out Dollars) is

-- This procedure gets the total of all U.S. accounts
--
-- Preconditions  : None
--
-- Postconditions : Total of all Dollar accounts is returned

   Account_Balance : Dollars;    -- The value of one account

begin
   Total := 0.0;    -- Initialize total
   Ada.Text_IO.Put ("Enter all of the U.S. bank account balances.");
   Ada.Text_IO.New_Line;
   Ada.Text_IO.Put ("Enter a zero balance after the last account.");
   Ada.Text_IO.New_Line;
   Account_Loop: -- Get all of the account balances
   loop          -- Each iteration, one account is processed
      Dollar_IO.Get (Account_Balance);
      exit Account_Loop when Account_Balance <= 0.0;
      Total := Total + Account_Balance;
   end loop Account_Loop;
end Get_Total_Dollars;

-----------------------------------------------
procedure Get_Total_Pounds (Total : out Pounds) is

-- This procedure gets the total of all English accounts
--
-- Preconditions  : None
--
-- Postconditions : Total of all Pound accounts is returned

   Account_Balance : Pounds;    -- The value of one account

begin
   Total := 0.0;    -- Initialize total
   Ada.Text_IO.Put ("Enter all of the English bank account balances.");
   Ada.Text_IO.New_Line;
   Ada.Text_IO.Put ("Enter a zero balance after the last account.");
   Ada.Text_IO.New_Line;
   Account_Loop: -- Get all of the account balances
   loop          -- Each iteration, one account is processed
      Pound_IO.Get (Account_Balance);
      exit Account_Loop when Account_Balance <= 0.0;
      Total := Total + Account_Balance;
   end loop Account_Loop;
end Get_Total_Pounds;
```

```
   ----------------------------------------
   procedure Get_Total_Yen (Total : out Yen) is

   -- This procedure gets the total of all Japanese accounts
   --
   -- Preconditions  : None
   --
   -- Postconditions : Total of all Yen accounts is returned

      Account_Balance : Yen;     -- The value of one account

   begin
      Total := 0.0;     -- Initialize total
      Ada.Text_IO.Put ("Enter all of the Japanese bank account balances.");
      Ada.Text_IO.New_Line;
      Ada.Text_IO.Put ("Enter a zero balance after the last account.");
      Ada.Text_IO.New_Line;
      Account_Loop: -- Get all of the account balances
      loop          -- Each iteration, one account is processed
         Yen_IO.Get (Account_Balance);
         exit Account_Loop when Account_Balance <= 0.0;
         Total := Total + Account_Balance;
      end loop Account_Loop;
   end Get_Total_Yen;

   ----------------------------------------
   function To_Dollars (Dollars_Per_Pound : in Rate_Type;
                        Total_Pounds      : in Pounds) return Dollars is
   -- Convert pounds to dollars
   begin
      return Dollars (Dollars_Per_Pound * Total_Pounds);
   end To_Dollars;

   ----------------------------------------
   function To_Dollars (Dollars_Per_Yen : in Rate_Type;
                        Total_Yen       : in Yen) return Dollars is
   -- Convert yen to dollars
   begin
      return Dollars (Dollars_Per_Yen * Total_Yen);
   end To_Dollars;


   -----------------------------------------
   -- Country totals
   Total_Dollars : Dollars;    -- The total of all accounts
   Total_Pounds  : Pounds;     -- The total of all English accounts
   Total_Yen     : Yen;        -- The total of all Japanese accounts
```

```
   -- Exchange Rates
   Rates_File        : Ada.Text_IO.File_Type;   -- File cotaining rates
   Dollars_Per_Pound : Rate_Type;               -- Rates for pounds
   Dollars_Per_Yen   : Rate_Type;               -- and yen

begin  -- Total Assets
   -- Get the exchange rates
   Ada.Text_IO.Open (File => Rates_File,
                     Name => "Rates.txt",
                     Mode => Ada.Text_IO.In_File);
   Rate_IO.Get (File => Rates_File, Item => Dollars_Per_Pound);
   Rate_IO.Get (File => Rates_File, Item => Dollars_Per_Yen);
   Ada.Text_IO.Close (Rates_File);

   -- Get the total of the U.S. accounts
   Get_Total_Dollars (Total_Dollars);

   -- Get the total of the English accounts and add to Dollar total
   Get_Total_Pounds (Total_Pounds);
   Total_Dollars := Total_Dollars +
                    To_Dollars (Dollars_Per_Pound, Total_Pounds);

   -- Get the total of the Japanese accounts and add to Dollar total
   Get_Total_Yen (Total_Yen);
   Total_Dollars := Total_Dollars +
                    To_Dollars (Dollars_Per_Yen, Total_Yen);

   Ada.Text_IO.Put ("The total value of all accounts is ');
   Dollar_IO.Put (Item => Total_Dollars,  Fore => 1,  Aft  => 2,  Exp  => 0);
   Ada.Text_IO.Put (" dollars.");
   Ada.Text_IO.New_Line;
end Total_Assets;
```

Testing Program Total_Assets has three identical loops to test. For each loop we need to try a data set with typical data, a single value, and no values (just the sentinel). We can test the conversion to dollars by entering data for the pound or yen accounts and no data for the other two account types.

Testing and Debugging

Most of this chapter describes Ada features that can make debugging easier. Subtypes and types are powerful mechanisms that help to detect errors. Several times in this book we have had programs test for invalid data and write an error message. By declaring subtypes and types appropriate for our data, Ada will automatically monitor the validity of the data for us. If at any time a value is not in the correct range, the program will stop with an error message.

This automatic error detection is called *passive error detection* because it is accomplished without our having to write any Ada statements to do the error detection. *Active error detection* means having the program check for possible errors rather than leaving it to the system. Active error detection usually involves writing numerous if and exit statements to check the validity of values.

An advantage of active error detection is that our program may determine an appropriate action if an error is encountered. For example, if a user enters an invalid number, we can repeat the prompt and give him or her another chance to enter the number. With passive error detection, the system identifies the error automatically, halts the program, and displays an error message. In Chapter 9 we will learn how our program can retain control when the system detects an error and raises an exception. Determining what happens when the system detects an error allows us to combine the best features of active and passive error detection.

If you use different types for values that should not be combined in the same expression, the Ada compiler will give a syntax error if you attempt to combine them without the necessary conversion functions. If you don't use different types, it is often difficult to find these kinds of errors when your only clue is an incorrect answer.

Testing and Debugging Hints

1. Use type Character rather than type String when processing individual characters.
2. Utilize programmer-defined types or subtypes to constrain the range variables can have.
3. Use types rather than subtypes to ensure that values that should not be combined are not combined.
4. Qualify an enumeration literal to make it clear which enumeration type it is.
5. Use attributes rather than literals when your program needs information on a type. Then if you modify the type definition, you won't have to make other changes in your program.

Summary

A data type is a set of values (domain) and the operations that can be applied to them. There are four commonly used predefined scalar types in Ada: Integer, Float, Character, and Boolean. Integer, Character, Boolean, and enumeration types are called discrete types; they have the property that a unique successor and a unique predecessor exist for all but the first and last items in the set of values.

Programmer-defined types and subtypes are extremely useful in the writing of clear, self-documenting programs. Both types and subtypes allow Ada to perform automatic range checking. Subtypes that share the same base type may be mixed freely in an expression. You may not mix different types in an expression without the use of explicit or programmer-written type conversion functions.

Attributes are operators used to obtain the characteristics of a type or subtype. The most commonly used attributes for scalar types are First, Last, Image, and Value. We can use the attributes Succ, Pred, Pos, and Val,with any discrete type. We can use the attribute Digits with floating-point and decimal types.

A string subtype definition includes a range to indicate how many characters a variable of that subtype holds. String subtypes declared in a variable declaration are called anonymous types because there is no name associated with the type. You may not use anonymous string subtypes as formal parameters. Named string subtypes make a program easier to read and allow us to use string parameters in our subprograms.

Quick Check

1. What is the result of each of these three expressions? (pp. 380–386)

```
Integer'Pos(23)     Character'Succ('J')     Boolean'Pred(True)
```

2. Declare a type called Atomic_Number_Type, consisting of the whole numbers making up the atomic numbers on the periodic table of the elements. You may need to consult a chemistry or physics book to find the range of atomic numbers. (pp. 392–397)
3. Declare a type called US_Gallons that is appropriate for the amount of gasoline pumped into a car. (pp. 392–396)
4. Write the statement to instantiate a package to do input and output with US_Gallons. (pp. 400–401)
5. Write a single statement to display the number of digits of precision used by the type My_Float_Type. (pp. 395–396)
6. True or False. It is legal to
   a. Multiply a Float number and an Integer number.
   b. Multiply a decimal number and an Integer number.
   c. Multiply two different decimal type numbers.
   d. Add a Float number and an Integer number.
   e. Add a decimal number and an Integer number
   f. Add two different decimal type numbers. (pp. 401–404)
7. Declare a subtype called Digit_Type, consisting of the characters ‘0’ through ‘9’. (pp. 405–407)
8. Using the subtype Digit_Type declared in question 6, write the Ada statements that display the contents of the Character variable Key_Value and either the string “is a digit” or “is not a digit”. (pp. 408–409)

9. Write an Ada loop to display all of the values in the subtype Digit_Type declared in question 6. Each value should be on a separate line. (pp. 405–409)
10. Declare a named number for the natural logarithm base called E with the value of 2.7182818285. (pp. 414–415)
11. a. Why are Ada programs that use the predefined types Integer or Float not portable? (p. 413)
    b. What can be done to overcome this lack of portability? (p. 413)
12. A subtype can be a base type for another subtype. (True or False) (pp. 405–407)
13. A subtype can be used as a subtype mark for declaring another subtype. (True or False) (pp. 405–407)
14. What is a universal type? (pp. 413–414)

Answers

1. 23, 'K', False **2.** `type Atomic_Number_Type is range 1 . . 110;` your chemistry book may have a larger value than 110. **3.** `type US_Gallons is digits 4 range 0.00 . . 20.00;` **4.** `package US_Gallons_IO is new Text_IO.Float_IO (Num => US_Gallons);` **5.** `Ada.Integer_Text_IO.Put (Item => My_Float_Type'Digits);` **6.** a) False b) True c) True d) False e) False f) False **7.** `subtype Digit_Type is Character range '0'..'9';`

8.
```
Ada.Text_IO.Put (Key_Value);
if Key_Value in Digit_Type then
   Text_IO.Put(" is a digit");
else
   Text_IO.Put(" is not a digit");
end if;
```
9.
```
Ch := Digit_Type'First;
Digit_Loop:
loop
   Ada.Text_IO.Put(Ch);
   Ada.Text_IO.New_Line;
   exit Digit_Loop when Ch=Digit_Type'Last;
   Ch := Digit_Type'Succ(Ch);
end loop Digit_Loop;<r>
```
10. `E : constant := 2.718_281_828_5;` **11.** a) Because the range of the predefined types Integer and Float vary from computer to computer. b) Use programmer-defined types and subtypes instead of the predefined types and subtypes. **12.** False **13.** True **14.** A universal type is the type used for all numeric literals. Integer literals are of type universal_integer, and real literals are of type universal_real.

Exam Preparation Exercises

1. Where do the formal descriptions for the domains of the standard data types Integer and Float come from?
2. Distinguish between a scalar and a discrete type.
3. a. List and define the four most commonly used attributes for scalar types.
   b. List and define an additional four attributes commonly used with discrete types.

4. Discrete types are ordered so that every variable must be less than, equal to, or greater than any other variable of that type. (True or False).
5. The successor of 5.2 is 5.3. (True or False).
6. Given the following declaration:

```
type Perfume_Type is (Poison, Dior_Essence, Chanel_No_5, Coty);
```

what is the value of each of the following expressions? (If an expression results in an exception, give the name of the exception.)
   a. `Perfume_Type'Pos(Poison)`
   b. `Perfume_Type'Succ(Poison)`
   c. `Perfume_Type'Succ(Coty)`
   d. `Perfume_Type'Pred(Chanel_No_5)`
   e. `Perfume_Type'Val(1)`
   f. `Perfume_Type'First`
   g. `Perfume_Type'Last`
   h. `Perfume_Type'Pred(Perfume_Type'Last)`
   i. `Perfume_Type.Image(Coty)`
7. Given the following declaration:

```
type Season_Type is (Winter, Spring, Summer, Fall);
```

what is the value of each of the following expressions? (If an expression results in an exception, give the name of the exception.)
   a. `Season_Type'First`
   b. `Season_Type'Last`
   c. `Season_Type'Succ(Winter)`
   d. `Season_Type'Pred(Winter)`
   e. `Season_Type'Pos(Fall)`
   f. `Season_Type'Val(4)`
   g. `Season_Type'Val(Season_Type'Pos(Winter)+2)`
   h. `Season_Type'Val(Season_Type'Pos(Fall) rem Season_Type'Pos(Season_Type'Last))`
8. What is the value of each of the following expressions? (If an expression results in an exception, give the name of the exception.)
   a. `Boolean'Pos(False)`
   b. `Character'Pred('C')`
   c. `Character'Pos('C')`
   d. `Character'Val(84)`
   e. `Integer'Pos(-45)`
   f. `Integer'Succ(Integer'Last)`
9. Given the following declarations:

```
subtype My_Type   is Float range 1.00..5.00;
subtype Your_Type is Float range 0.00..10.00;
```

What is the value of each of the following expressions? (If an expression results in an exception, give the name of the exception.)

a. `My_Type'First`
b. `My_Type'Last`
c. `7.5 in My_Type`
d. `7.5 in Your_Type`

10. Explain why the number 5.2 cannot be stored exactly as a floating-point type.
11. Use of decimal types eliminates all problems with the representation of real numbers. (True or False).
12. What is the range of the following type?

```
type Fathoms is delta 0.1 digits 6;
```

13. All numeric subtypes can be mixed together in expressions. (True or False)
14. All numeric subtypes with the same base type can be mixed together in expressions. (True or False)

Programming Warm-up Exercises

1. Declare a numeric type made up of the single-digit numbers.
2. Declare a type called Degrees with eight digits of precision and a range required for a circle.
3. Declare a type called Imperial_Gallons with the same range and precision as the type US_Gallons declared in Quick Check question 3. Then write a function called To_US_Gallons to convert imperial gallons to U.S. gallons. There are 1.25 U.S. gallons in an imperial gallon.
4. Given the following declaration:

```
type Season_Type is (Winter, Spring, Summer, Fall);
```

write a function called Next_Season that returns the season that follows a given season. (Remember that Winter follows Fall!)

5. Rewrite the following loop using the Succ attribute instead of adding 1 to the Integer loop control variable.

```
Loop_6:
loop
   exit Loop_6 when Count > Max_Count;
   Integer_IO.Put (Count);
   Count := Count + 1;
end Loop_6;
```

6. Declare a subtype called Item_String that holds 25 characters.
7. Declare a numeric subtype that is made up of the single-digit numbers.

8. Declare a subtype called Allowance_Dollars of the decimal type Dollars defined in this chapter with a range constrained between one and one hundred.
9. Complete the following procedure to display all the values in the range of Allowance_Dollars. You'll need to use attributes.

```
procedure Display_All_Values is
-- This procedure displays all the values that are represented exactly
-- in the type Allowance_Dollars
   Current : Dollars;           -- Current value
begin
   Current := ________________________;
   Display_Loop:   -- Display all the values in the range
   loop            -- Each iteration, one value is displayed
      exit Display_Loop when _____________________________;
      Dollar_IO.Put (Item => Current,
                     Fore => 4,
                     Aft  => 2,
                     Exp  => 0);
      Ada.Text_IO.New_Line;
      Current := Current + _________________________;
   end loop Display_Loop;
end Display_All_values;
```

10. Given the following declarations:

```
Max_Label : constant := 10;
subtype Label_Type is String (1..Max_Label);
```

write a procedure called Reverse that is passed a value of type Label_Type. This procedure should reverse the characters in the string parameter. Thus if the value "ABCDEFGHIJ" were passed in, the value "JIHGFEDCBA" would be passed out.

11. Given the following declarations:

```
Name_Length : constant := 12;
subtype Name_Type is String (1..Name_Length);
```

write a procedure called Fix_Case that takes a single parameter of subtype Name_Type and returns that parameter with the first character in the string capitalized and the remaining characters lowercased. You may use the function To_Lower given in this chapter and may assume that a function called To_Upper, which converts a lowercase character to an uppercase character, also exists.

Programming Problems

1. Write an Ada program that reads a character from 'A' to 'Z' as input to produce output in the shape of a pyramid composed of the letters up to and including the letter that is input. The top letter in the pyramid should be 'A' and, on each level, the next letter in the alphabet should fall between the letter that was introduced in the level above it. For example, if the input is 'E', the output will look like the following:

```
    A
   ABA
  ABCBA
 ABCDCBA
ABCDEDCBA
```

2. Read in a float number character by character, convert the number to its numeric form, and print the result in E-notation. Your algorithm should convert the whole number part to an integer and the fractional part to an integer and then combine the two integers as follows:

Set result to whole number + (fraction / (10 $^{\text{number of digits in fraction}}$))

For example, 34.216 would be converted into 34 + (216/1000). You may assume that the number has at least one digit on either side of the decimal point.

3. Rewrite Program Mileage in Chapter 3 so that it will accept any number of fill-ups. Also allow for fill-up amounts in imperial gallons, U.S. gallons, and liters. The mileage displayed should be expressed in miles per U.S. gallon.
4. Write an Ada program to determine the average time five racers took to complete a marathon. The input consists of five times, each on a separate line. The times are in the form HH:MM:SS. A time of 03:27:42 indicates that the runner finished the race in 3 hours, 27 minutes, and 42 seconds. The average of the five runners should be displayed in the same format.
5. Write an Ada program to calculate exam statistics. The file Exam_Data.txt contains an unknown number of exam scores. Each exam score is a whole number between 0 and 100. A negative value is used as a sentinel after the last exam score. Display the average exam score (rounded to one decimal place) and the number of A's (scores between 90 and 100), B's (80 to 89), C's (70 to 79), D's (60 to 69), and E's (scores less than 60).
6. In this problem you will design and implement a Roman numeral calculator. The subtractive Roman numeral notation commonly in use today (such as IV, meaning "4") was used only rarely during the time of the Roman Republic and Empire. For ease of calculation, the Romans most frequently used a purely additive notation in which a number was simply the sum of its digits (4 equals IIII, in this notation). Each number starts with the digit of highest value and ends with the one of smallest value. This is the notation we will use in this problem.

Your program will input two Roman numbers and an arithmetic operator and will print out the result of the operation, also as a Roman number. The values of the Roman digits are as follows:

I	1
V	5
X	10
L	50
C	100
D	500
M	1000

Thus the number MDCCCCLXXXXVI represents 1996. The arithmetic operators that your program should recognize in the input are +, −, *, and /. These should perform the Ada operations of integer addition, subtraction, multiplication, and division.

One way of approaching this problem is to convert the Roman numbers into integers, perform the required operation, and then convert the result back into a Roman number for printing. The following might be a sample run of the program.

```
Enter the first number:
MCCXXVI
The first number is 1226
Enter the second number:
LXVIIII
The second number is 69
Enter the desired arithmetic operation:
+
The sum of MCCXXVI and LXVIIII is MCCLXXXXV (1295)
```

Your program should use proper style and indentation, appropriate comments, and meaningful identifiers, and it should avoid side effects. It should also check for errors in the input, such as illegal digits or arithmetic operators, and take appropriate actions when these are found. The program also may double-check that the numbers are in purely additive form—digits are followed only by digits of the same or lower value.

7. Solve Programming Problem 1 in Chapter 6 using enumeration types for the names of the month and the days of the week. The user should enter the actual day of the week rather than a number for the first day of the year.

CHAPTER 8

Additional Control Structures

GOALS

After reading this chapter, you should be able to

- write a case statement to solve a given problem
- use a null statement
- write a for statement to solve a given problem
- write a while loop to solve a given problem
- select the appropriate loop statement to solve a given problem

In the preceding chapters, we introduced Ada statements for selection and looping. This chapter introduces a new statement for doing selection and two new statements for looping. The case statement makes it easier to write selection structures with many branches. The for and while statements make it easier to program certain types of loops. Although none of these statements is essential to programming in Ada, they each provide a convenient mechanism for implementing a particular control algorithm.

The Case Statement

The case statement is a control structure that allows us to select any one of a number of branches. It is similar to an if statement with elsifs. The value of the *case selector*, an expression whose result must match a choice attached to one of the alternatives, determines which one of the branches is to be executed. For example, look at the following code fragment:

```
type Day_Type is (Monday, Tuesday, Wednesday, Thursday,
                  Friday, Saturday, Sunday);
   .
   .
   .
Day : Day_Type;
   .
   .
   .
   case Day is

      when Monday =>
         Ada.Text_IO.Put ("I have to go back to work today.");
         Ada.Text_IO.New_Line;

      when Tuesday =>
         Ada.Text_IO.Put ("Tuesdays are easier than Mondays.");
         Ada.Text_IO.New_Line;

      when Wednesday =>
         Ada.Text_IO.Put ("Half way through the week.");
         Ada.Text_IO.New_Line;

      when Thursday =>
         Ada.Text_IO.Put ("Two days to go.");
         Ada.Text_IO.New_Line;
         Ada.Text_IO.Put ("The weekend is in sight.");
         Ada.Text_IO.New_Line;

      when Friday =>
         Ada.Text_IO.Put ("TGIF!");
         Ada.Text_IO.New_Line;
```

```
   when Saturday =>
      Ada.Text_IO.Put ("Sleep in today.");
      Ada.Text_IO.New_Line;

   when Sunday =>
      Ada.Text_IO.Put ("Better call Mom today.");
      Ada.Text_IO.New_Line;
      Ada.Text_IO.Put ("And get ready for Monday's presentation.");
      Ada.Text_IO.New_Line;
end case;

Ada.Text_IO.Put ("Done with case statement.");
Ada.Text_IO.New_Line;
```

In this example, Day is the case selector. There are seven alternatives, each introduced by the reserved word `when`. The value of the case selector determines which one of the seven choices of this case statement is selected. For example, if Day has the value Saturday, then the message "Sleep in today." is displayed. Execution of the case statement is then complete. The next statement prints "Done with case statement."

Here is a simplified EBNF definition of the case statement.

```
case_statement              ::= case expression is
                                   case_statement_alternative
                                   {case_statement_alternative}
                                end case;
case_statement_alternative  ::= when discrete_choice_list =>
                                   sequence_of_statements
discrete_choice_list        ::= choice { | choice}
choice                      ::= component_simple_name  |
                                discrete_range         |
                                subtype_indication     |
                                expression             |
                                others
```

We can see from the definition of case_statement_alternative that there may be more than one choice and that multiple choices are separated by vertical bars. Here is an example with more than one choice in an alternative.

```
case Day is
   when Monday | Tuesday | Wednesday | Thursday | Friday =>
      Ada.Text_IO.Put ("Today is a weekday.");
      Ada.Text_IO.New_Line;
   when Saturday | Sunday =>
      Ada.Text_IO.Put ("It's the weekend!");
      Ada.Text_IO.New_Line;
end case;
```

The vertical bar may be read as "or." If Day is Monday *or* Tuesday *or* Wednesday *or* Thursday *or* Friday, the message "Today is a weekday." is displayed. The EBNF definition of choice shows that choices may also be specified by a discrete range, as illustrated in this next code fragment.

```
case Day is
   when Monday..Friday =>
      Ada.Text_IO.Put ("Today is a weekday.");
      Ada.Text_IO.New_Line;
   when Saturday | Sunday =>
      Ada.Text_IO.Put ("It's the weekend!");
      Ada.Text_IO.New_Line;
end case;
```

This case statement is equivalent to the previous one. We have simply replaced the multiple choices with a range choice. A discrete range may also be supplied by a subtype name. Given the declaration

```
subtype Weekday_Type is Day_Type range Monday..Friday;
```

we can rewrite our case statement as

```
case Day is
   when Weekday_Type =>
      Ada.Text_IO.Put ("Today is a weekday.");
      Ada.Text_IO.New_Line;
   when Saturday | Sunday =>
      Ada.Text_IO.Put ("It's the weekend!");
      Ada.Text_IO.New_Line;
end case;
```

Ada's case statement has two restrictions.

1. The case selector (the expression after the reserved word `case`) must be a discrete type.
2. Each value in the domain of the case selector must appear once and only once in the set of choices of the statement.

The second restriction prevents us from leaving out one of the seven days of the week in our example. It also prevents us from including Friday as both a weekday and a weekend choice. This restriction might seem to be a problem for case selectors with large ranges. For example, if our case selector is type Integer, we must have a choice for every possible whole number from Integer'First to Integer'Last. Although we can use ranges to shorten the number of alternatives in our case statement, Ada gives us another option. We can give the choice "others" as the *only* choice of the *last* alternative. This choice stands for all values not given in the choices of previous alternatives. Here is an example that uses the others choice.

```
case Day is
   when Monday | Wednesday | Friday =>
      Ada.Text_IO.Put ("Classes today.");
   when Saturday  Sunday =>
      Ada.Text_IO.Put ("The weekend is here!");
   when others =>
      Ada.Text_IO.Put ("No classes today.");
end case;
```

Because it can hide an error made by omitting a particular choice, many Ada programmers consider it poor style to use the others alternative.

When to Use the Case Statement

We use both the case and if statements to write selection structures. There aren't any formal rules for determining when to use a case statement and when to use an if statement, but here are some guidelines:

1. If there are only two alternatives, use an if statement.
2. If the selection decision is not based on the value of a single discrete expression, use an if statement.
3. If there are many choices based on the value of a single discrete expression, use a case statement.
4. If there are only a few choices based on the value of a single discrete expression, use whichever statement makes the program easiest to read.

In the Rich Uncle Problem-Solving Case Study (Chapter 7), we used an if statement with membership tests to decide which of six counters to increment. Here is a fragment of the code from the program we developed.

```
-- Subtypes for checking membership
   subtype Uppercase is Character range 'A'..'Z';
   subtype Lowercase is Character range 'a'..'z';
   subtype Digit     is Character range '0'..'9';
   .
   .
   .
if A_Character in Uppercase then
      Uppercase_Count := Uppercase_Count + 1;
elsif A_Character in Lowercase then
      Lowercase_Count := Lowercase_Count + 1;
elsif A_Character in Digit then
      Digit_Count := Digit_Count + 1;
```

```
elsif A_Character = ' ' then
   Blank_Count := Blank_Count + 1;
elsif A_Character = '?' or
      A_Character = '!' or
      A_Character = '.'    then
   Punctuation_Count := Punctuation_Count + 1;
else
   Other_Count := Other_Count + 1;
end if;
```

The selection decision in this problem is based on a discrete type (the predefined type Character). There are six alternatives based on 256 different possibilities (the domain of type Character). Our guidelines suggest that a case statement is more appropriate than the if statement we used. Here is the equivalent case statement.

```
case A_Character is
   when Uppercase =>
      Upper_Count := Upper_Count + 1;
   when Lowercase =>
      Lower_Count := Lower_Count + 1;
   when Digit =>
      Digit_Count := Digit_Count + 1;
   when ' ' =>
      Blank_Count := Blank_Count + 1;
   when  '?'  |  '!'  |  '.'  =>
      Punct_Count := Punct_Count + 1;
   when others =>
      Other_Count := Other_Count + 1;
end case;
```

Which do you think is easier to read?

The Null Statement

There are times in which the program should take no action for certain situations. Suppose that we needed only five counters in the last case statement. That is, we only want to count uppercase and lowercase letters, decimal digits, and punctuation marks (?, !, and .). The program should ignore any other characters; no counter should be incremented. We cannot just remove the when others alternative from the case statement because Ada requires that there be a choice in the case statement for every possible value in the domain in the case selector. We cannot remove the statement

```
Other_Count := Other_Count + 1;
```

because there must be a sequence of statements for each alternative (see the EBNF definition). We need a statement that does nothing. That is exactly what the null statement does. We use a null statement whenever a sequence of statements is required but no actions should be taken. Here is the EBNF definition of the null statement.

null_statement ::= **null**;

Here is our case statement using a null statement so that nothing is done when the case selector does not match a choice in one of the earlier alternatives.

```
case A_Character is
   when Uppercase =>
      Upper_Count := Upper_Count + 1;
   when Lowercase =>
      Lower_Count := Lower_Count + 1;
   when Digit =>
      Digit_Count := Digit_Count + 1;
   when ' ' =>
      Blank_Count := Blank_Count + 1;
   when '?' | '!' | '.' =>
      Punct_Count := Punct_Count + 1;
   when others =>
      null;
end case;
```

There are a few other places where the null statement is useful. During program development it can act as a placeholder for code not yet written. This allows us to test part of our code without having to complete the entire program. We discussed this type of testing (stubs and drivers) at the end of Chapter 6.

The For Statement

The for statement is designed to simplify the writing of count-controlled loops. Let's look at a simple example.

```
Count_Loop:
for Count in 1..5 loop
   Ada.Integer_Text_IO.Put (Item => Count, Width => 4);
end loop Count_Loop;
```

This code fragment produces the following line of output.

```
   1   2   3   4   5
```

This loop iterates five times. The value of the identifier Count during the first iteration is 1. Its value during the second iteration is 2. The value of Count during the last iteration is 5. The identifier Count is called the *loop parameter*. The loop parameter values are determined by the range given after the reserved word in.

The range may be specified by any discrete values. Thus in addition to integer values, you can use a for statement with Character, Boolean, or enumeration values. For example, the following loop prints the 26 letters of the alphabet.

```
Letter_Loop:
for Letter in Character'('A').. Character'('Z') loop
   Ada.Text_IO.Put (Letter);
end loop Letter_Loop;
```

Notice that we had to qualify the character literals in this for statement. Without this qualification, the Ada compiler is unable to tell if 'A' is of type Character or of type Wide_Character.

Just like the loop statement, the for statement may be nested. For example, the nested for structure

```
Outer:
for End_Letter in Character'('A') .. Character'('G') loop
   Inner:
   for Printed_Letter in 'A'..End_Letter loop
      Ada.Text_IO.Put (Printed_Letter);
   end loop Inner;
   Ada.Text_IO.New_Line;
end loop Outer;
```

prints the following triangle of letters.

```
A
AB
ABC
ABCD
ABCDE
ABCDEF
ABCDEFG
```

Why didn't we have to qualify the literal 'A' in our inner loop? The values in this range are not ambiguous because End_Letter is of type Character. The type of End_Letter was set in the outer for statement. We could omit the qualification of the literal 'G' in the outer loop as well. The qualification of 'A' is sufficient to make the type of 'G' unambiguous.

You may specify the range of a for statement in several different forms, as shown in this simplified EBNF definition.

for_loop_statement	::=	[*loop*_simple_name:] **for** loop_parameter **in** [**reverse**] discrete_range **loop** sequence_of_statements **end** loop [*loop*_simple_name];
loop_parameter	::=	identifier
discrete_range	::=	*discrete*_subtype_indication | range
subtype_indication	::=	*type*_name | *subtype*_name
range	::=	simple_expression .. simple_expression

Here are some examples that illustrate some of the various ways the discrete range may be specified.

```
type  Day_Type    is (Sunday, Monday, Tuesday, Wednesday,
                      Thursday, Friday, Saturday);
type  ID_Type     is range 1..10;
subtype Year_Type is Integer range 1900..1950;
   .
   .
   .
for Day in Day_Type loop                  -- This loop iterates 7 times
   .                                      -- Day ranges from Sunday to
   .                                      -- Saturday
   .
for ID in ID_Type loop                    -- This loop iterates 10 times
   .                                      -- ID ranges from 1 to 10
   .
   .
for Year in Year_Type loop                -- This loop iterates 51 times
   .                                      -- Year ranges from 1900 to 1950
   .
   .
for Count in 5..17 loop                   -- This loop iterates 13 times
   .                                      -- Count ranges from 5 to 17
   .
   .
for Count in 14 rem 3 .. 14 / 3 loop      -- This loop iterates 3 times
   .                                      -- Count ranges from 2 to 4
   .
   .
```

When the reserved word `reverse` is used in a for statement, the loop identifier takes on values from the last value down to the first value in the range. For example, the output of the following for statement

```
Count_Down:
for Number in reverse 1..5 loop
   Ada.Integer_Text_IO.Put (Item => Number, Width => 4);
end loop Count_Down;
```

is

```
   5   4   3   2   1
```

In Chapter 3, we used ranges to define string slices. There we defined a null range as a range in which the starting value is greater than the ending value. A null range contains no values. If the discrete range of a for statement is a null range, the statements in the body of the loop are not executed at all, even when reverse is used. When the upper and lower bounds of the range are the same, the range contains a single value and the body is executed one time.

```
Limit := 3;
    .
    .
for Number in 10..Limit loop               -- Loop iterates 0 times.
    .
    .
    .
for Number in reverse 10..Limit loop       -- Loop iterates 0 times.
    .
    .
    .
for Number in 3..Limit loop                -- Loop iterates 1 time.
    .                                      -- Number has a value of 3.
    .
    .
```

The Loop Parameter

The loop parameter is a special object. It is declared automatically when we write the for statement. It is not declared in a declarative part. You must treat the loop parameter as a constant. You can use it but not change it within the loop; that is, the loop parameter may appear in an expression, but not on the left-hand side of an assignment statement. It may be given as an *in* parameter of a subprogram but never as an *out* or *in out* parameter.

Loop Parameter Scope Recall from Chapter 6 that the scope of an identifier is all the places from which it can be accessed. The scope of a loop parameter is the body of the for statement (see Figure 8-1). In Figure 8-1, X is a homograph (one of multiple declarations with identical names). It is declared as an Integer variable in the declarative part of procedure Example and as a loop parameter in the for statement Letter_Loop. When a homograph exists, the local identifier takes precedence over any global identifier. Therefore any references to X within the body of Letter_Loop refer to the loop parameter. Any references to X outside of this loop body refer to the Integer variable.

FIGURE 8-1
Scope of Loop Parameters

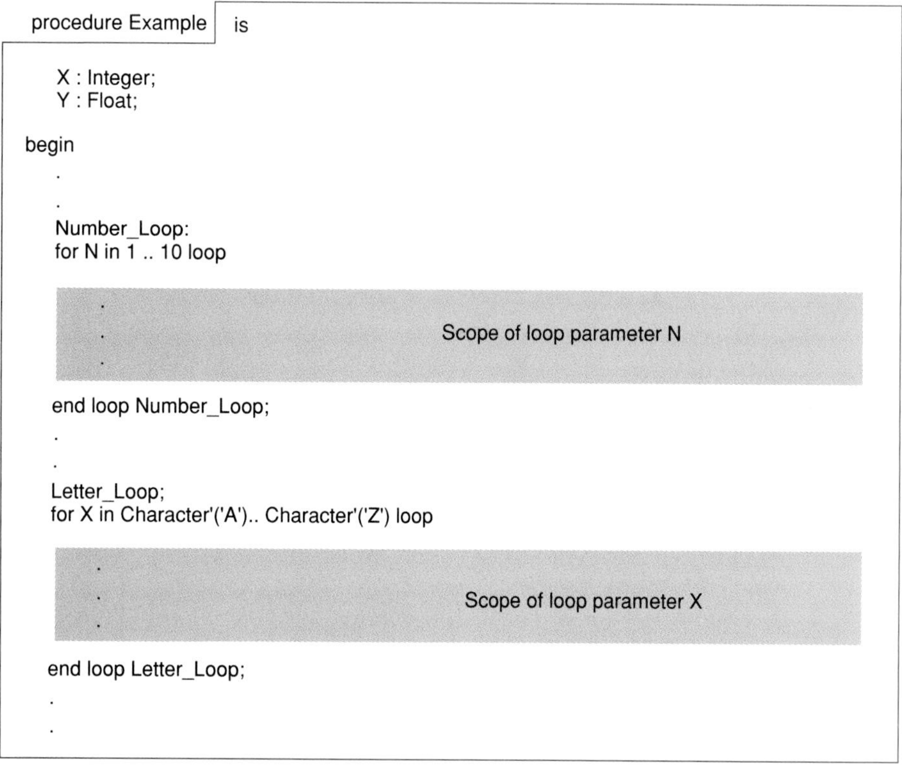

The scope of loop parameters in nested for statements follows that of identifiers in nested subprograms. Figure 8-2 shows a scope diagram for the nested loop given on page 446. The loop parameter End_Letter in loop Outer is available anywhere within the outer region including within the body of the inner loop. Loop parameter Printed_Letter is not available outside of the body of loop Inner.

Loop Parameter Type

The loop parameter is declared in the for statement. Unlike variable declarations, no type is explicitly given for a loop parameter. The type of the loop parameter is determined by the type of the discrete range defined in the for statement. Here are some examples that use the types we declared on page 447. Variable ID is type ID_Type, and variable Year is type Year_Type. Start and End are named numbers (constants of type universal_integer).

FIGURE 8-2 Scope of Nested Loop Parameters

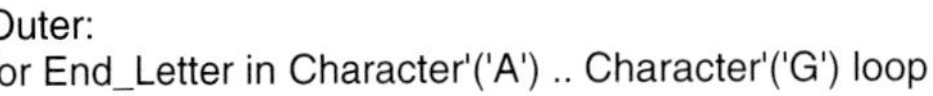
Outer:
for End_Letter in Character'('A') .. Character'('G') loop

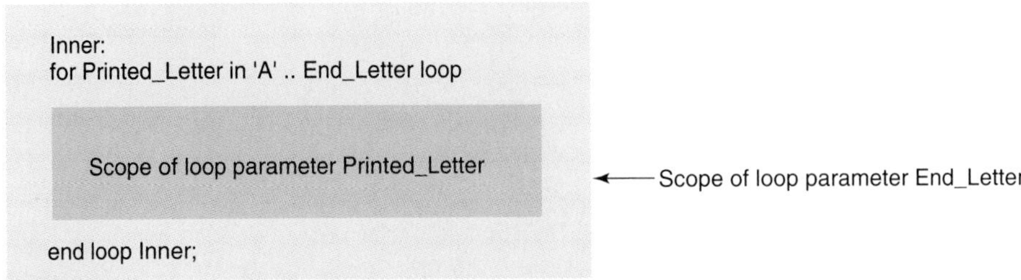
Inner:
for Printed_Letter in 'A' .. End_Letter loop
Scope of loop parameter Printed_Letter
Scope of loop parameter End_Letter
end loop Inner;

end loop Outer;

For Statement	Loop Parameter Type
for LP in Character loop	Character
for LP in Day_Type loop	Day_Type
for LP in Sunday .. Saturday loop	Day_Type
for LP in Year_Type loop	Year_Type
for LP in 1925 .. Year loop	Year_Type
for LP in ID_Type loop	ID_Type
for LP in ID .. 8 loop	ID_Type
for LP in 1 .. 10 loop	Integer
for LP in Start .. End loop	Integer
for LP in Start .. 25 loop	Integer

When the range of the loop is specified by a subtype or type name, the loop parameter type is that subtype or type. If the range is given by starting and ending values, the type of the loop parameter is the same as the type of these values. The last three examples in the list illustrate that if the starting and ending values are both numeric literals or named numbers, the loop parameter is type Integer.

For statements are convenient and many programmers tend to overuse them. Be warned: For statements are not general-purpose loops. They are designed exclusively for count-controlled loops. To use them intelligently, remember the following points.

1. The loop parameter may be used, but not changed, within the loop; that is, the loop parameter may appear in an expression, but not on the left-hand side of an assignment statement.
2. A numeric loop parameter always steps by 1 or −1. If you need to increment or decrement by another value, you should use a loop statement.
3. The loop parameter is only defined in the loop body.

4. The loop is executed with the loop parameter at the initial value (the first value in the range), the final value (the last value in the range), and all values in between.
5. If the initial value is equal to the final value, the loop body is executed once.
6. If the range is null, the loop body is not executed.
7. You should not use an exit statement in a for statement. If an additional termination condition is required, use a loop statement rather than a for statement.

Besides simplicity, another benefit of implementing count-controlled loops with a for statement is that it always terminates. You cannot write an infinite loop with a for statement.

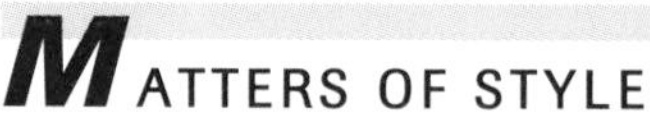

MATTERS OF STYLE

Loop Names

We have used loop names for all of our loop and for statements. However, Ada does not require them. We provide loop names to make it easier for people to understand the logic of the loop. In some situations the extra information supplied by a loop name does not add to the comprehensibility of the program and, in fact, may lessen it. In these cases it is better not to name the loop.

How can a loop name make a program more difficult to read? Primarily, the use of a loop name increases the number of lines of code. Also, as with all names in our program, we must be sure to choose a name that properly describes the purpose of the loop. A loop name that is not meaningful may be more harmful than no name at all.

You should use loop names when the loop body is so long that it cannot be examined in its entirety on a display screen. The name allows an easy match of the loop or for statement with the end statement as the program is scrolled up and down on the screen. Don't forget that a loop body will often grow in size as errors are corrected during testing or new features are added during the program's maintenance phase.

You should also name the loops when they are nested. Naming nested loops not only helps us understand the logic, it also allows the Ada compiler to check that the loops are nested correctly.

Finally, we recommend that you continue using loop names with the general loop statement because we can use the name in the exit statement and thus easily match the exit statement with the loop's end statement.

The While Loop

In Chapter 5 we defined a pretest loop as one in which the exit statement is the first statement. Here is a simple example using the general loop statement introduced in that chapter.

```
Decade := 10;                                              -- Initialize counter
Decade_Loop:
loop:
   exit Decade_Loop when Decade > 100                      -- Test counter
   Ada.Integer_Text_IO.Put (Item := Decade, Width => 5);
   Decade := Decade + 10;                                  -- Increment counter
end loop Decade_Loop;
```

This code fragment produces the following line of output.

```
   10   20   30   40   50   60   70   80   90  100
```

The while statement is designed to simplify the writing of pretest loops like this. The following code fragment uses a while statement to accomplish the same task as the general loop statement.

```
Decade := 10;                                              -- Initialize counter
Decade_Loop:
while Decade <= 100 loop                                   -- Test counter
   Ada.Integer_Text_IO.Put (Item := Decade, Width => 5);
   Decade := Decade + 10;                                  -- Increment counter
end loop Decade_Loop;
```

Both of these loops are count-controlled pretest loops using Decade as a loop control variable. The major difference between them is the logic of termination. The program exits the while loop when the condition given in the while statement is False. The exit condition is tested in the while statement itself. No separate exit statement is required. The program terminates execution of the general loop when the condition given in the exit statement is True. Figures 8-3 and 8-4 illustrate the flow of control in these two loops.

You can use the while loop in place of any *pretest* general loop. Just negate the condition you would use in the exit statement to determine the condition needed in the equivalent while statement.

While we have discussed the loop, for, and while statements as though they were distinct looping statements, Ada defines each of them as a variation of a single loop statement. Here is its EBNF definition.

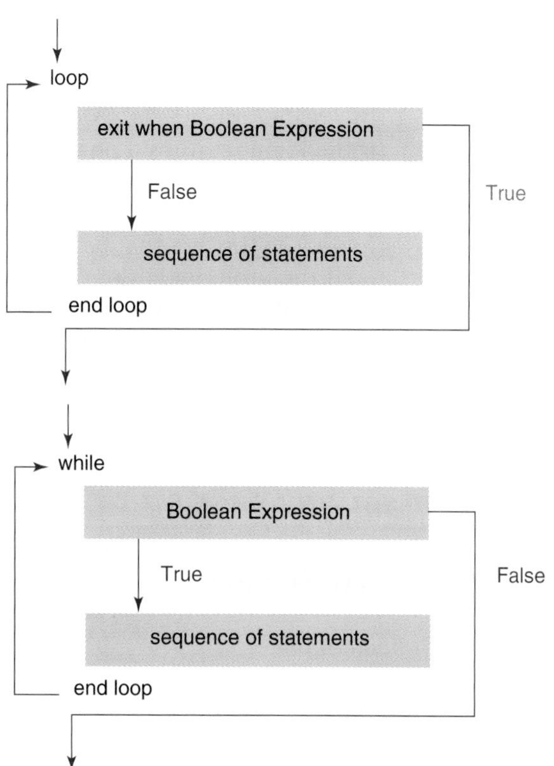

FIGURE 8-3 Flow of Control of a Pretest Loop Statement

FIGURE 8-4 Flow of Control of a While Statement

```
loop_statement                  ::=  [loop_identifier:]
                                     [iteration_scheme] loop
                                       sequence_of_statements
                                     end loop [loop_identifier];
iteration_scheme                ::=  while condition   |
                                     for loop_parameter_specification
loop_parameter_specification    ::=  identifier in [reverse] discrete_range
```

The exit statement does not appear in this definition because it is a separate statement that is written as part of the sequence of statements. Of course, a general loop is not required to contain an exit statement (remember the heart monitor loop given in Chapter 5).

Guidelines for Choosing a Looping Statement

Here are some guidelines to help you decide when to use each of the three looping statements.

1. If the loop is a simple count-controlled loop, use a for statement. It is the simplest loop and you cannot create an infinite loop with it.
2. If a counter and an event control the loop, or if the loop must count by a value other than 1 or −1, use a loop or while statement.
3. If the logic requires a posttest loop or a midtest loop, use the loop statement.
4. If the logic requires a pretest loop, use either a general loop or a while loop. Use the one that better reflects the semantics of the loop—that is, if the problem is stated in terms of when to stop looping, use a loop statement; if the problem is stated in terms of when to continue looping, use a while statement.
5. When in doubt, use a loop statement.

PROBLEM-SOLVING CASE STUDY

Solitaire Scoring

Specification

Problem In a simple solitaire game, a player picks cards out of a deck until an Ace is found. A score is calculated by adding the values of the cards drawn based on the following criteria.

Jack of Clubs and Jack of Spades	10 points
Jack of Diamonds and Jack of Hearts	15 points
Queen of Clubs and Queen of Spades	14 points
Queen of Diamonds and Queen of Hearts	18 points
King of Clubs and King of Spades	20 points
King of Diamonds and King of Hearts	22 points
Even non-face cards	0 points
Odd non-face cards	Value of card
Aces	0 points

Input All cards drawn. A card is specified by a name and a suit. Names are Ace, Two, Three, Four, Five, Six, Seven, Eight, Nine, Ten, Jack, Queen, and King. Suits are Spades, Clubs, Diamonds, and Hearts.

PROBLEM-SOLVING CASE STUDY cont'd.

Output Before reading the input, display the value of all cards in the deck. Prompt the user for each card and display the value of each card entered. After an Ace is read, display the total score.

Design In the game we draw cards until we come to an Ace. We can model this behavior with a sentinel-controlled loop in our program. On each iteration, one card is processed. Here is the main module.

```
Solitaire                                                          Level 0
Score := 0
Display Card Values
loop
   Get Card_Name
   exit when Card_Name is Ace
   Get Card_Suit
   Score := Score + Value Of Card (Card_Name, Card_Suit)
end loop
Display end of game message
Display Score
```

As there are only 13 different values for names of cards and 4 different suits, enumeration types provide a good way to model these values. Here are all of the objects in our level 0 module.

Name	Data Type	Role
Card_Name	Card_Type	The name of the card drawn
Card_Suit	Suit_Type	The suit of the card drawn
Score	Natural	The current score of the game

We could use 52 different Put statements to display the values of all of the cards in the deck at the start of the program. However, this seems like a lot of work. There must be a way to use a loop. Since we are using enumeration types for the card names and suits, we can use nested count-controlled loops to process every card. The for statement is probably best suited for these count-controlled loops. The problem did not specify an order to display the card values. We choose to display together the values of all cards with the same name. We can use the same function used in the main module to determine the value of the cards in these loops.

PROBLEM-SOLVING CASE STUDY cont'd.

```
Display Card Values                                          Level 1
for Name in Card_Type loop
   for Suit in Suit_Type loop
      Put Name
      Put Suit
      Put Value Of Card (Name, Suit)
   end loop
end loop
```

In both of the previous modules, we called a function to determine the value of a particular card. Given the card name and suit, it returns the value of the card. The algorithm for determining the value of a particular card is clearly a nested selection structure. As the selections are dependent on discrete (enumeration) types, the case statement is appropriate. We could use a case statement to determine the value of each odd non-face card. However, by ordering the enumeration literals properly, we can use the position of a name in the enumeration type to determine its value.

```
Value Of
   in        Name
   in        Suit
case Name is
   when Name is Three, Five, Seven, or Nine
      Value := position of Name in enumeration type + 1
   when Name is Jack
      case Suit is
         when Suit is Clubs or Spades
            Value := 10
         when Suit is Hearts or Diamonds
            Value := 15
      end case
   when Name is Queen
      case Suit is
         when Suit is Clubs or Spades
            Value := 14
         when Suit is Hearts or Diamonds
            Value := 18
      end case
   when Name is King
      case Suit is
         when Suit is Clubs or Spades
            Value := 20
         when Suit is Hearts or Diamonds
            Value := 22
         end case
   when others
      Value := 0
end case
return Value
```

PROBLEM-SOLVING CASE STUDY cont'd.

Module Structure Chart

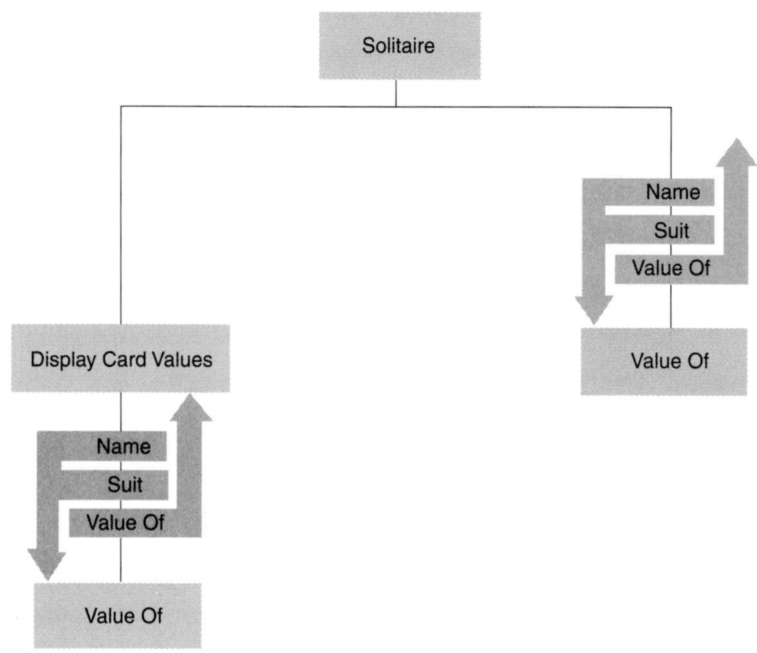

Implementation

```
with Ada.Text_IO;
with Ada.Integer_Text_IO;
procedure Solitaire is

   -- This program scores a simple game of solitaire.

   type Card_Name_Type is (Ace, Two, Three, Four, Five, Six, Seven,
                           Eight, Nine, Ten, Jack, Queen, King);
   type Card_Suit_Type is (Clubs, Spades, Diamonds, Hearts);

   package Name_IO is new Ada.Text_IO.Enumeration_IO (Enum => Card_Name_Type);
   package Suit_IO is new Ada.Text_IO.Enumeration_IO (Enum => Card_Suit_Type);
```

PROBLEM-SOLVING CASE STUDY cont'd.

```
---------------------------------------
function Value_Of (Name : in Card_Name_Type;
                   Suit : in Card_Suit_Type) return Natural is
-- This function determines the value of a particular card.

   Value : Natural;     -- Value of the given card

begin  -- Value_Of
   case Name is
      when Three | Five | Seven | Nine =>
         -- The value of these cards is one greater than its position
         -- in the enumeration type
         Value := Card_Name_Type'Pos (Name) + 1;
      when Jack =>
         case Suit is
            when Clubs | Spades =>
               Value := 10;
            when Diamonds | Hearts =>
               Value := 15;
         end case;
      when Queen =>
         case Suit is
            when Clubs | Spades =>
               Value := 14;
            when Diamonds | Hearts =>
               Value := 18;
         end case;
      when King =>
         case Suit is
            when Clubs | Spades =>
               Value := 20;
            when Diamonds | Hearts =>
               Value := 22;
         end case;
      when others =>
         Value := 0;
   end case;
   return Value;
end Value_Of;

---------------------------------------
procedure Display_Card_Values is

-- This procedure displays the value of all the cards in the deck
```

PROBLEM-SOLVING CASE STUDY *cont'd.*

```
   begin
      Ada.Text_IO.Put ("The value of the cards in this game are as follows:");
      Ada.Text_IO.New_Line;
      Ada.Text_IO.New_Line;

                     -- Display the value of all cards
      Name_Loop:  -- Each iteration, display all values for one card name
      for Name in Card_Name_Type loop

                        -- Display all values for the current card name
         Suit_Loop: -- Each iteration, display one card's value
         for Suit in Card_Suit_Type loop
            Name_IO.Put (Item => Name, Width => 6,
                         Set  => Ada.Text_IO.Lower_Case);
            Ada.Text_IO.Put (" of ");
            Suit_IO.Put (Item => Suit, Width => 8,
                         Set  => Ada.Text_IO.Lower_Case);
            Ada.Integer_Text_IO.Put (Item  => Value_Of (Name, Suit),
                                     Width => 4);
            Ada.Text_IO.Put (" points");
            Ada.Text_IO.New_Line;
         end loop Suit_Loop;
         Ada.Text_IO.New_Line;
      end loop Name_Loop;
   end Display_Card_Values;

----------------------------------------
   Name  : Card_Name_Type;    -- Name of current card
   Suit  : Card_Suit_Type;    -- Suit of current card
   Score : Natural;           -- Score from cards processed

begin  -- Solitaire
   Ada.Text_IO.Put ("This program scores a simple game of solitaire.");
   Ada.Text_IO.New_Line;
   Ada.Text_IO.New_Line;
   Score := 0;
   Display_Card_Values;
   Ada.Text_IO.New_Line;
   Input_Loop:
   loop
      Ada.Text_IO.Put ("Enter the name (two, eight, etc.) of your card:  ");
      Ada.Text_IO.New_Line;
      Name_IO.Get (Name);
      exit Input_Loop when Name = Ace;
      Ada.Text_IO.Put ("Enter the suit of your card:  ");
      Ada.Text_IO.New_Line;
      Suit_IO.Get (Suit);
```

PROBLEM-SOLVING CASE STUDY *cont'd.*

```
      Score := Score + Value_Of (Name, Suit);
   end loop Input_Loop;
   Ada.Text_IO.New_Line;
   Ada.Text_IO.New_Line;
   Ada.Text_IO.Put ("Ace ends the game.  Your score for this game is ");
   Ada.Integer_Text_IO.Put (Item => Score, Width => 1);
   Ada.Text_IO.New_Line;
end Solitaire;
```

Testing To test the Value_Of function in this program, we need to enter all 52 possible input values. To test our loop control and summing, enter Ace as the first card; then enter Ace after just one card, and again after a number of other cards have been entered. Here is the result of one test run.

```
This program scores a simple game of solitaire.

The value of the cards in this game are as follows:

ace    of clubs      0 points
ace    of spades     0 points
ace    of diamonds   0 points
ace    of hearts     0 points

two    of clubs      0 points
two    of spades     0 points
two    of diamonds   0 points
two    of hearts     0 points

three  of clubs      3 points
three  of spades     3 points
three  of diamonds   3 points
three  of hearts     3 points

four   of clubs      0 points
four   of spades     0 points
four   of diamonds   0 points
four   of hearts     0 points

five   of clubs      5 points
five   of spades     5 points
five   of diamonds   5 points
five   of hearts     5 points
```

PROBLEM-SOLVING CASE STUDY cont'd.

```
six    of clubs      0 points
six    of spades     0 points
six    of diamonds   0 points
six    of hearts     0 points

seven  of clubs      7 points
seven  of spades     7 points
seven  of diamonds   7 points
seven  of hearts     7 points

eight  of clubs      0 points
eight  of spades     0 points
eight  of diamonds   0 points
eight  of hearts     0 points

nine   of clubs      9 points
nine   of spades     9 points
nine   of diamonds   9 points
nine   of hearts     9 points

ten    of clubs      0 points
ten    of spades     0 points
ten    of diamonds   0 points
ten    of hearts     0 points

jack   of clubs     10 points
jack   of spades    10 points
jack   of diamonds  15 points
jack   of hearts    15 points

queen  of clubs     14 points
queen  of spades    14 points
queen  of diamonds  18 points
queen  of hearts    18 points

king   of clubs     20 points
king   of spades    20 points
king   of diamonds  22 points
king   of hearts    22 points


Enter the name (two, eight, etc.) of your card:
two
Enter the suit of your card:
hearts
Enter the name (two, eight, etc.) of your card:
five
```

PROBLEM-SOLVING CASE STUDY cont'd.

```
Enter the suit of your card:
diamonds
Enter the name (two, eight, etc.) of your card:
queen
Enter the suit of your card:
spades
Enter the name (two, eight, etc.) of your card:
jack
Enter the suit of your card:
diamonds
Enter the name (two, eight, etc.) of your card:
king
Enter the suit of your card:
clubs
Enter the name (two, eight, etc.) of your card:
three
Enter the suit of your card:
hearts
Enter the name (two, eight, etc.) of your card:
ace


Ace ends the game.  Your score for this game is 57
```

Testing and Debugging

The same testing techniques that we used with the loop statement apply to the for and while statements. With a data-dependent for statement, it is important to test for proper results when the loop executes zero times—when the range of the loop is a null range (a range in which the end value is less than the start value). We present a more formal approach to loop testing in the next two sections.

The Loop Invariant

In Chapter 4, we saw that we can use an algorithm trace to test a design before we implement it. Loops present some special problems in performing a trace because each iteration can behave differently. To test a data-dependent loop design, we would have to try every possible combination of input. In many cases this is not practical because the possibilities are too numerous, if not infinite.

What we would like to do is treat a loop as a separate module so that we can use the trace technique we developed in Chapter 4. But in order to establish a fixed set of preconditions and postconditions for a loop, we must determine those characteristics that do not vary from one iteration to the next. The collection of all these characteristics is called the **loop invariant** and is expressed as a set of assertions that always must be true in order for the loop to execute correctly.

Loop invariant Assertions about the characteristics of a loop that always must be true for a loop to execute properly. The assertions are true on loop entry, at the start of each loop iteration, and on exit from the loop. They are not necessarily true at each point in the body of the loop.

At first, you might think that the invariant is just the Boolean expression in the exit statement that controls the loop. But until a loop exits, this Boolean expression is always false. Here are some examples.

Exit Condition	Related Invariant Condition
Loop_Control_Variable > 365 (Loop_Control_Variable is initialized before the loop.)	The loop control variable can range from 1 to 366.
Odd_Count = 10 (Odd_Count is initialized before the loop.)	The event counter is equal to the number of odd numbers input; it can range from 0 to 10.
Data < 0 (Data is initialized first thing in the loop)	Only nonnegative data values are processed; the loop exits with a negative value in the input variable

You can see that an invariant condition is related to each exit condition. The loop invariant must be true and the exit condition must be false for the loop to execute. Both must be true after the loop exits. Also the loop invariant usually consists of other conditions as well as those related to the exit condition. It typically includes the ranges of all the variables used in the loop and the status of any files.

To create the invariant, we begin with our answer to the last question on the loop design checklist (*What is the state of the program on exiting the loop?*) because it forces us to determine the final condition of the variables and files. Then we work backward, answering the other questions on the checklist.

Let's write the invariant for the outer loop in Program Running in Chapter 6. We begin with the part of the invariant associated with the loop Member_Loop. We know that on loop exit, Club_Distance contains the sum of all the individual totals. Then we look at how the process is initialized and updated. Here's the related invariant condition.

- Club_Total can range from zero upward; at the start of each iteration it must equal the sum of all the individual totals that have been computed.

In the same way, we look at the termination condition, initialization, and update of Member_Count to determine the portion of the invariant that relates to it.

- Member_Count can range from zero upward; at the start of each iteration it contains the count of all the members processed so far.

Here are the invariant conditions for the other variables used in the loop.

- Member_ID is either undefined or contains a nonnegative Integer value. The loop exits with a negative value in this input variable. Member_ID contains the most recently input club-member identification number.
- Member_Distance is either undefined or contains a Float value. Member_Distance contains the sum of the seven daily distances run by the member processed in the most recently completed iteration.

In addition to the status of variables and files, most programs contain some general invariant conditions. For example:

- One line of member information should be printed for each loop iteration, and the number of lines output should be one less than the number input.

Loop Testing Strategy

The loop invariant is a good place to start in designing test data. The invariant tells us what the acceptable ranges of variables are and what sorts of I/O operations we should see. To test a loop, we try to devise data sets that could cause the variables to go out of range or leave the files in improper states that violate the postconditions of the module containing the loop.

To verify an algorithm, we use the loop invariant as a bridge between the statements that precede and follow the loop. We have to show that the invariant conditions are true before entering the loop. If the loop is designed correctly, they should still be true when the termination condition is reached.

To show that the invariant is true before loop entry, we compare the current set of conditions (the postconditions from the preceding statements) with the invariant. If the invariant is a subset of the current conditions, then the loop is ready to start. If the invariant contains an assertion that has not been established, then something is missing in our preparations for executing the loop.

Once we know that the invariant is true at loop entry, we must show that the invariant is true at the start of each iteration. We do this by tracing through the body of the loop and determining the postconditions of each statement. Then we compare the postconditions of the last statement in the loop to the invariant. If any part of the invariant is not satisfied by these conditions, there is something wrong with the loop. Otherwise we know that the invariant will be true at the beginning of the next iteration.

When the loop exits, its termination condition is true. The postcondition of the loop is the combination of the termination condition and the invariant. The postcondition also includes any conditions that existed before the loop that have not changed.

Let's tie all this together with an example: summing the integers 1 through 10.

```
with Ada.Text_IO;
procedure Sum_Up is

   Sum    : Integer;
   Number : Integer;

begin
   Sum := 0;
   Number := 1;
   Sum_Loop:
   loop
      exit Sum_Loop when Number > 10;
      Sum := Sum + Number;
      Number := Number + 1;
   end loop Sum_Loop;
end Sum_Up;
```

To verify this program, we have to do the following:

1. Define the loop invariant.
2. Show that the invariant is true before loop entry.
3. Show that the invariant is true at the start of each iteration.
4. Show that at loop exit the invariant is still true and the termination condition is true.

This is the loop invariant.

- Sum contains the sum of the integers from 0 to Number −1; Number is in the range 1 through 11 and is equal to the number of loop iterations executed plus 1.

We can state the last part of the invariant more concisely as follows:

Iterations = Number − 1

At loop entry, the following conditions have been established: Sum is equal to 0, and Number is equal to 1. Comparing these conditions to the invariant, we see that Sum is equal to the sum of the integers from 0 to Number −1; Number is in the range 1 through 11; and the number of iterations executed is 0, which equals Number −1.

Next we walk through the loop body. The first statement tests the loop exit condition. The next statement adds the value of Number to Sum, so Sum now contains the sum of the integers from 0 to Number. The next statement increments Number, which means that Sum now contains the sum of the integers from 0 to Number −1. At the end of this iteration, Number −1 also equals the number of iterations. Because Number cannot be greater than 11 at the start of an iteration, we also know that Number cannot be greater than 11 at this point (the exit statement's condition would have been true and the loop exited). So the invariant is true for the start of the next iteration.

We can tell that the loop terminates correctly from the fact that Number is initially less than 10 and is incremented in each loop iteration. So Number eventually will become greater than 10, and the loop will terminate.

This may seem like an awful lot of work to show something that's obvious anyway: The code *is* correct. But what is obvious in simple code may not be obvious in more complicated code. That's where verification methods are critically important.

Testing and Debugging Hints

1. The case statement is a selection control structure with multiple alternatives. There must be a choice for every possible value that the case selector can take. Each choice can appear only once.
2. The for statement is a special-purpose loop. It is a count-controlled loop in which the values that the loop control variable may take are listed in the statement itself. The increment is always 1 for the normal version and −1 when the reserved word `reverse` appears before the range.
3. When using the reverse form of the for statement, you still must give the range with the smaller value followed by the larger value. If the first value of the range is greater than the last value, the range is a

null range and the loop is executed zero times regardless of whether or not the word `reverse` is used.
4. Treat the loop parameter as a local constant—it may be used but not modified. The loop parameter is defined in the for statement and is local to the body of the loop.
5. The condition given in a while loop is the condition for which the loop continues execution. This logic is opposite that of the exit statement used in a general loop.

Summary

The case statement is a multiway selection statement. It allows the program to choose among a set of alternative branches. The case is less general than an if-elsif-else structure and can always be simulated by it. If case can be used, however, it usually makes the code shorter and more self-documenting. The case selector must be a discrete value, and there must be one and only one choice for every value in its domain.

Ada provides a special-purpose looping statement, the for statement, with a predefined range for the loop parameter and automatic incrementing or decrementing. If the range is a null range, the loop is not executed. The loop parameter is defined in the for statement and its type is determined by the range.

Ada also provides a special-purpose looping statement, the while statement, for pretest loops. When the condition in a while statement is True, the loop continues execution. Control exits a while loop when the condition is False. This is opposite of the logic used in the exit statement.

A loop invariant is a set of conditions that specify what must be true on loop entry, at the beginning of each iteration, and at loop exit in order for the loop to work properly. Writing out the loop invariant is a part of the verification process for programs that contain loops.

Quick Check

1. Write a case statement that, given an Integer selector called Name, will print your first name if Name = 1, your middle initial if Name = 2, your last name if Name = 3, and an error message if Name is not 1, 2, or 3. (pp. 440–443)
2. How would you change your answer to question 1 so that nothing is displayed if Name is not 1, 2, or 3? (pp. 444–445)
3. A certain problem requires a count-controlled loop that starts at 10 and counts down to 1. Which type of Ada loop should be used? Write the statement. (pp. 445–448)
4. The condition in a while loop is (Day < 1) or (Day > 31). What would be the equivalent condition in an exit statement? (pp. 453–453)
5. What is the major criterion for selecting a while statement over a loop statement? (p. 454)

6. With what kind of loop is the following invariant most likely associated? (pp. 462–466)

   Day may range from 1 to 365 and must indicate the number of the iteration that is about to be executed.

Answers

1.
```
case Name is
   when 1 =>
      Ada.Text_IO.Put ("Mildred");
   when 2 =>
      Ada.Text_IO.Put ("R.");
   when 3 =>
      Ada.Text_IO.Put ("Smedley");
   when others =>
      Ada.Text_IO.Put ("Invalid number");
end case;
```
2. Change `Ada.Text_IO.Put ("Invalid number");` to `null;`. **3.** A for statement: for Count in reverse 1 . . 10 loop **4.** (Day >= 1) and (Day <= 31) **5.** When the problem is stated in terms of when to continue looping. **6.** A count-controlled loop.

Exam Preparation Exercises

1. What is wrong with each of the following code fragments?

   a.
   ```
   Choice : Integer;
      .
      .
      .
   case Choice is
      when 1 | 3 | 5 | 7 | 9 =>
         Ada.Text_IO.Put ("Odd");
      when 2 | 4 | 6 | 8 | 10 =>
         Ada.Text_IO.Put ("Even");
   end case;
   ```
   b.
   ```
   Choice : String;
      .
      .
      .
   case Choice is
      when "Hello" | "Hi" =>
         Ada.Text_IO.Put ("Greeting");
      when others =>
         Ada.Text_IO.Put ("No greeting");
   end case;
   ```

c.
```
Choice : Integer;
   .
   .
   .
case Choice is
   when 1 | 3 | 5 | 7 | 9 =>
      Ada.Text_IO.Put ("Odd");
   when others =>
      Ada.Text_IO.Put ("Out of range");
   when 2 | 4 | 6 | 8 | 10 =>
      Ada.Text_IO.Put ("Even");
end case;
```

2. Given the following declarations

```
type Day_Type is (Monday, Tuesday, Wednesday, Thursday,
                  Friday, Saturday, Sunday);
package Day_IO is new Ada.Text_IO.Enumeration_IO (Enum => Day_Type);
```

what will be printed by each of the following code fragments?

a.
```
for Day in Tuesday..Friday loop
   Day_IO.Put (Day);
   Ada.Text_IO.New_Line;
end loop;
```

b.
```
for Day in reverse Tuesday..Friday loop
   Day_IO.Put (Day);
   Ada.Text_IO.New_Line;
end loop;
```

c.
```
for Day in Day_Type loop
   Day_IO.Put (Day);
   Ada.Text_IO.New_Line;
end loop;
```

d.
```
for Day in reverse Day_Type loop
   Day_IO.Put (Day);
   Ada.Text_IO.New_Line;
end loop;
```

3. How many lines will be displayed by each of the following for statements?

a.
```
for Index in 1..5 loop
   Ada.Text_IO.Put ("Hello Mildred.");
   Ada.Text_IO.New_Line;
end loop
```

b.
```
for Index in reverse 1..5 loop
   Ada.Text_IO.Put ("Hello Mildred.");
   Ada.Text_IO.New_Line;
end loop
```

c.
```
for Index in 5..1 loop
   Ada.Text_IO.Put ("Hello Mildred.");
   Ada.Text_IO.New_Line;
end loop
```
d.
```
for Index in reverse 5..1 loop
   Ada.Text_IO.Put ("Hello Mildred.");
   Ada.Text_IO.New_Line;
```
e.
```
for Index in 1..1 loop
   Ada.Text_IO.Put ("Hello Mildred.");
   Ada.Text_IO.New_Line;
end loop
```
f.
```
for Index in reverse 1..1 loop
   Ada.Text_IO.Put ("Hello Mildred.");
   Ada.Text_IO.New_Line;
end loop
```

4. a. You may change the value of the loop parameter within a for statement. (True or False)
   b. You must declare the loop parameter of a for statement before the for statement. (True or False)
   c. It is impossible to write an infinite loop using only the for statement. (True or False)
   d. The for statement is a general-purpose loop because we can rewrite any loop statement as a for statement. (True or False)
5. What will be displayed by the following program fragment?

```
for I in reverse 1..4 loop
   for J in reverse 1..I loop
      Ada.Integer_Text_IO.Put (I);
   end loop;
   Ada.Text_IO.New_Line;
end loop;
```

6. What will be displayed by the following program fragment?

```
for Row in  1..5  loop
   for Col in 1..(4 - Row) loop
      Ada.Text_IO.Put ('*');
   end loop;
   for Col in 1..(2 * Row -1) loop
      Ada.Text_IO.Put (' ');
   end loop;
   for Col in 1..(4 - Row) loop
      Ada.Text_IO.Put ('*');
   end loop;
   Ada.Text_IO.New_Line;
end loop;
```

7. What will be displayed by the following program fragment?

```
for M in 1..5 loop
   X := M;
   while X > 1 loop
      Ada.Integer_Text_IO.Put (X);
      X := X -1;
   end loop;
   Ada.Text_IO.New_Line;
end loop;
```

8. Is a while loop appropriate for writing a sentinel-controlled input loop? Explain your answer.
9. Must every while loop have a loop label? (*Hint:* Look at the EBNF definition.)
10. Write the invariant conditions for the following loop. (Sum and Count are of type Integer.)

```
Sum := 0;
Count := 0;
Exercise_Loop:
loop
   exit Exercise_Loop when Count >= 10;
   Sum   := Sum + Count;
   Count := Count + 1;
end loop Exercise_Loop;
```

Programming Warm-up Exercises

1. Write a case statement that does the following:

```
if the value of Grade is
   'A'  add 4 to Sum
   'B'  add 3 to Sum
   'C'  add 2 to Sum
   'D'  add 1 to Sum
   'F'  display "Student is on probation"
```

2. Rewrite the following for statements using general loop statements.

   a.
```
for Index in 1..5 loop
   Ada.Integer_Text_IO.Put (Index);
   Ada.Text_IO.New_Line;
end loop
```

b.
```
type Color_Type is (Red, Green, Blue,
                    Cyan, Magenta, Yellow);
   .
   .
   .
for Color in Color_Type loop
   Color_IO.Put (Color);
   Ada.Text_IO.New_Line;
end loop
```

3. Write a function that accepts an Integer parameter called Base and a Natural parameter called Exponent that returns Base raised to the Exponent power. Use a for statement instead of the ** operator.
4. Rewrite the following for statement as a while loop.

```
for M in reverse 5..93 loop
   Ada.Integer_Text_IO.Put (M);
   Ada.Text_IO.New_Line;
end loop;
```

5. Write a while loop that displays the following sequence of numbers.

```
1024 512 256 128  64  32  16   8   4   2   1
```

6. Rewrite the following code segment using a loop statement.

```
Sum := 0;
Ada.Integer_Text_IO.Get (Value);
Sentinel_Loop:
while Value /= 0 loop
   Sum := Sum + Value;
   Ada.Integer_Text_IO.Get (Value);
end loop Sentinel_Loop;
Ada.Integer_Text_IO.Put (Sum);
```

7. Rewrite the following code segment using a while statement.

```
Approx := X / 2.0;              -- Choose an initial approximation
Calculate_Square_Root:
loop
   exit Calculate_Square_Root when abs(Approx ** 2 - X) < Tolerance;
   Approx := 0.5 * (Approx + X / Approx);
end loop Calculate_Square_Root;
Ada.Float_Text_IO.Put (X);              -- Display value and
Ada.Float_Text_IO.Put (Approx);         -- its square root
```

Programming Problems

1. Develop a top-down design and write an Ada program that will input a two-letter abbreviation for one of the 50 states and print out the full name of the state. If the abbreviation isn't valid, the program should print an error message and ask for an abbreviation again. The names of the 50 states and their abbreviations are:

State	Abbreviation	State	Abbreviation
Alabama	AL	Alaska	AK
Arizona	AZ	Arkansas	AR
California	CA	Colorado	CO
Connecticut	CT	Delaware	DE
Florida	FL	Georgia	GA
Hawaii	HI	Idaho	ID
Illinois	IL	Indiana	IN
Iowa	IA	Kansas	KS
Kentucky	KY	Louisiana	LA
Maine	ME	Maryland	MD
Massachusetts	MA	Michigan	MI
Minnesota	MN	Mississippi	MS
Missouri	MO	Montana	MT
Nebraska	NE	Nevada	NV
New Hampshire	NH	New Jersey	NJ
New Mexico	NM	New York	NY
North Carolina	NC	North Dakota	ND
Ohio	OH	Oklahoma	OK
Oregon	OR	Pennsylvania	PA
Rhode Island	RI	South Carolina	SC
South Dakota	SD	Tennessee	TN
Texas	TX	Utah	UT
Vermont	VT	Virginia	VA
Washington	WA	West Virginia	WV
Wisconsin	WI	Wyoming	WY

Hint: Use nested case statements where the outer case statement uses the first letter of the abbreviation as its selector.

2. Write a top-down design and an Ada program that reads a date in numeric form and prints it in English. For example:

```
Enter a date in the form mm dd yyyy.
10 27 1942

October twenty-seventh, nineteen hundred and forty-two.
```

Here is another example.

```
Enter a date in the form of mm dd yyyy.
12 10 1910

December tenth, nineteen hundred and ten.
```

The program should work for any date in the twentieth century and should print an error message for a year outside of the century and for any invalid date, such as 2 29 1983 (1983 wasn't a leap year). Remember that 1901 is the first year of the twentieth century and 2000 is the last.

3. Write a top-down design and an Ada program that will convert letters of the alphabet into their corresponding digits on the telephone. The program should let the user enter letters repeatedly until a *Q* or a *Z* is entered. (*Q* and *Z* are the two letters that are not on the telephone.) An error message should be printed for any nonalphabetic character that is entered. The letters and digits on the telephone have the following correspondence.

```
ABC = 2    DEF = 3    GHI = 4

JKL = 5    MNO = 6    PRS = 7

TUV = 8    WXY = 9
```

Here is an example.

```
Enter a letter.
P
The letter P corresponds to 7 on the telephone.
Enter a letter.
A
The letter A corresponds to 2 on the telephone.
Enter a letter.
S
The letter S corresponds to 7 on the telephone.
Enter a letter.
C
The letter C corresponds to 2 on the telephone.
Enter a letter.
A
The letter A corresponds to 2 on the telephone.
Enter a letter.
L
The letter L corresponds to 5 on the telephone.
Enter a letter.
2
Invalid letter, enter Q or Z to quit.
Enter a letter.
Z
Quit.
```

4. Write a top-down design and an Ada program that performs a display test. The program should write lines containing the lowercase and uppercase characters. Each line should begin with the successor of the character that began the previous line and contain 80 characters. Prompt the user to enter the number of lines to display. Here is the output for 30 lines.

```
abcdefghijklmnopqrstuvwxyzABCDEFGHIJKLMNOPQRSTUVWXYZabcdefghijklmnopqrstuvwxyzAB
bcdefghijklmnopqrstuvwxyzABCDEFGHIJKLMNOPQRSTUVWXYZabcdefghijklmnopqrstuvwxyzABC
cdefghijklmnopqrstuvwxyzABCDEFGHIJKLMNOPQRSTUVWXYZabcdefghijklmnopqrstuvwxyzABCD
defghijklmnopqrstuvwxyzABCDEFGHIJKLMNOPQRSTUVWXYZabcdefghijklmnopqrstuvwxyzABCDE
efghijklmnopqrstuvwxyzABCDEFGHIJKLMNOPQRSTUVWXYZabcdefghijklmnopqrstuvwxyzABCDEF
fghijklmnopqrstuvwxyzABCDEFGHIJKLMNOPQRSTUVWXYZabcdefghijklmnopqrstuvwxyzABCDEFG
ghijklmnopqrstuvwxyzABCDEFGHIJKLMNOPQRSTUVWXYZabcdefghijklmnopqrstuvwxyzABCDEFGH
hijklmnopqrstuvwxyzABCDEFGHIJKLMNOPQRSTUVWXYZabcdefghijklmnopqrstuvwxyzABCDEFGHI
ijklmnopqrstuvwxyzABCDEFGHIJKLMNOPQRSTUVWXYZabcdefghijklmnopqrstuvwxyzABCDEFGHIJ
jklmnopqrstuvwxyzABCDEFGHIJKLMNOPQRSTUVWXYZabcdefghijklmnopqrstuvwxyzABCDEFGHIJK
klmnopqrstuvwxyzABCDEFGHIJKLMNOPQRSTUVWXYZabcdefghijklmnopqrstuvwxyzABCDEFGHIJKL
lmnopqrstuvwxyzABCDEFGHIJKLMNOPQRSTUVWXYZabcdefghijklmnopqrstuvwxyzABCDEFGHIJKLM
mnopqrstuvwxyzABCDEFGHIJKLMNOPQRSTUVWXYZabcdefghijklmnopqrstuvwxyzABCDEFGHIJKLMN
onpqrstuvwxyzABCDEFGHIJKLMNOPQRSTUVWXYZabcdefghijklmnopqrstuvwxyzABCDEFGHIJKLMNO
npqrstuvwxyzABCDEFGHIJKLMNOPQRSTUVWXYZabcdefghijklmnopqrstuvwxyzABCDEFGHIJKLMNOP
pqrstuvwxyzABCDEFGHIJKLMNOPQRSTUVWXYZabcdefghijklmnopqrstuvwxyzABCDEFGHIJKLMNOPQ
qrstuvwxyzABCDEFGHIJKLMNOPQRSTUVWXYZabcdefghijklmnopqrstuvwxyzABCDEFGHIJKLMNOPQR
rstuvwxyzABCDEFGHIJKLMNOPQRSTUVWXYZabcdefghijklmnopqrstuvwxyzABCDEFGHIJKLMNOPQRS
stuvwxyzABCDEFGHIJKLMNOPQRSTUVWXYZabcdefghijklmnopqrstuvwxyzABCDEFGHIJKLMNOPQRST
tuvwxyzABCDEFGHIJKLMNOPQRSTUVWXYZabcdefghijklmnopqrstuvwxyzABCDEFGHIJKLMNOPQRSTU
uvwxyzABCDEFGHIJKLMNOPQRSTUVWXYZabcdefghijklmnopqrstuvwxyzABCDEFGHIJKLMNOPQRSTUV
vwxyzABCDEFGHIJKLMNOPQRSTUVWXYZabcdefghijklmnopqrstuvwxyzABCDEFGHIJKLMNOPQRSTUVW
wxyzABCDEFGHIJKLMNOPQRSTUVWXYZabcdefghijklmnopqrstuvwxyzABCDEFGHIJKLMNOPQRSTUVWX
xyzABCDEFGHIJKLMNOPQRSTUVWXYZabcdefghijklmnopqrstuvwxyzABCDEFGHIJKLMNOPQRSTUVWXY
yzABCDEFGHIJKLMNOPQRSTUVWXYZabcdefghijklmnopqrstuvwxyzABCDEFGHIJKLMNOPQRSTUVWXYZ
zABCDEFGHIJKLMNOPQRSTUVWXYZabcdefghijklmnopqrstuvwxyzABCDEFGHIJKLMNOPQRSTUVWXYZa
ABCDEFGHIJKLMNOPQRSTUVWXYZabcdefghijklmnopqrstuvwxyzABCDEFGHIJKLMNOPQRSTUVWXYZab
BCDEFGHIJKLMNOPQRSTUVWXYZabcdefghijklmnopqrstuvwxyzABCDEFGHIJKLMNOPQRSTUVWXYZabc
CDEFGHIJKLMNOPQRSTUVWXYZabcdefghijklmnopqrstuvwxyzABCDEFGHIJKLMNOPQRSTUVWXYZabcd
DEFGHIJKLMNOPQRSTUVWXYZabcdefghijklmnopqrstuvwxyzABCDEFGHIJKLMNOPQRSTUVWXYZabcde
```

CHAPTER 9

The File Data Type and Handling Exceptions

GOALS

After reading this chapter, you should be able to

- understand how text files are organized
- use the End_Of_Line and End_Of_File functions
- explain the difference between text files and binary files
- understand and use sequential files
- understand and use direct access files
- explain what an exception is
- write an exception handler
- use the resources of package Calendar

At first glance this chapter may seem redundant, considering that you have been using files since Chapter 2. Files are so important that we had to describe how to use them from the beginning. You couldn't have run your first program if you hadn't learned to create a file. Your programs would have been trivial if you hadn't known how to read in data from a file.

In this chapter we look at the organization of the text file in more detail. We discuss some additional functions that you may use in the processing of text files. We define another type of file called a binary file and describe two different ways that you can access the values in a binary file.

In previous chapters we have used both passive and active error detection. Passive error handling takes little effort on our part. By declaring subtypes and types appropriate for our data, Ada automatically monitors the validity of the data for us. If at any time a value is not in the correct range, the program will stop with an error message. We have had no control of the program once the system detected an error. In this chapter we discuss how we can keep control when the system detects an error during the execution of the program.

Keeping track of time is an important human endeavor. We finish this chapter with a look at basic operations for dealing with time.

Files

In Ada, the **file data type** is a collection of like elements that are stored outside of the program. **Text files** are collections of Character elements organized into lines. Ada also allows us to use files where the elements are not organized into lines. This type of file is called a **binary file.** The binary file's elements may be any type, but all the elements in a particular binary file must be the same type. Binary files are created within one program to be read by another program or by the same program at a later date. Binary files store the data using the internal representation of the machine.

File data type A collection of elements, all of the same type, stored outside of the program.

Text file A file data type whose elements are characters organized as a collection of lines. A line terminator follows every line. A file terminator follows the last line in the file.

Binary file A file data type whose elements are stored in the internal binary representation of the machine. A file terminator follows the last element in the file.

We use files when the amount of data is too great to store in primary memory. We also use them when it is necessary to store data between runs of a program or when more than one program needs the data.

Text files are the most common type of file. Although there are many tools (like the editor) on your computer that work with text files, that is not the case with binary files. A binary file is used only with programs specifically written for the file. Don't attempt to display a binary file with your editor or print a binary file; the binary values it contains will show up as strange characters and may even disable your display or printer.

Text Files

A text file contains a sequence of characters. You have used an editor to create and modify text files containing Ada source programs since Chapter 2. In Chapter 3 you learned how a program could get data from a text file and put values into a text file.

The characters in a text file are grouped into lines. The end of each line is marked with a line terminator. The end of the file is marked with a file terminator. Ada also defines a page terminator, which we will not spend much time discussing. Figures 9-1 and 9-2 illustrate how a file is laid out. The symbols ¶ and § represent line terminators and file terminators. Figure 9-1 shows the logical view of a file. In actuality, the file is just a collection of characters as shown in Figure 9-2. Notice that the file terminator always follows the last line terminator because the file ends after the last line.

Figure 9-1
Logical Layout of a Text File

```
Mildred Smedley¶
40.5   12.39¶
Horace Beasley¶
35.83    8.90¶
Nell Dale¶
42.6    13.76¶
Jim Doherty¶
40.0     4.35¶
Chip Weems¶
39.5     9.72¶
Pamela Smith¶
20.7     4.35¶
Robert Berliner¶
40.0    14,92¶
John McCormick¶
72.4     9.85¶§
```

FIGURE 9-2 Physical Layout of a Text file

```
Mildred Smedley¶40.5 12.39¶Horace Beasley¶35.83  8.90¶Nell Dale¶42.6 13.76¶J
im Doherty¶40.0 4.35¶Chip Weems¶39.5 9.72¶Pamela Smith¶20.7 4.35¶Robert Berl
iner¶40.0 14.92¶John McCormick¶72.4 9.85¶§
```

In Chapter 3 we said that the line terminator is not defined by the Ada language. File terminators also are not defined by the Ada language. Both of these terminators are either nonprintable control characters or sequences of nonprintable control characters that the system recognizes. Because the procedures in Text_IO handle these terminators for us, we do not need to know exactly what they are.

When working at a keyboard, you generate a line terminator each time you hit the Return or Enter key. You also can generate a line terminator with a call to the New_Line procedure. New_Line outputs a line terminator when it tells the screen or printer to go to the next line.

File terminators are generated with a call to the Close procedure that we discussed in Chapter 3. You generate a file terminator when you save your work and end a session with the editor. Most systems allow you to use special keys or combinations of keys to generate file terminators from the keyboard.

All of the Get procedures we have used ignore line terminators. When prompted to enter several numbers, we can type them on one line or on separate lines because the line terminators between the numbers are ignored. Only the Get_Line procedure is affected by a line terminator. In contrast, our program cannot ignore file terminators. Because a file terminator marks the end of our file, attempting to Get a value after a file terminator will result in an END_ERROR. (If you have never encountered this error, try Programming Warm-up Exercise 7 in Chapter 2.)

The End_Of_Line and End_Of_File Functions

Package Text_IO contains Boolean functions that are commonly used to control loops processing text files. These functions include:

End_Of_Line	Returns True when the reading marker is on a line terminator or on the file terminator.
End_Of_File	Returns True when the reading marker is on the file terminator or on the line terminator that precedes the file terminator.

Remember the reading marker from Chapter 3? It works as a bookmark, but, instead of marking a place in a book, it keeps track of the point in the input data where the computer should continue reading. The reading marker indicates the next character in the text file to be read.

Appendix D contains the complete specification for these functions. You can use both of them with or without a parameter named File whose type is Ada.Text.IO.File_Type. This is the same File parameter name that we have used with all the other input and output procedures. If you do not give an actual parameter, the function operates with the standard input file.

End_Of_Line tells us whether the program has read the last character on a line of input. For example, the following loop gets and displays all of the characters on a line in file Story_File. Variable Char is of type Character.

```
Char_Echo:       -- Get and echo one line
loop             -- Each iteration, one character is read and displayed
   exit Char_Echo when Ada.Text_IO.End_Of_Line (Story_File);
   Ada.Text_IO.Get (File => Story_File,  Item => Char);
   Ada.Text_IO.Put (Char);
end loop Char_Echo;
Ada.Text_IO.New_Line;   -- End the output line
```

This loop continues until the reading marker is on the line terminator. At this point, End_Of_Line returns True and the loop is terminated. Using the sample data

```
Mildred¶
```

the following table traces the reading marker for the previous loop. We use a gray box to indicate the position of the reading marker and we draw a line through all the characters that have been processed at this point.

Operation	*Value of End_Of_Line*	*Marker Position*
Before the loop	False	Mildred¶
After the first pass	False	Mildred¶
After the second pass	False	Mildred¶
After the third pass	False	Mildred¶
After the fourth pass	False	Mildred¶
After the fifth pass	False	Mildred¶
After the sixth pass	False	Mildred¶
After the last pass	True	Mildred¶

End_Of_File tells us whether the program has read the last line in the file. The following code fragment uses two nested loops to get and display all of the characters in file Story_File. The inner loop processes the characters on a line, and the outer loop processes the lines in the file.

```
Line_Echo:   -- Read and display all of the lines in the file
loop         -- Each iteration, one line is read and displayed
   exit Line_Echo when Ada.Text_IO.End_Of_File(Story_File);

   Char_Echo:   -- Read and display one line of the file
   loop         -- Each iteration, one character is read and displayed
      exit Char_Echo when Ada.Text_IO.End_Of_Line (Story_File);
      Ada.Text_IO.Get (File => Story_File,
                       Item => Char);
      Ada.Text_IO.Put (Char);
   end loop Char_Echo;

   Ada.Text_IO.New_Line; -- End the output line
   -- Move the reading marker to the next line
   if not Ada.Text_IO.End_Of_File (Story_File) then
      Ada.Text_IO.Skip_Line (Story_File);
   end if;
end loop Line_Echo;
```

The New_Line call ends an output line after the end of the input line is detected. Without this call, the displayed characters would all be on one line.

In Chapter 3 we said that procedure Skip_Line advances the reading marker to the beginning of the next line. As no line follows the last one in the file, we must not call Skip_Line after processing it. The if statement that checks for the end of the file ensures that we do not call Skip_Line when there is no following line. If we call Skip_Line when there is no following line, it will raise the END_ERROR exception.

Here is a trace of this code showing the state of the program just before and just after each call to procedure Skip_Line.

Operation	*Values of End_Of_Line and End_Of_File*	*Marker Position*
Before the loops	False, False	Ada Lovelace¶ was born¶ in 1815.¶§
Before the first call to Ada.Text_IO.Skip_Line	True, False	Ada Lovelace¶ was born¶ in 1815.¶§
After the first call to Ada.Text_IO.Skip_Line	False, False	Ada Lovelace¶ was born¶ in 1815.¶§
Before the second call to Ada.Text_IO.Skip_Line	True, False	Ada Lovelace¶ was born¶ in 1815.¶§
After the second call to Ada.Text_IO.Skip_Line	False, False	Ada Lovelace¶ was born¶ in 1815.¶§
Before the third call to Ada.Text_IO.Skip_Line	True, True	Ada Lovelace¶ was born¶ in 1815.¶§

Because End_Of_File returns True before the third call to Skip_Line, the if statement ensures that we do not actually make the call and attempt to move the reading marker to the beginning of a nonexistent line.

Without the call to Skip_Line, the reading marker would remain on the first line terminator, and the exit condition of loop Char_Echo would always be True. Trace the code yourself to verify that removing the call to Skip_Line results in an infinite outer loop.

In both of these examples, we used the Get procedure for data type Character. Keep in mind that text files contain only characters. However, you can use a group of characters in a text file to represent a number or a string. The four characters '1', '8', '1', and '5' in the preceding table can be taken together and interpreted as the integer number 1815 or the four-character string "1815". Of course, we also can interpret them simply as four distinct characters. The Get procedures in packages Ada.Integer_Text_IO and Ada.Float_Text_IO read *groups* of characters and convert them to numeric types according to certain rules. The Put procedures in packages Ada.Integer_Text_IO and Ada.Float_Text_IO convert numeric values to groups of characters.

You must be careful when using the End_Of_Line and End_Of_File functions in combination with procedures that get numeric, enumeration, or string data types. Each call to a procedure that reads a number, an enumeration value, or a string usually reads more than one character. The following loop attempts to read and sum all the integers on a line of input from the standard input file.

```
Sum := 0;
Integer_Sum:     -- Sum the integers on a line
loop             -- Each iteration, one integer is read and added to the sum
   exit Integer_Sum when Ada.Text_IO.End_Of_Line;
   Ada.Integer_Text_IO.Get (Value);
   Sum := Sum + Value;
end loop Integer_Sum;
```

Given this line of input:

```
123 456 789
```

the loop behaves as expected.

Operation	*Value of End_of_Line*	*Marker Position*
Before the loop	False	123 456 789¶
After the first pass of loop Integer_Sum	False	123 456 789¶
After the second pass of loop Integer_Sum	False	123 456 789¶
After the third and last pass of loop Integer_Sum	True	123 456 789¶

However, if there is a blank after the last number on the line, the behavior of the loop is not as you might expect. The loop does not stop after echoing the values on the line; it continues to process values on subsequent lines of input.

Operation	*Value of End_of_Line*	*Marker Position*
Before the loop	False	123 456 789 ¶ 876 620 975 ¶
After the first pass of loop Integer_Sum	False	123 456 789 ¶ 876 620 975 ¶
After the second pass of loop Integer_Sum	False	123 456 789 ¶ 876 620 975 ¶
After the third pass of loop Integer_Sum	False	123 456 789 ¶ 876 620 975 ¶
After the fourth pass of loop Integer_Sum	False	123 456 789 ¶ 876 620 975 ¶

After processing the last number on the line, the reading marker is on the blank before the line terminator. Thus, End_Of_Line returns a value of False. When Integer_Text_IO.Get is called again, it skips over the line terminator and gets the next Integer value on the following line.

Because line terminators are skipped when using the Get procedure for enumeration values and strings, we encounter the same problem. In general, we recommend that you do *not* use End_Of_Line with string, enumeration, or numeric data types. If you must use End_Of_Line with numeric or enumeration types, write the program to read the individual characters into a string, and then use the 'Value attribute to convert them into numeric or enumeration values.

Additional Text File Operations

We have discussed only the major operations for text files. Appendix D lists all the types and operations for text files. We discuss a few more of these in this section.

Put_Line We use the procedure Put_Line to display strings. It is equivalent to a call to procedure Put followed by a call to procedure New_Line. The following two sequences of statements produce the same output.

```
Ada.Text_IO.Put ("Enter the amount of pasta required.");
Ada.Text_IO.New_Line;
Ada.Text_IO.Put ("(in pounds)");
Ada.Text_IO.New_Line;

Ada.Text_IO.Put_Line ("Enter the amount of pasta required.");
Ada.Text_IO.Put_Line ("(in pounds)");
```

Put_Line is available for string data only. There are no Put_Line procedures for other data types.

Delete Text_IO has the procedure Delete to remove the external file associated with the file variable. We need to have prepared the file with a call to Open or Create before we can call the Delete procedure. The given file is closed, and the external file ceases to exist. Here is an example call to procedure Delete.

```
Ada.Text_IO.Delete (File => Story_File);
```

Not all systems support the Delete procedure. The exception USE_ERROR occurs if the system does not support it. The exception STATUS_ERROR occurs if the file was not prepared prior to calling Delete.

Is_Open We can use the function Is_Open to determine whether or not a file has been prepared with a call to procedure Open or Create. Here is an example of this function.

```
-- Delete the story file
if Ada.Text_IO.Is_Open (Story_File)  then
   Ada.Text_IO.Delete (File => Story_File);
else
   Ada.Text_IO.Open (File => Story_File,                -- If the file is not
                     Mode => Ada.Text_IO.In_File,       -- currently open,
                     Name => "Story.Dat");              -- open it
   Ada.Text_IO.Delete (File => Story_File);             -- and then delete it.
end if;
```

New_Page The procedure New_Page is similar to procedure New_Line. However, it outputs a page terminator to the output file instead of a line terminator. Sending a page terminator to a printer will advance the paper to the top of the next page. Sending a page terminator to the screen usually will position the cursor at the beginning of a blank screen. In the following examples, a page terminator is sent to the standard output file (probably the screen) and to a file called Report.

```
Ada.Text_IO.New_Page;                    -- Send page terminator to standard output
Ada.Text_IO.New_Page (File => Report);   -- Send page terminator to file Report
```

New_Line You have used procedure New_Line to control the formatting of your output. You used two calls to this procedure whenever you wanted a blank line, three calls whenever you wanted two blank lines, and so on. New_Line has a parameter called Spacing that you may use to create blank lines. Here is an example of this parameter.

```
Ada.Text_IO.New_Line (Spacing => 4);     -- End current line and
                                         -- print 3 blank lines
```

Name We use the function Name to determine the name of the external file associated with a file variable. It returns a string value. But before we can use this function, the file must have been prepared with a call to procedure Open or Create. The exception STATUS_ERROR occurs if the file was not prepared. Here is a short example that uses it.

```
Ada.Text_IO.Open (File => Story_File,
                  Mode => Ada.Text_IO.In_File,
                  Name => "Story.Txt");
   .
   .
   .
-- This put will display the name of the file, Story.Txt
Ada.Text_IO.Put (Item => Ada.Text_IO.Name (Story_File) );
```

Reset The procedure Reset resets the given file so that reading or writing starts at the beginning of the file. It is used frequently in a program that writes data to a file and then needs to read it. Here is an example.

```
Ada.Text_IO.Put_Line (File => My_File,
                      Item => "This is the last line in the file.");
   .
   .
   .
Ada.Text_IO.Reset (File => My_File,                 -- Position marker at beginning
                   Mode => Ada.Text_IO.In_File);    -- of file for reading

Ada.Text_IO.Get_Line (File => My_File,              -- Read first line of file
                      Item => Line,
                      Last => Num_Characters):
```

Recall that the Get_Line procedure reads characters into a string variable until the string is filled or the line terminator is found. Because Get_Line may encounter the line terminator before the string is filled, it has an additional parameter, Last, that is assigned the position of the last character put into the string by Get_Line. For the String variables we've declared so far, this position also happens to be the number of characters read.

Some systems do not allow you to use the Reset procedure to change the mode of a file. These systems generate a USE_ERROR exception when you attempt to reset a file with a different mode. You can call procedure Close and then procedure Open to accomplish the same results as procedure Reset.

Package Ada.Text_IO contains many other operations for text files that you may find useful. Browse through Appendix D and try out the ones that look interesting to you.

BACKGROUND INFORMATION

Admiral Grace Murray Hopper

From 1943 until her death on New Year's Day in 1992, Admiral Hopper was intimately involved with computing. In 1991, she was awarded the National Medal of Technology "for her pioneering accomplishments in the development of computer programming languages that simplified computer technology and opened the door to a significantly larger universe of users."

Admiral Hopper was born Grace Brewster Murray in New York City on December 9, 1906. She attended Vassar and received a Ph.D. in mathematics from Yale. For the next 10 years she taught mathematics at Vassar.

In 1943 Admiral Hopper joined the Navy and was assigned to the Bureau of Ordnance Computation Project at Harvard University as a programmer on the Mark I, one of the first computers. After the war, she remained at Harvard as a faculty member and continued work on the Navy's Mark II and Mark III computers. In 1949 she joined the Eckert-Mauchly Computer Corporation and worked on the UNIVAC I. It was there that she made perhaps her best known contribution to computing: She discovered the first computer "bug." It was a moth caught in the hardware.

Admiral Hopper had a working compiler in 1952—the time when the conventional wisdom was that computers could only do arithmetic, and programming was done in machine or assembly language. Although not on the committee that designed the computer language COBOL, she was actively involved with its design, implementation, and use. COBOL is still one of the most commonly used languages for programs requiring a business orientation and powerful file-handling capabilities.

Admiral Hopper retired from the Navy in 1966 only to be recalled within a year to full-time active duty. She served with the Naval Data Automation Command until she retired again in 1986 with the rank of Rear Admiral. At the time of her death she was a senior consultant at Digital Equipment Corporation.

Admiral Hopper's mission in the Navy was to oversee the Navy's efforts at maintaining uniformity in programming languages. It has been said that, just as Admiral Hyman Rickover was the father of the nuclear Navy, Rear Admiral Hopper was the mother of computerized data automation in the Navy.

Admiral Hopper received honorary degrees from more than 40 colleges and universities. She was honored by her peers on several occasions including receiving the first Computer Sciences Man of the Year award given by the Data Processing Management Association and the Contributions to Computer Science Education Award given by the Special Interest Group for Computer Science Education of the ACM.

Admiral Hopper loved young people and enjoyed giving talks on college and university campuses. She always handed out colored wires that she called nanoseconds: They were cut to the length that electrons travel in a nanosecond. Her advice to the young was, "You manage things, you lead people. We went overboard on management and forgot about leadership."

When asked which of her many accomplishments she was the most proud, she answered, "All the young people I have trained over the years."

Binary Files

A binary file is a collection of like elements outside of the program. There are some important differences between binary files and text files.

- The elements of a binary file are not restricted to characters. They may be any type except File_Type.
- The elements of a binary file are not organized into lines. There are no line terminators in binary files. There is, however, a file terminator after the last element.
- The elements of a binary file are stored using the internal representation of the machine.

Input and output operations with binary files are usually much faster than with text files. This is because the elements of a binary file are stored using the internal format of the machine. When using Ada.Integer_Text_IO.Get to read an integer, the procedure must read individual characters from a text file. It must then translate these characters into an integer value. When reading from a binary file of integers, the procedure needs to read only a single element, and no translation is necessary.

In addition, binary files usually take up less space. For example, the integer value –14832 is stored as six character elements in a text file, but in a binary file it is stored as a single integer element.

Ada provides the package Text_IO for text files. It provides two different packages for binary files—Sequential_IO and Direct_IO.

Sequential Files Sequential files are binary files whose elements can be accessed sequentially. "Sequentially" means that individual elements are accessed in the order that they appear in the file. The elements in a text file also are accessed sequentially. Once a character has been processed, you cannot back up the reading marker to input it again.

Sequential file operations are very similar to the operations you have used with text files. For each sequential file we use, we declare a file variable, prepare it for reading or writing with a call to the appropriate Open or Create procedure, include its name in all operations, and close the sequential file when we have finished with it.

The operations for sequential files are in the generic library package Ada.Sequential_IO. The specification of Sequential_IO is given in Appendix E. To use this generic library package, we must add the following *with* clause to our program:

```
with Ada.Sequential_IO;
```

You must instantiate a separate package for each different type of sequential file. Specify the file element type in the instantiation statement. For example, the following instantiations

```
package Seq_Float_IO  is new Ada.Sequential_IO (Element_Type => Float);
package Seq_Weight_IO is new Ada.Sequential_IO (Element_Type => Weight_Type)
```

will construct packages for doing sequential input or output with binary files whose elements are Float and Weight_Type respectively. These newly created packages contain a type named File_Type that you may use to declare file variables.

```
Distances : Seq_Float_IO.File_Type;    -- A file of Float elements
Weights   : Seq_Weight_IO.File_Type;   -- A file of Weight_Type elements
```

These packages also contain the procedures Open and Create to prepare the files. As with text files, we use procedure Open to prepare a file for reading and procedure Create to create a new file for writing. The file modes available for sequential files are the same as for text files— In_File, Out_File, and Append_File. The packages also contain the procedure Close to sever the connection between our program and the file. To distinguish them from text file operations, the sequential packages use the procedure names Read and Write instead of Get and Put to do the actual input and output.

0034	0056	0371	0893	0005	1987	0002	....	0274	0978	1020	0319	§

FIGURE 9-3
A Sequential File of Integers

Let's look at a complete example. Here is an Ada program that takes 100 positive integer values from the keyboard and writes them to a sequential file.

```
with Ada.Sequential_IO;
with Ada.Text_IO;
with Ada.Integer_Text_IO;
procedure Copy_Nums is

   -- Package for output of integers to a sequential file
   package Seq_Integer_IO is new Ada.Sequential_IO (Element_Type => Integer);

   Value    : Integer;                   -- The value to be written to the file
   Int_File : Seq_Integer_IO.File_Type; -- The sequential file

begin -- Copy Nums
   -- Prepare the sequential file for output
   Seq_Integer_IO.Create (File => Int_File,
                          Name => "Integers.Dat");
   -- Get 100 numbers and write them to the sequential file
   for Count in 1..100 loop
      Ada.Integer_Text_IO.Get (Item => Value);       -- Get a value from
                                                      -- the keyboard
      Seq_Integer_IO.Write (File => Int_File,        -- Write the value to
                            Item => Value);           -- the file
   end loop;
   Seq_Integer_IO.Close (File => Int_File);   -- Sever the file connection
end Copy_Nums;
```

Figure 9-3 is an illustration of the file produced by program Copy_Nums. The file contains 100 integers. A file terminator follows the last value in the file. While the integers are shown as decimal values, they would be in binary form in the actual file.

Here is a second program that you can use later to display the values in the sequential file created by program Copy_Nums.

```
with Ada.Sequential_IO;
with Ada.Text_IO;
with Ada.Integer_Text_IO;
procedure Display_File is

   -- Package for input of integers from a sequential file
   package Seq_Integer_IO is new Ada.Sequential_IO (Element_Type => Integer);
```

```
   Value      : Integer;                    -- The value to be written
                                            -- to the screen
   Int_File : Seq_Integer_IO.File_Type;   -- The sequential file

begin -- Display File
   -- Prepare the sequential file for input
   Seq_Integer_IO.Open (File => Int_File,
                        Mode => Seq_Integer_IO.In_File,
                        Name => "Integers.Dat");
   -- Display all of the numbers in the sequential file
   Display_Loop:
   loop
      exit Display_Loop when Seq_Integer_IO.End_Of_File (Int_File);
      Seq_Integer_IO.Read (File => Int_File,       -- Get the next value
                           Item => Value);         -- from the file
      Ada.Integer_Text_IO.Put (Item => Value);    -- Display the value
      Ada.Text_IO.New_Line;
   end loop Display_Loop;
   Seq_Integer_IO.Close (Int_File);        -- Sever the file connection
end Display_File;
```

A sequential file has a reading marker that serves the same function as the reading marker used in a text file. The reading marker indicates the next element to be read. When we call the Read procedure, the element indicated by the reading marker is returned, and the reading marker advances to the next element. The End_Of_File function returns True when the reading marker is on the file terminator. Figure 9-4 illustrates the actions of Program Display_File on the file. Figure 9-4 part (a) shows the state of the file just after the call to Open. Part (b) of Figure 9-4 shows the file after three complete iterations of Display_Loop. Part (c) of Figure 9-4 shows the file after the program has read all 100 values and the exit condition of Display_Loop is True.

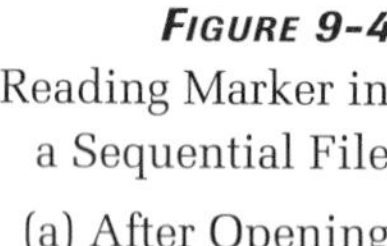

FIGURE 9-4 Reading Marker in a Sequential File (a) After Opening the File (b) After Reading Three Elements (c) After Reading All Elements

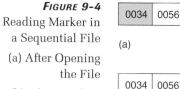

We have not discussed all of the operations available in Sequential_IO. Many of the operations like Reset, Delete, and Is_Open that we discussed for text files are also available for sequential files. See Appendix E for a complete listing of available operations for sequential files.

Direct Files Direct files, sometimes called *random access files*, are binary files. As with sequential files, the elements are stored using the internal representation of the machine. The difference between direct files and sequential files is how the elements are accessed. The elements of sequential files and text files are accessed sequentially. That is, they are accessed in the order given in the file. Once elements have been processed, you cannot back up the reading marker to access them again. However, Ada's direct files allow us to access the elements of a binary file in any order.

We can find the operations for direct files in the generic package Direct_IO. To use this generic library package, we must add the following with clause to our program.

```
with Ada.Direct_IO;
```

As with sequential files, you must instantiate a separate package for each different type of direct file. We specify the file element type in an instantiation statement. For example, the following instantiations

```
package Dir_Float_IO  is new Ada.Direct_IO (Element_Type => Float);
package Dir_Weight_IO is new Ada.Direct_IO (Element_Type => Weight_Type);
```

will construct packages to perform direct input or output with binary files whose elements are Float and Weight_Type respectively. These newly created packages contain a type named File_Type that we may use to declare file variables.

```
Distances : Dir_Float_IO.File_Type;    -- A file of Float elements
Weights   : Dir_Weight_IO.File_Type;   -- A file of Weight_Type elements
```

Direct_IO contains other declarations and operations that allow us to access the elements in a direct file in any order. The additional declarations include the following type and subtype.

```
type    Count          is       range 0..implementation_defined;
subtype Positive_Count is Count range 1..implementation_defined;
```

The elements in a direct file are numbered sequentially starting at 1 with values of subtype Positive_Count. Figure 9-5 illustrates a file that contains 67 elements numbered from 1 to 67. The upper bound of type Count specifies the maximum number of elements that a direct file can contain. As indicated in the previous declarations, Count'Last is defined by the particular system being used. For example, GNAT Ada specifies an upper bound of 2,147,483,647 ($2^{31} - 1$) for Count.

FIGURE 9-5
A Direct File

1	2	3	4	5	6	7	....	64	65	66	67	
												§

The operations for direct files include all of those available for sequential files. Thus we can access the elements of a direct file sequentially. We could change the programs Copy_Nums and Display_File given in the previous section to work with direct files simply by using Direct_IO in place of Sequential_IO.

In addition to the same Read and Write procedures contained in Sequential_IO, Direct_IO contains a Read procedure and a Write procedure that permit us to access any element in the file. These procedures have an additional parameter to specify which element is desired. In the following code fragment, the 12th element is read from the file, modified by doubling it, and written back.

```
Dir_Float_IO.Read (File => Distances,         -- The Direct file
                   Item => Trip_Length,       -- Trip_Length is type Float
                   From => 12);               -- Specifies the 12th element

Trip_Length := 2.0 * Trip_Length;             -- Modify the value

Dir_Float_IO.Write (File => Distances,        -- Put the modified value back
                    Item => Trip_Length,      -- to the 12th position in the
                    To   => 12);              -- file
```

The formal parameters From and To are used to indicate the position number of the element desired. These parameters are of subtype Positive_Count.

In order to read a file element, change it, and write it back to the file, we must be able to read and write to the same file. None of the file access modes we have seen, In_File, Out_File, or Append_File, permit *both* input and output operations. Direct_IO defines a new access mode, Inout_File, which permits this intermixing of input and output operations. Mode Append_File is not available for direct files. File Distances in the preceding example must be prepared (opened or created) with mode Inout_File.

Package Direct_IO contains a function called Size that returns the position number of the last element in the file. The following code fragment that sums all of the values in a file of Float values illustrates the use of this function in a count-controlled loop.

```
Total_Length : Float;
Trip_Length  : Float;
    .
    .
    .
Total_Length := 0.0;
            -- Add up all the distances recorded in the file
```

```
Sum_Loop:   -- Each iteration, one leg of the trip is added to the total
for Trip_Count in  1 .. Dir_Float_IO.Size (Distances)  loop
   Dir_Float_IO.Read (File => Distances,
                      Item => Trip_Length,
                      From => Trip_Count);
   Total_Length := Total_Length + Trip_Length;
end loop Sum_Loop;
```

The loop parameter Trip_Count in this code fragment has type Dir_Float_IO.Count. A loop parameter takes its type from the discrete range, and function Size used in Trip_Count's range returns a value of type Dir_Float_IO.Count.

Also note that this code fragment processes the elements sequentially. Such processing can be done more easily with the sequential operations available in Direct_IO. However, we must ensure that reading begins at the start of the file before we start our loop. Every direct file has an index value associated with it. This index indicates the number of the element that will be read from or written to with the next sequential Read or Write operation. We use the procedure Set_Index to set the index to whatever element number we desire. The following code fragment uses this procedure, the sequential Read procedure, and the End_Of_File function to sum the elements of the file Distances.

```
Total_Length := 0.0;
Dir_Float_IO.Set_Index (File => Distances,      -- Set file marker
                        To   => 1);             -- to first element
Sum_Loop:      -- Add up all the distances recorded in the file
loop           -- Each iteration, one leg of the trip is added to the total
   exit Sum_Loop when Dir_Float_IO.End_Of_File (Distances);
   Dir_Float_IO.Read (File => Distances,            -- Sequential Read has
                      Item => Trip_Length);         -- no From parameter
   Total_Length := Total_Length + Trip_Length;
end loop Sum_Loop;
```

Every call to procedure Read in this code fragment gets an element and increments the file's index by one. End_Of_File returns True when the file's index exceeds the size of the file. The file index is incremented by every call to Read or Write whether sequential or not. Thus the value of index after the following call is 42.

```
Dir_Float_IO.Write (File => Distances,
                    Item => Trip_Length,
                    To   => 41);
```

The exception END_ERROR occurs if a program attempts to read an element whose number is greater than the size of the file. Given the file illustrated in Figure 9-6 part (a), the following Read would result in an END_ERROR exception.

```
Dir_Float_IO.Read (File => Distances,
                   Item => Trip_Length,
                   From => 11);
```

However, an END_ERROR does not occur if a program *writes* an element whose number is greater than the current size of the file. We can write to any element location. Any elements that have not been written to have undefined values. The file terminator always follows the last element with a defined value. Figure 9-6 part (b) shows the same file as part (a) after the following call to procedure Write.

```
Dir_Float_IO.Write (File => Distances,
                    Item => 42.8,
                    To   => 11);
```

As with text files and sequential files, we have not discussed all of the operations available for direct files. See Appendix E for a complete listing of available operations.

The Use Type Clause As you learned in Chapter 2, we prefix the name of a library resource with the name of the package in which it is defined. This prefixing allows us to easily distinguish between identically named subprograms such as Dir_Float_IO.Write and Dir_Weight_IO.Write.

When a *type* is defined in a package, all of the *operations* available for objects of that type must also use the package name as a prefix. Let's look at the consequences of this requirement. Given the declaration

```
Distance_Location : Dir_Float_IO.Count;   -- Location of a distance in the file
```

for a variable that holds the index of an element in a direct access file, the following assignment statement is not legal.

```
Distance_Location := Distance_Location + 1;    -- Not legal
```

The + operator for values of type Count is automatically defined in the package Dir_Float_IO by the declaration of type Count. This operator, like

FIGURE 9-6
A Direct File
(a) Before Writing a Value to Location 11
(b) After Writing a Value to Location 11

1	2	3	4	5	6	7	
14.2	34.6	87.4	03.5	19.3	33.5	40.0	§

(a)

1	2	3	4	5	6	7	8	9	10	11	
14.2	34.6	87.4	03.5	19.3	33.5	40.0	????	????	????	42.8	§

(b)

a type name or subprogram name, must have the package name as a prefix. In order to prefix an operator (such as +, -, rem, *, and /) we must write the operator as a function call as in the following assignment statement.

```
Distance_Location := Dir_Float_IO."+"(Distance_Location, 1);  -- Legal
```

This syntax (called prefix notation) with the + operator before its two operands is not as clear as having it between its two operands (a notation called infix).

One solution to this problem is to include a *use clause* in our program. This clause allows us to use *any* resource in a package without prefixing. However, as we discussed in Chapter 2, the loss of prefixing information can make understanding a large program difficult. Ada has another solution to this problem—the *use type clause.* This clause allows us to write *operators* between operands without any prefixes. By adding the clause

```
use type Dir_Float_IO.Count;   -- Make operators for Count directly visible
```

just after the instantiation of package Dir_Float_IO, we can use all of the integer operators for Count objects without prefixing. We must continue to prefix other resources such as procedures, functions, and types from the package that we use in our program. In the Pasta case study at the end of this chapter we include a use type clause so we can write infix arithmetic expressions with operands that are direct file indices. We'll discuss the use type clause again in Chapter 12.

Exception Handling

A great deal of checking goes on automatically while an Ada program is running. Every time we assign a value to a variable, the system checks it to ensure that it is in the range established for that variable. Every time we get a value from a file, the system checks it to ensure that the data type is valid. We do not have to do anything to accomplish these checks. Whenever one of these checks determines that an abnormal condition has occurred, the system raises an exception. To **raise an exception** is to abandon normal program execution. Until now, we have simply allowed the system to take over execution from our program. In this section we'll see what really happens when an exception occurs.

Let's briefly review some of the exceptions that can occur. Ada predefines the following four exceptions.

Raise an exception To abandon normal program execution. The system raises exceptions when it detects abnormal conditions.

CONSTRAINT_ERROR	Raised during an attempt to assign a value to a variable when the value does not satisfy some limitation defined for that variable. Commonly raised when the value being assigned violates the range constraint for the variable's subtype. Also raised when an array index is out of range (covered in Chapter 11).
PROGRAM_ERROR	Raised upon an attempt to execute an action that is erroneous. One example of such an action is reaching the end of a function subprogram without encountering a return statement. There are other erroneous actions that are related to aspects of Ada beyond the scope of this text.
STORAGE_ERROR	Raised when the program requires more memory than is available.
TASKING_ERROR	Raised during intertask communication. As Ada's tasking features are beyond the scope of this text, you should not see this error in any of your programs associated with this book.

The package Ada.IO_ Exceptions defines eight exceptions that might be raised by the predefined input-output packages (such as Ada.Text_IO, Ada.Sequential_IO, and Ada.Direct_IO). The following exception descriptions relate only to the aspects of input/output we have discussed. Improper use of I/O operations available in Ada but not covered in this text can also raise these exceptions.

Ada.IO_Exceptions.DATA_ERROR	Raised by procedure Get if the input character sequence is not a valid literal of the type being input. Also raised if the value is out of the range of the type being input.
Ada.IO_Exceptions.DEVICE_ERROR	Raised if an I/O operation cannot be completed because of a malfunction of the computer system.
Ada.IO_Exceptions.END_ERROR	Raised by an attempt to read or skip past the end of a file.
Ada.IO_Exceptions.LAYOUT_ERROR	Raised by an attempt in text input-output to set the column or line numbers in excess of specified maximum line or page lengths.
Ada.IO_Exceptions.MODE_ ERROR	Raised by an attempt to use an I/O operation with a file whose current mode is not compatible with the operation. For example, for files whose current mode is Out_File or Append_File: reading from, testing for the end of a file, testing for the end of line, and calling Skip_Line. For files whose mode is In_File: writing to, calling New_Line, and calling New_Page.
Ada.IO_Exceptions.NAME_ERROR	Raised by a call to Open if the string given for the parameter Name does not uniquely identify an external file. It also is raised by a call to Create if the string given for the parameter Name is not a valid name for a file.

Ada.IO_Exceptions.STATUS_ERROR	Raised by an attempt to operate on a file that has not been prepared with a call to Open or Create. Also raised if an attempt is made to use Open or Create when the file has already been prepared.
Ada.IO_Exceptions.USE_ERROR	Raised if an operation is attempted that is not possible for reasons that depend on the characteristics of the external file. For example, a call to Open that attempts to open a file for input on a printer (a device that can only output).

As discussed earlier, we call the automatic detection of exceptional conditions *passive error handling*. Although passive error handling takes little effort on our part, up until now we have had no control of the program once the system has detected an error. Halting a program and displaying an error message is a useful tool for debugging. However, such behavior is often unacceptable when someone uses the program. Imagine the results if a program controlling a modern airliner were to halt suddenly with a CONSTRAINT_ERROR exception. (This example brings new meaning to the term *program crash*!)

Ada has facilities, called **exception handlers,** that allow us to specify what should be done when an exception is raised. An exception handler is a sequence of instructions that we write to be executed when an exception is raised. We can specify different exception handlers for the same exception raised in different parts of our program, allowing us to tailor the response to an exception to the particular processing that is going on when the exception is raised.

Exception handler A sequence of instructions that is executed when an exception is raised.

Exceptions and Block Statements

One way to associate an exception handler with a group of statements is to make use of a block statement. A simplified EBNF definition for a block statement is as follows:

```
block_statement     ::=  [block_identifier:]
                         begin
                            sequence_of_statements
                         [exception
                            exception_handler
                            {exception_handler} ]
                         end [block_identifier]
exception_handler   ::=  when exception_choice { | exception_choice} =>
                            sequence_of_statements
exception_choice    ::=  exception_name | others
```

We use the block statement in its simplest form to give a name to a group of statements. For example, the two input statements in the following code fragment

```
Ada.Text_IO.Put_Line ("Enter item price and sales tax rate.");

Ada.Float_Text_IO.Get (Price);
Ada.Float_Text_IO.Get (Tax_Rate);

Tax  := Price * Tax_Rate;
Total:= Price + Tax;
Ada.Float_Text_IO.Put (Item => Total,  Fore => 1,  Aft  => 2,  Exp  => 0);
```

may be grouped under the name Input_Block by using a block statement like this:

```
Ada.Text_IO.Put_Line ("Enter item price and sales tax rate.");

Input_Block:
begin
   Ada.Float_Text_IO.Get (Price);
   Ada.Float_Text_IO.Get (Tax_Rate);
end Input_Block;

Tax  := Price * Tax_Rate;
Total:= Price + Tax;
Ada.Float_Text_IO.Put (Item => Total,  Fore => 1,  Aft  => 2,  Exp  => 0);
```

The flow of control is identical in both of these examples. The block statement serves only to group the input statements together and give them a name. By adding the optional exception clause to this block, we also associate an exception handler with this group of statements.

```
Ada.Text_IO.Put_Line ("Enter item price and sales tax rate.");

Input_Block:
begin
   Ada.Float_Text_IO.Get (Price);
   Ada.Float_Text_IO.Get (Tax_Rate);
exception
   when Ada.IO_Exceptions.DATA_ERROR =>
      Ada.Text_IO.Put ("Data entered is not valid");
      Ada.Text_IO.New_Line;
end Input_Block;

Tax  := Price * Tax_Rate;
Total:= Price + Tax;
Ada.Float_Text_IO.Put (Item => Total,  Fore => 1,  Aft  => 2,  Exp  => 0);
```

If the system raises no exceptions, the flow of control in this third version is the same as the previous two: The system skips the statements between the line containing the reserved word `exception` and the line `end Input_Block`. However, if a DATA_ERROR exception occurs while executing one of the two input statements, the flow of control is different. When DATA_ERROR is raised in the block, execution of the statements in the block is abandoned, and control is transferred to the DATA_ERROR exception handler associated with the block. In this example, the exception handler displays an error message. Control then continues with the first statement after the block (the statement that calculates Tax). If DATA_ERROR is raised in one of the first two versions, there is no exception handler defined, so control transfers to a system exception handler that displays an error message and halts the program. Our exception handler isn't very realistic. This example and the next few do nothing but display our own error message. We would not normally go on to a calculation without somehow correcting the error. We'll see how to do that in the next section.

Only one exception handler is defined for block Input_Block. If an exception other than DATA_ERROR is raised in the block, control transfers to a system exception handler, which displays an error message and halts the program. We can add other exception handlers to the block. For additional flexibility, each exception handler can manage more than one exception. In the following version, two exception handlers cover three different exceptions.

```
Ada.Text_IO.Put_Line ("Enter item price and sales tax rate.");

Input_Block:
begin
   Ada.Float_Text_IO.Get (Price);
   Ada.Float_Text_IO.Get (Tax_Rate);
exception
   when Ada.IO_Exceptions.DATA_ERROR  |  CONSTRAINT_ERROR  =>
      Ada.Text_IO.Put ("Data entered is not valid.");
      Ada.Text_IO.New_Line;
   when Ada.IO_Exceptions.DEVICE_ERROR =>
      Ada.Text_IO.Put ("Input hardware has malfunctioned.");
      Ada.Text_IO.New_Line;
end Input_Block;

Tax  := Price * Tax_Rate;
Total:= Price + Tax;
Ada.Float_Text_IO.Put (Item => Total,  Fore => 1,  Aft  => 2,  Exp  => 0);
```

As it did in the case statement, the vertical bar symbol (|) means *or*. If Ada.IO_Exceptions.DATA_ERROR or CONSTRAINT_ERROR is raised in the block, the message "Data entered is not valid." is displayed. If Ada.IO_Exceptions.DEVICE_ERROR is raised, "Input hardware has malfunctioned." is displayed.

We can use the reserved word `others` instead of an exception name. If there is no exception handler defined for a particular exception when it occurs, the program will transfer control to the others handler. In the next version of our block, we have added an others handler so that the program will continue no matter what exception occurs in the block.

```
Ada.Text_IO.Put_Line ("Enter item price and sales tax rate.");

Input_Block:
begin
   Ada.Float_Text_IO.Get (Price);
   Ada.Float_Text_IO.Get (Tax_Rate);
exception
   when Ada.IO_Exceptions.DATA_ERROR  |  CONSTRAINT_ERROR  =>
      Ada.Text_IO.Put ("Data entered is not valid.");
      Ada.Text_IO.New_Line;
   when Ada.IO_Exceptions.DEVICE_ERROR =>
      Ada.Text_IO.Put ("Input hardware has malfunctioned.");
      Ada.Text_IO.New_Line;
   when others =>
      Ada.Text_IO.Put ("Some other exception was raised.");
      Ada.Text_IO.New_Line;
end Input_Block;

Tax  := Price * Tax_Rate;
Total:= Price + Tax;
Ada.Float_Text_IO.Put (Item => Total,  Fore => 1,  Aft  => 2,  Exp  => 0);
```

We could leave out the DATA_ERROR | CONSTRAINT_ERROR and the DEVICE_ERROR exception handlers. The others handler would then deal with all exceptions raised in the block. It is better to include distinct handlers for different exceptions so that the program will display the most meaningful error message. The message "Some other exception was raised." is not very useful for either the user of the program or the programmer trying to track down bugs.

Data Validation Loops The exception handlers in the previous section do nothing but display a message when the exception is raised. The program was not halted; it continued to execute the statements that follow the block. Because the exceptions are raised while obtaining data, it is certain that the variables do not contain the desired values. Our exception handlers do nothing to ensure that these variables are valid.

When a DATA_ERROR is raised during an interactive input operation, it is likely that the user made a mistake while entering the data. For example, we may have entered the letter O instead of the digit 0 in a float value. To correct such an error, the program should display an appropriate message and prompt the user to enter the data again. Here's an example.

```
Validation_Loop:
loop
   Ada.Text_IO.Put_Line ("Enter item price and sales tax rate.");
```

```
   Input_Block:
   begin
      Ada.Float_Text_IO.Get (Price);
      Ada.Float_Text_IO.Get (Tax_Rate);
      exit Validation_Loop;        -- Exit statement without a when clause
   exception
      when Ada.IO_Exceptions.DATA_ERROR =>
         Ada.Text_IO.Put_Line ("Data entered is not valid.");
         Ada.Text_IO.Skip_Line;     -- Skip over the bad data
   end Input_Block;

end loop Validation_Loop;

Tax  := Price * Tax_Rate;
Total:= Price + Tax;
Float_IO.Put (Item => Total,  Fore => 1,  Aft  => 2,  Exp  => 0);
```

This program fragment contains a posttest loop. The exit statement is the last statement in the loop body. Notice that the exit statement used here does not have a *when* clause. When this exit statement is executed, the loop is exited unconditionally.

Let's trace this loop for the case in which the user enters the two Float values correctly. First, the program displays the prompt. Next the user enters the two Float values. The program then exits the loop, calculates the Tax and Total, and displays the Total.

Now let's trace the loop and see what happens when the user makes an error in entering one of the values. First, the program displays the prompt. Next an attempt is made to obtain the two values from the user. When the user makes an error in entering either one of the values, the program raises a DATA_ERROR exception. The program abandons the execution of the remaining statements in the block and transfers control to the exception handler. Here the message "Data entered is not valid." is displayed. Control now continues to the statement after the end of the block—the end of the loop. We now begin the second iteration of the loop. The program displays the prompt and obtains the values from the user. If they are entered correctly this time, the program exits the loop. If another mistake is made, control transfers to the exception handler and the process repeats for the third time.

When a Get procedure raises the DATA_ERROR exception, it does not process the incorrect data. The call to Skip_Line in the exception handler for the DATA_ERROR exception is necessary to skip over this bad data. Without this call, the program would process the same bad data the next time it went through the loop and would raise the same exception, resulting in an infinite loop.

In this example we used one data validation loop for two values. If the user enters the first number correctly, the logic forces him or her to enter it again. We could improve upon this solution by using a separate data validation loop for each value obtained from the user.

When doing input data validation with a subtype, you should include handlers for both DATA_ERROR and CONSTRAINT_ERROR. Because we are using Float_Text_IO in our example, the program will raise a DATA_ERROR exception if the value entered is not a valid Float number (values that are greater than Float'Last or less than Float'First and non-numeric values). Get stops processing characters from the data set as soon as an abnormality is detected. Thus it is usually necessary to include a call to Skip_Line to skip over the offending characters before the next call to Get in the loop. The program will raise a CONSTRAINT_ERROR if an input value being copied to Get's actual parameter is not in the range of the parameter's subtype. Because, in this case, the Get procedure finishes without error (the CONSTRAINT_ERROR is raised when the value is copied from the formal to the actual parameter), there are no offending characters and there is no need to call Skip_Line. The Pasta House case study in this chapter illustrates the use of these two exceptions for data validation.

Exceptions and Subprograms

An exception handler can also be associated with a subprogram body. Chapter 6 contained simplified EBNF definitions for procedure and function bodies. Here is a more complete EBNF definition that shows the association of exception handlers with subprogram bodies.

subprogram_body ::= subprogram_specification **is**
  declarative_part
begin
  sequence_of_statements
[**exception**
  exception_handler
  {exception_handler}]
end *subprogram*_name;

Here is a code fragment that illustrates the placement of exception handlers associated with a procedure.

```
procedure Example (Oreo       : in  Float;          -- Procedure to do some
                   Fig_Newton : in  Float;          -- cookie calculations
                   Chips_Ahoy : out Integer) is

   Cookie : Float;

begin
   if Oreo > Fig_Newton then
      Cookie :=  1.437E+7 * Oreo;
   else
      Cookie := -2.862E+6 * Fig_Newton;
   end if;
```

```
   -- Convert the result to an integer
   Chips_Ahoy := Integer (Cookie);  -- Control returned to caller after
                                    -- this statement is executed
exception
   when CONSTRAINT_ERROR  =>
      if Oreo > Fig_Newton then
         Chips_Ahoy := Integer'Last;
      else
         Chips_Ahoy := Integer'First;
      end if;
   when others =>
      Chips_Ahoy := 0;
end Example;
```

During normal execution of this procedure, control returns to the caller after the statement that assigns the value to Chips_Ahoy. If the program raises an exception during the execution of the statements in the procedure, the normal flow of control is abandoned and control transfers to the appropriate exception handler associated with the procedure.

The exception handler can use any item that is accessible from the procedure body. In this example, the exception handlers can use the three parameters Oreo, Fig_Newton, and Chips_Ahoy; the local variable Cookie; and any other identifiers that are global to the procedure.

When the exception handler associated with a procedure is completed, control returns to the caller of the procedure. When using exception handlers in function subprograms, it is important to include a return statement in each handler so that a function result is returned. The system will raise PROGRAM_ERROR if a return is not executed before coming to the end of the handler.

Propagation of Exceptions

We typically do not associate an exception handler with every statement in our program. In this section we explore how an exception is handled when there is no exception handler directly associated with the statement that caused the exception.

We have associated exception handlers with block statements and subprograms. We use the term **frame** for any construct that can be associated with exception handlers. Thus block statements and subprograms are frames. There are other constructs beyond the scope of this text that also serve as frames for exception handlers. The syntax of all frames includes the following part:

begin
    sequence_of_statements
exception
    exception_handler
    {exception_handler}
end

Frame An Ada construct that can have an associated exception handler. Block statements and subprograms are examples of frames.

Whenever an exception is raised in a frame, the program abandons the execution of the statements in the frame. If there is an exception handler for this exception associated with the frame, control transfers to it. What happens after the exception handler completes the execution of its statements depends on the nature of the frame.

1. After the execution of an exception handler in a block, control continues with the first statement after the block.
2. After the execution of an exception handler in a subprogram, control returns to the caller of the subprogram.

Now let's see what happens when there is no exception handler in the frame that raised the exception. If there is no exception handler in a block when an exception is raised, control transfers to the first statement after the block. Here the same exception is raised again. In a similar way, if there is no exception handler in a subprogram when an exception is raised, control returns to the caller of the subprogram and the same exception is raised again. We refer to an exception that is raised again as a **propagated exception.**

Propagated exception An exception that is raised again when control leaves a frame.

We use procedures in the following example to illustrate the propagation of an exception.

```
with Ada.Text_IO;
with Ada.IO_Exceptions;
procedure Propagation is

   procedure A is
   begin
      .
      .
      .
   end A;

   procedure B is
   begin
      .
      .
      .
```

```
      A;    -- Call procedure A
      .
      .
      .
   end B;

   procedure C is
   begin
      .
      .
      .
      B;    -- Call procedure B
      .
      .
      .
   exception
      when CONSTRAINT_ERROR =>
         Ada.Text_IO.Put_Line ("Procedure C:  Out of bounds");
   end C;

begin -- Program Propagation
   .
   .
   .
   C;    -- Call procedure C
   .
   .
   .
exception
   when Ada.IO_Exceptions.END_ERROR =>
      Ada.Text_IO.Put_Line ("Program Propagation:  Out of data");
end Propagation;
```

In this example the main subprogram calls procedure C, which calls procedure B, which in turn calls procedure A. There is an exception handler for CONSTRAINT_ERROR associated with procedure C and an exception handler for END_ERROR associated with procedure Propagation (the main subprogram).

If CONSTRAINT_ERROR is raised in procedure A, the program abandons the execution of the statements in A's body. Because there is no exception handler for CONSTRAINT_ERROR associated with procedure A, control returns to procedure B. Here the exception is raised again—it has been propagated back to procedure B. Now, the program abandons execution of the statements in procedure B. Because there is no exception handler for CONSTRAINT_ERROR associated with procedure B, control returns to procedure C, where the exception is raised again. This time there is an exception handler for CONSTRAINT_ERROR associated with the frame (procedure C). The program abandons the execution of the statements in procedure C, and executes the handler. Control now returns normally to the main subprogram. The flow of control in this example is illustrated in Figure 9-7.

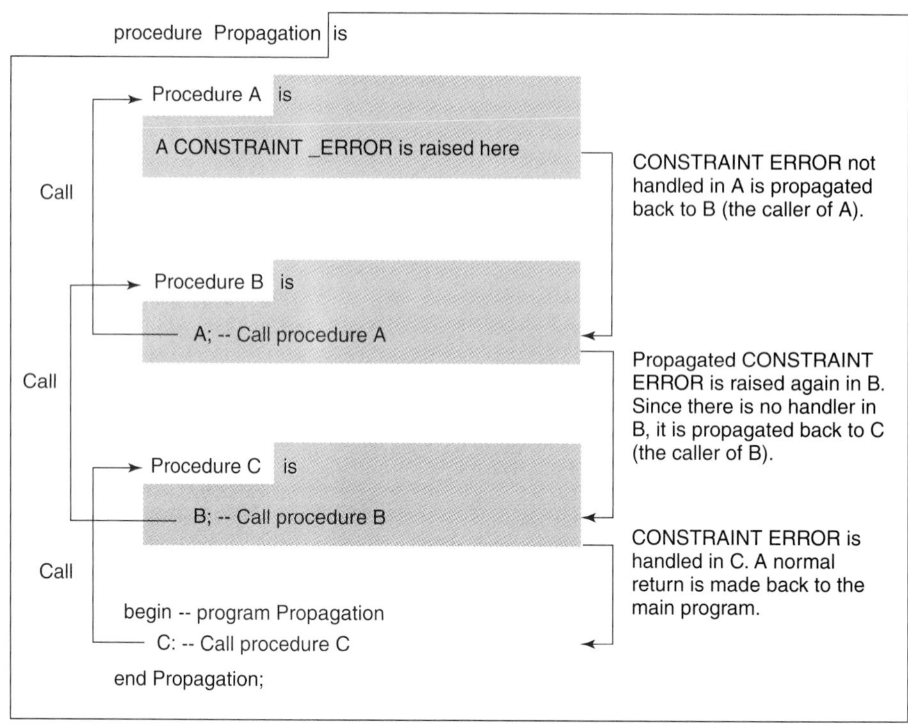

FIGURE 9-7 Propagation of CONSTRAINT_ERROR Raised in Procedure A

If DATA_ERROR is raised at any point in this example, it will be propagated all the way back to the main subprogram. Because there is no handler there, control returns to the caller of procedure Propagation. The caller of the main subprogram is the operating system of the computer. The exception is now propagated back to the operating system and the program terminates. The operating system has a standard handler for all possible exceptions that displays a message, usually including the exception name. These are the error messages that you have seen when you have run-time errors in your program. Figure 9-8 shows the flow of control when DATA_ERROR is raised in procedure A.

If END_ERROR is raised at any point in this example, it will be propagated all the way back to the main subprogram. Here the exception handler will be executed. Where is control transferred after this handler is completed? Control returns to the caller of procedure Propagation, the operating system. Because the main subprogram handled the exception, it is not propagated back to the operating system. No error message is displayed by the system. Figure 9-9 illustrates the flow of control for END_ERROR raised in procedure A.

We can choose to propagate an exception to the caller, even if we have a handler for it. To do so, just include the *raise* statement at the end of the handler. For example, we can modify procedure C as follows:

FIGURE 9-8 Propagation of DATA_ERROR Raised in Procedure A

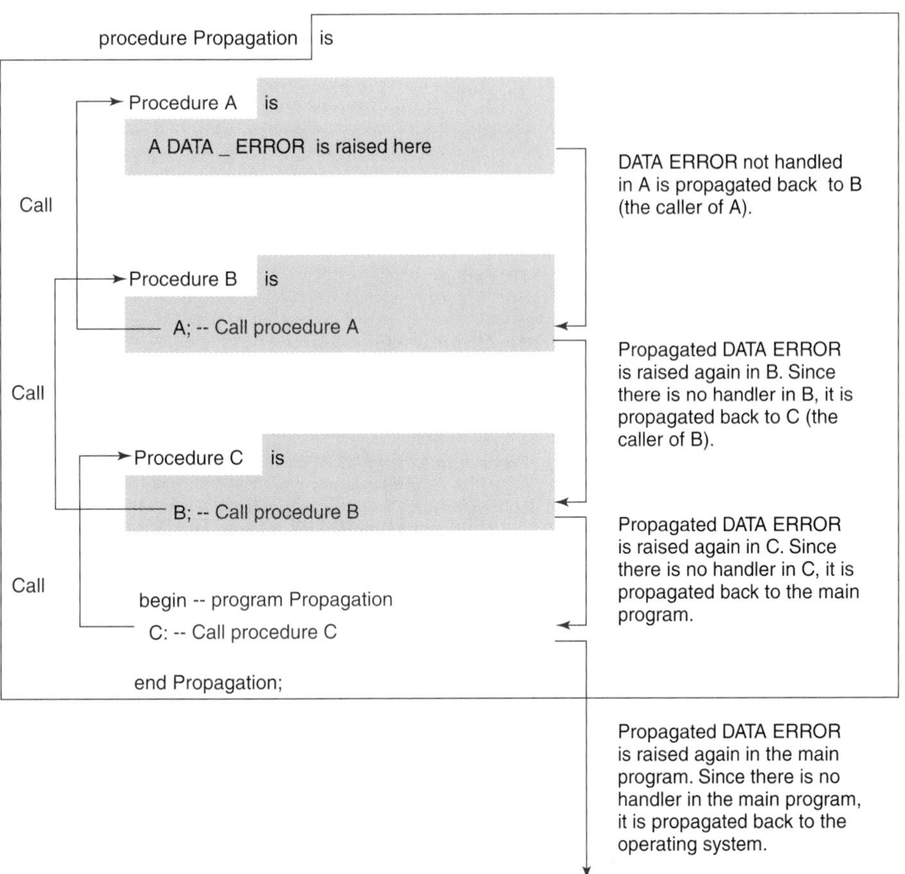


```
procedure C is
begin
   .
   .
   .
   B;    -- Call procedure B
   .
   .
   .
exception
   when CONSTRAINT_ERROR =>
      Ada.Text_IO.Put_Line ("Procedure C:  Out of bounds");
      raise;
end C;
```

As before, if a CONSTRAINT_ERROR is raised in procedure A, B, or C, it is handled in procedure C's handler. Now, however, because of the raise statement the exception is propagated back to the main subprogram and, in this example, back to the operating system.

FIGURE 9-9 Propagation of END_ERROR Raised in Procedure A

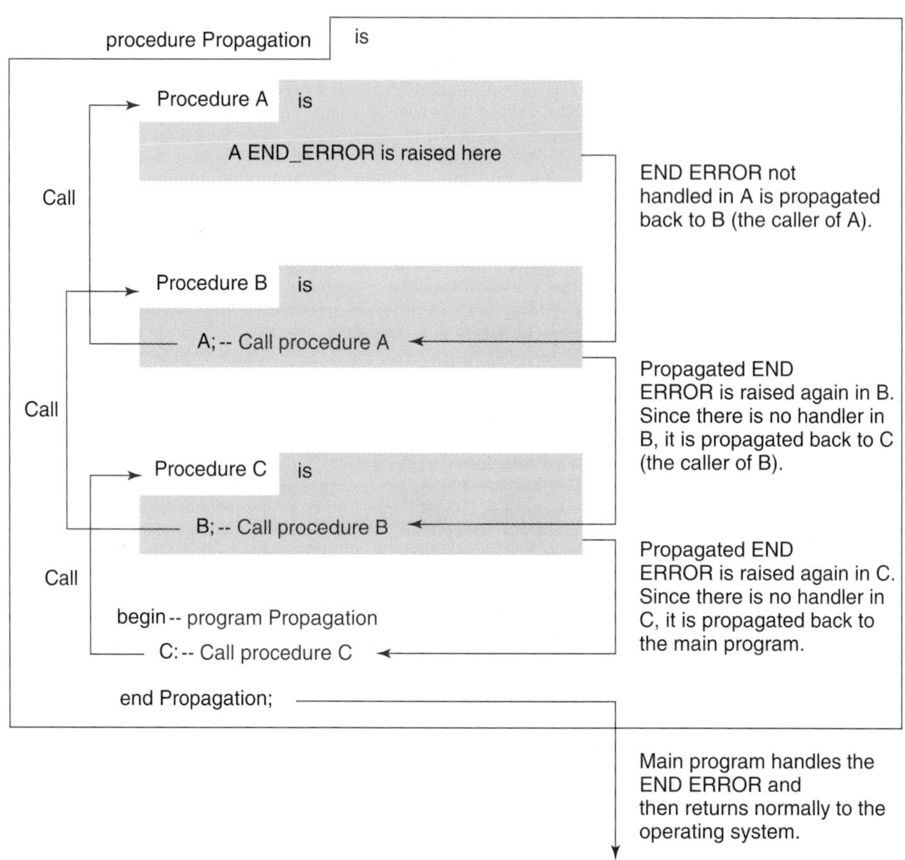

We illustrate a use for intentional propagation in the Testing and Debugging section of this chapter.

Exceptions For Exceptional Situations

Ada's exception handling provides a powerful mechanism for dealing with abnormal situations that require special processing. The active error-handling techniques discussed in previous chapters use if statements to check the state of the calculations at various places in the code. Because the error-checking statements are intermixed with the normal processing statements, such code can be difficult to read. Exception handlers permit us to separate the normal processing code from the code that handles exceptional events. Such separation generally results in programs that are easier to read.

Because Ada's exception handlers are so easy to write, many beginning programmers are tempted to use them to handle normal processing. Don't! Exception handlers that are invoked during normal processing defeat the reason for separating the handling of normal events and the handling of abnormal events. Such code can be as difficult to understand as the intertwined code of active error handling.

Programmers who do not understand the details of their own programs often add an exception handler to "fix" a program that crashes during testing. For example, here is a code fragment that gets and sums integer values.

```
Sum := 0;         -- END_ERROR is sometimes raised in this loop
Sum_Loop:
loop
   exit Sum_Loop when Ada.Text_IO.End_Of_File (Data_File);
   Ada.Integer_Text_IO.Get (File => Data_File,  Item => Value);
   Sum := Sum + Value;
end loop Sum_Loop;
```

This program fragment contains a loop whose termination condition is no more data left in the file. Reaching the end of the file is an expected event and therefore part of normal processing. When this code is tested, the program occasionally crashes with an END_ERROR exception. It is tempting to fix the problem by simply adding an exception handler for END_ERROR to the code as shown in the following example.

```
End_Block:        -- An example of a poor use of an exception handler
begin
   Sum := 0;
   Sum_Loop:
   loop
      exit Sum_Loop when Ada.Text_IO.End_Of_File (Data_File);
      Ada.Integer_Text_IO.Get (File => Data_File,  Item => Value);
      Sum := Sum + Value;
   end loop Sum_Loop;
exception
   when Ada.IO_Exceptions.END_ERROR =>
      null;                 -- We really don't need to do anything, but
end End_Block;              -- Ada requires a statement here.
```

Now the processing that takes place when all of the data in the file has been read is divided. Sometimes the exit statement handles the processing of the end of file and other times the exception handler does. Because end of file is processed in two different places, this code fragment is difficult to understand.

Have you determined what is really wrong with the original program fragment? It crashes whenever there are some blank characters after the last number in the file. In this case the End_Of_File function returns False after getting the last number. There are still some characters (the blanks) remaining in the file. Earlier in this chapter we discussed the use of the End_Of_File function with numeric and string data. We need a call to procedure Skip_Line to advance the reading marker past the line terminator.

After we add a call to Skip_Line to the loop, the program never terminates with an END_ERROR exception.

Because the End_Of_File function is always available to us, is there ever a need to write an exception handler for the END_ERROR exception? Yes, whenever reaching the end of a file is not expected. For example, we use an exception handler in the following program fragment for calculating the sum of 10 integers stored in a file.

```
Sum   := 0;
End_Block:
begin
   for Count in 1..10 loop
      Ada.Integer_Text_IO.Get (File => Data_File,  Item => Value);
      Sum := Sum + Value;
   end loop;
exception
   when Ada.IO_Exceptions.END_ERROR =>
      Ada.Text_IO.Put_Line ("Fewer than 10 numbers were added to the sum.");
end End_Block;
```

In this program we do not expect to run out of numbers in the file. The file is supposed to contain 10 numbers. Fewer than 10 numbers is an abnormal event suitable for processing in an exception handler.

Remember, when your program terminates because of an unhandled exception, don't just add an exception handler to patch it up. Look for the underlying cause of the error. If it truly is an exceptional situation, then writing an exception handler is an appropriate solution.

Package Calendar

Ada packages are the primary means for dividing the work required to solve a problem among different programmers. A package declaration defines the interface to the package. It describes what resources the package can supply to the rest of the program. As a member of a programming team, you need to be able to understand the package declarations written by your team members* or obtained from a public or private repository. If the package declaration was written by a team member who is still working on the project, you have the opportunity to ask any questions of that member directly. However, if the author of the package is not available, you must use the package declaration and perhaps some detective work or experimentation to answer your questions.

Let's look at the declaration of the predefined package Ada.Calendar. Like Ada.Text_IO, this package is part of every Ada system. We will use the resources of package Calendar in examples and case studies. Its declaration is given in Appendix F. Take a look at it now.

*We'll show you how to write packages in Chapter 12.

The first thing you might notice about this package declaration is the lack of comments. If you turned a package declaration like this one over to your fellow team members, they would be upset with you because it lacks documentation. To be fair to the authors of this predefined package, Calendar is described elsewhere in the *Ada 95 Reference Manual* (ARM).

The first declaration in package Calendar is for a type called Time. Time is a **private type,** which means that the details of this type are not available to us. The operations available for private types are assignment, the equality operators (= and /=), and any subprograms declared in the package. If you continue your study of Ada in a future course, you will learn how to write your own packages with private types. The package doesn't contain any comments about this type. From its name, we might deduce that it has something to do with the storage of the time of day. Let's look at some of the other declarations in the package to see whether they can give us additional information about this private type. The first three subtypes (Year_Number, Month_Number, and Day_Number) declared in Calendar obviously are meant for values involved with calendar dates. The fourth subtype (Day_Duration) is not as obvious. It is a subtype of the type Duration which is a standard type like Integer and Float. Duration is a measure of seconds of time. The range of Day_Duration may be familiar to those who have solved physics problems: 86,400 is the number of seconds in 24 hours. The subtype name also reveals its purpose. Day_Duration is a type of duration (seconds) with a maximum value of one day.

Private type A type whose details are not available to the user of the type (they are available to the programmer who defines and implements the type.) The *operations* available for private types are assignment, the equality operators (= and /=), and any subprograms declared in the package.

Function Clock has no parameters and returns a value of type Time, reinforcing our idea that type Time has something to do with the time of day. The next six subprogram declarations, however, suggest that Time is broader than the time of day. Function Year, for example, has a parameter of type Time and returns a Year_Number. Look at the declaration of procedure Split. This procedure has an *in* parameter of type Time and four *out* parameters of the four calendar date subtypes that we just looked at. Function Time_Of takes four *in* parameters, one for each of our subtypes, and returns a value of type Time. By looking at procedure Split and function Time_Of, it is apparent that type Time encapsulates a year, month, day, and a number of elapsed seconds.

The remaining functions overload well-understood arithmetic and relational operators. We can add values of type Time with values of type Duration. We cannot add two time values together. This restriction makes sense when you think about the nature of the types. It does not make any sense to add the dates 9/30/1948 and 12/20/1948. It does make sense to add an elapsed time (type Duration) to a date. For example 12/20/1948 +

259,200 seconds = 12/23/1948. We also can also subtract a Duration type from a Time type. The difference between two Time types is type Duration. What about the = and /= operators for type Time? Because time is defined as a private type, we can use the predefined operators = and /= so package Calendar does not need to supply them. To use the operators defined in package Calendar in infix expressions, we must include

```
with Ada.Calendar;
use type Ada.Calendar.Time;    -- Make operators available without prefixing
```

at the beginning of our program.

The final definition in this package declaration is of the exception TIME_ERROR. This exception can be raised by Time_Of, "+," "-," Split, Year, Month, and other Calendar operations. We can use our knowledge of integers to help us understand when a TIME_ERROR is raised. With integers, an exception is raised whenever a result is greater than Integer'Last or less than Integer'First. Like type Integer, type Time has a maximum and a minimum value. The four subtypes declared in this package specify these limits. We can use a TIME_ERROR exception handler with the Time_Of function to validate dates. Function Time_Of raises TIME_ERROR if its parameters do not form a valid date. For instance, 4/31/1995 is invalid because the last day possible in April is 30. We illustrate the use of this exception in the following program fragment that obtains a valid date from a user.

```
Year  : Ada.Calendar.Year_Number;
Month : Ada.Calendar.Month_Number;
Day   : Ada.Calendar.Day_Number;
Date  : Ada.Calendar.Time;
Slash : Character;
  .
  .
  .
Input_Validation_Loop:
loop
   Ada.Text_IO.Put_Line ("Enter a date in the form MM/DD/YYYY");
   Date_Validation:
   begin
      Ada.Integer_Text_IO.Get (Month);
      Ada.Text_IO.Get (Slash);
      Ada.Integer_Text_IO.Get (Day);
      Ada.Text_IO.Get (Slash);
      Ada.Integer_Text_IO.Get (Year);
      Date := Ada.Calendar.Time_Of (Year, Month, Day);
      exit Input_Validation_Loop;
   exception
      when CONSTRAINT_ERROR =>                -- values out of range like
                                              -- a month of 13
         Ada.Text_IO.Put_Line ("One of your numbers is not valid.");
      when Ada.Text_IO.DATA_ERROR =>          -- badly formed dates
```

```
                                                      -- like 12 / 20 / 1948
                                                      -- or Dec 20, 1948
            Ada.Text_IO.Put_Line ("Please separate numbers with a " &
                                  "single / character.");
            Ada.Text_IO.Skip_Line;
         when Ada.Calendar.TIME_ERROR =>        -- invalid dates like 2/30/1991
            Ada.Text_IO.Put_Line ("The date you entered is not valid.");
      end Date_Validation;
   end loop Input_Validation_Loop;
```

PROBLEM-SOLVING CASE STUDY

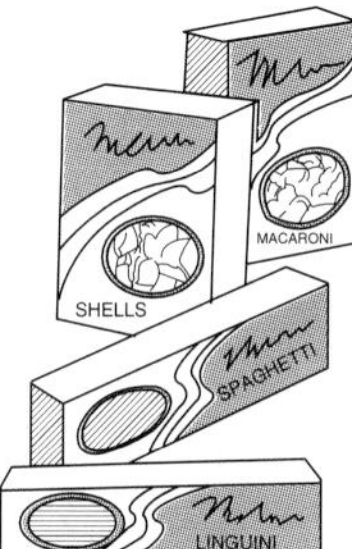

The Pasta House

Specification

Problem Write a program that keeps track of inventory for a large pasta manufacturing company. The company produces many different varieties of pasta, and the sales staff need to know exactly how much of each variety is available in the warehouse. The amounts change as new shipments arrive from the factory and as customer orders are shipped out. Each type of pasta has been assigned a unique number. Because the company has been a leader in the introduction of new pasta shapes, the number of different pastas will increase. When a new pasta variety is introduced, the program should assign it a new number. The program must process the following types of transactions:

Sale	A shipment of a particular variety of pasta to a customer
Shipment	An incoming shipment of a particular variety of pasta from the factory
New Pasta	The introduction of a new pasta variety
Amount	The number of pounds of a particular pasta in the warehouse
Total	The total amount of pasta in the warehouse

The company's shipping trucks can carry a maximum of 2000 pounds. The program must reject any sale or shipment greater than this amount; any sale or shipment less than one pound; and a sale if there is not enough of the pasta variety in the warehouse to fill the order. The warehouse has room to store only 20,000 pounds of each variety. Therefore, the program must reject any shipment into the warehouse that would result in exceeding this limit. The program should be robust. When invalid data is entered, it should display appropriate messages and continue to run.

PROBLEM-SOLVING CASE STUDY *cont'd.*

Input The type of transaction.

Depending on the type of the transaction, there are other input values required.

Sale	The pasta variety number and amount in pounds
Shipment	The pasta variety number and amount in pounds
New Pasta	No further input data
Amount	The pasta variety number
Total	No further input data

Output The output depends on the transaction.

Sale	No output
Shipment	No output
New Pasta	The number to be assigned to the new pasta
Amount	The pounds of the pasta variety in stock
Total	The total number of pounds of pasta in stock

Design This problem would be an easy one to solve by hand. We could keep a notebook with a page for each pasta variety. We would number the pages and use each page number as the identifying number for a particular pasta variety. On each page we would keep the total amount of that pasta in the warehouse. When a shipment of pasta #21 goes out to a customer, we subtract the amount from the total on page 21. When a shipment of pasta #92 arrives from the factory, we add the amount to the total on page 92. When a sales person wants to know how much of pasta #34 is in stock, we simply turn to page 34 of the notebook and read the total. When the company president wants to know the total amount of pasta in the inventory, we need only go through the notebook from beginning to end and add the values together. To add a new pasta variety, we turn to the page following the last pasta in the notebook and initialize its total to zero. The number of this page becomes the number for the new pasta.

The Ada equivalent of the notebook is the direct file. Package Direct_IO contains all of the necessary procedures and functions to mimic the notebook operations. We use the pasta number as an index to the file. Because we are using a file, the totals are kept even when our program is not running. However, because the totals are maintained external to our program, we have a little extra work to do when we need to change one. We must first read the total from the file into a variable. This variable now contains a copy of the total. We then change this copy by adding the amount of an incoming shipment or subtracting the amount of an outgoing shipment. Finally, we write this updated total back to the file, replacing the old total.

PROBLEM-SOLVING CASE STUDY cont'd.

By declaring appropriate subtypes, we can use exception handlers to control the program's actions when Ada's automatic checks detect data entry errors and weight limitation errors. We can also use exception handlers to solve a file-preparation problem. The first time we run the program we must prepare the file with a call to procedure Create. However, on subsequent runs of the program, we must call Open to access the existing file.

Here is our algorithm to solve this problem. Remember that we show only the final version of our algorithms here. We went through several versions of the Pasta House algorithm before settling on this one. We discovered errors in the earlier attempts by writing preconditions and postconditions for the modules and performing algorithm traces. Don't be discouraged if you don't get an algorithm right the first time.

```
Pasta House                                              Level 0
Prepare File
loop
   Get Transaction
   exit when Transaction = Done
   Process Transaction
end loop
Close File

Prepare File                                             Level 1
   out   Pasta File
Open Pasta File
if Open fails
   Create File

Get Transaction                                          Level 1
   out   Transaction
Display Transaction Menu
Get Transaction

Process Transaction                                      Level 1
   in       Which Transaction
   in out   Pasta File
case Which Transaction
   when Sale
      Process Sale
   when Shipment
      Process Shipment
   when New
      Process New Pasta
   when Amount
      Process Amount Query
   when Total
      Process Total Query
```

PROBLEM-SOLVING CASE STUDY cont'd.

```
Process Sale                                   Level 2
  in out   Pasta File
Get Pasta ID
Get Amount of Sale
Read Total for the Pasta ID
Subtract Sale Amount from Total
Write new Total

Process Shipment                               Level 2
  in out   Pasta File
Get Pasta ID
Get Amount of Shipment
Read Total for the Pasta ID
Add Shipment Amount to Total
Write new Total

Process New Pasta                              Level 2
  in out   Pasta File
New Pasta ID := Size of File + 1
Total := 0.0
Write Total

Process Amount Query                           Level 2
  in out   Pasta File
Get Pasta ID
Read Total for the Pasta ID
Display Total

Process Total Query                            Level 2
  in out   Pasta File
Grand Total := 0.0
Set File Index to 1
loop
  exit loop when End Of File
  Read Variety Total
  Add Variety Total to Grand Total
end loop
Display Grand Total

Get Pasta ID                                   Level 3
  in    Max Value
  out   Pasta Number
loop
  Get Pasta Number
  exit when Pasta Number is valid
end loop

Get Pounds                                     Level 3
  out   Amount
loop
  Get Pasta Amount
  exit when Pasta Amount is valid
end loop
```

PROBLEM-SOLVING CASE STUDY *cont'd.*

Module Structure Chart

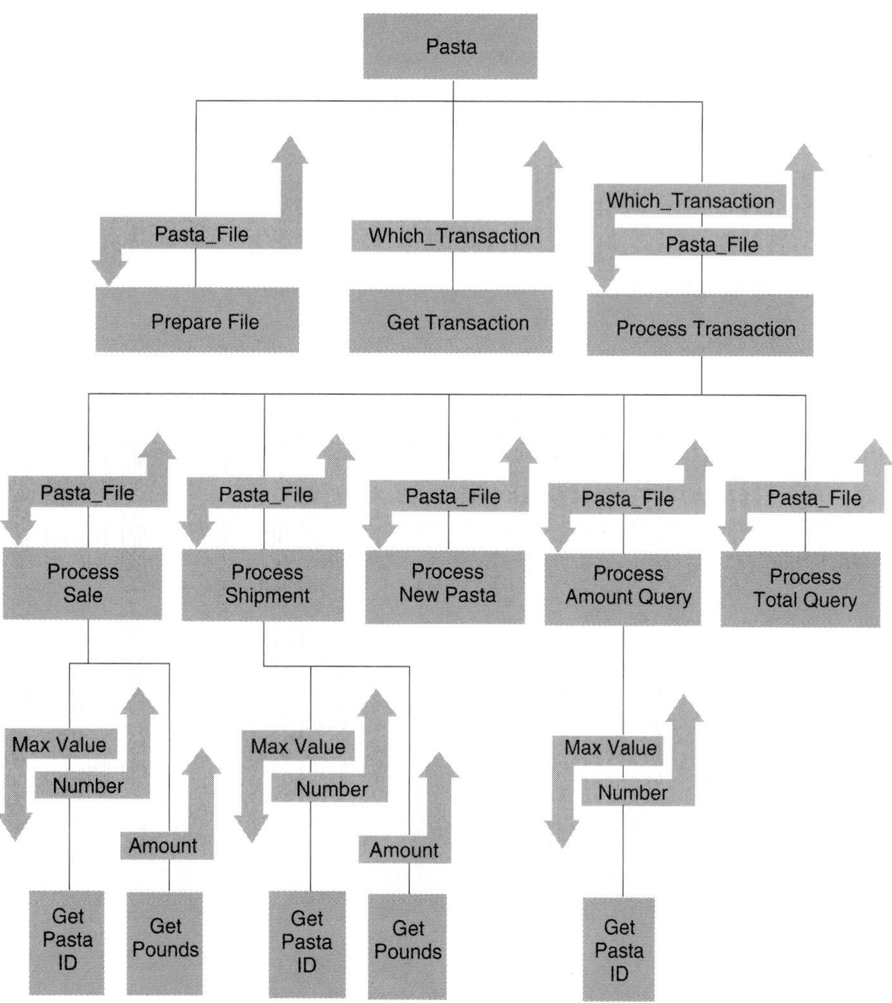

PROBLEM-SOLVING CASE STUDY cont'd.

Implementation

```
with Ada.Text_IO;
with Ada.Direct_IO;
with Ada.Float_Text_IO;
with Ada.IO_Exceptions;
procedure Pasta is

   -- This program maintains the warehouse inventory of different pasta varieties

   -- Name of inventory file
   Inventory_File_Name : constant String := "Pasta.Dat";

   -- Type for the different transactions
   type Transaction_Type is (Sale, Shipment, New_Pasta, Amount, Total, Done);

   -- Types for pasta amounts
   subtype Warehouse_Pounds is Float range 0.0..20_000.0;  -- Ten ton maximum
   subtype Shipping_Pounds  is Float range 1.0.. 2_000.0;  -- One pound minimum
                                                           -- One ton maximum
   -- Instantiations of I/O Packages
   package  Transaction_IO is new Ada.Text_IO.Enumeration_IO
                                  (Enum => Transaction_Type);

   package  Pasta_IO is new Ada.Direct_IO (Element_Type => Warehouse_Pounds);
   use type Pasta_IO.Count;  -- Make operators directly visible
   subtype  Pasta_ID_Type is Pasta_IO.Count;  -- A synonym for clarity

   package Pasta_ID_IO is new Ada.Text_IO.Integer_IO (Num => Pasta_IO.Count);

   ---------------------------------------------
   procedure Prepare_File (Pasta_File : out Pasta_IO.File_Type) is

   -- This procedure prepares the direct access file containing
   -- the company's pasta inventory information

   begin
      Pasta_IO.Open (File => Pasta_File,
                     Mode => Pasta_IO.InOut_File,
                     Name => Inventory_File_Name);
   exception
      when Ada.IO_Exceptions.NAME_ERROR =>
         Ada.Text_IO.Put_Line ("Inventory file does not exist");
         Ada.Text_IO.Put_Line ("Creating the inventory file Pasta.Dat");
         Pasta_IO.Create (File => Pasta_File,
                          Mode => Pasta_IO.InOut_File,
                          Name => Inventory_File_Name);
   end Prepare_File;
```

PROBLEM-SOLVING CASE STUDY cont'd.

```
-------------------------------------------
procedure Get_Transaction (Transaction : out Transaction_Type) is

-- This procedure asks users what type of transaction they want to
-- do and gets it from them. Handles invalid input.

begin
   Ada.Text_IO.New_Line (2);
   Ada.Text_IO.Put_Line ("The following operations are available:");
   Ada.Text_IO.Put_Line ("  Sale       - Update inventory for a shipment out");
   Ada.Text_IO.Put_Line ("  Shipment   - Update inventory for a shipment in");
   Ada.Text_IO.Put_Line ("  New_Pasta  - Obtain the number for a new pasta");
   Ada.Text_IO.Put_Line ("  Amount     - Amount of a pasta in the inventory");
   Ada.Text_IO.Put_Line ("  Total      - Total pasta in the inventory");
   Ada.Text_IO.Put_Line ("  Done       - Exit this program");
   Ada.Text_IO.New_Line;
   Input_Loop:  -- Get a transaction from the user
   loop         -- Each iteration, one input value is checked
      Ada.Text_IO.Put ("Enter your choice:   ");
      Validation_Block:  -- To handle invalid input values
      begin
         Transaction_IO.Get (Transaction);
         exit Input_Loop;
      exception
         when Ada.IO_Exceptions.DATA_ERROR =>
            Ada.Text_IO.Skip_Line;  -- Skip over bad data
            Ada.Text_IO.Put_Line ("Invalid choice, please try again.");
      end Validation_Block;
   end loop Input_Loop;
end Get_Transaction;

-------------------------------------------
procedure Get_Pasta_ID
         (Max_Value : in  Pasta_ID_Type;      -- The largest possible ID
          Pasta_ID  : out Pasta_ID_Type) is   -- The ID of the desired pasta

-- This procedure prompts for and gets a valid pasta identification number.
-- Handles invalid input.

begin
   Validation_Loop:     -- Get a valid pasta ID number
   loop                 -- Each iteration, one input value is checked
      Ada.Text_IO.Put ("Enter the Pasta Identification Number:  ");
      Validation_Block:
      begin
         Pasta_ID_IO.Get (Pasta_ID);
         exit Validation_Loop when Pasta_ID > 0 and Pasta_ID <= Max_Value;
```

PROBLEM-SOLVING CASE STUDY cont'd.

```
            Ada.Text_IO.Put_Line ("Invalid number.");
            Ada.Text_IO.Put ("Pasta number must be between 1 and ");
            Pasta_ID_IO.Put (Item => Max_Value, Width => 1);
            Ada.Text_IO.New_Line;
         exception
            when Ada.IO_Exceptions.DATA_ERROR =>
               Ada.Text_IO.Skip_Line;   -- Skip over bad data
               Ada.Text_IO.Put_Line ("Invalid number.  ");
            when CONSTRAINT_ERROR =>
               Ada.Text_IO.Put_Line ("Invalid number.  ");
               Ada.Text_IO.Put ("Pasta number must be between 1 and ");
               Pasta_ID_IO.Put (Item => Max_Value, Width => 1);
               Ada.Text_IO.New_Line;
            end Validation_Block;
      end loop Validation_Loop;
   end Get_Pasta_ID;

   ----------------------------------------
   procedure Get_Pounds (Amount : out Shipping_Pounds) is

   -- This procedure prompts for and gets a valid weight of a pasta shipment
   -- Handles invalid input.

   begin
      Validation_Loop:   -- Get a valid number of pounds for a truck
      loop               -- Each iteration, one input value is checked
         Ada.Text_IO.Put ("Enter the amount (pounds) of pasta in shipment:  ");
         Validation_Block:
         begin
            Ada.Float_Text_IO.Get (Amount);
            exit Validation_Loop;
         exception
            when Ada.IO_Exceptions.DATA_ERROR =>
               Ada.Text_IO.Skip_Line;   -- Skip over bad data
               Ada.Text_IO.Put_Line ("Data must be numeric.");
            when CONSTRAINT_ERROR =>
               Ada.Text_IO.Put_Line ("Invalid amount.");
               Ada.Text_IO.Put ("Enter a number between ");
               Ada.Float_Text_IO.Put (Item => Shipping_Pounds'First,
                                      Fore => 1, Aft  => 1, Exp  => 0);
               Ada.Text_IO.Put (" and ");
               Ada.Float_Text_IO.Put (Item => Shipping_Pounds'Last,
                                      Fore => 1, Aft  => 1, Exp  => 0);
               Ada.Text_IO.New_Line;
            end Validation_Block;
      end loop Validation_Loop;
   end Get_Pounds;
```

PROBLEM-SOLVING CASE STUDY cont'd.

```
-----------------------------------------------------------
procedure Process_Sale (Pasta_File : in out Pasta_IO.File_Type) is

-- This procedure gets sales information from the user and subtracts
-- the amount of pasta sold from the inventory.

   Pasta_Number : Pasta_ID_Type;      -- The pasta identification number
   Amount       : Shipping_Pounds;    -- The amount of pasta sold and shipped
   Total        : Warehouse_Pounds;   -- The total amount in inventory

begin
   -- Get a valid pasta ID number from the user
   -- The maximum legal value of a pasta ID number is the last index
   -- in the direct file of pasta weights
   Get_Pasta_ID (Max_Value => Pasta_IO.Size (Pasta_File),
                 Pasta_ID  => Pasta_Number);
   -- Get a valid amount from the user
   Get_Pounds (Amount);

   -- Update the inventory

   -- Get the total amount in inventory
   Pasta_IO.Read (File => Pasta_File,
                  Item => Total,
                  From => Pasta_Number);
   -- Calculate the new total
   Total := Total - Amount;
   -- Put the new total back in the inventory file
   Pasta_IO.Write (File => Pasta_File,
                   Item => Total,
                   To   => Pasta_Number);
exception
   when CONSTRAINT_ERROR =>    -- Negative total
      Ada.Text_IO.Put_Line ("Not enough Pasta in stock for this sale!");
end Process_Sale;

-----------------------------------------------------------
procedure Process_Shipment (Pasta_File : in out Pasta_IO.File_Type) is

-- This procedure gets factory production information from the user
-- and adds it to the inventory

   Pasta_Number : Pasta_ID_Type;      -- The pasta identification number
   Amount       : Shipping_Pounds;    -- The amount of pasta sold and shipped
   Total        : Warehouse_Pounds;   -- The total amount in inventory
```

PROBLEM-SOLVING CASE STUDY *cont'd.*

```
begin   -- Process Shipment
   -- Get the necessary data from the user
   -- The maximum legal value of a pasta ID number is the last index
   Get_Pasta_ID (Max_Value => Pasta_IO.Size (Pasta_File),
                 Pasta_ID  => Pasta_Number);
   -- Get a valid amount from the user
   Get_Pounds (Amount);

   -- Update the inventory

   -- Get the total amount in inventory
   Pasta_IO.Read (File => Pasta_File,
                  Item => Total,
                  From => Pasta_Number);

   -- Calculate the new total
   Total := Total + Amount;
   -- Put the new total back in the inventory file
   Pasta_IO.Write (File => Pasta_File,
                   Item => Total,
                   To   => Pasta_Number);
exception
   when CONSTRAINT_ERROR =>    -- Inventory exceeded Warehouse_Weight'Last
      Ada.Text_IO.Put_Line ("Not enough room in warehouse for shipment!");
end Process_Shipment;

 --------------------------------------------
procedure Process_New (Pasta_File : in out Pasta_IO.File_Type) is

-- This procedure determines and displays a unique identification
-- number for a new pasta variety. It also initializes the inventory
-- of that variety to zero.

   New_Pasta_Num : Pasta_ID_Type;   -- The ID number for the new variety

begin
   -- The ID of the new pasta is one greater than
   -- the size of the inventory file
   New_Pasta_Num := Pasta_IO.Size (Pasta_File) + 1;
   Ada.Text_IO.New_Line;
   Ada.Text_IO.Put ("The number assigned to the new pasta variety is ");
   Pasta_ID_IO.Put (Item => New_Pasta_Num,  Width => 1);

   -- Initialize the new pasta's inventory to zero
   Pasta_IO.Write (File => Pasta_File,
                   Item => 0.0,
                   To   => New_Pasta_Num);
```

PROBLEM-SOLVING CASE STUDY *cont'd.*

```
end Process_New;

  ------------------------------------------
procedure Process_Amount_Query (Pasta_File : in Pasta_IO.File_Type) is

-- This procedure displays the amount of a particular pasta in stock

   Pasta_Number : Pasta_ID_Type;      -- The pasta identification number
   Total        : Warehouse_Pounds;  -- The total amount in inventory

begin
   -- Get the necessary data from the user
   -- The maximum legal value of a pasta ID number is the last index
   Get_Pasta_ID (Max_Value => Pasta_IO.Size (Pasta_File),
                 Pasta_ID  => Pasta_Number);

   -- Get the total amount in inventory
   Pasta_IO.Read (File => Pasta_File,
                  Item => Total,
                  From => Pasta_Number);

   -- Display the total
   Ada.Text_IO.Put ("The amount of that pasta in stock is ");
   Ada.Float_Text_IO.Put (Item => Total, Fore => 1, Aft  => 1, Exp  => 0);
   Ada.Text_IO.Put_Line (" pounds.");
end Process_Amount_Query;

  ------------------------------------
procedure Process_Total_Query (Pasta_File : in Pasta_IO.File_Type) is

-- This procedure determines and displays the total amount of
-- pasta in the warehouse

   Total  : Float;                  -- The total amount of pasta in stock
   Amount : Warehouse_Pounds;       -- The amount of one pasta in stock

begin
   Total := 0.0;                             -- Initialize sum
   Pasta_IO.Set_Index (File => Pasta_File,   -- Initialize file index
                       To   => 1);

   Sum_Loop:     -- Each iteration, one pasta variety amount is read and
   loop          -- added to the total
      exit Sum_Loop when Pasta_IO.End_Of_File (Pasta_File);
      Pasta_IO.Read (File => Pasta_File,  Item => Amount);
      Total := Total + Amount;
   end loop Sum_Loop;
```

PROBLEM-SOLVING CASE STUDY *cont'd.*

```
      Ada.Text_IO.New_Line;
      Ada.Text_IO.Put ("Total amount of pasta in the warehouse is ");
      Ada.Float_Text_IO.Put (Item => Total, Fore => 1, Aft  => 1, Exp  => 0);
      Ada.Text_IO.Put_Line (" pounds.");
   end Process_Total_Query;

   ----------------------------------------

   procedure Process_Transaction
        (Which_Transaction : in     Transaction_Type;         -- Which kind
         Inventory_File    : in out Pasta_IO.File_Type) is   -- Inventory file
   -- This procedure carries out the appropriate actions
   -- for the given type of transaction.

   begin
      case Which_Transaction is
         when Sale =>
            Process_Sale (Inventory_File);
         when Shipment =>
            Process_Shipment (Inventory_File);
         when New_Pasta =>
            Process_New (Inventory_File);
         when Amount =>
            Process_Amount_Query (Inventory_File);
         when Total =>
            Process_Total_Query (Inventory_File);
         when Done =>
            null;
      end case;
   end Process_Transaction;

   ----------------------------------------

   Transaction : Transaction_Type;      -- Type of transaction being processed
   Pasta_File  : Pasta_IO.File_Type;    -- Pasta inventory totals

begin  -- Program Pasta
   Prepare_File (Pasta_File);

   Transaction_Loop:  -- Process all of the user's transactions
   loop               -- Each iteration, one transaction is processed
      Get_Transaction (Transaction);
      exit Transaction_Loop when Transaction = Done;
      Process_Transaction (Which_Transaction => Transaction,
                           Inventory_File    => Pasta_File);
   end loop Transaction_Loop;
   -- Close the file
   Pasta_IO.Close (Pasta_File);
exception
```

PROBLEM-SOLVING CASE STUDY *cont'd.*

```
   when others =>                    -- If any exception is not handled where
      Pasta_IO.Close (Pasta_File);   -- it occurs, close the file and propagate
      raise;                         -- the exception back to the system.
end Pasta;
```

Testing Most of the testing in this program involves the abnormal cases. Testing categories should include:

1. *Preparing files:* Test to ensure that the program opens the data file if it exists and creates it if it doesn't exist. Run the program several times and check the variety totals and warehouse total to make sure that the correct values are being stored between program runs.
2. *Transaction input:* Enter valid and invalid transaction types.
3. *Numeric input:* Enter invalid values for pasta identification numbers and amounts. Include out-of-range numbers and syntactically incorrect numbers such as numbers containing characters other than digits.
4. *Totals:* Test the warehouse total before any pasta varieties have been created. After obtaining a new pasta number, check to make sure that its total is zero. Test the warehouse total after adding new varieties but before any shipments have been entered. Enter several different shipments and sales, and check to make sure that the correct totals are maintained for the individual varieties and the warehouse total.
5. *Truck and warehouse limitations:* Enter sales or shipping amounts greater than 2000 pounds and less than one pound. Enter enough shipments to attempt to bring the total of one variety to over 20,000 pounds. Enter enough sales to attempt to take the total of one variety below zero.

Testing and Debugging

The error that programmers most commonly make when working with text files is they forget to include the File parameter in an Ada.Text_IO input or output procedure call. When there is no File parameter in an I/O procedure call, the standard input or output file is assumed. You will notice right away whether your program sends its output to the screen instead of a file. However, it is not easy to diagnose the problem if you forget to include a File parameter for an input operation. Your program will appear to "hang." It is waiting for input from the keyboard, and, because you designed it to take its input from a file, no prompt is displayed. All it takes is to omit the File parameter from a single input procedure. Don't forget to include the File parameter in all calls to Get, Get_Line, Skip_Line, and End_Of_File.

Another common mistake occurs when using the End_Of_File function. By neglecting to include a call to Skip_Line to move the reading marker beyond the line terminator, an End_Of_File loop can raise an END_ERROR exception.

Common sequential file problems include running out of data prematurely and losing the first or last elements in the file. The only advice that we can give you here is to be careful when designing the input section of your program. Always hand-simulate the input before you code it. When checking your output, be sure to check whether the first and last elements have been processed.

Attempting to read an element beyond the end of a direct file raises the exception END_ERROR. However, writing an element beyond the end of the same file does not. It may, however, produce a number of undefined elements between the old end of file and the newly written element. There is no file operation to determine whether an element in a direct file is undefined or not. It is up to our program to ensure that undefined elements are not read.

In previous chapters we have discussed how inserting debugging calls to Put can be useful in determining the values of variables at desired places in our program. Comparing the predicted value of a variable with its actual contents helps us to determine where a fault in our program lies. We can also place debugging Puts in exception handlers. It is easy to add such an exception handler to a procedure. When an exception occurs in the procedure, we can display the values of parameters and local variables.

Some systems display the procedure call chain when an exception occurs. Take, for example, the Program Propagation used earlier in this chapter. If an exception occurs in procedure A, the system would tell us that the exception occurred in procedure A, which was called by procedure B, which was called by procedure C, which was called by procedure Propagation. From this error display, we can determine whether the chain of calls is different than we expected. If your system does not give you such a call history, you can use exception handlers and the raise statement to obtain the same results. Simply include at least the `when others` exception handler with every procedure. In each of the handlers, display the name of the procedure and use the raise statement to propagate the exception to the caller. In this manner, the exception will be propagated all the way back, displaying the name of each procedure along the way.

Remember to call Skip_Line in the exception handler for DATA_ERROR in a data validation loop. If you don't, the same bad data will be used again, resulting in an infinite loop. Seeing your DATA_ERROR message displayed over and over probably means that you left out the call to Skip_Line.

Summary

Programs communicate with the outside world and with each other through files, which are composed of a number of like elements and reside external to the program. There are two kinds of files: text files and binary files.

The elements of text files are characters. The characters are organized as a collection of lines. A line terminator marks the end of each line of the file. A file terminator follows the last line and marks the end of the file. Your program may use the End_Of_Line and End_Of_File functions to detect these terminators.

The elements of a binary file can be any type other than another file. Input and output is usually faster with binary files than with text files because binary files require no translation between character and numeric values. Binary files usually take less storage space than the equivalent data in a text file.

The generic packages Ada.Sequential_IO and Ada.Direct_IO contain the necessary operations for processing binary files. The operations in Sequential_IO allow us to process the elements of a binary file in order, from beginning to end. The operations in Direct_IO allow us to process the elements of a binary file in any order. Direct_IO also permits us to easily mix read and write operations.

Exceptions are abnormal conditions that occur in a program. When the system detects an abnormal condition, it raises an exception. The program abandons the normal execution flow and transfers control to an exception handler. If there is no exception handler associated with the statement that caused the exception, the program propagates the exception back until it finds an exception handler.

We can place an exception handler at the end of a block statement or at the end of a subprogram. Exception handlers allow us to recover from abnormal conditions by giving our program control when an exception is raised. Ada's passive error checking combined with our own exception handlers are powerful tools for building robust programs.

Quick Check

1. You should avoid using End_Of_Line loops with numeric data. (True or False) (pp. 484–489)
2. You may treat the line terminator like any other character. (True or False) (p. 480)
3. There may be characters between the last line terminator in a file and the file terminator. (True or False) (p. 479)
4. End_Of_File may return True when the reading marker is on a file terminator. (True or False) (p. 480)
5. What procedure must you call at the end of the loop to use an End_Of_File loop with numeric data? (pp. 510–511)

6. What type of data does Put_Line display? (p. 486)
7. What does procedure New_Page do? (p. 486)
8. The elements of a binary file may be characters. (True or False) (p. 489)
9. Describe how the same number is stored differently in text and binary files. (p. 489)
10. What are the five things that you have to remember to do in order to use a sequential file? (p. 490)
11. What is the difference between sequential files and direct files? (p. 493)
12. What file modes are available with sequential files? With direct files? (p. 494)
13. What does the use type clause allow us to do? (pp. 496–497)
14. What occurs when an exception is raised? (p. 497)
15. Name two Ada constructs that can have exception handlers. (pp. 499–505)
16. What is a propagated exception? (pp. 505–506)
17. When is an exception propagated? (p. 506)

Answers

1. True. **2.** False. **3.** False. **4.** True. **5.** Procedure Skip_Line. **6.** String data. **7.** It sends a page terminator to the output file. When printed, the page terminator advances the paper to the top of a new page. When displayed on a screen, the page terminator usually clears the screen and positions the cursor at the beginning of the first line. **8.** True. Elements of a binary file may be any type except a file type. **9.** In a text file, a number is stored as a sequence of character elements. In a binary file, a number is stored as a single binary element. **10.** You must: *a.* Instantiate an I/O package for the element type. *b.* Declare a variable for each file. *c.* Prepare each file for reading or writing with a call to Open or Create. *d.* Include the file variable as a parameter in each call to a procedure in the sequential I/O package. *e.* Sever the connection to each file with a call to the Close procedure. **11.** The elements in a direct file may be accessed either sequentially or directly. The elements in a sequential file may only be accessed sequentially. **12.** The modes for sequential files are In_File, Out_File, and Append_File. The modes for direct files are In_File, Out_File, and Inout_File. **13.** The use type clause allows us to use operators for types declared in a package without having to prefix them with the package name. **14.** Normal program execution is abandoned. **15.** Block statements and subprograms. **16.** An exception that is raised again when control leaves a frame. **17.** When there is no exception handler for the exception in the frame where the exception occurred. Also when a raise statement is used in an exception handler.

Exam Preparation Exercises

1. Should the procedure Skip_Line be used in an End_Of_File loop with string data that is read with Get_Line?
2. The following code fragment processes strings of two characters.

```
Double : String (1..2);        -- A two-character string
   .
   .
   .
Double_Loop:
loop
```

```
   exit Double_Loop when End_Of_Line;
   Ada.Text_IO.Get (Double);              -- Get a two-character string
   Ada.Text_IO.Put (Double (1));          -- Display the first
                                          -- character of the string
end loop Double_Loop;
Ada.Text_IO.New_Line;
Ada.Text_IO.Put_Line ("All Done");
```

a. Will the program display the message "All Done" after the following line is entered at the keyboard?

```
Be careful when using End_Of_Line with strings¶
```

b. Will the program display the message "All Done" after the following line is entered at the keyboard? Note that this line is the same as that used in part a, but with a period added at the end.

```
Be careful when using End_Of_Line with strings.¶
```

3. The following code segment is supposed to copy the information from a text file to the standard output file. It contains an infinite loop. Correct the code so that it works as intended.

```
Line_Echo:          -- Display all the lines in the file
loop                -- Each iteration, one line is read and displayed
   exit Line_Echo when Ada.Text_IO.End_Of_File(Story_File);

   Char_Echo:    -- Display one line
   loop          -- Each iteration, one character is read and displayed
      exit Char_Echo when Ada.Text_IO.End_Of_Line (Story_File);
      Ada.Text_IO.Get (File => Story_File,
                       Item => Char);
      Ada.Text_IO.Put (Char);
   end loop Char_Echo;
   Ada.Text_IO.New_Line;         -- Output line terminator
end loop Line_Echo;
```

4. Given the following type

```
type Month_Type is (Jan, Feb, Mar, Apr, May, Jun,
                    Jul, Aug, Sep, Oct, Nov, Dec);
```

a. Write the declaration to instantiate a sequential file I/O package for files whose elements are type Month_Type.
b. Write the declaration to instantiate a direct file I/O package for files whose elements are type Month_Type.
c. Write the declaration for a sequential file called Birthdays whose elements are type Month_Type.

d. Write the declaration for a direct file called Renewals whose elements are type Month_Type.
e. Write the declaration for a numeric variable called Index that will be used as an actual parameter with the formal parameters To and From used in calls to the direct access Read and Write procedures.

5. A direct file contains 74 elements.
   a. What happens when a program reads the 82nd element in this file?
   b. What happens when a program writes the 82nd element of this file?
6. What output is produced by the following program segment

```
package Value_IO is new Direct_IO (Element_Type => Integer);
use type Value_IO.Count;
   .
   .
   .
Value_File : Value_IO.File_Type;
Value      : Integer;
Index      : Value_IO.Count;
   .
   .
   .
Value := 1;
Value_Loop:
loop
   Index := Value_IO.Count (Value);   -- Convert type Integer
                                      -- to type Count
   exit Value_Loop when Index > Value_IO.Size (Value_File);
   Value_IO.Read (File => Value_File,
                  Item => Value,
                  From => Index);
   Ada.Integer_Text_IO.Put (Value);
   Ada.Text_IO.New_Line;
end loop Value_Loop;
```

that uses the following direct file?

1	2	3	4	5	6	7	8	9	10	11	
0007	0008	0011	0001	0010	0012	0003	0001	0041	0003	0006	§

7. The following program does not compile. The error message indicates that the + operator in the line `Position := Position + 2;` is invalid. How can you correct this error?

```
with Ada.Direct_IO;
procedure Question is
   package Dir_Float_IO is new Ada.Direct_IO (Element_Type => Float);
   Float_File : Dir_Float_IO.File_Type;
   Position   : Dir_Float_IO.Count;
   Value      : Float;
   Sum        : Float;
```

```
begin
   Dir_Float_IO.Open (File => Float_File,
                      Mode => Dir_Float_IO.In_File,
                      Name => "MyData");
   Sum      := 0.0;
   Position := 12;
   Dir_Float_IO.Read (File => Float_File,
                      Item => Sum,
                      From => Position);
   Sum := Sum + Value;
   Position := Position + 2;
   Dir_Float_IO.Read (File => Float_File,
                      Item => Sum,
                      From => Position);
   Sum := Sum + Value;
end Question;
```

8. Given the following Ada code segment

```
type    Score_Type      is            range 0..100;
subtype Quiz_Score_Type is Score_Type range 0..10
   .
   .
   .
package Score_IO is new Ada.Text_IO.Integer_IO (Num => Score_Type);
   .
   .
   .
Score : .....................;    -- See question parts a through d
   .
   .
   .
Validation_Block:
begin
   Score_IO.Get (Item => Score);
   Ada.Text_IO.Put_Line ("No exception detected");
exception
   when Ada.IO_Exceptions.DATA_ERROR =>
      Ada.Text_IO.Put_Line ("DATA_ERROR detected");
   when CONSTRAINT_ERROR =>
      Ada.Text_IO.Put_Line ("CONSTRAINT_ERROR detected");
end Validation_Block;
```

a. What message is displayed if Score is Score_Type and the user enters a value of 50?
b. What message is displayed if Score is Score_Type and the user enters a value of 123?
c. What message is displayed if Score is Quiz_Score_Type and the user enters a value of 50?
d. What message is displayed if Score is Quiz_Score_Type and the user enters a value of 123?

9. Define the following terms:

text file	binary file
line terminator	file terminator
sequential access	direct Access
file index value	CONSTRAINT_ERROR
propagated exception	raise an exception
exception handler	frame
DATA_ERROR	

10. The following program skeleton contains three procedures. The main subprogram calls procedure Three, which calls procedure Two, which calls procedure One.

```
with Ada.Text_IO;
procedure Question_10 is

   procedure One is
      .
      .
      .
   begin
      .
      .
      .
   exception
      when CONSTRAINT_ERROR =>
         Ada.Text_IO.Put_Line ("Exception Handler Procedure One");
         raise;
   end One;

   procedure Two is
      .
      .
      .
   begin
      .
      .
      .
      One;        -- Call procedure One
      Ada.Text_IO.Put_Line ("Normal processing Procedure Two");
      .
      .
      .
   exception
      when CONSTRAINT_ERROR  | STORAGE_ERROR =>
         Ada.Text_IO.Put_Line ("Exception Handler Procedure Two");
   end Two;

   procedure Three is
      .
      .
      .
   begin
      .
      .
      .
```

```
      Two;        -- Call procedure Two
      Ada.Text_IO.Put_Line ("Normal processing Procedure Three");
      .
      .
      .
   exception
      when others =>
         Ada.Text_IO.Put_Line ("Exception Handler Procedure Three");
   end Three;

begin -- Program Question_10
   Three;        -- Call procedure Three
   Ada.Text_IO.Put_Line ("All Done");
end Question_10;
```

a. What is the output of this program if a CONSTRAINT_ERROR is raised in the body of procedure One?
b. What is the output of this program if a STORAGE_ERROR is raised in the body of procedure One?
c. What is the output of this program if a DATA_ERROR is raised in the body of procedure One?

Programming Warm-up Exercises

1. Write a program segment that determines and displays the number of blank characters in a line of input. Use the End_Of_Line function to terminate your loop.
2. Write a program segment that determines the average of the float numbers stored one per line in a text file. Use the End_Of_File function to terminate your loop.
3. Write a program segment that determines the average number of characters per line in a text file. Use the End_Of_Line and End_Of_File functions to terminate your nested loops.
4. Write a program segment that displays the last character on every line of input.
5. Using the declarations from Exam Preparation Exercise 4, write a program segment that determines and displays the total number of elements in file Birthdays that are May.
6. Using the declarations from Exam Preparation Exercise 4, write a program segment that determines and displays the total number of elements with an even index (that is, elements with file indices of 2, 4, 6, etc.) in file Renewals that are Aug. Take care in designing your loop termination condition.
7. Write a data validation loop that prompts the user and gets a value of type Month_Type (as declared in Exam Preparation Exercise 4). Use an exception handler to ensure that the program does not exit the loop until a valid month has been entered. Include the instantiation of the enumeration I/O package in your answer.
8. Using the following subtype declaration, an exit statement with a when clause, and an exception handler, write a data validation loop that prompts for and gets an even number between 0 and 100.

```
subtype Score_Type is Integer range 0..100;
```

9. Write a procedure called Delete_Text_File that prompts the user to enter the name of an external text file and then deletes that file. Use exception handlers to ensure a robust procedure that displays meaningful messages when an abnormal condition is detected.
10. Rewrite the function Factorial given in Chapter 6, page 322, with an exception handler so that Integer'Last is returned if the calculations in the function exceed Integer'Last.
11. The Pasta House case study has a flaw that could result in an infinite data validation loop. It occurs when a choice other than New_Pasta or Total is entered before *any* pasta varieties have been entered (that is, when the size of the file is 0). Confirm that this flaw exists and suggest how you could modify the program.

Programming Problems

1. (Extension of Chapter 4, Programming Problem 6) Write an Ada program that plays the game "rock, paper, scissors." In this game, two players choose simultaneously either rock, paper, or scissors. Whether a player wins or loses depends not only on that player's choice but also on the opponent's. The rules are:
   - Rock breaks scissors: rock wins.
   - Paper covers rock: paper wins.
   - Scissors cuts paper: scissors wins.
   - All matching combinations are ties.

   Each player uses the editor to prepare a text file containing his or her choices for a number of games. Choices are Rock, Paper, and Scissors. (In your program, use an enumeration type for these choices.) Each choice for a game is on a separate line. It may have blanks before and after it.

   Your program should read the choices from the two files and determine and display those choices and the winner of each game. After all games have been played, display the total number of games played, the number of games won by each player, and the number of tie games.

   Because the players have not agreed in advance on the number of games to play, your program should terminate when all of the choices in one file have been played. If a particular choice for a game is not spelled correctly, that player forfeits the game. If both players have invalid choices, it is considered a tie game. An appropriate message should be displayed if one or both players' choice is invalid. The invalid choice should not be displayed.

2. Readability statistics are one measure of how effectively a piece of writing communicates. Educators have devised a number of formulas to help judge the reading level of a piece of writing. These formulas make use of statistics such as average number of characters per word and average number of words per sentence. Write an Ada program to determine the following statistics from a piece of writing stored in a text file.
   - the average number of characters in a word
   - the average number of words in a sentence
   - the average number of sentences in a paragraph

   We make the following assumptions to simplify this problem:
   a. We define a word as a sequence of characters followed by a blank, punctuation mark, or line terminator.
   b. Punctuation marks include only commas, periods, exclamation marks, and question marks.
   c. We define a sentence as a sequence of words followed by a period, exclamation mark, or question mark.
   d. We define a paragraph as a sequence of sentences followed by a null line. This means that a paragraph is followed by two line terminators.
3. Write an interactive Ada program that prompts for and gets a number of daily high-temperature values. The user enters the word Done (or any other word) after the last temperature to signal the end of the data. After the data has been entered, the program should echo each value along with how many degrees that value is above or below the average of all the values. Use a sequential file to store the values. Delete the file when the program terminates.
4. The final exam in your psychology class is 50 multiple-choice questions. Your instructor says that, if you write the program to grade the finals, you won't have to take the exam.

   Input
   - A text file. The first data line contains the key to the exam. The correct answers are the first 50 characters; they are followed by an integer number that says how many students took the exam (call it N).
   - The next N lines contain student answers in the first 50 character positions, followed by the student's name in the next 10 character positions.

   Output
   - For each student—the student's name; followed by the number of correct answers; followed by PASS if the number correct is 60 percent or better, or FAIL otherwise.

   Hint: Because a student's answers are processed in order, store the exam key in a sequential file of 50 elements.

5. The local baseball team is computerizing its records. You are to write a program that maintains batting statistics between games. There are 20 players on the team, identified by the numbers 1 through 20. Their batting records for each game are coded on text files as follows—each line contains four numbers: the player's identification number and the number of hits, walks, and outs he or she made in a particular game.

   Example input line

```
3 2 1 1
```

   This example indicates that, during a game, player number 3 was at bat 4 times and made 2 hits, 1 walk, and 1 out. For each player there is one line in the text file for every game since the program was last run. The lines of data in the file are in no particular order.

   The team will run your program after every few games. It will take the statistics accumulated in the text file and add them to each player's totals. Then the program will print out each player's number and current batting average.

   Each player's batting average is computed by adding the player's total number of hits and dividing by the total number of times at bat. A walk does not count as either a hit or a time at bat when the batting average is being calculated. Your program prints a table showing each player's identification number, batting average, and number of walks.

   To solve this problem, use three direct files—one for hits, one for walks, and one for outs. Each file will have one element for each player (20 elements in each file). The player's number may be used to select the proper element from any of the files.

CHAPTER 10

Records

GOALS

After reading this chapter, you should be able to

- define a record data type
- access a component in a record object
- use files of records to solve a given problem
- define a hierarchical record structure
- access values stored in a hierarchical record object
- design an appropriate data structure for a given problem

A declaration associates an identifier with a process, object, or other entity. The processes are procedures and functions. Our objects have primarily been variables and constants. Because each of these objects has a single value, it is logical to think of an identifier as a synonym for its value. Objects, however, may contain many values. A file, for example, is an object that contains any number of values. In Chapter 7 we examined the concept of a data type and looked at how to define scalar data types. In this chapter we introduce a new data type, the record, that allows us to associate an identifier with a collection of values.

Throughout this book we have used top-down design for developing our programs. We work from the abstract (a list of the major steps in our solution) to the particular (algorithmic steps that we can translate directly into Ada code). The way we organize our data affects our algorithms. In this chapter we discuss how to design our algorithms and how to structure our data in parallel.

Record Types

A **record** is a data type that allows us to associate an identifier with a collection of values. Because a record is composed of several values, it is called a **composite data type.** Strings are also composite types; they are composed of several characters. Boolean, Character, Float, Integer, and all types and subtypes derived from them are referred to as **atomic data types.**

Record A composite data type with a number of components that are accessed by name. The components may be of different types.

Composite data type A data type that allows a collection of values to be associated with an identifier of that type.

Atomic data type A data type that allows only a single value to be associated with an identifier of that type.

The components of strings are all of the same type—Character. The components of a particular file are also of the same type. Composite types whose components are all of the same type are called *homogeneous* data types. The record is a *nonhomogeneous* data type. The components of a record do not have to be of the same type.

Records allow us to group related components together, regardless of their data types. We give each component in a record a name, sometimes referred to as a *field*, which is used to access the component. Here is an expansion of the simplified EBNF definition given in Chapter 7 for a type declaration which includes the record definition.

```
type_declaration        ::= type identifier is type_definition;
type_definition         ::= enumeration_type_definition  |
                            integer_type_definition      |
                            float_type_definition        |
                            record_type_definition
record_type_definition  ::= record
                              component_list
                            end record
component_list          ::= component_declaration
                            {component_declaration}
component_declaration   ::= component_identifier : subtype_mark;
subtype_mark            ::= type_name | subtype_name
```

As an example, let's use a record to describe a student in a class. We want to store the first and last name, the overall grade-point average (GPA) prior to this class, the grade on programming assignments, the grade on quizzes, the final exam grade, and the final course grade.

```
type    Letter_Grade_Type is (A, B, C, D, F);
subtype Percent           is Integer range 0..100;
subtype GPA_Type          is Float range 0.00..4.00;
subtype Name_String       is String (1..15);

type Student_Rec is
   record
      First_Name    : Name_String;
      Last_Name     : Name_String;
      GPA           : GPA_Type;
      Program_Grade : Percent;
      Quiz_Grade    : Percent;
      Final_Exam    : Percent;
      Course_Grade  : Letter_Grade_Type;
   end record;

-- Variables
First_Student : Student_Rec;
Student       : Student_Rec;
```

First_Name, Last_Name, GPA, Program_Grade, Quiz_Grade, Final_Exam, and Course_Grade are *component names* within the record type Student_Rec. These names make up the *component list*. Note that each component is given a type or subtype.

First_Name and Last_Name are of type Name_String, which is a string of 15 characters. GPA is of type GPA_Type, which is a float subtype with a range of 0.00 to 4.00. Program_Grade, Quiz_Grade, and Final_Exam are type Percent, which is an integer subtype with range 0 to 100. Course_Grade is an enumeration data type made up of the grades A through D and F.

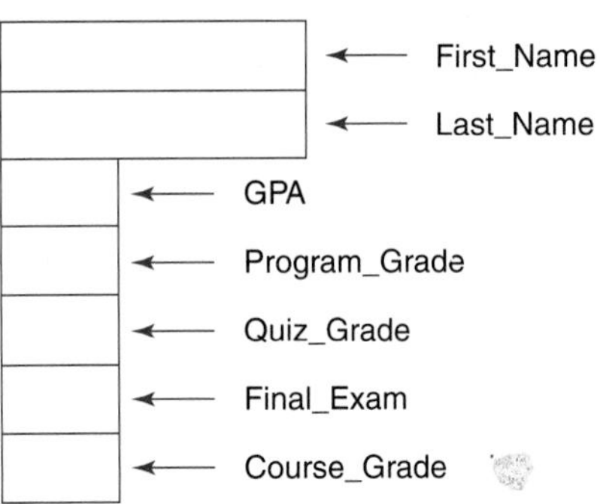

FIGURE 10-1
Pattern for Record Type Student_Rec

None of these components is associated with memory locations until we declare a variable of this record type. Student_Rec is merely a pattern for a record (see Figure 10-1). The variables First_Student and Student are of type Student_Rec.

We can access the components of a record variable by giving the name of the variable, followed by a period, and then the name of the component. This form of name is called a **selected component.** The simplified EBNF definition is:

selected_component ::= *record_*variable**.***component_*identifier

---

Selected component The form of name used to access components of a record object. It consists of the record object name followed by a period and the component identifier.

To access the GPA of First_Student, we would write

```
First_Student.GPA
```

To access the final exam score of Student, we would write

```
Student.Final_Exam
```

We treat the component of a record accessed by the selected component just like any other variable of the same type. We can use it in an assignment statement, pass it as a parameter, and so on. Figure 10-2 shows the record object Student with the selected component for each component. In this example, some processing already has taken place, so values are stored in some of the components.

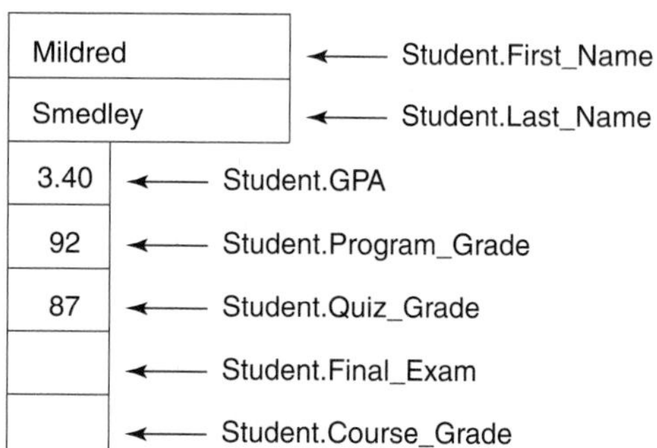

Figure 10-2
Record Variable Student with Selected Components

Let's demonstrate the use of these selected components. Using our example record, the following code segment reads in a final exam grade; calculates a weighted average of the program grade, the quiz grade, and the final exam grade; and then assigns a letter grade to the result. The variable Average is of type Percent.

```
Ada.Integer_Text_IO.Get (Item => Student.Final_Exam);
Average := (4 * Student.Final_Exam + 2 * Student.Program_Grade +
            3 * Student.Quiz_Grade) / 900;
if Average >= 90 then
   Student.Course_Grade := A;
elsif Average >= 80 then
   Student.Course_Grade := B;
elsif  ...
```

Just as we can read values into specific variables, we can read values into specific components of a record. For example the statement

```
Ada.Integer_Text_IO.Get (Item => Student.Final_Exam);
```

reads an integer value from the standard input file and stores the value into the Final_Exam component of Student. We used the selected component Student.Final_Exam as an actual parameter in the call to procedure Get. When using text files, we cannot read in whole records; we must read values into a record one component at a time.

The record component Student.Last_Name is a string. We access slices and the individual characters in this record component just as we would access the components in any other string: We give the name of the string followed by the character number or character range, enclosed in parentheses.

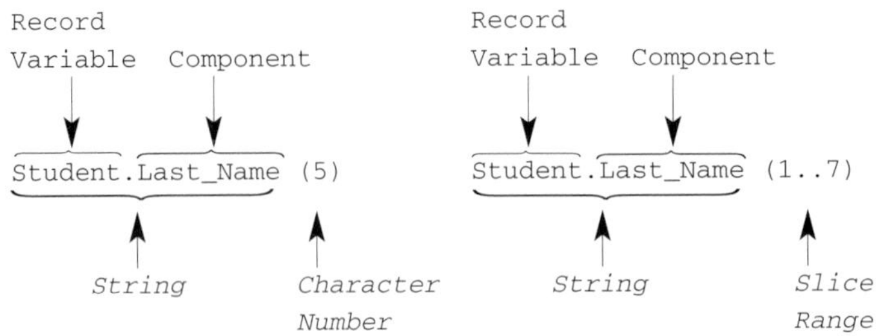

Student.Last_Name(5) would access the fifth letter in the last name, Student.First_Name(15) would access the last character in the first name, and so on. Student.Last_Name(1..7) is a string slice composed of the first seven characters of the last name component.

Operations on Entire Records

In addition to being able to access individual components of a record object, we can manipulate records as a whole. In the last section we showed how we can use a record *component* as an actual parameter. We can use entire records as actual parameters with procedures or functions whose formal parameters are of a record type. To illustrate, let's define a function that takes our example record as a parameter. The task of this function is to determine whether a student's grade in a course is consistent with his or her overall GPA. Consistent is defined to mean that the course grade is the same as the rounded GPA. We calculate the GPA on a 4-point scale, where A is 4, B is 3, C is 2, D is 1, and F is 0. If the rounded GPA is 4 and the course grade is A, then the function returns True. If the rounded GPA is 4 and the course grade is not A, then the function returns False. We test each of the other possible grades the same way. Function Consistent is coded here. The formal parameter Student is a record of type Student_Rec.

```
function Consistent (Student : in Student_Rec) return Boolean is

-- This function returns True if the student's course
-- grade is consistent with their overall GPA

   subtype Whole_GPA is Integer range 0..4;

   Rounded_GPA : Whole_GPA;                        -- Rounded GPA value

begin  -- Consistent
   Rounded_GPA := Whole_GPA (Student.GPA);         -- Round the GPA
   case Rounded_GPA is
```

```
      when 0 =>
         return  Student.Course_Grade = F;
      when 1 =>
         return  Student.Course_Grade = D;
      when 2 =>
         return  Student.Course_Grade = C;
      when 3 =>
         return  Student.Course_Grade = B;
      when 4 =>
         return  Student.Course_Grade = A;
   end case;
end Consistent;
```

Being able to manipulate records as a whole also means that we can assign one record object to a record variable of the same type. For example, if Another_Student is declared to be of Student_Rec, the statement

```
Another_Student := Student;
```

assigns the entire contents of the record variable Student to the record variable Another_Student.

Finally, entire record variables that have the same type can be compared with the = and /= operators. Two records are equal if all the components in one record are equal to the corresponding components in the other record. If a single component differs, the records are not equal. Here's an example that illustrates the comparison of two records. If First_Student and Student are both type Student_Rec, the if statement fragment

```
if First_Student = Student then    -- Are the two records exactly the same
      .
      .
      .
```

is equivalent to the if statement fragment

```
If First_Student.First_Name    = Student.First_Name     and
   First_Student.Last_Name     = Student.Last_Name      and
   First_Student.GPA           = Student.GPA            and
   First_Student.Program_Grade = Student.Program_Grade  and
   First_Student.Quiz_Grade    = Student.Quiz_Grade     and
   First_Student.Final_Exam    = Student.Final_Exam     and
   First_Student.Course_Grade  = Student.Course_Grade      then
      .
      .
      .
```

There are no predefined relational operators that we can use to compare one record variable with another. Scalar types like Float and Integer have an inherent order that you may use to determine whether one value is less than another. Strings also have an inherent order (alphabetical) that you may use to determine whether or not one string is greater than (comes after) another. Because there is no inherent ordering for records, operators like < and > make no sense with all record variables. There is no unique way to order two student records. We could order student records alphabetically by First_Name or by Last_Name or even numerically by GPA. We can write our own relational operator functions based on how we need to order records in a particular problem. We then can use these programmer-defined relational operators to compare two records. Here is a function that compares two student records based on the last name components followed by an example of its use.

```
function "<" (Left : in Student_Rec; Right : in Student_Rec) return
              Boolean is
-- Comparison of student records based on the last name component
begin
   return  Left.Last_Name < Right.Last_Name;
end "<";


if Student < Another_Student then
   .
   .
   .
```

Let's review the syntax and semantics of the record data type in the context of another example. A parts wholesaler wants to computerize her operation. Until now she has kept the inventory on handwritten 8 × 10-inch cards. A typical inventory card contains the following data.

```
Part number:        1A3321
Description:        cotter pin
Cost:               0.012
Quantity on hand:   2100
```

A record is a natural choice for describing a part. Each item on the inventory card can be a component of the record. The types necessary to declare a part record look like this:

```
subtype Part_Number_String      is String (1..6);
subtype Part_Description_String is String (1..20);
type    Dollars is delta 0.001 digits 6 range 0.000 .. 999.999;
```

```
type Part_Rec is
   record
      Number      : Part_Number_String;
      Description : Part_Description_String;
      Cost        : Dollars;
      Quantity    : Natural;
   end record;

Part : Part_Rec;
```

The reserved words `record` and `end record` bracket the component declarations. Each component name is followed by a colon and a type or subtype, just like the declaration of any variable. Component names must be unique within a record type, just as variable identifiers must be unique within a declarative region.

Once we have declared a record variable, we can treat and use the selected components of the record variable in the same way as any other declared variable. We can use selected components in expressions such as:

```
Part.Quantity := Part.Quantity + 24;
if Part.Cost < 5.00 then
   Ada.Text_IO.Put_Line (Item => Part.Number);
   Ada.Text_IO.Put_Line (Item => Part.Description);
   Ada.Integer_Text_IO.Put (Item => Part.Quantity, Width => 1);
   Ada.Text_IO.New_Line;
end if;
```

If the parts wholesaler supplied inventory data that looked like

```
2B3310Ring, piston                2.95   15
```

then the following procedure would read the data and store it in the appropriate components of the record *out* parameter.

```
procedure Get (Item : out Part_Rec) is
-- Our own Get procedure for Part records
begin
   Ada.Text_IO.Get (Item.Part_Number);
   Ada.Text_IO.Get (Item.Description);
   Dollar_IO.Get   (Item.Cost);
   Ada.Integer_Text_IO.Get (Item.Quantity);
end Get;
```

Item.Part_Number, Item.Description, Item.Cost, and Item.Quantity are selected components of the formal parameter Item. Dollar_IO is a package we instantiated for the input and output of values of the decimal type Dollars.

Default Initial Values

When we declare variables, their initial values are not defined. For example, because we have not assigned a value to Part.Quantity, we cannot predict what the following code fragment will display.

```
with Ada.Text_IO;
with Ada.Integer_Text_IO;
procedure Example_Program is

   subtype Part_Number_String      is String (1..6);
   subtype Part_Description_String is String (1..20);
   type    Dollars is delta 0.001 digits 6 range 0.000 .. 999.999;

   type Part_Rec is
      record
         Part_Number : Part_Number_String;
         Description : Part_Description_String;
         Cost        : Dollars;
         Quantity    : Natural;
      end record

   package Dollar_IO is new Ada.Text_IO.Decimal_IO (Num => Dollars);

   Part         : Part_Rec;
   Another_Part : Part_Rec;

begin  -- Example Program
   Ada.Integer_Text_IO.Put (Item => Part.Quantity,         Width => 5);
   Ada.Integer_Text_IO.Put (Item => Another_Part.Quantity, Width => 5);
   .
   .
   .
end Example_Program;
```

When we declare a record type, we can assign default initial values to each component of the record. Then when we declare a variable using that record type, the program automatically initializes the components in the variable to the values given in the record type declaration. Here is the same code fragment with default initial values supplied for each component in the Part_Rec record declaration.

```
with Ada.Text_IO;
with Ada.Integer_Text_IO;
procedure Example_Program is
```

```
   subtype Part_Number_String      is String (1..6);
   subtype Part_Description_String is String (1..20);
   type    Dollars is delta 0.001 digits 6 range 0.000 .. 999.999;

   type Part_Rec is
      record
         Part_Number : Part_Number_String      := "      ";
         Description : Part_Description_String := "                    ";
         Cost        : Dollars                 := 0.00;
         Quantity    : Natural                 := 0;
      end record

   package Dollar_IO is new Ada.Text_IO.Decimal_IO (Num => Dollars);

   Part         : Part_Rec;
   Another_Part : Part_Rec;

begin  -- Example Program
   Ada.Integer_Text_IO.Put (Item => Part.Quantity,         Width => 5);
   Ada.Integer_Text_IO.Put (Item => Another_Part.Quantity, Width => 5);
   .
   .
   .
end Example_Program;
```

For our record type declaration, we use the assignment symbol (:=) in the definition of each component to assign an initial value. Given these initial values assigned to Part_Rec, we can tell that the value 0 will be displayed for Part.Quantity. The value of Another_Part.Quantity is also 0. Default initial values are unique to record type declarations. There is *no* other type or subtype declaration in Ada that can contain default initial values.

Record Aggregates

Just as we can write integer literals and float literals, Ada allows us to write record literals. Record literals are called **aggregates.** An aggregate is a collection of values representing record components that are contained within parentheses. There must be a value in the aggregate for each component of the record.

Aggregate A collection of component values contained within parentheses.

Here is an example that assigns an aggregate to a variable of type Part_Rec.

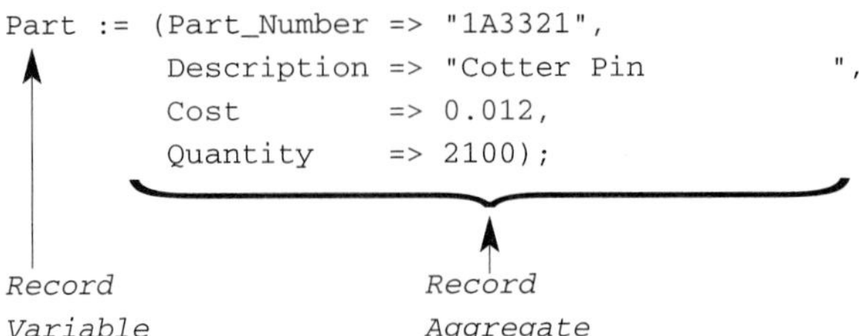
Part := (Part_Number => "1A3321",
Description => "Cotter Pin   ",
Cost   => 0.012,
Quantity   => 2100);
Record
Variable
Record
Aggregate

This one assignment statement is equivalent to the following four assignment statements.

```
Part.Part_Number := "1A3321";
Part.Description := "Cotter Pin          ";
Part.Cost        :=  0.012;
Part.Quantity    :=  2100;
```

The aggregate values in the first example are associated with the appropriate record components through *named association*. The order of the values in an aggregate that uses named association is not important. We can also make the association between values and components through *positional association* as illustrated here.

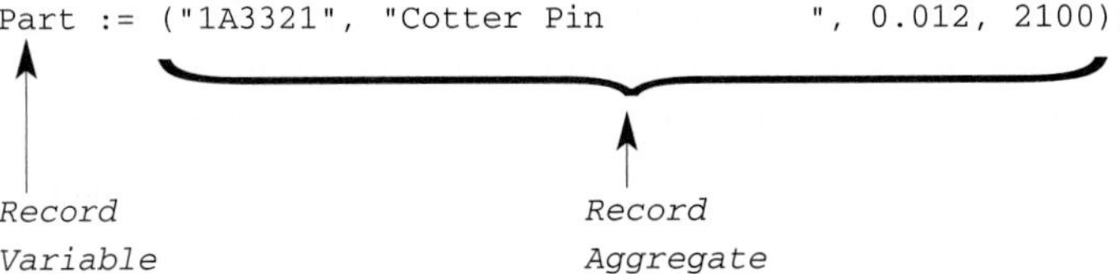
Part := ("1A3321", "Cotter Pin   ", 0.012, 2100);
Record
Variable
Record
Aggregate

With positional association, the first value of the aggregate is assigned to the first component of the record, the second value of the aggregate is assigned to the second component of the record, and so on.

We can use a record aggregate as an actual parameter for a function or procedure. The corresponding formal parameter must have mode *in* because there is no variable to which to copy a result back. Here is a code fragment that shows a call to a procedure that displays all the components of a part record.

```
procedure Put (Item: in Part_Rec) is
   -- Our own Put procedure for Part records
   -- This procedure displays all the components of the given Part
begin
   Ada.Text_IO.Put_Line ("Part number  : "  &  Item.Part_Number);
   Ada.Text_IO.Put_Line ("Description  : "  &  Item.Part_Description);
   Ada.Text_IO.Put      ("Cost         : ");
   Dollar_IO.Put        (Item => Item.Cost,  Fore => 3,
```

```
                          Aft  => 3,          Exp  => 0);
   Ada.Text_IO.New_Line;
   Ada.Text_IO.Put ("Quantity     : ");
   Ada.Integer_Text_IO.Put (Item => Item.Quantity,  Width => 1);
   Ada.Text_IO.New_Line;
end Put;

   .
   .
   .

-- Call procedure Put
Put (Item => (Part_Number => "1A3321",
              Description => "Cotter Pin          ",
              Cost        => 0.012,
              Quantity    => 2100) );

   Formal      Actual parameter is an aggregate
   parameter
```

Files of Records

Although single records can be useful, many applications require a collection of records. For example, a business needs a list of parts records, and a teacher needs a list of students in a class. Files are ideal for these applications. We simply define a sequential or direct file whose elements are records. Because each read or write operation with sequential and direct files transfers one element of the file, a program reads or writes an entire record with a single I/O call.

Let's define a grade book to be a list of students as follows:

```
-- Types
type    Letter_Grade_Type  is (A, B, C, D, F);
subtype Percent            is Integer range 0..100;
subtype GPA_Type           is Float   range 0.00..4.00;
subtype Name_String        is String (1..15);

type Student_Rec is
   record
      First_Name    : Name_String;
      Last_Name     : Name_String;
      GPA           : GPA_Type;
      Program_Grade : Percent;
      Quiz_Grade    : Percent;
      Final_Exam    : Percent;
      Course_Grade  : Letter_Grade_Type;
   end record;
```

```
-- Instantiate package for Student_Rec I/O
package Student_IO is new Ada.Direct_IO (Element_Type => Student_Rec);

-- Variables
New_GPA    : GPA_Type;
Student    : Student_Rec;
Grade_Book : Student_IO.File_Type;
```

Figure 10-3 illustrates the structure of the file Grade_Book.

The file in Figure 10-3 has 150 elements, each of which is a record. Figure 10-3 shows the layout of one record in the file. We access the elements in this file with the read and write procedures in package Student_IO. The following code fragment changes the sixth student's GPA without changing any of the other components in the record.

```
Student_IO.Read  (File => Grade_Book,    -- Obtain old student information
                  Item => Student,
                  From => 6);
Student.GPA := New_GPA;                  -- Modify the student's GPA
Student_IO.Write (File => Grade_Book,    -- Put the record back in the file
                  Item => Student,
                  To   => 6);
```

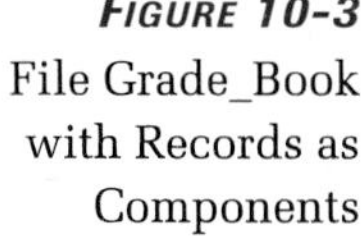

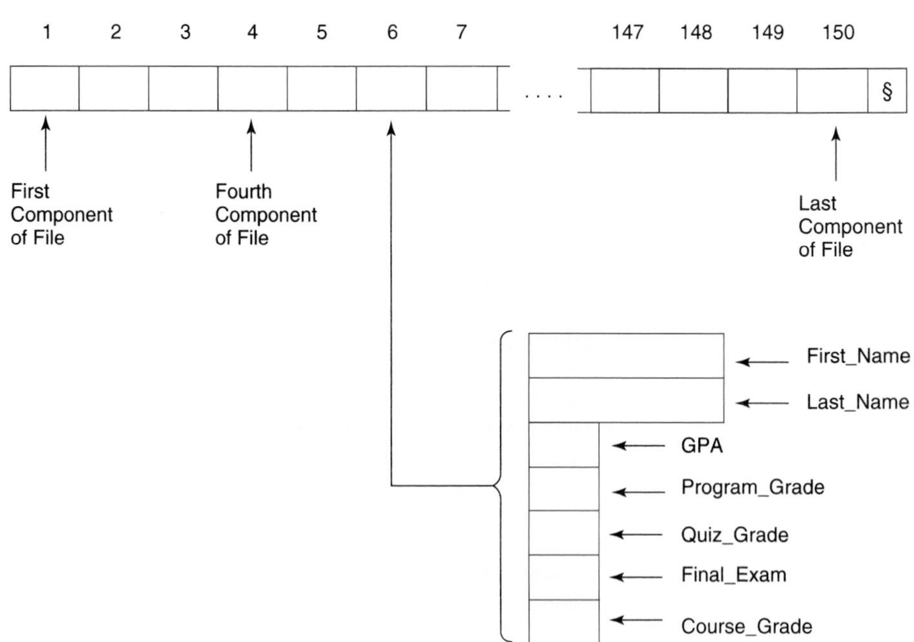

FIGURE 10-3 File Grade_Book with Records as Components

The following code fragment prints the first and last name of each student in the class by processing the record elements in the file Grade_Book sequentially.

```
Student_IO.Set_Index (File => Grade_Book  To => 1);
Print_Loop:          -- Display all the student names in the file
loop                 -- Each iteration, one student name is displayed
   exit Print_Loop when Student_IO.End_Of_File (Grade_Book);
   Student_IO.Read  (File => Grade_Book,          -- Obtain next student's
                     Item => Student);            -- information
   Ada.Text_IO.Put (Student.First_Name & ' ');  -- Display the student's
   Ada.Text_IO.Put_Line (Student.Last_Name);     -- name
end loop Print_Loop;
```

Don't forget that direct and sequential files are binary files and that binary files are stored using the internal representation of the machine. They must be built by a program. A text editor like the one you use to enter Ada programs only operates with text files. Do not use your text editor to view or edit binary files.

Hierarchical Records

Just as the components of a file can be of any type, so can the components of a record. A component of a record can also be another record. Records whose components are themselves records are called **hierarchical records.**

Hierarchical records Records in which at least one of the components is itself a record.

Let's look at an example where a hierarchical structure is appropriate. A small machine shop keeps information about each of its machines. There is descriptive information, such as the identification number, a description of the machine, the purchase date, and the cost. Statistical information is also kept, such as the number of down days, the failure rate, and the date of last service. What is a reasonable way to represent all this information? First, let's look at a flat (nonhierarchical) record structure that holds this information.

```
-- Types
subtype Description_String is String (1..40);
subtype ID_Range is Integer range 0..999_999;
subtype Percent  is Float range 0.0 .. 100.0;
type    Dollars  is delta 0.01 digits 7 range 0.00 .. 99_999.99;
```

```
type Machine_Rec is
   record
      ID_Number            : ID_Range;
      Description          : Description_String;
      Fail_Rate            : Percent;
      Last_Serviced_Month : Ada.Calendar.Month_Number;
      Last_Serviced_Day    : Ada.Calendar.Day_Number;
      Last_Serviced_Year   : Ada.Calendar.Year_Number;
      Down_Days            : Natural;
      Purchase_Date_Month : Ada.Calendar.Month_Number;
      Purchase_Date_Day    : Ada.Calendar.Day_Number;
      Purchase_Date_Year   : Ada.Calendar.Year_Number;
      Cost                 : Dollars;
   end record;

-- Variables
Machine : Machine_Rec;
```

Type Machine_Rec has 11 components. There is so much detailed information here that it is difficult to get a quick feeling for what the record represents.

Let's see if we can reorganize this lengthy record into a hierarchical structure that makes more sense. We can divide the information into two groups—information that changes and information that does not. We also need to keep two dates—date of purchase and date of last service. These observations suggest use of a record describing a date, a record describing the statistical data, and an overall record containing the other two as components. The following type declarations reflect this structure.

```
-- Types
subtype Description_String is String (1..40);
subtype ID_Range is Integer range 0..999_999;
subtype Percent  is Float range 0.0 .. 100.0;
type    Dollars  is delta 0.01 digits 7 range 0.00 .. 99_999.99;

type Date_Rec is
   record
      Month : Ada.Calendar.Month_Number;
      Day   : Ada.Calendar.Day_Number;
      Year  : Ada.Calendar.Year_Number;
   end record;

type Statistics_Rec is
   record
      Fail_Rate      : Percent;
      Last_Serviced : Date_Rec;
      Down_Days      : Natural;
   end record;

type Machine_Rec is
   record
```

```
      ID_Number      : ID_Range;
      Description    : Description_String;
      History        : Statistics_Rec;
      Purchase_Date  : Date_Rec;
      Cost           : Dollars;
   end record;

-- Instantiate package for Machine I/O
package Machine_IO is new Direct_IO (Element_Type => Machine_Rec);

-- Variables
Machine          : Machine_Rec;
Inventory_File   : Machine_IO.File_Type;
Today            : Ada.Calendar.Time;    -- Time and date from package calendar
Current_Year     : Ada.Calendar.Year;
No_Service_Count : Natural;
```

The contents of a machine record are now much more obvious. Two of the components of the record type Machine_Rec are themselves records. Purchase_Date is of record type Date_Rec, and History is of record type Statistics_Rec. One of the components of the record type Statistics_Rec is a record of type Date_Rec.

How do we access a hierarchical structure such as this one? We build the names (selected components) of the embedded records from left to right, beginning with the record variable name. Following are some selected component names and the components they access.

Name	**Component Accessed**
`Machine.Purchase_Date`	Date_Rec record variable
`Machine.Purchase_Date.Month`	Month component of a Date_Rec record variable
`Machine.Purchase_Date.Year`	Year component of a Date_Rec record variable
`Machine.History.Last_ Serviced.Year`	Year component of a Date_Rec record variable contained in a record of type Statistics_Rec

Figure 10-4 is a pictorial representation of Machine with values. Look carefully at how each component is accessed.

We can, of course, have a file of hierarchical records. Inventory_File is such a file. We can display the year that the first machine was purchased using the following code.

```
Machine_IO.Read (File => Inventory_File,
                 Item => Machine,
                 From => 1);
Ada.Integer_Text_IO.Put (Item => Machine.Purchase_Date.Year);
```

FIGURE 10-4
Hierarchical Records in Machine

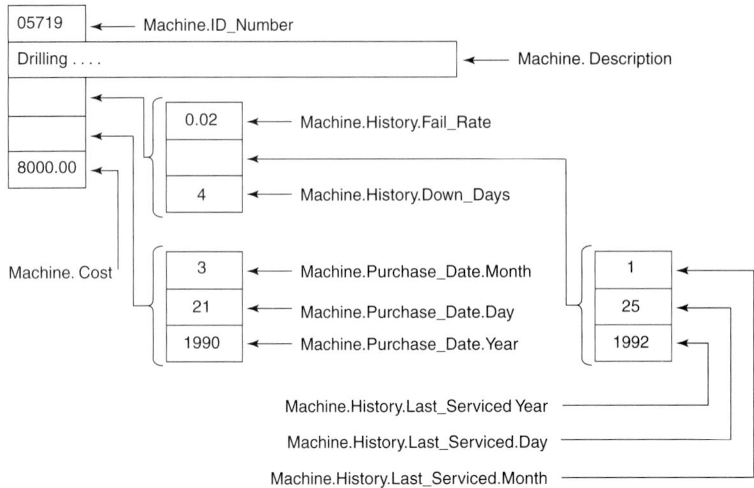

Let's look at another example using this file of hierarchical records. The following code fragment prints out the ID number and date of purchase of each machine with a failure rate of more than 8%. It also prints the total number of machines that have not been serviced within the current year.

```
-- Call function Clock to get the date and time from the computer's clock
Today := Ada.Calendar.Clock;
-- Call function Year to extract the year from the current date and time
Current_Year := Ada.Calendar.Year (Today);

No_Service_Count := 0;   -- Count of machines with no service this year
-- Start at the beginning of the file
Machine_IO.Set_Index (File => Inventory_File  To => 1);

Check_Failure_Loop:   -- Check every machine in the file
loop                  -- Each iteration, the failure rate and service
                      -- date of one machine is checked
   exit Check_Failure_Loop when Machine_IO.End_Of_File (Machine_File);
   Machine_IO.Read (File => Inventory_File,    -- Read a machine record
                    Item => Machine)
   if Machine.History.Fail_Rate > 0.08 then    -- Check failure rate
      Ada.Integer_Text_IO.Put (Item => Machine.ID_Number, Width => 1);
      Ada.Text_IO.Put ("    ");
      Put (Machine.Purchase_Date);             -- Call our Put for type Date_Rec
      Ada.Text_IO.New_Line;
   end if;
```

```
   -- Check to see whether the machine was serviced this year
   if Machine.History.Last_Serviced.Year /= Current_Year then
      No_Service_Count := No_Service_Count + 1;
   end if;
end loop Check_Failure_Loop;

Ada.Text_IO.Put ("The number of machines not requiring service this year: ");
Ada.Integer_Text_IO.Put (Item => No_Service_Count,  Width => 1);
Ada.Text_IO.New_Line;
```

This code fragment calls a Put procedure to display a date. The actual parameter used in this call is a component of the Machine_Rec that is itself a record. Here is the code for this Put procedure.

```
procedure Put (Item : in Date_Rec) is
   -- Display a date in the form mm/dd/yy
begin
   Ada.Integer_Text_IO.Put (Item => Item.Month,  Width => 1);
   Ada.Text_IO.Put ('/');
   Ada.Integer_Text_IO.Put (Item => Item.Day,  Width => 1);
   Ada.Text_IO.Put ('/');
   Ada.Integer_Text_IO.Put (Item => Item.Year rem 100,  Width => 1);
end Put;
```

Like simple records, hierarchical records may be used as parameters. Here, for example, is a call to a Put procedure that displays all the information in the hierarchical machine record variable Machine.

```
Put (Item => Machine);
```

And here is the code of this Put procedure.

```
procedure Put (Item : in Machine_Rec) is

-- This procedure displays the information in a machine record

begin
   Ada.Text_IO.Put_Line (Item.Description);
   Ada.Text_IO.Put ("   ID number       : ");
   Ada.Integer_Text_IO.Put (Item => Item.ID_Number, Width => 1);
   Ada.Text_IO.New_Line;
   Ada.Text_IO.Put ("   Failure rate    : ");
   Ada.Float_Text_IO.Put (Item => Item.History.Fail_Rate,
                          Fore => 1,  Aft  => 2,  Exp  => 0);
   Ada.Text_IO.New_Line;
   Ada.Text_IO.Put ("   Last serviced  : ");
   Put (Item.History.Last_Serviced);      -- Call Put for type Date_Rec
   Ada.Text_IO.New_Line;
```

```
   Ada.Text_IO.Put ("    Days down       : ");
   Ada.Integer_Text_IO.Put (Item => Item.History.Down_Days,  Width => 1);
   Ada.Text_IO.New_Line;
   Ada.Text_IO.Put ("    Purchased       : ");
   Put (Item.Purchase_Date);                  -- Call Put for type Date_Rec
   Ada.Text_IO.New_Line;
   Ada.Text_IO.Put ("    Purchase price : $");
   Dollar_IO.Put (Item => Item.Cost,   Fore => 1,
                  Aft  => 2,           Exp  => 0);
   Ada.Text_IO.New_Line;
end Put;
```

Hierarchical Record Aggregates

Just as a component in a record can be another record, the components of a record aggregate can be record aggregates. The following example uses the declarations of the previous section.

```
Machine  :=  (ID_Number      =>  174553,
              Description    => "Horizontal Boring Machine                ",
              History        => (Fail_Rate      => 0.012,
                                 Last_Serviced => (Month => 8,
                                                   Day   => 21,
                                                   Year  => 1997),
                                 Down_Days      => 5),

              Purchase_Date => (Month => 6,
                                Day   => 17,
                                Year  => 1971),
              Cost           => 8_450.00);
```

Machine.Purchase_Date is a record component that is assigned an aggregate value. Machine.History is a record component that contains another record component. The structure of the aggregate assigned to Machine.History matches that of the component. The following is an equivalent assignment statement that uses positional association rather than named association.

```
Machine := (174553, "Horizontal Boring Machine                ",
             (0.012, (8, 21, 1992), 5), (6, 17 1971), 8_450.00);
```

Although this assignment statement is considerably shorter, it is more difficult to read.

Data Structures

The record is a collection of data elements. As we saw in the last section, these elements also may be records. There are usually a number of different ways that we can organize the elements in a record. The way we structure the data affects how the individual data values are accessed. **Data structures** play an important role in the design process. The choice of data structure directly affects the design because it determines the algorithms used to process the data.

Data structure A collection of data elements whose organization determines the methods by which the individual elements are accessed.

Style Considerations in Choice of Data Structures

Just as there are style considerations in writing programs, there are also style considerations in choosing data structures. A program can produce a correct answer; but, if it is difficult to debug, read, or modify, it can still be a poor program. We can use a data structure to solve a problem, and yet it still may not reflect accurately the relationships within the problem. If the data structure does not reflect these relationships, it is not an effective structure for that program.

A data structure is a framework for holding data. We should tailor this framework to each particular problem by reflecting the relationships among data values, making it easy for users to see how the data items are related and how they should be processed to produce the required output. Because each problem is different, it is difficult to give a set of rules by which to judge an effective data structure. Instead, we examine the choices within a specific context, discuss the issues involved, and make some generalizations.

We have demonstrated how we design our algorithms and the structure of our data in parallel. We progress from the logical or abstract data structure envisioned at the top level through the refinement process until we reach the concrete coding in Ada. We have also shown two ways to represent the logical structure of a machine record in a shop inventory. The first used a record where all the components in an entry were defined at the same level. The second used a hierarchical record where the dates and statistics describing a machine's history were defined in lower-level records.

Let's look again at the two different structures we declared to represent our machine object.

```
-- Types
subtype Description_String is String (1..40);
subtype ID_Range is Integer range 0..999_999;
subtype Percent  is Float range 0.0 .. 100.0;
type    Dollars  is delta 0.01 digits 7 range 0.00 .. 99_999.99;
```

—1—

```
type Machine_Rec is
   record
      ID_Number            : ID_Range;
      Description          : Description_String;
      Fail_Rate            : Percent;
      Last_Serviced_Month  : Ada.Calendar.Month_Number;
      Last_Serviced_Day    : Ada.Calendar.Day_Number;
      Last_Serviced_Year   : Ada.Calendar.Year_Number;
      Down_Days            : Natural;
      Purchase_Date_Month  : Ada.Calendar.Month_Number;
      Purchase_Date_Day    : Ada.Calendar.Day_Number;
      Purchase_Date_Year   : Ada.Calendar.Year_Number;
      Cost                 : Dollars;
   end record;
```

—2—

```
type Date_Rec is
   record
      Month : Ada.Calendar.Month_Number;
      Day   : Ada.Calendar.Day_Number;
      Year  : Ada.Calendar.Year_Number;
   end record;

type Statistics_Rec is
   record
      Fail_Rate      : Percent;
      Last_Serviced  : Date_Rec;
      Down_Days      : Natural;
   end record;

type Machine_Rec is
record
      ID_Number      : ID_Range;
      Description    : Description_String;
      History        : Statistics_Rec;
      Purchase_Date  : Date_Rec;
      Cost           : Dollars;
   end record;
```

Which of these two representations is better? The second one is better for two reasons.

First, it groups elements together logically. The statistics and the dates are entities within themselves. We may want to have a date or a machine history in another record structure. If we define the dates and statistics only within Machine_Rec (as in the first structure), we would have to define them again for every other data structure that needs them, giving us multiple definitions of the same logical entity.

Second, the details of the objects (statistics and dates) are pushed down to a lower level in the second structure. The principle of deferring details to as low a level as possible should be applied to designing data structures as well as to designing algorithms. How a machine history or a date is represented is not relevant to our concept of a machine record, so the details need not be specified until it is time to write the algorithms to manipulate those components.

Pushing the implementation details of a data structure to a lower level separates the logical description from the implementation. This concept is analogous to control abstraction, which we discussed in Chapter 6. The separation of the logical properties of a data structure from its implementation details is called **data abstraction,** which is a goal of effective programming.

Data abstraction The separation of a data structure's logical properties from its implementation.

Eventually, we must define all the logical properties in terms of concrete data types and write routines to manipulate them. If we have designed the implementation properly, we can use the same routines to manipulate the structure in a wide variety of applications. For example, if we have a routine to compare dates, we can use that routine to compare dates representing days on which equipment was bought or maintained or dates representing people's birthdays.

Data structures that accurately reflect the relationships among the data values in a problem lead to effective programs. The logic of the program is easier to understand because the data structures mirror the problem. The code of the program is easier to maintain because the logic of the program is clearer. The program is easier to modify because the data structure accurately represents the problem.

We should make one additional point here. The best structure is the simplest one that accurately reflects the problem and the processing. Don't use a record if simple variables suffice.

PROBLEM-SOLVING CASE STUDY

Department Store Accounts

Specification

Problem The customer credit manager of the Chippendale Department Stores has requested a new program to perform the weekly update of the customer account file. This account file contains information on all of the customers who have charge accounts with the company. A customer's account must be changed when a purchase is charged or a payment is made. An account must also be changed when the credit manager raises or lowers a customer's credit limit. The data entry staff enters all changes into a text file. Once a week the items in this text file are used to bring the accounts up to date.

Input

- A sequential file (Old Master File) containing an account number, a name, an address, a credit limit, and a current balance for each customer.
- A text file (Transaction File). Each line in this file contains the information for a single customer transaction. This information includes
  - Account Number—A unique number that identifies the customer.
  - Transaction Type—The word Payment, Charge, or Limit.
  - Transaction Amount—A positive float value.

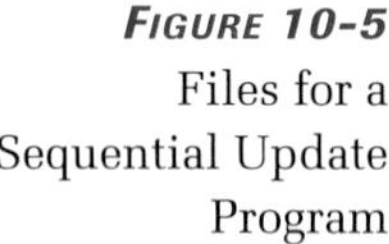
FIGURE 10-5 Files for a Sequential Update Program

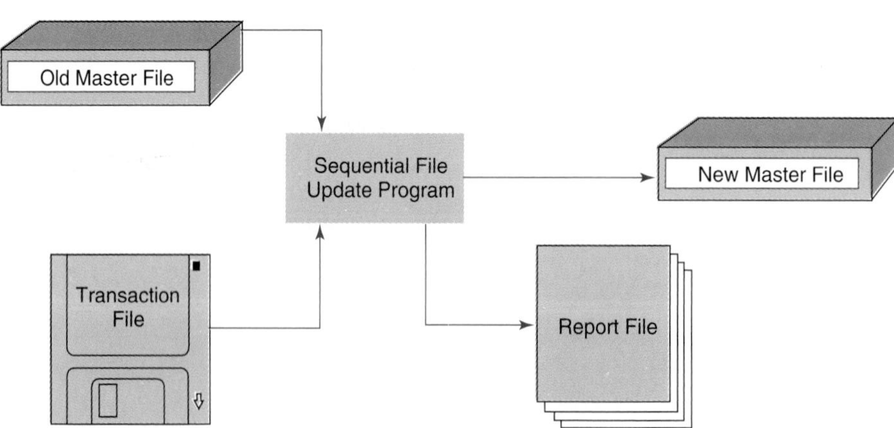

PROBLEM-SOLVING CASE STUDY cont'd.

Output

- A new sequential file (New Master) that contains all of the updated customer account information.
- A text file containing a line for each customer whose balance is over his or her assigned credit limit. This line should contain the account number, customer name, and the amount the balance is over the credit limit.

Discussion This is a classic problem in batch processing known as the *sequential file update* problem. Remember that, in batch processing, the user and the computer do not interact during the actual processing. Data for such processing comes from files, and the output is placed into files. Four files are used in updating a sequential file. The Old Master File contains the customer accounts from the last time the program was run. The

FIGURE 10-6A Sample Old Master File (Only Account Numbers and Balances Are Shown for Each Customer)

451	458	470	581		. . .		1951	2003	§
.	.	.	.				.	.	
.	.	.	.				.	.	
$0.00	$57.77	$184.64	$329.21				$896.75	$5.55	

FIGURE 10-6B Sample Transaction File

458	Payment	57.77
581	Charge	13.75
581	Charge	145.62
581	Charge	7.21
581	Payment	350.00
581	Charge	12.97
1951	Payment	100.00
1951	Charge	37.91
1951	Limit	500.00
1951	Payment	250.00

FIGURE 10-6C Sample New Master File (Only Account Numbers and Balances Are Shown for Each Customer)

451	458	470	581		. . .		1951	2003	§
.	.	.	.				.	.	
.	.	.	.				.	.	
$0.00	$0.00	$184.64	$158.76				$584.66	$5.55	

PROBLEM-SOLVING CASE STUDY cont'd.

Transaction File contains the changes to be made to the customer accounts. The New Master File contains the updated customer accounts. Finally, the Report File contains any messages about unusual cases (such as a customer being over his or her credit limit). Figure 10-5 shows these files in relation to the update program, and Figure 10-6 shows some sample contents of the Old Master File, Transaction File, and New Master File. The next time the update program is run, the New Master File becomes the Old Master File.

The components in the master files are in order by account number. The lines in the transaction file are also in order by account number. Although there is only one component for each customer in the master files, there may be none, one, or many transactions for a customer in the transaction file.

Because our program is reading an existing sequential file, we must know how the records are defined. Here are the types used in the program that created the original master file. The components in the file are of type Customer_Rec.

```
subtype Name_String    is String (1..20);
subtype Address_String is String (1..40);
subtype State_String   is String (1..2);
subtype Zip_String     is String (1..5);
type    Dollars is delta 0.01 digits 6 range 0.00 .. 9_999.99;

type Name_Rec is
   record
     First : Name_String;
     Last  : Name_String;
   end record;

type Address_Rec is
   record
      Street : Address_String;
      City   : Address_String;
      State  : State_String;
      Zip    : Zip_String;
   end record;

type Customer_Rec is
   record
      Account_Number : Positive;
      Name           : Name_Rec;
      Address        : Address_Rec;
      Credit_Limit   : Dollars;
      Balance        : Dollars;
   end record;
```

PROBLEM-SOLVING CASE STUDY cont'd.

We will need a loop to process the accounts in the Old Master File. Every record in this file must be copied over to the New Master File. This is the main loop of the program; the program terminates when we reach the end of the Old Master File. During each iteration of this loop, the program reads an account, processes all transactions for the account, and writes the updated account to the New Master File. If the new balance is over the customer's credit limit, a line for that customer is written to the Report File. This logic is expressed in Level 0 of our design.

Because there can be many transactions for a single account, we will need a second loop to process all the transactions for each account. If there are no transactions for a particular account, the program will execute the loop zero times. It must therefore be a pretest loop. This loop is an event-controlled loop; it terminates when a transaction for the next account is encountered. Thus a new account number acts as a sentinel value for the loop. Unlike previous sentinel loops, the sentinel value is also valid data. It must be saved and used to update a future account. A priming get is used to simplify the logic of saving the sentinel value.

If the last customers in the Old Master File do not have any transactions to process, we will reach end of file in the Transaction File before we reach end of file in the Old Master File. In this case, we must continue to process the accounts in the Old Master File. We check for the end of the Transaction File, and when it is encountered we assign a value to the transaction account number that will not be matched by a master account number.

Assumptions

- Each file is in order by account number.
- For every account number in the Transaction File there is a corresponding account in the Old Master file.
- All numbers in the Transaction File are valid.
- No customer has Integer'Last as an account number.

Design

Update **Level 0**

```
Prepare Files
Get the first Transaction Account Number
loop
   exit when end of Old Master File
   Read account from the Old Master
   Process all transactions for this one account
   Check Account Balance
   Write the modified account to the New Master
end loop
Close files
```

PROBLEM-SOLVING CASE STUDY *cont'd.*

Prepare Files **Level 1**

```
   in out    Old_Master
   in out    New_Master
   in out    Transaction
   in out    Report
Open Old Master File
Open Transaction File
Create New Master File
Create Report File
```

Process All Transactions for Account **Level 1**

```
   in out    Account_Number
   in out    Transaction_File
   in out    Customer
loop
   exit when Transaction Account Number /= Old Master Account Number
   Process One Transaction
   Get next Transaction Account Number
end loop
```

Check Account Balance **Level 1**

```
   in        Customer
   in out    Report_File
if Customer.Balance > Customer.Credit_Limit then
   Put Customer.Account_Number to Report_File
   Put Customer.Name to Report_File
   Put Amount Over Credit_Limit to Report_File
end if
```

Process One Transaction **Level 2**

```
   in out    Transact_File
   in out    Customer
Get Transaction Type
Get Transaction Amount
case Transaction Type is
   when Payment
      Customer.Balance := Customer.Balance - Amount
   when Charge
      Customer.Balance := Customer.Balance + Amount
   when Limit
      Customer.Credit_Limit := Amount
```

PROBLEM-SOLVING CASE STUDY cont'd.

Module Structure Chart

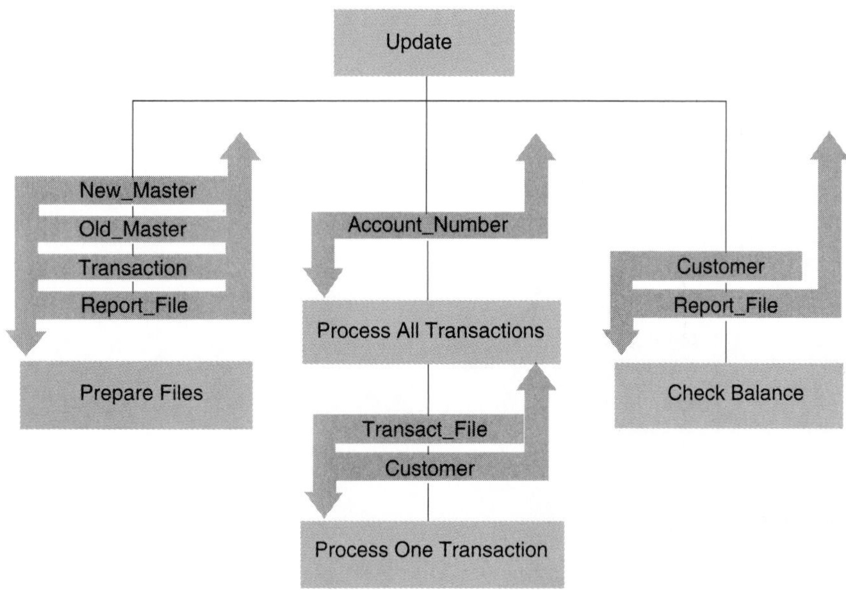

Implementation

```
with Ada.Sequential_IO;
with Ada.Integer_Text_IO;
with Ada.Text_IO;
procedure Update is

-- This program performs an update of a sequential master file

-- Assumptions: Each file is in order by account number.
--              For every account number in the transaction file there is
--                 a corresponding account in the Old Master file.
--              All numbers in the transaction file are valid.
--              No customer has Integer'Last as their account number.

   type    Transaction_Type is (Payment, Charge, Limit);
   subtype Name_String      is String (1..20);
   subtype Address_String   is String (1..40);
   subtype State_String     is String (1..2);
   subtype Zip_String       is String (1..5);
   type    Dollars          is delta 0.01 digits 6 range 0.00 .. 9_999.99;
```

```
type Name_Rec is
   record
     First : Name_String;
     Last  : Name_String;
   end record;

type Address_Rec is
record
   Street : Address_String;
   City   : Address_String;
   State  : State_String;
   Zip    : Zip_String;
end record;

type Customer_Rec is
   record
      Account_Number : Positive;
      Name           : Name_Rec;
      Address        : Address_Rec;
      Credit_Limit   : Dollars;
      Balance        : Dollars;
   end record;

-- Instantiate I/O Packages
package Customer_IO is new Ada.Sequential_IO
                           (Element_Type => Customer_Rec);
package Choice_IO   is new Ada.Text_IO.Enumeration_IO
                           (Enum => Transaction_Type);
package Dollar_IO   is new Ada.Text_IO.Decimal_IO
                           (Num => Dollars);

 -------------------------------------------
procedure Prepare_Files
   (Old_Master  : in out Customer_IO.File_Type;  -- Accounts before update
    New_Master  : in out Customer_IO.File_Type;  -- Accounts after update
    Transaction : in out Ada.Text_IO.File_Type;      -- Changes to accounts
    Report      : in out Ada.Text_IO.File_Type) is   -- Update report

-- This procedure prepares all of the files for the sequential file update

begin    -- Prepare Files
   Customer_IO.Open (File => Old_Master,
                     Mode => Customer_IO.In_File,
                     Name => "Old_Master.Dat");
   Customer_IO.Create (File => New_Master,
                       Mode => Customer_IO.Out_File,
                       Name => "New_Master.Dat");
   Ada.Text_IO.Open (File => Transaction,
                     Mode => Ada.Text_IO.In_File,
```

PROBLEM-SOLVING CASE STUDY cont'd.

```
                    Name => "Transaction.Txt");
   Ada.Text_IO.Create (File => Report,
                       Mode => Ada.Text_IO.Out_File,
                       Name => "Report.Txt");
end Prepare_Files;

-------------------------------------------
procedure Check_Account_Balance
   (Customer    : in     Customer_Rec;      -- Customer account information
    Report_File : in out Ada.Text_IO.File_Type) is      -- For messages

-- This procedure writes a message to the report file
-- if the customer has exceeded the credit limit.

begin    -- Check Account Balance
   if Customer.Balance > Customer.Credit_Limit then
      Ada.Integer_Text_IO.Put (File  => Report_File,
                               Item  => Customer.Account_Number,
                               Width => 10);
      Ada.Text_IO.Put (File => Report_File,
                       Item => ' ');
      Ada.Text_IO.Put (File => Report_File,
                       Item => Customer.Name.First);
      Ada.Text_IO.Put (File => Report_File,
                       Item => Customer.Name.Last);
      Dollar_IO.Put (File => Report_File,
                     Item => Customer.Balance - Customer.Credit_Limit,
                     Fore => 8,  Aft  => 2,  Exp  => 0);
      Ada.Text_IO.New_Line (Report_File);
   end if;
end Check_Account_Balance;

-------------------------------------------
procedure Process_One_Transaction
     (Transact_File  : in out Ada.Text_IO.File_Type;    -- Transactions
      Customer       : in out Customer_Rec) is          -- The account record

   Choice : Transaction_Type;   -- What kind of transaction
   Amount : Dollars;            -- The amount of the transaction

begin
      -- Get the kind and amount of transaction
      Choice_IO.Get (File => Transact_File, Item => Choice);
      Dollar_IO.Get (File => Transact_File, Item => Amount);
      Ada.Text_IO.Skip_Line (Transact_File);              -- Finish the line
```

PROBLEM-SOLVING CASE STUDY cont'd.

```
      -- Modify the customer record
      case Choice is
         when Payment =>
            Customer.Balance := Customer.Balance - Amount;
         when Charge =>
            Customer.Balance := Customer.Balance + Amount;
         when Limit =>
            Customer.Credit_Limit := Amount;
      end case;
   end Process_One_Transaction;

   ----------------------------------------
   procedure Process_All_Transactions
        (Account_Number : in out Positive; -- The account number being processed
         Transact_File  : in out Ada.Text_IO.File_Type;     -- Transactions
         Customer       : in out Customer_Rec) is           -- The account record

   -- This procedure processes all the transactions for one customer account

   begin    -- Process all transactions
      Transact_Loop:  -- Each iteration, one transaction is processed
      loop
         exit Transact_Loop when Account_Number /= Customer.Account_Number;
         -- Process a transaction for this customer
         Process_One_Transaction (Transact_File => Transact_File,
                                  Customer      => Customer);
         -- Get the account number of the next transaction
         if not Ada.Text_IO.End_Of_File (Transact_File) then
            Ada.Integer_Text_IO.Get (File => Transact_File,
                                     Item => Account_Number);
         else                                       -- No more transactions so assign
            Account_Number := Positive'Last;  -- an impossible account number
         end if;
      end loop Transact_Loop;
   end Process_All_Transactions;

----------------------------------------
   New_Master   : Customer_IO.File_Type;   -- Updated account records
   Old_Master   : Customer_IO.FIle_Type;   -- Old account records
   Transaction  : Ada.Text_IO.File_Type;   -- Changes to accounts
   Report       : Ada.Text_IO.File_Type;   -- Customers over their limits

   Account_Number : Positive;       -- The account number of the transaction
   Customer       : Customer_Rec;  -- The customer record for the current account
```

PROBLEM-SOLVING CASE STUDY cont'd.

```
begin    -- Program Update
   Prepare_Files (Old_Master  => Old_Master,
                  New_Master  => New_Master,
                  Transaction => Transaction,
                  Report      => Report);
   -- Priming read of first transaction
   if not Ada.Text_IO.End_Of_File (Transaction) then
      Ada.Integer_Text_IO.Get (File => Transaction, Item => Account_Number);
   else                                    -- No more transactions so assign
      Account_Number := Positive'Last;     -- an impossible account number
   end if;

   Acct_Loop:     -- Process all the accounts in the Old Master file
   loop           -- Each iteration, one old master account is processed
      exit Acct_Loop when Customer_IO.End_Of_File (Old_Master);
      -- Get the old account information for the next customer
      Customer_IO.Read (File => Old_Master, Item => Customer);
      -- Process all the transactions for this customer
      Process_All_Transactions (Account_Number => Account_Number,
                                Transact_File  => Transaction,
                                Customer       => Customer);
      -- Check to make sure the customer is not over the credit limit
      Check_Account_Balance (Customer    => Customer,
                             Report_File => Report);
      -- Put the updated account information into the new master file
      Customer_IO.Write (File => New_Master, Item => Customer);
   end loop Acct_Loop;

   -- Close all files
  Customer_IO.Close (Old_Master);
  Customer_IO.Close (New_Master);
  Ada.Text_IO.Close (Transaction);
  Ada.Text_IO.Close (Report);
end Update;
```

Testing Testing this program requires two input files—an Old Master File and a Transaction File. As a programmer working for the Chippendale Department Stores, we can just make a copy of the current master file to use as test data for an Old Master File. (Note that if no master file has been created previously, we must write a program to create such a file from data entered as text.) We can use an editor to prepare different transaction files for testing our update program.

Checking the output of our program requires some extra work. Because the report file is a text file, we can print it or display it on our screen. The New Master File, however, is a binary file, and we cannot print it or display it directly on the screen. We need to write a separate program to read

PROBLEM-SOLVING CASE STUDY cont'd.

and display the contents of a master file. Because the Old Master File and the New Master File contain the same type of components, we can use this display program to display the contents of either one. A sample display program is given in the Testing and Debugging section later in this chapter.

There are a number of different tests that we must carry out with this program.

1. We need to test that the three different transaction choices (Charge, Payment, and Limit) correctly update a customer record.
2. We need to test zero, one, and multiple transactions for a single account.
3. We need to test that accounts with no transactions are unchanged in the New Master File.
4. Finally, we need to test the termination of the program by running it with a Transaction File that contains transactions for the last account in the Old Master File and a Transaction File that does not contain any transactions for the last account.

Testing and Debugging

The record is one mechanism for associating a single identifier with a group of values. We use the same techniques for testing and debugging programs with records that we used with atomic data types. We just need to consider all the values that a particular record might take.

As we have demonstrated in several examples, hierarchical records simplify the logical design of a program, but they make the coding more complicated. The deeper the nesting of a structure, the longer the selected component becomes.

We commonly use records as components for sequential and direct files. Since we cannot display or print sequential and direct files, when working with files of records, it is often necessary to write our own programs to create and display the contents of a file. Here is a sample program to display the contents of the master files used in this chapter's Department Store example. You can use this program to print the contents of the old and new master files to confirm that the update program operates correctly.

```
with Ada.Sequential_IO;
with Ada.Integer_Text_IO;
with Ada.Text_IO;
procedure Display is
```

```
-- This program displays a master file of customer accounts

   type    Transaction_Type is (Payment, Charge, Limit);
   subtype Name_String      is String (1..20);
   subtype Address_String   is String (1..40);
   subtype State_String     is String (1..2);
   subtype Zip_String       is String (1..5);
   type    Dollars          is delta 0.01 digits 6 range 0.00 .. 9_999.99;

   type Name_Rec is
      record
        First : Name_String;
        Last  : Name_String;
      end record;

   type Address_Rec is
   record
      Street : Address_String;
      City   : Address_String;
      State  : State_String;
      Zip    : Zip_String;
   end record;

   type Customer_Rec is
      record
         Account_Number : Positive;
         Name           : Name_Rec;
         Address        : Address_Rec;
         Credit_Limit   : Dollars;
         Balance        : Dollars;
      end record;


   -- Instantiate I/O Packages

   package Customer_IO is new Ada.Sequential_IO
                              (Element_Type => Customer_Rec);
   package Choice_IO   is new Ada.Text_IO.Enumeration_IO
                              (Enum => Transaction_Type);
   package Dollar_IO   is new Ada.Text_IO.Decimal_IO
                              (Num => Dollars);

   -- Variables
   Master    : Customer_IO.File_Type;  -- File of account records
   Customer  : Customer_Rec;           -- One account record
   Count     : Integer;                -- Iteration counter
   File_Name : String (1..40);         -- External file name
```

```
begin  -- Program Display
   Ada.Text_IO.Put_Line ("Enter the name of the master file to display.");
   Ada.Text_IO.Get_Line (Item => File_Name, Last => Count);
   Customer_IO.Open (File => Master,
                     Mode => Customer_IO.In_File,
                     Name => File_Name (1..Count) );
   Ada.Text_IO.New_Line (2);
   Count := 1;
   Record_Loop:  -- Each iteration, one record is displayed
   loop
      exit Record_Loop when Customer_IO.End_Of_File (Master);
      Customer_IO.Read (File => Master, Item => Customer);
      Ada.Text_IO.Put ("Record #");
      Ada.Integer_Text_IO.Put (Item  => Count,
                               Width => 1);
      Ada.Text_IO.New_Line;
      Ada.Text_IO.Put_Line("---------");
      Ada.Text_IO.New_Line;
      Ada.Text_IO.Put_Line ("Account #");
      Ada.Text_IO.Put ("   ");
      Ada.Integer_Text_IO.Put (Item  => Customer.Account_Number,
                               Width => 1);
      Ada.Text_IO.New_Line;
      Ada.Text_IO.Put_Line ("Customer name");
      Ada.Text_IO.Put_Line ("   " & Customer.Name.First);
      Ada.Text_IO.Put_Line ("   " & Customer.Name.Last);
      Ada.Text_IO.Put_Line ("Customer address");
      Ada.Text_IO.Put_Line ("   " & Customer.Address.Street);
      Ada.Text_IO.Put_Line ("   " & Customer.Address.City);
      Ada.Text_IO.Put_Line ("   " & Customer.Address.State);
      Ada.Text_IO.Put ("   ");
      Ada.Text_IO.Put_Line (Customer.Address.Zip);
      Ada.Text_IO.Put_Line ("Credit Limit");
      Ada.Text_IO.Put ("   ");
      Dollar_IO.Put (Item  => Customer.Credit_Limit,
                     Fore  => 1,
                     Aft   => 2,
                     Exp   => 0);
      Ada.Text_IO.New_Line;
      Ada.Text_IO.Put_Line ("Balance");
      Ada.Text_IO.Put ("   ");
      Dollar_IO.Put (Item  => Customer.Balance,
                     Fore  => 1,
                     Aft   => 2,
                     Exp   => 0);
      Ada.Text_IO.New_Line;
      Ada.Text_IO.New_Line(2);
      Count := Count + 1;
```

```
      Ada.Text_IO.Put_Line ("Press Return to continue.");
      Ada.Text_IO.Skip_Line;    -- User must press Return to continue the display
   end loop Record_Loop;
end Display;
```

Testing and Debugging Hints

1. Be sure to specify the full selected component when referencing a component of a record variable.
2. Define subtypes for component types to take advantage of automatic range checking.
3. When using strings in records, be sure to include the index or range with the string name when accessing individual components or slices.
4. Process each component of a record separately, except when assigning one record variable to another, comparing two records for equality, or passing the record as a parameter.

Summary

The record is a useful data structure for grouping data relating to a single object. We can use a record variable to refer to the record as a whole, or we can use a selected component to access any individual component of the record. Records of the same type may be assigned directly to each other. We can compare records for equality with the = and /= operators. There are no other predefined relational operators available for record variables. Record I/O with text files must be done component by component. However, entire records are read from and written to sequential and direct files. Because the components of records can be of any type, we can build complex structures where the components of the records are themselves records.

We design our algorithms and data structures in parallel. Applying the top-down design techniques introduced in Chapter 3 to data structures is an example of data abstraction. The logical description of the data structure is at a higher level. The details of how the data structure is implemented are pushed down to a lower level.

Quick Check

1. Write the type definitions for a record data type called Clock_Time with three components called Hour, Minute, and Second. The data type for the Hour component is a subtype with a range from 0 through 23. The other two components contain subtypes with ranges from 0 through 59. (pp. 540–543)

2. Assume that a variable called Now, of type Clock_Time, has been defined. Write the assignment statements necessary to store the time 8:37:28 into Now. (pp. 542–543)
3. Define a hierarchical record data type called Interval that consists of two components of type Clock_Time. The components are called Past and Present. (pp. 553–557)
4. Assume that a variable called Channel_Crossing, of type Interval, has been defined. Write the assignment statements necessary to store the time 7:12:44 into the Past component of Channel_Crossing. Write the assignment statement that stores the value of variable Now into the Present component of Channel_Crossing. (pp. 553–557)
5. Define a variable called Boat_Times_File that is a direct file of Interval values. (pp. 551–552)
6. Decide what form of data structure is appropriate for the following problem. A card in a library catalog system must contain the call number, author, title, and description of a single book. (pp. 559–561)

Answers

1.
```
subtype Hour_Type   is Integer range 0..23;
subtype Minute_Type is Integer range 0..59;
subtype Second_Type is Integer range 0..59;
type Clock_Time is
   record
      Hour   : Hour_Type;
      Minute : Minute_Type;
      Second : Second_Type;
   end record;
```
2.
```
Now.Hour   := 8;
Now.Minute := 37;
Now.Second := 28;
```
3.
```
type Interval is
   record
      Past    : Clock_Time;
      Present : Clock_Time;
   end record;
```
4.
```
Channel_Crossing.Past.Hour   := 7;
Channel_Crossing.Past.Minute := 12;
Channel_Crossing.Past.Second := 44;
Channel_Crossing.Present     := Now;
```
5.
```
package Boat_Time_IO is new Direct_IO (Element_Type => Interval);
Boat_Times_File : Boat_Time_IO.File_Type;
```
6. A simple record with four components is sufficient.

Exam Preparation Exercises

1. Define the following terms:
   record
   component
   selected component
   hierarchical record
   data abstraction
2. Given the declarations

```
-- Types
type    Dept_Code_Type  is (ART, BIO, CSC, CHE, ENG,
                            MAT, PHI, PHY, PSY, SOC);
subtype Course_Num_Type is Integer range 100..499;
type Course_ID_Type is
   record
      Dept_Code : Dept_Code_Type;
      Number    : Course_Num_Type;
   end record;

subtype Building_String is String (1..25);
type Campus_Location is
   record
      Building : Building_String;
      Room     : Positive;
   end Record;

subtype Name_String   is String (1..30);
type Instructor_Type is
   record
      Name   : Name_String;
      Office : Campus_Location;
   end record;

subtype Course_String is String (1..45);
subtype Course_Credit_Type is Integer range 1..6;
type Course_Offering is
   record
      Course_ID    : Course_ID_Type;
      Name         : Course_String;
      Credit       : Course_Credit_Type;
      Instructor   : Instructor_Type;
      Class_Room   : Campus_Location;
      Prerequisite : Course_ID_Type;
   end record;
```

```
-- Variables
Required : Course_Offering;
Elective : Course_Offering;
Advisor  : Instructor_Type;
Room     : Campus_Location;
Course   : Course_ID_Type;
Same     : Boolean;
```

mark each of the following statements as valid or invalid. (Assume that the valid variables have defined values.)

a.
```
if Course_Offering.Course_ID.Number > 200 then
   Ada.Text_IO.Put_Line ("Not for freshmen.");
end if;
```
______

b. `Advisor := Required.Instructor;` ______

c.
```
if Required.Class_Room.Building = Advisor.Office.Building then
   Ada.Text_IO.Put_Line ("Same building.");
end if;
```
______

d. `Elective.Class_Room.Building(1) := 'H';` ______

e. `Required.Course_ID := (CSC, 221);` ______

f. `Required := Elective.Prerequisite;` ______

g. `Required.Course_ID := Required.Prerequisite;` ______

h. `Required.Instructor.Office := Campus_Location;` ______

i. `Required := Elective;` ______

3. Using the declarations in Exercise 2, write assignment statements to do the following:
   a. Assign the value of the Instructor component of the variable Required to the variable Advisor.
   b. Assign the value of the Building component of the Class_Room component of the variable Required to the Building component of the variable Advisor.
   c. Assign the variable Room to the Office component of the Instructor component of the variable Elective.
   d. Assign True to the variable Same if the Number component of the Course_ID component of the variable Required is the same as the Number component of the Course_ID component of the variable Elective. Otherwise, assign False to the variable Same. (Use an assignment statement, not an if statement.)
   e. Assign the string literal `"Redcay Hall                    "` and the integer literal 145 to the Office component of the Instructor component of the variable Required. (Use a single assignment statement.)
4. A hierarchical record structure may not contain another hierarchical record structure as a component. (True or False)
5. For each of the following descriptions of data, determine which general type of data structure (record, hierarchical record, or direct file of records) is appropriate.

a. A payroll entry with a name, address, and pay rate
b. A person's address
c. An inventory entry for a part
d. A list of addresses
e. A list of passengers on an airliner, including names, addresses, fare class, and seat assignment
f. A departmental telephone directory with last name and extension number

6. Given the declarations

```
-- Types
type Date_Rec is
   record
      Month  : Ada.Calendar.Month_Number;
      Day    : Ada.Calendar.Day_Number;
      Year   : Ada.Calendar.Year_Number;
   end record;

subtype Name_String is String (1..15);
type Person_Type is
   record
      First_Name : Name_String;
      Last_Name  : Name_String;
      Birth_Date : Date_Rec;
   end record;

-- Variables
Today  : Date_Rec;
A_Name : Name_String;
Friend : Person_Type;
Self   : Person_Type;
```

show the value of each variable after the following program segment is executed.

```
A_Name := "               ";
Friend.First_Name := A_Name;
Friend.Last_Name  := A_Name;
Today := (12, 21, 1979);
Friend.Birth_Date := Today;
Self := Friend;
```

7. Given the declarations in Exercise 6, explain why the following program segment is invalid.

```
if Friend.Birth_Date < Self.Birth_Date then
   Ada.Text_IO.Put_Line ("I am older than my friend.");
end if;
```

8. Declare a record type called Rec_Type to contain two integer variables and one Boolean variable.
9. Given the declarations

```
type Complex_Type is
   record
      Real_Part      : Float;
      Imaginary_Part : Float;
   end record;

package Complex_IO is new Direct_IO (Element_Type => Complex_Type);

C : Complex;
D : Complex_IO.File_Type;
```

   a. Write an assignment statement with a record aggregate using positional association to assign 5.7 to the component Real_Part and 7.2 to the component Imaginary_Part of the variable C.
   b. Write the same assignment statement using named association in the aggregate.
   c. Write the statement to read the 14th component of the File D into the variable C.
   d. Write the two statements to display the Real_Part and the Imaginary_Part components of the variable C.

10. Given the declarations

```
subtype Name_String  is String (1..12);
subtype City_String  is String (1..12);
subtype Zip_String   is String (1..5);
subtype State_String is String (1..2);

type Name_Rec is
   record
      First : Name_String;
      Last  : Name_string;
   end record;

type Place_Type is
   record
      City     : City_String;
      State    : State_String;
      Zip_Code : Zip_String;
   end record;
```

```
type Person_Type is
   record
      Name  : Name_Rec;
      Place : Place_Type;
   end record;

-- Variables
Person : Person_Type;
```

write Ada code that assigns information about yourself to Person.

Programming Warm-up Exercises

1. a. Write the necessary declarations for a record type to contain the following information about a student.

   Name (string)

   Social security number (string)

   Class (freshman, sophomore, junior, senior)

   GPA

   Sex (male, female)

   b. Declare a record variable of the type in part a.

   c. Write a program segment that prints the information in each component of the variable you declared in part b.

   d. Write the necessary declarations for a direct file called Roll that contains records of the type in part a.

2. a. Using the types declared in Exam Preparation Exercise 2, complete the following procedure body that gets the values of the components of record parameter Course_ID from the keyboard. You may assume that a package called Dept_Code_IO has been instantiated for Dept_Code's. You need not include prompts.

```
procedure Get (Item : out Course_ID_Type) is
```

   b. Using the types declared in Exam Preparation Exercise 2, complete the following procedure body that gets the values of the components of record parameter Location from the keyboard. You need not include prompts.

```
procedure Get (Item : out Campus_Location) is
```

   c. Using the types declared in Exam Preparation Exercise 2 and the procedure Get written in part b of this question, complete the following procedure body that gets the values of the components of record parameter Instructor. You need not include prompts.

```
procedure Get (Item : out Instructor_Type) is
```

d. Using the types declared in Exam Preparation Exercise 2 and the procedures from the previous parts of this question, complete the following procedure body that gets the values of the components of record parameter Course. Again, you need not include prompts.

```
procedure Get (Item : out Course_Offering) is
```

3. Write a hierarchical Ada record declaration to contain the following information about a student.

   Name (up to 30 characters)

   Student ID number

   Credit hours to date

   Number of courses taken

   Favorite course (20-character name and the grade received)

   Date first enrolled (month and year)

   Class (freshman, sophomore, junior, senior)

   GPA

4. a. Declare a record type called Apartment_Rec for an apartment locator service. The following information should be included.
      Landlord (a string of up to 20 characters)
      Address (a string of up to 20 characters)
      Bedrooms (Positive)
      Price (Dollars)
   b. Declare Available to be a direct file of records of type Apartment_Rec.
   c. Write a procedure to read values from the keyboard into the components of a variable of type Apartment_Rec. (The record variable should be passed as a parameter.) The order in which the data is read is the same as that of the items in the record. You need not include prompts.
5. You are designing an automated library catalog system. For each book, there is a catalog entry consisting of the call number (up to 10 characters), the number of copies in the library (a positive number), the author (up to 30 characters), the title (up to 100 characters), and a description of the contents (up to 300 characters).
   a. Write the type definitions necessary to contain this information in a direct file.
   b. Estimate how many characters of file space are required to hold all the catalog information for the library. (Assume that an integer value occupies the equivalent of four characters in the file and that the library has 50,000 book titles.)
   c. How many book records can a computer with 1,440,000 characters of file space hold?
6. Write a procedure that gets the information for a book from the keyboard and puts it into a record of the type defined in Exercise 5. Write another procedure that displays the information contained in a record of the type defined in Exercise 5. The record should be passed as a parameter to each of these procedures.

7. Complete the following procedure that prints out the names of all the book titles in the direct file Catalog.

```
procedure Put_All_Titles (Catalog : in out Book_IO.File_Type) is
```

8. You are writing the subscription renewal system for a magazine. For each subscriber, the system is to keep the following information.

   Name (first, last)

   Address (street, city, state, zip code)

   Expiration date (month, year)

   Date renewal notice was sent (month, day, year)

   Number of renewal notices sent so far

   Number of years for which subscription is being renewed (0 for renewal not yet received; otherwise 1, 2, or 3 years)

   Whether or not the subscriber's name may be included in a mailing list for sale to other companies

   Write a hierarchical record type definition to contain this information.

9. You are writing a program that keeps track of the over 200 terminals connected to a company computer. For each terminal, the following information must be kept:

   Brand and model (a string of up to 15 characters)

   Data rate (a range of 10 through 56,600 characters per second)

   Parity (Even, Odd, One, Zero, or None)

   Echoplex (Half or Full)

   Data bits (7 or 8)

   Stop bits (1 or 2)

   Design a data structure for this problem, and write the type definitions for all the data types that are needed to implement your design.

10. Write a record declaration to contain a string of not more than 20 characters and the length of the string (the position of the last character of interest). Then write a function that returns the length of a string stored in this record.

11. Write a function that concatenates (combines) two strings into a third string. Use the declaration you wrote in Exercise 10. You may assume that the combined length will not exceed 20 characters.

12. You are writing a program to keep track of a manufacturing company's inventory. For each part, the program needs to store the following information.

    Part Number (between 10000 and 99999)

    Cost (between $0.00 and $99,999.99)

    Quantity (Natural)

    a. Write all the declarations needed to declare a record type called Inventory_Rec that contains these three pieces of information.
    b. Write a procedure and the necessary declarations to get a variable of record type Inventory_Rec from the keyboard. You need not display prompts.

Programming Problems

1. Modify the Department Store case study given in this chapter so that it handles transactions to delete accounts from the store's files. A delete transaction contains the account number and the word Delete. An account is deleted by not writing the account record to the new master file. So that any outstanding balance can be billed to the proper person, all the account information should be written to the report file with an appropriate message. You may assume that there are no other transactions for an account following a delete transaction.
2. The Emerging Manufacturing Company has just installed its first computer and hired you as a junior programmer. Your first program is to read employee pay data and produce two reports: 1) an error report, and 2) a report on pay amounts. The second report must contain a line for each employee and a line of totals at the end of the report.

   INPUT

   Transaction File (Text File)
   One line for each employee containing ID number, job-site number, and number of hours worked.
   These data items have been sorted ahead of time by ID number.

   Master File (Text File) This file is ordered by ID number.
   ID number
   Name
   Pay rate per hour
   Number of dependents
   Type of employee (1 is management, 0 is union)
   Job site
   Sex (M, F)
   Note: 1) union members, unlike management, get time and a half for hours over 40; and 2) the tax formula for tax computation is as follows: if number of dependents is 1, tax rate is 15%. Otherwise, the tax rate is the greater of 2.5% or

$$\left[1 - \frac{\textit{Number of Dependents}}{\textit{Number of Dependents} + 6}\right] \times 15\%$$

   OUTPUT

   Error Report File (Text File)
   Lists the input lines for which there are no corresponding master records, or where the job-site numbers do not agree. Continues processing with the next line of data.

Gives the total number of employee records that were processed correctly during the run.

Payroll Report (Text File Labeled for Management)

Contains a line for each employee showing the name, ID number, job-site name, gross pay, and net pay.

Contains a total line showing the total amount of gross pay and total amount of net pay.

3. The Emerging Manufacturing Company has decided to use its new computer for parts inventory control as well as for payroll. You are writing a program that is to be run each night. It takes the stock tickets from the day's transactions, makes a list of the parts that need ordering, and prints an updated report that must be given to the five job-site managers each morning. Note that you are not being asked to update the file.

INPUT

Transaction File (Text File)

One line for each stock transaction containing part ID number, job-site number, and number of parts bought or sold (a negative number indicates that it has been sold).

This data has been sorted ahead of time by site number within part number.

Master File (Text File) This file is ordered by ID number.

Part ID number.

Part name (no embedded blanks).

Quantity on hand.

Order point.

Job site.

This file is also ordered by job-site number within part ID number. If a part is not in the master file and the transaction is a sale, an error message should be printed. If the transaction is a purchase, the part should be listed in the proper place in the parts report. Note that there is a separate entry in the master file for parts at each job site.

OUTPUT

Error Report File (Text File)

Contains error messages.

Lists the parts that need to be ordered (those for which quantity on hand is less than order point).

A Report for All the Parts in the Master File (Text File)

Contains the part number.

Contains the part name.

Contains the job-site name.

Contains the number on hand.

Remember, this report is for management. Be sure it is written so managers can read it.

4. You have taken a job with the IRS because you want to learn how to save on your income tax. They want you to write a toy tax-computing program so that they can get an idea of your programming abilities. The program reads in the names of the members of families and each person's income and computes the tax that the family owes. You may assume that people with the same last name who appear consecutively in input are in the same family. The number of deductions that a family can count is equal to the number of people listed in that family in the input data. Tax is computed as follows:

adjusted income = income − ($5,000 × number of deductions)
tax rate = adjusted income/100,000 if income < $60,000; 0.50, otherwise
tax = tax rate × adjusted income

There will be no refunds, so you must check for people whose tax would be negative and set it to 0. Input entries are as follows:

last name, first name. total income

Example:

```
Jones,      Ralph.       19,765.43
Jones,      Mary.         8,532.00
Jones,      Francis.          0.00
Atwell,     Humphrey.     5,678.12
Murphy,     Robert.      13,432.20
Murphy,     Ellen.            0.00
Murphy,     Paddy.            0.00
Murphy,     Eileen.           0.00
Murphy,     Conan.            0.00
Murphy,     Nora.             0.00
```

INPUT

The data as described previously, with an end of file indicating the end of the run.

OUTPUT

A table containing all the families, one family per line, with each line containing the last name of the family, their total income, and their computed tax.

CHAPTER 11

Arrays

GOALS

After reading this chapter, you should be able to

- define one-dimensional, two-dimensional, and multidimensional arrays for given problems
- assign a value to and access a value stored in an array component
- fill an array with data and process the data in the array
- apply subarray processing to a given problem
- define and use an array with index values that have semantic content
- use unconstrained array types, array attributes, and array slices to process subarrays
- select the correct array data structure for a problem

Sometimes it is necessary to show relationships among different variables or to store and reference variables as a group. This is difficult to do if each variable is named individually. The record data type is one way to store several values under a single name. Although the record type is appropriate for storing a small number of values under a single name, its syntax for naming and accessing individual values is awkward for large numbers of values. The array allows us to store many values under a single name easily.

Data structures play an important role in the design process. The choice of data structure directly affects the design because it determines the algorithms used to process the data. We start off this chapter with an examination of the one-dimensional array, which is useful when our data is best organized as a list or sequence.

Next we examine the two-dimensional array, which is useful when we need to organize data in the form of a table with rows and columns. Two-dimensional arrays also are useful for representing board games such as chess, tic-tac-toe, or Scrabble. We also introduce arrays of arrays and explain when they may be a better choice for representing a table.

Finally, we extend the definition of an array to allow arrays with any number of dimensions, which we call multidimensional arrays. Each dimension of such an array represents a different feature of a component.

One-Dimensional Arrays

Suppose that we have to print a set of values in reverse order. To do this, we must read and save all the values before we can print the last value. If there are 1000 values, we would have to define 1000 individual variables to hold the values and write 1000 different Get and Put procedure calls to input and output the values—an incredibly tedious task! A one-dimensional array is a composite data type that allows us to program operations of this sort with ease.

A program that reads a list of 1000 integer values and prints them in reverse order without using arrays might look like this:

```
with Ada.Text_IO;
with Ada.Integer_Text_IO;
procedure Reverse_List is

   Value1 : Integer;
   Value2 : Integer;
   Value3 : Integer;
    .
    .
    .
   Value1000 : Integer;
```

```
begin  -- Reverse_List
   Ada.Integer_Text_IO.Get (Item => Value1);          -- Get the 1st value
   Ada.Integer_Text_IO.Get (Item => Value2);
   Ada.Integer_Text_IO.Get (Item => Value3);
    .
    .
    .
   Ada.Integer_Text_IO.Get (Item => Value1000);       -- Get the 1000th value

   Ada.Integer_Text_IO.Put (Item => Value1000);     -- Display the 1000th value
   Ada.Text_IO.New_Line;
   Ada.Integer_Text_IO.Put (Item => Value999);
   Ada.Text_IO.New_Line;
   Ada.Integer_Text_IO.Put (Item => Value998);
   Ada.Text_IO.New_Line;
    .
    .
    .
   Ada.Integer_Text_IO.Put (Item => Value1);          -- Display the 1st value
   Ada.Text_IO.New_Line;
end Reverse_List;
```

This program would be over 4000 lines long! The problem is that we have to use 1000 separate variables. Although we could use a record to store all the values under a single variable name, it still would require 1000 different components and would not reduce the number of lines in the program. Note that all the variables have the same name except for an appended number that distinguishes them. Wouldn't it be convenient if we could put the number in a counter variable and use a for loop to go from 1 to 1000, and then from 1000 back down to 1? For example, if the counter variable is Number, we could write the body of the program as follows with Number enclosed in parentheses to set it apart from Value:

```
begin  -- Reverse_List
   Read_Loop:
   for Number in 1..1000 loop
      Ada.Integer_Text_IO.Get (Item => Value(Number) );
   end loop Read_Loop;

   Write_Loop:
   for Number in reverse 1..1000 loop
      Ada.Integer_Text_IO.Put (Item => Value(Number) );
      Ada.Text_IO.New_Line;
   end loop Write_Loop;
end Reverse_List;
```

This code fragment is correct Ada if we define Value to be a one-dimensional array: a collection of variables, all of the same type, where the first part of each variable name is the same, and the last part is an *index value* enclosed in parentheses. In this case, the value stored in Number is the index. We sometimes refer to the index as a *subscript* because we often use it as a subscript in a mathematical formula.

A one-dimensional array is a data type, so we must describe it in a declarative part before we define any variables of that type.

```
-- Types
subtype Index_Range is Integer range 1..1000;
type    Value_Array is array (Index_Range) of Integer;

-- Variable
Value : Value_Array;
```

The subtype Index_Range in this example is used in the declaration of the array type Value_Array to determine how many variables are contained in the array. The definition of Value_Array also indicates the data type of the variables (Integer).

The type definition describes the pattern for an array. To create an array, we must define a variable of type Value_Array, such as Value. We could also define other variables of type Value_Array. For example, if we defined Item and Quantity to be variables of type Value_Array, each one would be an array of 1000 integers. We could then access their individual components by writing Item(Number) and Quantity(Number).

Here is the complete program Reverse_List, using array notation and two for loops. This program is certainly much shorter than our first version.

```
with Ada.Text_IO;
with Ada.Integer_Text_IO;
procedure Reverse_List is

   -- Types
   subtype Index_Range is Integer range 1..1000;
   type    Value_Array is array (Index_Range) of Integer;

   -- Variable
   Value : Value_Array;

begin  -- Reverse_List
   for Number in Index_Range loop
      Ada.Integer_Text_IO.Get (Item => Value(Number) );
   end loop;

   for Number in reverse Index_Range loop
      Ada.Integer_Text_IO.Put (Item => Value(Number) );
      Ada.Text_IO.New_Line;
   end loop;
end Reverse_List;
```

Now that we have demonstrated how useful one-dimensional arrays can be, we define them formally and explain how to access individual components.

Defining Arrays

A **one-dimensional array** is a structured collection of components that we can access individually by specifying the position of a component with a single index value. Although both records and arrays are collections of components under a single name, there are two big differences. First, the array is a *homogeneous data type:* all components must have the same type. Each component of a record may be a different type. Second, components in an array are accessed by their position within the collection. We use names rather than position to access the individual components in a record.

One-dimensional array A structured collection of components, of the same type, given a single name. Each component is accessed by an index that indicates the component's position within the collection.

We now add the array type to our simplified EBNF definition of the type declaration. Recall that Ada's variant of the Backus-Naur form uses italics to give us additional information within the context of the definition. Names of syntactic elements that begin with an italicized part are equivalent to the name without the italicized portion.

type_declaration	::=	**type** identifier **is** type_definition;
type_definition	::=	enumeration_type_definition |
		integer_type_definition |
		float_type_definition |
		record_type_definition |
		array_type_definition
array_type_definition	::=	**array** index_constraint **of** *component*_subtype_indication
index_constraint	::=	(*discrete*_subtype_indication | range)
subtype_indication	::=	*type*_name | *subtype*_name
range	::=	simple_expression . . simple_expression |
		*range*_attribute

The index constraint gives the range of index values. The compiler uses it to determine how many components there are in this array type and how each individual component is accessed. The index type of an array must be a discrete type. The component type describes what is stored in each component of the array. Array components may be of any subtype or type. Let's look at some more examples of array declarations.

```
subtype Student_Range    is Integer range 1..25;
subtype Quiz_Score_Type is Float range 0.0..10.0;
type    Score_Array      is array (Student_Range) of Quiz_Score_Type;

subtype Grade_Type            is Character range 'A'..'E';
type    Grade_Frequency_Array is array (Grade_Type) of Natural;

type Grade_Rec is
   record
      Exam_Grade  : Grade_Type;
      Final_Grade : Grade_Type;
      Absences    : Natural;
   end record;
type Student_Array is array (Student_Range) of Grade_Rec;
```

Score_Array is an array type with 25 components. Each component is a float value between 0.0 and 10.0. Grade_Frequency_Array is an array type with 5 components (subtype Grade_Type's domain consists of 5 different character values). Each of these components is type Natural. Finally, Student_Array is an array type with 25 components. Each of the components in this array is a record (type Grade_Rec).

Accessing Individual Components

To access an individual array component, we write the name of an array variable, followed by an expression enclosed in parentheses. The expression specifies which component to access. The EBNF definition for accessing an array component is:

indexed_component ::= name (expression)

The index expression may be as simple as a constant or a variable name or as complex as a combination of variables, operators, and function calls. Whatever the form of the expression, it must result in a value that is compatible with the index type.

We can treat an array component as a single variable. We can assign it a value, read a value into it, write its contents, pass it as a parameter, and use it in an expression. Take, for example, the following two statements. We declared the array variable value on page 590.

```
Value(Counter) := 0;
if  Value(Number + 1) rem 10  /=  0   then
    .
    .
    .
```

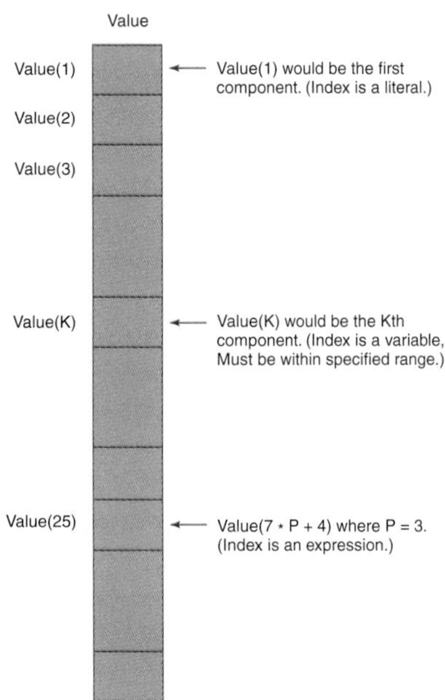

FIGURE 11-1 Index as a Literal, a Variable, and an Expression

In the first statement, 0 is stored into an array component. If Counter is 1, 0 is stored in the first component of the array. If Counter is 2, 0 is stored in the second place in the array. If Counter is 24, 0 is stored in the twenty fourth place in the array. If Counter has a value that is not within the index type, a CONSTRAINT_ERROR is raised. In our example, if Counter is 1001, trying to access Value(Counter) would cause a CONSTRAINT_ERROR exception.

In the second statement an array component is selected by the expression Number + 1. The specific array component accessed is divided by 10 and checked to see whether the remainder is nonzero. If Number + 1 is 1, the value in the first place is being tested; if Number + 1 is 2, the second place is tested; and so on. Figure 11-1 shows the indexing expression as a literal, a variable, and a more complex expression.

Accessing an Entire Array at Once

We can access an entire array at once simply by giving the array name *without* an index expression. Given the following declarations for the arrays Char_Count and Frequency

```
type Alpha_Array is array (Character) of Natural;

Char_Count : Alpha_Array;
Frequency  : Alpha_Array;
```

we could write the following assignment statement.

```
Char_Count := Frequency;
```

The effect is that each of the 256 integer values in the array Frequency are copied to the corresponding component of Char_Count.

We also can pass entire arrays as parameters, giving the procedure or function access to the entire array. If we define a procedure called Count_Line with a formal parameter called List of type Alpha_Array like this:

```
procedure Count_Line (List : in Alpha_Array) is
   .
   .
   .
```

we can call it and pass it the array Char_Count

```
Count_Line (List => Char_Count);     -- A call to procedure Count_Line
```

giving procedure Count_Line access to all 256 components in Char_Count. Within the procedure, we can access any component of the array parameter List, assign the entire array to another variable of type Alpha_Array, or pass it to another procedure.

Assignment of one array variable to another requires that the two array variables be declared using the same type name. Assignment is not allowed between array variables declared with different type names even if those types appear equivalent. Given the following array declarations

```
subtype Range_Type is Integer range 1..10;

type My_Array_Type   is array (Range_Type) of Character;
type Your_Array_Type is array (Range_Type) of Character;

A : My_Array_Type;          -- An array variable that holds 10 characters
B : Your_Array_Type;        -- An array variable that holds 10 characters
```

the assignment statement

```
A := B;                     -- Illegal assignment
```

is illegal because the two array variables are not the exact same type. Ada considers My_Array_Type and Your_Array_Type to be two different types, even though they are functionally equivalent. Ada does not permit assignment between two different types. Because of this incompatibility, we recommended in Chapter 7 that you declare and use subtypes rather than types for values that are used together. Later in this chapter, we show how to declare array subtypes.

The same restriction for array assignment is true for passing arrays as parameters: the data types of the formal and actual parameters must be identical. In addition, the data type of an array variable that is used as a formal parameter must have a named type rather than an anonymous type. The procedure declaration

```
procedure Pass (List : in out array (Character) of Integer);    -- Illegal
                              \_________________________________/
                                              ^
                                Anonymous type declaration
```

is illegal because we cannot write an anonymous type definition in a parameter list, whereas

```
procedure Pass (List : in out Alpha_Array);
```

is legal.

Although we can write an assignment statement containing a reference to an entire array, we cannot use the predefined arithmetic operators with entire arrays. For example, the following statement is illegal.

```
Frequency := Frequency + Char_Count;    -- Illegal
```

To add the components of one array to the corresponding components of another array, we must add each pair of components together individually using a loop that counts through the array indices. We can, of course, write our own "+" function that does just that.

```
function "+" (Left  : in Alpha_Array;
              Right : in Alpha_Array) return Alpha_Array is
-- Returns an array containing the sums of the corresponding components
   Result : Alpha_Array;
begin
                                      -- Go through all the components
   for Index in Character loop        -- Each iteration, add one pair of components
      Result(Index) := Left(Index) + Right(Index);
   end loop;
   return Result;    -- Return the array of component sums
end "+";
```

With this function in our program, the assignment of the sum to Frequency is now legal.

Array Aggregates

In Chapter 10 we showed how to use an *aggregate* as a record literal. We can also use aggregates for array literals. An array aggregate is a collection of values for the array components. These values are contained within parentheses. An array aggregate must contain a value for each component of the array. Let's look at some examples. Given the following types

```
subtype Index_Range    is Integer range 1..8;
type    Natural_Array  is array (Index_Range) of Natural;

type    Day_Type       is (Monday, Tuesday, Wednesday, Thursday,
                           Friday, Saturday, Sunday);
type Sales_Total_Array is array (Day_Type) of Float;

Score : Natural_Array;
Total : Sales_Total_Array;
```

we can make the following assignments

```
Score := (10, 20, 30, 40, 50, 60, 70, 80);

Total := (2_837.95,  3_589.39, 5_287.63, 4_459.29,
          5_503.23, 11_723.45, 8_450.32);
```

In these two assignment statements, we associate the values in the array aggregates with a particular array component by their *position* in the aggregate. Thus, the first assignment statement assigns a value of 10 to Score(1), a value of 20 to Score(2), a value of 30 to Score(3), and so on for all eight components in the array Score. The second assignment statement assigns a value of 2,837.95 to Total(Monday), a value of 3,589.39 to Total(Tuesday), and so on for all seven components of array Total.

We can associate the component values in an array aggregate with a particular array component by *name* as well as by position. In record aggregates, we use component names for this purpose. We use subscripts as names in array aggregates. The following two assignment statements are equivalent to the two shown previously. However, these use named association instead of positional association.

```
Score := (1 => 10,  2 => 20,  3 => 30,  4 => 40,
          5 => 50,  6 => 60,  7 => 70,  8 => 80);

Total := (Monday    => 2_837.95,  Tuesday  => 3_589.39,
          Wednesday => 5_287.63,  Thursday => 4_459.29,
          Friday    => 5_503.23,  Saturday => 11_723.45,
          Sunday    => 8_450.32,);
```

If every value in an array aggregate is different, as in these examples, positional association is probably easier to read than named association. Named association is useful when some or all of the values in the aggregate are the same. The following statement assigns 35 to all the array components with an odd index and 61 to all the array components with an even index.

```
Score := (1 | 3 | 5 | 7 => 35,  2 | 4 | 6 | 8 => 61);
```

The vertical bar separates the index values in the aggregate that are to be assigned the same value. We can also use ranges on the left side of the association symbol (=>). In the next example, we assign a value of 97 to the components with index values from 1 to 4 and a value of 42 to those from 5 to 8.

```
Score := (1..4 => 97,  5..8 => 42);
```

And here we have assigned every component of array Score a value of 0.

```
Score := (Index_Range => 0);
```

The reserved word `others` may appear as the *last* name in an aggregate. We use this special name to supply a value to any array components that have not already been associated with values in the aggregate. For example, the statement

```
Total := (Saturday | Sunday => 100.00,  others => 0.00);
```

assigns 100.00 to Total(Saturday) and Total(Sunday) and assigns 0.00 to the remaining five array components. We can use `others` by itself to assign a value to all array components.

```
Score := (others => 0);    -- Initialize all array components to 0
```

Programmers commonly use this form of the aggregate to initialize the values of an array to a single value.

When a program uses several similar array types, the compiler may not be able to determine the type of an aggregate in which `others` is used. In Chapter 7 we used qualification with ambiguous enumeration literals. We can also qualify an array aggregate with a type name. Here is our example using the array type name to qualify the array aggregate.

```
Score := Natural_Array'(others => 0);    -- Initialize all array
                                         -- components to 0
```

Type identifier used to qualify array aggregate

Examples of Defining and Accessing Arrays

We now look in detail at some specific examples of defining, declaring, and accessing arrays.

Arrays with Atomic Components

```
-- Constants
Num_Students : constant := 25;

-- Types
subtype Student_Range is Integer range 1..Num_Students;          -- Index type
type    Grade_Array   is array (Student_Range) of Character;     -- Array type

-- Variables
Grades      : Grade_Array;          -- Array of 25 character components
Student_Num : Student_Range;        -- A variable of the index type
One_Grade   : Character;            -- A variable of the component type
```

Grade_Array is a pattern for an array with 25 components, each of which can contain a character. Grades is an array variable of type Grade_Array. Each component of Grades is a Character variable, just like One_Grade or any other Character variable. Figure 11-2 illustrates these relationships.

When the index type is a subrange of the integers beginning with 1, it allows us to access the components by their position in the array—that is,

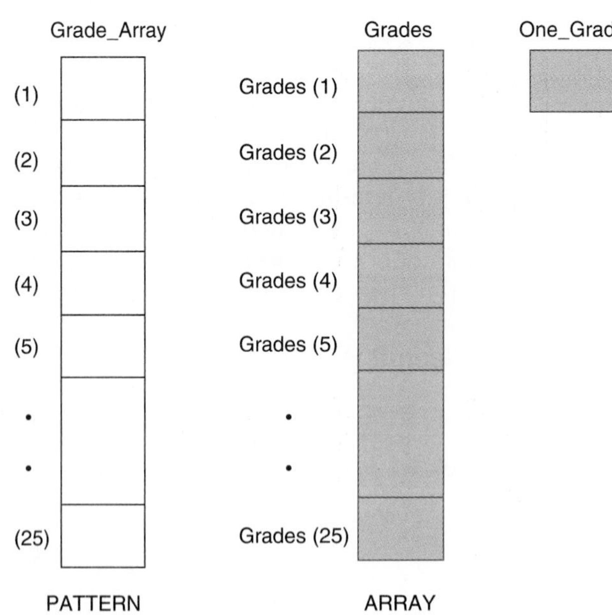

FIGURE 11-2 Array Pattern, Array Variable, and Array Component

the first, the second, the third, and so on, until the last. The correspondence of index and position is the most common way of thinking about an array. In fact, some programming languages allow only indices of this type. Ada, however, is much more flexible. We have already seen an array whose index type was an enumeration type. The next example shows an array in which the indices are characters.

```
-- Types
subtype Grade_Range       is Character range 'A'..'D';         -- Index type
type    Grade_Count_Array is array (Grade_Range) of Natural;  -- Array type

-- Variables
CSC221_Grades : Grade_Count_Array;      -- Array of four Naturals
CSC223_Grades : Grade_Count_Array;      -- Array of four Naturals
My_Grade      : Grade_Range;            -- Variable of the index type
```

Grade_Count_Array is a pattern for an array with four components, each a nonnegative integer. CSC221_Grades and CSC223_Grades are two array variables of this type. The first component in CSC221_Grades can be accessed by CSC221_Grades('A'), the second component by CSC221_Grades('B'), and so on as shown in Figure 11-3. The components in CSC223_Grades can be accessed by CSC223_Grades('A'), CSC223_Grades('B'), CSC223_Grades('C'), and CSC223_Grades('D').

Suppose we use CSC221_Grades('A') as a counter for the number of A's in the course CSC221, CSC221_Grades('B') to tally the B's in the course, and so on. Similarly, suppose we use CSC223_Grades('A') as a counter for the number of A's in the course CSC223, CSC223_Grades('B') to tally the B's in the course, and so on. Because the array components are variables, we must initialize the array components to 0 prior to counting, as in the following code fragment.

```
for Grade in Grade_Range loop
   CSC221_Grades(Grade) := 0;
   CSC223_Grades(Grade) := 0;
end loop;
```

FIGURE 11-3
Array Variable CSC221_Grades

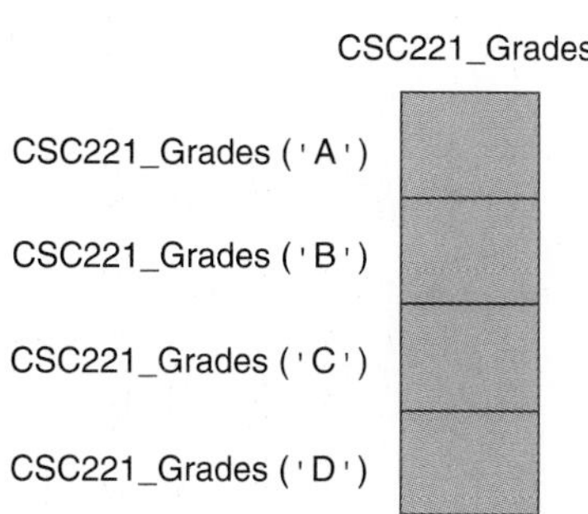

We can also accomplish this initialization with array aggregate assignments.

```
CSC221_Grades := (Grade_Range => 0);
CSC223_Grades := (Grade_Range => 0);
```

Let's look at another example. The index type in the following example is an enumeration type.

```
-- Index type
type Drink_Type is (Orange, Cola, Root_Beer, Ginger_Ale, Cherry, Lemon);

-- Component type
type Dollars is delta 0.01 digits 7 range 0.00 .. 99_999.99;

-- Array type
type Amount_Array is array (Drink_Type) of Dollars;

-- Variable
Amount : Amount_Array                -- Array of 6 Dollars values, indexed by Drink
```

Amount_Array is a pattern for a group of six components representing dollar sales figures. Amount is an array of this type (see Figure 11-4). The following code will print the six values in the array.

```
for Flavor in Drink_Type loop
   Dollar_IO.Put (Item => Amount(Flavor),
                  Fore => 1,
                  Aft  => 2,
                  Exp  => 0);
   Ada.Text_IO.New_Line;
end loop;
```

FIGURE 11-4 Array Variable Amount

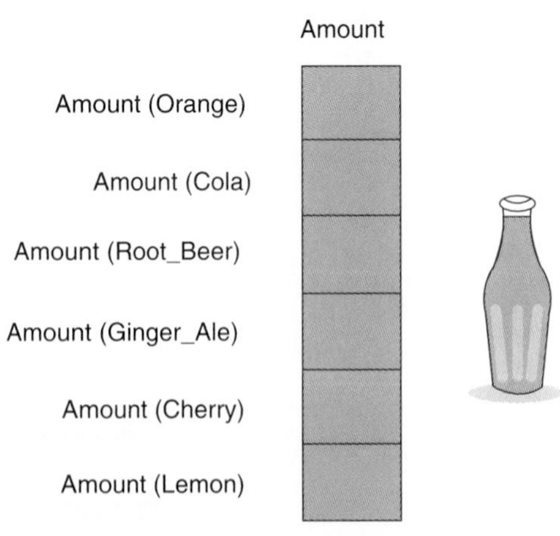

The next example is a little more complex. It might be used to analyze occupancy rates in an apartment building.

```
-- Constants
Building_Size : constant := 350;     -- Number of apartments
Max_People    : constant := 5;       -- Maximum people per apartment

-- Types
subtype Apartment_Range is Integer range 1..Building_Size;-- Index type
subtype Occupant_Range  is Integer range 0..Max_People;   -- Component type

   -- Array type
type Apartment_Array is array (Apartment_Range) of Occupant_Range;

-- Variables
Building     : Apartment_Array;      -- An array of 350 values between 0 and 5
Total_Number : Natural;              -- An integer for totaling the occupancy
```

Type Apartment_Array is a pattern for a group of 350 components. Its component type is an integer subtype called Occupant_Range. Building is an array of type Apartment_Array (see Figure 11-5). If values have been read into the array, then the following code will total the number of occupants in the 350 apartments in the building.

```
Total_Number := 0;
for Counter in Apartment_Range loop
   Total_Number := Total_Number + Building(Counter);
end loop;
```

Note how we used the named numbers Building_Size and Max_People in defining the type Apartment_Array. By using named numbers or constants in this manner, we can make changes easily.

FIGURE 11-5
Array Variable Building

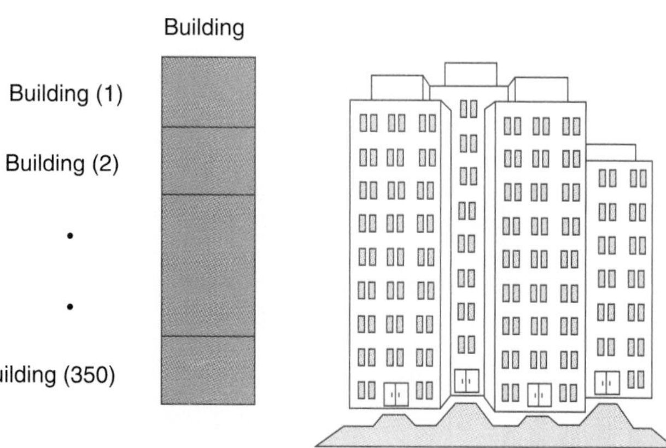

Here is one last example of arrays with atomic components.

```
Num_Students : constant := 10;

-- Types
subtype Grade_Range   is Character range 'A'..'E';        -- Component type
subtype Student_Range is Integer   range 1..Num_Students;    -- Index type
type    Student_Array is array (Student_Range) of Grade_Range;-- Array type

-- Variables
Students  : Student_Array;          -- Array of 10 student letter grades
ID_Number : Student_Range:          -- Variable of the index type
```

Figure 11-6 illustrates array Students. It shows values in the components, which implies that some processing of the array has occurred already. Here are some simple examples showing how this array may be used.

```
Ada.Text_IO.Get (File => Grade_File,
                 Item => Students(2) );
```

assigns the next character in file Grade_File to the second component in Students;

```
Students(4) := 'A';
```

assigns the character 'A' to the component in Students indexed by 4;

```
ID_Number := 6;
Students(ID_Number) := 'C';
```

assigns the character 'C' to the component of Students indexed by ID_Number (that is, by 6); and

```
for ID in Student_Range loop
   Ada.Text_IO.Put (Students(ID));
end loop;
```

loops through Students, printing each component. In this case, the output would be EBCAECAACB. And, finally

```
for ID in Student_Range loop
   Ada.Text_IO.Put ("Student ");
   Ada.Integer_Text_IO.Put (Item => ID,  Width => 2);
   Ada.Text_IO.Put ("  Grade ");
   Ada.Text_IO.Put (Students(ID));
end loop;
```

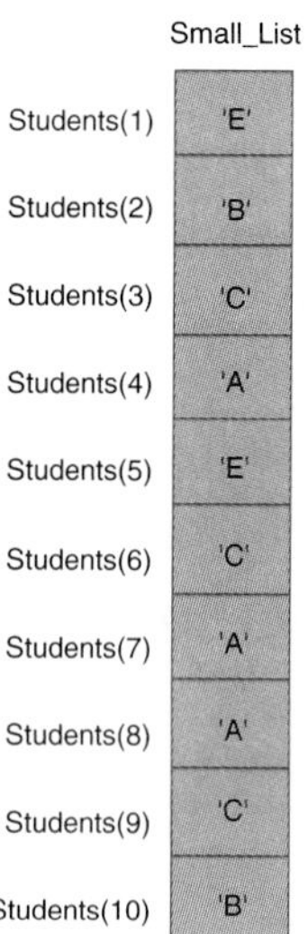

FIGURE 11-6 Array Variable Students with Values

loops through Students, printing each component in a more readable form. ID is used as the loop parameter, but it also has semantic content—it is the student's identification number. The output would be

```
Student  1  Grade E
Student  2  Grade B
Student  3  Grade C
.
.
.
Student  9  Grade C
Student 10  Grade B
```

Arrays with Record Components We introduced records in Chapter 10. There we found that, although individual records can be useful, many applications require a collection of records. To obtain such a collection, we declared sequential and direct files whose components were records. Arrays whose components are records give us another way to store collections of records. We use the following declarations to declare a collection of student records stored in an array instead of a file.

```
-- Types
type    Letter_Grade_Type is (A, B, C, D, F);
subtype Percent           is Integer range 0..100;
subtype GPA_Type          is Float   range 0.00..4.00;
subtype Name_String       is String (1..15);
```

```
type Student_Rec is                                          -- Component type
   record
      First_Name    : Name_String;
      Last_Name     : Name_String;
      GPA           : GPA_Type;
      Program_Grade : Percent;
      Quiz_Grade    : Percent;
      Final_Exam    : Percent;
      Course_Grade  : Letter_Grade_Type;
   end record;

subtype ID_Range    is Integer range 1..150;                 -- Index type
type    Grade_Array is array (ID_Range) of Student_Rec;      -- Array type

-- Variables
Student    : Student_Rec;      -- Information for one student
Grade_Book : Grade_Array;      -- Information for 150 students
```

Figure 11-7 illustrates this structure. Compare this figure to Figure 10-3 in which we used a direct access file to store a collection of records.

Recall that we access the components of a record by giving the record name, followed by a period, and then the component name. In this example, the record is a component within an array. We must use an index to select the desired record in the array. To access the course grade of the fourth student, we use the following.

Figure 11-7 Array Variable Grade_Book with Details of Its Fourth Component

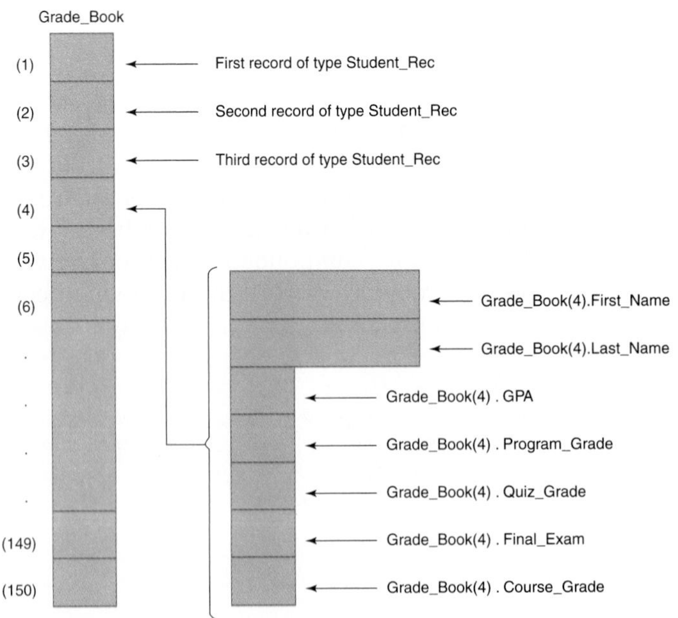

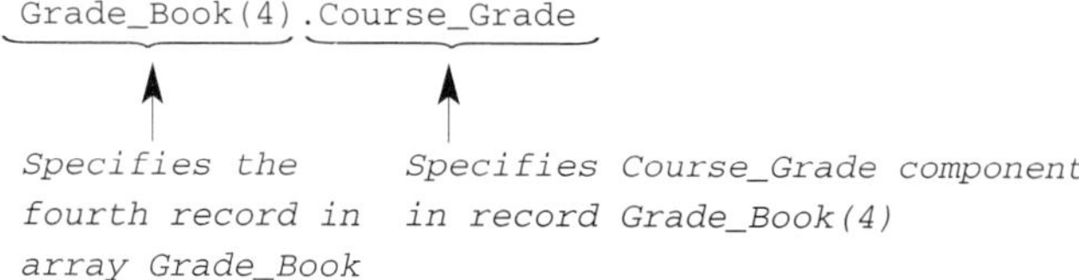

To access the first character in the last name of the fourth student, we use the following:

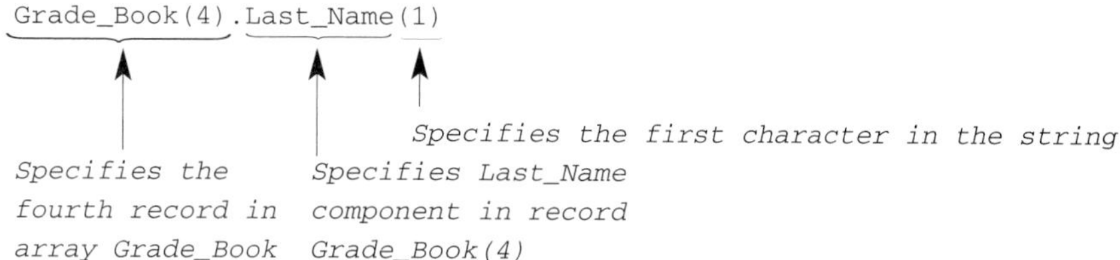

The following code fragment prints out the first and last name of each student in the class and a warning message if the grades in a student's record are not consistent. We use Boolean function Consistent (given on page 544 of Chapter 10) to determine whether or not the grades in a particular record are consistent. This function is passed one student record from the array.

```
for ID in ID_Range loop
   Ada.Text_IO.Put (Grade_Book(ID).First_Name  &  ' '  &
                    Grade_Book(ID).Last_Name);
   if not Consistent (Student => Grade_Book(ID)) then
      Ada.Text_IO.Put ("****  Information is not consistent  ****");
   end if;
   Ada.Text_IO.New_Line;
end loop;
```

Both arrays and files can store collections of records, so how do we decide which to use? The major difference between the two is that files are stored on auxiliary storage devices such as magnetic and optical disks while arrays are stored in the memory unit (the internal RAM storage) of the computer. Thus if you need speed, use an array. The time needed to access a component stored on an auxiliary storage device is thousands of times greater than the time required to access a component stored in the memory unit. If you have a large number of components or need to save the information between program runs, then use a file. The amount of storage available on auxiliary devices is much greater than that available in the memory unit. Information in files is kept until explicitly deleted, but the information in an array is lost as soon as its program terminates. Sometimes, it is possible to obtain the best of both by keeping information in an array while the program is running and writing it to a file after all processing has been completed. The data may be read back into an array the next time the program is executed.

Records with Array Components In Chapter 10 we showed that a record component can be any type or subtype. This includes array types. Suppose we need to keep track of a student's ID number and scores on each of 15 weekly quizzes. The following declarations organize this information in a single record.

```
subtype ID_Type          is Integer range 0..9999;
subtype Quiz_Num_Range   is Integer range 1..15;
subtype Quiz_Score_Type  is Integer range 1..10;
type    Quiz_Score_Array is array (Quiz_Num_Range) of Quiz_Score_Type;

type Student_Rec is                           -- Information for one student
   record
      ID         : ID_Type;                   -- Student ID
      Quiz_Score : Quiz_Score_Array;          -- List of Quiz scores
   end record;

Student : Student_Rec;
```

We can access the third quiz score for this student with the following:

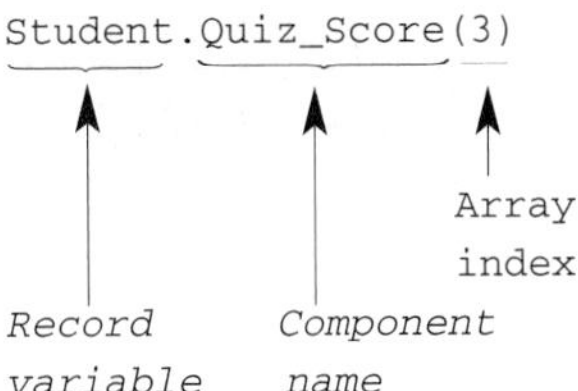

We also can declare an array of these student records to store the information for an entire class of students.

```
subtype Class_Index_Range is Integer range 1..100;
type    Class_Array       is array (Class_Index_Range) of Student_Rec;

Class : Class_Array;
```

We can access the third quiz score for the eighth student in this class as follows:

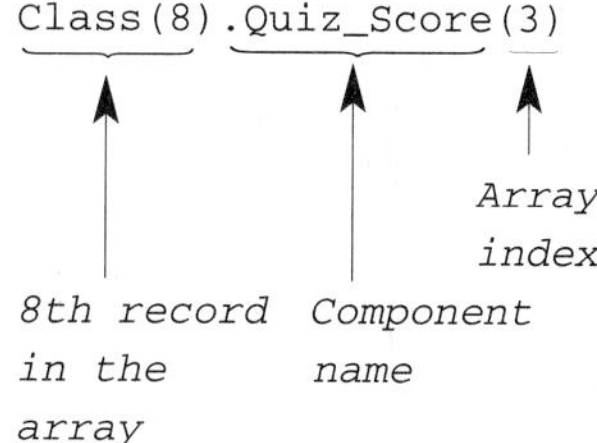

Processing Arrays

In Chapter 10 we demonstrated the need to design our algorithms and data structures in parallel. The best data representation for a particular problem is the one that reflects the emphasis of the processing within the problem. In this section we discuss some types of processing for which arrays are suited.

There are two types of array processing that come up most often: using index values that have specific meaning within the problem (indices with semantic content) and using part of the defined array (a subarray).

Indices with Semantic Content In some problems the index has meaning beyond simple position; that is, the index has semantic content. For example, the employees in a company might be given identification numbers ranging from 100 to 500. If an array of salary figures were defined as

```
subtype ID_Type      is Integer range 100..500;
type    Salary_Array is array (ID_Type) of Dollars;

Salary : Salary_Array;
```

the index of a specific salary would be the identification number of the person making that salary; that is, Salary(201) would be the salary for the employee whose identification number is 201.

The Frequency of Characters case study at the end of this chapter is another example of a problem with a solution that uses indices with semantic content given.

Subarray Processing Arrays are often used to store lists of values. The *length* of an array is established at compile time. We have to define it to be as big as it would ever need to be. Because the exact number of values to be put in the list is often dependent on the data itself, however, we may not fill all of the array components with values. The problem is that, to avoid processing empty ones, we must keep track of how many components are actually filled.

As values are put into the list, we keep a count of the array components that are filled. We then use this count to process only components that have values stored in them. We do not process any remaining places. For example, if there are 250 students in a class, a program to analyze test grades would set aside 250 locations for the grades. However, some students will surely be absent on the day of the test. So we would count the number of test grades, and we would use that number, rather than 250, to control the processing of the array.

We call the actual number of values in an array the *size* of the list. We typically use a separate variable to keep track of the size of our list. Let's look at an example.

```
subtype Score_Range is Float range 0.0..100.0;            -- Component type
type    Exam_Array  is array (1..250) of Score_Range;     -- Array type

Exams  : Exam_Array;        -- An array of 250 exam scores
Size   : Natural;           -- The number of exam scores stored in array Exams
```

Here an array of 250 components is used to store a list of student exam scores. The actual number of components in the list (its size) is kept in the variable Size. The following code fragment reads a list of exam scores from a text file and stores them in the array.

```
Size := 0;   -- At this point we haven't read any exam scores

Input_Loop:     -- Get all the exam scores from the file
loop            -- Each iteration, get one score from the file and
                -- store it in the array
   exit Input_Loop when Ada.Text_IO.End_Of_File (Score_File);
   Size := Size + 1;
   Ada.Float_Text_IO.Get (File => Score_File,
                          Item => Exams(Size));
end loop;
```

Figure 11-8 illustrates the array and the list that is stored in it after executing this code fragment. The value of Size indicates that 245 scores are stored in the array. The remaining five components of the array are not defined—they contain logical garbage.

Suppose we want to determine the highest exam grade in our list of scores. We can write a function to accomplish this task. We need to pass this function the array of scores and the number of values actually stored in this array (the list size). Here is such a function.

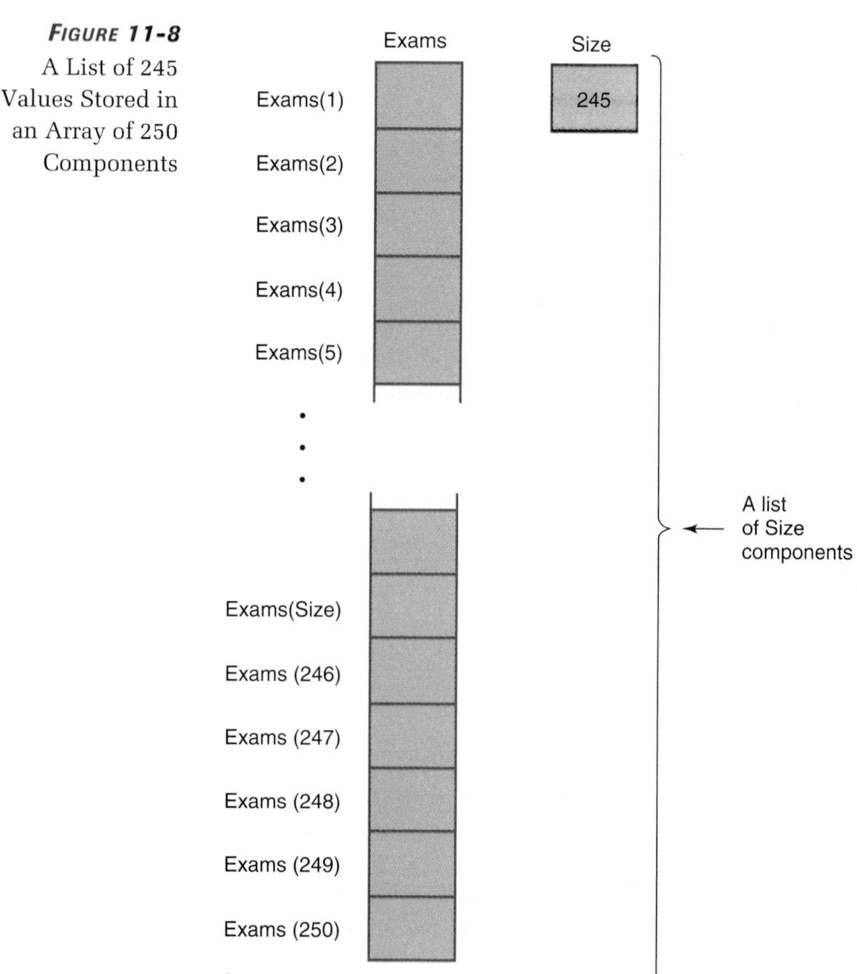

FIGURE 11-8 A List of 245 Values Stored in an Array of 250 Components

```
function Maximum (Class : in Exam_Array;
                  Size  : in Positive) return Score_Range is

-- Returns the largest value in the list of exam scores

   Result : Score_Range;     -- Largest exam score

begin
   Result := Class(1);     -- Initialize to the first score.
                            -- It is the largest "seen" so far.
```

```
   -- See if we can find a larger score than the first one

   for Index in 2..Size loop
      if Class(Index) > Result then   -- Is the current score greater than
         Result := Class(Index);      -- the largest we have seen so far?
      end if;
   end loop;
   return Result;    -- Return the largest score found
end Maximum;
```

This function does not process undefined array components. Size is the index of the last valid array component. Note that formal parameter Size is of type Positive. This function only works for a list containing at least one value.

Unconstrained Array Types

Suppose we have a lab section for which we want to keep a list of quiz scores.

```
type Quiz_Array is array (1..35) of Score_Range;

Quizzes        : Quiz_Array;
Quiz_List_Size : Natural;
```

The array Quizzes can hold up to 35 scores (its length). The variable Quiz_List_Size indicates the actual number of quiz scores stored in this array (its size).

Because Ada is a strongly typed language, we cannot use the function Maximum we presented in the previous section to determine the largest value stored in array Quizzes. Function Maximum only accepts an array parameter of type Exam_Array. In order to find the largest value in a Quiz_Array, we must write a second function that is almost identical to function Maximum. The only difference in these two functions would be the type of the array parameter. In this section, we present Ada features and techniques that allow us to use a single subprogram to process different length arrays.

We have been using constrained array types. A **constrained array type** is an array type with a range specified for its index. An **unconstrained array type** is an array type without a range specified for its index. Only the type of the index and the type of the component are given in the declaration of an unconstrained array.

Constrained array type An array type with a range specified for its index.

Unconstrained array type An array type without a range specified for its index.

Here is a simplified EBNF definition of the unconstrained array type definition.

unconstrained_array_definition ::= **array** (index_subtype_definition) **of** *component_*subtype_indication
index_subtype_definition ::= subtype_mark **range** <>

Here's an example of an unconstrained array declaration.

```
type Score_Array is array (Integer range <>) of Score_Range;
```

Score_Array is declared to be an array type whose components have type Score_Range. The type of the index is defined to be type Integer, but no range is given for the index. The < > symbol (called a *box*) stands for an undefined range. The two uses for unconstrained array types are:

1. Base types for constrained array subtypes
2. Formal parameters

We *cannot* use an unconstrained array type in the declaration of a variable.

```
Class : Score_Array;   -- Illegal declaration
```

The compiler needs to know how many memory locations to allocate to each variable. Because the number of components is not specified, we cannot use unconstrained array types in the declaration of variables.

Here are two examples of declaring constrained array subtypes from the unconstrained array type Score_Array.

```
-- Types
subtype Small_Range is Integer range 1..10;           -- Index subtype
subtype Small_Array is Score_Array (Small_Range);     -- Array subtype

subtype Large_Range is Integer range 1..1000;         -- Index subtype
subtype Large_Array is Score_Array (Large_Range);     -- Array subtype

-- Variables
Small_List : Small_Array;    -- An array of 10 scores
Large_List : Large_Array;    -- An array of 1000 scores
```

Small_Array and Large_Array are subtypes of Score_Array. We specified an index range in each of these array subtype declarations. Small_Array contains 10 components of type Score_Range, and Large_Array contains 1000 components of type Score_Range. Because an index range is specified for each array declaration, these are constrained array subtypes.

Here is an example of a subprogram with a formal parameter that is an unconstrained array type.

```
function Maximum (List : in Score_Array) return Score_Range is
.
.
.
```

With an unconstrained array formal parameter, the actual parameter in a call may be of *any* subtype that has this formal parameter's type as its base type. We can use this one function to find the largest value in Large_List or in Small_List.

The above function shows how unconstrained array types provide a mechanism for passing actual array parameters of different lengths. We also use this capability to eliminate passing, as a *separate* parameter, the list size (the actual number of values stored in the array) to a procedure or function. You may have noticed in contrast to the Maximum function on page 609, the Maximum function above does not have a formal parameter to specify the size of the list. To accomplish this parameter list simplification, we need to examine two more aspects of one-dimensional arrays: slices and attributes.

Array Slices You have been working with the String type since Chapter 2, and we introduced string slices in Chapter 3. By now you probably suspect that strings and arrays have a lot in common. In fact, the predefined type String is an unconstrained array type. It is declared within package Standard (Appendix G) as:

```
type String is array (Positive range <>) of Character;
```

We have used this unconstrained array type as a base type in our own string subtype declarations such as:

```
subtype Name_String is String (1..20);
```

Slices are not limited to string types. We can use slices with any one-dimensional array. A slice denotes a one-dimensional array formed by a sequence of consecutive components of a one-dimensional array. Let's look at some examples using the variable Small_List that we declared in the last section. These slices are illustrated in Figure 11-9.

Expression	**Description**
`Small_List`	An array of 10 scores. Index ranges from 1 to 10.
`Small_List(1..5)`	An array consisting of the first 5 components of Small_List. Index ranges from 1 to 5.
`Small_List(6..10)`	An array consisting of the last 5 components of Small_List. Index ranges from 6 to 10.
`Small_List(4..6)`	An array consisting of 3 components of Small_Array. Index ranges from 4 to 6.

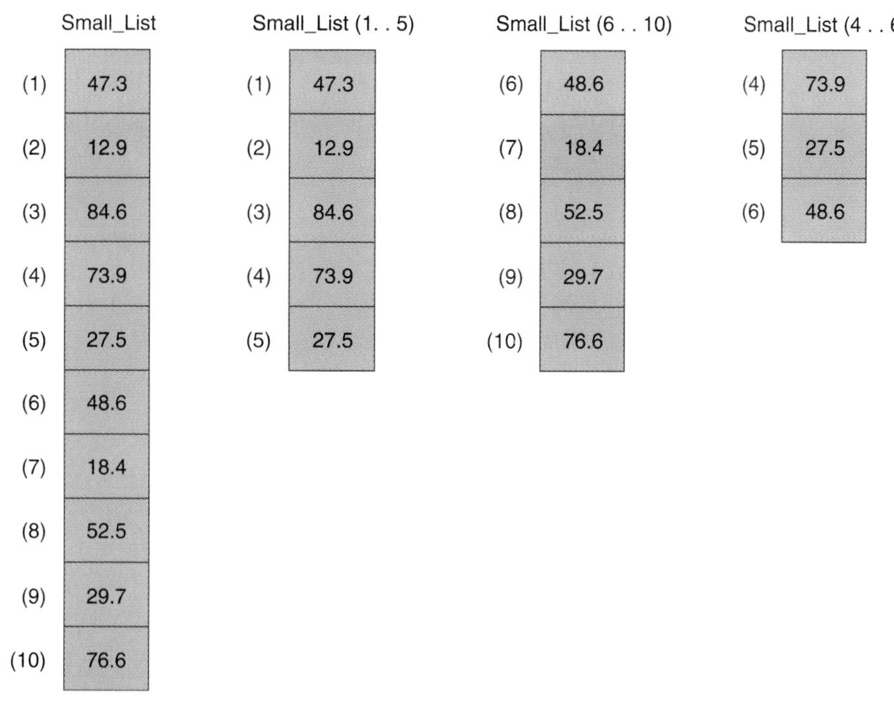

FIGURE 11-9 Slices of the Array Variable Small_List

We can use slices in expressions just as we use any other array variable. Here are some assignment statements that use slices.

```
Small_List(1..3)        :=  (72.4, 93.2, 85.7);
Large_List(221..230)    :=  Small_List;
Small_List              :=  Large_List(991..1000);
Small_List(1..3)        :=  Small_List(4..6);
Large_List (45..50)     :=  Large_List (46..51);
```

While the subscript ranges in these assignment statements may differ, the number of components in each must be the same. The following assignment statement will raise CONSTRAINT_ERROR because it attempts to assign four components to an array that holds three elements.

```
Small_List(1..3)  :=  Large_List(3..6);      -- Illegal assignment
```

The unconstrained array type Score_Array is the base type for all of these array slices. Because the formal parameter List in function Maximum on page 612 is type Score_Array, any slice of Small_List or Large_List can be an actual parameter for List. For example, the function call

```
Best := Maximum (List => Small_List(3..7) );
```

passes a one-dimensional array of five components to the function. Because slice ranges can contain variables, we can use the count of the components in the array (the list's size) to determine the upper index value of the array slice like this:

```
-- Determine the largest value in the first Size components of Small_List
Best := Maximum (List => Small_List(1..Size) );
```

Array Attributes We introduced attributes in Chapter 7 and showed how attributes can obtain information about scalar and discrete types. There are also attributes for array types. You can find descriptions of all attributes in the *Ada Reference Manual* (ARM). Here are four commonly used attributes for one-dimensional arrays.

Attribute	**Purpose**
First	Yields the lower bound of the index range.
Last	Yields the upper bound of the index range.
Length	Yields the number of components in the array. Equivalent to 'Last − 'First + 1
Range	Yields the index range of the array. Equivalent to 'First . . 'Last

The attributes for scalar and discrete types given in Chapter 7 can only be applied to type or subtype names. We can use array attributes with:

- constrained array type names
- constrained array subtype names
- array variable names
- formal array parameter names

Here are some examples with the array subtypes and variables declared on page 611.

Expression	**Result**
`Small_Array'First`	1
`Small_Array'Last`	10
`Small_Array'Length`	10
`Small_Array'Range`	1..10
`Small_List'First`	1
`Small_List'Last`	10
`Small_List'Length`	10
`Small_List'Range`	1..10
`Large_List'First`	1
`Large_List'Last`	1000
`Large_List'Length`	1000
`Large_List'Range`	1..1000
`Large_List(50..70)'First`	50
`Large_List(50..70)'Last`	70
`Large_List(50..70)'Length`	21
`Large_List(50..70)'Range`	50..70
`Large_List(16..15)'Length`	0

Array attributes are commonly used with unconstrained formal array parameters to determine the details of the actual array passed to the subprogram. The following program demonstrates subarray processing using an array slice, an unconstrained array formal parameter, and array attributes.

```
with Ada.Float_Text_IO;
with Ada.Text_IO;
procedure Example is

   subtype Score_Range is Float range 0.0..100.0;

   -- An unconstrained array type
   type Score_Array is array (Integer range <>) of Score_Range;

   -- A constrained array type
   subtype ID_Range   is Integer range 1..250;
   subtype Quiz_Array is Score_Array (ID_Range);

   ----------------------------------------------
   function Maximum (List : in Score_Array) return Score_Range is

   -- Returns the largest value in List
   -- Precondition : List'Length is greater than zero. (There is at least
   --                least one value in the list)

      Result : Score_Range;     -- Largest value
```

```
   begin
      Result := List(List'First);     -- Initialize to the first score.
                                      -- It is the largest "seen" so far.

      -- See if we can find a larger score than the first one

      for Index in List'First + 1 .. List'Last loop
         if List(Index) > Result then   -- Is the current score greater than
            Result := List(Index);      -- the largest we have seen so far?
         end if;
      end loop;
      return Result;    -- Return the largest score found
   end Maximum;

-----------------------------------------------
   Quizzes : Quiz_Array;       -- An array of 250 quiz scores
   Size    : Natural;          -- The number of values in Quizzes
   Best    : Score_Range;      -- Highest quiz score

   Score_File : Ada.Text_IO.File_Type;   -- File containing quiz scores

begin -- Example
   Ada.Text_IO.Open (File => Score_File,
                     Mode => Ada.Text_IO.In_File,
                     Name => "Quizzes.txt");
   Size := 0;   -- At this point we haven't read any exam scores

   Input_Loop:     -- Get all the exam scores from the file
   loop            -- Each iteration, get one score from the file and
                   -- store it in the array
      exit Input_Loop when Ada.Text_IO.End_Of_File (Score_File);
      Size := Size + 1;
      Ada.Float_Text_IO.Get (File => Score_File,
                             Item => Quizzes(Size));
   end loop Input_Loop;

   -- Display the largest score in the list of scores
   Best := Maximum (List => Quizzes(1..Size) );
   Ada.Float_Text_IO.Put (Item => Best, Fore => 2, Aft => 1, Exp => 0);
   Ada.Text_IO.New_Line;
end Example;
```

Notice that the variable Quizzes is a constrained array. We cannot use an unconstrained array type in the declaration of a variable. The variable Size contains the number of quiz scores actually stored in the array. When we call function Maximum, we use Size to slice off all of the logical garbage in the array Quizzes. Every element in the array passed to function Maximum is valid. The *length* of this array slice is equal to the *size* of the list of quiz scores.

Compare the code in the preceding version of function Maximum to that of our original version (page 609). The original code was written to find the largest value in a constrained array whose lower and upper bounds were fixed at 1 and 250. The number of actual values in the list was given by a second parameter, Size. Our new version uses a single parameter, List, which is an unconstrained array. Because the length of the actual array parameter is equal to the size of the list, we do not need to include the size as a separate parameter.

Why did we use List(List'First) instead of List(1) to initialize the value of Result in function Maximum? List(1) may not always be the first component of the array List. For example, we could use the following call to function Maximum to find the highest grade in the 5th through 20th student in the class.

```
Best := Maximum (List => Quizzes(5..20) );
```

If we use List(1) to initialize Result, this call would raise CONSTRAINT_ERROR—there is no component with an index of 1 in the slice passed to the function. By using List(List'First), Result will be initialized to List(5), the first component of the formal array parameter List. You should *never use literals as indices of unconstrained array parameters.* You never know what the range of the array indices might be. Use array attributes to determine the starting and ending indices.

The Mustard Yields case study in this chapter gives another complete example using unconstrained arrays, array slices, and array attributes.

Other Array Operations

Concatenation The concatenation operator, &, is not limited to strings. We can use it with any one-dimensional array type. Here are some example expressions using the array types declared on page 611.

```
Small_List := Small_List(6..10) & Small_List(1..5);      -- Reverse halves

Small_List := Small_List(10) & Small_List(1..9);         -- Rotate values

Small_List := 10.0 & 20.0 & 30.0 & 40.0 & 50.0 &         -- Combine ten values
              60.0 & 70.0 & 80.0 & 90.0 & 100.0;         -- to form an array

Best := Maximum (List => Small_List & Large_List);       -- Find largest in
                                                         -- combined arrays
```

Relational Operators We can use the equality operators (= and /=) to compare two array variables if they have the same base type. We consider two arrays equal if they contain the same number of components *and* the corresponding components in the arrays are equal. The following if statement illustrates comparing two arrays for equality (array variables Char_Count and Frequency are defined on page 593).

```
if  Char_Count = Frequency  then
   Ada.Text_IO.Put_Line ("The corresponding values in the " &
                         "two arrays are equal.");
else
   Ada.Text_IO.Put_Line ("At least one pair of corresponding values " &
                         "in the two arrays differ.");
end if;
```

We can also compare one-dimensional array variables of the same type with the remaining relational operators (<, <=, >, and >=). We can use these ordering operators if the two arrays have the same base type and the components in the array variables are a discrete type. Thus, although we may compare arrays of integers with the < operator, we cannot do the same with arrays of floats.

To determine the order of two unequal arrays, we compare corresponding components in the arrays beginning with the first component in each array and continuing until we find a pair of corresponding components that differ or until we run out of components in one array. If we find a difference, the array with the smaller component is considered less than the array with the larger component. If we run out of components in one array without finding a difference, the array with fewer components is considered less than the other array.

Let's look at some examples. In the following code fragment we declare an unconstrained array type, two constrained array subtypes, and two array variables.

```
type Integer_Array is array (Positive range <>) of Integer;

subtype Small_Int_Array is Integer_Array (1..5);
subtype Large_Int_Array is Integer_Array (1..15);
    .
    .
    .
S : Small_Int_Array;          -- An array of 5 integers
L : Large_Int_Array;          -- An array of 15 integers
    .
    .
    .
begin
   -- Use aggregates to assign values to variables S and L
   S := (31, 32, 33, 34, 35);
   L := (21, 22, 23, 24, 25, 31, 32, 33, 34, 35, 41, 42, 43, 44, 45);
```

The two subtypes Small_Int_Array and Large_Int_Array share the same base type (Integer_Array), and thus we can compare them with the relational operators. The following illustrates some of the possible comparisons and explains the results of these comparisons. There are array slices in several of these examples.

Expression	Value	Explanation
`S = L`	False	The number of components differ.
`S < L`	False	The first component of S is not less than the first component of L.
`S = L(1..5)`	False	The first component of S is not equal to the first component of L(1..5).
`S = L(6..10)`	True	The number of components are equal and the corresponding components are equal.
`S(1..4) < L(6..10)`	True	Ran out of components in S(1..4) before finding a difference.
`S(5..1) < L`	True	S(5..1) is a null array. Ran out of components in S(5..1) before finding a difference.

Because string types are one-dimensional array types, you have actually used relational operators with arrays since Chapter 2. Ordering strings (arrays of characters) is common. You will, however, find less opportunity to use the ordering operators with arrays of other discrete types.

Two-Dimensional Arrays

We use a one-dimensional array to represent a list. We use a **two-dimensional array** to represent a table with rows and columns, provided each item in the table is of the same data type. We can access a component in a two-dimensional array by specifying the row and column indices of the item in a table. This is a familiar task. For example, if you want to find a street on a map, you look up the street name on the back of the map to find the coordinates of the street, usually a letter and a number. The letter specifies a column to look on, and the number specifies a row. You find the street where the row and column meet.

Two-dimensional array A collection of components, all of the same type, structured in two dimensions. Each component is accessed by a pair of indices that represent the component's position in each dimension.

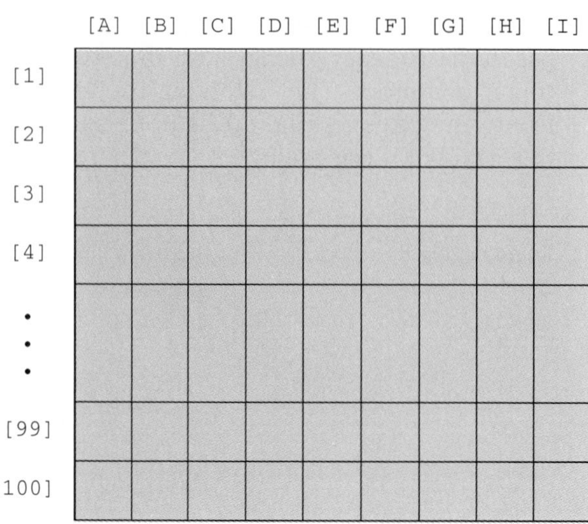

FIGURE 11-10 A Two-Dimensional Array

Figure 11-10 shows a two-dimensional array that has 100 rows and 9 columns. The rows are accessed by an integer ranging from 1 to 100; the columns are accessed by an uppercase letter ranging from *A* to *I*. Each component is accessed by a row-column pair: 1, *A*, for example.

Defining and Accessing Two-Dimensional Arrays

We define a two-dimensional array in exactly the same way as a one-dimensional array, except that two index types must be given. Here's how the array type for the table shown in Figure 11-10 might be declared.

```
-- Types
type    Row_Type    is range 1..100;
subtype Column_Type is Character range 'A'..'I';
type    Table_Type  is array (Row_Type, Column_Type) of Integer;

-- Variable
Map : Table_Type;
```

To access a component, we use two expressions (one for each dimension) to specify its position. These two expressions are listed in one pair of parentheses with a comma between them.

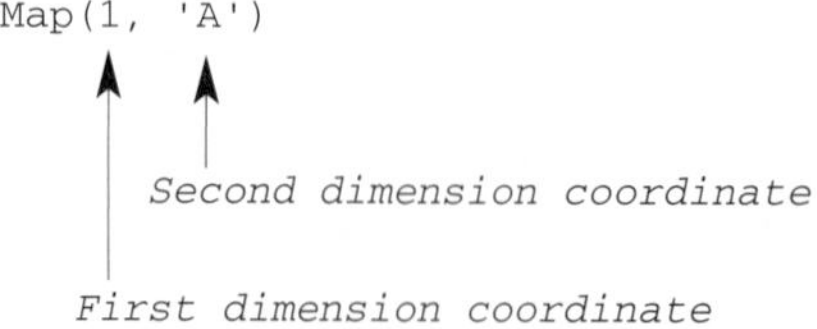

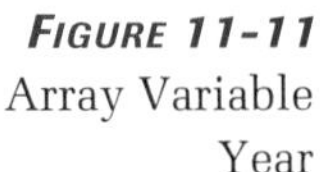

FIGURE 11-11
Array Variable Year

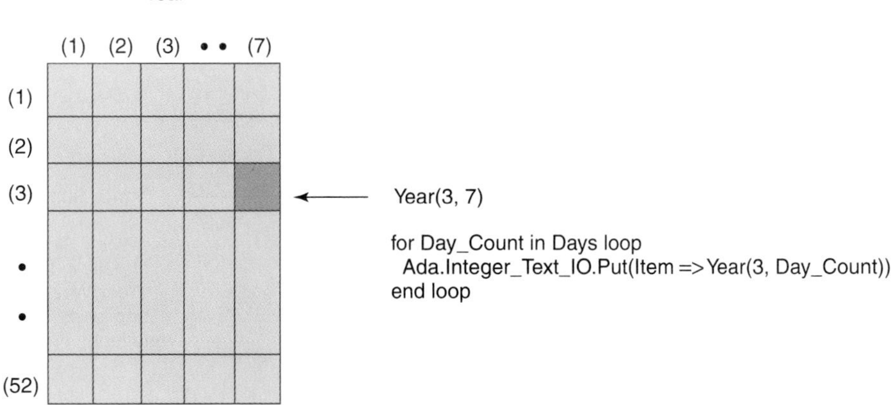

Let's look at some more examples.

```
-- Types
type Weeks     is range 1..52;
type Days      is range 1..7;
type Year_Type is array (Weeks, Days) of Integer;

-- Variable
Year : Year_Type;
```

Year_Type is a two-dimensional array type with 364 components. We can think of it as a table with 52 rows and 7 columns. The contents of each place in the table (each component) can be any Integer value. Year is an array variable of type Year_Type. Year(3, 7) refers to the Integer value in the third row and the seventh column. If the data represented high temperatures for each day in a year, Year(3, 7) would be the temperature for the seventh day of the third week. The code fragment shown in Figure 11-11 would print the temperature values for the third week.

Another representation for the same data might be as follows:

```
-- Types
type Day_Type  is (Monday, Tuesday, Wednesday, Thursday,
                   Friday, Saturday, Sunday);
type Weeks     is range 1..52;
type Year_Type is array (Weeks, Day_Type) of Integer;

-- Variable
Year : Year_Type;
```

Here, Year has the same number of rows and columns as our first representation, but we access the second component by an expression of type

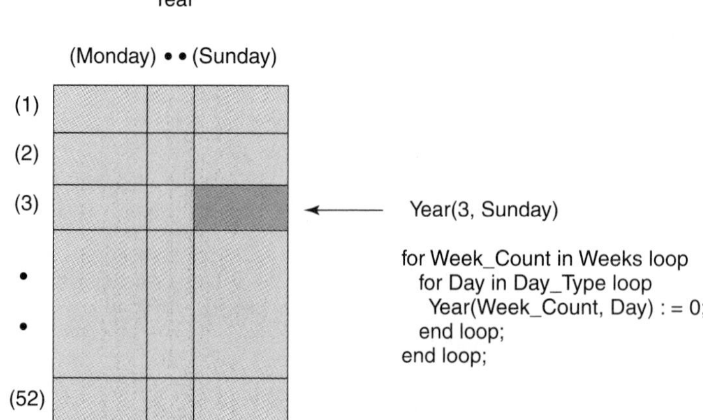

FIGURE 11-12 Array Variable Year (Alternate Form)

Day_Type. Year(3, Sunday) corresponds to the same component as Year(3, 7) in the first example. The code fragment shown in Figure 11-12 sets the entire array to 0.

Here is a third code fragment that defines another two-dimensional array structure that has 52 rows and 7 columns but different index and component types.

```
-- Types
subtype Number_Type is Integer   range -2..49;
subtype Letter_Type is Character range 'a'..'g';
type    Data_Type   is array (Number_Type, Letter_Type) of Character;

-- Variable
Data : Data_Type;
```

In this case, the accessing expression for the row must be in the range −2 . . 49, and for the column it must be in the range 'a' . . 'g'. Each component is a single character. The code fragment shown in Figure 11-13 would print the column whose index is Letter. If the index types were listed in reverse order, the rows and columns would be reversed; that is, if

```
type Data_Type is array (Letter_Type, Number_Type) of Character;
```

declares an array like that shown in Figure 11-14, the code fragment would print the row whose index is Letter.

Another way of looking at a two-dimensional array is to see it as a structure in which each component has two features. In the following definitions

```
-- Component type
subtype Probability is Float range 0.0 .. 1.0;
```

FIGURE 11-13 Array Variable Data

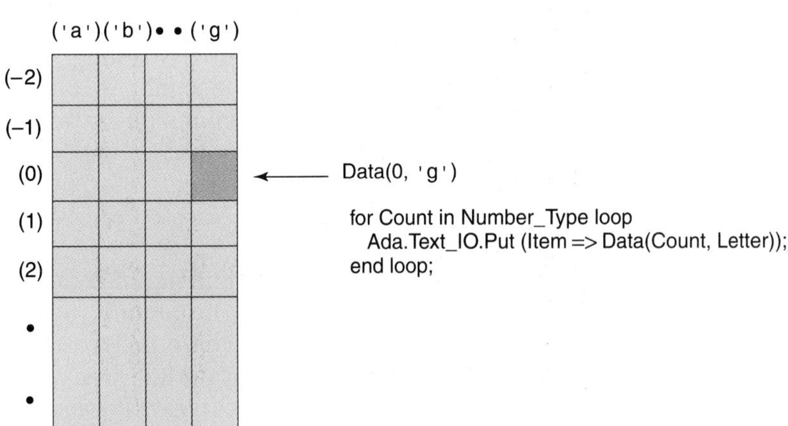


```
-- Index types
type Color_Type is (Red, Orange, Yellow, Green, Blue, Indigo, Violet);
type Make_Type  is (Ford, Toyota, Hyundai, Jaguar, Citroen, BMW, Subaru);
-- Array type
type Car_Type   is array (Color_Type, Make_Type) of Probability;

-- Variable
Crash_Rating : Car_Type;   -- Array of crash probabilities by color and make
```

the data structure uses one dimension to represent the color and the other to represent the make. In other words, both indices have semantic content.

The order in which we define the rows and columns doesn't matter to the computer as long as we're consistent. To help visualize a two-dimensional array, we use the common convention of letting the first dimension define the rows and the second dimension define the columns.

FIGURE 11-14 Array Variable Data (Second Definition)

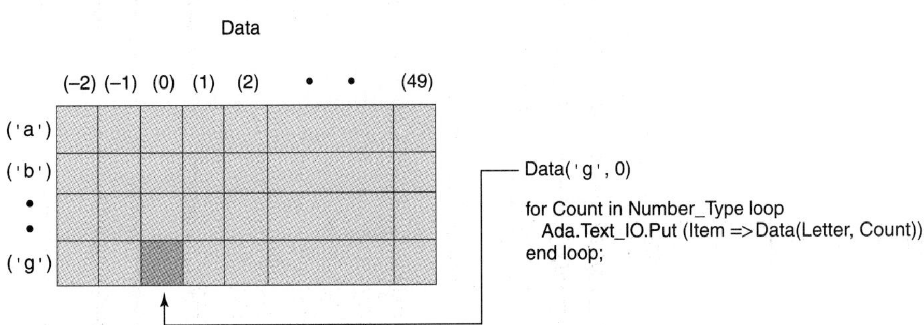

Processing Two-Dimensional Arrays

Processing data in a two-dimensional array generally means accessing the array in one of four patterns: randomly, along rows, along columns, or throughout the array. Each of these also may involve subarray processing.

The simplest way to access a component is to look in a given location. For example, a user enters map coordinates that we use as indices into an array of street names to access the sought-after name at those coordinates. We refer to this process as random access because the user may enter any set of coordinates at random.

There are many cases where we might wish to perform an operation on all the elements of a particular row or column in a table. Look back at the array Year defined on page 621, where the rows represent weeks of the year and the columns represent days of the week. The data represents the high temperatures for each day in a year. If we wanted the average high temperature for a given week, we would sum the values in that row and divide by 7. If we wanted the average for a given day of the week, we would sum the values in that column and divide by 52. The former case is access along rows; the latter case is access along columns.

Now, suppose that we wish to determine the average for the year. We must access every element in the array, sum them, and divide by 364. In this case, the order of access is not important. (The same is true when we initialize every element of an array to 0.) This is an example of access throughout the array.

There are situations in which we must access every element in an array in a particular order, either by rows or by columns. If we wanted the average for every week, we would run through the entire array, taking each row in turn. However, if we wanted the average for each day of the week, we would run through the array one column at a time.

Let's take a closer look at these patterns of access by considering four common examples of array processing.

1. Sum the rows.
2. Sum the columns.
3. Print the table.
4. Initialize the table to all zeros (or some special value).

First, let's define some types and variables using general identifiers, such as Row and Column, rather than problem-dependent identifiers. Then let's look at each algorithm in terms of generalized table processing.

```
-- Named Numbers
Number_Of_Rows    : constant := 4;
Number_Of_Columns : constant := 4;
```

```
-- Types
type Row_Range    is range 1..Number_Of_Rows;
type Column_Range is range 1..Number_Of_Columns;
type Table_Type   is array (Row_Range, Column_Range) of Integer;

-- Variables
Table       : Table_Type;       -- A two-dimensional array
Total       : Integer;          -- A variable for summing
Row_Size    : Row_Range;        -- For specifying a subrange
                                -- of rows to process
Column_Size : Column_Range;     -- For specifying a subrange of
                                -- columns to process
```

Notice our use of *type* declarations rather than *subtype* declarations for the row and column indices. A common error in processing two-dimensional arrays is to accidently reverse the order of the indices in an accessing expression. By using different types rather than subtypes for the two index types, the Ada compiler will give a syntax error if we write our indices in the wrong order.

Sum the Rows Suppose that we want to sum row number 3 in array Table and print the result. We can do this easily with a for statement.

```
Total := 0;
-- Find the sum of the values in row 3 of the table
-- Each iteration, add one of the values to the total
for Column in Column_Range loop
   Total := Total + Table(3, Column);
end loop;
Ada.Integer_Text_IO.Put (Item => Total,  Width => 1);
Ada.Text_IO.New_Line;
```

This loop runs through each column of Table, while keeping the row index equal to 3. Every value in row 3 is added to Total. Suppose that we wanted to sum and print two rows—row 2 and row 3. We could add a duplicate of the preceding code fragment, but with the index set to 2:

```
Total := 0;
-- Sum row 2
-- Each iteration, add one of the values in row 2 to the total
for Column in Column_Range loop
   Total := Total + Table(2, Column);
end loop;
Ada.Integer_Text_IO.Put (Item => Total,  Width => 1);
Ada.Text_IO.New_Line;


Total := 0;
```

```
-- Sum row 3
-- Each iteration, add one of the values in row 3 to the total
for Column in Column_Range loop
   Total := Total + Table(3, Column);
end loop;
Ada.Integer_Text_IO.Put (Item => Total,  Width => 1);
Ada.Text_IO.New_Line;
```

or we could use a nested loop and make the row index a variable:

```
-- Calculate and print the row totals for rows 2 and 3
-- Each iteration, process one row
for Row in 2..3 loop
   Total := 0;
   for Column in Column_Range loop  -- Each iteration, add one value to Total
      Total := Total + Table(Row, Column);
   end loop;
   Ada.Integer_Text_IO.Put (Item => Total,  Width => 1);
   Ada.Text_IO.New_Line;
end loop;
```

The second approach is shorter, but its real advantage is that we can easily modify it to process any range of rows.

The outer loop controls the rows and the inner loop controls the columns. For each value of Row, the program processes every column, then the outer loop moves to the next row. In the first iteration of the outer loop, Row holds at 2 and Column goes from 1 to Number_Of_Columns. Therefore, the array is accessed in the following order.

```
Table(2, 1)  Table(2, 2)  Table(2, 3)  Table(2, 4)
```

In the second iteration of the outer loop, the program increments Row to 3, and accesses the third row as follows:

```
Table(3, 1)  Table(3, 2)  Table(3, 3)  Table (3, 4)
```

We can generalize this row processing to run through every row of the table by having the outer loop run from 1 to Number_Of_Rows. However, if we want to access only part of the array (subarray processing), we write the code fragment as follows:

```
for Row in 1..Row_Size loop   -- Each iteration, display one row sum
   Total := 0;
   for Column in 1..Column_Size loop -- Each iteration, add one value to total
      Total := Total + Table(Row, Column);
   end loop;
   Ada.Integer_Text_IO.Put (Item => Total,  Width => 1);
   Ada.Text_IO.New_Line;
end loop;
```

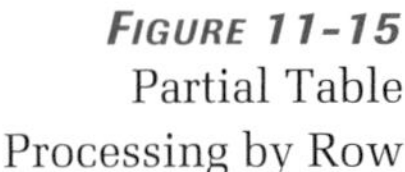
FIGURE 11-15
Partial Table Processing by Row

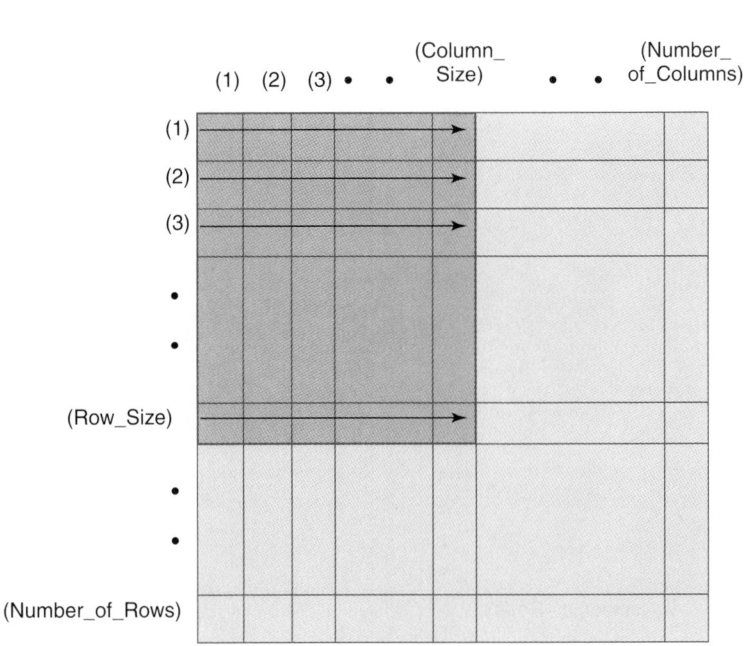

Figure 11-15 illustrates subarray processing by row.

Sum the Columns Suppose that we want to sum and print each column. The following code will perform this task. Again we have generalized the code to sum only the portion of the array that contains valid data.

```
for Column in 1..Column_Size loop    -- Each iteration, display one column sum
   Total := 0;
   for Row in 1..Row_Size loop    -- Each iteration, add one value to the total
      Total := Total + Table(Row, Column);
   end loop;
   Ada.Integer_Text_IO.Put (Item => Total,  Width => 1);
   Ada.Text_IO.New_Line;
end loop;
```

In this case, the outer loop controls the column, and the inner loop controls the row. The program accesses and sums all the components in the first column before the outer loop index changes and the components in the second column are accessed. Figure 11-16 illustrates subarray processing by column.

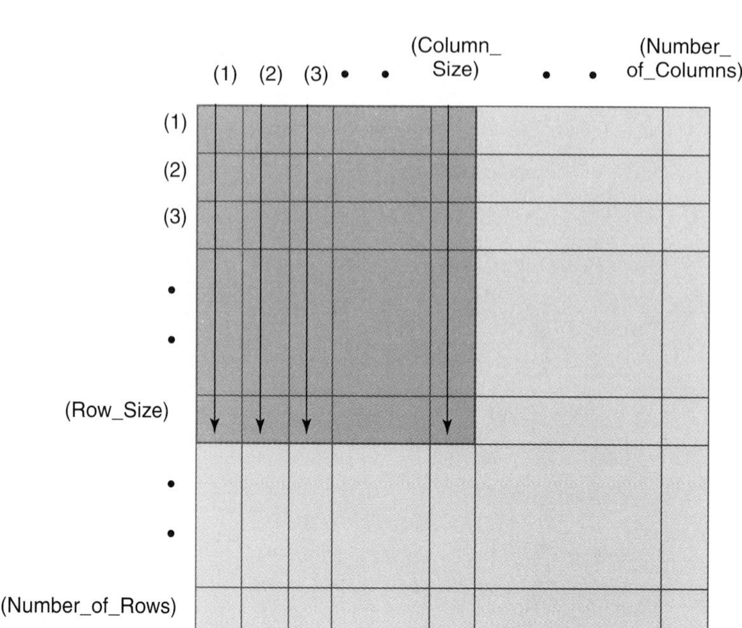

FIGURE 11-16 Partial Table Processing by Column

Print the Table If we wish to print out a table with one row per line, then we have another case of row processing.

```
for Row in 1..Row_Size loop
   for Column in 1..Column_Size loop
      Ada.Integer_Text_IO.Put (Item => Table(Row, Column),  Width => 8);
   end loop;
   Ada.Text_IO.New_Line;
end loop;
```

This code fragment prints the values of the table in columns that are 8 characters wide. As a matter of proper style, we should precede this fragment with code that prints headings over the columns to identify their contents.

There's no rule that we have to print each row on a line. We could turn the table sideways and print each column on one line simply by exchanging the two for loops. When you are printing a table, you must consider which order of presentation makes the most sense and how the table fits on the page. A table with 6 columns and 100 rows would best be printed as 6 columns, 100 lines long.

Almost all processing of data stored in a two-dimensional array involves either processing by row or processing by column. In our examples, the index type has been an integer type, but the pattern of operation of the loops is the same no matter what types the indices are.

The looping patterns for row processing and column processing are so useful that we have summarized them in the following code fragments. Remember that row processing has the row index in the outer loop, and column processing has the column index in the outer loop.

Row Processing

```
for Row in Row_Range loop
   for Column in Column_Range loop
      -- Whatever processing is required
   end loop;
end loop;
```

Column Processing

```
for Column in Column_Range loop
   for Row in Row_Range loop
      -- Whatever processing is required
   end loop;
end loop;
```

Initialize the Table Initializing a table is the same as initializing any other array variable: each element is set to some special value, such as 0. Here is some code that implements this task.

```
for Row in Row_Range loop
   for Column in Column_Range loop
      Table(Row, Column) := 0;
   end loop;
end loop;
```

In this case, we initialized the table a row at a time, but we could just as easily have run through each column instead. The order doesn't matter as long as we access every element.

Aggregates We may use array aggregates with two-dimensional arrays. As with one-dimensional array aggregates, two-dimensional array aggregates must contain a value for each component of the array. In a two-dimensional array aggregate, *every row is enclosed in parentheses*. Values may be associated with a particular array component by position or by name. Using the declarations given for Table on page 625 in which Table has 4 rows and 4 columns, we can use the following aggregates to initialize all components in Table to 0.

All Elements by Position

```
Table := ((0, 0, 0, 0),        -- 1st row
          (0, 0, 0, 0),        -- 2nd row
          (0, 0, 0, 0),        -- 3rd row
          (0, 0, 0, 0));       -- 4th row

Table := ((0, 0, 0, 0),  (0, 0, 0, 0),  (0, 0, 0, 0),  (0, 0, 0, 0));
```

Rows by Name, Columns by Position

```
Table := (1 => (0, 0, 0, 0),        -- 1st row
          2 => (0, 0, 0, 0),        -- 2nd row
          3 => (0, 0, 0, 0),        -- 3rd row
          4 => (0, 0, 0, 0));       -- 4th row

Table := (1..4 => (0, 0, 0, 0));
```

Rows by Position, Columns by Name

```
Table := ((1 => 0, 2 => 0, 3 => 0, 4 => 0),        -- 1st row
          (1 => 0, 2 => 0, 3 => 0, 4 => 0),        -- 2nd row
          (1 => 0, 2 => 0, 3 => 0, 4 => 0),        -- 3rd row
          (1 => 0, 2 => 0, 3 => 0, 4 => 0));       -- 4th row

Table := ((1..4 => 0)        -- 1st row
          (1..4 => 0)        -- 2nd row
          (1..4 => 0)        -- 3rd row
          (1..4 => 0));      -- 4th row
```

All Elements by Name

```
Table := (1 => (1 => 0, 2 => 0, 3 => 0, 4 => 0),        -- 1st row
          2 => (1 => 0, 2 => 0, 3 => 0, 4 => 0),        -- 2nd row
          3 => (1 => 0, 2 => 0, 3 => 0, 4 => 0),        -- 3rd row
          4 => (1 => 0, 2 => 0, 3 => 0, 4 => 0));       -- 4th row

Table := (1 => (1..4 => 0),        -- 1st row
          2 => (1..4 => 0),        -- 2nd row
          3 => (1..4 => 0),        -- 3rd row
          4 => (1..4 => 0));       -- 4th row

Table := (1..4 => (1..4 => 0));

Table := (Row_Range => (Column_Range => 0));
```

The reserved word `others` may appear as the last name in any parenthesized list of the aggregate. Here are some examples using `others`.

```
Table := (1 => (2 | 3 => 34, others => 17)        -- 1st row
          3 => (1 => 58, others => 26)            -- 3rd row
          others => (0, 0, 0, 0));                -- 2nd and 4th rows

Table := (others => (others => 0));
```

When a program uses several similar two-dimensional array types, the compiler may not be able to determine the type of the aggregate in which `others` is used. As we did with one-dimensional array aggregates, we can qualify the aggregate with the type name as illustrated here.

```
Table := Table_Type'(others => (others => 0));
```

Arrays of Arrays

In Ada, we can also define a two-dimensional array as an array of arrays. The declaration of an array type includes an index type (or types) and a component type. Although an index type must be a discrete type, the component of an array may be of any type. Thus, a component type may even be another array type. The following statements declare a one-dimensional array type of 24 hourly temperatures.

```
Hours_Per_Day : constant := 24;

subtype Degrees             is Integer range -40 .. 140;
subtype Hour_Index          is Integer range 1..Hours_Per_Day;
type    Hourly_Temperatures is array (Hour_Index) of Degrees;
```

The array type Hourly_Temperatures is a list of 24 temperatures. It may be used as the component type in the declaration of another array type and an array variable like this:

```
Days_Per_Week : constant := 7;

type Day_Type is (Monday, Tuesday, Wednesday, Thursday,
                  Friday, Saturday, Sunday);
type Daily_Temperatures is array (Day_Type) of Hourly_Temperatures;

Week : Daily_Temperatures;
```

Array variable Week is illustrated in Figure 11-17. It contains seven components indexed by Day_Type. Each of these components is an array of 24 temperatures. The array Week may be used like any other one-dimensional array.

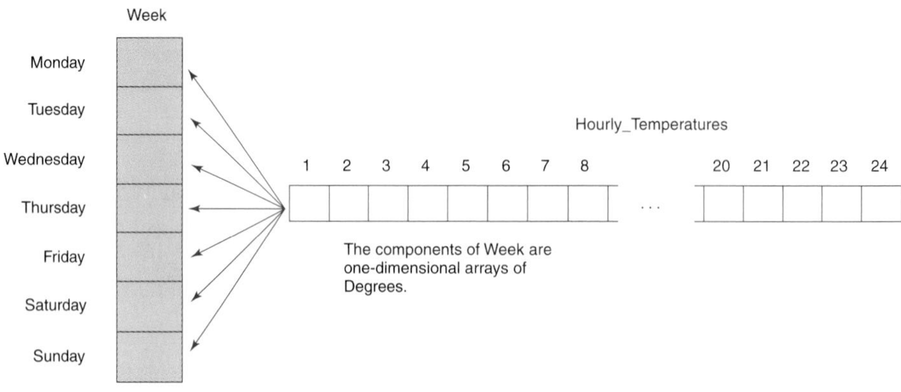

FIGURE 11-17
An Array of Arrays

```
Week ◄────────────────────── The entire array of seven components
Week(Wednesday) ◄─────────── The third component of the array Week
Week(Monday..Friday) ◄─── A slice consisting of five components
```

Because each component in Week is itself an array of temperatures, we use a second index to select one of the 24 temperatures. For example, the following references the eighth temperature on Wednesday.

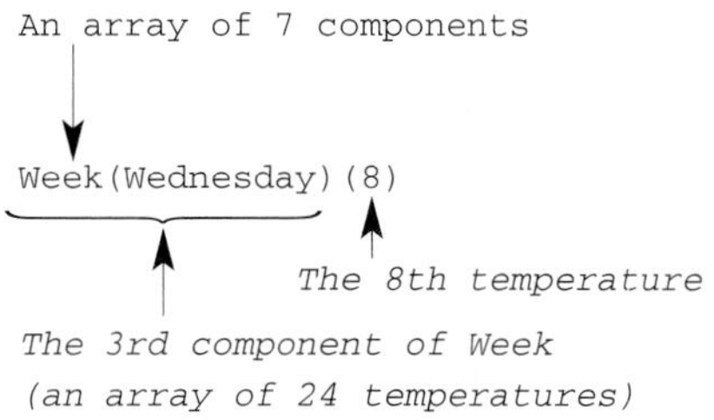

We can even use slices of the hourly temperature array such as this:

```
Week(Tuesday)(13..24) ◄──Tuesday's p.m. temperatures
```

The processing of an array of arrays is nearly identical to the processing of a two-dimensional array. Just make sure that each index is enclosed in its own set of parentheses. Here's a code fragment that illustrates how we can access the components in Week. It calculates the average hourly temperature for the data stored in array Week.

```
Sum := 0;
for Day in Day_Type loop   -- Each iteration, process one day's temperatures
   for Hour in Hour_Index loop   -- Each iteration, sum one hourly temperature
      Sum := Sum + Week(Day)(Hour);
   end loop;
end loop;
Average_Daily_Temperature := Sum / (Days_Per_Week * Hours_Per_Day);
```

Except for enclosing each index value in its own set of parentheses, this processing is the same as the processing used to access all the components of a two-dimensional array.

Here's a way to calculate a different average temperature. First we average the 24 temperatures of a day to calculate the average temperature for that day. Then we average the seven daily averages.

```
function Average_For_Day (Readings : in Hourly_Temperatures)
                          return Degrees is
   Sum : Integer;
begin
   Sum := 0;
   for Hour in Hour_Index loop    -- Each iteration, add one temperature to Sum
      Sum := Sum + Readings (Hour);
   end loop;
   return  Sum / Hours_Per_Day;
end Average_For_Day;
         .
         .
         .
Total := 0;
-- Find the average of the average daily temperatures
-- Each iteration, add one daily average to Total
for Day in Day_Type loop
   Total := Total + Average_For_Day (Readings => Week (Day));
end loop;
Average_Daily_Temperature := Total / Days_Per_Week;
```

The Day loop sums the average temperatures for each day. It calls the function Average_For_Day to determine the average temperature for one day. The formal parameter, Readings, of the function is a one-dimensional array of Degrees. The actual parameter in the call to the function is a single component of Week (a one-dimensional array of Degrees).

This code fragment illustrates one of the advantages of using an array of arrays instead of a two-dimensional array. If we had declared Week to be a two-dimensional array like this

```
-- Alternative declaration of Week
type Daily_Temperatures is array (Day_Type, Hour_Index) of Degrees;

Week : Daily_Temperatures;      -- A two-dimensional array of temperatures
```

we could not pass a row of this table to a procedure. We would have to pass the entire table.

Slices would seem a way to pass a single row of a table. However, slices are available only for one-dimensional arrays; we can't use them with two-dimensional arrays. The availability of slices is a second advantage of using an array of arrays instead of a two-dimensional array.

Unconstrained Two-Dimensional Array Types

Recall that a constrained array type is an array type with a range specified for its index, and an unconstrained array type is an array type without a range specified for its index. Only the type of the index and the type of the component are given in the declaration of an unconstrained array type. Unconstrained array types are used for formal parameters and serve as base types for constrained array subtypes.

As with one-dimensional arrays, two-dimensional array types may be constrained or unconstrained. Here are some example declarations of unconstrained and constrained one-dimensional arrays, arrays of arrays, and two-dimensional arrays.

```
subtype Degrees    is Integer    range -40 .. 140;
subtype Hour_Index is Integer    range 1..Hours_Per_Day;
subtype Hour_Index is Integer    range  1..24;
subtype AM_Range   is Hour_Index range  1..12;
subtype PM_Range   is Hour_Index range 13..24
type    Day_Type   is (Monday, Tuesday, Wednesday, Thursday,
                       Friday, Saturday, Sunday);

subtype Month_Range is Integer range 1..12;

-- One-dimensional unconstrained array type
type Hourly_Array is array (Hour_Index range <>) of Degrees;

-- One-dimensional constrained array types
subtype Morning_Temperatures is Hourly_Array (AM_Range);
subtype Daily_Temperatures   is Hourly_Array (Hour_Index);

-- Unconstrained arrays of arrays
type Daily_Array   is array (Day_Type range <>) of Daily_Temperatures;
type Morning_Array is array (Day_Type range <>) of Hourly_Array (AM_Range);

-- Constrained array of arrays
subtype Daily_Temperatures is Daily_Array (Day_Type);

-- Unconstrained two-dimensional array
type Temperature_Array is
     array (Integer range <>, Integer range <>) of Degrees;

-- Constrained two-dimensional arrays
subtype XX_Century_Temps  is Temperature_Array (1..12, 1901..2000);
subtype XIX_Century_Temps is Temperature_Array (1..12, 1801..1900);
```

If an array component is an array, then it must be a constrained array. Thus, while the declaration of the array of arrays types Daily_Array and Morning_Array given in the previous examples are legal, the following array declaration is not.

```
-- Illegal declaration
type Weather_Array is array (Day_Type range <>) of Hourly_Array;
```

The component Hourly_Array is an unconstrained array type. The declaration of Morning_Array uses the unconstrained type Hourly_Array in its definition along with a range that constrains it.

Array Attributes

A very important use of unconstrained array types is the declaration of formal parameters of subprograms. Earlier in this chapter, we used the attributes 'First, 'Last, 'Range, and 'Length with unconstrained one-dimensional array parameters. The same attributes are available with two-dimensional arrays. However, we must now specify for which index of the array we desire the low bound, high bound, and so on. We indicate the index we want by giving its dimension number in parentheses after the attribute. The first index of a two-dimensional array is dimension number 1, the second index is dimension number 2. The attribute to determine the lower bound of the second dimension of the array Table is written as

```
Table'First(2)          -- The lower bound of the 2nd index
```

The following function to determine the average of the values in a two-dimensional array illustrates the use of attributes with an unconstrained multidimensional array parameter. Type Temperature_Array is declared on the previous page.

```
function Average (Temperatures : in Temperature_Array) return Degrees is
   Sum : Integer;
begin
   Sum := 0.0;
   for Row in Temperatures'Range(1) loop                -- Row loop
      for Column in Temperatures'Range(2) loop          -- Column loop
         Sum := Sum + Temperatures(Row, Column);
      end loop;
   end loop;
   return Sum / (Temperatures'Length(1) * Temperatures'Length(2));
end Average;
```

We can call this function with any actual array parameter whose base type is Score_Array. For example:

```
Twentieth  : XX_Century_Temps;
Nineteenth : XIX_Century_Temps;

Twentieth_Average   : Degrees;
Nineteenth_Average : Degrees;
   .
   .
   .
Twentieth_Average   := Average (Temperatures => Twentieth);
Nineteenth_Average := Average (Temperatures => Nineteenth);
```

We frequently use array slices as actual parameters with unconstrained one-dimensional array formal parameters. Remember that slices are not available for two-dimensional arrays. Use an array of arrays if you need to use slices.

Multidimensional Arrays

Ada does not place a limit on the number of dimensions that an array can have. We can generalize our definition of an **array** to cover all cases. Here is a more complete EBNF definition for an array type.

array_type_definition	::=	unconstrained_array_definition | constrained_array_definition
constrained_array_definition	::=	**array** index_constraint **of** *component*_subtype_indication
index_constraint	::=	(discrete_range {, discrete_range})
discrete_range	::=	*discrete*_subtype_indication | range
subtype_indication	::=	*type*_name | *subtype*_name
range	::=	simple_expression .. simple expression | *range*_attribute
unconstrained_array_definition	::=	**array** (index_subtype_definition {, index_subtype_definition}) **of** *component*_subtype_indication
index_subtype_definition	::=	subtype_mark **range** <>

Each discrete range in the index constraint establishes a different dimension. You can give an array as many dimensions as you want. How many should you have in a particular case? As many as there are features that describe the components in the array.

Array A collection of components, all of the same type, ordered on N dimensions ($N \geq 1$). Each component is accessed by N indices, each of which represents the component's position within that dimension.

Take, for instance, a chain of department stores. Each store must keep monthly sales figures for each item. There are three important pieces of information about each item: the month in which it was sold, the store from which it was purchased, and the item number. We can define an array to summarize this data as follows:

```
-- Constants
Number_Of_Items  : constant := 100;
Number_Of_Stores : constant := 10;

-- Types
type    Item_Range  is range 1..Number_Of_Items;
type    Store_Range is range 1..Number_Of_Stores;
subtype Month_Range is Ada.Calendar.Month_Number;

type Sales_Array is array (Store_Range, Month_Range, Item_Range)
                           of Natural;

--I/O Package instantiations
package Item_IO  is new Ada.Text_IO.Integer_IO (Num => Item_Range);
package Store_IO is new Ada.Text_IO.Integer_IO (Num => Store_Range);

-- Variables
Sales         : Sales_Array;
Current_Month : Month_Range;
Number_Sold   : Natural;
```

A graphic representation of the array variable Sales is shown in Figure 11-18. The number of components in Sales is 12,000 ($10 \times 12 \times 100$). If it is only June (Current_Month = 6), then part of the array (July through December) is empty. If we want to process the data in the array, we must use subarray processing. The following program fragment sums and prints the total number of each item sold this year to date by all stores.

```
-- Get the current month from the computer's clock
Current_Month := Ada.Calendar.Month (Ada.Calendar.Clock);

for Item in Item_Range loop  -- Each iteration, process one Item
   Number_Sold := 0;
   for Store in Store_Range loop  -- Each iteration, process one Store
      for Month in 1..Current_Month loop  -- Each iteration, process one Month
         Number_Sold := Number_Sold + Sales(Store, Month, Item);
      end loop;
   end loop;
```

```
   Ada.Text_IO.Put ("Item #");
   Item_IO.Put (Item => Item,  Width => 3);
   Ada.Text_IO.Put ("Sales to date = ");
   Ada.Integer_Text_IO.Put (Item => Number_Sold,  Width => 6);
   Ada.Text_IO.New_Line;
end loop;
```

Because Item is controlled by the outer for loop, we are summing each item's sales by Store and Month. If we want to find the total sales for each store, we control Store in the outer for loop, summing its sales by Month and Item with the inner loops.

```
-- Get the current month from the computer's clock
Current_Month := Ada.Calendar.Month (Ada.Calendar.Clock);

for Store in Store_Range loop  -- Each iteration, process one store
   Number_Sold := 0;
   for Item in Item_Range loop;  -- Each iteration, process one item
      for Month in 1..Current_Month loop  -- Each iteration, process one month
         Number_Sold := Number_Sold + Sales(Store, Month, Item);
      end loop;
   end loop;
   Ada.Text_IO.Put ("Store #");
   Store_IO.Put (Item => Store,  Width => 3);
   Ada.Text_IO.Put ("Sales to date = ");
   Ada.Integer_Text_IO.Put (Item => Number_Sold,  Width => 6);
   Ada.Text_IO.New_Line;
end loop;
```

It takes two loops to access each component in a two-dimensional array; it takes three loops to access each component in a three-dimensional array. In a three-dimensional array, the job to be done determines which index controls the outer loop, the middle loop, and the inner loop. If we

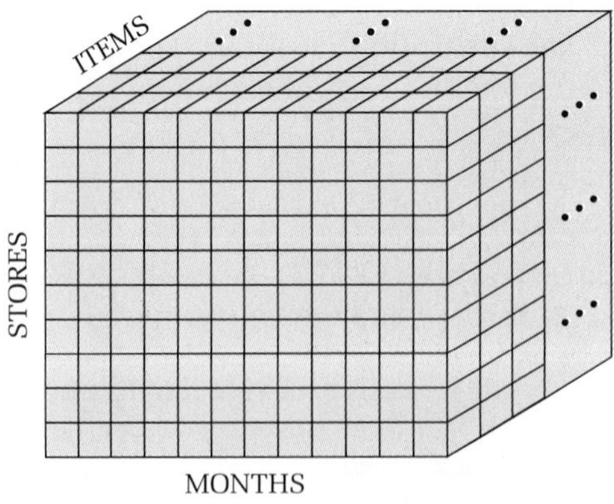

FIGURE 11-18 Graphical Representation of Array Variable Sales

want to calculate monthly sales by store, Month controls the outer loop and Store controls the middle loop. If we want to calculate monthly sales by item, Month controls the outer loop and Item controls the middle loop.

If we want to keep track of the departments that sell each item, we can add a fourth dimension.

```
subtype Dept_Range  is Character range 'A'..'G';
type    Sales_Array is
        array (Store_Range, Month_Range, Item_Range, Dept_Range)
              of Natural;
```

How would we visualize this new structure? Not very easily! Fortunately, we do not have to visualize a structure to use it. If we want the number of sales in store 1, during May (the fifth month), for item number 4, in department C, we simply write

```
Sales(1, 5, 4, 'C')
```

SOFTWARE ENGINEERING TIP

Choosing a Data Structure

We use arrays and records to associate an identifier with a collection of values. We use arrays when all the values are the same type and records when the values have differing types. We nest and combine arrays and records to create more complex data structures.

Data structures that accurately reflect the relationships among the data values in a problem lead to effective programs. The logic of the program is easier to understand because the data structures mirror the problem. The code of the program is easier to maintain because the logic of the program is clearer. The program is easier to modify because the data structure accurately represents the problem.

We should make one additional point here. The best structure is the simplest one that accurately reflects the problem and the processing. For example, don't use either arrays or records if simple variables suffice.

One-dimensional arrays are useful for storing lists. When your problem requires a table, the two-dimensional array is likely a good data structure. If your table processing demands that individual rows of the table be processed by subprograms, the array of arrays is probably a better choice for storing the data. Arrays with dimensions greater than two are most useful when the indices have semantic content or for implementing mathematical algorithms that involve *n*-dimensional space.

This discussion presupposes that you know where to begin. What if you look at a problem and don't even know what the choices are? Go back and carefully examine the problem statement. Do you understand what is being asked? Can you do what is being asked by hand? If so, what sorts of forms would you use? Would you set up a table with rows and columns on a sheet of paper? Would you set up a column and make hash marks? More than likely, the appropriate data structure resembles the forms you would create to do the job by hand.

If you cannot do the job by hand, your problem is more fundamental than the choice of a data structure–you need to clarify the problem. Try writing down everything you know about the problem. Then write down what your output must be and what you must have as input to produce that output. If necessary, refer to the problem-solving techniques in Chapter 1.

PROBLEM-SOLVING CASE STUDY

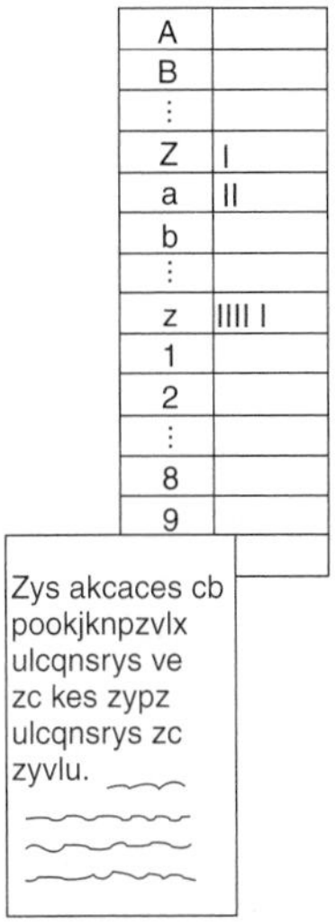

Frequency of Characters

Specification

Problem You've found a secret message written in some sort of code. After doing some research, you decide to see whether it is a simple substitution cipher—a code in which each letter is replaced by a different letter. Your research tells you that the way to break this type of code is to count the occurrences of each letter in the text and compare them to the average occurrence of letters in any English text. For example, the most common letter is probably a substitute for *e*. You decide to write a program to count the occurrences of each character in a text file.

Input

- The name of a text file.
- The text file.

Output Each printable character in the character set that occurred at least one time in the message followed by the number of times it occurred.

Discussion To do this by hand, you would make a list of all the characters. Then you would process the text by taking each character and making a mark on the list beside that character. When you are finished with the text, the number of marks beside each character in the list tells you how many times that character occurred in the text.

Ada already has a built-in list of all the characters—type Character. Ada also allows us to use any discrete type as an index type. By using the characters themselves as the indices in a counting array, we can increment the proper counter for a particular character by using that character as the index.

PROBLEM-SOLVING CASE STUDY cont'd.

The ISO 8859-1 character set used by Ada has nonprinting characters and characters we know are not found in English text. We need to set up our array to count only those characters. Fortunately, these characters are all grouped together, so we can define a subtype of the characters to be our index type. From Appendix C we find that the space character and the tilde (~) are the first and last characters in the set of interest. If we use Frequency_Count as the name of our array variable,

- Frequency_Count('A') is the counter for A's.
- Frequency_Count(Frequency_Count'First) is the counter for spaces.
- Frequency_Count(Frequency_Count'Last) is the counter for tildes.
- Frequency_Count(Char) is the counter for whatever character variable Char contained.

The fact that the array index itself has meaning simplifies this problem. Figure 11-19 shows the array.

Assumptions

- The name of the file contains no more than 80 characters.
- The text file containing the secret message exists.
- The text file contains only characters from blank to tilde in the character set.

Design

Character Counts **Level 0**

```
Get the name of the data file
Open Data File
Set all components of Frequency_Count to zero
Loop
   Exit when End of File
   Get Char from Data_File
   Increment Frequency_Count(Char) by 1
end loop
Display counts
Close Data File
```

Zero Frequency Count **Level 1**

```
   out      Frequency_Count
Frequency_Count := (others => 0)
```

PROBLEM-SOLVING CASE STUDY *cont'd.*

FIGURE 11-19 An Array of 95 Components Used to Store the Frequencies of Characters Found

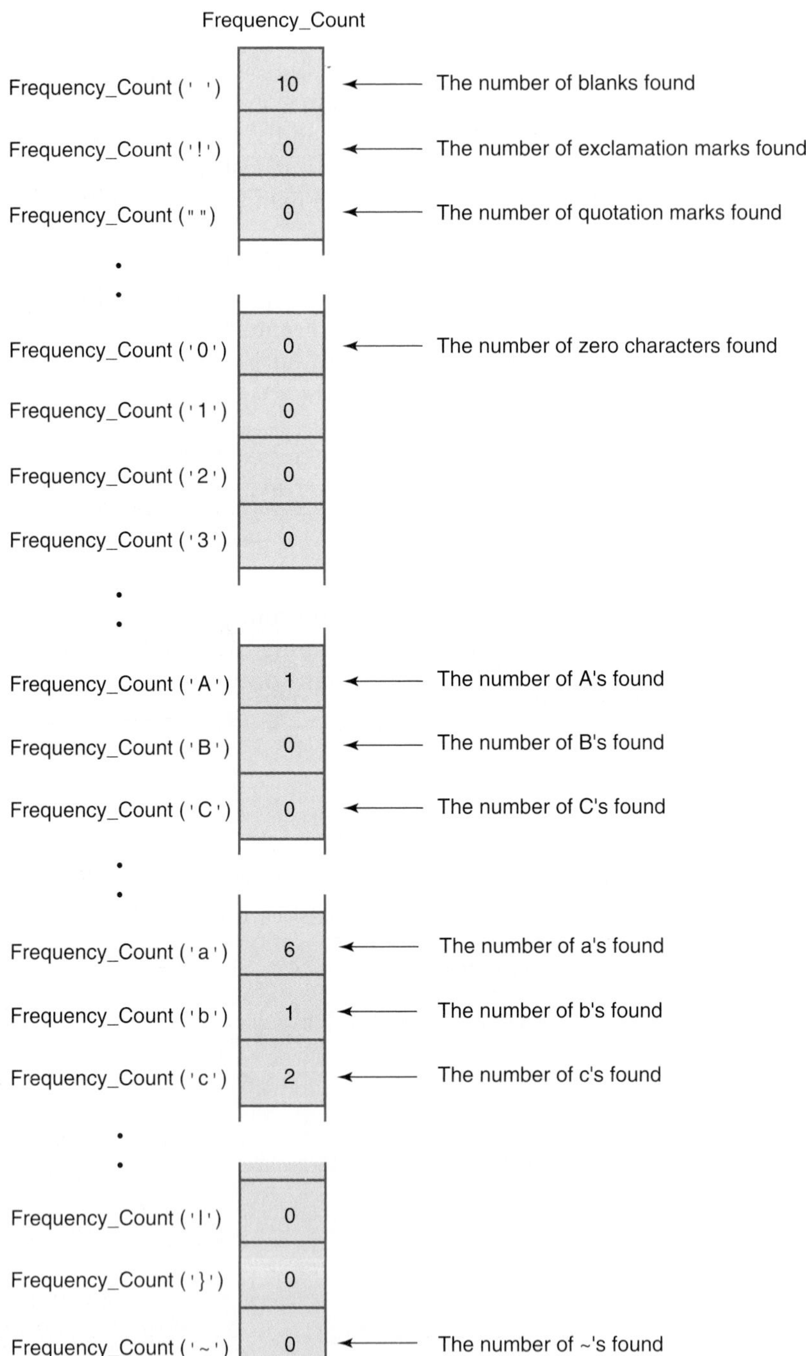

PROBLEM-SOLVING CASE STUDY *cont'd.*

Display Counts **Level 1**

in Frequency_Count

For Index going from Min_Char to Max_Char loop
  If Frequency_Count(Index) > 0
    Put Index
    Put Frequency_Count(Index)
  end if
end loop

Module Structure Chart

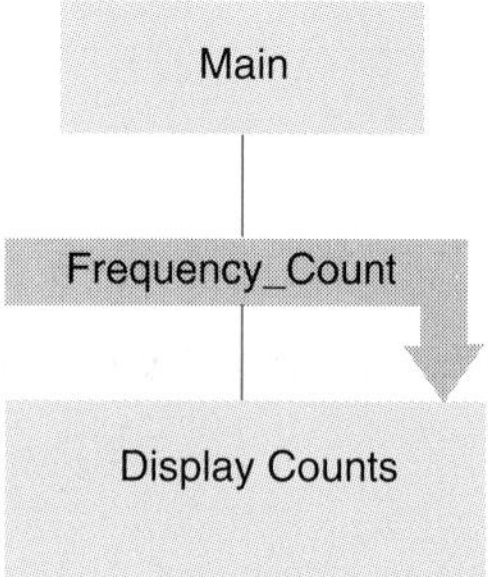

Implementation

```
with Ada.Text_IO;
with Ada.Integer_Text_IO;
procedure Character_Counts is

-- Program to count frequency of occurrence of all printable characters
-- in a text file.

-- Assumptions
--    1. The name of the file contains no more than 80 characters.
--    2. The text file containing the secret message exists.
--    3. The text file contains only printable characters
--          (from blank to tilde in the character set).

   -- Types for an array of character counters
   subtype Index_Range is Character range ' '..'~';
   type    Count_Type  is array (Index_Range) of Natural;

   subtype File_Name_String is String (1..80);

   --------------------------------------------

   procedure Display_Counts (Frequency_Count : in Count_Type) is

   -- Prints each character with a frequency count greater than zero along
   -- with its count
```

PROBLEM-SOLVING CASE STUDY cont'd.

```
   begin  -- Display Counts
      for Index in Frequency_Count'Range loop
         if Frequency_Count(Index) > 0 then
            Ada.Text_IO.Put(Index);
            Ada.Text_IO.Put (" OCCURRED ");
            Ada.Integer_Text_IO.Put (Item => Frequency_Count(Index), Width => 3);
            Ada.Text_IO.Put_Line (" TIMES");
         end if;
      end loop;
   end Display_Counts;

----------------------------------------------
   Frequency_Count : Count_Type;             -- List of character frequencies
   Char            : Index_Range;            -- Character read
   Data_File       : Ada.Text_IO.File_Type;  -- File with text
   File_Name       : File_Name_String;       -- Name of the input file
   Length          : Natural;                -- Size of File_Name

begin  -- Character Counts

   Ada.Text_IO.Put_Line ("Enter the name of your data file");
   Ada.Text_IO.Get_Line (Item => File_Name, Last => Length);
   Ada.Text_IO.Open (File => Data_File,
                     Mode => Ada.Text_IO.In_File,
                     Name => File_Name(1..Length));

   Frequency_Count := (others => 0);      -- Initialize all frequency counts

   Input_Loop:  -- Process all of the characters in the file
   loop         -- Each iteration, get and count one character
      exit Input_Loop when Ada.Text_IO.End_Of_File (Data_File);
      Ada.Text_IO.Get (File => Data_File, Item => Char);
      Frequency_Count(Char) := Frequency_Count(Char) + 1;
   end loop Input_Loop;

   Display_Counts (Frequency_Count);
   Ada.Text_IO.Close (Data_File);
end Character_Counts;
```

PROBLEM-SOLVING CASE STUDY *cont'd.*

Testing Using an input file containing the following text:

Roses are red, violets are blue.
If I can learn Ada, so can you.

we get the following output from program Count_All.

```
  OCCURRED  12 TIMES
, OCCURRED   2 TIMES
. OCCURRED   2 TIMES
A OCCURRED   1 TIMES
I OCCURRED   2 TIMES
R OCCURRED   1 TIMES
a OCCURRED   6 TIMES
b OCCURRED   1 TIMES
c OCCURRED   2 TIMES
d OCCURRED   2 TIMES
e OCCURRED   7 TIMES
f OCCURRED   1 TIMES
i OCCURRED   1 TIMES
l OCCURRED   3 TIMES
n OCCURRED   3 TIMES
o OCCURRED   4 TIMES
r OCCURRED   4 TIMES
s OCCURRED   4 TIMES
t OCCURRED   1 TIMES
u OCCURRED   2 TIMES
v OCCURRED   1 TIMES
y OCCURRED   1 TIMES
```

We must test two things in this program: 1) Does it count the characters correctly, and 2) can it handle data files of different sizes? To test whether this program counts characters correctly, we create a data file that contains all of the printable characters at least once and some of them more than once. To make sure that the program runs correctly on files of different sizes, we test the program with an empty file, a file with one character, and a file with many characters. We also test it with files containing one line and those with many lines of characters.

PROBLEM-SOLVING CASE STUDY

Mustard Yields

Specification

Problem The Yellow Jacket Mustard Seed Company is always trying to improve the mustard it grows. Currently it is testing a new variety of mountain mustard on 35 different 100-acre test plots. The company harvests the mustard in each test plot and trucks it to its processing plant. As each truck arrives at the plant, someone records the test-plot number (1 through 35) and pounds of mustard in the truck. The test plots are located at different altitudes on the mountains and are numbered from lowest altitude (plot #1) to highest altitude (plot #35). The Yellow Jacket Company needs a program that can calculate the average yields of *different groups* of adjacent test plots.

Input A text file containing one line of data for each truck that arrives at the grain elevator. Each line contains the test-plot number (1 through 35) and the number of pounds (a whole number) of mustard in the truck.
Pairs of numbers entered from the keyboard to specify a range of adjacent test plots whose average the program is to calculate. For example, if a mustard yield analyst enters the numbers 7 and 13, the program should calculate and display the average yield of mustard grown in plots 7 through 13. The program is terminated when the low plot number entered is greater than the high plot number entered.

Output A prompt for a range of test plots whose average yield is desired. For each pair of plot numbers entered, display the average yield per acre with one decimal place.

Discussion We need to keep a sum for each of the 35 different test plots. Each time the program reads the data for a truck, it adds the number of pounds in the truck to the sum for the given plot. We can calculate the average for a range of test plots by adding the total production for each plot in the range and dividing by the total number of acres.

We need a sum for each of the 35 test plots. We can use a one-dimensional array of 35 components to store these totals. We'll call this array Harvest. We can use a plot number as an index to select the desired sum in this array. We can pass a slice of this array to a subprogram to calculate the average yield of a range of test plots.

PROBLEM-SOLVING CASE STUDY *cont'd.*

Design

```
Mustard Yields                                              Level 0
Get Harvest Totals from file
loop
   Get Low and High
   exit loop when Low > High
   Put Average of Harvest(Low . . High)
end loop

Get Harvest Totals                                          Level 1
   out     Harvest
Open file
Set all components of Harvest to zero
loop
   exit loop when end of file
   get Plot Number from file
   get Amount from file
   Harvest (Plot_Number) := Harvest (Plot_Number) + Amount
end loop
close file

Average Yield                                               Level 1
   in      Harvest
Sum := 0
For Index in Harvest'Range loop
   Sum := Sum + Harvest(Index)
end loop
return Sum / (Number of Plots * Number Acres per Plot)
```

Module Structure Chart

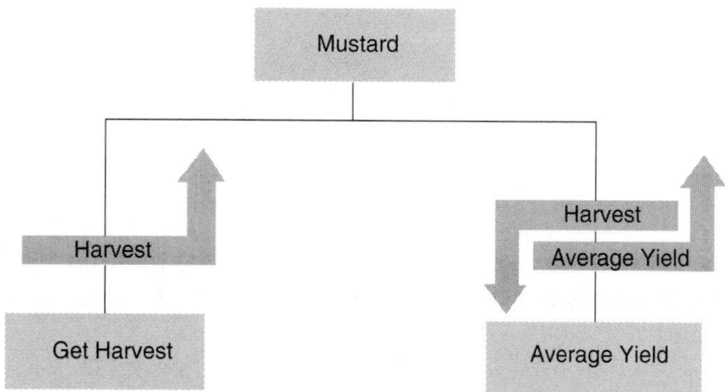

PROBLEM-SOLVING CASE STUDY cont'd.

Implementation

```
with Ada.Text_IO;
with Ada.Integer_Text_IO;
with Ada.Float_Text_IO;
procedure Mustard_Yields is

   -- Named Numbers
   Number_Of_Test_Plots : constant := 35;
   Acres_Per_Test_Plot  : constant := 100;

   -- Types
   type    Natural_Array     is array (Integer range <>) of Natural;
   subtype Plot_Number_Range is Integer range 1..Number_Of_Test_Plots;
   subtype Harvest_Array     is Natural_Array (Plot_Number_Range);

   ----------------------------------------------------
   procedure Get_Harvest (Harvest : out Harvest_Array) is

   -- This procedure calculates the total yield of all test plots
   -- by summing the amounts delivered to the processing plant

      Plot_Number : Plot_Number_Range;   -- Used as index for array Sum
      Amount      : Natural;             -- Amount of mustard in one delivery
      Truck_File  : Ada.Text_IO.File_Type;  -- File containing data for truck
                                            -- deliveries

   begin  -- Get Harvest
      Harvest := (Plot_Number_Range => 0);    -- Initialize all totals to zero

      Ada.Text_IO.Open (File => Truck_File,
                        Mode => Ada.Text_IO.In_File,
                        Name => "Harvest.txt");

      Input_Loop:   -- Get and sum all deliveries of mustard
      loop          -- Each iteration, the amount of one delivery is
                    -- added to the proper sum
         exit Input_Loop when Ada.Text_IO.End_Of_File (Truck_File);

         -- Get the data for one delivery
         Ada.Integer_Text_IO.Get (File => Truck_File, Item => Plot_Number);
         Ada.Integer_Text_IO.Get (File => Truck_File, Item => Amount);

         -- Advance the reading marker to the next line
         if not Ada.Text_IO.End_Of_File (Truck_File) then
            Ada.Text_IO.Skip_Line (Truck_File);
         end if;
```

PROBLEM-SOLVING CASE STUDY *cont'd.*

```
         -- Add the delivery to the proper total
         Harvest(Plot_Number) := Harvest(Plot_Number) + Amount;
      end loop Input_Loop;

      Ada.Text_IO.Close (Truck_File);
   end Get_Harvest;

   ----------------------------------------
   function Average_Yield (Harvest : in Natural_Array) return Float is

   -- This function determines the average yield (pounds per acre)
   -- of the plots in the Harvest array

      Sum : Natural;     -- The sum of the values in the array Harvest

   begin  -- Average_Yield
      Sum := 0;
      -- Sum all of the yields in the Harvest array
      for Index in Harvest'Range loop
         Sum := Sum + Harvest(Index);
      end loop;
         -- Harvest'Length equals the number of test plots being averaged
      return Float (Sum) / Float (Harvest'Length * Acres_Per_Test_Plot);
   end Average_Yield;

----------------------------------------
   Harvest : Harvest_Array;          -- The total yields of all the test plots
   Low     : Plot_Number_Range;  -- Lower bound of a test plot range
   High    : Plot_Number_Range;  -- Upper bound of a test plot range
   Average : Float;                  -- Average yield for a range of test plots

begin -- Program Mustard Yields
   Get_Harvest (Harvest);   -- Get the yields for each of the plots
   Range_Loop:   -- Analyze several ranges of test plots
   loop          -- Each iteration, calculate the average yield of one range of
                 -- test plots
      Ada.Text_IO.Put_Line ("Enter the plot range of interest.");
      Ada.Text_IO.Put_Line ("   (Enter a null range to terminate program)");
      Ada.Integer_Text_IO.Get (Low);
      Ada.Integer_Text_IO.Get (High);
      exit Range_Loop when Low > High;
```

PROBLEM-SOLVING CASE STUDY *cont'd.*

```
      -- Calculate and display the average yield of the range of test plots
      Average := Average_Yield (Harvest(Low..High));
      Ada.Text_IO.New_Line;
      Ada.Text_IO.Put ("Average yield is ");
      Ada.Float_Text_IO.Put (Item => Average,
                             Fore => 1,
                             Aft  => 1,
                             Exp  => 0);
      Ada.Text_IO.Put_Line (" pounds per acre");
      Ada.Text_IO.New_Line;
   end loop Range_Loop;
end Mustard_Yields;
```

Testing This program has two sources of data: the file of deliveries made by trucks to the processing plant and the range values entered on the keyboard. We should test the program with a single line of data for a particular test plot, using several lines of data for a particular plot. Using a file with simple data, we can easily calculate averages by hand to check against those computed by the program. Test different ranges and compare results to the hand-calculated results.

PROBLEM-SOLVING CASE STUDY

City Council Election

Specification

Problem Recently there has been a hotly contested city council election. Let's analyze the votes for the four candidates by precinct. We want to know how many votes each candidate received in each precinct, how many total votes each candidate received, and how many total votes were cast in each precinct.

Input For each vote recorded: the precinct number and ballot position of candidate (available in the text file Votes.txt, formatted one vote per line). The candidate names, which are entered from the keyboard (to be used for printing the output).

Output A text file containing a table showing how many votes each candidate received in each precinct, the total number of votes for each candidate, and the total number of votes in each precinct.

PROBLEM-SOLVING CASE STUDY cont'd.

FIGURE 11-20
By-Hand Analysis of Vote

Precinct	Smith	Jones	Adams	Smiley
1	𝍸 𝍷𝍷	𝍷𝍷	𝍸 𝍸 𝍷𝍷	𝍸
2	𝍸 𝍸	𝍷𝍷	𝍸	𝍷𝍷𝍷
3	𝍷𝍷	𝍸 𝍷𝍷𝍷	𝍸 𝍸 𝍸	𝍷𝍷𝍷
4	𝍸	𝍸 𝍷𝍷𝍷	𝍸 𝍸	𝍷𝍷

Discussion The data is available in the form of a pair of numbers for each vote. The first number is the precinct number; the second number is the ballot position of the candidate for whom the vote was cast.

If we were doing the analysis by hand, our first task would be to go through the data, counting how many people in each precinct voted for each candidate. We probably would create a table with precincts down the side and candidates across the top. We would record each vote as a mark in the appropriate column and row (see Figure 11-20). With all the votes recorded, a sum of each column would tell us how many votes each candidate received. A sum of each row would tell us how many people voted in each precinct.

As is so often the case, we can use this by-hand algorithm directly in our program. We can create a two-dimensional array in which each component is a counter for the number of votes for a particular candidate in each precinct; that is, the value indexed by (2, 1) would be the counter for the votes in precinct 2 for candidate 1.

How can we store the candidates names? If we were doing this problem by hand, we would write a list of names in the order they appear on the ballot. We can implement this list as a one-dimensional array in which each component is a string. Figure 11-21 shows the two data structures for our election analysis.

Note that we store each candidate's name in the slot in the array corresponding to his or her position on the ballot. This correspondence will be useful when the totals are printed: The index has semantic content; it represents the candidate's place on the ballot.

Design

Election Analysis **Level 0**

Prepare Files
Get Candidate Names
Initialize all components of Votes to Zero

PROBLEM-SOLVING CASE STUDY *cont'd.*

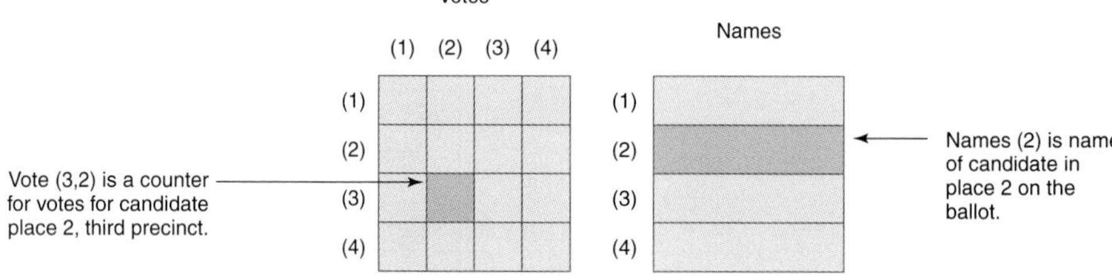

Figure 11-21 Data Structures for Analysis of Election Results

```
Loop
   Exit when end of file
   Get Precinct and Candidate
   Increment Votes(Precinct, Candidate)
end Loop
Write Table (of votes) to the Report File
Write Totals per Candidate to the Report File
Write Totals per Precinct to the Report File
Close Files
```

Get Candidate Names **Level 1**

```
   out      Names
Display   "Enter the names of the candidates, one name per line,
           in the order in which they appear on the ballot."
for Candidate going from 1 to the number of candidates
   Get a Name from the keyboard and put it into Names(Candidate)
end loop
```

Write Table **Level 1**

```
   in      Names
   in      Votes
   in out  Report File
for all candidates
   Put Names(Candidate) to Report File
end Loop
for all precincts loop
   for all candidates loop
      Put Votes(Precincts, Candidates) to Report File
   end Loop
end Loop
```

PROBLEM-SOLVING CASE STUDY *cont'd.*

Write Totals per Candidate **Level 1**

in Votes
in Names
in out Report
– Calculate column sums
for all candidates loop
Initialize Total to 0
for all precincts loop
Add Votes(Precincts, Candidates) to Total
end Loop
Put "Total votes for," Names(Candidate), and Total to Report File
end Loop

Write Totals per Precinct **Level 1**

in votes
in out Report File
– Calculate row sums
for all precincts loop
Initialize Total to 0
For all candidates loop
Add Votes(Precincts, Candidate) to Total
end Loop
Write "Total votes for precinct," and Precinct, Total to Report File
end Loop

Get A Name **Level 2**

out Name
Get Name
Pad unused characters in Name with blanks

Module Structure Chart

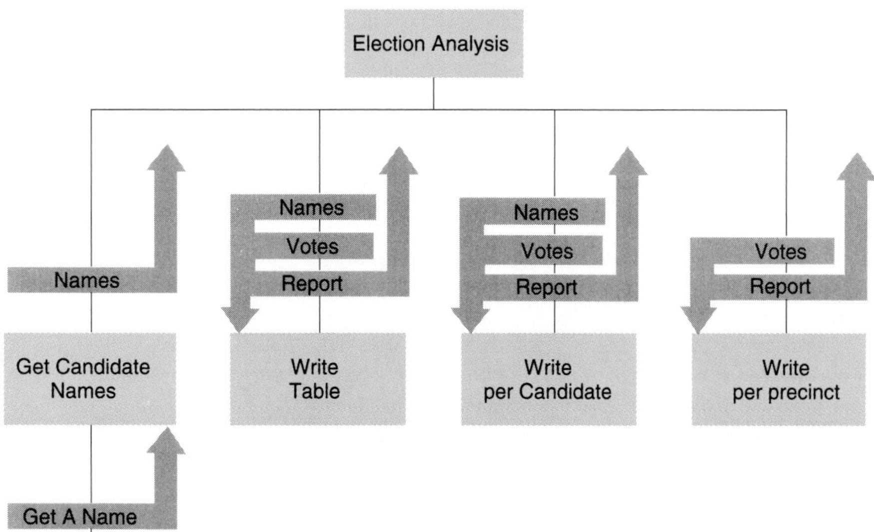

PROBLEM-SOLVING CASE STUDY *cont'd.*

Implementation

```
with Ada.Integer_Text_IO;
with Ada.Text_IO;
procedure Election_Analysis is

   -- Named numbers
   Number_Of_Precincts  : constant := 4;
   Number_Of_Candidates : constant := 4;

   subtype Name_String is String (1..10);   -- For candidate names

   -- Index types
   type Precinct_Range   is range 1..Number_Of_Precincts;
   type Candidate_Range  is range 1..Number_Of_Candidates;
   -- Array types
   type Vote_Count_Array is array (Precinct_Range, Candidate_Range) of Natural;
   type Name_Array       is array (Candidate_Range) of Name_String;

   -- I/O Package instantiations
   package Precinct_IO  is new Ada.Text_IO.Integer_IO (Num => Precinct_Range);
   package Candidate_IO is new Ada.Text_IO.Integer_IO (Num => Candidate_Range);


   ---------------------------------------------
   procedure Get_A_Name (Name : out Name_String) is

   -- A name is obtained from the keyboard and padded with blanks.

      Last : Natural;    -- Actual parameter for Ada.Text_IO.Get_Line

   begin
      Ada.Text_IO.Get_Line (Item => Name, Last => Last);        -- Get a string
      Name (Last+1..Name'Last) := (Last+1..Name'Last => ' '); -- Pad with blanks
   end Get_A_Name;

   ---------------------------------------------
   procedure Get_Candidate_Names (Names : out Name_Array) is

   -- This procedure prompts for and gets a list of candidate names

   begin
      Ada.Text_IO.Put_Line ("Enter the names of the candidates one per line,");
      Ada.Text_IO.Put_Line ("in the order they appear on the ballot.");
      for Candidate in Names'Range loop
         Get_A_Name (Name => Names(Candidate));
      end loop;
   end Get_Candidate_Names;
```

PROBLEM-SOLVING CASE STUDY cont'd.

```
----------------------------------------
procedure Write_Table (Votes  : in     Vote_Count_Array; -- Vote totals
                       Names  : in     Name_Array;       -- Candidates
                       Report : in out Ada.Text_IO.File_Type) is

-- Report votes by precinct and candidate

begin
   Ada.Text_IO.Set_Col (File => Report, To => 20);        -- Set up headings
   -- Write all of the candidates' names
   for Candidate in Candidate_Range loop
      Ada.Text_IO.Put (File => Report, Item => Names (Candidate) & "   ");
   end loop;
   Ada.Text_IO.New_Line (Report);

  -- Write votes for all candidates in all precincts
  -- Each iteration, the votes for one precinct are written
  for Precinct in Precinct_Range loop
     Ada.Text_IO.Put (File => Report, Item => "Precinct");
     Precinct_IO.Put (File => Report, Item => Precinct , Width => 4);

     -- Write votes for all the candidates in one precinct
     -- Each iteration, the votes for one candidate are written
     for Candidate in Candidate_Range loop
        Ada.Integer_Text_IO.Put (File  => Report,
                                 Item  => Votes(Precinct, Candidate),
                                 Width => 12);
     end loop;
     Ada.Text_IO.New_Line (Report);
  end loop;
  Ada.Text_IO.New_Line (Report);
end Write_Table;

----------------------------------------
procedure Write_Per_Candidate
             (Votes  : in     Vote_Count_Array;      -- Vote totals
              Names  : in     Name_Array;            -- Candidates
              Report : in out Ada.Text_IO.File_Type) is

-- Votes per person are totaled and reported

   Total : Natural; -- Total votes for a candidate

begin
   -- Write the total votes for all candidates
   -- Each iteration, the votes for one candidate are written
   for Candidate in Candidate_Range loop
      Total := 0;
```

PROBLEM-SOLVING CASE STUDY cont'd.

```
      -- Sum the votes for one candidate
      -- Each iteration, the votes for one precinct are added to the sum
      for Precinct in Precinct_Range loop
         Total := Total + Votes (Precinct, Candidate);
      end loop;
      Ada.Text_IO.Put (File => Report,
                       Item => "Total votes for " & Names(Candidate) & "  ");
      Ada.Integer_Text_IO.Put (File  => Report,
                               Item  => Total,
                               Width => 3);
      Ada.Text_IO.New_Line (Report);
   end loop;
end Write_Per_Candidate;

-----------------------------------------

procedure Write_Per_Precinct
             (Votes  : in     Vote_Count_Array;           -- Vote totals
              Report : in out Ada.Text_IO.File_Type) is

-- Votes per person are totaled and reported

   Total : Natural;   -- Total votes for a precinct

begin
   -- Write the total votes for all precincts
   -- Each iteration, the votes for one precinct are written
   for Precinct in Precinct_Range loop
      Total := 0;
      -- Sum the votes for each precinct
      -- Each iteration, the votes for one candidate are added to the sum
      for Candidate in Candidate_Range loop
         Total := Total + Votes (Precinct, Candidate);
      end loop;
      Ada.Text_IO.Put (File => Report, Item => "Total votes for precinct");
      Precinct_IO.Put (File => Report, Item => Precinct, Width => 3);
      Ada.Text_IO.Put (File => Report, Item => ':');
      Ada.Integer_Text_IO.Put (File => Report, Item => Total, Width => 3);
      Ada.Text_IO.New_Line (Report);
   end loop;
end Write_Per_Precinct;

-----------------------------------------
```

PROBLEM-SOLVING CASE STUDY *cont'd.*

```
   Votes       : Vote_Count_Array;        -- Totals for precincts versus candidates
   Names       : Name_Array;              -- List of candidate names
   Candidate   : Candidate_Range;         -- Candidate number from file Vote_File
   Precinct    : Precinct_Range;          -- Precinct number from file Vote_File
   Vote_File   : Ada.Text_IO.File_Type;   -- Input file of precincts and candidates
   Report_File : Ada.Text_IO.File_Type;   -- Output file receiving summaries

begin  -- Election Analysis
   -- Prepare the files
   Ada.Text_IO.Create (File => Report_File, Name => "Results.Txt");
   Ada.Text_IO.Open   (File => Vote_File,   Name => "Votes.Txt",
                       Mode => Ada.Text_IO.In_File);

   Get_Candidate_Names (Names);
   Votes := (Precinct_Range => (Candidate_Range => 0)); -- Initialize counters

   Input_Loop:  -- Read and tally votes
   loop         -- Each iteration, one vote is tallied
      exit Input_Loop when Ada.Text_IO.End_Of_File (Vote_File);
      Precinct_IO.Get  (File => Vote_File, Item => Precinct);
      Candidate_IO.Get (File => Vote_File, Item => Candidate);
      if not Ada.Text_IO.End_Of_File (Vote_File) then
         Ada.Text_IO.Skip_Line (Vote_File);
      end if;
      -- Increment the counter in the 2-D array
      Votes (Precinct, Candidate) := Votes (Precinct, Candidate) + 1;
   end loop Input_Loop;
   Write_Table (Votes  => Votes,
                Names  => Names,
                Report => Report_File);
   Write_Per_Candidate (Votes  => Votes,
                        Names  => Names,
                        Report => Report_File);
   Ada.Text_IO.New_Line (Report_File);
   Write_Per_Precinct  (Votes  => Votes,
                        Report => Report_File);
   Ada.Text_IO.Close (Vote_File);
   Ada.Text_IO.Close (Report_File);
end Election_Analysis;
```

Testing We ran this program with the following data list. (We list it in three columns to save space.) The names of the candidates entered from the keyboard were Jones, Beasley, Adams, and Smedley. In this data set, there is at least one vote for each candidate in each precinct.

PROBLEM-SOLVING CASE STUDY cont'd.

Input Data

```
1 1      3 1      3 3
1 1      4 3      4 4
1 2      3 4      4 4
1 2      3 2      4 3
1 3      3 3      4 4
1 4      2 1      4 4
2 2      2 3      4 1
2 2      4 3      4 2
2 3      4 4      2 4
2 1      3 2      4 4
```

The output, which was written on file Report_File, is listed as:

```
                     Jones        Beasley     Adams        Smedley
Precinct   1             2              2         1              1
Precinct   2             2              2         2              1
Precinct   3             1              2         2              1
Precinct   4             1              1         3              6

Total votes for Jones          6
Total votes for Beasley        7
Total votes for Adams          8
Total votes for Smedley        9

Total votes for precinct  1:  6
Total votes for precinct  2:  7
Total votes for precinct  3:  6
Total votes for precinct  4: 11
```

Testing and Debugging

The most common error that you will encounter in processing arrays is the CONSTRAINT_ERROR. This means that your program attempted to access a component using an index outside the range of indices defined for the array. For example, given the declarations

```
subtype Index_Range is Integer range 1..100;
type    Table       is array (Index_Range) of Character;

Counter : Integer;
Line    : Table;
```

the following for loop would print the contents of array Line and then cause the program to stop with a CONSTRAINT_ERROR exception.

```
for Index in 1..101 loop
   Ada.Text_IO.Put (Line(Index));
end loop;
```

This example is trivial to debug, but you won't always use a simple for loop in accessing arrays. Suppose that we read data into array Line in another part of the program. We use a loop statement that reads to the end of the line.

```
Counter := 0;
Input_Loop:
loop
   exit Input_Loop when Ada.Text_IO.End_Of_Line;
   Counter := Counter + 1;
   Ada.Text_IO.Get (Line(Counter));
end loop Input_Loop;
```

This logic seems reasonable enough, but what if the input contains a line with more than 100 characters? After the hundredth character is read, the loop continues to execute, and on the next iteration the program terminates because the array index is out of range.

The moral is: When processing arrays, give special attention to the design of loop termination conditions. Always ask yourself whether there is any possibility that the loop could keep running after the last array component has been processed.

Whenever a program with arrays stops with a CONSTRAINT_ERROR message, the first suspicion should be an array processing loop that fails to terminate properly. The second thing to check for is any array access involving an index that is based on input data or a calculation. When an array index is input as data, then a data validation check (active with if statements or passive with exception handlers) is an absolute necessity. Finally, make sure that the type of the loop control variable is adequate for the loop. In some cases the loop control variable must take a value one greater than the maximum value of the array index.

As the number of dimensions increases, so does the likelihood of a subtle logic error. The syntax of your nested loop structure may be valid, but what you intended to happen may not be what you coded. Using meaningful identifiers for your loop control variables will help. If you were to use *I* and *J* as the loop control variables in the City Council Election example, it would be easy to interchange them by mistake. If you use Precinct and Candidate, you are less likely to confuse the indices. Also, if you use distinct types rather than subtypes for indices, the compiler will find any interchanged index variables.

Testing and Debugging Hints

1. Be consistent when using arrays. We describe the pattern of an array and give it a name in a type declaration; we declare array variables with an array type. We store values in the individual components of an array variable during execution of the program. These three actions—describing, declaring, using—must all be consistent.
2. The individual components of an array are themselves variables of the component type. When values are stored into an array, they must be of the component type; otherwise, the compiler will issue a type-conflict syntax error.
3. When an individual component in an array is accessed, the index must be within the index range. Attempting to use an index value that is not within the defined index range will raise a CONSTRAINT_ERROR.
4. You declare the length of an array, but its actual size is determined at run time. This means that you must declare an array to be as large as it could ever be for the particular problem. We use subarray processing to process only the components that have data in them.
5. Pass a slice of the array with no logical garbage to procedures and functions when subarray processing is to take place within them. The array attributes 'First, 'Last, 'Length, and 'Range provide the means for processing the data in unconstrained array parameters.
6. Never use literal or constant values for unconstrained array parameter indices. Determine the index range with the array attributes 'First, and 'Last, and limit processing to components within this range.
7. Use distinct types rather than subtypes for indices; then the compiler will find any interchanged index variables.
8. Be careful when passing parameters to avoid array index range errors.
9. Use meaningful identifiers for index variables.
10. Use the proper number of indices with array names when referencing an array component.

Summary

In addition to being able to create programmer-defined atomic and nonhomogeneous composite data types, we can create homogeneous composite data types. In both records and arrays, we can give a name to a group of components that have a specific arrangement. We can access the group as a whole, or we can access each individual component separately.

The one-dimensional array data type gives a name to a sequential group of components. You can access each component by its relative position within the group, and each component is a variable of the component type. To access a particular component, we give the name of the array and an index that specifies which one of the group we want. The index must be of the index type, which can be any discrete type. Therefore, a program can access the components in an array sequentially by stepping through the values of the index type.

A constrained array type has a range specified for its index and an unconstrained array type does not. We use unconstrained array types as a base type for declaring constrained array subtypes and for declaring formal array parameters. Unconstrained parameters allow a subprogram to accept different lengths of actual array parameters. We use the array attributes 'First, 'Last, 'Length, and 'Range with unconstrained array parameters.

We can compare entire arrays for equality. We also can compare arrays whose components are a discrete type with the remaining relational operators. We use slices to obtain a portion of an array and concatenation to combine arrays.

Two-dimensional arrays are useful for processing information that is represented naturally in table form. Processing data in two-dimensional arrays usually takes one of two forms: processing by row or processing by column. An array of arrays, which is useful if you must pass rows of the array as parameters, is an alternative way of defining a two-dimensional array.

A multidimensional array is a collection of like components, ordered on more than one dimension. Each component is accessed by a set of indices, one for each dimension, that represents the component's position on the various dimensions. You can think of each index as describing a feature of a given array component.

You should select data structures to reflect accurately the relationships inherent in the data itself. You can use two-dimensional arrays and arrays of arrays to hold the same data. An analysis of what the data means can help you to make the appropriate choice.

Quick Check

1. Define an array data type called Quiz_Array that will contain 12 components indexed by the integers 21 through 32. The component type is Boolean. (pp. 591–603)
2. If an array is to hold the number of correct answers given by students to each question on a 20-question multiple choice quiz, what data types should you use for the indices and components of the array? Assume a class size of 50. (pp. 591–603)
3. Given the declarations

```
Max_Size : constant : = 30;

subtype Index_Range is Integer range 1..Max_Size;
type    Name_String is array (Index_Range) of Character;

First_Name : Name_String;
```

write an assignment statement that will store 'A' in the first component of array First_Name. (pp. 592–603)

4. Given the declarations in question 3, write a call to Put that will print the value of the fourteenth component of array First_Name. (pp. 592–603)
5. Given the declarations in question 3,
   a. Write a for loop that will fill array First_Name with blanks. (pp. 592–603)
   b. Write an assignment statement that uses an aggregate to assign all blanks to the array First_Name. (pp. 595–597)
6. Given the declarations in question 3 and the following program fragment, which reads characters into array First_Name until a blank is encountered, write a for loop that will print out the portion of the array that is filled with input data. (pp. 592–603)

```
Size := 0;
Input_Loop:
loop
   Ada.Text_IO.Get (Letter);
   exit Input_Loop when Letter = ' ';
   Size := Size + 1;
   First_Name(Size) := Letter;
end loop Input_Loop;
```

7. Define an array data type in which the index values represent the musical notes A through G (excluding sharps and flats), and the component type is Float. (pp. 597–603)
8. Differentiate between the length of an array and the size of a list. (pp. 607–604)
9. What are the two major uses of unconstrained array types? (p. 611)
10. Why can't we use an unconstrained array type in the declaration of a variable? (p. 611)
11. Given the declarations

```
subtype Weight_Type  is Float range 0.0..350.0;
type    Weight_Array is array (Integer range <>) of Weight_Type;
subtype Index_Range  is Integer range 1..100;
subtype Player_List  is Weight_Array (Index_Range);

Players : Player_List;   -- An array of weights
Size    : Index_Type;    -- The number of components in Players
```

   a. Write a procedure that displays all values stored in an array parameter of type Weight_Array; (pp. 614–617)
   b. Write a call statement to the procedure that you wrote in part a to display the values of the first Size values in array Players. (pp. 614–617)
12. Define a two-dimensional array data type called Chart with 30 rows and 10 columns. The component type of the array is type Float. (pp. 619–623)
13. Assign the value 27.3 to the component in row 13, column 7 of an array variable called Plan of type Chart. (pp. 619–623)

14. You can use nested for loops to sum the values in each row of array Plan. What range of values would the *outer* for loop count through to do this? (pp. 624–626)
15. You can use nested for loops to sum the values in each column of array Plan. What range of values would the *outer* for loop count through to do this? (pp. 627–628)
16. Write a program fragment that uses for loops to initialize array Plan from questions to all zeros. (pp. 624–629)
17. Write a program fragment that uses an array aggregate to initialize array Plan from question 12 to all zeros. (pp. 629–631)
18. Write a program fragment that prints the contents of array Plan from question 12. (p. 629)
19. Given the type definitions

```
subtype Row_Index is Character range 'A'..'Z';
type    Col_Index is range 1..100;
type    Two_Dim_Array is array (Row_Index, Col_Index) of Integer;
```

    rewrite the definition of type Two_Dim_Array as an array of arrays. (pp. 631–633)
20. You may use slices with two-dimensional arrays. (True or False) (p. 633)
21. You may use slices with any index of an array of arrays. (True or False) (p. 633)
22. Given the type definitions

```
type Index_Range is range -5 .. 5;
type Four_Dim is
     array (Index_Range, Index_Range, Index_Range, Index_Range) of
Float;
```

    how many components does Four_Dim contain? (pp. 636–639)
23. Write a program fragment using for loops that fills a variable of type Four_Dim called Quick with zeros. (pp. 637–639)
24. Write a program fragment using an array aggregate with `others` clauses that fills a variable of type Four_Dim called Quick with blanks. (pp. 629–631)
25. Suppose that you are writing a program to process a table of employee numbers, names, and pay rates. Is a two-dimensional array an appropriate data structure for this problem? Explain. (pp. 639–640)

Answers

1.
```
subtype Index_Range is Integer range 21..32;
type Quiz_Array     is array (Index_Range) of Boolean;
```
2.
```
subtype Index_Type  is Integer range 1..20;    -- Index type
subtype Count_Type is Integer range 0..50;     -- Component type
```
3. `First_Name(1) := 'A';` **4.** `Ada.Text_IO.Put (First_Name(14));`

5. a. `for Index in Index_Range loop`

```
   First_Name(Index) := ' ';
end loop;
```

b. `First_Name := (Index_Range => ' ');`

6.
```
for Index in 1..Size loop
   Ada.Text_IO.Put (First_Name(Index));
end loop;
```

7.
```
subtype Note_Range is Character range 'A'..'G';
type    Note_List  is array (Note_Range) of Float;
```

8. The length of an array is the number of components in the array as set in its declaration. The size of a list is the number of the array components that contain valid data—the remaining components contain logical garbage. The size of a list is less than or equal to the length of the array in which it is stored. **9.** The declaration of formal parameters and the declaration of constrained array subtypes. **10.** The number of components is not specified in an unconstrained type. The compiler needs to know how many memory locations to allocate to each variable.

11. a.
```
procedure Display_Weights (Weights : in Weight_Array) is
begin
   for Index in  Weights'Range  loop
      Ada.Float_Text_IO.Put (Item => Weights(Index), Fore => 5,
                             Aft  => 1, Exp  => 0);
      Ada.Text_IO.New_Line;
   end loop;
end Display_Weights;
```

b. `Display_Weights (Weights => Players(1..Size));`

12.
```
type Row_Index    is range 1..30;
type Column_Index is range 1..10;
type Chart        is array (Row_Index, Column_Index) of Float;
```

13. `Plan(13, 7) := 27.3;` **14.** `for Row in Row_Index loop` **15.** `for Column in Column_Index loop`

16.
```
for Row in Row_Index loop
   for Column in Column_Index loop
      Plan(Row, Column) := 0.0;
   end loop;
end loop;
```

17. `Plan := (Row_Index => (Column_Index => 0.0));`

18.
```
for Row in Row_Index loop
   for Column in Column_Index loop
      Ada.Float_Text_IO.Put (Item => Plan(Row, Column),
                             Fore => 5, Aft => 1, Exp => 0);
   end loop;
   Ada.Text_IO.New_Line;
end loop;
```

19.
```
type One_Dim_Array is array (Col_Index) of Integer;
type Two_Dim_Array is array (Row_Index) of One_Dim_Array;
```

20. False. **21.** True. **22.** 14,641 (11 * 11 * 11 * 11)

23.
```
for Dim1 in Index_Range loop
   for Dim2 in Index_Range loop
      for Dim3 in Index_Range loop
         for Dim4 in Index_Range loop
            Quick(Dim1, Dim2, Dim3, Dim4) := 0.0;
         end loop;
      end loop;
   end loop;
end loop;
```

24. `Quick := (others => (others => (others => (others => ' '))));` **25.** A two-dimensional array is *not* appropriate because the data types of the columns are not the same. A one-dimensional array of records is appropriate in this case.

Exam Preparation Exercises

1. Every component in an array must have the same type, which is fixed at compile time, but the type of the indices may vary during execution. (True or False)
2. Both the indices and the components of an array must have discrete types. (True or False)
3. Write a code fragment to do the following.
   a. Define a subtype Score_Range to be from 0 to 100.
   b. Define an array data type Student_Scores of length Max_Length. The components are of type Score_Range.
   c. Declare an array variable Quiz_One to be of the type Student_Scores.
4. Write a code fragment to do the following.
   a. Define an enumerated type Bird_Type made up of bird names.
   b. Define an integer component array data type Siting_Type indexed by Bird_Type.
   c. Declare an array variable Sitings of type Siting_Type.
5. Given the declarations

```
Max_Size : constant := 100;

type    Color_Type   is (Red, Green, Blue, Cyan, Magenta, Yellow);
subtype Index_Range  is Integer range 1..Max_Size;
type    Rainbow_Type is array (Index_Range) of Color_Type;
type    Count_Type   is array (Color_Type)  of Natural;

Count   : Count_Type;
Rainbow : Rainbow_Type;
```

   a. What is the index type of the array variable Count?
   b. What is the index type of the array variable Rainbow?
   c. How many components are there in the array variable Count?
   d. How many components are there in the array variable Rainbow?

e. How many variables are there of type Color_Type? Count each array component as a separate variable.
f. How many Natural variables are there?

6. Using the declarations in Exercise 5, write code fragments to do the following.
   a. Initialize Count to all zeros (two different ways).
   b. Initialize Rainbow to all Blue (two different ways).
   c. Count the number of times Green appears in Rainbow.
   d. Print the value in Count indexed by Blue.
   e. Total the values in Count.
7. What is the output of the following program? The data for the program is given after it.

```
with Ada.Text_IO;
with Ada.Integer_Text_IO;
procedure Exercise is

   subtype Index_Range is Integer range 1..100;
   type    List_Type   is array (Index_Range) of Natural;

   A              : List_Type;
   B              : List_Type;
   M              : Index_Range;
   Sum_A          : Natural;
   Sum_B          : Natural;
   Sum_Difference : Integer;

begin
   Sum_Difference := 0;
   Sum_A := 0;
   Sum_B := 0;
   Ada.Integer_Text_IO.Get (M);
   Ada.Text_IO.Skip_Line;
   for J in 1..M loop
      Ada.Integer_Text_IO.Get (A(J));
      Ada.Integer_Text_IO.Get (B(J));
      Ada.Text_IO.Skip_Line;
      Sum_A := Sum_A + A(J);
      Sum_B := Sum_B + B(J);
      Sum_Difference := Sum_Difference + (A(J) - B(J));
   end loop;
   for J in 1..M loop
      Ada.Integer_Text_IO.Put (A(J));
      Ada.Integer_Text_IO.Put (B(J));
      Ada.Integer_Text_IO.Put (A(J) - B(J));
      Ada.Text_IO.New_Line;
   end loop;
   Ada.Text_IO.New_Line;
   Ada.Integer_Text_IO.Put (Sum_A);
   Ada.Integer_Text_IO.Put (Sum_B);
```

```
   Ada.Integer_Text_IO.Put (Sum_Difference);
   Ada.Text_IO.New_Line;
end Exercise;
```

Data

```
  5
11  15
19  14
 4   2
17   6
 1   3
```

8. Declare the necessary subtypes, array types, and array variables for each of the following situations.
   a. A 24-component Float array for which the index goes from 1 to 24.
   b. A 24-component Integer array for which the index goes from 24 to 47.
   c. A 26-component Boolean array for which the index goes from 'A' to 'Z'.
   d. A 10-component Character array for which the index goes from -10 to -1.
9. Given the declarations

```
subtype Index_Range is Integer range 1..8;
type    Array_Type  is array (Index_Range) of Integer;

Sample : Array_Type;
```

   show the contents of the array Sample after the following code segment is executed. Use a question mark to indicate any undefined elements.

```
for K in Index_Range loop
   Sample(K) := 10 - K;
end loop;
```

10. Using the same declarations given for Exercise 9, show the contents of the array Sample after the following code segment is executed.

```
for I in Index_Range loop
   if I <= 3 then
      Sample(I) := 1;
   else
      Sample(I) := -1;
   end if;
end loop;
```

11. Both files and arrays may be used to store a collection of records.
    a. Give a reason to use an array instead of a file.
    b. Give two reasons to use a file instead of an array.

12. Given the following declarations:

```
subtype Hour_Type   is Integer range 0..23;
subtype Minute_Type is Integer range 0..59
subtype Second_Type is Integer range 0..59
type Clock_Time is
   record
      Hour   : Hour_Type;
      Minute : Minute_Type;
      Second : Second_Type;
   end record;

type Job_Rec is
   record
      Start  : Clock_Time;
      Finish : Clock_Time;
   end record;

subtype Index_Type is Integer range 1..100;
type    Job_Array is array (Index_Type) of Job_Rec;

Jobs : Job_Array;
```

   a. Write an assignment statement that sets the hour of the start time of the 43rd record in Jobs to 18.
   b. Use a record aggregate to write a single assignment statement that sets the start time of the 18th record in Jobs to the time 10:52:17.
   c. Use a hierarchical record aggregate to write a single assignment statement that sets the start time of the 12th record in Jobs to the time 10:52:17 and the stop time of the 12th record in Jobs to the time 11:31:00.
   d. Use record and array aggregates to write a single assignment statement that sets the start and stop times of all the records in Jobs to 00:00:00.

13. Given the following declarations:

```
subtype Hours_Type is Float range 0.0..12.0;
type    Day_Type   is (Monday, Tuesday, Wednesday, Thursday, Friday,
                       Saturday, Sunday);
type    Work_Array is array (Day_Type) of Hours_Type;

type    Wage_Type   is delta 0.01 digits 4 range 5.35 .. 99.99;
subtype Name_String is String (1..20);
type Work_Rec is
   record
      Name : Name_String;
      Wage : Wage_Type;
      Week : Work_Array;
   end record;
```

```
subtype ID_Type is Integer range 100..999;
type    Employee_Array is array (ID_Type) of Work_Rec;

Time_Cards : Employee_Array;
```

   a. Write an assignment statement that sets the wage to $6.25 of the employee in Time_Cards whose ID is 353.
   b. Write an assignment statement that sets the hours worked on Thursday to 8.3 of the employee in Time_Cards whose ID is ID 772.
   c. Write a call to procedure Ada.Text_IO.Put_Line that displays the name of the employee in Time_Cards whose ID is 444.
   d. Write a call to procedure Ada.Text_IO.Put that displays the 3rd character in the name of the employee in Time_Cards whose ID is 621.

14. Declare an unconstrained array type for each of the following.
   a. An array type with Float components and Integer indices.
   b. An array type with Integer components and Integer indices.
   c. An array type with Boolean components and Character indices.
   d. An array type with Character components and Integer indices.
15. Using the types you declared in the previous exercise, declare the subtypes necessary for each of the following.
   a. A 24-component Float array for which the index goes from 1 to 24.
   b. A 24-component Integer array for which the index goes from 24 to 47.
   c. A 26-component Boolean array for which the index goes from 'A' to 'Z'.
   d. A 10-component Character array for which the index goes from −10 to −1.
16. Given the declaration

```
type Score_Array is array (Character range <>) of Float;
```

   complete the following function to sum all of the components in the array parameter List.

```
function Sum (List :  in Score_Array) return Float is
   Result  : Float;
begin
   Result := 0.0;    -- Initialize sum
```

17. a. Reorder the following string literals so that they are listed in ascending order.

   "Mildred"

   "Horace"

   "Mild"

   "mild"

   "Mildred Smedley"

b. Reorder the following array aggregates so that they are listed in ascending order.

(5, 7, 6, 8)
(5, 7, 5, 9)
(5, 6, 7, 8)
(5, 6)
(5, 6, 7, 8, 9)
(3, 8, 9, 10)

18. Given the declarations

```
Number_Of_Weeks : constant := 5;
Number_Of_Teams : constant := 6;

type Week_Range is range 1..Number_Of_Weeks;
type Team_Range is range 1..Number_Of_Teams;
type Sold_Array is array (Team_Range, Week_Range] of Integer;

Weeks   : Week_Range;
Teams   : Team_Range;
Tickets : Sold_Array;
```

answer the following:

a. What is the number of rows in Tickets?
b. What is the number of columns in Tickets?
c. How many Integer variables have been declared? Count each array component as a separate variable.
d. What kind of processing (row or column) would be needed to total the ticket sales by weeks?
e. What kind of processing (row or column) would be needed to total the ticket sales by teams?

19. Given the declarations

```
Number_Of_Schools : constant := 10;

type School_Index     is range 1..Number_Of_Schools;
type Sport_Type       is (Football, Basketball, Volleyball);
type Participant_Type is array (School_Index, Sport_Type) of Integer;
type Money_Type       is array (Sport_Type, School_Index] of Float;

Kids_In_Sports : Participant_Type;
Cost_Of_Sports : Money_Type;
Schools        : School_Index;
Sports         : Sport_Type;
```

answer the following:

a. What is the number of rows in Kids_In_Sports?

b. What is the number of columns in Kids_In_Sports?
c. What is the number of rows in Cost_Of_Sports?
d. What is the number of columns in Cost_Of_Sports?
e. How many Integer variables have been declared? Count each array component as a separate variable.
f. How many Float variables have been declared? Count each array component as a separate variable.
g. What kind of processing (row or column) would be needed to total the amount of money spent on each sport?
h. What kind of processing (row or column) would be needed to total the number of children participating in sports at a particular school?

20. Given the following code segments, draw the arrays and their contents after the code is executed. Indicate any undefined positions with a question mark.

a.
```
type ExA is array (1..4, 1..3) of Integer;
ExampleA : ExA;
 .
 .
 .
for I in 1..4 loop
   for J in 1..3 loop
      ExampleA(I, J) := I * J;
   end loop;
end loop;
```

b.
```
type ExB is array (1..4, 1..3) of Integer;
ExampleB: ExB;
 .
 .
 .
for I in 1..4 loop
   for J in 1..3 loop
      ExampleA(I, J) := (I + J) rem 3;
   end loop;
end loop;
```

c.
```
type ExC is array (1..8, 1..2) of Integer;
ExampleC : ExC;
 .
 .
 .
ExampleC(8, 1) := 4;
ExampleC(8, 2) := 5;
for I in 1..7 loop
   ExampleC(I, 1) := 2;
   ExampleC(I, 2) := 3;
end loop;
```

21. a. Define an enumeration type Teams made up of the clubs on your campus.
b. Define an array type Team_Record_Array with Integer components indexed by Teams.
c. Declare an array variable Win_Loss to be of type Team_Record_Array.

22. Given the following declarations

```
subtype Name_String is String (1..20);
type    T_List is array (1..50) of Name_String;

One_Name : Name_String;
List     : T_List;
Size     : Natural;
```

indicate whether each of the following is valid or invalid.

a. `List(3) := One_Name;`
b. `List(14, 17) := 'z';`
c. `List(3)(7) := 'y';`
d. `Ada.Text_IO.Get_Line (Item => List(7), Last => Size);`
e. `Ada.Text_IO.Put (Item => List(9));`
f. `Ada.Text_IO.Put (Item => List (9)(7));`

23. Write all of the declarations needed to declare the following array variables.
    a. A table with five rows and six columns that contains Boolean values.
    b. A table indexed from −5 to 0 and 'A' to 'F' that contains Float values.
    c. A table with rows indexed by uppercase letters and columns indexed by lowercase letters that contains Boolean values.
24. Indicate which of the following would be represented best by a two-dimensional array and which would be represented best by an array of arrays.
    a. A board for the game of checkers.
    b. A list of sales totals for each salesperson in the company. Each yearly sales total consists of 12 monthly sales totals.
    c. A page of text consisting of 64 lines of text. Each line contains 132 characters.
    d. A page of text with 64 rows and 132 columns.
25. A logging operation keeps records of 37 loggers' monthly production for purposes of analysis, using the following array structure.

```
Number_Loggers : constant := 37;

type Logger_Index is range 1..Number_Loggers;
type Month_Type   is range 1..12;   -- 1 = January, 12 = December
type Cut_Table     is array (Logger_Index, Month_Type) of Natural;

Logs_Cut       : Cut_Table;
Monthly_High   : Natural;
Monthly_Total  : Natural;
Yearly_Total   : Natural;
High           : Natural;
Month          : Month_Type;
Best_Month     : Month_Type;
Logger         : Logger_Index;
Best_Logger    : Logger_Index;
```

a. The following statement would assign the January log total for logger number 7 to Monthly Total. (True or False)

```
Monthly_Total := Logs_Cut(7, 1);
```

b. The following statements would compute the yearly total for logger number 11. (True or False)

```
Yearly_Total := 0;
For Month in Logger_Index loop
   Yearly_Total := Yearly_Total + Logs_Cut(Month, 11);
end loop;
```

c. The following statements would find the Best_Logger (most logs cut) in March. (True or False)

```
Best_Logger  := Logger_Index'Fist;
Monthly_High := Logs_Cut (Logger_Index'First, 3);
for Logger in Logger_Index'First + 1 .. Logger_Index'Last loop
   if Logs_Cut(Logger, 3) > Monthly_High then
       Best_Logger := Logger;
       Monthly_High := Logs_Cut(Logger, 3);
   end if;
end loop;
```

d. The following statements would find the logger with the highest monthly production and that logger's best month. (True or False)

```
High := 0;
for Month in Month_Index loop
   for Logger in Logger_Index loop
      if Logs_Cut(Logger, Month) > High then
         High := Logs_Cut(Logger, Month);
         Best_Logger := Logger;
         Best_Month := Month;
      end if;
   end loop;
end loop;
```

26. Write all of the declarations needed to declare the following array variables. Use Float as the component type in each array.
    a. A three-dimensional array where the first dimension is indexed from −1 to +3, the second dimension is indexed from 'A' to 'Z', and the third dimension is indexed from 1 to 20.
    b. A four-dimensional array where the first two dimensions are indexed from 1 to 10, and the third and fourth are indexed from 'a' to 'f'.
27. Why is it better to declare and use distinct types rather than subtypes or predefined types for indices in two-dimensional or multidimensional arrays?

28. We used a two-dimensional array in the City Council Election case study. What advantages would there be in using an array of arrays instead of the two-dimensional array?

Programming Warm-up Exercises

Use the following declarations in Exercises 1-4.

```
Max_Length : constant := 100;

subtype Index_Type is Integer range 1..Max_Length;
type    Pass_Array  is array (Index_Type) of Boolean;
type    Score_Array is array (Index_Type) of Natural;

Passing    : Pass_Array;
Scores     : Score_Array;
Num_Scores : Natural;
```

1. Write an assignment statement that will initialize all of the components in the array Passing to True.
2. Complete the following procedure that reads in a number of scores from the keyboard and returns them in the array parameter Scores. The end of the data is indicated with a negative sentinel. Return the number of scores read in the parameter Num_Scores.

```
procedure Get_Scores (Scores     : out Score_Array;
                      Num_Scores : out Natural) is
   Value : Integer;
begin
```

3. Write an Ada main subprogram that calls procedure Get_Scores from the previous question and then displays the number of A's (scores from 90 to 100), B's (scores from 80 to 89), C's (scores from 70 to 79), D's (scores from 60 to 69), and F's (scores less than 60).
4. Write an Ada code fragment that reverses the order of the components in array Scores; that is, Scores(1) and Scores(100) are swapped, Scores(2) and Scores(99) are swapped, and so on.
5. Using the types given in Exam Preparation Exercise 13, complete the following function that totals the hours worked on a particular day in one week by all employees.

```
function Total_Hours (Time_Cards : in Employee_Array;
                      Day        : in Day_Type) return Float is
   Result : Float;
begin
```

Use the following declarations in Exercises 6–10.

```
subtype Score_Range is Integer range 0..100;

type Grade_Rec is
   record
      Pass  : Boolean;
      Score : Score_Range;
   end record;
type Grade_Array is array (Positive range <>) of Grade_Rec;
```

6. Write an Ada procedure called Set_Status that has a parameter called Grade_List of type Grade_Array. For every component of this array, set field Pass to False wherever value of field Score is less than 60 and to True whenever the value of field Score is greater than or equal to 60.
7. Write an Ada function called Talley_Pass that takes a parameter called Grade_List of type Grade_Array and returns the number of components in the array in which the field Pass is True.
8. Write an Ada function called Tally that takes a parameter called Grade_List of type Grade_Array and a parameter called Score of type Score_Range. The function should return the number of values in Grade_List that have field Score greater than or equal to parameter Score.
9. Write an Ada function called Minimum that takes a parameter called Grade_List of type Grade_Array and returns the value of the lowest score in Grade_List.
10. Write an Ada procedure called Reverse_List that takes a parameter called Grade_List of type Grade_Array and reverses the order of the record components in Grade_List; that is, Grade_List(Grade_List'First) goes into Grade_List(Grade_List'Last), Grade_List (Grade_List'First+1) goes into Grade_List(Grade_List'Last-1), and so on.
11. Complete the following function that returns True if all the integer values in the unconstrained two-dimensional array Table are positive and False otherwise.

```
function All_Positive (Table : in Integer_Array) return Boolean is
```

12. Complete the following procedure to set the diagonals of an unconstrained square (number of rows equals the number of columns) two-dimensional array Table to the character specified by parameter To.

```
procedure Set_Diagonal (Table : in out Character_Array;
                        To    : in     Character) is
```

13. Complete the following function that finds the largest value in a two-dimensional unconstrained array of integers.

```
function Largest (Table : in Integer_Array) return Integer is
```

14. Using the declarations in Exam Preparation Exercise 18 in this chapter, write subprograms to do the following:
    a. Determine the team that sold the most tickets during the first week of ticket sales.
    b. Determine the week in which the second team sold the most tickets.
    c. Determine the week in which the most tickets were sold.
    d. Determine the team that sold the most tickets.
15. Using the declarations in Exam Preparation Exercise 19 in this chapter, write subprograms to do the following:
    a. Determine which school spent the most money on football.
    b. Determine which sport the last school spent the most money on.
    c. Determine which school has the most students playing basketball.
    d. Determine in which sport the third school had the most students participating.
    e. Determine the total amount spent by all the schools on volleyball.
    f. Determine the total number of students playing all sports. (Assume that each student plays only one sport.)
    g. Determine which school had the most students participating in sports. (Assume that each student plays only one sport.)
    h. Determine which was the most popular sport in terms of money spent.
    i. Determine which was the most popular sport in terms of student participation. (Assume that each student plays only one sport.)
16. Given the following declarations

```
Number_Of_Items  : constant := 100;
Number_Of_Stores : constant := 10;

type Item_Number_Type  is range 1..Number_Of_Items;
type Store_Number_Type is range 1..Number_Of_Stores;
type Month_Type        is range 1..12;
type Sales_Array is array (Item_Number_Type  range <>,
                           Store_Number_Type range <>,
                           Month_Type        range <>)  of Natural;
```

write an Ada procedure to initialize an array of type Sales_Array to 0 using nested for loops.

17. Given the following declarations

```
Number_Of_Salespeople : constant := 100;

type Dollars is delta 0.01 digits 7 range 0.00 .. 99_999.99;
type Salesperson_Index    is range 1..Number_Of_Salespeople;
type Month_Index          is range 1..12;
type Monthly_Sales_Array is array (Month_Index) of Dollars;
type Total_Sales_Array    is
     array (Salesperson_Index range <>) of Monthly_Sales_Array;
```

Write an Ada procedure that displays the average sales for each salesperson. This procedure should call a function (which you also must write) that sums the 12 monthly sales totals of each salesperson.

18. A set of libraries on a big campus is similar to a five-dimensional array of books. There are several libraries, each with several floors, each floor a rectangular array of stacks. Each stack is made of shelves.
    a. Write the types necessary to describe the storage of library books according to this scheme. Use a string of 80 characters for the components (books) in your array. This string will hold the title of the book.
    b. Write a code fragment to print out a list of book titles in a given library.
    c. Write a code fragment to print out a list of book titles on the third floor of all libraries.

Programming Problems

1. The local baseball team is computerizing its records. You are to write a program that computes batting averages. There are 20 players on the team, identified by the numbers 1 through 20. Their batting records are coded on a file as follows. Each line contains four numbers: the player's identification number and the number of hits, walks, and outs he or she made in a particular game.

Example Input Line

```
3  2  1  1
```

The example indicates that, during this game, player number 3 was at bat 4 times and made 2 hits, 1 walk, and 1 out. For each player there are many lines in the file—one for each game played. Each player's batting average is computed by adding the player's total number of hits and dividing by the total number of times at bat. A walk does not count as either a hit or a time at bat when you calculate the batting average. Your program prints a table showing each player's identification number, batting average, and number of walks.

This problem also appeared in Chapter 9 where you were to solve it with files. Which solution is best?

2. An advertising company wants to send a letter to all its clients announcing a new fee schedule. The clients' names are on several different lists in the company. The company merges the various lists to form one file, Client_Names, but obviously the company does not want to send the same letter twice to anyone.

   Write a program that removes any clients appearing in the file more than once. On each line of data there is a four-digit code number (with no leading zeros), followed by a blank, and then the client's name. For example, Amalgamated Steel is listed as:

```
5031 Amalgamated Steel
```

   Your program should create a new file that contains the same information (not necessarily in the same order) as the old file but without duplicates. Use an array indexed by four-digit code numbers in your solution.

3. Write a program that calculates the mean and standard deviation of integers stored in a file. The output should be of type Float and should be properly labeled and formatted to two decimal places. The formula for calculating the mean of a series of integers is to add all the numbers, then to divide by the number of integers. Expressed in mathematical terms, this is

$$\bar{X} = \frac{\sum_{i=1}^{N} X_i}{N}$$

   To calculate the standard deviation of a series of integers, subtract the mean from each integer (you may get a negative number) and square the result; add all these squared differences; divide by the number of integers minus one; then take the square root of the result. Expressed in mathematical terms, this is

$$S = \sqrt{\frac{\sum_{i=1}^{N} (X_i - \bar{X})^2}{N - 1}}$$

   Use the Sqrt function in package Ada.Numerics.Elementary_Functions to calculate square roots.

4. One of the local banks is gearing up for a big advertising campaign and would like to see how long its customers are waiting for service at drive-in windows. The bank has asked several employees to keep accurate records for the 24-hour drive-in service. The collected information, which is read from a file, consists of the time when the customer arrived in hours, minutes, and seconds; the time when the customer was actually served; and the ID number of the teller. Write a program that does the following:
   a. Reads in the wait data.
   b. Computes the wait time in seconds.

c. Calculates the mean, standard deviation (the square root of the sum of the squares of the differences between each value and the average divided by the number of values minus one—see formulas in previous problem), and range.
d. Prints a single-page summary showing the values calculated in c.

Input

The first data line contains a title.

The remaining lines each contain a teller ID, an arrival time, and a service time. The times are broken up into hours, minutes, and seconds according to a 24-hour clock.

Processing

Calculate the mean and the standard deviation.

Locate the shortest wait time and the longest wait time for any number of records up to 100.

Output

The input data (echo print).

The title.

The following values, all properly labeled: number of records, mean, standard deviation, and range (minimum and maximum).

5. Your history professor has so many students in her class that she has trouble determining how well the class does on exams. She has found out that you are a computer whiz and has asked you to write a program to do some simple statistical analyses on exam scores. Your program must work for any class size up to 100 ($0 < N <= 100$). Write and test a program that does the following:
   a. Reads the test grades from a file.
   b. Calculates the class mean, standard deviation (see formulas in Problem 3), and percentage of the test scores falling into the ranges: <10, 10–19, 20–29, 30–39,…,80–89, and 90–100.
   c. Prints a summary showing the mean and standard deviation, as well as a histogram showing the percentage distribution of test scores.

Input

The first data line contains the number of exams to be analyzed and a title for the report.

The remaining lines have 10 test scores on each line until the last, and 1–10 scores on the last.

The scores are all nonnegative integers.

Output

The input data as they are read.

A report consisting of the title that was read from data, the number of scores, the mean, the standard deviation (labeled), and the histogram.

6. A small postal system ships parcels within your state. Acceptance of parcels is subject to the following constraints:
   a. Parcels are not to exceed a weight of 50 pounds.
   b. Parcels are not to exceed 3 feet in length, width, or depth, and may not have a combined length and girth exceeding 6 feet. (The girth of a parcel is the circumference of the parcel around its two smallest sides; the mathematical formula is

$$\text{Girth} = 2 \times (S1 + S2 + S3 - \text{Largest})$$

   where Largest is the largest of the three parcel dimensions, S1, S2, and S3.)

   Your program should process a transaction file containing one entry for each box mailed during the week. Each entry contains a transaction number followed by the weight of the box and its dimensions (in no particular order). The program should print the transaction number, weight, and postal charge for all accepted parcels, as well as the transaction number and weight for all rejected parcels. At the end of the report, the program must print the number of parcels processed and the number rejected.

   Input

   Parcel post table—weight and cost (contains 25 pairs of values). Store this table in a one-dimensional array of records. You can then determine the postal cost of each parcel by searching the Weight fields and then using the Cost field. If a parcel weight falls between weight categories in the table, your program should use the cost for the higher weight.

   Transaction file—transaction number, weight, and three dimensions for an arbitrary number of transactions. Assume that all weights are whole numbers, and that all dimensions are given to the nearest inch.

   Output

   First line—appropriate headings.

   Next *N* records—transaction number, whether accepted or rejected, weight, and cost.

   Last line—number of parcels processed, number of parcels rejected.

7. The final exam in your psychology class is 30 multiple-choice questions. Your instructor says that if you write the program to grade the finals, you won't have to take it.

Input

The first data line contains the key to the exam. The correct answers are the first 30 characters; they are followed by an integer number that says how many students took the exam (call it *N*).

The next *N* lines contain student answers in the first 30 character positions followed by the student's name in the next 10 character positions.

Output

For each student—the student's name; followed by the number of correct answers; followed by PASS if the number correct is 60 percent or better, or FAIL otherwise.

8. Design and implement an Ada program to determine whether or not any two consecutive lines typed at the keyboard are anagrams of one another. Two lines are anagrams of one another if they contain exactly the same characters in (perhaps) different order. For example, the following two lines are anagrams.

   Mildred Smedley

   slid remedy meld

   Echo the two lines after both have been read. Then print one of the following messages followed by three blank lines:

   The above two lines are anagrams!

   The above two lines are not anagrams!

   You may assume that no line contains more than 80 characters. You may also assume that the only characters in the lines are the 26 uppercase and lowercase characters of the alphabet and the blank character. Ignore blanks in the input. Consider equivalent uppercase and lowercase letters to be equal. Terminate your program when the first line of the pair contains less than two characters.

9. We can represent a deck of playing cards as a two-dimensional array, where the first dimension is rank and the second dimension is suit. Read in a bridge hand (13 cards) and determine whether the player should pass or bid. Input each card on a line by itself with the suit given first and rank next. The decision to pass or bid is based on the number of points the hand is worth. Count points as follows:

   An ace is worth 4 points.

   A king is worth 3 points.

   A queen is worth 2 points.

   A jack is worth 1 point.

   Add up the points in the hand and print one of the following messages.

Below 13 points,	"Pass"
Between 13 and 16 points,	"Bid one of a suit"
Between 17 and 19 points,	"Bid one no trump"
Between 20 and 22 points,	"Bid one of a suit"
Over 22 points,	"Bid two of a suit"

10. Write an interactive program that plays tic-tac-toe. Represent the board as a three-by-three character array. Initialize the array to blanks and ask each player in turn to input a position. The first player's position will be marked on the board with an O, and the second player's position will be marked with an X. Continue the process until a player wins or the game is a draw. To win, a player must have three marks in a row, in a column, or on a diagonal. A draw occurs when the board is full and no one has won.

    Input each player's position in the form of an index into the tic-tac-toe board; that is, a row number, space, and column number. Make the program user friendly.

    After each game, print out a diagram of the board showing the ending positions. Keep a count of the number of games each player has won and the number of draws. Before the beginning of each game, ask each player whether he or she wishes to continue. If either player wishes to quit, print out the statistics and stop.

11. The Galileo spacecraft sends photos taken in space back to Earth as a stream of numbers. Your job is to take a matrix (two-dimensional array) of the numbers and print it as a negative picture.

    If the numbers received represent levels of brightness, then one approach to generating a picture is to print a dark character (such as $) when the brightness level is low and print a light character (such as a blank or a period) when the level is high. Unfortunately, errors in transmission sometimes occur. Thus, your program should first attempt to find and correct these errors. Assume that a value is in error if it differs by more than one from each of its four neighboring values. Correct the erroneous value by giving it the average of its neighboring values, rounding it to the nearest integer. For example:

```
  5         Regard the 2 as an error and
4 2 5       give it a corrected value of 5.
  4
```

    Note that values on the corners or boundaries of the matrix have to be processed differently from the values on the interior. Your program should print a negative image of the corrected picture on a new page.

12. You work for the Jet Propulsion Laboratory. Your supervisor wants you to write a program that takes an array containing the digitized representation of a picture of the night sky and locates the stars on it. Each element of the array represents the amount of light hitting that portion of the image when the picture was taken. Intensities range from 0 to 20.

    Sample Input

```
0   3  4   0  0  0   6  8
5  13  6   0  0  0   2  3
2   6  2   7  3  0  10  0
0   0  4  15  4  1   6  0
0   0  7  12  6  9  10  4
5   0  6  10  6  4   8  0
```

A star probably is located in the area covered by the array element Row, Column, if the following is the case: (A(Row, Column) + sum of the 4 surrounding intensities) / 5 > 6.0

Ignore possible stars along the edges of the array.

Input

A title

An array of intensities

Output

The desired output is a star map containing asterisks where you have found a star and blanks elsewhere, such as:

```
- - - - - - - - - - - - - - - - - - - - - - - -
:
:      *
:
:              *
:
:              *        *    *
:
:
```

Display two blanks for the "no star" case. Indicate the presence of a star by a blank, followed by an asterisk. Give the chart a border and label it with the title.

13. Design and write a program that reads a 4 × 4 array of integers from the keyboard and determines whether or not these form a magic square. A magic square is a matrix of numbers in which the sum of each row and the sum of each column are identical.

    Optional: Add the criterion that the sum of the two diagonals of the square must be the same as the sum of every row and the sum of every column in the matrix for it to be a magic square.

CHAPTER 12

Packages, Searching, and Sorting

GOALS

After reading this chapter, you should be able to

- understand what a package is and why packages are important
- write a package declaration and a package body
- explain what a compilation and a compilation unit are
- determine the order in which program units can be compiled
- search an array for a component with a given value
- sort the components of an array into ascending or descending order
- insert a value into an ordered array
- search an ordered array using the binary search algorithm

You have been using packages since the Get and Put procedures in the predefined package Ada.Text_IO were introduced in Chapter 2. Since then you have used functions, procedures, types, and constants that are defined in the predefined packages Ada.Text_IO, Ada.Sequential_IO, Ada.Direct_IO, and Ada.Calendar. By now you should be comfortable with *using* packages. In this chapter we explain why you might want to define your own packages and show you how to create them.

Chapter 11 introduced the concept of a one-dimensional array—a data structure that is a collection of components of the same type given a single name. In this chapter, we examine some common algorithms that are applied again and again to data stored in a one-dimensional array.

An Overview of Packages

Information hiding is what we do in the top-down design process when we postpone the solution of a difficult subproblem. Information hiding does not mean that information is not available; it is just kept out of sight when not required. Information hiding is not limited to programming. Try to list all of the operations and information required to make a ham and cheese sandwich. We normally don't consider the details of raising hogs and dairy cows; producing cheese; or growing wheat, mustard, tomatoes, and lettuce as part of making a sandwich. Information hiding lets us deal only with the operations and information needed at a particular level in the solution of a problem.

Encapsulation is a programming language feature that lets a compiler enforce information hiding. It is like the case around a watch that prevents us from accessing the works. The case is provided by the watchmaker, who can easily open it when repairs become necessary. Encapsulation lets us use code reliably and with less worry. Most programming languages provide the subprogram and hierarchical record for encapsulation. You call the various predefined Get and Put procedures without worrying about what the code for these operations looks like. Although these methods of isolating modules and data have been adequate for our programs thus far, they are insufficient for larger programs, particularly for programs that are complex enough to require a team of programmers. Ada was designed for developing large programs. Packages, both predefined and programmer-written, are Ada's principal method of encapsulation for complex programs. With packages, we can concentrate our efforts on one level of the problem while our fellow team members concentrate on other levels. The programming process becomes more like making a sandwich. One person concentrates on combining the meat, cheese, and bread; someone else is responsible for raising the pigs.

Encapsulation A programming language feature that allows a compiler to enforce information hiding.

Information hiding The management of access to the details of control and data structures.

In Chapter 1 we defined a package as an Ada tool that allows programmers to implement a subproblem separately from the solutions to other subproblems. We also can use this statement to define the subprogram. Given what we know now, it's clear that a package is much more. A **package** is a group of logically related entities that may include types and subtypes, objects of those types and subtypes, and subprograms with parameters of those types and subtypes. Once we have written and thoroughly tested a package, we can use it with confidence in later programs simply by including an appropriate with clause.

Package A group of logically related entities that may include types and subtypes, objects of those types and subtypes, and subprograms with parameters of those types and subtypes.

We write packages in two parts: the package declaration and the package body. The package declaration defines the interface to the package. It is like the face and stems on a watch. The declaration describes what *resources* the package can supply to the program. Resources supplied by a watch might include the value of the current time and operations to set the current time. In a package, resources can include types, subtypes, constants, and subprograms. The package body provides the implementation of the resources defined in the package declaration (the insides of the watch).

There are significant advantages to separating the declaration of a package from its implementation. A clear interface is important, particularly when a package is used by other members of a programming team. Any ambiguities in an interface will result in problems when the team members' efforts are combined. By separating the declaration of the package from its implementation, we have the opportunity to concentrate our efforts on the design of the interface without needing to worry about implementation details.

By using separate declarations and interfaces for our packages, we can save time during the development of our programs. When we find an error in a body, we need only correct and recompile the package body that contained the error. We do not have to recompile the entire program—a time-consuming process when our programs are large. We discuss the issues of separate compilation in a later section of this chapter.

Another advantage of this separation is that we can change the implementation (the body) at any time without affecting the work done by other programmers. We can make changes when we discover a better algorithm or when there is a change in the environment in which the program is run. For example, suppose we need to control how text is displayed in a window. Text control operations may include moving the cursor to a particular location and setting text characteristics like bold, blink, and underline. The algorithms required for controlling these characteristics usually differ from one computer system to another. By defining an interface and encapsulating the algorithms in the package body, we can easily move our program to a different system simply by rewriting one package body. We do not have to change the rest of the program.

Child Packages

Every Ada compiler vendor provides over 30 packages defined and required by the Ada standard. These include the packages we have used throughout this book, such as Ada.Text_IO, Ada.Direct_IO, Ada.Sequential_IO, and Ada.Calendar. The compiler vendors also provide many other specialized packages that are defined by the standard but not required by it. For example, a vendor who sells Ada compilers to customers who develop financial applications will include the packages defined in the Ada standard's Information Systems annex that provide resources for processing financial data. In addition, compiler vendors, other vendors, and public and private organizations furnish a wide variety of packages to provide a wealth of other resources to Ada programmers. These resources are typically not defined by the Ada standard. You may find hundreds of packages available on the computer system you are using to complete your Ada programming assignments.

Ada provides a hierarchical structure to organize the large numbers of packages found in an Ada development environment. This structure is based on the concept of the child package. As we mentioned in Chapter 2, all standard packages are organized under three parent packages: Ada, Interfaces, and System. The package named Ada serves as the parent of most other standard library packages. Resources for combining Ada statements with statements written in other programming languages in the same program are found in the package Interfaces and its children. Finally package System and its children provide the definitions of characteristics of the particular environment in which the program runs.

Child packages can also have children. The standard package Elementary_Functions is a child of package Numerics, which is a child of package Ada. The prefixed name of this package is Ada.Numerics. Elementary_Functions.

While the hierarchical package structure is crucial to the development of large software systems, we do not develop any child packages in this book. You may do so in later courses as the size of your problems grow and you begin to develop your own set of resources.

Package Syntax

Here is a simplified EBNF definition of the package declaration.

```
package_declaration          ::= package_specification;
package_specification        ::= package defining_program_unit_name is
                                    {basic_declarative_item}
                                 end [defining_program_unit_name]
defining_program_unit_name   ::= [parent_unit_name.]identifier
basic_declarative_item       ::= type_declaration            |
                                 subtype_declaration         |
                                 object_declaration          |
                                 subprogram_declaration      |
                                 generic_instantiation
```

Ada's formal syntax has different definitions for package declaration and package specification. However, most programmers use the two terms interchangeably. Notice that the package specification can contain subprogram declarations but not subprogram bodies. Because the package declaration serves as the interface to the package, all of the declarations that it contains are available to the rest of the program. If the package declaration contained the subprogram bodies, the implementations of the subprograms would not be hidden from the program.

Here is a simplified EBNF definition of the package body.

```
package_body      ::= package body defining_program_unit_name is
                         [declarative_part]
                      end [defining_program_unit_name];
declarative_part  ::= {basic_declarative_item | subprogram_body}
```

The package body contains the implementation details for items declared in the package declaration. It can also contain additional subtypes, types, constants, generic instantiations, and subprograms that we need for these implementations. The contents of a package body are not available to the rest of the program.

In order to access the resources of Ada.Text_IO, Ada.Direct_IO, Ada.Sequential_IO, or Ada.Calendar from our program, we included a with clause that named the package. We use this same mechanism to access a programmer-written package.

Kinds of Packages

Although there are many different ways to define and use packages, most packages fall into one of three categories: definition packages, service packages, and data-abstraction packages. We'll take a closer look at each of these in the following sections. This classification system is not strict—its purpose is to give a beginner guidance in the development of packages. Some packages have the properties of more than one of these categories, and a few have properties not found in any of them.

Definition Packages

A definition package groups together related constants and types. Definition packages are useful when the same types must be used in several programs or by different programmers working on different parts of one large program. For example, the sequential-file update program written for the Department Store Account case study in Chapter 10 had to use the same type declarations as the program that originally created the master file. The program given at the end of that chapter to display a master file also needed to use these same type declarations. In our examples, the type declarations were duplicated in each program. By grouping these declarations into a single package, we can eliminate the extra effort involved in typing the declarations over and over again. More importantly, we ensure that all the programs use the exact same declarations. Here is the specification for a package that can be used by all the programs that work with customer accounts.

```
package Customer_Accounts is

-- This package contains the types used to declare customer account records

   subtype Name_String    is String (1..20);
   subtype Address_String is String (1..40);
   subtype State_String   is String (1..2);
   subtype Zip_String     is String (1..5);
   type    Dollars        is delta 0.01 digits 6 range 0.00 .. 9_999.99;

   type Name_Rec is
      record
        First : Name_String;
        Last  : Name_String;
      end record;

   type Address_Rec is
      record
         Street : Address_String;
```

```
         City   : Address_String;
         State  : State_String;
         Zip    : Zip_String;
      end record;

   type Customer_Rec is
      record
         Account_Number : Positive;
         Name           : Name_Rec;
         Address        : Address_Rec;
         Credit_Limit   : Dollars;
         Balance        : Dollars;
      end record;

end Customer_Accounts;
```

Here is a portion of the Update Program from Chapter 10 to illustrate the use of the Customer_Rec type declared in package Customer_Accounts.

```
with Customer_Accounts;           -- We use resources from our definition package
with Ada.Sequential_IO;
with Ada.Integer_Text_IO;
with Ada.Text_IO;
procedure Update is

-- This program performs an update of a sequential master file

.
.
.

   -- Instantiate I/O Packages
   package Customer_IO is new Ada.Sequential_IO
                    (Element_Type => Customer_Accounts.Customer_Rec);

.
.
.

   Customer : Customer_Accounts.Customer_Rec;    -- The customer record for
                                                 -- the current account

.
.
.
```

There are two things you should notice in this program fragment. First, it has a with clause naming our previously written definition package Customer_Accounts. Second, the type name Customer_Rec is prefixed with the name of the package in which we declared it. Although we used only the type Customer_Rec in this code fragment, we could use any of the other subtype or type declarations of package Customer_Accounts in a similar way.

Package declarations that contain only subtype, type, and constant declarations are considered a simple form of a package and cannot have a package body. There is nothing to implement; everything is in the package declaration.

Service Packages

A service package groups together the constants, types, subtypes, and subprograms necessary to provide some particular service. Every Ada compiler comes with a predefined service package called Ada.Numerics.Elementary_Functions that contains 29 mathematical subprograms. This package includes functions such as square root, the trigonometric functions (sine, cosine, tangent, and so on), and logarithms for Float values. The predefined package Ada.Numerics.Generic_ Elementary_Functions is a generic template that we instantiate to obtain the same mathematical functions for other real types.

The predefined package Ada.Text_IO is another example of a service package. It provides us with all the resources required to work with text files. In Appendix D you will find the complete package declaration for Text_IO. This package declaration contains four type declarations, three subtype declarations, one constant declaration, and 77 subprogram declarations. It also contains the package declarations for generic packages Integer_IO, Float_IO, Decimal_IO, Enumeration_IO, Fixed_IO, and Modular_IO. When we include `with Ada.Text_IO` at the beginning of our program, we can use any of the resources declared in Text_IO's package declaration.

The service-package specification contains the declarations of all the subprograms needed by the rest of the program. The bodies of these subprograms are written in the package body. The package body often includes additional procedures required to carry out the desired operations. Any declarations in the package body are not available to the rest of the program.

As an example of a service package, we present a package with operations that allow us to have more control over output displayed on a display screen than is available through Ada.Text_IO. Here is the package declaration.

```
package Display_Control is

-- This service package contains a group of operations
-- for controlling the display screen.
```

```
   -- Types
   type     Erase_Area  is (Current_Line, Screen);   -- Area to erase
   subtype Row_Type     is Integer range 1..24;    -- Screen has 24 rows
   subtype Column_Type is Integer range 1..80;     -- Screen has 80 columns

   ---------------------------------------------
   procedure Put_Cursor (Row     : in Row_Type;        -- The desired row
                         Column : in Column_type); -- The desired column
   -- Move the cursor to the given row and column

   ---------------------------------------------
   procedure Erase (Area : in Erase_Area);      -- The area to be erased
   -- Erase either the entire screen or the line that
   -- currently contains the cursor

   ---------------------------------------------
   procedure Bold_On;
   -- Everything sent to the screen after this procedure is called will
   -- be displayed in bold characters

   ---------------------------------------------
   procedure Blink_On;
   -- Everything sent to the screen after this procedure is called will
   -- be blinking

   ---------------------------------------------
   procedure Normal;
   -- Everything sent to the screen after this procedure is called will
   -- be displayed normally

end Display_Control;
```

Everything in this package declaration is available to our program. There are three types/subtypes and five operations in the declaration. Put_Cursor moves the cursor to a given position on the screen. Erase clears either the entire screen or the current line. After calling procedure Bold_On, the program will display everything put to the screen in bold characters. After calling procedure Blink_On, the program will display everything put to the screen in blinking characters. Calling procedure Normal will return the output to normal characters, turning off both bold and blinking for subsequent puts.

Here is a program fragment that uses the operations in this service package.

```
with Display_Control;
with Ada.Text_IO;
procedure Example is
   .
   .
   .
```

```
-- Clear the entire display screen
Display_Control.Erase (Area => Display_Control.Screen);

-- Display a title in bold characters on the 5th line
Display_Control.Bold_On;
Display_Control.Put_Cursor (Row => 5,  Column => 31);
Ada.Text_IO.Put_Line ("Mildred's Secrets");

-- Display a blinking prompt (not bold) on the 10th line
Display_Control.Normal;                                    -- Turn off bold
Display_Control.Blink_On;                                  -- Turn on blink
Display_Control.Put_Cursor (Row => 10,  Column => 1);
-- The following Put_Line moves cursor to row 11
Ada.Text_IO.Put_Line ("Enter the secret number");
Display_Control.Normal;                                    -- Turn off blink
Ada.Integer_Text_IO.Get (Number);
-- If the number is the secret number,
-- erase the line so no one else can see it
if Number = Secret_Number then
   Display_Control.Put_Cursor (Row => 11, Column => 1);
   Display_Control.Erase (Area => Display_Control.Current_Line);
   Ada.Text_IO.New_Line;
else
   .
   .
   .
```

As with Ada.Text_IO, we do not need to know how these operations actually work in order to use them. The implementation of these operations is in the package body. Here is a sample body for the Display_Control package. This body is written for systems that accept ANSI control codes. Many different systems use these control codes.

```
with Ada.Text_IO;
with Ada.Characters.Latin_1;
package body Display_Control is

-- This service package contains a group of operations
-- for controlling the display screen.

-- Assumption: The display accepts and processes American
-- National Standards Institute (ANSI) escape sequences.

   -- Code to start an ANSI control string (consists of
   -- the Escape control character and the left bracket character)
   ANSI_Start : constant String := Ada.Characters.Latin_1.ESC & '[';

   ----------------------------------------------------------------
   function To_String (Value : in Natural) return String is
```

```
-- Convert a nonnegative number to a string of digit characters.
-- Handles a maximum of Max_Size digits

   -- Position of the zero character in the collating sequence
   Zero_Char : constant := Character'Pos ('0');
   Max_Size  : constant := 10;  -- Maximum digits in number

   subtype Digit_Type   is Integer range 0..9;
   subtype Digit_String is String (1..Max_Size);

   Number : Natural;          -- Local copy of parameter
   Result : Digit_String;     -- String representation of Value
   Index  : Positive;         -- Index for array Result
   Digit  : Digit_Type;       -- One digit in the number

begin -- To_String
   Number := Value;          -- Make local copy of the parameter
   Index  := Result'Last;  -- First digit placed at end of Result
   Digit_Loop:  -- Converts Number to a string
   loop         -- Each iteration, one digit of Number is converted
      Digit := Number rem 10;  -- Get the least significant digit
      -- Convert the digit to a character and assign to the array
      Result(Index) := Character'Val (Digit + Zero_Char);

      Number := Number / 10; -- Go to the next significant digit in Number
      exit Digit_Loop when Number = 0;
      Index := Index - 1;      -- Move left one place in Result
   end loop Digit_Loop;
   -- Return the slice of Result containing the number
   return Result (Index..Result'Last);
end To_String;

--------------------------------------------
procedure Put_Cursor (Row    : in Row_Type;        -- The desired row
                      Column : in Column_type) is -- and column
begin
   -- Send the string "ESC[r;cH" where r is the desired row
   -- number and c is the desired column number. For example,
   -- sending the string "ESC[12;32H" would position the cursor
   -- on row 12, column 32
   Ada.Text_IO.Put (ANSI_Start & To_String (Row)    & ';' &
                                  To_String (Column) & 'H');
   Ada.Text_IO.Flush;  -- Send any buffered characters to the display
end Put_Cursor;

--------------------------------------------
procedure Erase (Area : in Erase_Area) is   -- The area to be erased
begin
   if Area = Current_Line then
```

```
         Ada.Text_IO.Put (ANSI_Start & "2K");   -- "ESC[2K" erases line
      else
         Ada.Text_IO.Put (ANSI_Start & "2J");   -- "ESC[2J" erases screen
      end if;
      Ada.Text_IO.Flush;  -- Send any buffered characters to the display
   end Erase;

   ---------------------------------------------
   procedure Bold_On is
   begin
      Ada.Text_IO.Put(ANSI_Start & "1m");   -- "ESC[1m" turns on Bold
      Ada.Text_IO.Flush;  -- Send any buffered characters to the display
   end Bold_On;

   ---------------------------------------------
   procedure Blink_On is
   begin
      Ada.Text_IO.Put(ANSI_Start & "5m");   -- "ESC[5m" turns on Blink
      Ada.Text_IO.Flush;  -- Send any buffered characters to the display
   end Blink_On;

   ---------------------------------------------
   procedure Normal is
   begin
      Ada.Text_IO.Put(ANSI_Start & "0m");   -- "ESC[0m" turns off all attributes
      Ada.Text_IO.Flush;  -- Send any buffered characters to the display
   end Normal;

end Display_Control;
```

Everything in the package declaration is automatically visible to the package body; the package body does *not* need a with clause to use its own declaration. We need the with clauses here for Ada.Text_IO and Ada.Characters.Latin_1 because procedures in the package *body* use resources from these two packages. We didn't need these with clauses in the package *declaration* because none of these packages resources are used in that declaration.

The package body includes a procedure body for each procedure declared in the package declaration. The function To_String is not declared in the package declaration. It is local to the package body and cannot be used outside. Similarly, the constant ANSI_Start is only available to the procedures in the package body. This constant is defined with a control character value from the predefined package Ada.Characters. Latin_1 (discussed in Chapter 7).

The implementation of the display control procedures in this package body is written for display windows that use the ANSI control codes. This implementation will not work for display terminals that use other methods. However, by encapsulating the display operations in a package like this, we can run our program on other kinds of displays simply by writing a different package body. We will not have to make any modifications to the package declaration or to any program that uses the package.

Data Abstraction Packages

In Chapter 10 we defined data abstraction as the separation of a data structure's logical properties from its implementation. Because we write the package as two separate parts, it is an ideal mechanism for data abstraction.

A data type is a formal description of a set of values (called the *domain*) and the basic operations that can be applied to these values. Ada's subtype and type declarations allow us to define the domain of new data types. However, these declarations do not define any new operations for the data types. Each new data type we define comes with a predefined set of operations. For example, a new integer type or subtype has the same operations available as type Integer.

Data abstraction packages allow us to define additional operations for a new data type. In the package declaration we declare the domain of the type and any operations that are not already predefined for that type. The following package declaration is for a data type for the colors used in a primitive color display screen that can display eight different colors.

```
package Pixel is

-- This package implements a data type for the colors available on a
-- primitive RGB color display screen. Note that mixing colored lights is
-- different than mixing colored pigments like paints.

   type     Color_Type            is (Red, Green, Blue, Magenta,
                                      Cyan, Yellow, White, Black);
   subtype Primary_Color_Type    is Color_Type range Red..Blue;
   subtype Secondary_Color_Type is Color_Type range Magenta..Yellow;
   subtype Neutral_Color_Type    is Color_Type range White..Black;

   ------------------------------------
   function "+" (Color_1 : in Primary_Color_Type;
                 Color_2 : in Primary_Color_Type) return
                                                 Secondary_Color_Type;
   -- This function returns the color resulting from the mixing of
   -- two different primary colored lights
```

```
   -- Precondition : Color_1 and Color_2 are different

   ----------------------------------------
   procedure Find_Components (A_Color : in  Secondary_Color_Type;
                              Color_1 : out Primary_Color_Type;
                              Color_2 : out Primary_Color_Type);
   -- This procedure returns the two primary colors making up a secondary color

end Pixel;
```

We declare the enumeration type Color_Type and three subtypes of Color_Type in this package. We also declare two operations for these types in the package. These operations supplement those predefined for any enumeration type. Function "+" returns the result of mixing two different primary colors. Procedure Find_Components returns the two primary colors that make up a secondary color. These operations are not available for any enumeration type; they are specific to type Color_Type.

Here is the body of the package Pixel. Remember, everything in the package declaration is automatically visible here; we do not have to include a with clause to use the declarations in package Pixel's own declaration.

```
package body Pixel is

   ----------------------------------------
   function "+" (Color_1 : Primary_Color_Type;
                 Color_2 : Primary_Color_Type) return
                                                Secondary_Color_Type is
   begin
      if Color_1 /= Blue and Color_2 /= Blue then
         return Yellow;                         -- Mixing Red and Green
      elsif Color_1 /= Green and Color_2 /= Green then
         return Magenta;                        -- Mixing Red and Blue
      else
         return Cyan;                           -- Mixing Green and Blue
      end if;
   end "+";

   ----------------------------------------
   procedure Find_Components (A_Color : in  Secondary_Color_Type;
                              Color_1 : out Primary_Color_Type;
                              Color_2 : out Primary_Color_Type) is
   begin
      case A_Color is
         when Yellow =>
            Color_1 := Red;
            Color_2 := Green;
         when Magenta =>
            Color_1 := Red;
```

```
            Color_2 := Blue;
         when Cyan =>
            Color_1 := Green;
            Color_2 := Blue;
      end case;
   end Find_Components;

end Pixel;
```

The distinction between service packages and data abstraction packages is not always clear. Some people classify package Ada.Text_IO as a data abstraction package rather than a service package. The data type defined is File_Type. All of the functions and procedures in the package are operations for this type. We classify packages as service packages when the operations seem more significant than the data types and as data abstraction packages when the data types seem more significant than the operations. Thus we classify Ada.Text_IO as a service package.

Compilation of Programs and Packages

A programming language would not be very suitable for team programming if the team had to share one source file. Ada provides facilities for compiling different parts of a program separately. In this section we look at Ada's facilities for separate compilation in more detail.

An Ada program is a collection of compilation units submitted to a compiler in one or more compilations. A **compilation** is the Ada term for a source file submitted to an Ada compiler. A portion of an Ada program that can be compiled by itself is called a **compilation unit.** A compilation contains one or more compilation units.

Compilation A source file containing one or more compilation units submitted to an Ada compiler.

Compilation unit A portion of an Ada program that can be compiled by itself.

For greatest flexibility, we restrict our examples to one compilation unit per compilation and recommend that you do the same. Ada does not specify any rules for naming our source files. Each different Ada development environment has its own conventions. Check the manual that comes with your Ada compiler to learn how to name the files in which you store your Ada code.

Here is a simplified EBNF definition that defines what portions of an Ada program may be compiled by themselves.

```
compilation               ::=  {compilation_unit}
compilation_unit          ::=  context_clause library_item
context_clause            ::=  {context_item}
context_item              ::=  with_clause                    |
                               use_clause
library_Item              ::=  library_unit_declaration       |
                               library_unit_body
library_unit_declaration  ::=  package_declaration            |
                               subprogram_declaration
library_unit_body         ::=  package_body                   |
                               subprogram_body
```

A compilation unit may contain zero or more with clauses. These clauses tell what other units this compilation unit depends upon. For example, nearly all of our compilation units have depended upon Ada.Text_IO. It has probably become an automatic reflex for you to type `with Ada.Text_IO;` each time you begin a new program. The with clause makes a library unit available within the compilation unit. This means that once we have included Ada.Text_IO in a context clause, we can use Ada.Text_IO anywhere within the compilation unit. We will discuss the use clause later in this chapter.

What we defined in Chapter 2 as an Ada *main* subprogram is really a procedure body. Because they are compilation units, we could put many of the procedures and functions that a main subprogram uses in their own files and compile them individually. We would then need to include a with clause for every procedure and function used by our program. We will, however, continue our practice of writing the procedures we need within our program or within packages that we write ourselves.

The Program Library

Ada requires that the language rules be enforced in the same manner for a program made up of multiple compilations as for a single compilation program. This requirement means that, whether a procedure is defined within the main subprogram file or in an independently compiled package, the Ada compiler must ensure that the actual parameters of any calls to the procedure are compatible with the formal parameters. To enforce the language rules for programs composed of multiple compilation units, the Ada compiler uses a program library to keep track of all of the units making up a program.

Ada does not specify the manner by which a unit is added to the library. Some Ada environments add a unit to the library when we compile it or issue specific library commands. The existence of a unit's source code in a directory is all that is required by other environments to have the unit *in* the library. The nature of the information stored in the library for each compilation unit and when this information is placed in the library varies from system to system. The information might include such things as:

1. the unit name and location of the source file containing the unit
2. the date and time the unit was compiled
3. a list of all units that this unit depends on (named by with clauses)
4. a symbol table for library units (a list of identifiers declared in the library unit that may be used by other units)
5. the object code created for library unit bodies

When we submit a compilation unit to the Ada compiler, it accesses the program library as part of the process of checking the validity of the new code. For example, if Ada.Text_IO.Put is used in the compilation unit, the Ada compiler checks the Ada.Text_IO unit entry in the program library to ensure that the Ada.Text_IO.Put parameter list is valid.

Order of Compilation

The following two rules define the order in which units must be compiled. They are based on the visibility of units established by context (with) clauses.

1. A compilation unit cannot be compiled until all library unit declarations named in its context clause are available in the library.
2. A library unit body (package body or subprogram body) cannot be compiled until its corresponding declaration is available in the library.

Let's look at an example. Each of the following boxes represents a single file to be submitted to the compiler (a compilation). Each of these compilations contains a single compilation unit.

```
with Apple;
with Pear;
with Ada.Text_IO;
procedure Fruit is   -- This is a library unit body
   .
   .                 -- This is the main subprogram.
   .
end Fruit;
```

```
package Apple is     -- This is a package declaration
   .
   .
   .
end Apple;
```

```
with Banana;
package body Apple is     -- This is a package body
   .
   .
   .
end Apple;
```

```
package Banana is       -- This is a package declaration
   .
   .
   .
end Banana;
```

```
package body Banana is     -- This is a package body
   .
   .
   .
end Banana;
```

```
with Apple;          -- This is a package declaration
package Pear is
   .
   .
   .
end Pear;
```

```
package body Pear is      -- This is a package body
   .
   .
   .
end Pear;
```

FIGURE 12-1
The Dependencies Among the Units Making up an Ada Program

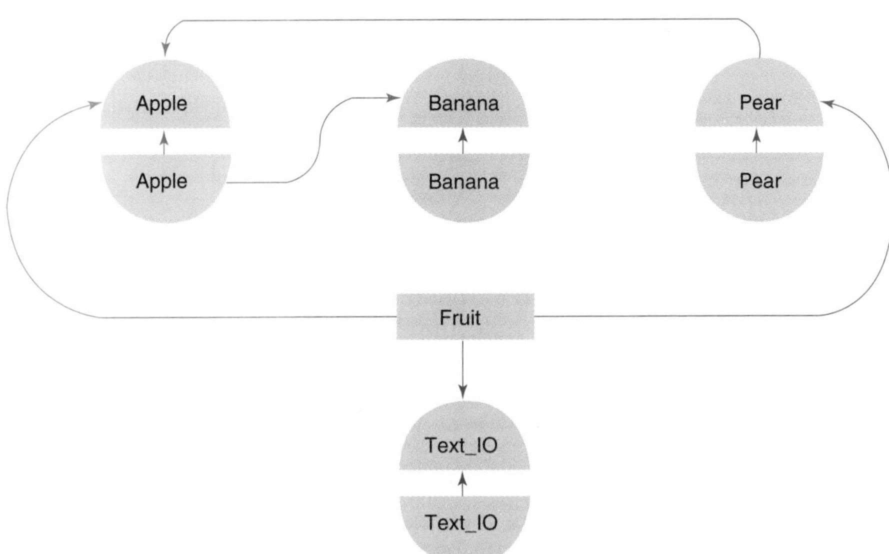

Compilation unit body Fruit depends upon three library unit declarations: Apple, Pear, and Ada.Text_IO. All three of these library unit declarations must be compiled* before Fruit can be compiled. Because Ada.Text_IO is a predefined package, it is already available in the program library.

The library unit declarations Apple, Banana, and Pear must be compiled before their corresponding package bodies. Because there are no with clauses in library unit declarations Apple and Banana, they do not depend on any other library units. However, library unit declaration Pear is dependent on library unit declaration Apple. Therefore library unit declaration Apple must be compiled before library unit declaration Pear can be compiled.

Library unit body Apple depends on library unit declaration Banana. Apple's body cannot be compiled until Banana's declaration has been compiled. No other library unit bodies in this example have with clauses.

Figure 12-1 is a dependency graph that is used to illustrate the dependencies among all the compilation units in this example. Each arrow indicates a dependency on the unit to which it points. A circle represents a package, with the upper and lower halves representing the declaration and body. A rectangle represents a procedure.

There are many different orders of entering units into the library that meet the restrictions of the dependencies specified in the with clauses and shown in the dependency graph of Figure 12-1. Here are three valid orders.

*We are assuming throughout this example that compilation is the method for adding a unit to the program library.

Order A	**Order B**	**Order C**
Banana (declaration)	Apple (declaration)	Banana (declaration)
Banana (body)	Pear (declaration)	Apple (declaration)
Apple (declaration)	Banana (declaration)	Pear (declaration)
Apple (body)	Apple (body)	Fruit
Pear (declaration)	Pear (body)	Apple (body)
Pear (body)	Banana (body)	Banana (body)
Fruit	Fruit	Pear (body)

After all of the units have been compiled, the linking process combines the object code into the executable program. Figure 12-2 illustrates this program development process.

If a library unit is changed and compiled again, all of the units that depend on it become **obsolete** and must be recompiled. The linker will issue an error message if a required unit is either missing from the program library or obsolete. For example, if the package declaration for Apple is changed and recompiled, Apple's body, Pear's declaration and body, and procedure Fruit become obsolete; they must be recompiled. In Figure 12-1 you can see that these units depend on Apple's declaration. Apple's body, Pear's declaration, and procedure Fruit depend directly on Apple's declaration. Pear's body has an indirect dependency on Apple; it depends on Pear's declaration that depends on Apple's declaration. Dependency graphs like the one in Figure 12-1 are a good way to determine what units become obsolete when another unit is recompiled.

Figure 12-2
Compiling and Linking an Ada Program Made up of Multiple Units

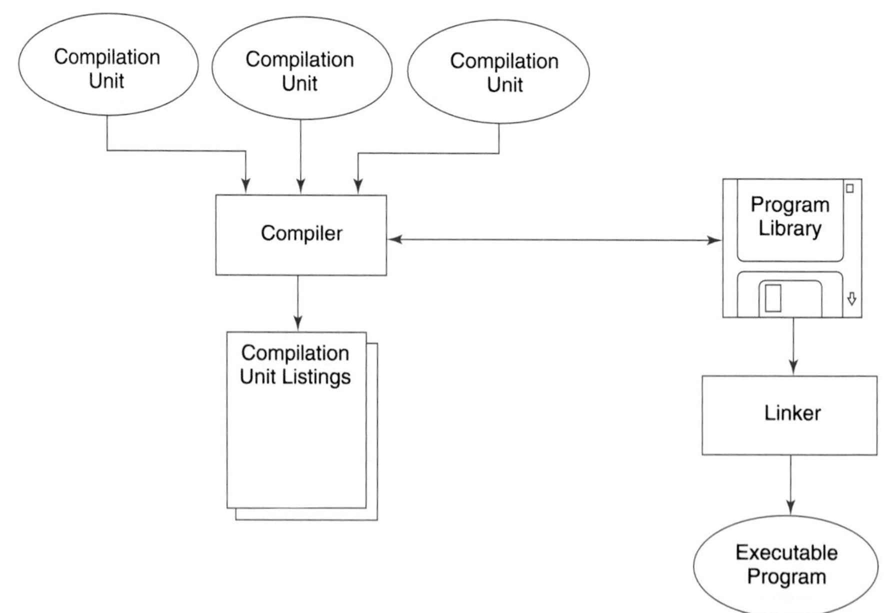

Obsolete unit A compilation unit that has not been recompiled after a unit on which it depends has been recompiled. The linker will issue an error if an attempt is made to use an obsolete unit to form an executable program.

The programming environment in which an Ada compiler is used includes commands for manipulating the program library. Many systems include commands for determining whether any units in the library are obsolete as well as commands that automatically will compile or recompile the units making up a program in the correct order. Such program development tools are necessary for programs with large numbers of units.

BACKGROUND INFORMATION

Reusable Components and Software Repositories

Because we can easily use packages in different programs, the package is the principal mechanism for reusing Ada code. We reuse Ada code at many levels. As you develop packages, you will probably save them for possible reuse in future programs. Your class may reuse packages prepared by your instructor or classmates in assignments and projects. Universities and corporations using Ada often maintain collections of packages so that the same programming tasks need not be repeated over and over.

Throughout the world there are large collections of Ada software known as repositories. Many of these repositories allow free access to anyone. As with most other public-domain software, the Ada programs and packages available through these repositories come as is, without warranty. Other repositories are commercial enterprises that sell Ada packages with guarantees. Many government and military agencies also maintain Ada repositories that are available to authorized personnel. The categories of software in these repositories include:

- Ada Tools (for developing Ada programs)
- Metrics (for measuring the quality of Ada programs)
- Language Translation
- Abstract Data Types (data abstraction packages)
- Text Manipulation
- User Interface
- Image Processing
- Computer-Aided Instruction (including interactive Ada tutorials)
- Data Management
- Math Routines
- Computer System Support

- Simulation
- Artificial Intelligence and Expert Systems
- Operations Research

The largest collection of public-domain Ada-related software is available from the Public Ada Library (PAL). You can access all of it on the World Wide Web at http://wuarchive.wustl.edu/languages/ada/. Other Web sites with links to repositories of Ada materials include:

ACM SIGAda	www.acm.org/sigada/
Ada Home	www.adahome.com/
Ada Power	www.adapower.com/

The Use Clause

Throughout this book, we always prefix our use of an identifier from a package by preceding the identifier with the appropriate package name. For example, we use the statement

```
Ada.Text_IO.New_Line;
```

to call the procedure New_Line contained in package Ada.Text_IO. In Chapter 2 we mentioned that Ada's use clause permits us to use package identifiers without prefixing. Here is a simplified EBNF definition of the use clause.

use_clause	::=	use_package_clause | use_type_clause
use_package_clause	::=	**use** *package*_name;
use_type_clause	::=	**use type** *subtype*_name;

As indicated by the EBNF definition on page 700, we can place a use clause at the beginning of any compilation unit. We can also place use clauses in any declarative part. When we have child packages, we can use the use clause to eliminate the need for parent package names. The following program illustrates these placements and uses of the use package clause.

```
with Ada.Text_IO;             -- Make Ada.Text_IO available
use  Ada;                     -- Make all entities in parent package Ada
                              --    available without prefixing

with Ada.Integer_Text_IO;     -- Make Ada.Integer_Text_IO available
use  Ada.Integer_Text_IO;     -- Make all symbols in package Ada.Integer_Text_IO
                              --    available without prefixing
```

```
procedure Use_Example is

   type Chess_Piece_Type  is (Pawn, Rook, Knight, Bishop, Queen, King);

   -- Instantiate package for Chess_Piece_Type input and output
   package Chess_Piece_IO is new Text_IO.Enumeration_IO
                                 (Enum => Chess_Piece_Type);
   use Chess_Piece_IO;                     -- Make all entities in the new package
                                           -- available without prefixing
begin

   Text_IO.Put ("Mildred Smedley");        -- Call to Ada.Text_IO.Put
   Text_IO.New_Line;                       -- Call to Ada.Text_IO.New_Line
   Put (Item => 5 + 3, Width => 12);       -- Call to Ada.Integer_Text_IO.Put
   Put (Item => Queen);                    -- Call to Chess_Piece_IO.Put
   Ada.Text_IO.New_Line;                   -- Prefixed Call

end Use_Example;
```

All of the use clauses in this sample program are use *package* clauses. The use Ada clause on the second line of this program permits calls to procedures Put and New_Line from package Ada.Text_IO without the parent package name (Ada). The other two use clauses in the program allow us to call procedure Put from package Ada.Integer_Text_IO and Chess_Piece_IO without any prefixing. The second call to procedure New_Line shows that prefixing may still be used even when a use clause makes it unnecessary.

The Use Package Clause

It is generally accepted that programs that use prefixing are easier to understand and debug than programs that use use package clauses. Programs are read more often than they are written. Recall how many times you read through the code you wrote for a single programming assignment looking for an error. Because we have stressed programming methods that make programs easier to comprehend, we avoid the use package clause.

Although, in general, we recommend that you avoid using use *package* clauses, there are some circumstances where they are better than prefixing. With them, you can shorten statements and expressions. In some situations, the shortened code makes the program easier to understand. Calls to package functions within lengthy expressions may be easier to read without prefixing. For example, the second of these two equivalent assignment statements that uses trigonometric functions is easier to read than the first.

```
Result := Ada.Numerics.Elementary_Functions.Sin(A) *
          Ada.Numerics.Elementary_Functions.Cos(B) +
          Ada.Numerics.Elementary_Functions.Cos(A) *
          Ada.Numerics.Elementary_Functions.Sin(B);

Result := Sin(A) * Cos(B)  +  Cos(A) * Sin(B);
```

If you use a use package clause to make particular expressions easier to read, you should continue to prefix all other resources even though the Ada compiler does not require you to do so. It is also good practice to put use package clauses in the declarative parts of procedures rather than at the beginning of the program to localize the area in which prefixing is not required.

The Use Type Clause

While we strongly discourage using the use *package* clause in your programs, we encourage the use of use *type* clauses. The use type clause allows us to use infix notation with operators defined in packages.

Operator Functions The most obvious way to define an operator in a package is to use it as the name of a function. For example, we defined a function called "+" in package Pixel on page 697 that added two primary colors together to form a secondary color. The following program fragment illustrates the traditional way to call a function.

```
with Pixel;
program Paint is
   My_Color   : Pixel.Color_Type;
   Your_Color : Pixel.Color_Type;
   Our_Color  : Pixel.Color_Type;

      .
      .
      .

   -- Determine the result of combining my and your colors
   Our_Color := Pixel."+" (My_Color, Your_Color);
```

The notation of writing the operator ("+") before its two operands (My_Color and Your_Color) is called prefix notation. Infix notation is the usual notation we use for writing expressions with the operator in between its two operands. Ada does not permit prefixing of operators in infix expressions. We can use a *use type clause* to eliminate prefixing of all *operators* for a given type. The following program fragment illustrates this technique.

```
with Pixel;
use  type Pixel.Color_Type;      -- Make all operators for Color_Type
                                 -- available without prefixing
program Paint is
   My_Color   : Pixel.Color_Type;
   Your_Color : Pixel.Color_Type;
   Our_Color  : Pixel.Color_Type;

      .
      .
      .

   -- Determine the result of combining my and your colors
   Our_Color := My_Color + Your_Color;
```

We think that you will agree that this use of infix notation is more natural and easier to read than the prefix notation used in the first code fragment.

Types and Operators There is a more subtle way to define an operator in a package—declare a data type. As we discussed in Chapter 7, a data type is a formal description of a set of values (called the domain) and the basic operations that we can apply to these values. When we declare a new type, the Ada compiler produces a new set of operators for it. This new set of operators is created according to the category of the type. We illustrate this creation of new operators with a definition package in which three types and two subtypes are declared.

```
package Grade_Definitions is

   type     Quiz_Score_Type is range 0..10;
   type     Exam_Score_Type is range 0..100;
   type     Grade_Type      is (A, B, C, D, F);
   subtype  Passing_Type    is Grade_Type range A..D;
   subtype  Percent         is Integer    range 0..100;

end Grade_Definitions;
```

The Ada compiler produces a *new* set of operators for Quiz_Score_Type, Exam_Score_Type, and Grade_Type. Because Quiz_Score_Type and Exam_Score_Type are integer types, their operators are equivalent to those available with the predefined type Integer (+, -, *, /, rem, =, <, and so on). Grade_Type is an enumeration type, so the operators defined in the package for it are equivalent to those of any new enumeration type (=, <, and so on). When a new type is defined in a package declaration, the operators, like the type itself, are not directly visible outside of the package. They must either be prefixed or made available through a use clause.

First we give a code fragment that does not employ a use type clause to make the operators directly available. We must prefix every operator used with the types defined in this package.

```
with Grade_Definitions;
with Ada.Text_IO;
procedure  Grade_Example_1 is

   Quiz_1 : Grade_Definitions.Quiz_Score_Type;
   Quiz_2 : Grade_Definitions.Quiz_Score_Type;
   .
   .
   .
   -- We must prefix the > operator for Quiz_Score_Type with the package name
   -- so it must be written in prefix notation rather than infix notation
   if Grade_Definitions.">" (Quiz_1, Quiz_2) then
      Ada.Text_IO.Put_Line ("Did better on first quiz.");
   end if;
   .
   .
   .
```

If we insert a use type clause, we may use the > operator for Quiz_Score_Type directly.

```
with Ada.Text_IO;
with Grade_Definitions;
use type Grade_Definitions.Quiz_Score_Type;     -- Make the operators for
use type Grade_Definitions.Exam_Score_Type;     -- these three types directly
use type Grade_Definitions.Grade_Type;          -- visible.
procedure  Grade_Example_2 is

   Quiz_1 : Grade_Definitions.Quiz_Score_Type;
   Quiz_2 : Grade_Definitions.Quiz_Score_Type;
   .
   .
   .
   -- We can now use infix notation with quiz score operators
   if Quiz_1 > Quiz_2 then
      Ada.Text_IO.Put_Line ("Did better on first quiz.");
   end if;
   .
   .
   .
```

Subtypes A subtype is a subset of a base type. No new operators are created when we declare a subtype; the operators of its base type are used. Because every subtype with the same base type shares the same operators, we can freely mix subtypes with the same base type in an expression.

What does this sharing of base type operators mean for subtypes declared in a package? Let's look at the subtype Percent declared in the definition package Grade_Definitions. Because the base type of Percent is type Integer, the operators for Percent values are the type Integer operators. Now, because the operators for type Integer are available everywhere, we don't need prefixes or use clauses to work directly with operators for subtype Percent.

Subtype Passing_Type is another story. Because its base type is Grade_Type, it uses the same operators as Grade_Type. Since Grade_Type is declared in the definition package, its operators are not directly visible outside of the package. Grade_Type's operators must either be prefixed or made available with a use type clause.

The Predefined Package Standard

We have used predefined entities like Boolean, Integer, and Float in all of our programs. All of the predefined entities in Ada are defined in a package called Standard. Package Standard is the part of the predefined language environment that is automatically available to every compilation unit. It is as if the context clauses

```
with Standard;      -- We do not need to include
use  Standard;      -- these clauses in our programs
```

were added automatically by the Ada compiler to the beginning of every compilation unit.

Appendix G contains the declaration of package Standard. Let's look at some of the declarations in this appendix. The first declaration is that of type Boolean. We see that Boolean is an enumeration type with the possible values of True and False. Following the declaration of Boolean are the definitions for the operators that may be used with Boolean values. The operators that are predefined for Boolean are given in comments because they are implicitly defined.

Type Integer is defined next. Its actual declaration is dependent on the specific Ada system being used. For example, some computers can store integers as large as 2,147,483,647. Others are limited to a maximum integer value of 32,767. As with type Boolean, the operators that are predefined for type Integer are given in comments in package Standard. Following the definition of type Integer is the definition of type Float. Again, its details are dependent on the system being used.

The predefined subtypes Natural and Positive are defined after Integer. Because they are subtypes of type Integer, no operations are defined for them. They use the operations of their base type, Integer.

Type Character is an enumeration type with 256 different values. Certain characters, called control characters, cannot be written on paper. An example is the *bel* character. When this character is sent to the display screen, it causes a bell to ring. Early Teletype terminals actually had a bell.

Today's display terminals typically use an electronic beep. No actual character is displayed on the screen when the *bel* character is received. The first 32 characters and the characters in positions 127 through 159 given in the definition of type Character are shown in italics to indicate that they are control characters.

Type Wide_Character is an enumeration type with 65,536 different values which include the characters used in many different alphabets around the world. They are not all listed in the appendix.

We discussed the predefined type String in Chapter 11. The operations for this predefined type follow its definition in the appendix.

The predefined type Duration declared after type String is also a type that we discussed briefly in Chapter 9. Duration is a measure of elapsed time. A Duration value has units of seconds associated with it. A duration value of 5.2 represents five and two-tenths seconds. The final declarations in package Standard are the four predefined exceptions we described in Chapter 9.

Because Standard is a package, we can use it to prefix identifiers and operators. The following short program illustrates this.

```
with Ada.Integer_Text_IO;
with Ada.Text_IO;
procedure Illustrate_Standard is

   I : Standard.Integer;          -- Prefix the predefined type Integer
   J : Standard.Integer;

begin
   Ada.Integer_Text_IO.Get (I);
   Ada.Integer_Text_IO.Get (J);
   if Standard."<" (I, J) then   -- < operator written in prefix form
      Ada.Text_IO.Put ("First number is smaller.");
   else
      Ada.Text_IO.Put ("First number is not smaller.");
   end if;
end Illustrate_Standard;
```

Searching and Sorting

Scanning a list to find a particular value is part of many everyday tasks. We scan the television guide to see what time a program is aired. We scan a course syllabus to locate the current reading assignment. It is usually faster to find an item in a list if the items are in order. In the last sections of this chapter, we examine some algorithms for the searching and sorting of lists stored in arrays.

FIGURE 12-3 An Array of Winning Lottery Numbers

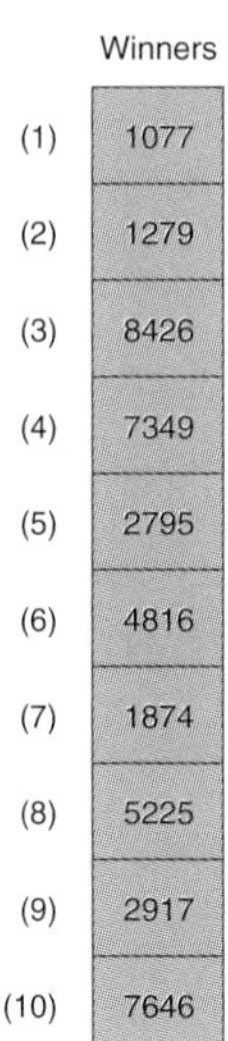

Sequential Search in an Unordered List

Suppose we have stored the winning numbers of a lottery in an array such as the one illustrated in Figure 12-3. We would like to search this array to see if our ticket number is a winner. If we were searching this list of winning numbers by hand, we would probably compare our number to the first number in the list, then to the second number, then to the third number, and so on. We stop our search as soon as we find our number in the list of winners. We also stop our search if we reach the end of the list without finding our number. Here is a more formal description of this algorithm.

Sequential Search

```
   in   List       -- An array of winning lottery numbers
   in   Number     -- Our number
   out  Found
Found   := False
Index   := First Index of List
loop
   Exit loop when No More Components In List or Found
   If Our Ticket Number = Winners(Index) Then
      Found := True
   else
      Increment Index
   end if
end loop
```

Here is an Ada implementation of this algorithm.

```
type Winner_Array is array (Integer range <>) of Positive;
     .
     .
     .
procedure Search (List  : in  Winner_Array;      -- The array to search
                  Number: in  Positive;          -- The number to search for
                  Found : out Boolean) is        -- True if number is found

   Index : Integer;

begin
   Found := False;
   Index := List'First;        -- Start search with first component

   Search_Loop:                -- Search for Number in List
   loop                        -- Each iteration, check one value in List
      exit Search_Loop when  Index > List'Last  or  Found;
      if Number = List(Index) then
         Found := True;
      else
         Index := Index + 1;  -- Didn't find it, go to next component
      end if;
   end loop Search_Loop;
end Search;
```

Short-Circuit Logical Operators Why did we need to use an if statement to test whether our number is at the current position? Why not just perform this test as part of the exit statement?

```
   Search_Loop:
   loop
      exit Search_Loop when  (Index > List'Last)     or
                             (Number = List(Index));
      Index := Index + 1;
   end loop Search_Loop;
```

A problem occurs in this exit statement's Boolean expression when the item is not in the list. Then, the loop is supposed to stop when Index is greater than List'Last. The first portion of the Boolean expression, (Index > List'Last), evaluates to True. The second portion, however, raises a CONSTRAINT_ERROR because Index is out of the array's index range; it is greater than List'Last. By using the if statement after the exit, an array component is not checked unless Index is in the range of the array index. CONSTRAINT_ERROR will not be raised.

Although necessary to prevent a CONSTRAINT_ERROR, the if statement complicates the logic of this algorithm. Ada has other logical operators, called short-circuit operators, that allow us to use the simpler logic of the second loop without the risk of CONSTRAINT_ERRORs. **Short-circuit operators** stop the evaluation of additional terms in a Boolean expression as soon as the result is known. The two short-circuit operators are `and then` and `or else`.

Short-circuit operator A logical operator (either `or else` or `and then`) that stops the evaluation of additional terms in a Boolean expression as soon as the result is known.

How can we determine the result of a Boolean expression without evaluating all of the terms? The `and` operator requires both operands to be True in order for the overall result to be True. If either or both of the operands are False, `and` makes the entire result False. Thus, if the first operand is False, we don't even need to look at the second term. We already know that the expression is False. If either of the operands with an `or` operator is True, then the expression is True. So if the first operand is True, we don't need to look at the second operand. This logic is exactly what the `and then` and `or else` operators perform. The following tables summarize these two logical operators. We use the question marks for Y to indicate that we have not yet looked at Y's value.

X	**Y**	**X and then Y**
False	????	False
True	False	False
True	True	True

X	**Y**	**X or else Y**
True	????	True
False	True	True
False	False	False

Here is the loop from procedure Search written with a short-circuit operator rather than an if statement.

```
Search_Loop:
loop
   exit Search_Loop when  (Index > List'Last)      or else
                          (Number = List(Index));
   Index := Index + 1;
end loop Search_Loop;
```

Now when Index becomes greater than the number of items in the list, the evaluation of the Boolean expression in the exit statement stops before the second term is evaluated. A CONSTRAINT_ERROR is not raised.

We now recode procedure Search as a general-purpose sequential search package that we can use in any program that requires searching a list of values stored in an array. To make it more general, we replace the problem-dependent variable names of our lottery ticket example with general ones. We also return the location of the item in the array if it is found.

```
package List_Ops is

-- This package contains an array type used for a list. Throughout
-- this chapter we will add various procedures for searching and
-- sorting to this package.

   subtype Item_Type  is Positive;
   type    Item_Array is array (Integer range <>) of Item_Type;

   procedure Search (List  : in  Item_Array;
                     Item  : in  Item_Type;
                     Found : out Boolean;
                     Index : out Integer);
   -- Search List for the given Item
   --
   -- Preconditions : None
   --
   -- Postconditions : If Item is in List
   --                     Found is True
   --                     Index is the location of Item in List
   --                   If Item is not in List
   --                     Found is False
   --                     Index is List'Last + 1
end List_Ops;
```

The **in** parameters for the search procedure are the array to be searched (List) and the item we are searching for (Item). The Boolean *out* parameter Found tells whether the item is in the list and, if it is in the list, *out* parameter Index gives the location of the item in the list. Here is the package body.

```
package body List_Ops is

   procedure Search (List  : in  Item_Array;
                     Item  : in  Item_Type;
                     Found : out Boolean;
                     Index : out Integer) is
```

```
   begin
      Index := List'First;    -- Start searching at the first component
      Search_Loop:       -- Search for Item in List
      loop               -- Each iteration, check one value in List
         exit Search_Loop when  (Index > List'Last)    or  else
                                (Item = List(Index));
         Index := Index + 1;
      end loop Search_Loop;
      -- Determine whether Item was found or not.
      -- Item is not in the list if Index > List'Last
      Found := Index <= List'Last;
   end Search;

end List_Ops;
```

We can modify this sequential search procedure for any program requiring a list search. In this form, it will search an array of any type (Item_Type) that can be compared with the = operator (see Figure 12-4). In a later course you will learn how to build generic units to make reuse of packages like this one even easier.

If Item is not unique, this algorithm finds the first occurrence of the searched-for item. How can we modify it to find the last occurrence? We initialize Index to List'Last and decrement Index each time through the loop, stopping when we find the item that we want or when index becomes less than List'First.

FIGURE 12-4 Generalized Sequential Search

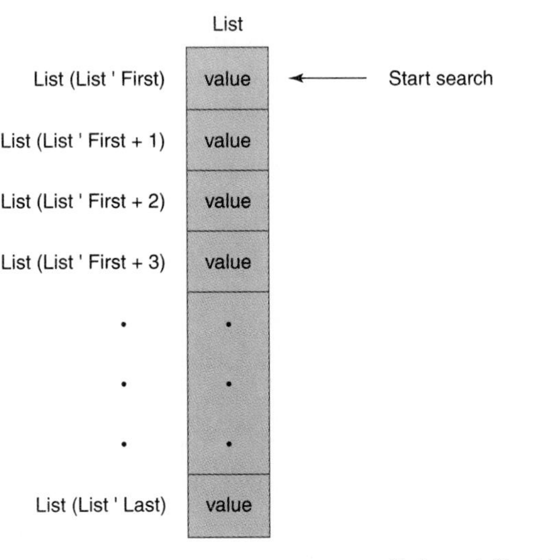

Selection Sort

Another task commonly performed on an array is ordering its components. For example, we might want to put a list of stock numbers in either ascending or descending order, a list of student records in order by student identification numbers, or a list of words in alphabetical order. Arranging values in order is known as sorting. In Chapter 7 we discussed the ordering inherent in any scalar data type. Because of this ordering, we can compare and sort, in ascending or descending order, values of any scalar type.

If you were given a sheet of paper with a column of 20 numbers on it and were asked to write the numbers in ascending order, you would probably:

1. Look for the smallest number.
2. Write it on the paper in a second column.
3. Cross the number off the original list.
4. Repeat the process, always looking for the smallest number remaining on the original list.
5. Stop when all the numbers had been crossed off.

We can implement this algorithm directly in Ada, but we need two arrays: one for the original list and a second for the ordered list. If the list is large, we might not have enough memory for two copies of it. It is also difficult to "cross off" a component. We would have to simulate this process with some dummy value. We could set the value of the crossed-off variable to something that would not interfere with the processing of the rest of the components, such as Integer'Last. A slight variation on this hand-done algorithm allows us to sort the components *in place*. In place means that we do not have to use a second array because we can put a value in its proper place in the original list by having it swap places with the component that is there.

If we use an unconstrained array called List that contains a number of components, we can state the algorithm as follows:

```
for Pass_Count in List'Range loop
   Find Minimum in List(Pass_Count .. List'Last)
   Swap Minimum with List(Pass_Count)
end loop
```

Figure 12-5 illustrates how this algorithm works. Try tracing it yourself.

This sort, known as straight selection, belongs to a class of sorts called selection sorts. There are many types of sorting algorithms. Selection sorts are characterized by searching for the smallest or largest value in the unsorted portion of the list and exchanging it with another value until the list is all sorted. Here is the Ada code that implements our selection sort algorithm.

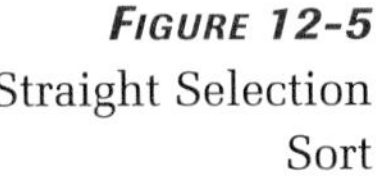

Figure 12-5 Straight Selection Sort

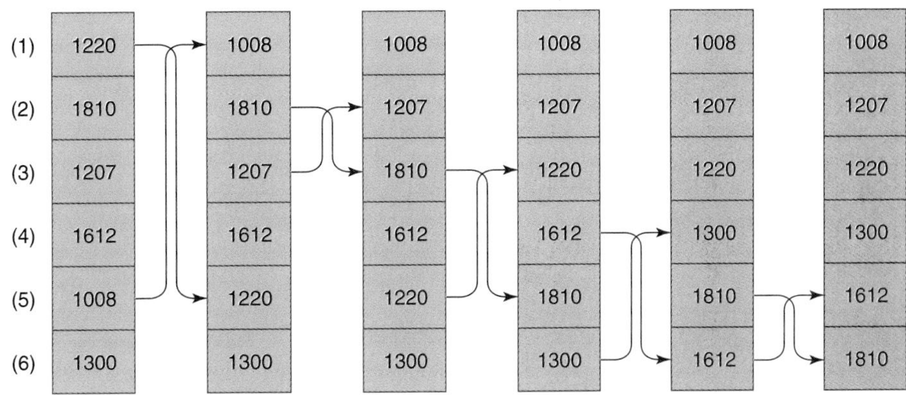


```
procedure Selection_Sort (List : in out Item_Array) is

   Min_Index : Integer;          -- Index of smallest value

begin
   for Pass_Count in  List'First .. List'Last - 1  loop
      Min_Index := Position_of_Smallest (List(Pass_Count..List'Last));
      Swap (Left => List(Min_Index), Right => List(Pass_Count));
   end loop;
end Selection_Sort;
```

Note that the loop runs from List'First to List'Last −1. Because the last item, List(List'Last), is in its proper place if the rest of the array is sorted, the loop does not need to be executed when Pass_Count = List'Last.

Another point to note is that we may swap a component with itself. We could avoid such an unnecessary swap by checking to see whether Min_Index is equal to Pass_Count. Because this comparison would have to be made during each iteration of the loop, it may be more efficient not to check for this possibility and just to swap something with itself occasionally. If the components we are sorting are much more complex than simple numbers (such as a large record), we might reconsider this decision.

We can modify the algorithm we developed in Chapter 11 to find the maximum value in an array to create a function that finds the position of the smallest value in an array. Here is the resulting Ada code.

```
function Position_of_Smallest (List : in Item_Array) return Integer is

-- Search for the smallest item in List and return its index
-- Precondition : List'Length > 0

   Result : Integer;   -- Index of smallest value in List

begin
   Result := List'First;   -- Initialize result to 1st index of List

   -- Search the rest of the array for a smaller value
   -- Each iteration, check one value in the array
   for Index in List'First + 1 .. List'Last loop
      if List(Index) < List(Result) then
         Result := Index;
      end if;
   end loop;

   return Result;
end Position_Of_Smallest;
```

Exchanging the contents of two variables—two components in an array—requires a temporary variable so that no values are lost (see Figure 12-6). Here is a procedure that we can call to accomplish this swap.

```
procedure Swap (Left : in out Item_Type; Right : in out Item_Type) is
   Temp : Item_Type;
begin
   Temp  := Left;
   Left  := Right;
   Right := Temp;
end Swap;
```

We add our selection sort, our function to find the position of the smallest value, and our swap procedures to the package List_Ops. We encapsulate the find position function and the swap procedure as local subprograms in the body of List_Ops—they are not accessible outside of our package. Because we want to use the selection sort in other programs, we include its declaration in the package specification and its body in the package body. Our final version of package List_Ops with these and other operations developed in the next few sections is given on page 734.

Our selection sort algorithm sorts the components into ascending order. To sort them into descending order, we need to search for the maximum value instead of the minimum value. Of course, Min_Index would no longer be a meaningful identifier and should be changed to Max_Index. Similarly, we would need to change the comments to reflect our new logic.

FIGURE 12-6 Exchanging the Contents of Two Places

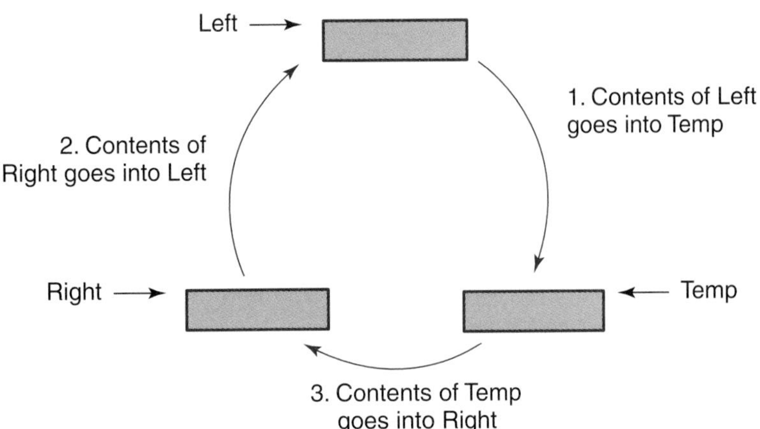

Let's look at a complete program that uses our selection sort procedure to sort and display a list of integers read from a file. Although our unconstrained array type can be used for the formal list parameters, we need a constrained array variable to hold the actual list. We also need to keep track of the length of this actual list. Because the length and the array of items are closely related, we include both in a record.

```
with List_Ops;
with Ada.Text_IO;
with Ada.Integer_Text_IO;
procedure Test_Selection_Sort is

   Max_List : constant := 100;   -- Maximum number of values in the list

   -- Constrained array of Positives
   subtype Index_Type is Integer range 1..Max_List;
   subtype List_Array is List_Ops.Item_Array(Index_Type);

   -- A list of positive numbers
   subtype Length_Type is Integer range 0..Max_List;
   type List_Type is
      record
         Length : Length_Type := 0;     -- The number of components in list
         Items  : List_Array;           -- The components
      end record;

   Number_List : List_Type;
   Data_File   : Ada.Text_IO.File_Type;
```

```
begin
   Ada.Text_IO.Open (File => Data_File,
                     Mode => Ada.Text_IO.In_File,
                     Name => "Numbers.txt");

   Input_Loop:    -- Read all the numbers into the list
   loop           -- Each iteration, one number is read from
                  -- the file and put into the list's array
      exit Input_Loop when Ada.Text_IO.End_Of_File (Data_File);
      Number_List.Length := Number_List.Length + 1;
      Ada.Integer_Text_IO.Get (File => Data_File,
                               Item => Number_List.Items(Number_List.Length));
   end loop Input_Loop;
   Ada.Text_IO.Close (Data_File);

   -- Pass a slice of the array to the sort procedure
   List_Ops.Selection_Sort (Number_List.Items (1..Number_List.Length));

   -- Display the sorted list
   for Index in 1..Number_List.Length loop
      Ada.Integer_Text_IO.Put (Item => Number_List.Items(Index));
      Ada.Text_IO.New_Line;
   end loop;
end Test_Selection_Sort;
```

Figure 12-7 illustrates the list record. We use the Length field of the record as an iteration counter in the input loop and as the index of the array field Items in the get statement. Only a portion of the array in the list record is passed to the selection sort procedure. We use the Length field to specify the slice of the array passed.

Sequential Search in an Ordered List

When we search for an item in an unordered list, we won't discover that the item is missing until we reach the end of the list. If the list is ordered, we know that an item is missing when we pass its correct place in the list. For example, if a list contains the values

```
  7
 11
 13
 76
 98
102
238
267
321
416
```

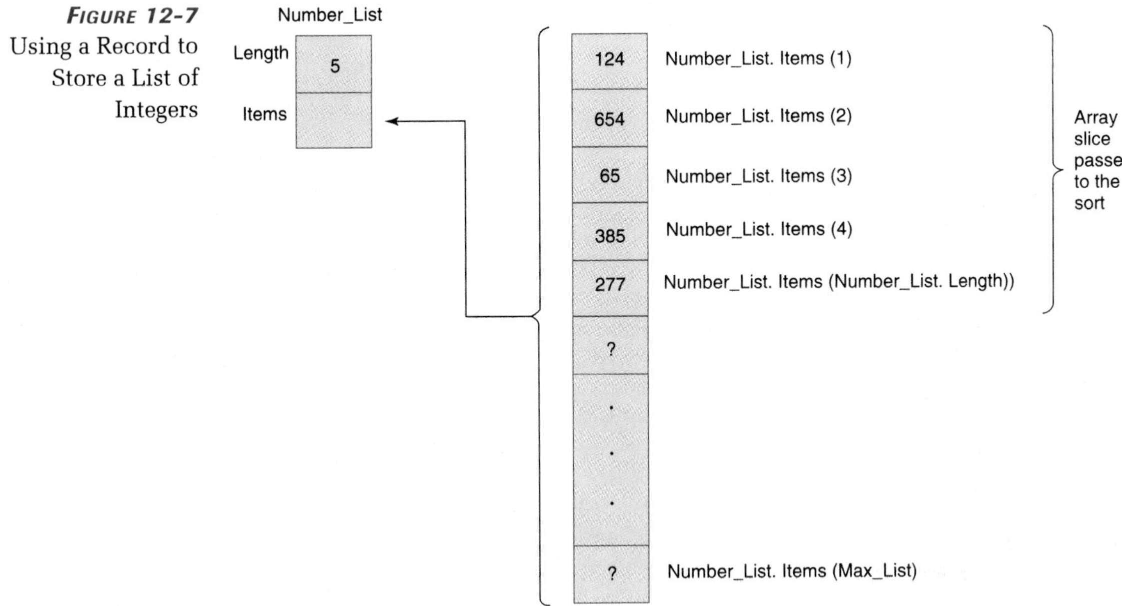

FIGURE 12-7 Using a Record to Store a List of Integers

and we are looking for 12, we need only compare 12 with 7, 11, and 13 to know that 12 is not in the list.

If the item we are searching for is greater than the current list component, we move on to the next component. If the item is equal to the current component, we have found what we are looking for. If the item is less than the current component, then we know that the item is not in the list. In either of the last two cases, we stop looking. We can restate this algorithm as follows:

```
Current Place := First Place in List
loop
   exit when No More Places Left in List or Item <= current component in List
   increment Current Place
end loop
if Item = the value at the Current Place
   Found := True
else
   Found := False
end if
```

Here is the procedure body that implements this algorithm. We include its declaration in the specification of package List_Ops (page 734) and its body in the package body.

```
procedure Search_Ordered (List  : in  Item_Array;
                          Item  : in  Item_Type;
                          Found : out Boolean;
                          Index : out Integer) is
-- Search List for the given Item
--
-- Preconditions : Items in List are in ascending order
--
-- Postconditions : If Item is in List
--                        Found is True
--                        Index is the location of Item in List
--                     If Item is not in List
--                        Found is False
--                        Index is the location of where Item would be
--                        if it were in List
begin
   Index :=  List'First;   -- Start searching at the first component
   Search_Loop:      -- Search for Item in List
   loop              -- Each iteration, check one value in List
      exit Search_Loop when  (Index > List'Last)   or else
                             (Item <= List(Index));
      Index := Index + 1;
   end loop Search_Loop;

   -- Determine whether or not the item was found
   Found := (Index <= List'Last) and then (Item = List(Index));
end Search_Ordered;
```

Notice how we have replaced the if statement in our algorithm with a simple assignment statement. The short-circuit operator `and then` is used to ensure that we don't compare an item beyond the end of the list.

On average, searching an ordered list in this way takes the same number of iterations to find an item as searching an unordered list. The advantage of this new algorithm is that we find out sooner if an item is missing. It is thus slightly more efficient; however, it works only on a sorted list.

Inserting into an Ordered List

What if we want to add a new value to an already sorted list like Number_List (used in our program on page 721)? We can place the new value at the end of the list (increment Number_List.Length and store the new value at Number_List(Number_List.Length)) and sort the array again. However, such a solution is an inefficient way to solve the problem. Let's develop an algorithm that inserts a value into the proper place in a sorted list.

If we were to insert a value by hand into a sorted list, we would write the new value out to the side and draw a line showing where it belongs.

We do this by scanning the list until we find a value greater than the one we are inserting. The new value goes in the list just before that point. How do we actually insert our new value into this location? We have to shift all of the values larger than the new one down one place to make room for it. Here is the algorithm.

```
Insert Value into Sorted List
Index := first place in list
loop
   exit when no more places to look or place found
   increment Index
end loop
Shift remainder of List down
Insert Item
Increment Length
```

Figure 12-8 illustrates this algorithm. The algorithm for Shift remainder of List down (Index is the place found) is:

```
Shift remainder of List down
Items(Length + 1)  := Items(Length)
Items(Length)      := Items(Length - 1)
Items(Length - 1)  := Items(Length - 2)
Items(Length - 2)  := Items(Length - 3)
  .
  .
  .
Items(Index + 1)  := Items(Index)
```

FIGURE 12-8
Inserting into an Ordered List

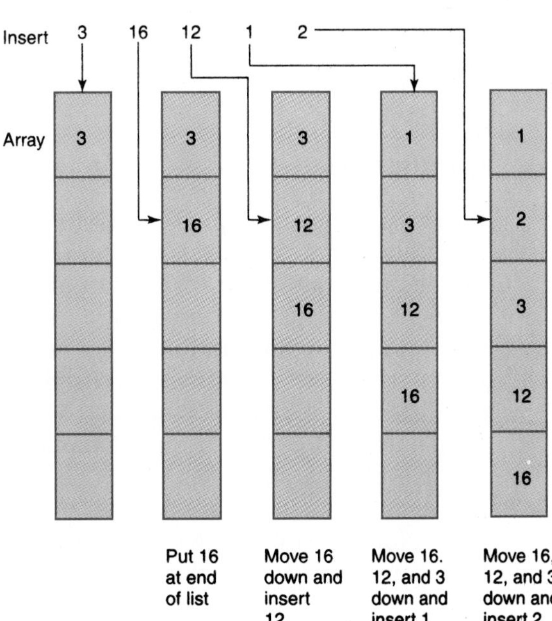

There are two shorter ways to accomplish this shift. We can use a reverse version of the for loop like this:

```
for Count in reverse Index .. Length loop
   Items(Count + 1) := Items(Count);
end loop;
```

or a single assignment statement with array slices like this:

```
Items(Index+1 .. Length+1) := Items(Index .. Length);
```

On many computers, slice assignments such as this are much faster than using for loops to move portions of an array.

There is something familiar about the loop in our algorithm that searches for the place to insert our new item. It is logically like the loop in Search_Ordered. In Search_Ordered we leave the loop either when we find Item or when we pass the place in the list where Item belongs. We can simply use Search_Ordered to find the insertion place for us. On return from Search_Ordered, if Found is False, Index is the place in List where Item should be inserted. If Found is True, we can either insert a second copy or skip the insertion, as we choose, as long as we document clearly what we've done. Inserting a second copy seems more reasonable. Therefore, Index is the insertion point, whether or not Item already exists in the list.

Notice that this algorithm works even if the list is empty. When Search_Ordered is passed a null array (range of slice is 1. .0), it returns Found as False and Index as 1. The two array slices in the assignment statement to shift the components down are both null arrays. Therefore, nothing is copied. Item is then stored in the first position of the array, and its length is incremented to 1. This algorithm also works if Item is larger than any component in the list. When this happens, Index is List.Length + 1 and Item is placed at the end of the list.

Insertion Sort

We can use the algorithm we developed in the previous section as the basis of an algorithm that sorts an unordered list. To accomplish this sort, we divide our array into a sorted part and an unsorted part. To sort our array, we repeatedly take the first value out of the unsorted part and insert it at the appropriate place in the sorted part. Figure 12-9 illustrates this process. Figure 12-9, Part (a) shows the original unordered list. We have divided this list into a sorted part (element 1) shown shaded, and an unordered list (elements 2–5). A list of one element is always ordered. In our first iteration we use the algorithm developed in the previous section to insert the top element of the unsorted list into the sorted list. The arrow in Figure 12-9, Part (a) shows where we need to insert the element and Figure 12-9, Part (b) shows the results of the insertion—the sorted list's length has increased by one and the unsorted list's length has decreased by one. The rest of the figure shows the remaining repetitions of the process needed to sort the list Here is the algorithm:

Insertion Sort

```
First_Unsorted := Info'First + 1
loop
   exit when there are no elements left in the unsorted portion
   Search the sorted portion of the array for the insertion Location
   Make room for the first unsorted value by moving array elements down.
   Insert the first unsorted value into List(Location)
   Shrink the unsorted part of the list by incrementing First_Unsorted
end loop
```

And here is the body of the insertion sort procedure we have added to our List_Ops package body.

```
procedure Insertion_Sort (List : in out Item_Array) is

   First_Unsorted : Integer;    -- Index of first element of unsorted list
   Location       : Integer;    -- Insertion location in sorted list
   Value          : Item_Type;  -- Copy of first element of unsorted list
   Found          : Boolean;    -- Not used, needed for call to Search_ordered

begin  -- Insertion_Sort
   First_Unsorted := List'First + 1;   -- Sorted part has one element at start
   loop  -- Each iteration, the first element in the unsorted part of the
         -- array is inserted into the sorted part of the array
      exit when First_Unsorted > List'Last;
      -- Find where in the sorted portion of the array to insert
      Search_Ordered (List  => List(List'First .. First_Unsorted - 1),
                      Item  => List(First_Unsorted),
                      Found => Found,
                      Index => Location);
      -- Make a copy of List(First_Unsorted) so slide won't destroy it
      Value := List(First_Unsorted);
      -- Open up a space for the element by sliding all below it down
      List(Location + 1 .. First_Unsorted) :=
           List(Location .. First_Unsorted - 1);
      -- Insert the current value
      List(Location) := Value;
      -- Shrink the unsorted part of the array
      First_Unsorted := First_Unsorted + 1;
   end loop;
end Insertion_Sort;
```

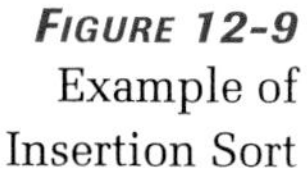
FIGURE 12-9 Example of Insertion Sort

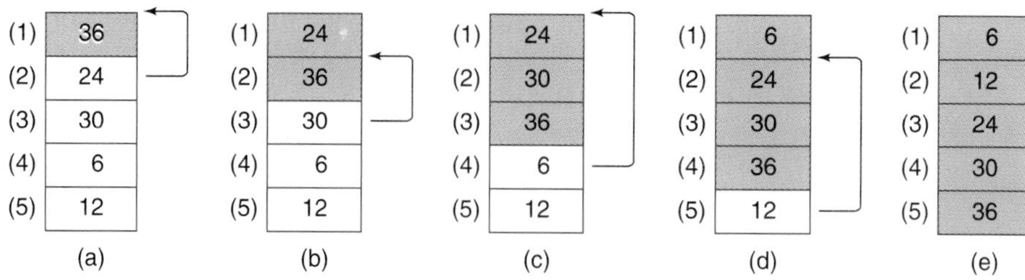

Binary Search in an Ordered List

There is a second search algorithm on a sorted list that is considerably faster both for finding an item and for discovering that an item is missing. This algorithm is called a binary search. A binary search is based on the principle of divide and conquer. It involves dividing the list in half (dividing by 2—that's why it's called *binary* search) and deciding which half to look in next. Division of the selected portion of the list is repeated until the item is found or it is determined that the item is not in the list.

This method is similar to the way we look up a name in a phone book. We open the phone book in the middle and compare the name with one on the page that we turned to. If the name we're looking for comes before this page, we continue our search with the left-hand section of the phone book. Otherwise, we continue with the right-hand section. We do this repeatedly until we find the name. If it is not there, we realize that either we have misspelled the name or the person isn't listed.

Here is a general description of binary searching.

1. Compare Item to the middle element of List. If Item is equal to the middle element, then we have found it.
2. Stop when we have found Item or know it is missing. We know it's missing when the list to search is empty.
3. Redefine List to be that half of List that we look in next. If Item is less than the middle element, choose the first half of List. If Item is greater than the middle element, choose the second half of List.
4. Go back to step 1.

With each comparison, at best, we find the item for which we are searching; at worst, we eliminate one-half of the remaining List from consideration.

We need to keep track of the first possible place to look (First) and the last possible place to look (Last). At any one time we are looking in List(First . . Last). Middle is halfway between First and Last. The list is empty when First > Last. Here is the body of the binary search procedure we have added to our list package body.

```
procedure Binary_Search (List   : in  Item_Array;
                         Item   : in  Item_Type;
                         Found  : out Boolean;
                         Index  : out Integer) is
-- Search List for the given Item
--
-- Preconditions : Items in List are in ascending order
--
-- Postconditions : If Item is in List
--                      Found is True
--                      Index is the location of Item in List
--                  If Item in not in List
--                      Found is False
--                      Index is undefined

   First  : Integer;   -- Lower index bound of list
   Last   : Integer;   -- Upper index bound of list
   Middle : Integer;   -- Middle index

begin
   First := List'First;     -- Set up initial
   Last  := List'Last;      --     list bounds
   Found := False;

   Search_Loop:    -- Search for Item in List (First..Last)
   loop            -- Each iteration, check the middle value and half list
      exit Search_Loop when  Found          or     -- We found item
                             First > Last;         -- No items left in list
      Middle := (First + Last) / 2;
      if Item < List(Middle) then
         -- Item is not in List(Middle..Last)
         Last := Middle - 1;    -- Redefine list to 1st half
      elsif Item > List(Middle) then
         -- Item is not in List(First..Middle)
         First := Middle + 1; -- Redefine list to 2nd half
      else
         Found := True;
         Index := Middle;
      end if;
   end loop Search_Loop;
end Binary_Search;
```

Let's do a code trace of this algorithm. The value being searched for is 24. Figure 12-10, Part (a) shows the values of First, Last, and Middle during the first iteration. In this iteration, 24 is compared with 103, the value in List(Middle). Because 24 is less than 103, Last becomes Middle −1 and

FIGURE 12-10
Code Trace of Procedure Binary_Search (Item is 24)
(a) First Iteration, 24 < 103
(b) Second Iteration, 24 < 72
(c) Third Iteration, 24 > 12
(d) Fourth Iteration, 24 < 64, Last becomes < First

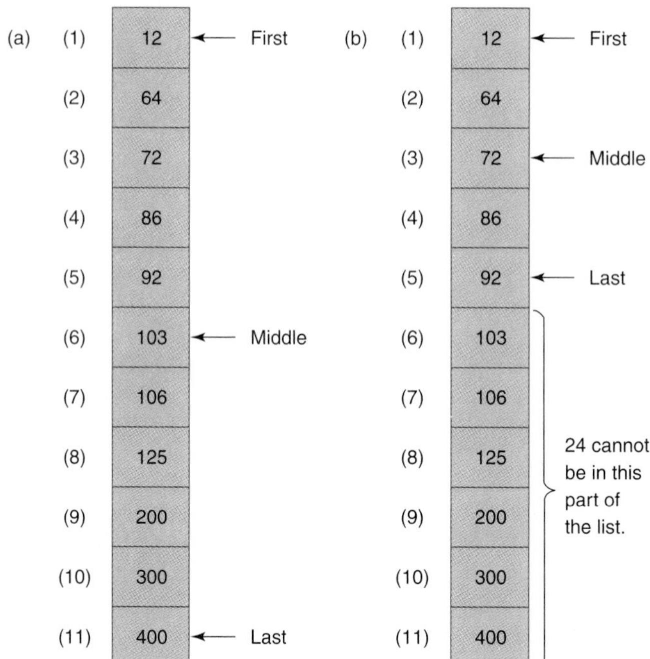

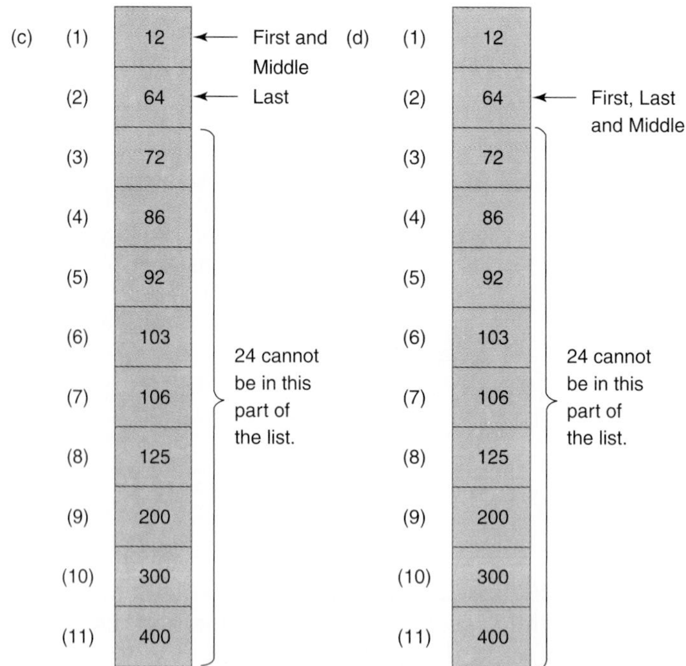

First stays the same. Figure 12-10, Part (b) shows the situation during the second iteration. This time 24 is compared with 72, the value in List(Middle). Because 24 is less than 72, Last becmes Middle −1 and First again stays the same.

In the third iteration of Figure 12-10, Part (c), Middle and First are both 1. The value 24 is compared with 12, the value in List(Middle). Because 24 is greater than 12, First becomes Middle + 1. In the fourth iteration Part (d), First, Last, and Middle are all the same. Again, 24 is compared with the value in List(Middle). Because 24 is less than 64, Last becomes Middle −1. Now Last is less than First, and the process stops. Found is False.

The binary search algorithm may be the most complex algorithm that we have examined so far. The following table shows First, Last, Middle, and List(Middle) for searches of 106, 400, and 406, using the same data as in the previous example. Go over the results shown in this table carefully.

Item	First	Last	Middle	List(Middle)	Termination of Loop
106	1	11	6	103	
	7	11	9	200	
	7	8	7	106	Found = True
400	1	11	6	103	
	7	11	9	200	
	10	11	10	300	
	11	11	11	400	Found = True
406	1	11	6	103	
	7	11	9	200	
	10	11	10	300	
	11	11	11	400	
	12	11			Last < First Found = False

Notice that the loop never executed more than four times. It will never execute more than four times in a list of 11 components because the list is being cut in half each time through the loop. The next table compares a sequential search and a binary search in terms of the average number of iterations needed to find an item.

	Average Number of Iterations	
Length of List	**Sequential Search**	**Binary Search**
10	5.5	2.9
100	50.5	5.8
1000	500.5	9.0
10,000	5000.5	12.4

If the binary search is so much faster, why not use it all the time? It is certainly faster in terms of the number of times through the loop, but more computations are done within the binary search loop than in the other search algorithms. Therefore, if the number of components in the list is small (say, under 20), the sequential search algorithms are faster because they do less work at each iteration. As the number of components in the list increases, the binary search algorithm becomes relatively more efficient. Remember, however, that the binary search requires that the list be sorted, and sorting itself takes time. Keep three factors in mind when you are deciding which search algorithm to use:

1. The length of the list to be searched.
2. Whether or not the list is already ordered.
3. The number of times the list is to be searched.

THEORETICAL FOUNDATIONS

Complexity of Searching and Sorting

We introduced Big-O notation in Chapter 5 as a way of comparing the work done by different algorithms. Let's apply it to the algorithms that we've developed in this chapter and see how they compare to each other. In each algorithm we start with a list containing some number of values. We'll refer to the number of values as N.

In the worst case, procedure Search scans all N values to locate an item. It requires N steps to execute. On average, Search takes roughly $N/2$ steps to find an item; however, recall that in Big-O notation we ignore constant factors (as well as lower-order terms). Thus, procedure Search is an order N algorithm.

What about Search_Ordered? The number of iterations is decreased for the case in which the item is missing from the list. However, all we have done is to take a case that would require N steps and reduced its time, on average, to $N/2$ steps. So, Search_Ordered is also order N.

Now consider Binary_Search. In the worst case, it eliminates half of the remaining array components on each iteration. Thus, the worst-case number of iterations is equal to the number of times N must be divided by 2 to eliminate all but one value. This number is computed by taking the logarithm, base 2, of N [written $\log_2(N)$]. Here are some examples of $\log_2(N)$ for different values of N:

N	$\log_2(N)$
2	1
4	2
8	3
16	4
32	5
1,024	10
32,768	15
1,048,576	20
33,554,432	25
1,073,741,824	30

As you can see, even for a list of over 1 billion values, Binary_Search takes only 30 iterations. It is definitely the best choice for searching large lists. Algorithms such as Binary_Search are said to be of *logarithmic order.*

Now let's turn to sorting. Procedure Selection_Sort contains a nested for loop. The total number of iterations is the product of the iterations performed by the two loops. The for loop in procedure Selection_Sort executes $N - 1$ times. The for loop in the function to find the position of the smallest value also starts out executing $N - 1$ times, but steadily decreases until it performs just one iteration. This loop executes an average of $N / 2$ iterations. The total number of iterations is:

$$\frac{(N-1) \times N}{2}$$

Ignoring the constant factors, this expression reduces to N^2 iterations, and Selection_Sort is an order N^2 algorithm. Consider that, although Binary_Search takes only 30 iterations to search an ordered array of 1 billion values, putting the array into order takes Selection_Sort one billion times one billion iterations!

Procedure Insertion_Sort also contains two nested loops. The outer loop executes $N - 1$ times. On the average, the inner loop (procedure Search_Ordered) executes $N / 2$ iterations. So on the average, Insertion_Sort is also an order N^2 algorithm.

Is every sorting algorithm order N^2? Most of the simpler ones are, but there are sorting algorithms with order $N * \log_2(N)$. Algorithms that are order $N * \log_2(N)$ are much closer in performance to order N algorithms than are order N^2 algorithms. For example, if N is 1 million, then an N^2 algorithm takes 1 million times 1 million (1 trillion) iterations, but an $N * \log_2(N)$ algorithm takes only 20 million iterations—it is 20 times slower than the order N algorithm but 50,000 times faster than the order N^2 algorithm.

Package List_Ops

Here is the declaration and body of package List_Ops with all of the operations we developed in the previous sections.

Declaration

```
package List_Ops is

-- This package contains an array type for a list of Positive numbers
-- and various searching and sorting operations for the list.

   subtype Item_Type  is Positive;
   type    Item_Array is array (Integer range <>) of Item_Type;

   ------------------------------------------
   procedure Search (List  : in  Item_Array;
                     Item  : in  Item_Type;
                     Found : out Boolean;
                     Index : out Integer);
   -- Search List for the given Item
   --
   -- Preconditions : None
   --
   -- Postconditions : If Item is in List
   --                     Found is True
   --                     Index is the location of Item in List
   --                  If Item is not in List
   --                     Found is False
   --                     Index is List'Last + 1

   ------------------------------------------
   procedure Search_Ordered (List  : in  Item_Array;
                             Item  : in  Item_Type;
                             Found : out Boolean;
                             Index : out Integer);
   -- Search List for the given Item
   --
   -- Preconditions : Items in List are in ascending order
   --
   -- Postconditions : If Item is in List
   --                     Found is True
   --                     Index is the location of Item in List
   --                  If Item is not in List
   --                     Found is False
   --                     Index is the location of where Item would be
   --                     if it were in List
```

```
   ----------------------------------------
   procedure Binary_Search (List  : in  Item_Array;
                            Item  : in  Item_Type;
                            Found : out Boolean;
                            Index : out Integer);
   -- Search List for the given Item
   --
   -- Preconditions : Items in List are in ascending order
   --
   -- Postconditions : If Item is in List
   --                       Found is True
   --                       Index is the location of Item in List
   --                    If Item is not in List
   --                       Found is False
   --                       Index is undefined

   ----------------------------------------
   procedure Selection_Sort (List : in out Item_Array);
   -- Sort List into ascending order
   --
   -- Preconditions : none
   --
   -- Postconditions : Items in List are sorted in ascending order

   ----------------------------------------
   procedure Insertion_Sort (List : in out Item_Array);
   -- Sort List into ascending order
   --
   -- Preconditions : none
   --
   -- Postconditions : Items in List are sorted in ascending order

end List_Ops;
```

Body

```
package body List_Ops is

   procedure Search (List  : in  Item_Array;
                     Item  : in  Item_Type;
                     Found : out Boolean;
                     Index : out Integer) is
   begin
      Index := List'First;     -- Start searching at the first component
      Search_Loop:       -- Search for Item in List
      loop               -- Each iteration, check one value in List
         exit Search_Loop when  (Index > List'Last)    or  else
                                (Item = List(Index));
         Index := Index + 1;
      end loop Search_Loop;
```

```
   -- Determine whether Item was found or not.
   -- Item is not in the list if Index > List'Last
   Found := Index <= List'Last;
end Search;

 ----------------------------------------
procedure Search_Ordered (List   : in  Item_Array;
                          Item   : in  Item_Type;
                          Found  : out Boolean;
                          Index  : out Integer) is
begin
   Index :=  List'First;   -- Start searching at the first component
   Search_Loop:        -- Search for Item in List
   loop                -- Each iteration, check one value in List
      exit Search_Loop when  (Index > List'Last)   or else
                             (Item <= List(Index));
      Index := Index + 1;
   end loop Search_Loop;

   -- Determine whether or not the item was found
   Found := (Index <= List'Last) and then (Item = List(Index));
end Search_Ordered;

 ----------------------------------------
procedure Binary_Search (List   : in  Item_Array;
                         Item   : in  Item_Type;
                         Found  : out Boolean;
                         Index  : out Integer) is

   First  : Integer;   -- Lower index bound of list
   Last   : Integer;   -- Upper index bound of list
   Middle : Integer;   -- Middle index

begin
   First := List'First;     -- Set up initial
   Last  := List'Last;      --    list bounds
   Found := False;

   Search_Loop:     -- Search for Item in List (First..Last)
   loop             -- Each iteration, check the middle value and half list
      exit Search_Loop when  Found        or      -- We found item
                             First > Last;        -- No items left in list
      Middle := (First + Last) / 2;
      if Item < List(Middle) then
         -- Item is not in List(Middle..Last)
         Last := Middle - 1;   -- Redefine list to 1st half
      elsif Item > List(Middle) then
```

```
         -- Item is not in List(First..Middle)
         First := Middle + 1; -- Redefine list to 2nd half
      else
         Found := True;
         Index := Middle;
      end if;
   end loop Search_Loop;

end Binary_Search;

---------------------------------------------
function Position_of_Smallest (List : in Item_Array) return Integer is

-- Search for the smallest item in List and return its index
-- Precondition : List'Length > 0

   Result : Integer;  -- Index of smallest value in List

begin
   Result := List'First;  -- Initialize result to 1st index of List

   -- Search the rest of the array for a smaller value
   -- Each iteration, check one value in the array
   for Index in List'First + 1 .. List'Last loop
      if List(Index) < List(Result) then
         Result := Index;
      end if;
   end loop;

   return Result;
end Position_Of_Smallest;

---------------------------------------------
procedure Swap (Left : in out Item_Type; Right : in out Item_Type) is
   Temp : Item_Type;
begin
   Temp  := Left;
   Left  := Right;
   Right := Temp;
end Swap;

---------------------------------------------
procedure Selection_Sort (List : in out Item_Array) is

-- An unordered list is taken as input. The same list
-- with the components in ascending order is returned
```

```
      Min_Index : Integer;         -- Index of smallest value

   begin
      for Pass_Count in  List'First .. List'Last - 1  loop

         -- Assertion: At this point, the components in
         -- List(List'First..Pass_Count - 1) are already "sorted."
         -- That is, the components are in their proper places.

         -- Find the index of the smallest item in List(Pass_Count..List'Last)
         Min_Index := Position_of_Smallest (List(Pass_Count..List'Last));

         -- Swap the smallest value and the "top" value
         Swap (Left => List(Min_Index), Right => List(Pass_Count));
      end loop;
   end Selection_Sort;

   ----------------------------------------

   procedure Insertion_Sort (List : in out Item_Array) is

      First_Unsorted : Integer;    -- Index of first element of unsorted list
      Location       : Integer;    -- Insertion location in sorted list
      Value          : Item_Type;  -- Copy of first element of unsorted list
      Found          : Boolean;    -- Not used, needed for call to Search_ordered

   begin  -- Insertion_Sort
      First_Unsorted := List'First + 1;   -- Sorted part has one element at start
      loop   -- Each iteration, the first element in the unsorted part of the
             -- array is inserted into the sorted part of the array
         exit when First_Unsorted > List'Last;
         -- Find where in the sorted portion of the array to insert
         Search_Ordered (List  => List(List'First .. First_Unsorted - 1),
                         Item  => List(First_Unsorted),
                         Found => Found,
                         Index => Location);
         -- Make a copy of List(First_Unsorted) so slide won't destroy it
         Value := List(First_Unsorted);
         -- Open up a space for the element by sliding all below it down
         List(Location + 1 .. First_Unsorted) :=
              List(Location .. First_Unsorted - 1);
         -- Insert the current value
         List(Location) := Value;
         -- Shrink the unsorted part of the array
         First_Unsorted := First_Unsorted + 1;
      end loop;
   end Insertion_Sort;

end List_Ops;
```

PROBLEM-SOLVING CASE STUDY

A Data Abstraction Package for Vectors

Specification

Problem Most of the software for the international space station is written in Ada. Your company has just received a contract to produce some support packages for this project. You are assigned to develop a very basic data abstraction package for vectors in three-dimensional space that NASA engineers will use in writing the attitude control software.

Design Like most programming languages, Ada does not have a predefined type for vectors. We need to design a new type for vectors. In our design we must define the domain and the operations for the new type. We use a data abstraction package to implement our new type.

Domain Many quantities in the world are completely specified by a single number called a magnitude. For example, we can specify the height of a building by a number of stories and the weight of a bag of sugar by a number of pounds. Other quantities require a direction as well as a magnitude. Such quantities are called vectors. An example of a vector is the movement of a space craft. To describe this movement we must specify both a direction and a distance.

From our mathematics books we find that we can represent a vector as a collection of values. We use two values to represent a vector in two-dimensional space, three values to represent a vector in three-dimensional space, four values to represent a vector in four-dimensional space, and so on. Here are some example representations of vectors:

```
(1.31, 4.25)      (7.32, -6.11, 5.00)     (0.25, 1.00, 6.25, -2.10)
```

Our problem is restricted to three-dimensional space. Each of our vectors consist of a collection of three values. Ada provides two predefined types that allow us to store multiple values under a single name—the record and the array. With a record, we select a particular value through a field name. We use a position rather than a name to select a particular value in an array. As the components in a vector are not named, we choose to use a one-dimensional array of three values to store a vector.

```
subtype Index_Type  is Integer range 1..3;
type    Vector_Type is array (Index_Type) of Component_Type;
```

Operations Our contract specifies the following vector operations:

PROBLEM-SOLVING CASE STUDY *cont'd.*

- Addition of two vectors
- Subtraction of two vectors
- Multiplication of a vector and a scalar
- Multiplication of two vectors (also called the dot product)

These basic operations for vectors are described in our mathematics books. From these descriptions we develop the algorithms for Ada functions that carry out these operations. We use operators for function names so that the programmers who use our package can write infix expressions with our vectors.

Addition and subtraction are done by adding and subtracting the corresponding components in each vector to form the result vector.

```
"+"
  in   Left     -- a vector
  in   Right    -- a vector
for Index in 1 to 3 loop
  Result (Index) := Left (Index) + Right (Index)
end loop
return Result
```

```
"-"
  in   Left     -- a vector
  in   Right    -- a vector
for Index in 1 to 3 loop
  Result (Index) := Left (Index) - Right (Index)
end loop
return Result
```

Multiplication of a vector and a scalar is done by multiplying each vector component by the scalar value. So that the multiplication can be done in either order (vector times scalar or scalar times vector) we write two different functions. The second function simply reverses the order of its parameters and calls the first one.

```
"*"
  in   Left     -- a vector
  in   Right    -- a scalar
for Index in 1 to 3 loop
  Result (Index) := Left (Index) * Right
end loop
return Result
```

PROBLEM-SOLVING CASE STUDY *cont'd.*

```
"*"
  in    Left      -- a scalar
  in    Right     -- a vector
return Right * Left    -- Call the * function we just wrote
```

Our mathematics book defines the dot product as the sum of the products of the corresponding components as given by the following formula for calculating the dot product of vectors *A* and *B*.

$$\text{DotProduct} = \sum_{i=1}^{3} A_i \times B_i$$

```
"*"
  in    Left      -- a vector
  in    Right     -- a vector
Sum := 0.0
for Index in 1 to 3 loop
  Sum := Sum + Left (Index) * Right (Index)
end loop
return Sum
```

Implementation We implement our data abstraction package in two parts: the declaration and the body. Here is the declaration.

```
package Vector_ADT is

-- This data abstraction package implements the basic operations for vectors
-- in three-dimensional space.

   -- Types that define the domain of a vector

   subtype Component_Type is Float;     -- Vector components

   subtype Index_Type is Integer range 1..3;
   type    Vector     is array (Index_Type) of Component_Type;


   -- Operations for vectors

   function "+" (Left : in Vector; Right : in Vector) return Vector;
   -- Returns the sum of two vectors

   function "-" (Left : in Vector; Right : in Vector) return Vector;
   -- Returns the difference of two vectors

   function "*" (Left : in Vector; Right : in Component_Type) return Vector;
   -- Returns the product of a vector and a scalar
```

PROBLEM-SOLVING CASE STUDY cont'd.

```
   function "*" (Left : in Component_Type; Right : in Vector) return Vector;
   -- Returns the product of a scalar and a vector

   function "*" (Left : in Vector; Right : in Vector) return Component_Type;
   -- Returns the dot product of two vectors

end Vector_ADT;
```

Here is the body of the package.

```
package body Vector_ADT is

   ----------------------------------------
   function "+" (Left : in Vector; Right : in Vector) return Vector is
      Result : Vector;
   begin
      for Index in Index_Type loop
         Result(Index) := Left(Index) + Right(Index);
      end loop;
      return Result;
   end "+";

   ----------------------------------------
   function "-" (Left : in Vector; Right : in Vector) return Vector is
      Result : Vector;
   begin
      for Index in Index_Type loop
         Result(Index) := Left(Index) - Right(Index);
      end loop;
      return Result;
   end "-";

   ----------------------------------------
   function "*" (Left : in Vector; Right : in Component_Type) return Vector is
      Result : Vector;
   begin
      for Index in Index_Type loop
         Result(Index) := Left(Index) * Right;
      end loop;
      return Result;
   end "*";

   ----------------------------------------
   function "*" (Left : in Component_Type; Right : in Vector) return Vector is
   begin
      return Right * Left;  -- Reverse the order and call the procedure above
   end "*";
```

PROBLEM-SOLVING CASE STUDY *cont'd.*

```
   ----------------------------------------
   function "*" (Left : in Vector; Right : in Vector) return Component_Type is
      Sum : Component_Type;
   begin
      Sum := 0.0;
      for Index in Index_Type loop
         Sum := Sum + Left(Index) * Right(Index);
      end loop;
      return Sum;
   end "*";

end Vector_ADT;
```

Testing To test our data abstraction package we must write a separate test program that uses it. The following program reads in two vectors and a scalar from the keyboard, calls all the operations in our package, and displays the results. We can compare the output of this test program to values we calculate by hand. Notice how the use type clause allows us to use infix notation with the vector operators.

```
with Vector_ADT;
use type Vector_ADT.Vector;   -- Make operators available without prefixing
with Ada.Text_IO;
with Ada.Float_Text_IO;
procedure Test_Vector is

-- This program reads in two vectors and a scalar from the keyboard,
-- calls all the operations in the vector package, and displays the results.

   ----------------------------------------
   procedure Get (Item : out Vector_ADT.Vector) is
   -- Gets one vector
   begin
      for Index in Vector_ADT.Index_Type loop
         Ada.Float_Text_IO.Get (Item => Item(Index));
      end loop;
   end Get;

   ----------------------------------------
   procedure Put (Item : in Vector_ADT.Vector;
                  Fore : in Natural;
                  Aft  : in Natural;
                  Exp  : in Natural) is
```

PROBLEM-SOLVING CASE STUDY *cont'd.*

```
      -- Puts one vector
      begin
         Ada.Text_IO.Put ('(');
         for Index in Vector_ADT.Index_Type loop
            Ada.Float_Text_IO.Put (Item => Item(Index),
                                   Fore => Fore,
                                   Aft  => Aft,
                                   Exp  => Exp);
            -- Add a comma and blank between the components
            if Index < Vector_ADT.Index_Type'Last then
               Ada.Text_IO.Put (", ");
            end if;
         end loop;
         Ada.Text_IO.Put (')');
      end Put;

      ----------------------------------------------

      First  : Vector_ADT.Vector;   -- The two
      Second : Vector_ADT.Vector;   -- vectors
      Value  : Float;               -- One scalar

   begin -- Test Vector
      -- Get the test data
      Ada.Text_IO.Put_Line ("Enter the first vector.");
      Get (First);
      Ada.Text_IO.Put_Line ("Enter the second vector.");
      Get (Second);
      Ada.Text_IO.Put_Line ("Enter a scalar value.");
      Ada.Float_Text_IO.Get (Value);

      -- Display the results of each vector operation

      Ada.Text_IO.Put ("The sum of the two vectors is             ");
      Put (Item => First + Second,
           Fore => 1, Aft => 2, Exp => 0);
      Ada.Text_IO.New_Line;
      Ada.Text_IO.Put ("The difference between the two vectors is ");
      Put (Item => First - Second,
           Fore => 1, Aft => 2, Exp => 0);
      Ada.Text_IO.New_Line;
      Ada.Text_IO.Put ("The scalar times the first vector is      ");
      Put (Item => Value * First,
           Fore => 1, Aft => 2, Exp => 0);
```

PROBLEM-SOLVING CASE STUDY *cont'd.*

```
   Ada.Text_IO.New_Line;
   Ada.Text_IO.Put ("The first vector times the scalar is      ");
   Put (Item => First * Value,
        Fore => 1, Aft => 2, Exp => 0);
   Ada.Text_IO.New_Line;
   Ada.Text_IO.Put ("The dot product of the two vectors is     ");
   Ada.Float_Text_IO.Put (Item => First * Second,
                          Fore => 1, Aft => 2, Exp => 0);
   Ada.Text_IO.New_Line;

end Test_Vector;
```

PROBLEM-SOLVING CASE STUDY

Exam Attendance

Specification

Problem You are the grader for a U.S. government class. The teacher has asked you to prepare two lists: students who took an exam and students who missed it. The catch is that she wants the lists before the exam is over. You decide to write a program for your notebook computer that prints the lists of absentees and attendees after receiving the name of each student who entered the exam room.

Input

- A file containing a list of the last names of students in the class, one name per line, not ordered alphabetically, not more than 800 names.
- Each student's last name as he or she enters the room.

Output

- An alphabetical listing of those students taking the exam.
- An alphabetical listing of those students who are absent.

Assumptions

- There are no two students with the same last name in the class.

Design How would you do this by hand? You would stand at the door with a class roster. As each student came in, you would check off his or her name. When all the students had entered, you would go through the roster, making a list of those present. Then you would do the same for those who are absent.

This by-hand algorithm can serve as a model for our program. We will use a list package to model the class roster. We need to study the problem some more to define the details of the list and to see what operations are required for this package.

As each student enters the room, you enter his or her name at the keyboard. Our program scans the list of students for that name and marks that the student is present. When the last student has entered, you can enter a special name, perhaps blank, to signal the program to print the lists.

The size of the list and the speed required to process the large number of students arriving at the exam suggest that we should use a binary search to find the names. This binary search requires that the list be sorted alphabetically by name. But names in the file we have are not ordered. We will have to create a sorted list of these names before we can process the students. We can input all the names at once and sort them using one of the sort algorithms we developed in this chapter, or we could put each name into its proper place as it is read and inserted into the list. Let's take the second approach.

We have now identified three operations needed in the list package. We need to *insert* a student into an ordered list and to *search* that list quickly for a student. We also need to *display* those students who are at the exam and those who are absent.

What information do we need to store in the list for each student? Obviously we need a name which we can store as a string. We can simulate "mark that the student is present" by having an enumeration field Here. This field is initialized to Absent for all students. Then, when a name is found in the list of students, we set the field for that student to Present.

We can modify the list package developed in this chapter for this problem. We need an array of records, each record having two fields: a name field (type String) and an attendance field (an enumeration type). We define the actual list as a record containing a length field and our array of records. Figure 12-11 shows this data structure.

In the following algorithm, we use italics to highlight the three abstract steps in the algorithm that are carried out by subprograms in the attendance list package.

Exam Attendance **Level 0**

Get Class Roster
Check in Students
Display Present List
Display Absent List

PROBLEM-SOLVING CASE STUDY *cont'd.*

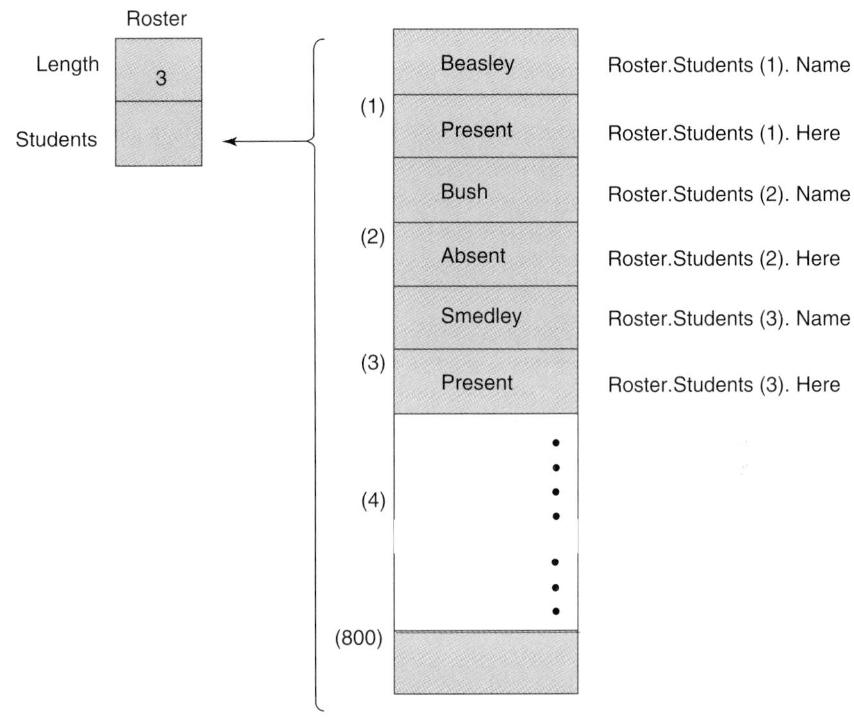

FIGURE 12-11 Data Structure for the Exam Attendance List

Get Class Roster **Level 1**

out Roster
Prepare File
loop
exit when no more names on roster
Get Name from file
Insert Name into Roster
end loop
Close File

Check in Students **Level 1**

in out Roster
loop
Display prompt
Get Name from keyboard
exit when Name is blank
Process Name
end loop

PROBLEM-SOLVING CASE STUDY cont'd.

Get Name **Level 2**

in File
out Name

Get Name from File
pad Name with blanks

Process Name **Level 2**

in Name
in out Roster

Search for Name on Roster
if Name is on Roster then
   Mark that student as present
else
   Put Name & " is not registered in this course"
end if

Module Structure Chart The dashed boxes in the following chart indicate modules in the attendance list package.

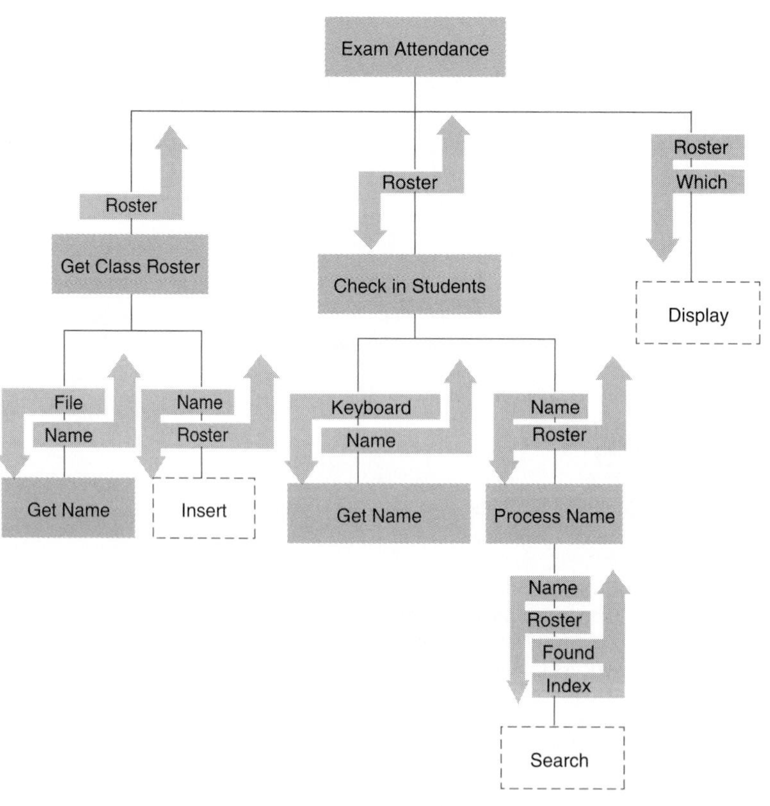

PROBLEM-SOLVING CASE STUDY *cont'd.*

Implementation Because our program is dependent on the attendance list package, we write its declaration first. It contains the types for the list of student records that we use to declare our class roster and three operations for this list.

```
package Attendance_List is

   Max_Class_Size : constant := 800;

   -- Declarations for the items in the list
   Max_Name_Length : constant := 15;
   subtype Name_String     is String (1..Max_Name_Length);
   type    Attendance_Type is (Absent, Present);
   type Student_Rec is
      record
         Name : Name_String;
         Here : Attendance_Type := Absent;
      end record;

   -- Array types for the list
   type    Student_Array is array (Positive range <>) of Student_Rec;
   subtype Student_Index is Integer range 1..Max_Class_Size;
   subtype Class_Array   is Student_Array (Student_Index);

   -- The list type
   subtype Length_Type is Integer range 0..Max_Class_Size;
   type Student_List   is
      record
         Length   : Length_Type := 0;   -- The number of components in list
         Students : Class_Array;        -- The components
      end record;

   ------------------------------------------
   procedure Insert (Roster : in out Student_List;
                     Name   : in     Name_String);
   -- Insert the Name into the class Roster
   --
   -- Preconditions : Length of Roster is less than Max_Class_Size
   --                 Names in Roster are in ascending order
   --                 Name is not already on Roster
   --
   -- Postconditions : Name is added to Roster
   --                  Names in Roster are in ascending order
```

<u>*PROBLEM-SOLVING CASE STUDY cont'd.*</u>

```
   ----------------------------------------
   procedure Display (Roster : in Student_List;
                      Which  : in Attendance_Type);
   -- Display a list of student names
   --
   -- Preconditions : none
   --
   -- Postconditions : If Which = Present
   --                       display students in Roster who are marked present
   --                  If Which = Absent
   --                       display students in Roster who are marked absent


   ----------------------------------------
   procedure Search (Roster : in  Student_List;
                     Name   : in  Name_String;
                     Found  : out Boolean;
                     Index  : out Integer);
   -- Search Roster for the given Name
   --
   -- Preconditions : Names in Roster are in ascending order
   --
   -- Postconditions : If Name is in Roster
   --                       Found is True
   --                       Index is the location of Name in Roster
   --                  If Name is not in Roster
   --                       Found is False
   --                       Index is undefined

end Attendance_List;
```

Here is the program that uses the attendance list package in the implementation of our algorithm.

```
with Attendance_List;
with Ada.Text_IO;
procedure Exam_Attendance is

   ----------------------------------------
   procedure Get_Name (File : in  Ada.Text_IO.File_Type;
                       Name : out String) is
   -- Gets a name from the given file and pads it with blanks

      Length : Natural;   -- Number of characters in Name
   begin
```

PROBLEM-SOLVING CASE STUDY cont'd.

```
   -- Get the Name from the file
   Ada.Text_IO.Get_Line (File => File,
                         Item => Name,
                         Last => Length);

   if Length = Name'Last then   -- Did we fill the string?
      Ada.Text_IO.Skip_Line (File);   -- Skip over remaining characters
   else
      -- Use an array aggregate to pad the Name with blanks
      Name(Length + 1 .. Name'Last) := (Length + 1 .. Name'Last => ' ');
   end if;
end Get_Name;

 ----------------------------------------
procedure Get_Class_Roster (Roster : out Attendance_List.Student_List) is
-- Set up the class roster from information in a file

   -- Data file from the registrar with the names of all students.
   -- The names are not in alphabetical order.
   Registration_File : Ada.Text_IO.File_Type;
   File_Name         : constant String:= "Registration.txt";

   Name : Attendance_List.Name_String;  -- One student name

begin
   Ada.Text_IO.Open (File => Registration_File,
                     Mode => Ada.Text_IO.In_File,
                     Name => File_Name);
   Input_Loop:    -- Process all of the names in the file
   loop           -- Each iteration, get one name and insert in Roster
      exit Input_Loop when Ada.Text_IO.End_Of_File (Registration_File);
      Get_Name (File => Registration_File, Name => Name);
      Attendance_List.Insert (Roster => Roster, Name => Name);
   end loop Input_Loop;
   Ada.Text_IO.Close (Registration_File);
end Get_Class_Roster;

 ----------------------------------------
procedure Process_Name (Name   : in     Attendance_List.Name_String;
                        Roster : in out Attendance_List.Student_List) is
-- Marks one student as present at the exam
```

PROBLEM-SOLVING CASE STUDY *cont'd.*

```
      On_Roster : Boolean;     -- True if Name is on class Roster
      Location  : Integer;     -- Location of Name on class Roster

   begin
      Attendance_List.Search (Roster => Roster,
                              Name   => Name,
                              Found  => On_Roster,
                              Index  => Location);
      if On_Roster then
         -- Mark student as present
         Roster.Students(Location).Here := Attendance_List.Present;
      else
         Ada.Text_IO.Put_Line (Name & " is not registered in this course");
      end if;
   end Process_Name;

   ------------------------------------------
   procedure Check_in_Students (Roster : in out Attendance_List.Student_List) is
   -- Check in all students attending exam

      Blank : constant Attendance_List.Name_String := (others => ' ');
      Name  : Attendance_List.Name_String; -- One student name

   begin
      Input_Loop:   -- Mark all students attending as present
      loop          -- Each iteration, mark one student as present
         Ada.Text_IO.Put ("Enter last name (blank name to exit)  ");
         Get_Name (File => Ada.Text_IO.Standard_Input,     -- Keyboard "file"
                   Name => Name);
         exit Input_Loop when Name = Blank;
         Process_Name (Name => Name, Roster => Roster);
      end loop Input_Loop;
   end Check_in_Students;

----------------------------------------------
   Roster : Attendance_List.Student_List;   -- The class roster

begin  -- Exam Attendance
   Get_Class_Roster  (Roster);
   Check_in_Students (Roster);
   Ada.Text_IO.Put_Line ("The following students were present at the exam.");
   Ada.Text_IO.New_Line;
   Attendance_List.Display (Roster => Roster,
                            Which  => Attendance_List.Present);
```

PROBLEM-SOLVING CASE STUDY cont'd.

```
   Ada.Text_IO.New_Line (2);
   Ada.Text_IO.Put_Line ("The following students were absent from the exam.");
   Ada.Text_IO.New_Line;
   Attendance_List.Display (Roster => Roster,
                            Which  => Attendance_List.Absent);
end Exam_Attendance;
```

As the roster is a record containing an array of records, this program is good practice for array and record syntax. Use the picture in Figure 12-11 to help you interpret the assignment statement in procedure Process_Name that sets one student's attendance to Present.

The procedure Get_Name is called to get names from both the registrar's text file and the keyboard. To read from the keyboard, Get_Name's parameter File is assigned a value by a call to the function Text_IO. Standard_Input.

Here is the package body of our attendance list package.

```
with Ada.Text_IO;
package body Attendance_List is

   ----------------------------------------

   procedure Search_Ordered (List    : in  Student_Array;
                             Name    : in  Name_String;
                             Index   : out Integer) is
   -- Search array of student records for the given Name
   --
   -- Preconditions : Items in List are in ascending order
   --
   -- Postconditions : Index is the location of Name in List or the location
   --                  of where Name would be if it were in List
   begin
      Index :=  List'First;  -- Start searching at the first component
      Search_Loop:       -- Search for Name in List
      loop               -- Each iteration, check one name in List
         exit Search_Loop when  (Index > List'Last)   or else
                                (Name <= List(Index).Name);
         Index := Index + 1;
      end loop Search_Loop;
   end Search_Ordered;

   ----------------------------------------

   procedure Insert (Roster : in out Student_List;
                     Name   : in     Name_String) is

      Location : Integer;  -- Place to insert Name
   begin
```

PROBLEM-SOLVING CASE STUDY cont'd.

```
   -- Search the array for the insert location
   Search_Ordered (List  => Roster.Students(1..Roster.Length),
                   Name  => Name,
                   Index => Location);
   -- Shift records in the list to make room for new student
   Roster.Students(Location + 1 .. Roster.Length + 1) :=
         Roster.Students(Location .. Roster.Length);
   -- Insert a new record (with name and presence set to Absent) to the array
   Roster.Students(Location) := (Name => Name,      -- Note the use of a
                                 Here => Absent); -- record aggregate
   -- Update the list's length
   Roster.Length := Roster.Length + 1;
end Insert;

---------------------------------------------
procedure Display (Roster : in Student_List;
                   Which  : in Attendance_Type) is
begin
   for Index in 1..Roster.Length loop
      if Roster.Students(Index).Here = Which then
         Ada.Text_IO.Put_Line (Roster.Students(Index).Name);
      end if;
   end loop;
end Display;

---------------------------------------------
procedure Search (Roster : in  Student_List;
                  Name   : in  Name_String;
                  Found  : out Boolean;
                  Index  : out Integer) is

   First  : Integer;  -- Lower index bound of list
   Last   : Integer;  -- Upper index bound of list
   Middle : Integer;  -- Middle index

begin
   First := 1;                  -- Set up initial
   Last  := Roster.Length;      -- list bounds
   Found := False;
```

PROBLEM-SOLVING CASE STUDY cont'd.

```
      Search_Loop:   -- Search for Name in Roster.Students(First..Last)
      loop           -- Each iteration, check the middle value and half list
         exit Search_Loop when  Found          or   -- We found item
                                First > Last;      -- No items left in list
         Middle := (First + Last) / 2;
         if Name < Roster.Students(Middle).Name then
            -- Item is not in Roster.Students(Middle..Last)
            Last := Middle - 1;  -- Redefine list to 1st half
         elsif Name > Roster.Students(Middle).Name then
            -- Item is not in Roster.Students(First..Middle)
            First := Middle + 1; -- Redefine list to 2nd half
         else
            Found := True;
            Index := Middle;
         end if;
      end loop Search_Loop;
   end Search;
end Attendance_List;
```

The procedure Search_Ordered is not available outside of the package body. It is used locally by Insert. Notice that we do not duplicate the comments written in the package declaration in the body, but we did document the local procedure.

Except for the Display procedure, all of the algorithms in this package body were developed earlier in this chapter. In a later course, you will learn how to create generic packages that can be instantiated to create custom packages without the need for the copying, pasting, and editing we used to create the attendance list package.

Testing We must test the program with names that are more than 15 characters, exactly 15 characters, and less than 15 characters. We must spell names from the keyboard incorrectly as well as correctly. The following data was used in our tests.

File Registration.txt contained the following names

Dale	Jones
McCormick	Kirshen
Weems	NameLongerThanFifteenCharacters
Vitek	Gleason
Westby	Thompson
Smith	Ripley
Jamison	Lilly

PROBLEM-SOLVING CASE STUDY *cont'd.*

Output from one test run

```
Enter last name (blank name to exit)  Weems
Enter last name (blank name to exit)  Dale
Enter last name (blank name to exit)  McCormack
McCormack       is not registered in this course
Enter last name (blank name to exit)  McCormick
Enter last name (blank name to exit)  Vitek
Enter last name (blank name to exit)  Westby
Enter last name (blank name to exit)  NameLongerThanFifteenCharacters
Enter last name (blank name to exit)  Gleason
Enter last name (blank name to exit)
The following students were present at the exam.

Dale
Gleason
McCormick
NameLongerThanF
Vitek
Weems
Westby


The following students were absent from the exam.

Jamison
Jones
Kirshen
Lilly
Ripley
Smith
Thompson
```

Testing and Debugging

Packages are collections of related types, constants, and subprograms. We can apply the techniques that we used to test and debug these Ada features in earlier chapters to packages. As we saw in the vector case study and with our List package, separate programs are frequently used to test package subprograms.

The dependencies among packages introduce the possibility of obsolescence errors: errors arising from the changing of a library unit on which another unit depends. However, the program library allows the Ada development system to detect obsolete packages. When such a package is detected, it is only a matter of recompiling it. Many Ada environments determine which units are obsolete and recompile them automatically.

Once we have tested and debugged a package, we can reuse it in other programs without testing it again. In this way packages contribute to more cost-effective development of reliable programs.

We discussed and coded five general-purpose procedures: two sequential searches, a binary search, a selection sort, and an insertion sort. These were all encapsulated into a single service package. We can write one or more programs to test these procedures. The program on page 721 tests the selection sort procedure. We need change only one line of this program to test the insertion sort. Following is the algorithm for a driver to test procedure Search:

```
Test Search
Get List of components
Loop
  Get Item
  exit when a sentinel item is entered
  Search (List, Item, Found, Index)
  if Found then
    Put Item, "found at index position," Index
  else
    Put Item, "not found in list"
  end if
end Loop
```

The driver would have to be run with several sets of test data to test procedure Search thoroughly. The minimum set of lists of components would be:

- a list of no components
- a list of one component
- a list of many components

The minimum set of items being searched for would be

- Item in List(1)
- Item in List(Length)
- Item between List(1) and List(Length)
- Item < List(1)
- Item > List(Length)
- Item between List(1) and List(Length) but not there

By adding a call to one of our sorting algorithms after getting the list of components, we can use the same program to test procedure Binary_Search. We can also reuse the test cases developed for procedure Search.

Testing and Debugging Hints

1. Beware of the dependencies resulting from with clauses that determine the order in which to compile units. The compiler will give error messages if units are compiled in an incorrect order. The linker will give error messages if units are missing or obsolete.
2. Draw a dependency graph to reveal the dependencies in a program with many units.
3. If an error is found and corrected in a library unit, all units that depend on that library unit become obsolete and must be recompiled. To prevent large numbers of recompilations, design your package declarations carefully.
4. If an error is found in a body, you need to recompile only that body. By designing your program in packages, you can save time through smaller compilations.
5. Employ use type clauses to allow the use of infix notation with operators defined in packages.
6. Employ use package clauses only when they markedly improve the readability of your program. Do not use them to cut down on the amount of typing.
7. When you use a use package clause, continue to prefix other identifiers from the library unit that do not benefit from removing the prefixing.

Summary

Packages are Ada's principal method of encapsulation for complex programs. They are also important tools for the reuse of Ada code. Although they are particularly important for programming teams, packages are also valuable for individual programming projects.

We write packages in two parts: the package declaration and the package body. The package declaration defines the interface to the package; the body supplies the implementation of operations declared in the declaration. By separating the declarations from its body we allow programmers to concentrate on interface design without needing to worry about implementation details. When an error is found and corrected, we do not have to recompile the entire program, only the offending package body. Finally, we can change the implementation of operations declared in the interface at any time without affecting the remainder of the program.

Most packages fall into one of three categories. A definition package groups related constants and types. A service package groups together the constants, types, and subprograms necessary to provide some particular service. Data abstraction packages encapsulate the domain and operations of new data types. Because this classification is not a strict one, you will find some packages that fit in several of these categories.

We can compile an Ada program in separate parts called compilation units. A compilation is the source file submitted to an Ada compiler. Although a compilation may contain one or more compilation units, it is good programming style to limit a compilation to a single compilation unit. Compilation units are either declarations or bodies. Ada keeps track of all the units making up a program through the program library. When a unit is compiled, Ada uses information from library units in the program library to ensure enforcement of language rules.

Context clauses indicate what library units are available for use by a compilation unit. The order in which compilation units are submitted to the compiler is based on the visibility of units established by these context clauses. The Ada compiler cannot compile a compilation unit until all library units named in its context clause have been entered into the library. It also cannot compile a package body or subprogram body until its corresponding declaration has been entered into the library. If a declaration is changed and reentered into the library, all of the units that depend on it become obsolete and must be recompiled.

The use *type* clause allows us to use operators defined in a package for a particular type without prefixing. A major benefit of the use type clause is the ability to use infix notation in expressions involving operators declared in packages. Operators are defined by new type declarations and functions with operator names.

The use *package* clause allows us to employ identifiers declared in packages without prefixing. It is generally accepted that programs that use prefixing are easier to understand and debug than programs that employ use package clauses. However, use package clauses can make a program more comprehensible by shortening expressions containing calls to functions.

Finally, this chapter provided practice in working with lists represented by one-dimensional arrays. We examined algorithms that search and sort data stored in a list, and we have written procedures to implement these algorithms. We can use these procedures again and again in different contexts because we have written them in a general fashion.

Quick Check

1. What is an Ada package? (p. 687)
2. Why are packages important? (p. 687)
3. Ada packages have two parts: a declaration and a body. List three advantages of separating the declaration from the body. (pp. 687–688)
4. Define the following terms:
   a. definition package (p. 690)
   b. service package (p. 692)
   c. data abstraction package (p. 697)
   d. compilation (p. 699)
   e. compilation unit (p. 699)

5. Package bodies can use anything declared in the package declaration. (True or False) (p. 696)
6. Package declarations may contain procedure bodies. (True or False) (p. 689)
7. Package bodies may contain subprograms not declared in the package declaration. (True or False) (p. 696)
8. Package bodies may contain constants and types not declared in the package declaration. (True or False) (p. 696)
9. Label each of the following as a declaration, a body, or both. (p. 700)

   Package declaration

   Package body

   Procedure body (with no previously compiled procedure declaration)

   Procedure body (with a previously compiled procedure declaration)

   Procedure declaration

   Function declaration
10. Bodies may be named in a with clause. (True or False) (p. 703)
11. What is the purpose of the Ada program library? (pp. 700–701)
12. When does a unit become obsolete? (p. 704)
13. What does the use *package* clause allow us to do? (pp. 708–709)
14. What does the use *type* clause allow us to do? (p. 709)
15. Name two ways in which operators are defined in a package.
16. In a search of an unordered array of 1000 values, what will be the average number of loop iterations required to find a value? What is the maximum number of iterations required to find a value? (p. 732)
17. The following program fragment sorts a list into descending order. Change it to sort in ascending order. (p. 720)

```
for Pass_Count in  List'First .. List'Last - 1  loop
   Min_Index := Pass_Count;
   for Index in Pass_Count + 1 .. List'Last loop
      if List(Index) < List(Min_Index) then
         Min_Index := Index;
      end if;
   end loop;
   Swap (Left => List(Min_Index), Right => List(Pass_Count));
end loop;
```

18. Describe the basic principle behind the binary search algorithm. (pp. 728–729)
19. Describe how the list insertion operation could be used to build a sorted list from unordered input data. (pp. 724–725)

Answers

1. A group of logically related entities that may include types and subtypes, objects of those types and subtypes, and subprograms with parameters of those types and subtypes. **2.** Packages are important for the development of large programs. They are Ada's principal method of encapsulation and reuse. **3.** a. They allow programmers to concentrate on interface design without needing to worry about implementation details. b. When an error is found and corrected, the entire program does not have to be recompiled, only the offending package body. c. The implementation of the interface can be changed at any time without affecting the remainder of the program. **4.** a. A package that groups together related constants and types. b. A package that groups together the constants, types, and subprograms necessary to provide some particular service. c. A package that defines a new type and any operations that are not already predefined for that type. d. A source file containing one or more compilation units submitted to an Ada compiler. e. A portion of an Ada program that can be compiled by itself. **5.** True. **6.** False. **7.** True. **8.** True. **9.** Package declarations, procedure declarations, and function declarations are declarations. Package bodies, and procedure bodies (with separate procedure declarations) are bodies. Procedure bodies (with no separate procedure declarations) are both. **10.** False. Only declarations may be named in a with clause. **11.** To ensure that the Ada language rules are enforced in the same manner for a program submitted through several compilations as for a program submitted as a single compilation. **12.** Whenever a library unit on which it depends is recompiled. **13.** To use package symbols without prefixing. **14.** To use operators defined in a package without prefixing so that we can use them in infix notation expressions. **15.** a. As functions that use an operator as a name. b. As operators that are automatically defined in the declaration of a new type. **16.** The average number is 500 iterations. The maximum is 1000 iterations. **17.** The only required change is to replace the < symbol in the inner loop with a >. As a matter of style, Min_Index should be changed to Max_Index. **18.** The binary search takes advantage of ordered array values, looking at a component in the middle of the array and deciding whether the sought-after value precedes or follows the midpoint. The search is then repeated on the appropriate half, quarter, eighth, and so on, of the array until the value is located. **19.** The list is initialized with a length of 0. Each time a data value is read, insertion adds the value to the list in its correct position. When all the data has been read, it will be stored in order in the array.

Exam Preparation Exercises

1. Define the following:

package	obsolete unit
child package	compilation unit
package declaration	compilation
package body	library declaration
definition package	library body
service package	program library
data abstraction package	

2. Subprogram declarations and package declarations each serve to define an interface. Why are clear interfaces so important?
3. When is a definition package useful?

4. Using the definition package Customer_Accounts on page 690.
   a. Declare a variable called Name whose type is Name_Rec.
   b. Instantiate a package for sequential I/O of components of type Name_Rec.
   c. Write a Boolean function that takes two parameters of type Customer_Rec and returns True if the Account_Number of the first parameter is greater than that of the second parameter.
5. Using the service package Display_Control on page 692, write an Ada code fragment that clears the screen and displays your name in bold, centered on the display screen. You may assume that the display has 24 rows and 80 columns.
6. Using the data abstraction package Pixel on page 697,
   a. Instantiate a package to do input and output with display colors.
   b. Write an Ada code fragment that gets two display colors from the keyboard and uses a case statement to display whether each is a primary color, secondary color, or neutral color. If both are primary colors, display what color results from mixing them.
7. Name all the compilation units and indicate whether each is a library unit or a secondary unit.
8. Give the rules for defining the order in which units must be compiled.
9. Using the example units Apple, Banana, Pear, and Fruit on page 701–702, determine whether the compilation orders of the units in the following lists are valid or invalid. For each invalid compilation order, explain why the order is invalid. *Hint:* Use the dependency graph given in Figure 12-1.
   a. Apple (declaration)
      Apple (body)
      Banana (declaration)
      Banana (body)
      Pear (declaration)
      Pear (body)
      Fruit
   b. Pear (declaration)
      Apple (declaration)
      Banana (declaration)
      Pear (body)
      Apple (body)
      Banana (body)
      Fruit
   c. Apple (declaration)
      Banana (declaration)
      Pear (declaration)
      Pear (body)
      Apple (body)
      Banana (body)
      Fruit

d. Banana (body)
   Pear (body)
   Apple (declaration)
   Banana (declaration)
   Pear (declaration)
   Apple (body)
   Fruit

10. Assuming that the units of the previous question have all been compiled successfully, what units, if any, become obsolete if the following units are recompiled?
    a. Fruit
    b. Pear (declaration)
    c. Pear (body)
    d. Apple (declaration)
    e. Apple (body)
    f. Banana (declaration)
    g. Banana (body)
11. Explain what the with and use clauses do.
12. Compare the use package clause and the use type clause.
13. Why should Ada programmers avoid the use package clause?
14. The following Ada program fragment requires package Pixel given on page 697. It does not compile. The compiler gives a syntax error on the Boolean expression in the if statement.

```
with Pixel;
procedure Question_14 is
      .
      .
      .
   My_Color    : Pixel.Color_Type;
   Your_Color : Pixel.Color_Type;
      .
      .
      .
   if Your_Color < My_Color then
      .
      .
      .
```

    a. Why does the compiler reject the Boolean expression in this if statement?
    b. Give two ways to correct the problem in this code fragment.
15. Draw a dependency graph for the program Test_Vector on page 743.
16. The following values are stored in an array in ascending order.

    28 45 97 103 107 162 196 202 257

    Apply procedures Search and Search_Ordered to this array, search for the following values, and indicate how many comparisons are required either to find the number or to find that it is not in the list.

a. 28
b. 32
c. 196
d. 194

17. The following values are stored in an array in ascending order.

    29 57 63 72 79 83 96 104 114 136

    Apply procedure Bin_Search with Item = 114 to this list, and trace the values of First, Last, and Middle. Indicate any undefined values with a U.

Programming Warm-up Exercises

1. Write the declaration for a service package to do input and output of vectors (use package Vector_ADT on page 741). Include a procedure called Get to read in a vector value from the keyboard and a procedure called Put to display a vector value. Both procedures should have a parameter called Item to pass the value. The Put procedure should have parameters called Fore, Aft, and Exp that specify the layout of each component in a vector.
2. Write an Ada code fragment that uses the operations in the package declared in the previous question to read and echo print vectors until a vector whose components are all zero is entered. Then display the sum of the vectors.
3. Write the body of the package you declared in question 1. The Put procedure should enclose the three vector components within parentheses and separate them with a comma and a space.
4. Extend the Vector_ADT package to include a negation operator ("-") function that returns a vector whose components are the negations of the corresponding *in* parameter vector's components.
5. Extend the Vector_ADT package to include a less than operator ("<") function that returns true if the magnitude of the left operand is less than the magnitude of the right operand and false otherwise. The magnitude of a vector is equal to the dot product of the vector with itself.
6. Write a Boolean function called Has_Greater_Than that searches an unconstrained array, List, of Float values for a Float value greater than the value of Item. If such a value is found, the function returns True; otherwise, it returns False.

Programming Problems

1. Write a service package (declaration and body) called My_Math_Library that contains a single function called Sqrt that returns the square root of a Float value. Use the function for calculating square roots given in Chapter 6. However, instead of declaring the tolerance as a local constant in the function, declare it in the package body. Use a tolerance value of 0.00001.

   Write an Ada program to test your service package. In this program prompt the user to enter a Float value. Then display its square root calculated by your service package, its square root calculated by the square root in

Ada.Numerics.Elementary_Functions, and the difference between the two calculated square roots.

2. Write a data abstraction package that defines a type for complex numbers and functions for operators +, -, *, /, <, and >. The package should also include a function that returns the conjugate of a complex number.

   Also write a service package that provides input and output procedures for these complex numbers. Include Get and Put procedures that allow for interactive input and output and Get and Put procedures with a File parameter that allow for file input and output. Finally, write a driver program to test these two packages.

   A complex number consists of two parts, a real part and an imaginary part. In algebra, a complex number is represented as a quantity of two values often enclosed in parentheses like this:

$$(5.27 + 17.34i)$$

   where 5.27 is the real part of the complex number and 17.34 is the imaginary part. We obtain the conjugate of a complex number simply by changing the sign of the imaginary part of the number. For example, the conjugate of (5.27 + 17.34*i*) is (5.27 − 17.34*i*).

   Addition and subtraction of complex numbers is done by separately adding and subtracting the real and imaginary parts. For example:

$$(5.27 + 17.34i) + (6.11 - 5.30i) = (11.38 + 12.04i)$$

$$(5.27 + 17.34i) - (6.11 - 5.30i) = (-0.84 + 22.64i)$$

   To multiply two complex numbers, apply the following formula:

$$(a + bi)(c + di) = (e + fi)$$

   where

$$e = ac - bd$$

$$f = bc + ad$$

   For example:

$$(5.27 + 17.34i)(6.11 - 5.30i) = (124.10 + 78.02i)$$

The formula for division of two complex numbers is

$$(a + bi) \div (c + di) = (e + fi)$$

where

$$e = (ac + bd) \div (c^2 + d^2)$$

$$f = (bc - ad) \div (c^2 + d^2)$$

For example

$$(5.27 + 17.34i) \div (6.11 - 5.30i) = (-0.91 + 2.05i)$$

Comparisons of complex numbers using the relational operators < and > are done by comparing the magnitudes of the numbers. The magnitude of a complex number is calculated by taking the square root of the sum of the squares of its real part and its imaginary part. For example, the magnitude of (5.27 + 17.34*i*) is 18.12 and the magnitude of (6.11 − 5.30*i*) is 8.09. Thus (5.27 + 17.34*i*) is greater than (6.11 − 5.30*i*).

The form of input and output values for the service I/O package should be that used in our examples: two numbers separated by a sign enclosed in parentheses. The second number should have an *i* immediately after it. The Put procedure should have Fore, Aft, and Exp parameters to specify the layout of both components in the complex value.

3. Write a data abstraction package for the colors used in a sophisticated color monitor that can display 262,144 different colors. Unlike the example given on page 697, we cannot give different names to each of these colors. Instead, a particular color on the screen is specified by the intensity of each of the primary colors (red, green, and blue) forming the color. The intensity of each of the three primary colors on this display range from 0 to 63, yielding $64 \times 64 \times 64 = 262{,}144$ different colors.

   Your data abstraction package should include the following operations.

```
function "+" (Left : in Color_Type; Right : in Color_Type) return Color_Type;
   -- This function returns the color that is the sum of two colors.
   -- If the sum of two primary component intensities is greater than 63,
   -- the sum is set to 63.

function "-" (Left : in Color_Type; Right : in Color_Type) return Color_Type;
   -- This function returns the color that is the difference between two
   -- colors. If the difference of two primary component intensities is
   -- less than 0, the difference is set to 0.

function "*" (Left : in Natural ; Right : in Color_Type) return Color_Type;
   -- This function multiplies the components of a color by a
   -- dimensionless value. If a product of a component is greater
   -- than 63, the product is set to 63.

function "*" (Left : in Color_Type; Right : in Natural) return Color_Type;
   -- This function multiplies the components of a color by a
   -- dimensionless value. If a product of a component is greater
   -- than 63, the product is set to 63.

function Is_Neutral (Color : in Color_Type) return Boolean;
   -- This function returns True if the intensity values of the three
   -- primary components making up this color are all equal.

function Is_Primary (Color : in Color_Type) return Boolean;
   -- This function returns True if the intensity values of two of the
   -- three components are zero and the third is non-zero.

function Is_Secondary (Color : in Color_Type) return Boolean;
   -- This function returns True if the intensity values of two of the
   -- three components are equal and non-zero and the third is zero.

function Is_Pastel (Color : in Color_Type) return Boolean;
   -- This function returns True if the intensity values of all three
   -- components are greater than one half their maximum intensities.
```

Write a driver program to test your package.

4. Write a package that contains floating-point types for inches, feet, miles, centimeters, meters, and kilometers. The package should also contain conversion functions to convert values from one length type to another. Write a driver program to test your package. Why do we use types instead of subtypes for these six units? How would you classify this package?

CHAPTER

13

Recursion

GOALS

After reading this chapter, you should be able to

- explain what recursion is
- identify the base case(s) and the general case in a recursive definition
- write a recursive algorithm for a problem involving only simple variables
- write a recursive algorithm for a problem involving array variables

When we used scope tables in Chapter 6 to document the scope of identifiers, we noted that a statement in a procedure can call that same procedure. We discuss this process, called recursion, in this chapter. Recursion is a powerful technique that can often be used in place of iteration (loops). Some problems lend themselves to simple, elegant, recursive solutions that are exceedingly cumbersome to solve using loops.

Many of the older programming languages, such as FORTRAN, BASIC, and COBOL, do not allow recursion. Some languages are especially oriented to recursive algorithms—LISP is one of these. Ada lets us take our choice: We can implement both iterative and recursive algorithms in Ada.

Our examples are broken into two groups: problems that use only simple variables and problems that use array variables. If you are studying recursion before reading Chapter 11 on array types, then cover only the first set of examples and leave the rest until you have completed the chapter on array types.

What Is Recursion?

You may have seen a set of gaily painted Russian matryoshka dolls that fit inside one another. Inside the first doll is a smaller doll, inside of which is an even smaller doll, inside of which is yet a smaller doll, and so on. A recursive algorithm is like such a set of Russian dolls. It reproduces itself

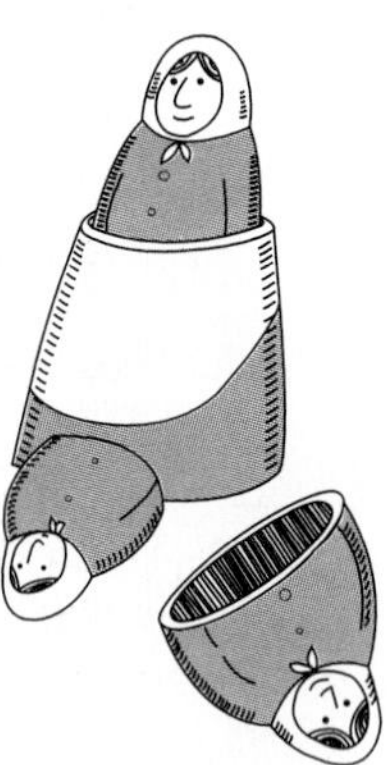

with smaller and smaller examples of itself until a solution is found (there are no more dolls).

In our discussion of scope in Chapter 6, we said that the ability of a function or a procedure to call itself was a process known as recursion. The call that a function or procedure makes to itself is a **recursive call.** The word *recursive* means "having the characteristic of coming up again, or repeating." In this case, a subprogram call is being repeated by the subprogram itself. Let's look at an example. We use the ** operator in Ada to raise a number to a given power. Some programming languages do not have such an operator. In these languages, we usually write a function whenever a program requires exponentiation. Here's what such a function might look like in Ada using iteration (a loop).

```
function Power (A : in Float;           -- Base number
               (N : in Positive)        -- Power to raise base to
                return Float is

-- This function computes X to the N power.  It is equivalent to A ** N.

   Result : Float;           -- Holds intermediate powers of A
   Count  : Positive;        -- Iteration counter
begin
   Result := 1.0;          -- Initialize product
   Count  := 1;            -- Initialize iteration counter
   Product_Loop:           -- Calculate A ** N
   loop                    -- Each iteration, multiply one more term
      exit Product_Loop when Count > N;
      Result := Result * A;
      Count := Count + 1;
   end loop Product_Loop;
   return Result;
end Power;
```

Recursive call A subprogram call in which the subprogram being called is the same as the one making the call.

Let's rewrite function Power using recursion. To compute

$$A^N$$

where N is a nonzero positive integer, the formula is

$$A^N = A \times A \times A \times \ldots \times A$$

Another way of writing this relationship is

$$A^N = A \times (A \times A \times \ldots \times A)$$

or

$$A^N = A \times (A^{N-1})$$

If we know what A^{N-1} is, we can calculate A^N, because $A^N = A \times (A^{N-1})$. We can reduce A^{N-1} further.

$$A^N = A \times (A \times (A \times \ldots \times A))$$

or

$$A^N = A \times (A \times (A^{N-2}))$$

If we know the value of A^{N-2}, we can calculate A^{N-1} and thus calculate A^N, since $A^N = A(A(A^{N-2}))$. We can continue this process until the innermost expression becomes A^1. We know the value of A^1 without needing to perform any calculation; it's A.

We express this reasoning in the following recursive function Power, which has the same two parameters as the iterative function, A and N. (In Programming Warm-up Exercise 1, you will be asked to rewrite this function so that it works when N = 0.) Compare this implementation with the iterative version.

```
function Power (A : in Float;          -- Base number
                (N : in Positive)      -- Power to raise base to
                 return Float is

-- This function computes A to the N power.  It is equivalent to A ** N.

   Result : Float;

begin
   if N = 1 then
      Result := A;
   else
      Result := A * Power (A, N-1);
   end if;
   return Result;
end Power;
```

Each call to function Power in the statement Result := A * Power (A, N − 1) passes the actual parameters to a new call of the function. The value of A remains the same for each call of Power, but the value for N is decreased by 1 for each call until N − 1 becomes 1. The call to function Power where N is 1 stops the calling chain because we can now return an answer, A. The value A is passed back to the invocation of function Power that made the last call. The value of Power for that call can then be calculated and passed back to the invocation that made the call. This process continues until the value of Power can be passed back to the original call.

Let's see what happens with a call to Power when A = 2.0 and N = 3. The statement

```
Num := Power (2.0, 3);
```

in the body of the calling program assigns the value returned by the call to the variable Num. The value returned by Power and assigned to Num should be 8.0 (2.0 to the third power, or 2.0 × 2.0 × 2.0).

For illustrative purposes let's assume that each call to Power creates a complete new version of Power. Each box in Figure 13-1 represents the code for Power listed above it, along with the values of the actual parameters for that version. The figure and the code illustrate that the Power function does what it is supposed to do. Each version of Power gets its parameters from the function call in the version above it in the diagram. There is no confusion as to which N is being used because N is a formal parameter.

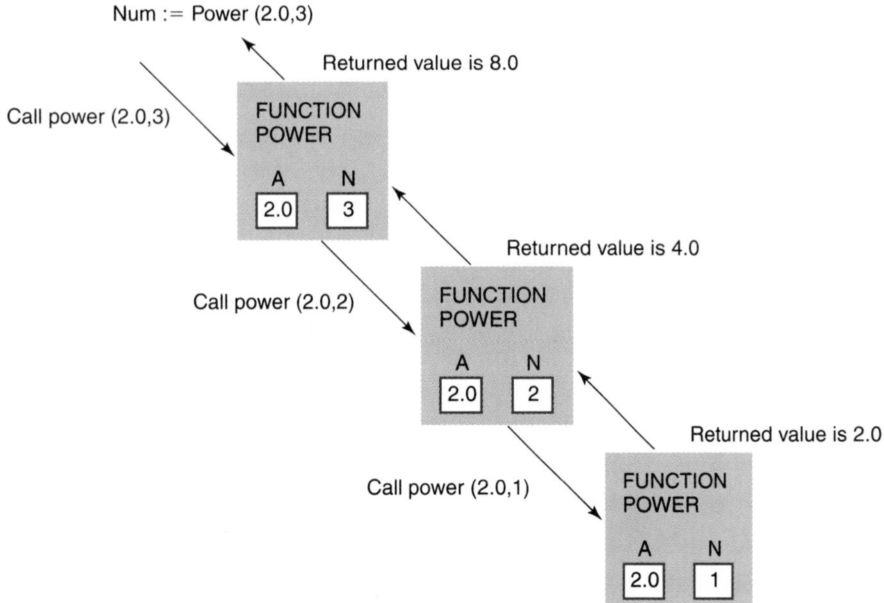

Figure 13-1 Recursion in Power (2.0, 3)

An accidental use of recursion occurs when the function name is used within the function as a variable name. Such use usually results in a syntax error because most functions have a parameter list, and, if you mistakenly use the function name as a variable in an expression, the compiler spots the absence of parameters. If no syntax error is present, however, the likely result is a condition called **infinite recursion,** which is the recursive equivalent of an infinite loop. In actuality, recursive calls can't go on forever. Each time a subprogram calls itself, it uses a little more of the computer's memory space to store the old values of the variables. Eventually, all the memory space will be used and the exception STORAGE_ERROR is raised.

Infinite recursion The situation in which a subprogram calls itself over and over continuously.

Let's use our example to illustrate the important concepts of programming with recursion. The problem is to calculate the result of taking a float value to a positive power. We noted that the formula for exponentiation could be rewritten successively as follows:

$A^N = A \times A \times A \times A \times \ldots \times A$ *N times*

$A^N = A \times (A \times A \times A \times \ldots \times A)$ $(N - 1)$ *times*

$A^N = A \times A \times (A \times A \times \ldots \times A)$ $(N - 2)$ *times*

Another way of writing the formula would be

$A^N = A \times (A^{N-1})$

This definition is a classic **recursive definition:** The definition is given in terms of a simpler version of itself.

A^N is defined in terms of multiplying A times A^{N-1}. How is A^{N-1} defined? Why, as $A \times A^{N-2}$, of course! And A^{N-2} is $A \times A^{N-3}$, A^{N-3} is $A \times A^{N-4}$, and so on. In this example, "in terms of simpler versions of itself" means that the exponent is decremented each time.

Recursive definition A definition in which something is defined in terms of simpler versions of itself.

When does the process stop? When we have reached a case where we know the answer without resorting to a recursive definition. In this example, it is the case where N equals 1: A^1 is A. The case (or cases) for which an answer is explicitly known is called the **base case;** the case for which the solution is expressed in terms of a smaller version of itself is called the **recursive** or **general case.** A **recursive algorithm** is an algorithm that expresses the solution in terms of a call to itself—a recursive call. A recursive algorithm must terminate; that is, it must have a base case.

Base case The case for which the solution can be stated nonrecursively.

General case The case for which the solution is expressed in terms of a smaller version of itself. Also known as *recursive case.*

Recursive algorithm A solution that is expressed in terms of a) smaller instances of itself and b) a base case.

The following program reads in a number and an exponent, calls function Power to calculate the value of the number raised to the exponent, and prints the result. It shows function Power with the base case and the recursive call marked.

```
with Ada.Float_Text_IO;
with Ada.Integer_Text_IO;
with Ada.Text_IO;
procedure Exponentiation is

   function Power (A : in Float;          -- Base number
                   N : in Positive)       -- Power to raise base to
                   return Float is
      Result : Float;
   begin
      if N = 1 then
         Result := A;  <------------------------------------ Base case
      else
         Result := A * Power (A => A, N => N-1);  <-------- Recursive call
      end if;
      return Result;
   end Power;

----------------------------------------------

   Number   : Float;          -- Number that is being raised to power
   Exponent : Positive;       -- Power the number is raised to
   Answer   : Float;          -- Result of raising the number to the power
```

```
begin  -- Program Exponentiation
   Ada.Text_IO.Put_Line ("Enter a float number and exponent");
   Ada.Float_Text_IO.Get (Number);
   Ada.Integer_Text_IO.Get (Exponent);
   Answer := Power (A => Number, N => Exponent); <------ Nonrecursive call
   Ada.Float_Text_IO.Put (Answer);
end Exponentiation;
```

Let's trace the execution of this recursive function, with Number equal to 2.0 and Exponent equal to 3. We use a new format to trace recursive routines: We number the calls and then discuss what is happening in paragraph form. For illustrative purposes, we assume that each call creates a new copy of the function Power.

Call 1: Power is called with actual parameters Number (equal to 2.0) and Exponent (equal to 3). These are copied to the formal parameters A and N, respectively. Therefore, A is equal to 2.0 and N is equal to 3. N is not equal to 1, so Power is called with A and N − 1 as actual parameters. Execution of Call 1 to the function halts until an answer is sent back from this recursive call.

Call 2: A is equal to 2.0 and N is equal to 2. Because N is not equal to 1, the function Power is called again, this time with A and N − 1 as actual parameters. Execution of Call 2 to the function halts until an answer is sent back from this recursive call.

Call 3: A is equal to 2.0 and N is equal to 1. Because N is equal to 1, the value of A is stored in Result. Execution of the return statement ends the execution of Call 3 to the function and Result (2.0) is returned back to the place in the statement from which the call was made.

Call 2: This call to the function can now complete the statement that contained the recursive call because Power now has a value. This value (which is 2.0) is multiplied by A and stored in Result. Call 2 to the function has finished executing, and Result (4.0) is returned to the place in the statement from which the call was made.

Call 1: This call to the function can now complete the statement that contained the recursive call because Power now has a value. This value (which is 4.0) is multiplied by A and stored in Result. Call 1 to the function has finished executing, and Result (8.0) is returned to the place in the statement from which the call was made. Because the first call (the nonrecursive call) has now been completed, this Result is the final value of the function Power.

This trace is summarized in Figure 13-2. Each box represents a call to the function Power. The values for the parameters for that call are shown in each box.

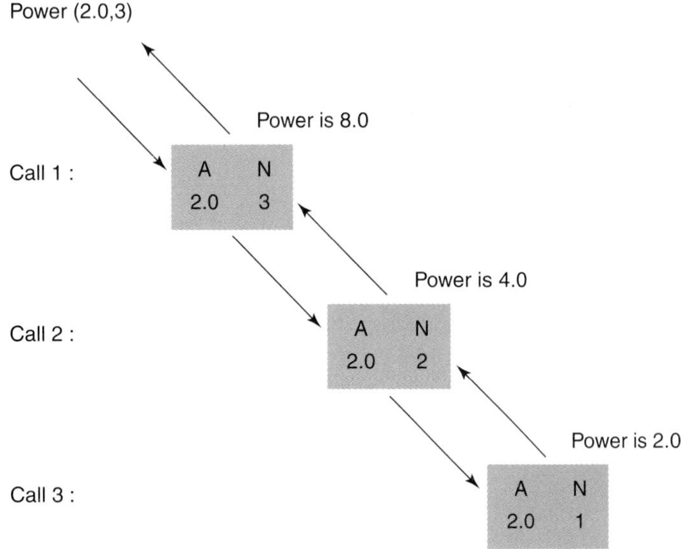

FIGURE 13-2 Execution of Power (2.0, 3)

What happens if there is no base case? We have infinite recursion, the equivalent of an infinite loop. For example, if the statement

```
if N = 1 then
```

were omitted, Power would be called over and over again. Eventually, the program would halt with a STORAGE_ERROR exception.

Recursive Algorithms with Simple Variables

Let's look at the classic example for learning recursion—calculating a factorial. In Chapter 6 we wrote a function that used a loop to calculate factorial. Recall that the factorial of a number N (written $N!$) is N multiplied by $N - 1$, $N - 2$, $N - 3$, and so on. Another way of expressing factorial is

$$N! = N \times (N-1)!$$

This expression looks like a recursive definition. $(N - 1)!$ is a smaller instance of $N!$—it takes one less multiplication to calculate $(N - 1)!$ than it does to calculate $N!$. If we can find a base case, we can write a recursive algorithm. Fortunately, we don't have to look too far; 0! is defined to be 1.

```
Factorial
if N is 0 then
  the result is 1
else
  the result is N * Factorial (N-1)
end if
```

We can code this algorithm directly as a function.

```
function Factorial (N : in Natural) return Positive is
   Result : Positive;
begin
   if N = 0 then
      Result := 1;
   else
      Result := N * Factorial (N - 1);
   end if;
   return Result;
end Factorial;
```

Let's trace this function with an original N of 4.

Call 1: N is 4. Because N is not 0, the else branch is taken. The assignment statement cannot be completed until the recursive call to function Factorial with N − 1 as the actual parameter has been completed.

Call 2: N is 3. Because N is not 0, the else branch is taken. The assignment statement cannot be completed until the recursive call to function Factorial with N − 1 as the actual parameter has been completed.

Call 3: N is 2. Because N is not 0, the else branch is taken. The assignment statement cannot be completed until the recursive call to function Factorial with N − 1 as the actual parameter has been completed.

Call 4: N is 1. Because N is not 0, the else branch is taken. The assignment statement cannot be completed until the recursive call to function Factorial with N − 1 as the actual parameter has been completed.

Call 5: N is 0. Because N is equal to 0, Result is set to 1. Result is returned by Call 5.

Call 4: The assignment statement in Call 4 can now be completed. Result is Factorial times N. Because a value of 1 was returned for Factorial and N in this call has a value of 1, Result is assigned the value 1 and returned. Call 4 is finished.

Call 3: The assignment statement in Call 3 can now be completed. Result is Factorial times N. Because a value of 1 was returned for Factorial and N in this call has a value of 2, Result is assigned the value 2 and returned. Call 3 is finished.

Call 2: The assignment statement in Call 2 can now be completed. Result is Factorial times N. Because a value of 2 was returned for Factorial and N in this call has a value of 3, Result is assigned the value 6 and returned. Call 2 is finished.

Call 1: The assignment statement in Call 1 can now be completed. Result is Factorial times N. Because a value of 6 was returned for Factorial and N in this call has a value of 4, Result is assigned the value 24 and returned. Because this is the last of the calls to Factorial, the recursive process is over. The value 24 is returned as the final value of the call to function Factorial with an actual parameter of 4. Figure 13-3 summarizes the execution of function Factorial with an actual parameter of 4.

Let's organize what we have done in these two solutions into an outline for writing recursive algorithms.

1. Understand the problem. (We threw this step in for good measure: It is always the first step.)
2. Determine the base case(s).
3. Determine the recursive case(s).

In the next section we'll apply this outline to obtain a recursive solution to another simple problem.

Fibonacci Numbers

Understand the Problem The following sequence of numbers is called the Fibonacci sequence.

1, 1, 2, 3, 5, 8, 13, 21, 34, 55, . . .

FIGURE 13-3 Execution of Factorial (4)

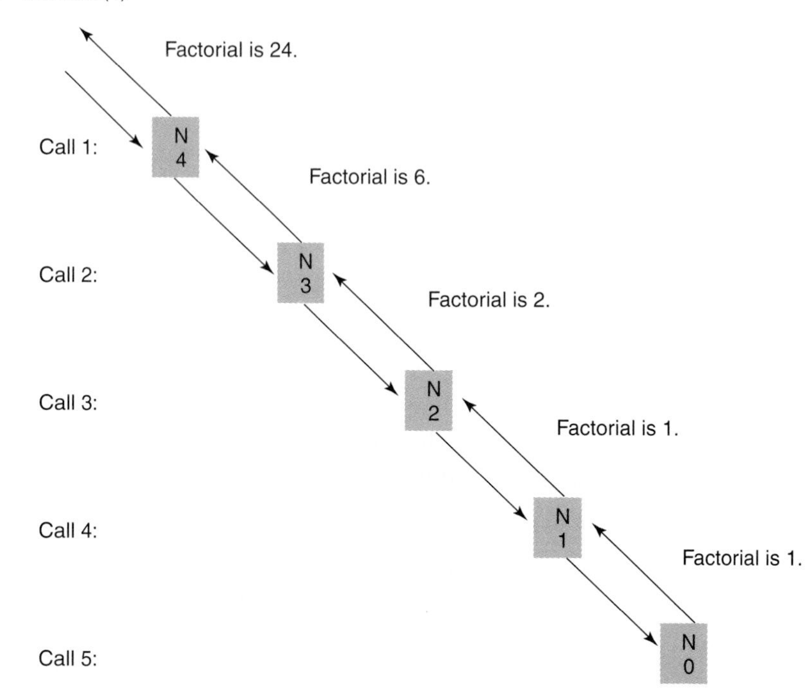

The numbers in this sequence are called Fibonacci numbers. Each Fibonacci number in this sequence is the sum of the two previous numbers. Fibonacci numbers are often found in nature. In fact the sequence was first used by Leonardo Fibonacci of Pisa, a medieval mathematician, to determine the number of rabbits that would be produced in a hutch in *N* months starting with a single pair of newborn rabbits. Leonardo made the following assumptions in this problem.

1. Newborn rabbits become adults (are able to breed) one month after birth.
2. There are an equal number of male and female rabbits.
3. Each pair of adult rabbits produces one pair of newborn rabbits each month.
4. No rabbits die.

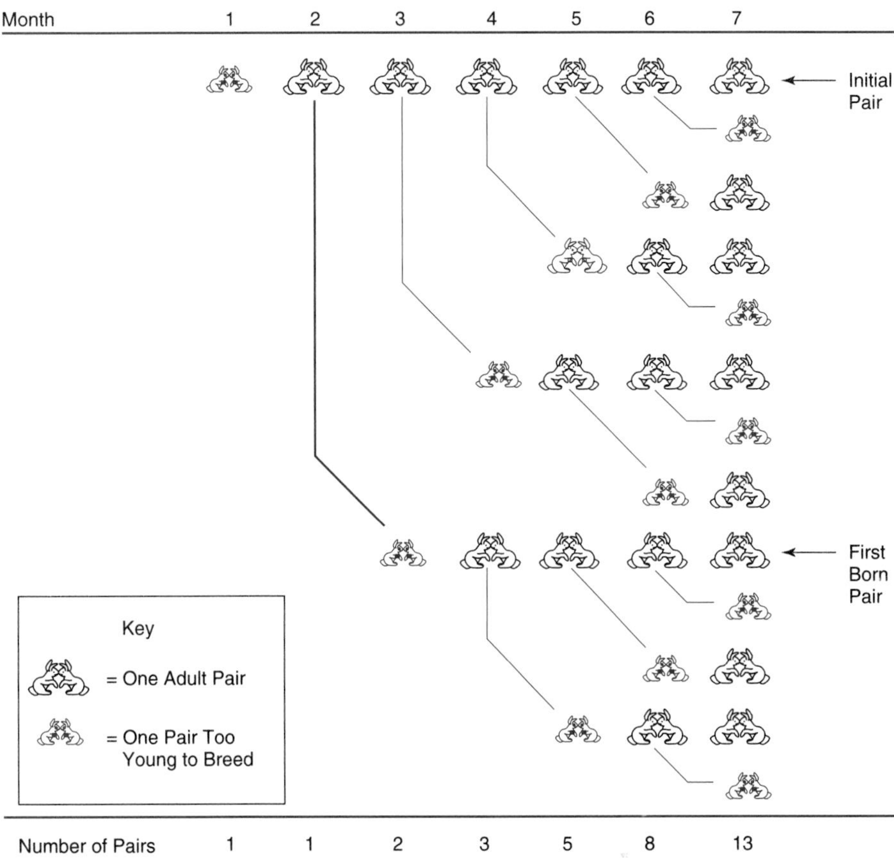

FIGURE 13-4 The Pattern of Rabbit Reproduction over Seven Months

Figure 13-4 illustrates the pattern of reproduction in the hutch for seven months. Each row of the figure traces one pair of rabbits through the months. The first row traces the initial pair of rabbits. The pair is young during month 1 and adult in the remaining months. The ninth row traces the first pair of offspring of the initial pair. They are juvenile in month 3 and adult in the remaining months. The number of rows under any given month is the number of pairs in the hutch that month. The monthly totals are listed at the bottom of the figure.

The number of pairs of rabbits each month is equal to the number of pairs last month plus the number of pairs born this month (which is equal to the number of pairs two months previous). This is a Fibonacci sequence. To know how many rabbits are in the hutch after a year, we just determine the 13th Fibonacci number.

Determine the Base Case The first number in the Fibonacci sequence is always 1. This number looks like a good base case. We can state it as:

$$F_1 = 1$$

Determine the Recursive Case The value of the *n*th Fibonacci number is equal to the sum of the two previous Fibonacci numbers. We can state this relation as:

$$F_n = F_{n-1} + F_{n-2}$$

F_n is calculated from two smaller Fibonacci numbers. For example, F_5 is calculated from F_4 and F_3.

There is a problem in using this recursive case for calculating F_2. Calculating F_2 requires the value of the first Fibonacci number and the zeroth Fibonacci number, a number that is not defined. The solution to this problem is to add a second base case. Both the first and second Fibonacci numbers are 1. Here is a summary of our base cases and recursive case.

Fibonacci
if *N* is 1 or 2 then
  the result is 1
else
  the result is Fibonacci (N − 1) + Fibonacci (N − 2)
end if

And here is an Ada function to determine a particular Fibonacci number.

```
function Fibonacci (N : in Positive ) return Positive is
   Result : Positive;
begin
   if N <= 2 then
      Result := 1;
   else
      Result := Fibonacci (N-1) + Fibonacci (N-2);
   end if;
end Fibonacci;
```

We have used the power, factorial, and Fibonacci algorithms to demonstrate recursion because they are easy to visualize. In practice, one would never want to calculate any of these functions using the recursive solution. The iterative solutions are more efficient because starting a new iteration of a loop is a faster operation than calling a function or a procedure. Each call to a function or procedure also requires additional memory. The recursive Fibonacci algorithm is particularly inefficient because the calculations to determine F_{n-2} have already been done once when F_{n-1} was determined.

In the next section we examine a more complicated problem—one in which the recursive solution is much simpler than the iterative solution.

Towers of Hanoi

One of your first toys may have been three pegs with colored disks of different diameters. If so, you probably spent countless hours moving the disks from one peg to another. If we put some constraints on how the disks can be moved, we have a game called the Towers of Hanoi. When the game begins, all the disks are on the first peg in order by size, with the smallest on the top. The object of the game is to move the disks, one at a time, to the third peg. The catch is that you cannot place a disk on top of one that is smaller in diameter. You can use the middle peg as an auxiliary peg, but it must be empty at the beginning and the end of the game.

To get a feel for how this might be done, let's look at some sketches of what the configuration must be at certain points if a solution is possible. We use four disks. The beginning configuration is

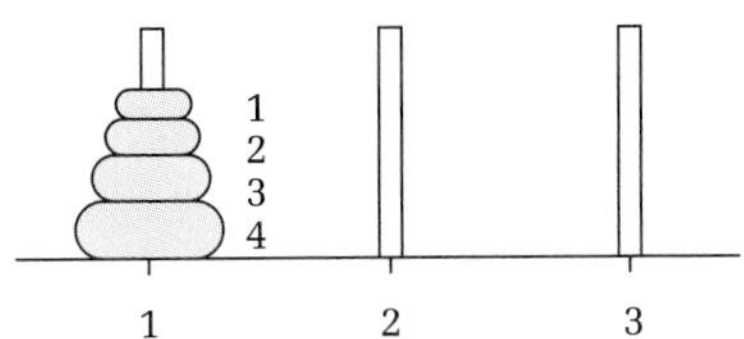

To move the largest disk (disk 4) to peg 3, we must move the three smaller disks to peg 2. Then disk 4 can be moved into its final place.

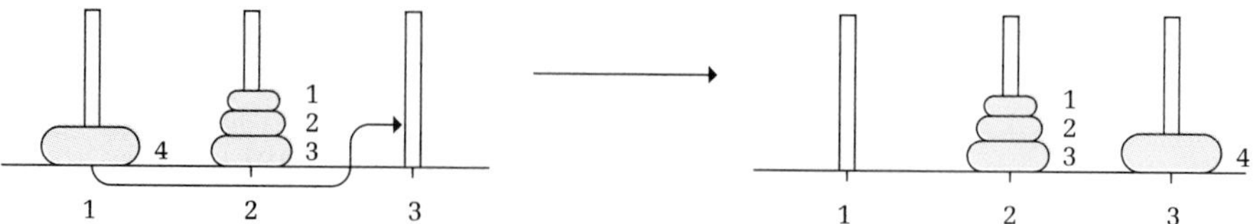

Let's assume that we can do this. Now, to move the next largest disk (disk 3) into place, we must move the two disks on top of it onto an auxiliary peg (peg 1 in this case).

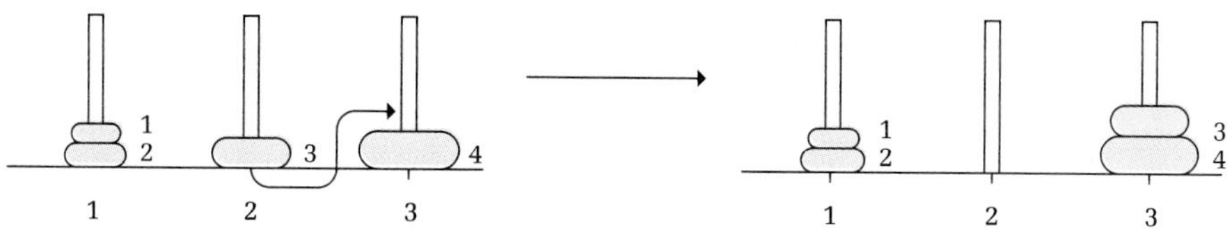

To get disk 2 into place, we must move disk 1 to another peg, freeing disk 2 to be moved to its place on peg 3.

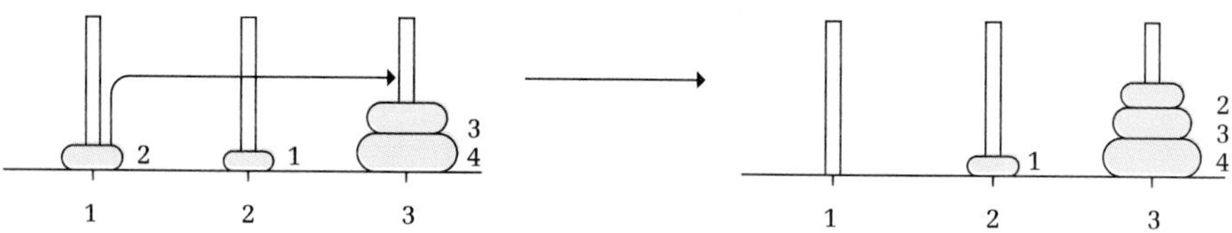

We can now move the last disk (disk 1) into its final place, finishing the game.

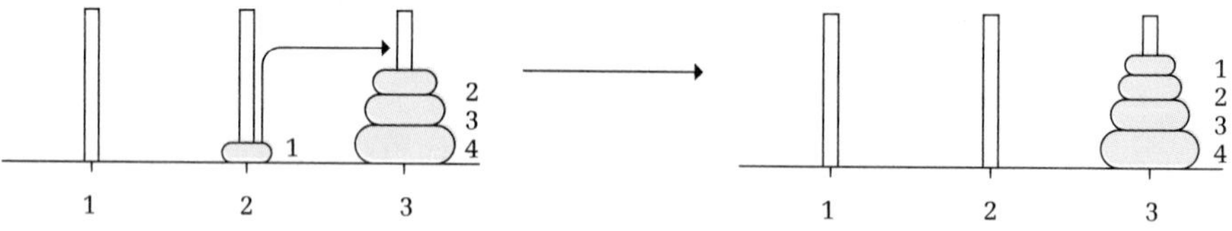

Notice that, to free disk 4, we had to move three disks to another peg. To free disk 3, we had to move two disks to another peg. To free disk 2, we had to move one disk to another peg. This sounds like a recursive algorithm: To free the *N*th disk, we have to move $N - 1$ disks. We can think of each stage as beginning again with three pegs, but with one fewer disk each time. Let's see whether we can summarize this process, using N instead of an actual number.

To Move *N* Disks from Peg 1 to Peg 3
Move $N - 1$ disks from peg 1 to peg 2
Move N^{th} disk from peg 1 to peg 3
Move $N - 1$ disks from peg 2 to peg 3

This algorithm certainly sounds simple; we would think there must be more, but this is really all there is to it.

Let's write a recursive procedure that implements this algorithm. We can't actually move disks, of course, but we can print out a message to do so. Notice that the beginning peg, the ending peg, and the auxiliary peg keep changing during the algorithm. To make the algorithm easier to follow, we call the pegs Begin_Peg, End_Peg, and Aux_Peg. These three pegs, along with the number of disks on the beginning peg, are the parameters of the procedure.

We have the recursive or general case; what about a base case? How do we know when to stop the recursive process? The clue is in the expression "Move *N* disks." If we don't have any disks to move, we don't have anything to do. We are finished with that stage. Therefore, when the number of disks equals 0, we do nothing (that is, return).

```
subtype Peg_Num is Integer range 1..3;
   .
   .
   .
procedure Towers
           (Disks     : in Natural;      -- Number of disks to move
            Begin_Peg : in Peg_Num;      -- Peg containing disks to move
            Aux_Peg   : in Peg_Num;      -- Peg used to hold disks temporarily
            End_Peg   : in Peg_Num) is   -- Peg receiving disks being moved
begin
   if Disks > 0 then                   -- Check for base case

      -- Move Disks-1 disks from Begin_Peg to Aux_Peg using End_Peg
      -- to hold disks temporarily
      Towers (Disks     => Disks - 1,
              Begin_Peg => Begin_Peg,
              Aux_Peg   => End_Peg,
              End_Peg   => Aux_Peg);
```

```
      -- Display instructions to move one disk
      Ada.Text_IO.Put ("Move disk ");
      Ada.Integer_Text_IO.Put (Item => Disks, Width => 2);
      Ada.Text_IO.Put (" from ");
      Ada.Integer_Text_IO.Put (Item => Begin_Peg, Width => 2);
      Ada.Text_IO.Put (" to ");
      Ada.Integer_Text_IO.Put (Item => End_Peg, Width => 2);
      Ada.Text_IO.New_Line;

      -- Move Disks-1 disks from Aux_Peg to End_Peg using Begin_Peg
      -- to hold disks temporarily
      Towers (Disks     => Disks - 1,
              Begin_Peg => Aux_Peg,
              Aux_Peg   => Begin_Peg,
              End_Peg   => End_Peg);
   end if;
end Towers;
```

It's hard to believe that such a simple algorithm actually works, but we'll prove it to you. Following is a driver program that calls procedure Towers. We have added some Put statements to procedure Towers so that you can see the values of the actual parameters with each recursive call. Because there are two recursive calls within procedure Towers, we have indicated which recursive statement issued the call.

```
with Ada.Integer_Text_IO;
with Ada.Text_IO;
procedure Test_Towers is

   -- This program reads in a number of disks from the console and calls
   -- procedure Towers to move them from Peg #1 to Peg #3.

   subtype Peg_Num is Integer range 1..3;

   ----------------------------------------------------------------------
   procedure Towers
           (Disks     : in Natural;        -- Number of disks to move
            Begin_Peg : in Peg_Num;        -- Peg containing disks to move
            Aux_Peg   : in Peg_Num;        -- Peg used to hold disks temporarily
            End_Peg   : in Peg_Num) is     -- Peg receiving disks being moved

   -- This recursive procedure moves the number of disks in Disks
   -- from Begin_Peg to End_Peg. All but one of the disks are moved
   -- from Begin_Peg to Aux_Peg, the last disk is moved from Begin_Peg
   -- to End_Peg, then the disks are moved from Aux_Peg to End_Peg.
   -- The subgoals of moving disks to and from Aux_Peg are what involve
   -- recursion.
```

```
   begin
      -- Display the parameters to aid in tracing this recursive procedure
      Ada.Integer_Text_IO.Put (Item => Disks,      Width => 7);
      Ada.Integer_Text_IO.Put (Item => Begin_Peg, Width => 9);
      Ada.Integer_Text_IO.Put (Item => Aux_Peg,    Width => 7);
      Ada.Integer_Text_IO.Put (Item => End_Peg,    Width => 7);
      Ada.Text_IO.New_Line;

      if Disks > 0 then                          -- Check for base case

         -- Move Disks-1 disks from Begin_Peg to Aux_Peg
         Ada.Text_IO.Put ("From  first:");  -- Display call location
         Towers (Disks     => Disks - 1,
                 Begin_Peg => Begin_Peg,
                 Aux_Peg   => End_Peg,
                 End_Peg   => Aux_Peg);

         -- Display instructions to move one disk
         Ada.Text_IO.Set_Col (To => 47);
         Ada.Text_IO.Put (" move disk ");
         Ada.Integer_Text_IO.Put (Item => Disks, Width => 2);
         Ada.Text_IO.Put (" from ");
         Ada.Integer_Text_IO.Put (Item => Begin_Peg, Width => 2);
         Ada.Text_IO.Put (" to ");
         Ada.Integer_Text_IO.Put (Item => End_Peg, Width => 2);
         Ada.Text_IO.New_Line;

         -- Move Disks-1 disks from Aux_Peg to End_Peg
         Ada.Text_IO.Put ("From second:");  -- Display call location
         Towers (Disks    => Disks - 1,
                 Begin_Peg => Aux_Peg,
                 Aux_Peg   => Begin_Peg,
                 End_Peg   => End_Peg);
      end if;
   end Towers;

-----------------------------------------------
   Disks : Natural;     -- Number of disks on starting peg

begin -- Test_Towers
   Ada.Text_IO.Put_Line ("Enter number of Disks you have on Peg #1.");
   Ada.Integer_Text_IO.Get (Disks);
   Ada.Text_IO.Put ("OUTPUT WITH ");
   Ada.Integer_Text_IO.Put (Item => Disks, Width => 3);
   Ada.Text_IO.Put_Line (" DISKS");
   Ada.Text_IO.New_Line;
   Ada.Text_IO.Put_Line
        ("CALLED FROM    DISKS    BEGIN  AUXIL.   END   INSTRUCTIONS");
   Ada.Text_IO.New_Line;
```

```
      Ada.Text_IO.Put ("Original   :");
      Towers (Disks    => Disks,
              Begin_Peg => 1,
              Aux_Peg   => 2,
              End_Peg   => 3);
   end Test_Towers;
```

The output from a run with three disks follows. "Original:" means that the actual parameters listed beside it are from the nonrecursive call, which is the first call to procedure Towers. "From first:" means that the parameters listed are for a call issued from the first recursive call statement in the procedure. "From second:" means that the parameters listed are for a call issued from the second recursive call statement in the procedure. A call cannot be issued from the second recursive statement until the preceding call from the first recursive statement has completed execution.

```
OUTPUT WITH   3 DISKS

CALLED FROM     DISKS    BEGIN  AUXIL.   END    INSTRUCTIONS

Original   :      3        1      2       3
From  first:      2        1      3       2
From  first:      1        1      2       3
From  first:      0        1      3       2
                                                 move disk  1 from  1 to  3
From second:      0        2      1       3
                                                 move disk  2 from  1 to  2
From second:      1        3      1       2
From  first:      0        3      2       1
                                                 move disk  1 from  3 to  2
From second:      0        1      3       2
                                                 move disk  3 from  1 to  3
From second:      2        2      1       3
From  first:      1        2      3       1
From  first:      0        2      1       3
                                                 move disk  1 from  2 to  1
From second:      0        3      2       1
                                                 move disk  2 from  2 to  3
From second:      1        1      2       3
From  first:      0        1      3       2
                                                 move disk  1 from  1 to  3
From second:      0        2      1       3
```

Recursive Algorithms with Array Variables

In our definition of a recursive algorithm, we said there were two cases: the recursive or general case and the base case for which an answer can be expressed nonrecursively. In the general case for all our algorithms so far, a parameter was expressed in terms of a smaller value each time. When structured variables are used, the recursive case is often in terms of a smaller structure rather than a smaller value; the base case occurs when there are no values left to process in the structure.

To show what we mean, let's examine the recursive definition for printing the components in a one-dimensional array of *N* components.

Print Array

```
if the array contains components
  Display the value of the first component in the array
  Print array of N - 1 components
else
  Do nothing
end if
```

The recursive case is to print the values in an array that is one component smaller; that is, the size of the array gets smaller with each recursive call. The base case is when the length of the array becomes 0; there are no more components to print.

By using an unconstrained array type, array attributes, and array slices, the procedure takes just one parameter.

```
procedure Print (List: Integer_Array) is
begin
   if List'Length > 0 then
      -- Display the value of the first component in the array
      Ada.Integer_Text_IO.Put (Item => List (List'First));
      -- Display the rest of the array
      Print (List=> List (List'First+1 .. List'Last));
   end if;
end Print;
```

Here is a code walk-through with the array shown at the top of page 790.

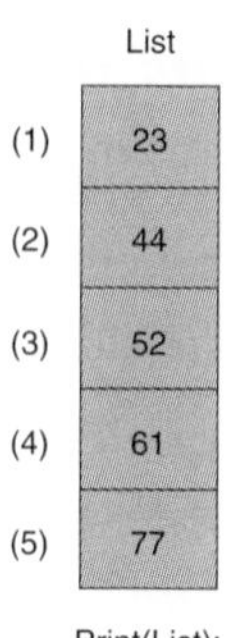

Call 1: List'First is 1 and List'Last is 5. Because List'Length is 5, the value in List(List'First) (which is 23) is printed. Execution of Call 1 halts while the array from List'First + 1 (which is 2) to List'Last (which is 5) is printed.

Call 2: List'First is 2 and List'Last is 5. Because List'Length is 4, the value in List(List'First) (which is 44) is printed. Execution of Call 2 halts while the array from List'First + 1 (which is 3) to List'Last (which is 5) is printed.

Call 3: List'First is 3 and List'Last is 5. Because List'Length is 3, the value in List(List'First) (which is 52) is printed. Execution of Call 3 halts while the array from List'First + 1 (which is 4) to List'Last (which is 5) is printed.

Call 4: List'First is 4 and List'Last is 5. Because List'Length is 2, the value in List(List'First) (which is 61) is printed. Execution of this call halts while the array from List'First + 1 (which is 5) to List'Last (which is 5) is printed.

Call 5: List'First is 5 and List'Last is 5. Because List'Length is 1, the value in List(List'First) (which is 77) is printed. Execution of this call halts while the array from List'First + 1 (which is 6) to List'Last (which is 5) is printed.

Call 6: List'First is 6 and List'Last is 5. Because List'Length is now 0, the execution of this call is now complete.

Call 5: Execution of Call 5 is now complete.

Call 4: Execution of Call 4 is now complete.

Call 3: Execution of Call 3 is now complete.

Call 2: Execution of Call 2 is now complete.

Call 1: Execution of Call 1 is now complete.

Figure 13-5 shows the execution of procedure Print with the values of the parameter's attributes for each call.

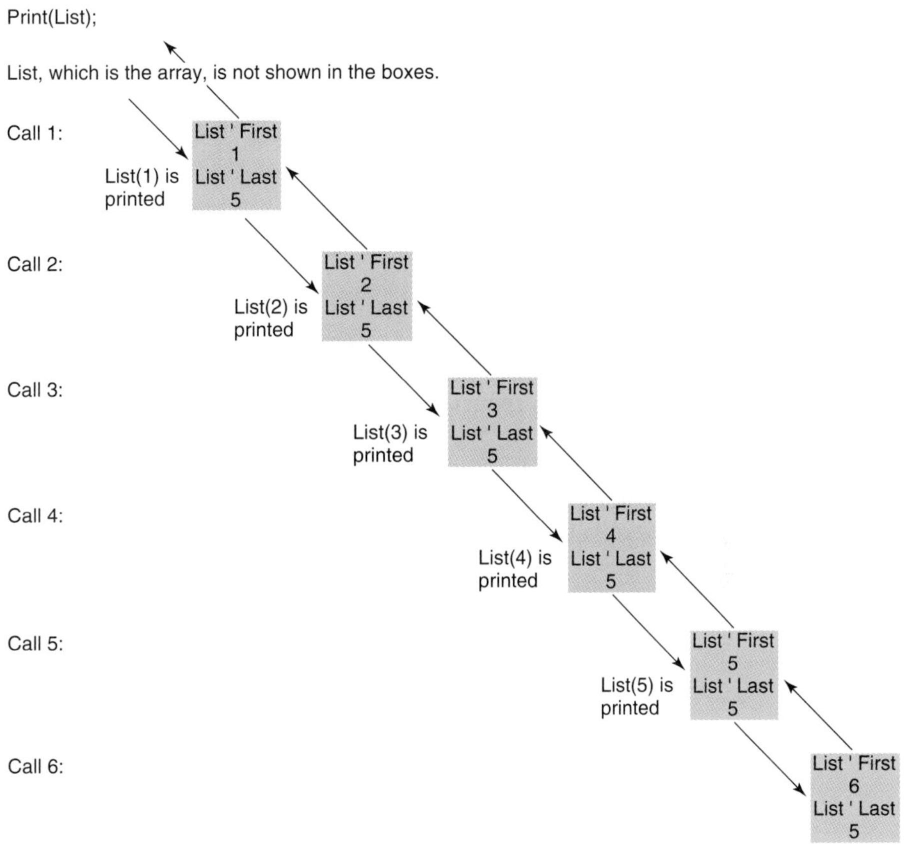

FIGURE 13-5 Execution of Print (List)

Print(List);

List, which is the array, is not shown in the boxes.

Call 1: List'First 1, List'Last 5 — List(1) is printed

Call 2: List'First 2, List'Last 5 — List(2) is printed

Call 3: List'First 3, List'Last 5 — List(3) is printed

Call 4: List'First 4, List'Last 5 — List(4) is printed

Call 5: List'First 5, List'Last 5 — List(5) is printed

Call 6: List'First 6, List'Last 5

Notice that, once the deepest call (the call with the highest number) was reached, each of the calls before it returned without doing anything. When no statements are executed after the return from the recursive call to the procedure or function, the recursion is known as *tail recursion*. Tail recursion usually indicates that we can easily solve the problem with iteration. We used the array example because it made the recursive process easy to visualize; in practice, an array should be printed iteratively.

What happens if we interchange the order of the two statements in the if statement in procedure Print? In this version there is something to do after the recursive call. Exam Preparation Exercise 13 asks you to trace this new version.

In the next sections we look at other examples of recursion involving arrays.

Sequential Search

There were several iterative search algorithms in Chapter 12 that could be done with recursion. As an example, we look at the sequential search of an unordered list. The general case in such an algorithm is the same as that used in the recursive print array algorithm. We search (rather than print) a smaller array. There are two base cases that we must include. Recursion is terminated if we find the item that we are looking for or if the array we are searching is empty. In the second base case, the item is not in the array. Here is the code for a recursive search of an unordered array.

```
procedure Search (List  : in  Item_Array;     -- List to be searched
                  Item  : in  Item_Type;      -- The item being searched for
                  Found : out Boolean;        -- True if the item is found
                  Index : out Integer) is     -- Location of item if found

   -- List is searched for Item.  If Item is found, Found is True and
   -- Index gives the location.  Otherwise Found is False and Index
   -- is List'Last + 1.

begin
   if List'Length = 0 then                   -- 1st base case, list is empty
      Found := False;
      Index := List'Last + 1;
   elsif List (List'First) = Item then       -- 2nd base case, the first
      Found := True;                         -- component contains the item
      Index := List'First;
   else                                                        -- Didn't find
      Search (List  => List (List'First+1..List'Last),         -- item; search
              Item  => Item,                                   -- rest of list
              Found => Found,
              Index => Index);
   end if;
end Search;
```

Try tracing this procedure using the array of five components that we used to trace procedure Print. Try cases in which the item is the first in the list, in the middle of the list, at the end of the list, and not in the list.

This procedure uses tail recursion, an indication that the iterative solution given in Chapter 12 is as good.

Binary Search

When the list is ordered, a binary search is usually much faster than a sequential search. The recursive binary search algorithm is simpler than the iterative version you learned in Chapter 12. The base cases in this algorithm are the same as the sequential search. The search terminates when we find the item we are looking for or the list contains no items. However, instead of checking to see whether the first component in the list matches our item, we check the middle element of the list. If the middle element is not the one we are looking for, we search either the lower half or the upper half. Here's the code.

```
procedure Binary_Search
                 (List  : in  Item_Array;      -- List to be searched
                  Item  : in  Item_Type;       -- The item being searched for
                  Found : out Boolean;         -- True if the item is found
                  Index : out Integer) is      -- Location of item if found

-- List is searched for Item.  If Item is found, Found is True
-- and Index gives the location.  Otherwise Found is False.
-- Assumption:  List is sorted in ascending order

   Middle : Integer;           -- Middle index

begin
   Middle := (List'First + List'Last) / 2;
   if List'Length = 0 then                 -- 1st base case, list is empty
      Found := False;
   elsif List(Middle) = Item then          -- 2nd base case, the middle
      Found := True;                       -- component contains the item
      Index := Middle;
   elsif Item < List(Middle) then
```

```
      -- Item is not in List(Middle..Last); search the bottom half
      Binary_Search (List => List (List'First..Middle-1),
                     Item  => Item,
                     Found => Found,
                     Index => Index);
   else
      -- Item is not in List(First..Middle); search the top half
      Binay_Search (List  => List (Middle+1..List'Last),
                    Item  => Item,
                    Found => Found,
                    Index => Index);
   end if;
end Binary_Search;
```

Notice that the array is reduced in size by half each time the procedure is called. Compare this to the sequential search, in which the list is reduced in size by a single component in each call of the sequential search. Figure 13-6 shows the execution of procedure Binary_Search with the values of the *in* mode parameters shown.

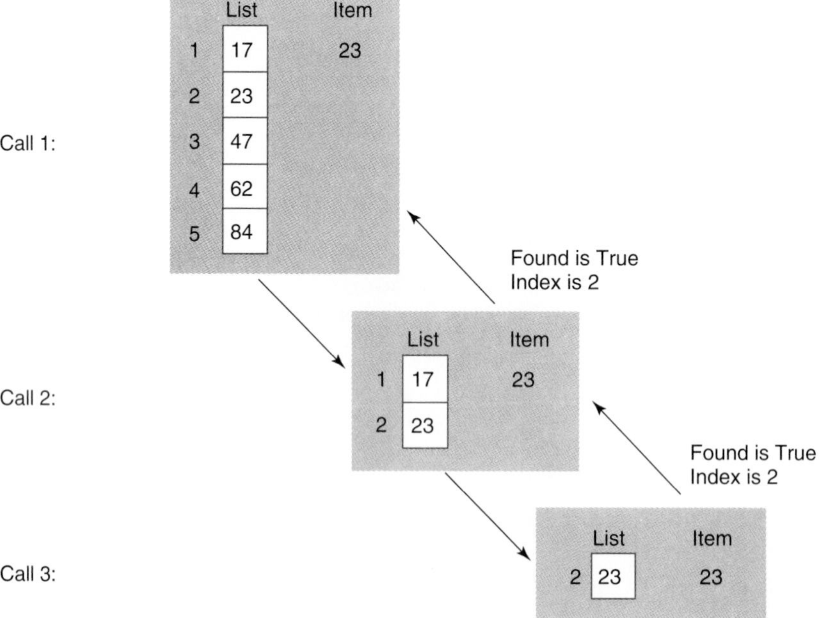

FIGURE 13-6 Execution of Binary_Search (List, Item, Found, Index)

Recursion or Iteration?

Recursion is an alternative form of program control. When we use iterative control structures, we make processes repeat by embedding code in a looping structure. In recursion, we make a process repeat by having a procedure or function call itself. We use a selection statement to control the repeated calls.

Each time the program makes a recursive call, it must assign space for all local variables and parameters copied. The overhead involved in any procedure or function call is often time consuming. If an iterative solution is obvious, use it—it will generally be more efficient. There are problems for which the recursive solution is clearer, such as the Towers of Hanoi problem. In these problems, use recursion—you'll finish your program faster and with fewer errors. Of course, if the definition of a problem is inherently recursive, then you should use a recursive solution.

Let's compare the code for the iterative and recursive versions of the binary search algorithm.

```
-- Iterative Solution
procedure Binary_Search
          (List  : in  Item_Array;
           Item  : in  Item_Type;
           Found : out Boolean;
           Index : out Integer) is

  First  : Integer;
  Last   : Integer;
  Middle : Integer;

begin
  First := List'First
  Last  := List'Last;
  Found := False;
  Search_Loop:
  loop
    exit Search_Loop when Found
                     or   First > Last;
```

```
-- Recursive Solution
procedure Binary_Search
          (List  : in  Item_Array;
           Item  : in  Item_Type;
           Found : out Boolean;
           Index : out Integer) is

  Middle : Integer;

begin
  Middle := (List'First + List'Last) / 2;
  if List'Length = 0 then
    Found := False;
  elsif List(Middle) = Item then
    Found := True;
    Index := Middle;
  elsif Item < List(Middle) then
```

```
    Middle := (First + Last) / 2;
    if Item < List(Middle) then
      Last := Middle - 1;
    elsif Item > List(Middle) then
      First := Middle + 1;
    else
      Found := True;
      Index := Middle;
    end if;
  end loop Search_Loop;
end Binary_Search;
```

```
    Found := False;     Binary_Search
  (List(List'First..Middle-1),
                        Item, Found, Index);
  else
    Binary_Search (List(Middle+1..List'Last),
                        Item, Found, Index);
  end if;
end Binary_Search;
```

The iterative version has three local variables; the recursive version has one. There are usually fewer local variables in a recursive routine than in an iterative routine. Also the iterative version always has a loop; the recursive always has a branch. Although the recursive version is shorter, the iterative version may be more efficient. The shortness and small number of local variables in the recursive version, however, make it easier to write.

PROBLEM-SOLVING CASE STUDY

Converting Decimal Integers to Binary Integers

Specification

Problem Convert a positive decimal integer (base 10) to a binary integer (base 2).

Design The algorithm for this conversion is as follows:

1. Take the decimal number and divide it by 2.
2. Make the remainder the rightmost digit in the answer.
3. Replace the original dividend with the quotient.
4. Repeat, placing each new remainder to the left of the previous one.
5. Stop when the quotient is 0.

This is clearly an algorithm we need to try out with paper and pencil. We certainly cannot directly implement expressions such as "to the left of" in Ada. Let's do an example—convert 43 from base 10 to base 2—and get a feel for the algorithm before we try to write a computer solution. Remember, the quotient from one step becomes the dividend in the next.

PROBLEM-SOLVING CASE STUDY cont'd.

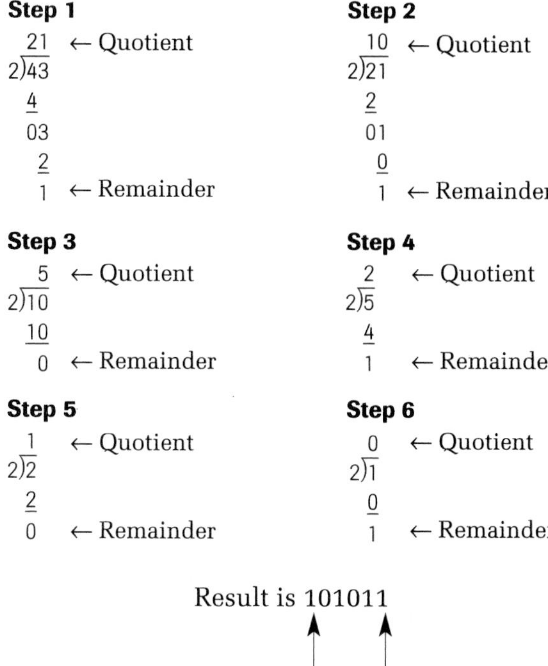

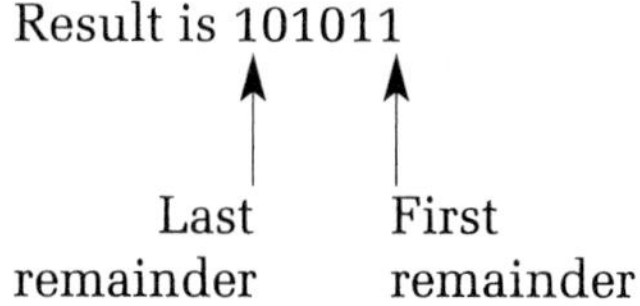

It looks as though we can implement the problem with a straightforward iterative algorithm. The remainder is, of course, the rem operation, and the quotient is the / operation.

```
loop
   exit when Number=0
   Remainder := Number rem 2
   Put Remainder
   Number := Number / 2
end loop
```

Let's do a trace to test this algorithm.

PROBLEM-SOLVING CASE STUDY *cont'd.*

Number	**Remainder**
43	1
21	1
10	0
5	1
2	0
1	1

Answer: 1 1 0 1 0 1

(remainder from step 1 2 3 4 5 6)

The answer is backwards! An iterative solution using only simple variables doesn't work. We need to print the last remainder first. The first remainder should be printed only after the rest of the remainders have been calculated and printed.

In the case of our example, this means that we should print 43 rem 2 after (43 / 2) rem 2 has been printed. But this in turn means that we should print (43 / 2) rem 2 after ((43 / 2) / 2) rem 2 has been printed. Now this begins to look like a recursive definition. We can summarize by saying that, for any given number, we should print Number rem 2 after (Number / 2) rem 2 has been printed. This becomes the following algorithm.

```
Convert
if Number > 0 then
  Convert Number / 2
  Put Number rem 2
else
  Do nothing
end if
```

If Number is 0, we have called Convert as many times as we need to and can begin printing the answer. The base case is simply when we stop making recursive calls.

Implementation The recursive solution to this problem is encoded in procedure Convert.

```
procedure Convert (Number : Natural) is -- Number being converted to binary
begin
   if Number > 0 then
      Convert (Number => Number / 2);
      Ada.Integer_Text_IO.Put (Item  => Number rem 2,
                               Width => 1);
   end if;
end Convert;
```

PROBLEM-SOLVING CASE STUDY cont'd.

Testing Let's do a code trace of Convert (10).

Call 1: Convert is called with an actual parameter of 10. Because Number is not equal to 0, execution of Call 1 halts until the recursive call to Convert with an actual parameter of Number / 2 has been completed.

Call 2: Number is 5. Because Number is not equal to 0, execution of Call 2 halts until the recursive call to Convert with an actual parameter of Number / 2 has been completed.

Call 3: Number is 2. Because Number is not equal to 0, execution of Call 3 halts until the recursive call to Convert with an actual parameter of Number / 2 has been completed.

Call 4: Number is 1. Because Number is not equal to 0, execution of Call 4 halts until the recursive call to Convert with an actual parameter of Number / 2 has been completed.

Call 5: Number is 0. Execution of this call to Convert is completed. Nothing is printed and control is passed back to the preceding call.

Call 4: Execution of Call 4 resumes with the statement following the recursive call to Convert. From the previous description of Call 4 you can see that Number in this call is 1. Number rem 2 (which is 1) is printed. Execution of Call 4 to Convert is completed.

Call 3: Execution of Call 3 resumes with the statement following the recursive call to Convert. From the previous description of Call 3 you can see that Number in this call is 2. Number rem 2 (which is 0) is printed. Execution of Call 3 to Convert is completed.

Call 2: Execution of Call 2 resumes with the statement following the recursive call to Convert. From the previous description of Call 2 you can see that Number in this call is 5. Number rem 2 (which is 1) is printed. Execution of Call 2 to Convert is completed.

Call 1: Execution of Call 1 resumes with the statement following the recursive call to Convert. From the previous description of Call 1 you can see that Number in this call is 10. Number rem 2 (which is 0) is printed. Execution of Call 1 to Convert is completed. Since this is the initial nonrecursive call, execution resumes with the statement immediately following that original call.

Figure 13-7 shows the execution of procedure Convert with the values of the actual parameters.

PROBLEM-SOLVING CASE STUDY *cont'd.*

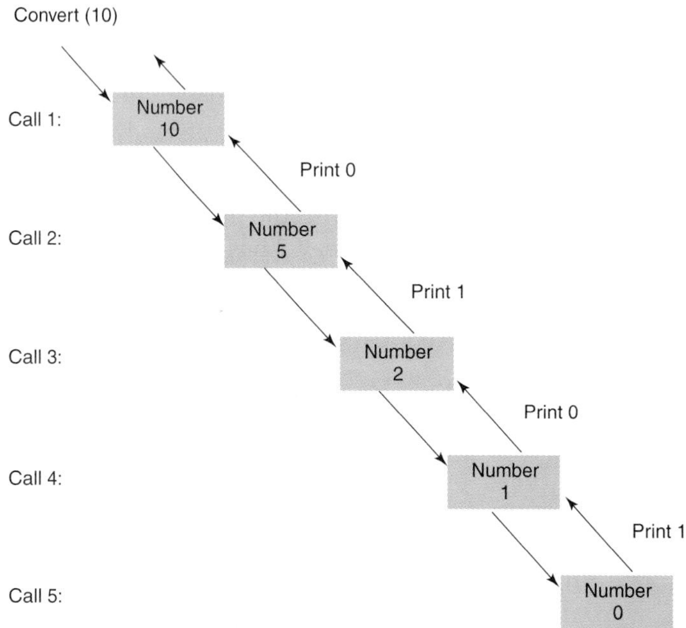

Figure 13-7 Execution of Convert (10)

Problem-Solving Case Study

Minimum Value in an Integer Array

Specification

Problem Find the minimum value in an array of integers.

Design In Chapter 11 we used iteration to solve a similar problem—finding the maximum value in an array. We could use the same approach to find the minimum, but the objective here is to think recursively. The problem has to be stated in terms of a smaller case of itself. Because this is a problem using an array, a smaller case probably involves a smaller array. Here's one way of looking at it. The minimum value in an array is the smaller of two values: the last value in the array and the smallest value in the rest of the array. Finding the smallest value in the rest of the array is a smaller version of the original problem. What about base cases? It is a trivial matter to find the minimum value in an array containing only one component.

```
Minimum
   in      List
   out     Result
if Length of List = 1 then
   Result := First component in List
else
   Minimum In Rest of List := Minimum of all of List except the Last Value
   if Last Value < Minimum in Rest of List then
      Result := Last Value
   else
      Result := Minimum In Rest of List
   end if
end if
```

Implementation Here is the Ada function that implements our algorithm.

```
type Integer_Array is array (Integer range <>) of Integer;
.
.
.
function Minimum (List : in Integer_Array) return Integer is
-- Returns the smallest value in the array
--
-- Preconditions : There is at least one element in List

   Result          : Integer;  -- The answer we return
   Minimum_In_Rest : Integer;  -- The minimum in the rest of the array

begin
   if List'Length = 1 then
      Result := List (List'First);
   else
      -- Calculate the minimum in all of list except the last value
      Minimum_In_Rest := Minimum (List(List'First .. List'Last - 1));
      -- Compare the last value to the smallest in the rest of the list
      if List(List'Last) < Minimum_In_Rest then
         Result := List (List'Last);
      else
         Result := Minimum_In_Rest;
      end if;
   end if;
   return Result;
end Minimum;
```

Testing We do not provide a code trace for this function. A diagram showing the actual parameters for each call appears in Figure 13-8.

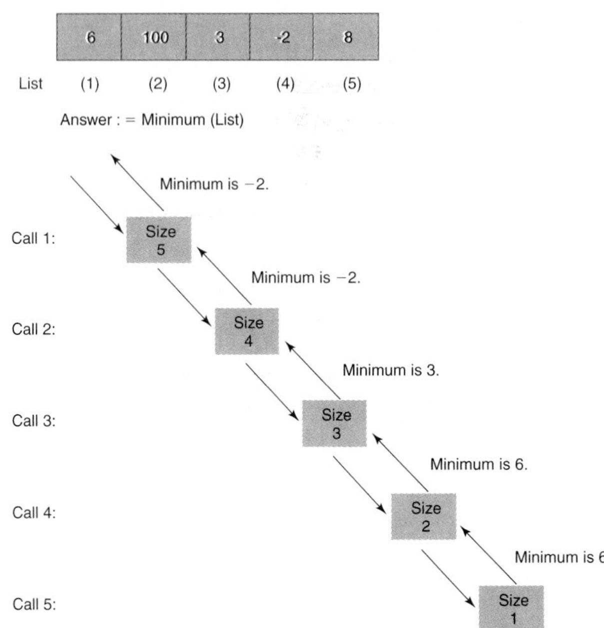

Figure 13-8 Execution of Minimum (List)

To test this function, we need a driver program that reads values into an array, calls the function, and prints the results. The cases to be tested are the end cases (smallest element is first in the array and then last in the array) and several cases between. We also should test it with different length arrays, including an array of length 1.

Testing and Debugging

Recursion is a powerful technique when used correctly. Improperly used, recursion can cause bugs that are difficult to diagnose. The best way to debug a recursive algorithm is to construct it correctly in the first place. To be realistic, however, we give a few hints about where to look if an error occurs.

Testing and Debugging Hints

1. Be sure there is a base case. If there is no base case, the algorithm continues to issue recursive calls until all the memory has been used. Each time the procedure or function is called, either recursively or nonrecursively, more memory space is used. If there is no base case to end the recursive calls, eventually all the memory will be assigned. A STORAGE_ERROR exception indicates that the base case is missing.

2. Be sure you have not used a loop structure. The basic control structure in a recursive algorithm is the if-then-else. There must be at least two cases: a recursive case and a base case. The base case may do nothing, and thus the else branch is not present. The branching structure, however, must be there. If you use a loop statement in a recursive algorithm, the loop statement usually should not contain a recursive call.
3. Do not reference global variables directly within a recursive procedure or function.
4. Formal parameters that relate to the size of the problem should generally be *in* mode parameters. Actual parameters that relate to the size of the problem are usually expressions. Only *in* mode parameters can be passed expressions.

Summary

A recursive algorithm is expressed in terms of a simpler instance of itself. It must include a recursive case, for which the algorithm is expressed in terms of itself, and a base case, for which the algorithm is expressed in nonrecursive terms.

In many recursive problems, the smaller instance refers to a numeric parameter that is being reduced with each call. In other problems, the smaller instance refers to the size of the data structure being manipulated. The base case is the one in which the size of the problem (value or structure) reaches a point where an explicit answer is known or trivial to calculate.

In the Towers of Hanoi game, the size of the problem was the number of disks to be moved. When there was only one left on the beginning peg, we could move it to its final destination.

In the case study for finding the minimum using recursion, the size of the problem was the size of the array being searched. When the array size became 1, we knew the solution. If there is only one component, it must be the minimum (as well as the maximum).

Quick Check

1. What is a recursive call? (p. 771)
2. What distinguishes the base case in a recursive algorithm? (p. 775)
3. What is the base case in the Towers of Hanoi algorithm? (p. 785)
4. In working with simple variables, the recursive case is often in terms of a smaller value. What is typical of the recursive case in working with structured variables? (p. 789)
5. In printing the components of an array recursively, what is the base case? (p. 789)
6. What are the base cases for the recursive binary search algorithm? (p. 793)

Answers

1. A subprogram call to itself. **2.** The base case is the simplest case: the case where the solution can be stated nonrecursively. **3.** When there are no more disks left to move. **4.** It often is stated in terms of a smaller structure. **5.** When the length of the array parameter is 0. **6.** When the length of the array parameter is 0 or the middle element is the one desired.

Exam Preparation Exercises

1. Recursion is an example of:
   a. selection
   b. a data structure
   c. repetition
   d. data-flow programming
2. A procedure can be recursive and a function cannot. (True or False)
3. When a procedure is called recursively, the actual parameters and local variables of the calling version are saved until its execution is resumed. (True or False)
4. Given the recursive formula $F(N) = -F(N - 2)$, with base case $F(0)=1$, what are the values of $F(4)$ and $F(6)$? What is the value of $F(5)$?
5. When can one have infinite recursion?
6. What control structure appears most commonly in a recursive procedure?
7. If you develop a recursive algorithm that employs tail recursion, what alternative control structure should you consider?
8. A recursive algorithm depends on making something smaller. When the algorithm works on a data structure, what may become smaller?
   a. Distance from a position in the structure
   b. The data structure
   c. The number of variables in the recursive procedure
9. What are the base cases of a recursive procedure that searches an array?
10. Given the input data

    ABCDE¶

    a. What is the output of the following program?

```
with Ada.Text_IO;
procedure Exercise_10 is
```

```
   procedure Do_It is
      Ch : Character;
   begin
      if not Ada.Text_IO.End_Of_Line then
         Ada.Text_IO.Get (Ch);
         Do_It;
         Ada.Text_IO.Put (Ch);
      end if;
   end Do_It;

begin
   Do_It;
end Exercise_10;
```

b. What is the base case in this program?

11. Given the following input
    15
    23
    21
    19
    a. What is the output of the following code?

```
with Ada.Integer_Text_IO;
with Ada.Text_IO;
procedure Exercise_11 is

   procedure Numbers is

      N : Integer;

   begin
      if not Ada.Text_IO.End_Of_File then
         Ada.Integer_Text_IO.Get (N);
         Ada.Text_IO.Skip_Line;
         Ada.Integer_Text_IO.Put (N);
         Numbers;
         Ada.Integer_Text_IO.Put (N);
      end if;
   end Numbers;

begin
   Numbers;
end Exercise_11;
```

b. What is the base case in this program?

12. What is the output produced by each of the following three versions of procedure Numbers if called with

```
Numbers (Low => 0, High => 8, Power => 3);?
```

a. Version 1

```
procedure Numbers (Low   : in Natural;
                   High  : in Natural;
                   Power : in Natural) is

   Middle : Natural;

begin
   if Power > 0 then
      Middle := (Low + High) / 2;
      Ada.Integer_Text_IO.Put (Middle);
      Ada.Text_IO.New_Line;
      Numbers (Low => Low,    High => Middle, Power => Power - 1);
      Numbers (Low => Middle, High => High,   Power => Power - 1);
   end if;
end Numbers;
```

b. Version 2

```
procedure Numbers (Low   : in Natural;
                   High  : in Natural;
                   Power : in Natural) is

   Middle : Natural;

begin
   if Power > 0 then
      Middle := (Low + High) / 2;
      Numbers (Low => Low,    High => Middle, Power => Power - 1);
      Ada.Integer_Text_IO.Put (Middle);
      Ada.Text_IO.New_Line;
      Numbers (Low => Middle, High => High,   Power => Power - 1);
   end if;
end Numbers;
```

c. Version 3

```
procedure Numbers (Low   : in Natural;
                   High  : in Natural;
                   Power : in Natural) is

   Middle : Natural;

begin
   if Power > 0 then
      Middle := (Low + High) / 2;
      Numbers (Low => Low,     High => Middle, Power => Power - 1);
      Numbers (Low => Middle, High => High,   Power => Power - 1);
      Ada.Integer_Text_IO.Put (Middle);
      Ada.Text_IO.New_Line;
   end if;
end Numbers;
```

13. What is the output of the following procedure if called with List equal to (23, 44, 52, 61, 77)?

```
procedure Print (List: Integer_Array) is
begin
   if List'Length > 0 then
      -- Display the rest of the array
      Print (List=> List (List'First+1 .. List'Last));
      -- Display the value of the first component in the array
      Ada.Integer_Text_IO.Put (Item => List (List'First));
   end if;
end Print;
```

Programming Warm-up Exercises

1. The recursive definition of function Power requires a positive value for an exponent, yet A^0 is simply 1. Change the function so that the parameter N is type Natural rather than Positive and returns the correct value when N is 0.
2. Write an Ada function that implements the recursive formula: $F(N) = F(N-1) - F(N-2) + F(N-3)$ with base cases $F(0) = 1$, $F(1) = 2$, and $F(2) = 3$.
3. Add whatever is necessary to fix the following function so that $F(3) = 10$. Do not replace the recursion with iteration.

```
function Funct (N : in Integer) return Integer is
   Result : Integer;
begin
   Result := Funct (N-1) + 3;
   return Result;
end Funct;
```

4. Procedure Line_Print uses tail recursion. Rewrite it using iteration instead of recursion.

```
procedure Line_Print (In_File : in out Ada.Text_IO.File_Type) is
   Ch : Character;
begin
   if not Ada.Text_IO.End_Of_File (In_File) then
      if not Ada.Text_IO.End_Of_Line (In_File) then
         Ada.Text_IO.Get (File => In_File, Item => Ch);
         Ada.Text_IO.Put (Ch);
      else
         Ada.Text_IO.Skip_Line (In_File);
         Ada.Text_IO.New_Line;
      end if;
      Line_Print (In_File);
   end if;
end Line_Print;
```

5. Rewrite procedure Square_Print using recursion.

```
procedure Square_Print is
   Count : Integer;
begin
   Count := 1;
   loop
      exit when Count > 10;
      Ada.Integer_Text_IO.Put (Count);
      Ada.Integer_Text_IO.Put (Count ** 2);
      Count := Count + 1;
   end loop;
end Square_Print;
```

6. Modify function Factorial of this chapter to print its parameter and returned value indented two spaces for each level of call to the function. The call Factorial(3) should produce the output:

```
3
  2
    1
      0
      1
    1
  2
6
```

7. Write a recursive function that sums the numbers from 1 to *N*.

8. Rewrite the following procedure so that it is recursive.

```
procedure Halves (N : in Integer) is
   Count : Integer;
begin
   Count := N;
   loop
      exit when Count < 1;
      Ada.Integer_Text_IO.Put (Count);
      Ada.Integer_Text_IO.Put (Count / 2);
      Ada.Text_IO.New_Line;
      Count := Count - 1;
end Halves;
```

Use the following function in questions 9 and 10.

```
function Puzzle (Base  : in Natural;
                 Limit : in Natural) return Integer is
   Result : Integer;
begin
   if Base > Limit then
      Result := -1;
   elsif Base = Limit then
      Result := 1;
   else
      Result := Base * Puzzle (Base + 1, Limit);
   end if;
   return Result;
end Puzzle;
```

9. Identify
   a. the base case(s) of function Puzzle
   b. the general case(s) of function Puzzle
10. Show what would be displayed by each of the following calls to the recursive function Puzzle.
    a. `Ada.Integer_Text_IO.Put (Item => Puzzle (14, 10));`
    b. `Ada.Integer_Text_IO.Put (Item => Puzzle (4, 7));`
    c. `Ada.Integer_Text_IO.Put (Item => Puzzle (0, 0));`
11. Rewrite procedure Print (page 789) so that it displays the contents of the array in reverse order.

Programming Problems

1. The greatest common divisor of two positive whole numbers is the largest integer that divides both numbers exactly. For example, the greatest common divisor of 12 and 18 is 6; the greatest common divisor of 12 and 17 is 1; and the greatest common divisor of 12 and 22 is 2. A recursive formula for calculating the greatest common divisor of two positive whole numbers, *m* and *n*, is

```
GCD (m, n)   =  m                    if n = 0
             =  GCD (n, m rem n)     if n > 0
```

   Implement this recursive formula as a recursive Ada function and write a program to test it.
2. Every week you and your friends divide the assigned group of study questions among yourselves. If there are 20 different questions to pass out to four students, we can easily see that—to be equitable—we should assign each student five questions. But how many different combinations of five questions can be made out of the 20 questions? There is a recursive mathematical formula that you can use to solve this problem. Given that C is the number of combinations (what we want to determine), Group is the total size of the group to pick from (20 questions in our example), and Members is the size of each subgroup (five questions in our example), this formula can be written as

```
C (Group, Members) = Group                          if Members = 1

                   = 1                              if Members = Group

                  = C (Group - 1, Members - 1) +    if Members > Group > 1
                     C (Group - 1, Members)
```

   Write an Ada program that reads in the number of study questions and the number of questions to be assigned to each student and prints out the number of combinations possible. End the program when a 0 is entered for the total number of study questions.
3. Extend the recursive decimal to binary conversion program developed in the first case study of this chapter so that a decimal whole number can be displayed in any base between 2 and 10. Pass in the desired base as a second parameter. To check your answers, use the Base parameter available in the predefined procedure Ada.Integer_Text_IO.Put. For example, the following displays the decimal number 42 in base 8.

```
Ada.Integer_Text_IO.Put (Item => 42, Width => 5, Base => 8);
```

4. A *palindrome* is a string of characters that reads the same forward and backward. Write a program that reads in lines of characters and then calls a recursive Boolean function for each line that determines whether or not the string is a palindrome. Use End_Of_Line to determine the end of each string and End_Of_File to determine when all lines have been processed. Echo print each line within quotation marks followed by " is a palindrome." if the line is a palindrome or " is not a palindrome." if the line is not a palindrome. For example, given the following input line

```
Able was I ere I saw Elba
```

   the output should be

```
"Able was I ere I saw Elba" is a palindrome.
```

   Consider uppercase and lowercase letters to be the same.

5. A maze is to be represented by a 10×10 array of an enumerated data type composed of three values: Path, Hedge, and Exit. There is one exit from the maze. Write a program to determine whether it is possible to exit the maze from a given starting point. You may move vertically or horizontally in any direction that contains Path; you may not move to a square that contains Hedge. If you move into a square that contains Exit, you have exited.

   The input data consists of two parts: the maze and a series of starting points. The maze is entered as 10 lines of 10 characters (P, H, and E). Each succeeding line contains a pair of integers that represents a starting point (that is, row and column numbers). Continue processing entry points until end of file.

Appendices

APPENDIX A

Ada Reserved Words

Ada has 69 words that are reserved for special purposes. Programmer-defined identifiers may not be reserved words. Certain attributes are identical to some reserved words.

abort
abs
abstract
accept
access
aliased
all
and
array
at

begin
body

case
constant

declare
delay
delta
digits
do

else
elsif
end
entry
exception
exit

for
function

generic
goto

if
in
is

limited
loop

mod

new
not
null

of
or
others
out

package
pragma
private
procedure
protected

raise
range
record
rem
renames
requeue

return
reverse

select
separate
subtype

tagged
task
terminate
then
type

until
use

when
while
with

xor

APPENDIX B

Ada Syntax (EBNF)

One of the oldest computer-oriented metalanguages is the Backus-Naur Form (BNF), which is named for John Backus and Peter Naur, who developed it in 1960. The *Ada Language Reference Manual* uses a simple variant of BNF, called Extended Backus-Naur Form (EBNF) to define the syntax of Ada. These syntax definitions are written out using letters, numbers, and four special symbols. The special symbols are:

::= Stands for "is defined as"
[ ] Used to enclose an optional item
{ } Used to enclose an item that may be repeated zero or more times
| Stands for "or" (used to separate alternative items)

All other symbols in the definitions are for use in Ada programs.

Boldface items denote literals, that is, symbols or words that should be written exactly as shown. Lowercase words, called nonterminal symbols, are those further defined in a separate EBNF rule. Names that begin with an *italicized* part are equivalent to the name without the italicized part. The italicized part simply conveys additional meaning within the context of the definition. Think of the italicized part as a comment, not actually part of the definition.

Here is the complete syntax of Ada in EBNF. Entries are in alphabetical order.

A

abort_statement ::= **abort** *task*_name {, *task*_name};
abortable_part ::= sequence_of_statements
abstract_subprogram_declaration ::= subprogram_specification is **abstract**;
accept_alternative ::= accept_statement [sequence_of_statements]
accept_statement ::= **accept** entry_direct_name [(entry_index)] parameter_profile [**do**
handled_sequence_of_statements
end [*entry*_identifier]];
access_definition ::= **access** subtype_mark
access_to_object_definition ::= **access** [general_access_modifier] subtype_indication
access_to_subprogram_definition ::= **access** [**protected**] **procedure** parameter_profile
| **access** [**protected**] **function** parameter_and_result_profile
access_type_definition ::= access_to_object_definition | access_to_subprogram_definition
actual_parameter_part ::= (parameter_association {, parameter_association})
aggregate ::= record_aggregate | extension_aggregate | array_aggregate

```
allocator                        ::= new subtype_indication | new qualified_expression
ancestor_part                    ::= expression | subtype_mark
assignment_statement             ::= variable_name := expression;
asynchronous_select              ::= select
                                       triggering_alternative
                                     then abort
                                       abortable_part
                                     end select;
array_aggregate                  ::= positional_array_aggregate | named_array_aggregate
array_component_association      ::= discrete_choice_list => expression
array_type_definition            ::= unconstrained_array_definition | constrained_array_definition
at_clause                        ::= for direct_name use at expression;
attribute_definition_clause      ::= for local_name'attribute_designator use expression;
                                     | for local_name'attribute_designator use name;
attribute_designator             ::= identifier[(static_expression)] | Access | Delta | Digits
attribute_reference              ::= prefix'attribute_designator
```

B

```
base                             ::= numeral
based_literal                    ::= base # based_numeral [.based_numeral] # [exponent]
based_numeral                    ::= extended_digit {[underline] extended_digit}
basic_declaration                ::=   type_declaration          | subtype_declaration
                                     | object_declaration        | number_declaration
                                     | subprogram_declaration    | abstract_subprogram_declaration
                                     | package_declaration       | renaming_declaration
                                     | exception_declaration     | generic_declaration
                                     | generic_instantiation
basic_declarative_item           ::= basic_declaration | representation_clause | use_clause
binary_adding_operator           ::= + | - | &
block_statement                  ::= [block_statement_identifier:]
                                     [declare
                                       declarative_part]
                                     begin
                                       handled_sequence_of_statements
                                     end [block_identifier];
body                             ::= proper_body | body_stub
body_stub                        :=  subprogram_body_stub        | package_body_stub
                                     | task_body_stub            | protected_body_stub
```

C

```
case_statement                   ::= case expression is
                                       case_statement_alternative
                                       {case_statement_alternative}
                                     end case;
case_statement_alternative       ::= when discrete_choice_list =>
                                       sequence_of_statements
character                        ::= graphic_character | format_effector | other_control_function
character_literal                ::= 'graphic_character'
choice_parameter_specification   ::= defining_identifier
```

code_statement	::= qualified_expression;
comment	::= --{*non_end_of_line*_character}
compilation	::= {compilation_unit}
compilation_unit	::= context_clause library_item
	| context_clause subunit
component_choice_list	::= component_selector_name {| component_selector_ name} | **others**
component_clause	::= component_local_name **at** position **range** first_bit .. last_bit;
component_declaration	::= defining_identifier_list : component_definition [:= default_expression];
component_definition	::= [**aliased**] subtype_indication
component_item	::= component_declaration | representation_clause
component_list	::= component_item {component_item}
	| {component_item} variant_part
	| **null**;
composite_constraint	::= index_constraint | discriminant_constraint
compound_statement	::= if_statement | case_statement
	| loop_statement | block_statement
	| accept_statement | select_statement
condition	::= *boolean*_expression
conditional_entry_call	::= **select**
	entry_call_alternative
	else
	sequence_of_statements
	end select;
constrained_array_definition	::= **array** (discrete_subtype_definition {, discrete_subtype_definition}) **of** component_definition
constraint	::= scalar_constraint | composite_constraint
context_clause	::= {context_item}
xt_item	::= with_clause | use_clause

D

decimal_fixed_point_definition	::= **delta** *static*_expression **digits** *static*_expression [real_range_specification]
decimal_literal	::= numeral [.numeral] [exponent]
declarative_item	::= basic_declarative_item | body
declarative_part	::= {declarative_item}
default_expression	::= expression
default_name	::= name
defining_character_literal	::= character_literal
defining_designator	::= defining_program_unit_name | defining_operator_symbol
defining_identifier	::= identifier
defining_identifier_list	::= defining_identifier {, defining_identifier}
defining_operator_symbol	::= operator_symbol
defining_program_unit_name	::= [parent_unit_name .]defining_identifier
delay_alternative	::= delay_statement [sequence_of_statements]
delay_statement	::= delay_until_statement | delay_relative_statement
delay_relative_statement	::= **delay** *delay*_expression;
delay_until_statement	::= **delay until** *delay*_expression;
delta_constraint	::= **delta** *static*_expression [range_constraint]
derived_type_definition	::= [**abstract**] **new** *parent*_subtype_indication [record_extension_part]
designator	::= [parent_unit_name .]identifier | operator_symbol
digits_constraint	::= **digits** *static*_expression [range_constraint]
direct_name	::= identifier | operator_symbol
discrete_choice	::= expression | discrete_range | **others**

discrete_choice_list	::= discrete_choice {| discrete_choice}
discrete_range	::= *discrete*_subtype_indication | range
discrete_subtype_definition	::= *discrete*_subtype_indication | range
discriminant_association	::= [*discriminant*_selector_name {| *discriminant*_selector_name} =>] expression
discriminant_constraint	::= (discriminant_association {, discriminant_association})
discriminant_part	::= unknown_discriminant_part | known_discriminant_part
discriminant_specification	::= defining_identifier_list : subtype_mark [:= default_expression] | defining_identifier_list : access_definition [:= default_expression]

E

entry_barrier	::= **when** condition
entry_body	::= **entry** defining_identifier entry_body_formal_part entry_barrier **is** declarative_part **begin** handled_sequence_of_statements **end** [*entry*_identifier];
entry_body_formal_part	::= [(entry_index_specification)] parameter_profile
entry_call_alternative	::= entry_call_statement [sequence_of_statements]
entry_call_statement	::= *entry*_name [actual_parameter_part];
entry_declaration	::= **entry** defining_identifier [(discrete_subtype_definition)] parameter_profile;
entry_index	::= expression
entry_index_specification	::= **for** defining_identifier **in** discrete_subtype_definition
enumeration_aggregate	::= array_aggregate
enumeration_literal_specification	::= defining_identifier | defining_character_literal
enumeration_representation_clause	::= **for** first_subtype_local_name **use** enumeration_aggregate;
enumeration_type_definition	::= (enumeration_literal_specification {, enumeration_literal_specification})
exception_choice	::= *exception*_name | **others**
exception_declaration	::= defining_identifier_list : **exception**;
exception_handler	::= **when** [choice_parameter_specification:] exception_choice {| exception_choice} => sequence_of_statements
exception_renaming_declaration	::= defining_identifier : **exception renames** *exception*_name;
exit_statement	::= **exit** [*loop*_name] [**when** condition];
explicit_actual_parameter	::= expression | *variable*_name
explicit_dereference	::= name.**all**
explicit_generic_actual_parameter	::= expression | *variable*_name | *subprogram*_name | *entry*_name | subtype_mark | *package_instance*_name
exponent	::= **E** [+] numeral | **E** - numeral
expression	::= relation {**and** relation} | relation {**and then** relation} | relation {**or** relation} | relation {**or else** relation} | relation {**xor** relation}
extended_digit	::= digit | A | B | C | D | E | F
extension_aggregate	::= (ancestor_part **with** record_component_association_list)

F

factor	::= primary [** primary] | **abs** primary | **not** primary
first_bit	::= *static*_simple_expression
fixed_point_definition	::= ordinary_fixed_point_definition | decimal_fixed_point_definition
floating_point_definition	::= **digits** *static*_expression [real_range_specification]

formal_access_type_definition ::= access_type_definition

formal_array_type_definition ::= array_type_definition

formal_decimal_fixed_point_definition ::= **delta** <> **digits** <>

formal_derived_type_definition ::= [**abstract**] **new** subtype_mark [**with private**]

formal_discrete_type_definition ::= (<>)

formal_floating_point_definition ::= **digits** <>

formal_modular_type_definition ::= **mod** <>

formal_object_declaration ::= defining_identifier_list : mode subtype_mark [:= default_expression];

formal_ordinary_fixed_point_definition ::= **delta** <>

formal_package_actual_part ::= (<>) | [generic_actual_part]

formal_package_declaration ::= **with** package defining_identifier **is new** *generic_package*_name
formal_package_actual_part;

formal_part ::= (parameter_specification {; parameter_specification})

formal_private_type_definition ::= [[**abstract**] **tagged**] [**limited**] **private**

formal_signed_integer_type_definition ::= **range** <>

formal_subprogram_declaration ::= **with** subprogram_specification [**is** subprogram_default];

formal_type_declaration ::= **type** defining_identifier[discriminant_part] **is** formal_type_definition;

formal_type_definition ::= formal_private_type_definition
| formal_derived_type_definition
| formal_discrete_type_definition
| formal_signed_integer_type_definition
| formal_modular_type_definition
| formal_floating_point_definition
| formal_ordinary_fixed_point_definition
| formal_decimal_fixed_point_definition
| formal_array_type_definition
| formal_access_type_definition

full_type_declaration ::= **type** defining_identifier [known_discriminant_part] **is** type_definition;
| task_type_declaration
| protected_type_declaration

function_call ::= *function*_name
| *function*_prefix actual_parameter_part

G

general_access_modifier ::= **all** | **constant**

generic_actual_part ::= (generic_association {, generic_association})

generic_association ::= [*generic_formal_parameter*_selector_name =>] explicit_generic_actual_parameter

generic_declaration ::= generic_subprogram_declaration | generic_package_declaration

generic_formal_parameter_declaration ::= formal_object_declaration
| formal_type_declaration
| formal_subprogram_declaration
| formal_package_declaration

generic_formal_part ::= **generic** {generic_formal_parameter_declaration | use_clause}

generic_instantiation ::= **package** defining_program_unit_name **is**
new generic_package_name [generic_actual_part];
| **procedure** defining_program_unit_name **is**
new generic_procedure_name [generic_actual_part];
| **function** defining_designator **is**
new generic_function_name [generic_actual_part];

generic_package_declaration ::= generic_formal_part package_specification;

generic_renaming_declaration ::= **generic package**
defining_program_unit_name **renames** *generic_package*_name;
| **generic procedure**
defining_program_unit_name **renames** *generic_procedure*_name;
| **generic function**
defining_program_unit_name **renames** *generic_function*_name;

generic_subprogram_declaration ::= generic_formal_part subprogram_specification;

goto_statement ::= **goto** *label*_name;

graphic_character ::= identifier_letter | digit | space_character | special_character

guard ::= **when** condition =>

H

handled_sequence_of_statements ::= sequence_of_statements
[**exception**
exception_handler
{exception_handler}]

highest_precedence_operator ::= ** | **abs** | **not**

I

identifier ::= identifier_letter {[underline] letter_or_digit}

if_statement ::= **if** condition **then**
sequence_of_statements
{**elsif** condition **then**
sequence_of_statements}
[**else**
sequence_of_statements]
end if;

implicit_dereference ::= name

incomplete_type_declaration ::= **type** defining_identifier [discriminant_part];

index_constraint ::= (discrete_range {, discrete_range})

index_subtype_definition ::= subtype_mark **range** <>

indexed_component ::= prefix(expression {, expression})

integer_type_definition ::= signed_integer_type_definition | modular_type_definition

iteration_scheme ::= **while** condition | **for** loop_parameter_specification

K

known_discriminant_part ::= (discriminant_specification {; discriminant_specification})

L

label ::= <<*label*_statement_identifier>>

last_bit ::= *static*_simple_expression

letter_or_digit ::= identifier_letter | digit

```
library_item                        ::=   [private] library_unit_declaration
                                        | library_unit_body
                                        | [private] library_unit_renaming_declaration
library_unit_body                   ::= subprogram_body | package_body
library_unit_declaration            ::=   subprogram_declaration     | package_declaration
                                        | generic_declaration        | generic_instantiation
library_unit_renaming_declaration   ::=   package_renaming_declaration
                                        | generic_renaming_declaration
                                        | subprogram_renaming_declaration
local_name                          ::=   direct_name
                                        | direct_name'attribute_designator
                                        | library_unit_name
logical_operator                    ::= and | or | xor
loop_parameter_specification        ::= defining_identifier in [reverse] discrete_subtype_definition
loop_statement                      ::= [loop_statement_identifier:]
                                        [iteration_scheme] loop
                                          sequence_of_statements
                                        end loop [loop_identifier];
```

M

```
mode                                ::= [in] | in out | out
mod_clause                          ::= at mod static_expression;
modular_type_definition             ::= mod static_expression
multiplying_operator                ::= * | / | mod | rem
```

N

```
name                                ::=   direct_name                | explicit_dereference
                                        | indexed_component          | slice
                                        | selected_component         | attribute_reference
                                        | type_conversion            | function_call
                                        | character_literal
named_array_aggregate               ::= (array_component_association {, array_component_association})
null_statement                      ::= null;
number_declaration                  ::= defining_identifier_list : constant := static_expression;
numeral                             ::= digit {[underline] digit}
numeric_literal                     ::= decimal_literal | based_literal
```

O

```
object_declaration                  ::=   defining_identifier_list : [aliased] [constant] subtype_indication [:= expression];
                                        | defining_identifier_list : [aliased] [constant] array_type_definition [:= expression];
                                        | single_task_declaration
                                        | single_protected_declaration
object_renaming_declaration         ::= defining_identifier : subtype_mark renames object_name;
operator_symbol                     ::= string_literal
ordinary_fixed_point_definition     ::= delta static_expression  real_range_specification
```

P

package_body ::= **package body** defining_program_unit_name is
    declarative_part
  [**begin**
    handled_sequence_of_statements]
  end [[parent_unit_name.]identifier];

package_body_stub ::= package body defining_identifier **is separate**;

package_declaration ::= package_specification;

package_renaming_declaration ::= **package** defining_program_unit_name **renames** *package_*name;

package_specification ::= **package** defining_program_unit_name **is**
    {basic_declarative_item}
  [**private**
    {basic_declarative_item}]
  end [[parent_unit_name.]identifier]

parameter_and_result_profile ::= [formal_part] **return** subtype_mark

parameter_association ::= [*formal_parameter_*selector_name =>] explicit_actual_parameter

parameter_profile ::= [formal_part]

parameter_specification ::= defining_identifier_list : mode subtype_mark [:= default_expression]
  | defining_identifier_list : access_definition [:= default_expression]

parent_unit_name ::= name

position ::= *static_*expression

positional_array_aggregate ::= (expression, expression {, expression})
  | (expression {, expression}, **others** => expression)

pragma ::= pragma identifier [(pragma_argument_association {, pragma_argument_association})];

pragma_argument_association ::= [*pragma_argument_*identifier =>] name
  | [*pragma_argument_*identifier =>] expression

prefix ::= name | implicit_dereference

primary ::= numeric_literal | **null** | string_literal | aggregate
  | name | qualified_expression | allocator | (expression)

private_extension_declaration ::= **type** defining_identifier [discriminant_part] **is**
  [**abstract**] **new** *ancestor_*subtype_indication **with private**;

private_type_declaration ::= **type** defining_identifier [discriminant_part] **is** [[**abstract**] **tagged**] [**limited**] **private**;

procedure_call_statement ::= *procedure_*name;
  | *procedure_*prefix actual_parameter_part;

proper_body ::= subprogram_body | package_body | task_body | protected_body

protected_body ::= **protected body** defining_identifier is
    { protected_operation_item }
  end [*protected_*identifier];

protected_body_stub ::= **protected body** defining_identifier **is separate**;

protected_definition ::= { protected_operation_declaration }
  [**private**
  { protected_element_declaration }]
  end [*protected_*identifier]

protected_element_declaration ::= protected_operation_declaration
  | component_declaration

protected_operation_declaration ::= subprogram_declaration
  | entry_declaration
  | representation_clause

protected_operation_item ::= subprogram_declaration
  | subprogram_body
  | entry_body
  | representation_clause

protected_type_declaration ::= **protected type** defining_identifier [known_discriminant_part] **is** protected_definition;

Q

qualified_expression	::= subtype_mark'(expression) | subtype_mark'aggregate

R

raise_statement	::= **raise** [*exception*_name];
range	::= range_attribute_reference | simple_expression .. simple_expression
range_attribute_designator	::= Range[(*static*_expression)]
range_attribute_reference	::= prefix'range_attribute_designator
range_constraint	::= **range** range
real_range_specification	::= **range** *static*_simple_expression .. *static*_simple_expression
real_type_definition	::= floating_point_definition | fixed_point_definition
record_aggregate	::= (record_component_association_list)
record_component_association	::= [component_choice_list =>] expression
record_component_association_list	::= record_component_association {, record_component_association} | **null record**
record_definition	::= **record** component_list **end record** | **null record**
record_extension_part	::= **with** record_definition
record_representation_clause	::= **for** first_subtype_local_name **use** **record** [mod_clause] {component_clause} **end record**;
record_type_definition	::= [[**abstract**] **tagged**] [**limited**] record_definition
relation	::= simple_expression [relational_operator simple_expression] | simple_expression [**not**] **in** range | simple_expression [**not**] **in** subtype_mark
relational_operator	::= = | /= | < | <= | > | >=
renaming_declaration	::= object_renaming_declaration | exception_renaming_declaration | package_renaming_declaration | subprogram_renaming_declaration | generic_renaming_declaration
representation_clause	::= attribute_definition_clause | enumeration_representation_clause | record_representation_clause | at_clause
requeue_statement	::= **requeue** *entry*_name [**with abort**];
return_statement	::= **return** [expression];
restriction	::= *restriction*_identifier | *restriction_parameter*_identifier => expression

S

```
scalar_constraint               ::= range_constraint | digits_constraint | delta_constraint
select_alternative              ::=   accept_alternative
                                    | delay_alternative
                                    | terminate_alternative
select_statement                ::=   selective_accept
                                    | timed_entry_call
                                    | conditional_entry_call
                                    | asynchronous_select
selected_component              ::= prefix . selector_name
selective_accept                ::= select
                                      [guard]
                                      select_alternative
                                    { or
                                      [guard]
                                      select_alternative }
                                    [ else
                                    sequence_of_statements ]
                                    end select;
selector_name                   ::= identifier | character_literal | operator_symbol
sequence_of_statements          ::= statement {statement}
signed_integer_type_definition  ::= range static_simple_expression .. static_simple_expression
simple_expression               ::= [unary_adding_operator] term {binary_adding_operator term}
simple_statement                ::=   null_statement
                                    | assignment_statement     | exit_statement
                                    | goto_statement           | procedure_call_statement
                                    | return_statement         | entry_call_statement
                                    | requeue_statement        | delay_statement
                                    | abort_statement          | raise_statement
                                    | code_statement
single_protected_declaration    ::= protected defining_identifier is protected_definition;
single_task_declaration         ::= task defining_identifier [is task_definition];
slice                           ::= prefix(discrete_range)
statement                       ::= {label} simple_statement | {label} compound_statement
statement_identifier            ::= direct_name
string_element                  ::= ""| non_quotation_mark_graphic_character
string_literal                  ::= "{string_element}"
subprogram_body                 ::= subprogram_specification is
                                      declarative_part
                                    begin
                                      handled_sequence_of_statements
                                    end [designator];
subprogram_body_stub            ::= subprogram_specification is separate;
subprogram_declaration          ::= subprogram_specification;
subprogram_default              ::= default_name | <>
subprogram_renaming_declaration ::= subprogram_specification renames callable_entity_name;
subprogram_specification        ::=   procedure defining_program_unit_name  parameter_profile
                                    | function defining_designator  parameter_and_result_profile
subtype_declaration             ::= subtype defining_identifier is subtype_indication;
subtype_indication              ::= subtype_mark [constraint]
subtype_mark                    ::= subtype_name
subunit                         ::= separate (parent_unit_name) proper_body
```

T

task_body	::= **task body** defining_identifier is
	  declarative_part
	begin
	  handled_sequence_of_statements
	end [*task*_identifier];

task_body_stub	::= **task body** defining_identifier **is separate**;
task_definition	::= {task_item} [**private** {task_item}] **end** [*task*_identifier]
task_item	::= entry_declaration | representation_clause
task_type_declaration	::= **task type** defining_identifier [known_discriminant_part] [**is** task_definition];
term	::= factor {multiplying_operator factor}
terminate_alternative	::= **terminate**;

timed_entry_call	::= **select**
	  entry_call_alternative
	or
	  delay_alternative
	  end select;

triggering_alternative	::= triggering_statement [sequence_of_statements]
triggering_statement	::= entry_call_statement | delay_statement
type_conversion	::= subtype_mark(expression) | subtype_mark(name)
type_declaration	::= full_type_declaration | incomplete_type_declaration | private_type_declaration | private_extension_declaration
type_definition	::= enumeration_type_definition | integer_type_definition | real_type_definition | array_type_definition | record_type_definition | access_type_definition | derived_type_definition

U

unary_adding_operator	::= + | -
unconstrained_array_definition	::= **array**(index_subtype_definition {, index_subtype_definition}) **of** component_definition
unknown_discriminant_part	::= (<>)
use_clause	::= use_package_clause | use_type_clause
use_package_clause	::= **use** *package*_name {, *package*_name};
use_type_clause	::= **use type** subtype_mark {, subtype_mark};

V

variant ::= **when** discrete_choice_list =>
    component_list

variant_part ::= **case** *discriminant*_direct_name is
    variant
    {variant}
  end case;

W

with_clause ::= **with** *library_unit*_name {, *library_unit*_name};

APPENDIX C

Character Sets

Ada's type Character is made up of the 256 characters of the ISO 8859-1 character set. The first 128 characters of this set are commonly known as the ASCII (American Standard Code for Information Interchange) character set. The ASCII character set contains most of the graphic (printable) characters used in English. The following ASCII chart shows the ordering of the 128 characters in the set. The ordinal position of each character is shown in decimal. For example, the 65th character is the letter *A* and the 32nd character is the blank (denoted by "❑").

Left Digit(s) / *Right Digit*	*ASCII* 0	1	2	3	4	5	6	7	8	9
0	NUL	SOH	STX	ETX	EOT	ENQ	ACK	BEL	BS	HT
1	LF	VT	FF	CR	SO	SI	DLE	DC1	DC2	DC3
2	DC4	NAK	SYN	ETB	CAN	EM	SUB	ESC	FS	GS
3	RS	US	□	!	"	#	$	%	&	'
4	(	)	*	+	,	–	.	/	0	1
5	2	3	4	5	6	7	8	9	:	;
6	<	=	>	?	@	A	B	C	D	E
7	F	G	H	I	J	K	L	M	N	O
8	P	Q	R	S	T	U	V	W	X	Y
9	Z	[	\	]	^	_	`	a	b	c
10	d	e	f	g	h	i	j	k	l	m
11	n	o	p	q	r	s	t	u	v	w
12	x	y	z	{	|	}	~	DEL		

Codes 00–31 and 127 are the following nonprintable control characters:

NUL	Null character	VT	Vertical tab	SYN	Synchronous idle
SOH	Start of header	FF	Form feed	ETB	End of transmitted block
STX	Start of text	CR	Carriage return	CAN	Cancel
ETX	End of text	SO	Shift out	EM	End of medium
EOT	End of transmission	SI	Shift in	SUB	Substitute
ENQ	Enquiry	DLE	Data link escape	ESC	Escape
ACK	Acknowledge	DC1	Device control one	FS	File separator
BEL	Bell character (beep)	DC2	Device control two	GS	Group separator
BS	Back space	DC3	Device control three	RS	Record separator
HT	Horizontal tab	DC4	Device control four	US	Unit separator
LF	Line feed	NAK	Negative acknowledge	DEL	Delete

The following package defines constants for all nonprintable and some printable characters in the ISO 8859-1 character set.

```
package Ada.Characters.Latin_1 is
   pragma Pure(Latin_1);

   -- Control characters:

   NUL                    : constant Character := Character'Val(0);
   SOH                    : constant Character := Character'Val(1);
   STX                    : constant Character := Character'Val(2);
   ETX                    : constant Character := Character'Val(3);
   EOT                    : constant Character := Character'Val(4);
   ENQ                    : constant Character := Character'Val(5);
   ACK                    : constant Character := Character'Val(6);
   BEL                    : constant Character := Character'Val(7);
   BS                     : constant Character := Character'Val(8);
   HT                     : constant Character := Character'Val(9);
   LF                     : constant Character := Character'Val(10);
   VT                     : constant Character := Character'Val(11);
   FF                     : constant Character := Character'Val(12);
   CR                     : constant Character := Character'Val(13);
   SO                     : constant Character := Character'Val(14);
   SI                     : constant Character := Character'Val(15);

   DLE                    : constant Character := Character'Val(16);
   DC1                    : constant Character := Character'Val(17);
   DC2                    : constant Character := Character'Val(18);
   DC3                    : constant Character := Character'Val(19);
   DC4                    : constant Character := Character'Val(20);
   NAK                    : constant Character := Character'Val(21);
   SYN                    : constant Character := Character'Val(22);
```

```
ETB                    : constant Character := Character'Val(23);
CAN                    : constant Character := Character'Val(24);
EM                     : constant Character := Character'Val(25);
SUB                    : constant Character := Character'Val(26);
ESC                    : constant Character := Character'Val(27);
FS                     : constant Character := Character'Val(28);
GS                     : constant Character := Character'Val(29);
RS                     : constant Character := Character'Val(30);
US                     : constant Character := Character'Val(31);

    -- ISO 646 graphic characters:

Space                  : constant Character := ' ';   -- Character'Val(32)
Exclamation            : constant Character := '!';   -- Character'Val(33)
Quotation              : constant Character := '"';   -- Character'Val(34)
Number_Sign            : constant Character := '#';   -- Character'Val(35)
Dollar_Sign            : constant Character := '$';   -- Character'Val(36)
Percent_Sign           : constant Character := '%';   -- Character'Val(37)
Ampersand              : constant Character := '&';   -- Character'Val(38)
Apostrophe             : constant Character := ''';   -- Character'Val(39)
Left_Parenthesis       : constant Character := '(';   -- Character'Val(40)
Right_Parenthesis      : constant Character := ')';   -- Character'Val(41)
Asterisk               : constant Character := '*';   -- Character'Val(42)
Plus_Sign              : constant Character := '+';   -- Character'Val(43)
Comma                  : constant Character := ',';   -- Character'Val(44)
Hyphen                 : constant Character := '-';   -- Character'Val(45)
Minus_Sign             : Character renames Hyphen;
Full_Stop              : constant Character := '.';   -- Character'Val(46)
Solidus                : constant Character := '/';   -- Character'Val(47)

-- Decimal digits '0' though '9' are at positions 48 through 57

Colon                  : constant Character := ':';   -- Character'Val(58)
Semicolon              : constant Character := ';';   -- Character'Val(59)
Less_Than_Sign         : constant Character := '<';   -- Character'Val(60)
Equals_Sign            : constant Character := '=';   -- Character'Val(61)
Greater_Than_Sign      : constant Character := '>';   -- Character'Val(62)
Question               : constant Character := '?';   -- Character'Val(63)
Commercial_At          : constant Character := '@';   -- Character'Val(64)

-- Letters 'A' through 'Z' are at positions 65 through 90

Left_Square_Bracket    : constant Character := '[';   -- Character'Val(91)
Reverse_Solidus        : constant Character := '\';   -- Character'Val(92)
Right_Square_Bracket   : constant Character := ']';   -- Character'Val(93)
Circumflex             : constant Character := '^';   -- Character'Val(94)
Low_Line               : constant Character := '_';   -- Character'Val(95)
```

```
Grave               : constant Character := '`';  -- Character'Val(96)
LC_A                : constant Character := 'a';  -- Character'Val(97)
LC_B                : constant Character := 'b';  -- Character'Val(98)
LC_C                : constant Character := 'c';  -- Character'Val(99)
LC_D                : constant Character := 'd';  -- Character'Val(100)
LC_E                : constant Character := 'e';  -- Character'Val(101)
LC_F                : constant Character := 'f';  -- Character'Val(102)
LC_G                : constant Character := 'g';  -- Character'Val(103)
LC_H                : constant Character := 'h';  -- Character'Val(104)
LC_I                : constant Character := 'i';  -- Character'Val(105)
LC_J                : constant Character := 'j';  -- Character'Val(106)
LC_K                : constant Character := 'k';  -- Character'Val(107)
LC_L                : constant Character := 'l';  -- Character'Val(108)
LC_M                : constant Character := 'm';  -- Character'Val(109)
LC_N                : constant Character := 'n';  -- Character'Val(110)
LC_O                : constant Character := 'o';  -- Character'Val(111)

LC_P                : constant Character := 'p';  -- Character'Val(112)
LC_Q                : constant Character := 'q';  -- Character'Val(113)
LC_R                : constant Character := 'r';  -- Character'Val(114)
LC_S                : constant Character := 's';  -- Character'Val(115)
LC_T                : constant Character := 't';  -- Character'Val(116)
LC_U                : constant Character := 'u';  -- Character'Val(117)
LC_V                : constant Character := 'v';  -- Character'Val(118)
LC_W                : constant Character := 'w';  -- Character'Val(119)
LC_X                : constant Character := 'x';  -- Character'Val(120)
LC_Y                : constant Character := 'y';  -- Character'Val(121)
LC_Z                : constant Character := 'z';  -- Character'Val(122)
Left_Curly_Bracket  : constant Character := '{';  -- Character'Val(123)
Vertical_Line       : constant Character := '|';  -- Character'Val(124)
Right_Curly_Bracket : constant Character := '}';  -- Character'Val(125)
Tilde               : constant Character := '~';  -- Character'Val(126)
DEL                 : constant Character := Character'Val(127);

-- ISO 6429 control characters:

IS4                 : Character renames FS;
IS3                 : Character renames GS;
IS2                 : Character renames RS;
IS1                 : Character renames US;

Reserved_128        : constant Character := Character'Val(128);
Reserved_129        : constant Character := Character'Val(129);
BPH                 : constant Character := Character'Val(130);
NBH                 : constant Character := Character'Val(131);
Reserved_132        : constant Character := Character'Val(132);
NEL                 : constant Character := Character'Val(133);
SSA                 : constant Character := Character'Val(134);
ESA                 : constant Character := Character'Val(135);
HTS                 : constant Character := Character'Val(136);
```

```
HTJ                : constant Character := Character'Val(137);
VTS                : constant Character := Character'Val(138);
PLD                : constant Character := Character'Val(139);
PLU                : constant Character := Character'Val(140);
RI                 : constant Character := Character'Val(141);
SS2                : constant Character := Character'Val(142);
SS3                : constant Character := Character'Val(143);

DCS                : constant Character := Character'Val(144);
PU1                : constant Character := Character'Val(145);
PU2                : constant Character := Character'Val(146);
STS                : constant Character := Character'Val(147);
CCH                : constant Character := Character'Val(148);
MW                 : constant Character := Character'Val(149);
SPA                : constant Character := Character'Val(150);
EPA                : constant Character := Character'Val(151);

SOS                : constant Character := Character'Val(152);
Reserved_153       : constant Character := Character'Val(153);
SCI                : constant Character := Character'Val(154);
CSI                : constant Character := Character'Val(155);
ST                 : constant Character := Character'Val(156);
OSC                : constant Character := Character'Val(157);
PM                 : constant Character := Character'Val(158);
APC                : constant Character := Character'Val(159);

-- Other graphic characters:

-- Character positions 160 (16#A0#) .. 175 (16#AF#):

                                                 -- Character'Val(160)
No_Break_Space               : constant Character := ' ';

NBSP                         : Character renames No_Break_Space;
Inverted_Exclamation         : constant Character := Character'Val(161);
Cent_Sign                    : constant Character := Character'Val(162);
Pound_Sign                   : constant Character := Character'Val(163);
Currency_Sign                : constant Character := Character'Val(164);
Yen_Sign                     : constant Character := Character'Val(165);
Broken_Bar                   : constant Character := Character'Val(166);
Section_Sign                 : constant Character := Character'Val(167);
Diaeresis                    : constant Character := Character'Val(168);
Copyright_Sign               : constant Character := Character'Val(169);
Feminine_Ordinal_Indicator   : constant Character := Character'Val(170);
Left_Angle_Quotation         : constant Character := Character'Val(171);
Not_Sign                     : constant Character := Character'Val(172);
Soft_Hyphen                  : constant Character := Character'Val(173);
Registered_Trade_Mark_Sign   : constant Character := Character'Val(174);
Macron                       : constant Character := Character'Val(175);
```

```
-- Character positions 176 (16#B0#) .. 191 (16#BF#):
Degree_Sign                  : constant Character := Character'Val(176);
Ring_Above                   : Character renames Degree_Sign;
Plus_Minus_Sign              : constant Character := Character'Val(177);
Superscript_Two              : constant Character := Character'Val(178);
Superscript_Three            : constant Character := Character'Val(179);
Acute                        : constant Character := Character'Val(180);
Micro_Sign                   : constant Character := Character'Val(181);
Pilcrow_Sign                 : constant Character := Character'Val(182);
Paragraph_Sign               : Character renames Pilcrow_Sign;
Middle_Dot                   : constant Character := Character'Val(183);
Cedilla                      : constant Character := Character'Val(184);
Superscript_One              : constant Character := Character'Val(185);
Masculine_Ordinal_Indicator  : constant Character := Character'Val(186);
Right_Angle_Quotation        : constant Character := Character'Val(187);
Fraction_One_Quarter         : constant Character := Character'Val(188);
Fraction_One_Half            : constant Character := Character'Val(189);
Fraction_Three_Quarters      : constant Character := Character'Val(190);
Inverted_Question            : constant Character := Character'Val(191);

-- Character positions 192 (16#C0#) .. 207 (16#CF#):
UC_A_Grave                   : constant Character := Character'Val(192);
UC_A_Acute                   : constant Character := Character'Val(193);
UC_A_Circumflex              : constant Character := Character'Val(194);
UC_A_Tilde                   : constant Character := Character'Val(195);
UC_A_Diaeresis               : constant Character := Character'Val(196);
UC_A_Ring                    : constant Character := Character'Val(197);
UC_AE_Diphthong              : constant Character := Character'Val(198);
UC_C_Cedilla                 : constant Character := Character'Val(199);
UC_E_Grave                   : constant Character := Character'Val(200);
UC_E_Acute                   : constant Character := Character'Val(201);
UC_E_Circumflex              : constant Character := Character'Val(202);
UC_E_Diaeresis               : constant Character := Character'Val(203);
UC_I_Grave                   : constant Character := Character'Val(204);
UC_I_Acute                   : constant Character := Character'Val(205);
UC_I_Circumflex              : constant Character := Character'Val(206);
UC_I_Diaeresis               : constant Character := Character'Val(207);

    -- Character positions 208 (16#D0#) .. 223 (16#DF#):
UC_Icelandic_Eth             : constant Character := Character'Val(208);
UC_N_Tilde                   : constant Character := Character'Val(209);
UC_O_Grave                   : constant Character := Character'Val(210);
UC_O_Acute                   : constant Character := Character'Val(211);
UC_O_Circumflex              : constant Character := Character'Val(212);
UC_O_Tilde                   : constant Character := Character'Val(213);
UC_O_Diaeresis               : constant Character := Character'Val(214);
Multiplication_Sign          : constant Character := Character'Val(215);
UC_O_Oblique_Stroke          : constant Character := Character'Val(216);
UC_U_Grave                   : constant Character := Character'Val(217);
```

```
   UC_U_Acute                    : constant Character := Character'Val(218);
   UC_U_Circumflex               : constant Character := Character'Val(219);
   UC_U_Diaeresis                : constant Character := Character'Val(220);
   UC_Y_Acute                    : constant Character := Character'Val(221);
   UC_Icelandic_Thorn            : constant Character := Character'Val(222);
   LC_German_Sharp_S             : constant Character := Character'Val(223);

       -- Character positions 224 (16#E0#) .. 239 (16#EF#):
   LC_A_Grave                    : constant Character := Character'Val(224);
   LC_A_Acute                    : constant Character := Character'Val(225);
   LC_A_Circumflex               : constant Character := Character'Val(226);
   LC_A_Tilde                    : constant Character := Character'Val(227);
   LC_A_Diaeresis                : constant Character := Character'Val(228);
   LC_A_Ring                     : constant Character := Character'Val(229);
   LC_AE_Diphthong               : constant Character := Character'Val(230);
   LC_C_Cedilla                  : constant Character := Character'Val(231);
   LC_E_Grave                    : constant Character := Character'Val(232);
   LC_E_Acute                    : constant Character := Character'Val(233);
   LC_E_Circumflex               : constant Character := Character'Val(234);
   LC_E_Diaeresis                : constant Character := Character'Val(235);
   LC_I_Grave                    : constant Character := Character'Val(236);
   LC_I_Acute                    : constant Character := Character'Val(237);
   LC_I_Circumflex               : constant Character := Character'Val(238);
   LC_I_Diaeresis                : constant Character := Character'Val(239);

       -- Character positions 240 (16#F0#) .. 255 (16#FF#):
   LC_Icelandic_Eth              : constant Character := Character'Val(240);
   LC_N_Tilde                    : constant Character := Character'Val(241);
   LC_O_Grave                    : constant Character := Character'Val(242);
   LC_O_Acute                    : constant Character := Character'Val(243);
   LC_O_Circumflex               : constant Character := Character'Val(244);
   LC_O_Tilde                    : constant Character := Character'Val(245);
   LC_O_Diaeresis                : constant Character := Character'Val(246);
   Division_Sign                 : constant Character := Character'Val(247);
   LC_O_Oblique_Stroke           : constant Character := Character'Val(248);
   LC_U_Grave                    : constant Character := Character'Val(249);
   LC_U_Acute                    : constant Character := Character'Val(250);
   LC_U_Circumflex               : constant Character := Character'Val(251);
   LC_U_Diaeresis                : constant Character := Character'Val(252);
   LC_Y_Acute                    : constant Character := Character'Val(253);
   LC_Icelandic_Thorn            : constant Character := Character'Val(254);
   LC_Y_Diaeresis                : constant Character := Character'Val(255);
end Ada.Characters.Latin_1;
```

APPENDIX D

Specification of the Package Text_IO

This appendix contains the specification of the predefined package Text_IO. It is taken directly from the *Ada Language Reference Manual* which contains detailed descriptions of the resources in the package.

```
with Ada.IO_Exceptions;
package Ada.Text_IO is

   type File_Type is limited private;

   type File_Mode is (In_File, Out_File, Append_File);

   type Count is range 0 ..implementation-defined;
   subtype Positive_Count is Count range 1 .. Count'Last;
   Unbounded : constant Count := 0;    line and page length

   subtype Field       is Integer range 0 .. implementation-defined;
   subtype Number_Base is Integer range 2 .. 16;

   type Type_Set is (Lower_Case, Upper_Case);

   -- File Management

   procedure Create (File : in out File_Type;
                     Mode : in File_Mode := Out_File;
                     Name : in String    := "";
                     Form : in String    := "");

   procedure Open   (File : in out File_Type;
                     Mode : in File_Mode;
                     Name : in String;
                     Form : in String := "");
```

```
procedure Close  (File : in out File_Type);
procedure Delete (File : in out File_Type);
procedure Reset  (File : in out File_Type; Mode : in File_Mode);
procedure Reset  (File : in out File_Type);

function  Mode   (File : in File_Type) return File_Mode;
function  Name   (File : in File_Type) return String;
function  Form   (File : in File_Type) return String;

function  Is_Open(File : in File_Type) return Boolean;

-- Control of default input and output files

procedure Set_Input (File : in File_Type);
procedure Set_Output(File : in File_Type);
procedure Set_Error (File : in File_Type);

function Standard_Input  return File_Type;
function Standard_Output return File_Type;
function Standard_Error  return File_Type;

function Current_Input   return File_Type;
function Current_Output  return File_Type;
function Current_Error   return File_Type;

type File_Access is access constant File_Type;

function Standard_Input  return File_Access;
function Standard_Output return File_Access;
function Standard_Error  return File_Access;

function Current_Input   return File_Access;
function Current_Output  return File_Access;
function Current_Error   return File_Access;

-- Buffer control
procedure Flush (File : in out File_Type);
procedure Flush;

-- Specification of line and page lengths

procedure Set_Line_Length(File : in File_Type; To : in Count);
procedure Set_Line_Length(To   : in Count);

procedure Set_Page_Length(File : in File_Type; To : in Count);
procedure Set_Page_Length(To   : in Count);
```

```
function  Line_Length(File : in File_Type) return Count;
function  Line_Length return Count;

function  Page_Length(File : in File_Type) return Count;
function  Page_Length return Count;

-- Column, Line, and Page Control

procedure New_Line   (File    : in File_Type;
                      Spacing : in Positive_Count := 1);
procedure New_Line   (Spacing : in Positive_Count := 1);

procedure Skip_Line  (File    : in File_Type;
                      Spacing : in Positive_Count := 1);
procedure Skip_Line  (Spacing : in Positive_Count := 1);

function  End_Of_Line(File : in File_Type) return Boolean;
function  End_Of_Line return Boolean;

procedure New_Page   (File : in File_Type);
procedure New_Page;

procedure Skip_Page  (File : in File_Type);
procedure Skip_Page;

function  End_Of_Page(File : in File_Type) return Boolean;
function  End_Of_Page return Boolean;

function  End_Of_File(File : in File_Type) return Boolean;
function  End_Of_File return Boolean;

procedure Set_Col (File : in File_Type; To : in Positive_Count);
procedure Set_Col (To   : in Positive_Count);

procedure Set_Line(File : in File_Type; To : in Positive_Count);
procedure Set_Line(To   : in Positive_Count);

function Col (File : in File_Type) return Positive_Count;
function Col  return Positive_Count;

function Line(File : in File_Type) return Positive_Count;
function Line return Positive_Count;

function Page(File : in File_Type) return Positive_Count;
function Page return Positive_Count;
```

```
-- Character Input-Output

procedure Get(File : in  File_Type; Item : out Character);
procedure Get(Item : out Character);

procedure Put(File : in  File_Type; Item : in Character);
procedure Put(Item : in  Character);

procedure Look_Ahead (File        : in  File_Type;
                      Item        : out Character;
                      End_Of_Line : out Boolean);
procedure Look_Ahead (Item        : out Character;
                      End_Of_Line : out Boolean);

procedure Get_Immediate(File      : in  File_Type;
                        Item      : out Character);
procedure Get_Immediate(Item      : out Character);

procedure Get_Immediate(File      : in  File_Type;
                        Item      : out Character;
                        Available : out Boolean);
procedure Get_Immediate(Item      : out Character;
                        Available : out Boolean);

-- String Input-Output

procedure Get(File : in  File_Type; Item : out String);
procedure Get(Item : out String);

procedure Put(File : in  File_Type; Item : in String);
procedure Put(Item : in  String);

procedure Get_Line(File : in  File_Type;
                   Item : out String;
                   Last : out Natural);
procedure Get_Line(Item : out String; Last : out Natural);

procedure Put_Line(File : in  File_Type; Item : in String);
procedure Put_Line(Item : in  String);

    -- Generic packages for Input-Output of Integer Types

generic
   type Num is range <>;
package Integer_IO is

   Default_Width : Field := Num'Width;
   Default_Base  : Number_Base := 10;
```

```
   procedure Get(File  : in  File_Type;
                 Item  : out Num;
                 Width : in Field := 0);
   procedure Get(Item  : out Num;
                 Width : in  Field := 0);

   procedure Put(File  : in File_Type;
                 Item  : in Num;
                 Width : in Field := Default_Width;
                 Base  : in Number_Base := Default_Base);
   procedure Put(Item  : in Num;
                 Width : in Field := Default_Width;
                 Base  : in Number_Base := Default_Base);
   procedure Get(From : in  String;
                 Item : out Num;
                 Last : out Positive);
   procedure Put(To   : out String;
                 Item : in Num;
                 Base : in Number_Base := Default_Base);

end Integer_IO;

generic
   type Num is mod <>;
package Modular_IO is

   Default_Width : Field := Num'Width;
   Default_Base  : Number_Base := 10;

   procedure Get(File  : in  File_Type;
                 Item  : out Num;
                 Width : in Field := 0);
   procedure Get(Item  : out Num;
                 Width : in  Field := 0);

   procedure Put(File  : in File_Type;
                 Item  : in Num;
                 Width : in Field := Default_Width;
                 Base  : in Number_Base := Default_Base);
   procedure Put(Item  : in Num;
                 Width : in Field := Default_Width;
                 Base  : in Number_Base := Default_Base);
   procedure Get(From : in  String;
                 Item : out Num;
                 Last : out Positive);
   procedure Put(To   : out String;
                 Item : in Num;
                 Base : in Number_Base := Default_Base);
```

```
end Modular_IO;

-- Generic packages for Input-Output of Real Types

generic
   type Num is digits <>;
package Float_IO is

   Default_Fore : Field := 2;
   Default_Aft  : Field := Num'Digits-1;
   Default_Exp  : Field := 3;

   procedure Get(File  : in  File_Type;
                 Item  : out Num;
                 Width : in  Field := 0);
   procedure Get(Item  : out Num;
                 Width : in  Field := 0);

   procedure Put(File : in File_Type;
                 Item : in Num;
                 Fore : in Field := Default_Fore;
                 Aft  : in Field := Default_Aft;
                 Exp  : in Field := Default_Exp);
   procedure Put(Item : in Num;
                 Fore : in Field := Default_Fore;
                 Aft  : in Field := Default_Aft;
                 Exp  : in Field := Default_Exp);

   procedure Get(From : in String;
                 Item : out Num;
                 Last : out Positive);
   procedure Put(To   : out String;
                 Item : in Num;
                 Aft  : in Field := Default_Aft;
                 Exp  : in Field := Default_Exp);
end Float_IO;

generic
   type Num is delta <>;
package Fixed_IO is

   Default_Fore : Field := Num'Fore;
   Default_Aft  : Field := Num'Aft;
   Default_Exp  : Field := 0;

   procedure Get(File  : in  File_Type;
                 Item  : out Num;
                 Width : in  Field := 0);
   procedure Get(Item  : out Num;
                 Width : in  Field := 0);
```

```
   procedure Put(File : in File_Type;
                 Item : in Num;
                 Fore : in Field := Default_Fore;
                 Aft  : in Field := Default_Aft;
                 Exp  : in Field := Default_Exp);
   procedure Put(Item : in Num;
                 Fore : in Field := Default_Fore;
                 Aft  : in Field := Default_Aft;
                 Exp  : in Field := Default_Exp);

   procedure Get(From : in  String;
                 Item : out Num;
                 Last : out Positive);
   procedure Put(To   : out String;
                 Item : in Num;
                 Aft  : in Field := Default_Aft;
                 Exp  : in Field := Default_Exp);
end Fixed_IO;

generic
   type Num is delta <> digits <>;
package Decimal_IO is

   Default_Fore : Field := Num'Fore;
   Default_Aft  : Field := Num'Aft;
   Default_Exp  : Field := 0;

   procedure Get(File  : in  File_Type;
                 Item  : out Num;
                 Width : in  Field := 0);
   procedure Get(Item  : out Num;
                 Width : in  Field := 0);

   procedure Put(File : in File_Type;
                 Item : in Num;
                 Fore : in Field := Default_Fore;
                 Aft  : in Field := Default_Aft;
                 Exp  : in Field := Default_Exp);
   procedure Put(Item : in Num;
                 Fore : in Field := Default_Fore;
                 Aft  : in Field := Default_Aft;
                 Exp  : in Field := Default_Exp);

   procedure Get(From : in  String;
                 Item : out Num;
                 Last : out Positive);
   procedure Put(To   : out String;
                 Item : in Num;
                 Aft  : in Field := Default_Aft;
```

```
                  Exp  : in Field := Default_Exp);
   end Decimal_IO;

   -- Generic package for Input-Output of Enumeration Types

   generic
      type Enum is (<>);
   package Enumeration_IO is

      Default_Width   : Field := 0;
      Default_Setting : Type_Set := Upper_Case;

      procedure Get(File : in  File_Type;
                    Item : out Enum);
      procedure Get(Item : out Enum);

      procedure Put(File  : in File_Type;
                    Item  : in Enum;
                    Width : in Field    := Default_Width;
                    Set   : in Type_Set := Default_Setting);
      procedure Put(Item  : in Enum;
                    Width : in Field    := Default_Width;
                    Set   : in Type_Set := Default_Setting);

      procedure Get(From : in  String;
                    Item : out Enum;
                    Last : out Positive);
      procedure Put(To   : out String;
                    Item : in  Enum;
                    Set  : in  Type_Set := Default_Setting);
   end Enumeration_IO;

   -- Exceptions

   Status_Error : exception renames IO_Exceptions.Status_Error;
   Mode_Error   : exception renames IO_Exceptions.Mode_Error;
   Name_Error   : exception renames IO_Exceptions.Name_Error;
   Use_Error    : exception renames IO_Exceptions.Use_Error;
   Device_Error : exception renames IO_Exceptions.Device_Error;
   End_Error    : exception renames IO_Exceptions.End_Error;
   Data_Error   : exception renames IO_Exceptions.Data_Error;
   Layout_Error : exception renames IO_Exceptions.Layout_Error;

private
   ... -- not specified by the language
end Ada.Text_IO;
```

APPENDIX E

Specifications of the Packages Sequential_IO and Direct_IO

This appendix contains the specification of the predefined packages Sequential_IO and Direct_IO. It is taken directly from the *Ada Language Reference Manual*, which contains detailed descriptions of the resources in the packages.

```
with Ada.IO_Exceptions;
generic
   type Element_Type(<>) is private;
package Ada.Sequential_IO is

   type File_Type is limited private;

   type File_Mode is (In_File, Out_File, Append_File);

   -- File management

   procedure Create(File : in out File_Type;
                    Mode : in File_Mode := Out_File;
                    Name : in String := "";
                    Form : in String := "");

   procedure Open  (File : in out File_Type;
                    Mode : in File_Mode;
                    Name : in String;
                    Form : in String := "");

   procedure Close (File : in out File_Type);
   procedure Delete(File : in out File_Type);
   procedure Reset (File : in out File_Type; Mode : in File_Mode);
   procedure Reset (File : in out File_Type);

   function Mode    (File : in File_Type) return File_Mode;
   function Name    (File : in File_Type) return String;
   function Form    (File : in File_Type) return String;

   function Is_Open(File : in File_Type) return Boolean;
```

```
   -- Input and output operations

   procedure Read  (File : in File_Type; Item : out Element_Type);
   procedure Write (File : in File_Type; Item : in Element_Type);

   function End_Of_File(File : in File_Type) return Boolean;

   -- Exceptions

   Status_Error : exception renames IO_Exceptions.Status_Error;
   Mode_Error   : exception renames IO_Exceptions.Mode_Error;
   Name_Error   : exception renames IO_Exceptions.Name_Error;
   Use_Error    : exception renames IO_Exceptions.Use_Error;
   Device_Error : exception renames IO_Exceptions.Device_Error;
   End_Error    : exception renames IO_Exceptions.End_Error;
   Data_Error   : exception renames IO_Exceptions.Data_Error;

private
   ... — not specified by the language
end Ada.Sequential_IO;
```

```
with Ada.IO_Exceptions;
generic
   type Element_Type is private;
package Ada.Direct_IO is

   type File_Type is limited private;

   type File_Mode is (In_File, Inout_File, Out_File);
   type Count     is range 0 .. implementation-defined;
   subtype Positive_Count is Count range 1 .. Count'Last;

   -- File management

   procedure Create(File : in out File_Type;
                    Mode : in File_Mode := Inout_File;
                    Name : in String := "";
                    Form : in String := "");

   procedure Open  (File : in out File_Type;
                    Mode : in File_Mode;
                    Name : in String;
                    Form : in String := "");
```

```
   procedure Close (File : in out File_Type);
   procedure Delete(File : in out File_Type);
   procedure Reset (File : in out File_Type; Mode : in File_Mode);
   procedure Reset (File : in out File_Type);

   function Mode   (File : in File_Type) return File_Mode;
   function Name   (File : in File_Type) return String;
   function Form   (File : in File_Type) return String;

   function Is_Open(File : in File_Type) return Boolean;

   -- Input and output operations

   procedure Read (File : in File_Type; Item : out Element_Type;
                                        From : in Positive_Count);
   procedure Read (File : in File_Type; Item : out Element_Type);

   procedure Write(File : in File_Type; Item : in  Element_Type;
                                        To   : in Positive_Count);
   procedure Write(File : in File_Type; Item : in Element_Type);

   procedure Set_Index(File : in File_Type; To : in Positive_Count);

   function Index(File : in File_Type) return Positive_Count;
   function Size (File : in File_Type) return Count;

   function End_Of_File(File : in File_Type) return Boolean;

   -- Exceptions

   Status_Error : exception renames IO_Exceptions.Status_Error;
   Mode_Error   : exception renames IO_Exceptions.Mode_Error;
   Name_Error   : exception renames IO_Exceptions.Name_Error;
   Use_Error    : exception renames IO_Exceptions.Use_Error;
   Device_Error : exception renames IO_Exceptions.Device_Error;
   End_Error    : exception renames IO_Exceptions.End_Error;
   Data_Error   : exception renames IO_Exceptions.Data_Error;

private
   . . .  — not specified by the language
end Ada.Direct_IO;
```

APPENDIX F

Specification of the Package Calendar

This appendix contains the specification of the standard package Calendar. It is taken directly from the *Ada Language Reference Manual.*

```
package Ada.Calendar is

   type Time is private;

   subtype Year_Number  is Integer  range 1901 ..  2099;
   subtype Month_Number is Integer  range 1 ..  12;
   subtype Day_Number   is Integer  range 1 ..  31;
   subtype Day_Duration is Duration range 0.0 ..  86_400.0;

   function Clock return Time;

   function Year    (Date : Time) return Year_Number;
   function Month   (Date : Time) return Month_Number;
   function Day     (Date : Time) return Day_Number;
   function Seconds (Date : Time) return Day_Duration;

   procedure Split (Date    : in  Time;
                    Year    : out Year_Number;
                    Month   : out Month_Number;
                    Day     : out Day_Number;
                    Seconds : out Day_Duration);

   function Time_Of (Year    : Year_Number;
                     Month   : Month_Number;
                     Day     : Day_Number;
                     Seconds : Day_Duration := 0.0)
     return Time;

   function "+" (Left : Time;     Right : Duration) return Time;
   function "+" (Left : Duration; Right : Time)     return Time;
   function "-" (Left : Time;     Right : Duration) return Time;
   function "-" (Left : Time;     Right : Time)     return Duration;
```

```
   function "<" (Left, Right : Time) return Boolean;
   function "<="(Left, Right : Time) return Boolean;
   function ">" (Left, Right : Time) return Boolean;
   function ">="(Left, Right : Time) return Boolean;

   Time_Error : exception;

private
   ... -- not specified by the language
end Ada.Calendar;
```

APPENDIX G

Specification of the Package Standard

This appendix contains the specification of the predefined package Standard containing all predefined identifiers in the language. It is taken directly from the *Ada Language Reference Manual.* The operators that are predefined for the types declared in the package Standard are given in comments since they are implicitly declared. Italics are used for pseudonames of anonymous types (such as root_real) and for undefined information (such as *implementation-defined*).

```
package Standard is
   pragma Pure(Standard);

   type Boolean is (False, True);

   -- The predefined relational operators for this type are as follows:

   -- function "=" (Left, Right : Boolean) return Boolean;
   -- function "/=" (Left, Right : Boolean) return Boolean;
   -- function "<" (Left, Right : Boolean) return Boolean;
   -- function "<=" (Left, Right : Boolean) return Boolean;
   -- function ">" (Left, Right : Boolean) return Boolean;
   -- function ">=" (Left, Right : Boolean) return Boolean;

   -- The predefined logical operators and the predefined logical
   -- negation operator are as follows:

   -- function "and" (Left, Right : Boolean) return Boolean;
   -- function "or" (Left, Right : Boolean) return Boolean;
   -- function "xor" (Left, Right : Boolean) return Boolean;
   -- function "not" (Right : Boolean) return Boolean;

   -- The integer type root_integer is predefined.
   -- The corresponding universal type is universal_integer.

   type Integer is range implementation-defined;

   subtype Natural  is Integer range 0 .. Integer'Last;
   subtype Positive is Integer range 1 .. Integer'Last;
```

```
-- The predefined operators for type Integer are as follows:

-- function "=" (Left, Right : Integer'Base) return Boolean;
-- function "/=" (Left, Right : Integer'Base) return Boolean;
-- function "<" (Left, Right : Integer'Base) return Boolean;
-- function "<=" (Left, Right : Integer'Base) return Boolean;
-- function ">" (Left, Right : Integer'Base) return Boolean;
-- function ">=" (Left, Right : Integer'Base) return Boolean;

-- function "+" (Right : Integer'Base) return Integer'Base;
-- function "-" (Right : Integer'Base) return Integer'Base;
-- function "abs" (Right : Integer'Base) return Integer'Base;

-- function "+" (Left, Right : Integer'Base) return Integer'Base;
-- function "-" (Left, Right : Integer'Base) return Integer'Base;
-- function "*" (Left, Right : Integer'Base) return Integer'Base;
-- function "/" (Left, Right : Integer'Base) return Integer'Base;
-- function "rem" (Left, Right : Integer'Base) return Integer'Base;
-- function "mod" (Left, Right : Integer'Base) return Integer'Base;

-- function "**" (Left : Integer'Base; Right : Natural)
                  return Integer'Base;

-- The specification of each operator for the type root_integer, or for
-- any additional predefined integer type, is obtained by replacing
-- Integer by the name of the type in the specification of the
-- corresponding operator of the Integer. The right operand of the
-- exponentiation remains as subtype Natural.

-- The floating point type root_real is predefined.
-- The corresponding universal type is universal_real.

type Float is digits implementation-defined;

-- The predefined operators for this type are as follows:

-- function "=" (Left, Right : Float) return Boolean;
-- function "/=" (Left, Right : Float) return Boolean;
-- function "<" (Left, Right : Float) return Boolean;
-- function "<=" (Left, Right : Float) return Boolean;
-- function ">" (Left, Right : Float) return Boolean;
-- function ">=" (Left, Right : Float) return Boolean;

-- function "+" (Right : Float) return Float;
-- function "-" (Right : Float) return Float;
-- function "abs" (Right : Float) return Float;
```

```
-- function "+" (Left, Right : Float) return Float;
-- function "-" (Left, Right : Float) return Float;
-- function "*" (Left, Right : Float) return Float;
-- function "/" (Left, Right : Float) return Float;

-- function "**" (Left : Float; Right : Integer'Base) return Float;

-- The specification of each operator for the type root_real, or for
-- any additional predefined floating point type, is obtained by
-- replacing Float by the name of the type in the specification of the
-- corresponding operator of the type Float.

-- In addition, the following operators are predefined for the root
-- numeric types:

function "*" (Left : root_integer; Right : root_real)
  return root_real;

function "*" (Left : root_real;    Right : root_integer)
  return root_real;

function "/" (Left : root_real;    Right : root_integer)
  return root_real;

-- The type universal_fixed is predefined.
-- The only multiplying operators defined between
-- fixed point types are

function "*" (Left : universal_fixed; Right : universal_fixed)
  return universal_fixed;

function "/" (Left : universal_fixed; Right : universal_fixed)
  return universal_fixed;


-- The declaration of type Character is based on the
-- standard ISO 8859-1 character set.

-- There are no character literals corresponding to the positions
-- for control characters. They are indicated in italics in this
-- definition. See 3.5.2.

type Character is

  (nul, soh, stx, etx,     eot, enq, ack, bel,
   bs,  ht,  lf,  vt,      ff,  cr,  so,  si,

   dle, dc1, dc2, dc3,     dc4, nak, syn, etb,
   can, em,  sub, esc,     fs,  gs,  rs,  us,
```

```
' ',   '!',   '"',   '#',      '$',   '%',   '&',   ''',
'(',   ')',   '*',   '+',      ',',   '-',   '.',   '/',

'0',   '1',   '2',   '3',      '4',   '5',   '6',   '7',
'8',   '9',   ':',   ';',      '<',   '=',   '>',   '?',

'@',   'A',   'B',   'C',      'D',   'E',   'F',   'G',
'H',   'I',   'J',   'K',      'L',   'M',   'N',   'O',

'P',   'Q',   'R',   'S',      'T',   'U',   'V',   'W',
'X',   'Y',   'Z',   '[',      '\',   ']',   '^',   '_',

'`',   'a',   'b',   'c',      'd',   'e',   'f',   'g',
'h',   'i',   'j',   'k',      'l',   'm',   'n',   'o',

'p',   'q',   'r',   's',      't',   'u',   'v',   'w',
'x',   'y',   'z',   '{',      '|',   '}',   '~',   del,

reserved_128,   reserved_129,   bph,   nbh,
reserved_132,   nel,   ssa,   esa,

hts,   htj,   vts,   pld,      plu,   ri,   ss2,   ss3,

dcs,   pu1,   pu2,   sts,      cch,   mw,   spa,   epa,

sos,   reserved_153,   sci,    csi,
st,    osc,   pm,    apc,

 ... );

-- The predefined operators for the type Character are the same as for
-- any enumeration type.

-- The declaration of type Wide_Character is based on the standard ISO
-- 10646 BMP character   The first 256 positions have the same contents
-- as type Character. See 3.5.2.

type Wide_Character is (nul, soh ... FFFE, FFFF);

package ASCII is ... end ASCII;   —Obsolescent; see J.5

-- Predefined string types:

type String is array(Positive range <>) of Character;
pragma Pack(String);

-- The predefined operators for this type are as follows:
```

```
   -- function "=" (Left, Right: String) return Boolean;
   -- function "/=" (Left, Right: String) return Boolean;
   -- function "<" (Left, Right: String) return Boolean;
   -- function "<=" (Left, Right: String) return Boolean;
   -- function ">" (Left, Right: String) return Boolean;
   -- function ">=" (Left, Right: String) return Boolean;

   -- function "&" (Left: String; Right: String) return String;
   -- function "&" (Left: Character; Right: String) return String;
   -- function "&" (Left: String; Right: Character) return String;
   -- function "&" (Left: Character; Right: Character) return String;

   type Wide_String is array(Positive range <>) of Wide_Character;
   pragma Pack(Wide_String);

   -- The predefined operators for this type correspond to those for String

   type Duration is delta implementation-defined
                    range implementation-defined;

      -- The predefined operators for the type Duration are the same as
      -- for any fixed point type.

   -- The predefined exceptions:

   Constraint_Error: exception;
   Program_Error   : exception;
   Storage_Error   : exception;
   Tasking_Error   : exception;

end Standard;
```

APPENDIX H

The Numerics Packages

Package Numerics

The library package Numerics is the parent of several child units that provide facilities for mathematical computation. This appendix includes the specification of package Numerics and three of its child packages: Generic_Elementary_Functions, Float_Random, and Discrete_Random. For further explanations of these specifications, consult the *Ada Language Reference Manual.*

```
package Ada.Numerics is
   pragma Pure(Numerics);
   ARGUMENT_ERROR : exception;
   Pi  : constant :=
        3.14159_26535_89793_23846_26433_83279_50288_41971_69399_37511;
   e   : constant :=
        2.71828_18284_59045_23536_02874_71352_66249_77572_47093_69996;
end Ada.Numerics;
```

The ARGUMENT_ERROR exception is raised by a subprogram in a child unit of Numerics to signal that one or more of the actual subprogram parameters are outside the domain of the corresponding mathematical function.

Elementary Functions

Implementation-defined approximations to the mathematical functions known as the "elementary functions" are provided by the subprograms in package Numerics.Generic_Elementary_Functions. The library package Numerics.Elementary_Functions defines the same subprograms as Numerics.Generic_Elementary_Functions, except that the predefined type Float is systematically substituted for Float_Type'Base throughout.

```
generic
   type Float_Type is digits <>;
package Ada.Numerics.Generic_Elementary_Functions is
   pragma Pure(Generic_Elementary_Functions);
```

```
   function Sqrt     (X           : Float_Type'Base) return Float_Type'Base;
   function Log      (X           : Float_Type'Base) return Float_Type'Base;
   function Log      (X, Base     : Float_Type'Base) return Float_Type'Base;
   function Exp      (X           : Float_Type'Base) return Float_Type'Base;
   function "**"     (Left, Right : Float_Type'Base) return Float_Type'Base;

   function Sin      (X           : Float_Type'Base) return Float_Type'Base;
   function Sin      (X, Cycle    : Float_Type'Base) return Float_Type'Base;
   function Cos      (X           : Float_Type'Base) return Float_Type'Base;
   function Cos      (X, Cycle    : Float_Type'Base) return Float_Type'Base;
   function Tan      (X           : Float_Type'Base) return Float_Type'Base;
   function Tan      (X, Cycle    : Float_Type'Base) return Float_Type'Base;
   function Cot      (X           : Float_Type'Base) return Float_Type'Base;
   function Cot      (X, Cycle    : Float_Type'Base) return Float_Type'Base;

   function Arcsin   (X           : Float_Type'Base) return Float_Type'Base;
   function Arcsin   (X, Cycle    : Float_Type'Base) return Float_Type'Base;
   function Arccos   (X           : Float_Type'Base) return Float_Type'Base;
   function Arccos   (X, Cycle    : Float_Type'Base) return Float_Type'Base;
   function Arctan   (Y           : Float_Type'Base;
                      X           : Float_Type'Base := 1.0) return
                                              Float_Type'Base;
   function Arctan   (Y           : Float_Type'Base;
                      X           : Float_Type'Base := 1.0;
                      Cycle       : Float_Type'Base) return Float_Type'Base;
   function Arccot   (X           : Float_Type'Base;
                      Y           : Float_Type'Base := 1.0) return
                                              Float_Type'Base;
   function Arccot   (X           : Float_Type'Base;
                      Y           : Float_Type'Base := 1.0;
                      Cycle       : Float_Type'Base) return Float_Type'Base;

   function Sinh     (X           : Float_Type'Base) return Float_Type'Base;
   function Cosh     (X           : Float_Type'Base) return Float_Type'Base;
   function Tanh     (X           : Float_Type'Base) return Float_Type'Base;
   function Coth     (X           : Float_Type'Base) return Float_Type'Base;
   function Arcsinh  (X           : Float_Type'Base) return Float_Type'Base;
   function Arccosh  (X           : Float_Type'Base) return Float_Type'Base;
   function Arctanh  (X           : Float_Type'Base) return Float_Type'Base;
   function Arccoth  (X           : Float_Type'Base) return Float_Type'Base;

end Ada.Numerics.Generic_Elementary_Functions;
```

Random Number Generation

Facilities for the generation of pseudo-random floating-point numbers are provided in the package Numerics.Float_Random. The generic package Numerics.Discrete_Random provides similar facilities for the generation of pseudo-random integers and pseudo-random values of enumeration types.

```
package Ada.Numerics.Float_Random is

   -- Basic facilities

   type Generator is limited private;

   subtype Uniformly_Distributed is Float range 0.0 .. 1.0;
   function Random (Gen : Generator) return Uniformly_Distributed;

   procedure Reset (Gen       : in Generator;
                    Initiator : in Integer);
   procedure Reset (Gen       : in Generator);

   -- Advanced facilities

   type State is private;

   procedure Save  (Gen        : in  Generator;
                    To_State   : out State);
   procedure Reset (Gen        : in  Generator;
                    From_State : in  State);

   Max_Image_Width : constant := implementation-defined integer value;

   function Image (Of_State    : State)  return String;
   function Value (Coded_State : String) return State;

private
   ... -- not specified by the language
end Ada.Numerics.Float_Random;
```

```
generic
   type Result_Subtype is (<>);
package Ada.Numerics.Discrete_Random is
```

```
   -- Basic facilities

   type Generator is limited private;

   function Random (Gen : Generator) return Result_Subtype;

   procedure Reset (Gen       : in Generator;
                    Initiator : in Integer);
   procedure Reset (Gen       : in Generator);

   -- Advanced facilities

   type State is private;

   procedure Save  (Gen        : in  Generator;
                    To_State   : out State);
   procedure Reset (Gen        : in  Generator;
                    From_State : in  State);

   Max_Image_Width : constant := implementation-defined integer value;

   function Image (Of_State    : State)  return String;
   function Value (Coded_State : String) return State;

private
   ... -- not specified by the language
end Ada.Numerics.Discrete_Random;
```

APPENDIX I

Program Style, Formatting, and Documentation

Throughout this text we encourage the use of good programming style and documentation. Although the programs you write for class assignments may not be looked at by anyone except the person grading your work, outside of class you will write programs that will be used by others.

Useful programs have very long lifetimes, during which they must be modified and updated. When maintenance work must be done, either you or another programmer will have to do it. Good style and documentation are essential if another programmer is to understand and work with your program. You will also discover that, after not working with your own program for a few months, you'll forget many of the details.

General Guidelines

The style used in the programs and fragments throughout this text provides a good starting point for developing your own style. Our goals in creating this style were to make it simple, consistent, and easy to read.

Style is of benefit only for a human reader of your program—differences in style make no difference to the computer. Good style includes the use of meaningful identifiers, comments, and indentation of control structures, all of which help others to understand and work with your program. Perhaps the most important aspect of program style is consistency. If the style within a program is not consistent, then it becomes misleading and confusing.

Sometimes, your instructor or the company you work for will specify a particular style. When you are modifying someone else's code, you will use his or her style in order to maintain consistency within the program. However, you will also develop your own personal programming style based on what you've been taught, your experience, and your personal taste.

Comments

Comments are extra information included to make a program easier to understand. You should include a comment wherever the code is difficult to understand. However, don't overcomment. Too many comments in a program will obscure the code and be a source of distraction.

In our style, there are five basic types of comments: headers, definitions, inline, sidebar, and subprogram.

1. *Header comments* appear at the top of the program immediately following the specification and should include your name, the date that the program was written, and its purpose. Also include the input, output, and assumptions sections from your top-down design. Think of the header comments as the reader's introduction to your program. Here is an example.

```
--
-- This program computes the sidereal
-- time for a given date and solar time.
--
-- Written By:      Your Name
--
-- Date Completed:  4/8/99
--
-- Input:  A date and time in the form of MM DD YYYY HH MM SS
--
-- Output:  Sidereal time in the form of HH MM SS
--
-- Assumptions:  Solar time is specified for a longitude of 0
--               degrees (GMT, UT, or Z time zone)
--
```

2. *Definition comments* accompany all declarations and definitions in the program. Wherever an identifier is declared, you should include a comment that explains its purpose. In programs in the text, definition comments appear to the right of the identifier being declared. For example:

```
E : constant := 2.718281828459      -- The base of the natural logarithms

Delta_X : Float;                    -- The difference in the X direction
Delta_Y : Float;                    -- The difference in the Y direction
```

   Notice that aligning the comments gives the code a neater appearance and is less distracting.

3. *Inline comments* are used to break long sections of code into shorter, more comprehensible fragments. These include comments that explain the purpose of a group of related Ada statements. When an

algorithm module is implemented as inline code rather than a subprogram, you should include the module name as an inline comment before the code. You should surround inline comments with blank lines to make them stand out. We have not always done this in this text. To save space, we have used color instead. He are some examples of inline comments.

```
begin  -- Main Subprogram

   -- Initialize

   Ada.Text_IO.Open (File => In_File,
                     Mode => Ada.Text_IO.In_File,
                     Name => "TEMP.DAT");
   Min_Temp := Integer'First;

   -- Get Data

   Ada.Text_IO.Get (File => In_File, Item => Num_Temps);
```

Even if you don't include an inline comment, you should insert blank lines wherever there is a logical break in the code that you would like to emphasize.

4. *Sidebar comments* appear to the right of statements in the body of the program and are used to shed light on the function of the statement. Sidebar comments are often pseudocode statements from the lowest levels of your top-down design. If a complicated Ada statement requires some explanation, you should write the pseudocode statement to the right of the Ada statement. For example:

```
if Ada.Text_IO.End_Of_File (File1) /=           -- If one of the files is empty
   Ada.Text_IO.End_Of_File (File2)   then
    .
    .
    .
```

5. *Subprogram comments* are used to describe the design module you have implemented as a procedure or function. These comments include a brief description of what the subprogram does and the lists of preconditions and postconditions developed when you verify your design (see Chapter 4). Include additional comments for any parameters that are not described in the context of the subprogram description or the lists of preconditions and postconditions. Finally, a row of dashes should appear before each procedure or function to help it to stand out. The following fragment illustrates subprogram comments.

```
-----------------------------------------
procedure Get_Next_Odd (File        : in  Ada.Text_IO.File_Type;
                        Odd         : out Integer;
                        End_Of_File : out Boolean) is

-- Get the next odd number from the File
--
-- Preconditions  : File is open for input
--                  File contains only whole numbers
--
-- Postconditions : If there is an odd number remaining in the file
--                    Odd is the next odd number in File
--                    End_Of_File is False
--                    The reading marker is on the non-digit
--                      character or terminator that
--                      marked the end of the odd number.
--                  Otherwise
--                    Odd is undefined
--                    End_Of_File is True
--                    The reading marker designates the file terminator
```

Identifiers and Reserved Words

The most important consideration in choosing a name for an object or process in a program is that the name convey as much information as possible about what the object is or what the process does. The name should also be readable in the context in which it is used. For example, the following names convey the same information, but one is more readable than the other:

Date_Of_Invc   Invoice_Date

In addition to picking an informative name for each identifier, you should choose names for different identifiers that are psychologically distant* enough to avoid confusion. Words that look alike or have similar meanings are not psychologically distant. The following table ranks some example identifier name pairs in terms of their psychological distance.

*The application of psychological principles to programming was first discussed by Gerald Weinberg in his classic book, *The Psychology of Computer Programming*. New York: John Wiley & Sons, 1971.

First Identifier	Second Identifier	Psychological Distance
Sum_1	Sum_2	Very little (look alike)
Sum	Total	Little (same meaning)
Male_Total	Female_Total	Big (very informative)

Use nouns as identifiers for types, constants, or variables and verbs as names of procedures. Because of the way that functions are called, use nouns or occasionally adjectives as function names. To distinguish them from variables and constants, it is usually best to end programmer-defined type identifiers with the word Type, Rec, or Array. In some cases, such as the name of a unit of measurement, it is clearer when the word Type is not added to the end of the type identifier. Here are some examples.

Variables	Name, Car_Make, Price, Hours, Month, Paper_Length
Constants	Pi, Tax_Rate, String_Length, Array_Size
Data Types	Name_Type, Car_Make_Type, Month_Type, Inches, Customer_Rec, Score_Array
Procedures	Get_Data, Clear_Table, Print_Bar_Chart
Functions	Cube_Root, Greatest, Color, Area_Of, To_Inches

Although an identifier may be a series of words, very long identifiers can become quite tedious, making the program difficult to read. One way to shorten long identifiers is to use acronyms or abbreviations. Use capital letters for acronyms (DNA_Weight, for example). An abbreviation should be significantly shorter than the word it abbreviates. Try to use only standard abbreviations such as those listed in the back of most dictionaries. Be consistent with your abbreviations. Don't, for example, use both Num and Nmbr as abbreviations of Number in the same program.

Capitalization is another consideration when choosing an identifier. In this text's programs, the first letter of every word in an identifier is capitalized, and Ada reserved words are lowercase letters to distinguish them from identifiers.

The best approach to designing an identifier is to try writing out different names until you reach an acceptable compromise, and then write an especially informative definition comment next to the declaration.

Declaration Order

Declarations for named numbers, constants, variables, subprograms, types, and subtypes are made in the declarative part of each subprogram (including the main subprogram). The instantiation of generic packages also is done in this part of our program. Ada allows flexibility in the order of declarations. Generally, you need only declare something before it is used. To maintain a consistent style, we generally make our declarations in the following order.

1. Declaration of named numbers
2. Declaration of programmer-defined types and subtypes
3. Declaration of constants of programmer-defined types and subtypes
4. Instantiations of generic packages
5. Declaration of procedures and functions
6. Declaration of variables

However, because we must define an identifier before we can use it, there are situations in which we cannot group all similar declarations together in this order. In such cases, we modify the order of declarations or mix different kinds of declarations. There is no particular advantage of this ordering over others. Consistency is the key to readable programs.

Some programmers precede each of these declaration categories by an inline comment. We indent them all in the same way. We list each identifier, one per line, and indent it by three spaces from the level of the procedure, function, or package specification with a defining comment to the right. Here is an example.

```
procedure Declaration_Example is

   -- Named Numbers

   Pi : constant := 3.141592654;  -- Ratio of circumference to diameter
   E  : constant := 2.718281828;  -- Base of the natural logarithms

   -- Types

   type Product_Type is (Lumber, Plywood);         -- Products offered
   type Hours_Type   is range 0..100;               -- Hours worked

   subtype Name_Type is String(1..30);              -- For names

   type Time_Rec is
      record                        -- Time clock data
         First : Name_Type;            -- Employee first name
         Last  : Name_Type;            -- Employee last name
```

```
      Hours : Hours_Type;        -- Hours worked this week
   end record;

-- Constants

Max_Hours : constant Hours_Type := 40;    -- Hours worked before overtime
                                          -- must be paid

-- Instantiated Packages

package Product_IO is
               new Ada.Text_IO.Enumeration_IO (Enum => Product_Type);
package Hour_IO is new Ada.Text_IO.Integer_IO (Num => Hours_Type);

-- Subprograms

procedure Display_Headings is
.
.
.
end Display_Headings;

-- Variables for main subprogram

Radius   : Float;                -- Radius of a circle
Diameter : Float;                -- Diameter of a circle
Area     : Float;                -- Area of a circle
Count      : Integer;            -- Example number
Max_Circle : Integer;            -- Number of greatest circle
Min_Circle : Integer;            -- Number of smallest circle
.
.
.
```

In the text, we use two different indentation styles in procedure and function declarations. When space permits, the parameter list begins on the same line as the procedure or function name. Each formal parameter is on a separate line, in a style similar to that used for variable declarations as shown in the following example.

```
procedure Get_Sum (Number : in  Integer;       -- Number of values to be read
                   Sum    : out Float) is      -- Sum of values read
```

Occasionally, we need more room for the comments. In such a case, we use a second style in which the parameter list appears on lines following the procedure or function name. In the following example, note that the parameter list is indented under the procedure name specification.

```
procedure Get_Data_Average
   (In_file    : in out Ada.Text_IO.File_Type; -- File of test scores
    Num_Scores : in     Integer;               -- Number of scores to read
    Average:   : out    Float); is             -- Average of the test scores
```

The local declarations and body of a procedure or function follow the same guidelines as the declarations and body of the main subprogram. The only difference is that nested procedures or functions should be indented by three spaces for each level of nesting.

Formatting Lines and Expressions

In general, it is best never to include more than one statement or declaration on a line. When you must break a long statement in the middle and continue it on the next line, it's important to choose a breaking point that is logical and readable. Compare the readability of the following code fragments.

```
Ada.Text_IO.Put ("When you use strings that are too long to fit on a sin" &
                 "gle line, break them at natural boundaries.");

Ada.Text_IO.Put ("When you use strings that are too long to fit on a " &
                 "single line, break them at natural boundaries.");
```

When you must split an expression across multiple lines, try to end each line with an operator. Also, try to take advantage of any repeating patterns in the expression. For example:

```
Mean_Of_Maxima := (Maximum(Set1_Value1, Set1_Value2, Set1_Value3)  +
                   Maximum(Set2_Value1, Set2_Value2, Set2_Value3)  +
                   Maximum(Set3_Value1, Set3_Value2, Set3_Value3)) / 3.0;


Total_Amount := 0.0;    -- These three assignment statements are
Num          := 0;      -- aligned at the assignment operator (:=)
Male_Count   := 0;      -- for easier reading
```

When writing expressions, also keep in mind that spaces improve readability. Usually you should include one space on either side of the := and most operators. Occasionally spaces are left out to emphasize the order in which operations are performed. Here are some examples.

```
if X+Y > Y+Z  then
   Maximum := X + Y
else
   Maximum := Y + Z;
end if

Poly_Result := 3.8*X**3 - 4.5*X**2 - 2.3*X + 7.2
```

Indentation

The purpose of indenting statements in a program is to provide visual cues to the reader and to make the program easier to debug. When a program is properly indented, the way the statements are grouped is immediately obvious. Compare the following two program fragments.

```
Count_Loop:
loop
exit Count_Loop when Count > 10
Ada.Integer_Text_IO.Get (Num);
if Num = 0 then
Count := Count + 1;
Num := 1;
end if;
Ada.Integer_Text_IO.Put (Item => Num,
                         Width => 1);
Ada.Integer_Text_IO.Put (Item => Count,
                         Width => 1);
end loop Count_Loop;
```

```
Count_Loop:
loop
   exit Count_Loop when Count > 10
   Ada.Integer_Text_IO.Get (Num);
   if Num = 0 then
      Count := Count + 1;
      Num := 1;
   end if;
   Ada.Integer_Text_IO.Put (Item => Num,
                            Width => 1);
   Ada.Integer_Text_IO.Put (Item => Count,
                            Width => 1);
end loop Count_Loop;
```

As a basic rule in this text, we have indented each nested or lower-level item by three spaces. Exceptions to this rule are formal parameters and statements that are split across two or more lines. Indenting by three spaces is really just a minimum. Many people prefer to indent by four or even five spaces.

Statements

In general, you should indent any statement that is part of another statement, including assignment statements, procedure calls, and nested statements. The following example Ada statements follow these indentation guidelines.

```
if Sex = Male then
   Male_Salary := Male_Salary + Salary;
   Male_Count  := Male_Count  + 1;
else
   Female_Salary := Female_Salary + Salary;
end if;

if Count > 0 then
   Average := Total / Count;
end if;

if Month = "Jan" then
   Month_Num := 1;
elsif Month = "Feb" then
   Month_Num := 2;
elsif Month = "Mar" then
   Month_Num := 3;
   .
   .
   .
elsif Month = "Nov" then
   Month_Num := 11;
else
   Month_Num := 12;
end if;

case Color is
   when Red | Blue | Green  =>
      Color_IO.Put (Color);
      Ada.Text_IO.Put (" is an additive primary.");
   when Cyan | Magenta | Yellow  =>
      Color_IO.Put (Color);
      Ada.Text_IO.Put (" is a subtractive primary.");
   when White | Black  =>
      Ada.Text_IO.Put ("Not valid color.");
   when others  =>
      Ada.Text_IO.Put ("Not a primary color.");
end case;

Basic_Loop:
loop
   exit Basic_Loop when Count >= 10;
```

```
   Ada.Integer_Text_IO.Get (Value);
   Total := Total + Value;
   Count := Count + 1;
end loop Basic_Loop;

While_Loop:
while Count < 10 loop
   Ada.Integer_Text_IO.Get (Value);
   Total := Total + Value;
end loop While_Loop;

For_Loop:
for Count in 1..9 loop
   Ada.Integer_Text_IO.Get (Value);
   Total := Total + Value;
end loop For_Loop;
```

Glossary

abstract data type A class of data objects with a defined set of properties and a set of operations that process the data objects while maintaining the properties.

abstract step An algorithmic step for which some implementation details remain unspecified.

actual parameter An expression associated with a formal parameter name in a call to a subprogram; an expression associated with a formal parameter in the instantiation of a generic package.

aggregate A collection of component values contained within parentheses representing the value of an array or record.

algorithm A step-by-step finite procedure for solving a problem; a verbal or written description of a logical sequence of actions.

algorithm trace A process for verifying an algorithm by establishing a set of preconditions and postconditions for each module and then examining the algorithm step by step to check that the preconditions and postconditions are preserved.

ALU See *arithmetic/logic unit*.

anonymous type A type or subtype defined in the declaration of a variable, so called because it does not have an identifier (a name) associated with it.

arithmetic/logic unit (ALU) The component of the central processing unit that performs arithmetic and logical operations.

array A collection of components, all of the same type, ordered on N dimensions ($N \geq 1$); each component is accessed by N indices, each of which represents the component's position within that dimension.

assembler A program that translates an assembly language program into machine code.

assembly language A low-level programming language in which a mnemonic is used to represent each of the machine language instructions for a particular computer.

assignment statement A statement that gives the value of an expression to a variable.

atomic data type A data type that allows only a single value to be associated with an identifier of that type.

attribute An operator that yields a characteristic of an identifier; some attributes are functions, requiring a parameter.

automatic range-checking The automatic detection of the assignment of an out-of-range value to a variable.

auxiliary storage device A device that stores data in encoded form outside the computer's memory.

base case The case for which the solution can be stated nonrecursively.

base type The type from which the operations and values for a subtype are taken.

batch processing A technique for entering data and executing programs without intermediate user interaction with the computer.

binary Expressed in terms of combinations of the numbers 1 and 0 only.

binary file A file data type whose components are stored in the internal binary representation of the machine; a file terminator follows the last component in the file.

binary search A search algorithm for sorted lists that involves dividing the list in half and determining, by value comparison, whether the item would be in the upper or lower half; the process is performed repeatedly until either the item is found or it is determined that an item is not in the list.

bit Short for binary digit; a single 1 or 0.

body See *loop body, package body,* or *subprogram body.*

Boolean data Type consisting of only two values: True and False.

Boolean expression An assertion that can be evaluated as being either True or False, the only values of the Boolean data type.

booting the system The process of starting up a computer by loading the operating system into its main memory.

branch See *selection control structure.*

bus A set of wires that connect multiple subsystems.

byte Eight bits.

case selector The expression whose value determines which case alternative is selected.

central processing unit (CPU) The part of the computer that executes the instructions (program) stored in memory; consists of the arithmetic/logic unit and the control unit.

character set A standard set of alphanumeric characters with a given collating sequence and binary representation.

chief architect The leader of a programming team; determines the basic structure of the program and then delegates responsibility to implement the major modules.

code coverage A testing procedure designed by looking at the code of the program; see *minimum complete coverage* and *path coverage.*

code trace A verification process for a program in which each statement is examined to check that it faithfully implements the corresponding algorithmic step, and that the preconditions and postconditions of each module are preserved.

coding Translating an algorithm into a programming language; the process of assigning bit patterns to pieces of information.

collating sequence The ordering of the elements of a set or series, such as the characters (values) in a character set.

compilation A source file containing one or more compilation units submitted to an Ada compiler.

compilation unit A portion of an Ada program that can be compiled by itself.

compiler A program that translates a high-level language (such as Ada, C++, Java, Pascal, COBOL, or FORTRAN) into machine code.

compiler listing A copy of a program output by the compiler into which have been inserted messages from the compiler (indicating errors in the program that prevent its translation into machine language if appropriate).

composite data type A data type that allows a collection of values to be associated with an identifier of that type.

computer A programmable device that can store, retrieve, and process data.

computer program A list of instructions to be performed by a computer.

computer programming The process of planning a sequence of steps for a computer to follow.

concrete step A step for which the implementation details are fully specified.

conditional test The point at which the Boolean expression is evaluated and the decision is made to either begin a new iteration or skip to the first statement following the loop.

constant An item in a program whose value is fixed at compile time and cannot be changed during execution; see *literal* and *named number*.

constant time An algorithm whose Big-O work expression is a constant.

constrained array type An array type with a range specified for its index.

control abstraction The separation of the logical properties of a control structure from its implementation; also called procedural abstraction.

control character A character that is interpreted with special meaning by a peripheral device; used to control the device.

control structure A statement used to alter the normally sequential flow of control.

control unit The component of the central processing unit that controls actions of other components so that instructions (the program) are executed in sequence.

convergent The property of a calculation-controlled loop that each calculation (iteration) brings us closer to the termination condition.

conversion function A function that converts a value of one type to another type so that it can be assigned to a variable of the second type.

count-controlled loop A loop that executes a predetermined number of times.

counter A variable whose value is incremented to keep track of the number of times a process or event occurs.

CPU See *central processing unit.*

crash The cessation of a computer's operations as a result of the failure of one of its components; cessation of program execution due to an error.

cursor control keys A special set of keys on a computer keyboard that allows the user to move the cursor up, down, right, and left to any point on the screen.

data Information that has been put into a form a computer can use.

data abstraction The separation of the logical properties of a data structure from its implementation.

data coverage A testing procedure based on input data values without regard to the program code.

data structure A collection of data elements whose organization determines the methods by which the individual elements are accessed.

data type The general form of a class of data items; a formal description of the set of values (called the domain) and the basic set of operations that can be applied to it.

data validation A test procedure that checks for errors in the data; may be done actively with if statements or passively with exceptions.

debugging The process by which errors are removed from a program so that it does exactly what it is supposed to do.

declaration The association of a name with an entity.

declarative part A sequence of declarations in a program unit or block statement.

declarative region The portion of a subprogram that begins immediately after the subprogram name and goes through the end of its body; used to determine scope of access.

designator The name that identifies a function; may be an identifier or operator symbol.

direct file A binary file whose components can be accessed sequentially or randomly (in any order).

discrete data type An atomic data type in which each value (except the first) has a unique predecessor and each value (except the last) has a unique successor.

documentation The written text and comments that make a program easier for the programmer and others to understand, use, and modify.

down A descriptive term applied to a computer when it is not in a usable condition.

driver A simple dummy main program that is used to call a procedure or function being tested.

echo printing Printing the data values input to a program to verify that they are correct.

editor An interactive program used to create and modify source programs or data.

elaboration The run-time processing of declarations.

embedded computer system A computer system that is only a part of a larger piece of equipment.

encapsulation A programming language feature that allows a compiler to enforce information hiding.

enumeration data type An ordered set of literal values (identifiers) defined as a data type.

event-controlled loop A loop that terminates when something happens inside the loop body to signal that the loop should be exited.

event counter A variable that is incremented each time a particular event occurs.

exception handler A sequence of instructions that is executed when an exception is raised.

exception report A set of messages in a program that explains the actions taken when an invalid data item is encountered during execution.

executing The action of a computer performing as instructed by a given program.

execution summary A computer-generated list of all commands processed and any system messages generated during batch processing.

execution trace A testing procedure that involves simulating by hand the computer executing a program.

explicit type conversion The conversion of one numeric type to another; accomplished by enclosing an expression in parentheses and preceding it with the name of the desired type.

fetch-execute cycle The sequence of steps performed by the central processing unit for each machine language instruction.

field The name of a component in a record.

field selector See *selected component*

file A named area in secondary storage that is used to hold a collection of data; the collection of data itself.

file data type A collection of components, all of the same data type, accessed one component at a time.

file terminator A nonprintable control character or a sequence of nonprintable control characters that the system recognizes as marking the end of a file; not defined by the Ada language.

finite state machine An idealized model of a simple computer consisting of a set of states, the rules that specify when states are changed, and a set of actions that are performed when changing states.

flag A Boolean variable that is set in one part of the program and tested in another to control the logical flow of a program.

flat implementation The hierarchical structure of a solution written as one long sequence of steps; also called inline implementation.

floating-point type A type used to approximate real numbers; uses a fixed number of digits (the mantissa) and a base raised to a power (the exponent).

flow of control The order of execution of the statements in a program.

formal parameter A parameter declared in a procedure specification, function specification, or generic declaration.

formatting The planned positioning of statements or declarations and blanks on a line of a program; the arranging of program output so that it is neatly spaced and aligned.

frame A section of code with which an exception handler is associated; most commonly block statements and subprograms.

function A subprogram that is called from within an expression, and in which a single value (for example, the square root of a number) is computed and returned through the function name.

functional cohesion A property of a module in which all concrete steps are directed toward solving just one problem, and any significant subproblems are written as abstract steps; the principle that a module should perform exactly one abstract action.

functional equivalence A property of a module that it performs exactly the same operation as the abstract step it defines. A pair of modules are functionally equivalent to each other if they each accomplish the same abstract operation.

functional problem description A description that clearly states what a program is to do.

function call An expression requiring the computer to execute a function subprogram.

function declaration See *subprogram declaration.*

function result The value computed by the function subprogram and then returned to the expression containing the function name; often referred to simply as the result.

function result type The data type of the result returned by a function; often referred to simply as function type.

function type See *function result type.*

general case In a recursive definition, the case for which the solution is expressed in terms of a smaller version of itself; also called recursive case.

generic formal parameter A parameter defined in a generic unit declaration; used to customize a generic unit for a specific problem.

generic unit A template for constructing packages and subprograms; a reusable software component.

global Any identifier declared outside of but accessible from a given declarative region.

graphic character A character that may be used as a character literal; a character other than a control character.

hardware The physical components of a computer.

heuristics Assorted problem-solving strategies.

hierarchical implementation A process in which a modular solution is implemented by subprograms that duplicate the hierarchical structure of the solution.

hierarchical records Records in which at least one of the fields is itself a record.

high-level programming language Any programming language in which a single statement translates into one or more machine language instructions.

homogeneous A descriptive term applied to structures in which all components are of the same data type (such as an array).

homograph Each of multiple declarations with identical names; see *name precedence.*

identifier A name associated with a process or object and used to refer to that process or object.

implementation phase The second set of steps in programming a computer: translating (coding) the algorithm into a programming language; testing the resulting program by running it on a computer, checking for accuracy, and making any necessary corrections; using the program.

implementing Coding and testing an algorithm.

index A value that selects a component of an array.

infinite loop A loop that has no termination conditions or whose termination condition is never reached; the loop is never exited without intervention from outside of the program.

infinite recursion The situation in which a subprogram calls itself continuously.

information Any knowledge that can be communicated.

information hiding The management of access to the details of control and data structures.

inheritance Extending a previously developed general solution by adding only the information that distinguishes the specific from the general solution.

inline implementation See *flat implementation*.

in mode A parameter passing mode; the value of the actual parameter is copied into the formal parameter when the subprogram is called; used when a subprogram requires a value.

in out mode A parameter passing mode; the value of the actual parameter is copied into the formal parameter when the subprogram is called and the value of the formal parameter is copied back to the actual parameter when control is returned; used when a subprogram must change a value.

in place Describes a kind of sorting algorithm in which the components in an array are sorted without the use of a second array.

input The process of placing values from an outside data set into variables in a program; the data may come from either an input device (keyboard) or an auxiliary storage device (disk or tape).

input/output (I/O) devices The parts of a computer that accept data to be processed (input) and present the results of that processing (output).

input prompts Messages printed by an interactive program, explaining what data is to be entered.

insertion sort A sorting algorithm in which values are placed one at a time into their proper position within a list that was originally empty.

instantiation The construction of an instance of a package, procedure, or function from a generic unit.

integer number A positive or negative whole number made up of a sign and digits (when the sign is omitted, a positive sign is assumed).

interactive system A system that allows direct communication between the user and the computer.

interface A connecting link (such as a computer keyboard) at a shared boundary that allows independent systems (such as the user and the computer) to meet and act on or communicate with each other; the formal definition of the function of a subprogram or package and the mechanism for communicating with it.

interpreter A program that inputs a program in a high-level language and directs the computer to perform the actions specified in each statement; unlike a compiler, an interpreter does not produce a machine language version of the program.

invoke To call on a subprogram, causing the subprogram to execute before control is returned to the statement following the call.

iteration An individual pass through, or repetition of, the body of a loop.

iteration counter A counter variable that is incremented with each iteration of a loop.

iterator An operation that allows us to process all the components in an abstract data type.

length (of an array) The physical space reserved for an array; the number of components in an array.

library unit A package declaration, subprogram declaration, package instantiation, or subprogram body with no corresponding declaration.

life cycle See *software life cycle*.

linear time For an algorithm, when the Big-O work expression can be expressed in terms of a constant times *N*, where *N* is the number of values in a data set.

line terminator A nonprintable control character or a sequence of nonprintable control characters that the system recognizes as marking the end of a line of data; not defined by the Ada language.

linker A system program that combines program units (stored in the program library) into an executable program.

listing See *compiler listing*.

literal Any value written directly in a program.

local variable A variable declared within a subprogram that is not accessible outside of the subprogram in which it's defined.

logarithmic order For an algorithm, when the Big-O work expression can be expressed in terms of the logarithm of *N*, where *N* is the number of values in a data set.

logging off Informing a computer—usually through a simple command—that no further commands will follow.

logging on Taking the preliminary steps necessary to identify oneself to a computer so that it will accept one's commands.

logical operators Operations applied to values of the type Boolean; in Ada these are the special symbols used: *and, or, not, and then*, and *or else*.

logical order The order in which the user wants the statements in a program to be executed, which may differ from the physical order in which they appear.

loop A method of structuring statements so that they are repeated until certain conditions are met.

loop body The sequence of statements in a loop.

loop control variable A variable whose value is used to determine whether the loop will execute another iteration or exit.

loop entry The point at which the flow of control first passes to a statement inside a loop.

loop exit That point when the repetition of the loop body ends and control passes to the first statement following the loop.

loop invariant Assertions about the characteristics of a loop that must always be true for a loop to execute properly; the assertions are true on loop entry, at the start of each loop iteration, and on exit from the loop, but are not necessarily true at each point in the body of the loop.

loop parameter The identifier defined in a for loop statement that acts as an iteration counter and loop control variable; its scope is the loop body.

machine language The language, made up of binary-coded instructions, that is used directly by the computer.

mainframe A large computing system designed for high-volume processing or for use by many people at once.

maintenance phase The modification of a program, after it has been completed, in order to meet changing requirements or to take care of any errors that occur.

mantissa With respect to floating-point numbers, the digits representing a number itself and not its exponent.

membership test An operation that determines whether or not a value belongs to the domain of a range or subtype.

memory unit Internal data storage in a computer.

metalanguage A language used to describe another language.

microcomputer See *personal computer.*

midtest loop A loop in which the conditional test is made at some place other than at the beginning or end of the loop.

minicomputer A computer system larger than a personal computer but smaller than a mainframe; sometimes called an entry-level mainframe.

minimum complete coverage A testing strategy in which every branch in the program is executed at least once.

mixed mode arithmetic An arithmetic expression that contains different numeric data types; not permitted in Ada.

mnemonic An assembly language instruction used to represent a machine language instruction.

modular programming See *top-down design.*

module A self-contained collection of steps that solves a problem or subproblem; can contain both concrete and abstract steps.

named association An association made between the actual and formal parameters by specifying the name of the formal parameter, an arrow symbol, =>, and the name of the actual parameter; also used in aggregates.

named number A named constant of type universal_integer or universal_real.

named type A type defined in the declarative part of a package, procedure, or function.

name precedence When a homograph exists, the local identifier in a procedure takes precedence over any global identifier in any references that the procedure makes to that identifier.

nested control structure A program structure consisting of one control statement (selection, iteration, or procedure) embedded within another control statement.

nested if An if statement that is within another if statement.

nested loop A loop that is within another loop.

nested procedure A procedure that is defined within another procedure.

nonlocal A descriptive term applied to any identifier declared outside of a given declarative region.

nonlocal access Access by a subprogram of any identifier declared outside of its own declarative region.

null range A range that contains no values; the beginning value of the range is greater than the ending value.

null string A string containing no characters.

nybble Four bits; half of a byte.

object In Ada, a value stored at some location in memory; variables and named constants; in object-oriented design, an entity that is a natural part of the problem and has a state and defined set of operations.

object-oriented design A program design methodology based on defining classes of objects, entities that make sense in the context of the problem being solved.

object package A package used to implement an object, see *object* and *object-oriented design.*

object program The machine language version of a source program.

obsolete unit A compilation unit that has not been recompiled after a unit on which it depends has been recompiled; an error is issued if an attempt is made to use an obsolete unit to form an executable program.

one-dimensional array A structured collection of components of the same type given a single name; each component is accessed by an index that indicates its position within the collection.

operating system A set of programs that manages all of the computer's resources.

ordinal data type See *discrete data type.*

out mode A parameter passing mode; the value of the formal parameter is copied into the actual parameter when control is returned; used when a subprogram returns a result.

overflow The condition that arises when the value of a calculation is too large to be represented.

overloading The ability of an identifier to have several different meanings; subprogram names and enumeration literals are commonly overloaded.

package A group of logically related entities that may include types and subtypes, objects of those types and subtypes, and subprograms with parameters of those types and subtypes; Ada's principal means of encapsulation.

package body The implementation of a package; its contents cannot be accessed by other program units.

package declaration The visible portion of a package; specifies what resources (types, objects, subprograms) are supplied by the package.

parallel processing computer A computer that contains many central processing units working together to solve a problem.

parameter declaration The code that associates a formal parameter identifier with a data type and a passing mode.

parameter list A mechanism for communicating with a subprogram, via which data may be given to the subprogram and/or results received from it.

password A unique series of letters assigned to a user (and known only by that user) by which that user identifies himself or herself to a computer during the logging on procedure; a password system protects information stored in a computer from being tampered with or destroyed.

path The sequence of statements executed in a run of a program.

path coverage A testing strategy in which as many paths as possible in the program are tested.

PC See *personal computer.*

peripheral device An input, output, or auxiliary storage device attached to a computer.

personal computer (PC) A small computer system (usually intended to fit on a desktop) that is designed to be used primarily by a single person.

portable program A program that can be moved from one computer to another without having to make any changes.

positional association A method of matching actual and formal parameters by their relative positions in the two parameter lists; also used in aggregates.

postconditions Assertions that must be true after a module is executed.

posttest loop A loop in which the conditional test is performed at the end of the loop body.

precedence rules Rules that establish the order of importance of operators in a programming language.

precision The number of significant digits in a float type.

preconditions Assertions that must be true before a module begins execution.

prefixing Designating an identifier with the hierarchy of names of packages in which it is declared.

pretest loop A loop in which the conditional test is performed at the beginning of the loop body.

priming read Getting a data value before entry into a loop in order to establish values for the variables; useful when a program must keep track of prior values.

private part The part of a package declaration containing declarations that are not available outside of the package.

private type A type declared in the visible part of a package declaration whose details (record fields, array index and component types, etc.) are declared in the private part of the package declaration; the type may be used outside of the package, but its internal components may not.

problem-solving phase The first set of steps in programming a computer: analyzing the problem; developing an algorithm; testing the algorithm for accuracy.

procedure A structure that allows replacement of a group of statements with a single statement; often called a subprogram or subroutine, it is used by writing a statement consisting of the subprogram name, often followed by a parameter list.

procedure call A statement that transfers control to a procedure; in Ada, this statement is the name of the procedure followed by a list of parameters.

procedure declaration See *subprogram declaration.*

process A program, procedure, or function; any independent collection of executable statements.

programming Planning, scheduling, or performing a task or an event; see *computer programming.*

programming in the large The design and implementation of solutions to problems at a scale too large to be carried out by a single programmer or even a small group of programmers.

programming in the small The design and implementation of solutions to problems at a scale small enough to be carried out by a single programmer or a small group of programmers.

programming language A set of rules, symbols, and special words used to construct a program.

program unit A procedure, function, package, or generic unit.

project director See *chief architect.*

prompts See *input prompts.*

propagated exception An exception that is raised again when control leaves a frame.

pseudocode A mixture of English statements and Ada-like control structures that can easily be translated into a programming language.

qualified expression An expression preceded by an indication of its type or subtype; used when an expression's type is ambiguous.

raise an exception To abandon normal program execution; done when the system or program detects an abnormal condition.

range The set of values between a specified first and last value, including those values.

reading marker An indicator of the next component to be read.

real number A number that has a whole and a fractional part and no imaginary part; in Ada, approximated by floating-point or fixed-point types.

record A structured data type with a fixed number of components that are accessed by name, not by an index; the components may be of different types.

recursion The situation in which a subprogram calls itself.

recursive algorithm A solution that is expressed in terms of (a) smaller instances of itself and (b) a base case.

recursive call A subprogram call in which the subprogram being called is the same as the one making the call.

recursive case See *general case.*

recursive definition A definition in which something is defined in terms of simpler versions of itself.

refinement In top-down design, the expansion of a module specification to form a new module that solves a major step in the computer solution of a problem.

relational operators Operators that state that a relationship exists between two values; in Ada, symbols that cause the computer to perform operations to verify whether or not the indicated relationship exists.

relative error The absolute error divided by the true value of the number.

reliable A descriptive term for a program that can work consistently and without errors regardless of whether the input data is valid or invalid.

reserved word A word that has special meaning in Ada; it cannot be used as a programmer-defined identifier.

result See *function result.*

return The point at which execution of a subprogram is completed and execution resumes with the statement immediately following the call.

robust A descriptive term for a program that can recover from erroneous inputs and keep running.

scalar data type A data type in which the values are ordered and each value is atomic (indivisible).

scope See *scope of access.*

scope of access All of the places from which an identifier can be accessed; often referred to just as its scope.

scope rules The rules that determine where in a program a given identifier may be accessed.

secondary storage device See *auxiliary storage device.*

secondary unit A package body, subunit, or subprogram body whose declaration has been compiled.

selected component The form of name used to access components of a record object. It consists of the record object name followed by a period and the component identifier.

selection control structure A form of program structure allowing the computer to select one among possible actions to perform based on given circumstances; also called branching.

self-documenting code A program containing meaningful identifiers as well as judiciously used clarifying comments.

semantics The set of rules that gives the meaning of instructions written in a programming language.

semihierarchical implementation A modular solution implemented by procedures and functions in a manner that preserves the hierarchical design, except that a subprogram used by multiple modules is implemented once, outside of the hierarchy, and called in each place it is needed.

sentinel A special data value used in certain event-controlled loops as a signal that the loop should be exited.

sequence A structure in which statements are executed one after another.

sequential file A binary file whose components can be accessed sequentially.

short-circuit operators A logical operator (either *or else* or *and then*) that stops the evaluation of additional terms in a Boolean expression as soon as the result is known.

side effect Any effect of one module on another module that is not a part of the explicitly defined interface between them.

significant digits Those digits from the first nonzero digit on the left to the last nonzero digit on the right (plus any zero digits that are exact).

simulation A problem solution that has been arrived at through the application of an algorithm designed to model the behavior of physical systems, materials, or processes.

size The actual number of values stored in an array (less than or equal to its length).

slice A contiguous portion of a one-dimensional array indicated by an index range; frequently used with strings.

software The computer programs; the set of all programs available on a computer.

software engineering A disciplined approach to the design, production, and maintenance of computer software that is developed on time and within cost estimates, using tools that help manage the size and complexity of the resulting software products.

software life cycle The phases in the life of a large software project, including requirements analysis, specification, design, implementation, testing, and maintenance.

sorting Arranging the components of a list in order (for instance, words in alphabetical order, numbers in ascending or descending order).

source program A program written in a high-level language.

standardized Made uniform; most high-level languages are standardized, as official descriptions of them exist.

stepwise refinement See *top-down design*.

structured data type A collection of components whose organization is characterized by the method used to access individual components; also called a data structure.

stub A dummy procedure or function that assists in testing part of a program; it has the same name and interface as a procedure or function that would actually be called by the part of the program being tested, but it is usually much simpler.

style The individual manner in which computer programmers translate algorithms into a programming language.

subprogram A procedure or function.

subprogram body The implementation of a subprogram; its specification can act as the subprogram declaration if a declaration is not already in the program library.

subprogram declaration A specification of a subprogram; commonly written in a package declaration to specify operations provided by the package.

subroutine See *subprogram.*

subscript See *index.*

subtype A subset of a type determined by a constraint on the type.

subunit A separately compiled body that is declared in the declarative part of another program unit.

supercomputer The most powerful class of computers.

syntax The formal rules governing how valid instructions (constructs) are written in a programming language.

system software A set of programs—including the compiler, the operating system, and the editor—that improves the efficiency and convenience of the computer's processing.

tail recursion A recursive algorithm in which no statements are executed after the return from the recursive call; often indicates the problem could be solved easily with iteration.

team programming The use of two or more programmers to design a program that would take one programmer too long to complete; the type of programming for which Ada was designed.

termination condition The condition that causes a loop to be exited.

testing Checking a program's output by comparing it to hand-calculated results; running a program with data sets designed to discover any errors.

text file A file data type whose components are characters organized as a collection of lines; a line terminator follows every line; a file terminator follows the last line in the file.

top-down design A technique for developing a program in which the problem is divided into more easily handled subproblems, the solutions of which create a solution to the overall problem; also called stepwise refinement and modular programming.

two-dimensional array A collection of components, all of the same type, structured in two dimensions; each component is accessed by a pair of indices that represent the component's position within each dimension.

type cast See *explicit type conversion.*

type coercion An automatic assignment of a value of one type to a variable of another type; in Ada, available only with universal types.

type definition The association of a type identifier with the definition of a new type or subtype in a declarative region.

unconstrained array type An array type without a range specified for its index; only the index type and component type are specified.

underflow The condition that arises when the value of a calculation is too small to be represented.

universal types The types of numeric literals; integer literals are type universal_integer and float literals are type universal_real.

user name The name by which a computer recognizes the user, and which must be entered to log onto a mainframe.

validated Ada An Ada implementation that has successfully passed the testing procedures of the Ada Validation Office and received a certificate of validation.

variable A location in memory, referenced by an identifier, in which a data value that can be changed is stored.

visible Accessible; a term used in describing a scope of access.

visible part The part of a package declaration containing declarations that can be used outside of the package.

walk-through An algorithm or code trace performed by a team of program developers.

word Groups of 16, 32, or 64 bits; a group of bits processed by the arithmetic logic unit in a single instruction.

work A measure of the effort expended by the computer in performing a computation.

workstation A minicomputer designed to be used primarily by one person at a time.

Answers to Selected Exercises

Chapter 1

Exam Preparation Exercises

1. The following are peripheral devices: disk drive, tape drive, printer, card reader, auxiliary storage, and terminal. The arithmetic logic unit and the control unit are not peripherals.
4. a. The source file and the object file.
   b. The source file.
   c. A listing of the program with any errors found in the source and other information relevant to the programmer.

Chapter 2

Exam Preparation Exercises

1. a. Invalid
   b. Valid
   c. Valid
   d. Invalid
   e. Valid
   f. Invalid
   g. Valid
   h. Invalid
   i. Valid
3. a. Invalid
   b. Invalid
   c. Valid
   d. Invalid
   e. Valid
5. a. Valid
   b. Invalid

c. Invalid
d. Invalid
e. Valid
f. Invalid
g. Invalid
h. Valid
i. Invalid
j. Invalid
k. Invalid

7. False

10. a. 13.33333
 c. 5
 e. –4
 g. 0

11. a. 3
 c. 37
 e. 23

19. a. 0
 c. 44.2
 e. 0
 g. 2
 i. 1

Programming Warm-up Exercises

1.
```
with Ada.Ada.Text_IO;
with Ada.Integer_Ada.Text_IO;

procedure Exercise_17 is

   Pounds : constant := 15;

   Price  : Integer;
   Cost   : Integer;
   Ch     : String (1..1);
begin   -- Exercise_17
   Price := 30;
   Cost  := Price * Pounds;
   Ch := "A";
   Ada.Ada.Text_IO.Put (Item => "Cost is ");
   Ada.Ada.Text_IO.New_Line;
   Ada.Integer_Ada.Text_IO.Put (Item => Cost);
   Ada.Ada.Text_IO.New_Line;
   Ada.Ada.Text_IO.Put (Item => "Price is ");
   Ada.Integer_Ada.Text_IO.Put (Item => Price);
   Ada.Ada.Text_IO.Put (Item => "Cost is ");
   Ada.Integer_Ada.Text_IO.Put (Item => Cost);
   Ada.Ada.Text_IO.New_Line;
   Ada.Ada.Text_IO.Put (Item => "Grade ");
```

```
      Ada.Ada.Text_IO.Put (Item => Ch);
      Ada.Ada.Text_IO.Put (Item => " costs ");
      Ada.Ada.Text_IO.New_Line;
      Ada.Integer_Ada.Text_IO.Put (Item => Cost);
      Ada.Ada.Text_IO.New_Line;
   end Exercise_17;
```

2. `2.0 * Pi * E ** (-N) * Float(N) ** N`

Chapter 3

Exam Preparation Exercises

2. a. Variable E will contain 17; variable F will contain 13.
   b. Leftover values 7 and 3 will be skipped over and lost.
3. a. By pressing the Return or Enter key.
   b. By calling the procedure Ada.Ada.Text_IO.New_Line.
5. a. True
   b. True
9. The following lines will raise a DATA_ERROR.

```
5  8.0  9.0
2.0  Hello
```

12. a. Severs the connection between the file variable and the file.
    b. The file may be altered or deleted by the system.

Programming Warm-up Exercises

1.
```
Ada.Float_Text_IO.Get (Item => Length);
Ada.Float_Text_IO.Get (Item => Height);
Ada.Float_Text_IO.Get (Item => Width);
```

2.
```
Ada.Float_Text_IO.Get (Item => Length1);
Ada.Float_Text_IO.Get (Item => Height1);
Ada.Text_IO.Skip_Line;
Ada.Float_Text_IO.Get (Item => Length2);
Ada.Float_Text_IO.Get (Item => Height2);
Ada.Text_IO.Skip_Line;
```

3.
```
Num1  : Integer;
Num2  : Float;
Num3  : Integer;
Name1 : String (1..7);
Name2 : String (1..6);

Ada.Integer_Text_IO.Get (Item => Num1);
Ada.Text_IO.Get (Item => Name1);
Ada.Float_Text_IO.Get (Item => Num2);
Ada.Integer_Text_IO.Get (Item => Num3);
Ada.Text_IO.Get (Item => Name2);
```

9. Starting an automobile with a manual transmission and an automatic choke. Note that the problem statement said nothing about getting into the car, adjusting seat belts, checking the mirror, or driving away. Presumably those tasks, along with starting the car, are subtasks of a larger design like "Go to the store." Here we are concerned only with starting the car itself.

Main Module
Ensure car won't roll.
Disengage gears.
Attempt ignition.

Ensure car won't roll.
Engage parking brake.
Turn wheels into curb.

Disengage gears.
Push in clutch with left foot.
Move gearshift to neutral.
Release clutch.

Attempt ignition.
Insert key into ignition slot.
Turn key to ON position.
Pump accelerator once.
Turn key to START position.
Release key after engine catches or 5 seconds, whichever comes first.

11.
```
with Ada.Text_IO;
with Ada.Integer_Text_IO
procedure Copy is

   A        : Integer;
   In_Data  : Ada.Text_IO.File_Type
   Out_Data : Ada.Text_IO.File_Type

begin
   Ada.Text_IO.Open   (File => In_Data,
                       Mode => Ada.Text_IO.In_File
```

```
                               Name => "Numbers.Dat");

   Ada.Text_IO.Create (File => Out_Data,
                       Name => "RESULTS");
   Ada.Integer_Text_IO.Get (File => In_Data,  Item => A);
   Ada.Integer_Text_IO.Put (File => Out_Data, Item => A);
   Ada.Text_IO.New_Line (File => Out_Data);
   Ada.Integer_Text_IO.Get (File => In_Data,  Item => A);
   Ada.Integer_Text_IO.Put (File => Out_Data, Item => A);
   Ada.Text_IO.New_Line (File => Out_Data);
   Ada.Text_IO.Close (File => In_Data);
   Ada.Text_IO.Close (File => Out_Data);
end Copy;
```

Chapter 4

Exam Preparation Exercises

1. a. True
   c. True
2. a. `Change >= 1.00`
   c. `First_Name /= "Mildred"  and  Last_Name /= "Smedley"`
5. a.
   ```
   10
   10
   ```
   c.
   ```
   3
   7
   6
   ```
8. a. `(X < Y)  and  (Y <= Z)`
   b. `(X > 0)  and  (Y > 0)  and  (Z > 0)`
10. a. if-then-else
    c. if-then
    e. if-then-else
13. No one wins the game.
15. a.
    ```
    package Suit_IO is new Ada.Text_IO.Enumeration_IO
      (Enum => Suit_Type);
    ```
    b. `Suit_IO.Put (Item => Card_1);`
    c. `Suit_IO.Get (Item => Card_2);`
    d. `DATA_ERROR`

Programming Warm-up Exercises

1. `Available := Number_Ordered <= (Number_On_Hand - Number_Reserved);`
4. `Left_Page := (Page_Number rem 2) = 0;`

6.
```
if  Year rem 4 = 0  then
   Ada.Integer_Text_IO.Put (Item => Year, Width => 4);
   Ada.Text_IO.Put         (Item => " is a leap year.");
   Ada.Text_IO.New Line;
end if;

if  Year rem 4 /= 0  then
   Year := Year + 4 - Year rem 4;
   Ada.Integer_Text_IO.Put (Item => Year, Width => 4);
   Ada.Text_IO.Put         (Item => " is the next leap year.");
   Ada.Text_IO.New Line;
end if;
```

8.
```
if Age > 64 then
   Ada.Text_IO.Put (Item => "Senior voter");
elsif Age < 18 then
   Ada.Text_IO.Put (Item =>  "Under age");
else
   Ada.Text_IO.Put (Item => "Regular voter");
end if;
```

10. a.
```
package Suit_IO is new Ada.Text_IO.Enumeration_IO (Enum =>
Suit_Type);
```

b.
```
Suit_IO.Put (Item => Card_1,
             Set  => Ada.Text_IO.Lower_Case);
Ada.Text_IO.New_Line;
Suit_IO.Put (Item => Card_2,
             Set  => Ada.Text_IO.Lower_Case);
Ada.Text_IO.New_Line;
Suit_IO.Put (Item => Card_3,
             Set  => Ada.Text_IO.Lower_Case);
Ada.Text_IO.New_Line;
```

Chapter 5

Exam Preparation Exercises

3.
```
Number := 1;
Exercise_Loop:
loop
   Ada.Integer_Text_IO.Put (Item => Number);
   Ada.Text_IO.New_Line;
   Number := Number + 1;
   exit Exercise_Loop when Number > 10;
end loop Exercise_Loop;
```

4. The number of iterations executed by the loop is 6.

Programming Warm-up Exercises

1.
```
Check_Pressure:
loop
   Ada.Float_Text_IO.Get (Item => Pressure);
   exit Check_Pressure when Pressure > 510.0;
end loop Check_Pressure;
Danger := True;
```

2.
```
Interation_Count := 1;
Count_Of_28      := 0;
Count_Loop:
   exit Count_Loop when Iteration_Count > 100;
   Ada.Integer_Text_IO.Get (Item => Number);
   if Number = 28 then
      Count_Of_28 := Count_Of_28 + 1;
   end if;
   Iteration_Count := Iteration_Count + 1;
end loop Count_Loop;
```

5.
```
Iteration_Count := 1;
Positive_Count  := 0;
Negative_Count  := 0;
Sign_Loop:
loop
   exit Sign_Loop when Iteration_Count > 100;
   Ada.Integer_Text_IO.Get (Item => Number);
   if Number > 0 then
      Positive_Count := Positive_Count + 1;
   elsif Number < 0 then
      Negative _Count := Negative _Count + 1;
   end if;
   Iteration_Count := Iteration_Count + 1;
end loop Sign_Loop;
```

6.
```
Sum    := 0;
Number := 16;
Even_Sum:
   exit Even_Sum when Number > 26;
   Sum := Sum + Number;
   Number := Number + 2;
end loop Even_Sum;
```

8.
```
Hour := 1;
AM   := True;
Hour_Loop:
loop
   Minute := 0;
   Minute_Loop:
   loop
      exit Minute_Loop when Minute = 60;
      Ada.Integer_Text_IO.Put (Item => Hour, Width => 1);
      Ada.Text_IO.Put (":");
      if Minute < 10 then
         Ada.Text_IO.Put (Item => "0");
      end if;
      Ada.Integer_Text_IO.Put (Item => Minute, Width => 1);
      if AM then
         Ada.Text_IO.Put (Item => " A.M.");
      else
         Ada.Text_IO.Put (Item => " P.M.");
      end if;
      Ada.Text_IO.New_Line;
      Minute := Minute + 1;
   end loop Minute_Loop;
   if Hour = 12 then
      Hour := 1;
      AM   := not AM;
   else
      Hour := Hour + 1;
   end if;
   exit Hour_Loop when (Hour = 1)  and  AM
end loop Hour_Loop;
```

Chapter 6

Exam Preparation Exercises

3. 3 2 4
6. Only one of the statements is not a procedure call.
8. a.
```
procedure One (Squirrel : out Integer;
               Rabbit   : out Integer) is
```
c.
```
procedure Three (Squirrel : in Integer;
                 Rabbit   : in Integer) is
```
e.
```
procedure Five (Squirrel :  in Integer;
                Chipmunk :  in Integer;
                Rabbit   : out Integer) is
```

g.
```
procedure Seven (Squirrel : in     Integer;
                 Chipmunk : in out Integer;
                 Rabbit   : in out Integer) is
```
i.
```
procedure Nine (Squirrel :  in Integer;
                 Chipmunk : out Integer;
                 Rabbit   : out Integer) is
```

10. False. An identifier is not accessible to statements in the declarative region that are *before* the declaration of that identifier.

12. a. False. Variable A declared immediately within Scope_Rules is not available with Region_2 since there is a local variable A declared in that region.
    c. False. Identifiers declared within a region cannot be accessed from outside of that region.
    e. False. Variable B2 is local to procedure Region_2.
    g. False. Variable A1 is not accessible within procedure Region_3.
    i. True

14. a.
```
X equals 3
X equals 3
X equals 7
```

18. True

22. a. True
    c. True

23. a. iv
    c. i
    e. ii

Programming Warm-up Exercises

3.
```
procedure Increment (Number : in out Integer) is
begin
   Number := Number + 15;
end Increment;
```

5. There is a semicolon following the procedure specification instead of the reserved word `is` that is required in a procedure body. The semicolon in this position makes this line a procedure declaration rather than the start of a procedure body.

7. b.
```
function Circumference (Radius : in Float) returns Float is
begin
   return 2.0 * Ada.Numerics.Pi * Radius;
end Circumference;
```

9.
```
procedure Get_Mean (Of : in Integer; Mean : out Float) is
   Count : Integer;
   Sum   : Float;
   Value : Float;
begin
   Count := 0;
   Sum_Loop:
   loop
```

```
      exit Sum_Loop when Count >= Of;
      Ada.Float_Text_IO.Get (Value);
      Sum := Sum + Value;
      Count := Count + 1;
   end loop Sum_Loop;
   Mean := Sum / Float (Of);
end Get_Mean;
```

11.
```
procedure Get_Average (Dept_Num  : in  Integer;
                       Avg_Sales : out Float) is
```

15.
```
function Equal (Num_1      : in Float;
                Num_2      : in Float;
                Difference : in Float) return Boolean is
```

17.
```
function Compass_Heading (True_Course    : in Float;
                          Wind_Corr_Angle : in Float;
                          Variance        : in Float;
                          Deviation       : in Float) return Float is
begin
   return (True_Course + Wind_Corr_Angle +
           Variance + Deviation) / 4.0;
end Compass_Heading;
```

Chapter 7

Exam Preparation Exercises

6. a. 0
   c. CONSTRAINT_ERROR
   e. Dior_Essence
   g. Coty
8. a. 0
   c. 67
   e. −45
13. False. Only numeric subtypes that share the same base type can be mixed together in expressions.

Programming Warm-up Exercises

2.
```
type Degrees is digits 8 range 0.0..360.0
```

3.
```
type Imperial_Gallons is digits 4 range 0.00..20.0
function To_US_Gallons (Gallons : in Imperial_Gallons
                        return US_Gallons is
begin
   return US_Gallons (1.25 * Gallons);
end To_US_Gallons;
```

5.
```
Loop_6:
loop
   exit Loop_6 when Count > Max_Count;
```

```
   Ada.Integer_Text_IO.Put (Count);
   Count := Integer'Succ (Count);
end loop Loop_6;
```

8. `subtype Allowance_Dollars is Dollars range 1.00 .. 100.00;`

Chapter 8

Exam Preparation Exercises

1. a. There must be a choice for *every* value in the domain of type Integer.
   c. The choice `others` must be the last alternative.
3. a. 5
   c. 0
   e. 1
5.
```
4    4    4    4
3    3    3
2    2
1
```
7.
```
2
3    2
4    3    2
5    4    3    2
```
8. No. Sentinel-controlled input requires a midtest loop. A while loop is a pretest loop.

Programming Warm-up Exercises

2. b.
```
Color : Color_Type;

Color := Color_Type'First;
loop
   Color_IO.Put (Color);
   exit when Color = Color_Type'Last;
   Color := Color_Type'Succ (Color);
end loop;
```
4.
```
M : Integer;

M := 93;
while M > 4 loop
   Ada.Integer_Text_IO.Put (M);
   Ada.Text_IO.New_Line;
   M := M - 1;
end loop;
```
6.
```
Sum := 0;
Sentinel_Loop:
loop
```

```
   Ada.Integer_Text_IO.Get (Value);
   exit Sentinel_Loop when Value = 0;
   Sum := Sum + Value;
end loop Sentinel_Loop;
Ada.Integer_Text_IO.Put (Sum);
```

Chapter 9

Exam Preparation Exercises

1. Usually not. The Get_Line procedure moves the reading marker past the line terminator. However, if the string variable is filled before the line terminator is found, the reading marker is not advanced past the line terminator. It is best to test the value of Last to determine whether or not you should call Skip_Line.
3. Add a call to procedure Skip_Line just before or after the call to procedure New_Line.
5. a. END_ERROR is raised.
   b. The write succeeds. The file will contain 82 components. File components 75 to 81 contain undefined values.
7. Because the type Count is defined in package Dir_Float_IO, so is its + operator. You can either prefix this operator with the name of the package in which it is declared (`Dir_Float_IO."+"`) or you can use a use type statement (`use type Dir_Float_IO.Count`), which allows us to write the + operator without prefixing.

Programming Warm-up Exercises

2.
```
Sum       : Float
Average   : Float;
Value     : Float;
Count     : Integer;
Data_File : Ada.Text_IO.File_Type;

Sum   := 0.0;
Count := 0;
Sum_Loop:
loop
   exit Sum_Loop when Ada.Text_IO.End_Of_File (Data_File);
   Ada.Float_Text_IO.Get (Item => Value, File => Data_File);
   if not Ada.Text_IO.End_Of_File (Data_File) then
      Ada.Text_IO.Skip_Line (Data_File);
   end if;
   Sum   := Sum + Value;
   Count := Count + 1;
end loop Sum_Loop;
Average := Sum / Float (Count);
```

4.
```
Char : Character;
```

```
Line_Loop:
loop
   exit Line_Loop when Ada.Text_IO.End_Of_File (Data_File);
   Char_Loop:
   loop
      exit Char_Loop when Ada.Text_IO.End_Of_Line (Data_File);
      Ada.Text_IO.Get (Item => Letter, File => Data_File);
   end loop Char_Loop;
   Ada.Text_IO.Put (Char);
   Ada.Text_IO.New_Line;
   if not Ada.Text_IO.End_Of_File (Data_File) then
      Ada.Text_IO.Skip_Line (Data_File);
   end if;
end loop Line_Loop;
```

8.

```
Value : Score_Type;

Validation_Loop:
loop
   Ada.Text_IO.Put_Line ("Enter an even number between 0 and 100");
   Input_Block:
   begin
      Ada.Integer_Text_IO.Get (Value);
      exit Validation_Loop when (Value rem 2) = 0;
      Ada.Text_IO.Put_Line ("The number is not even.");
   exception
      when Ada.IO_Exceptions.DATA_ERROR =>
         Ada.Text_IO.Put_Line ("Data entered is not a valid number.");
         Ada.Text_IO.Skip_Line;     -- Skip over the bad data
      when CONSTRAINT_ERROR =>
         Ada.Text_IO.Put_Line ("The number is not between 0 and 100");
   end Input_Block;
end loop Validation_Loop;
```

10.

```
function Factorial (X : in Integer) return Integer is
   Result     : Integer;
   Multiplier : Integer;
begin
   Multiplier := X
   Result     := 1
   Multiply_Loop:
   loop
      exit Multiply_Loop when Multiplier <= 1
      Result     := Result * Multiplier;
      Multiplier := Multiplier - 1;
   end loop Multiply_Loop;
   return Result
exception
   when CONSTRAINT_ERROR =>
```

```
      return Integer'Last;
   end Factorial;
```

Chapter 10

Exam Preparation Exercises

2. a. Invalid
   c. Valid
   e. Valid
   g. Valid
   i. Valid
4. False
7. You cannot use the < operator with record variables.
9. a. `C := (5.7, 7.2);`
   c. `Complex_IO.Read (File => D, Item => C, From => 14);`

Programming Warm-up Exercises

2. a.
```
procedure Get (Course_ID : out Course_ID_Type) is
begin
   Dept_Code_IO.Get (Course_ID.Dept_Code);
   Ada.Integer_Text_IO.Get (Course_ID.Number);
end Get;
```
   c.
```
procedure Get (Instructor : out Instructor_Type) is
   Last : Natural;
begin
   Ada.Text_IO.Get_Line (Item => Instructor.Name, Last => Last);
   for Index in Last + 1 .. 30 loop
      Instructor.Name(Index) := ' ';
   end loop;
   Get (Instructor.Office);
end Get;
```
4. a.
```
subtype String20 is String (1..20);
type Apt_Type is
   record
      Landlord : String20;
      Address  : String20;
      Bedrooms : Positive;
      Price    : Dollars;
   end record;
```
   c.
```
procedure Get (Apartment : Apt_Type) is
   Blank_String : constant := "                    ";
   Last : Natural;
begin
   Apartment.Landlord := Blank_String;
   Ada.Text_IO.Get_Line (Item => Apartment.Landlord,
```

```
                              Last => Last);
         Apartment.Address := Blank_String;
         Ada.Text_IO.Get_Line (Item => Apartment.Address,
                              Last => Last);
         Ada.Integer_Text_IO.Get (Apartment.Bedrooms);
         Dollar_IO.Get (Apartment.Price);
      end Get;
```

7.
```
procedure Put_All_Titles (Catalog : in out Book_IO.File_Type) is
   One_Book : Book_Rec;
begin
   Book_IO.Set_Index (File => Catalog, To => 1);
   Display_Loop:
   loop
      exit Display_Loop when Book_IO.End_Of_File (Catalog);
      Book_IO.Read (File => Catalog, Item => One_Book);
      Ada.Text_IO.Put_Line (One_Book.Title);
   end loop Display_Loop;
```

10.
```
subtype String20 is String (1..20);

type String_Rec is
   record
      Count : Natural  := 0;
      Value : String20;
   end record

function Length (Str : in String_Rec) return Natural is
begin
   return Str.Count;
end Length;
```

Chapter 11

Exam Preparation Exercises

2. False. The components of an array may be any type.
4. a. `type Bird_Type is (Sparrow, Robin, Chickadee, Nuthatch);`
   b. `type Siting_Type is array (Bird_Type) of Integer;`
   c. `Sitings : Siting_Type;`
6. a.
```
for Color in Color_Type loop
   Count (Color) := 0;
end loop;
```
   or
```
Count := (Color_Type => 0);
```
   c.
```
Green_Count := 0;
for Index in Index_Range loop
   if Rainbow (Index) = Green then
```

```
      Green_Count := Green_Count + 1;
   end if;
end loop;
```

e.
```
Total := 0;
for Color in Color_Type loop
   Total := Total + Count (Color);
end loop;
```

8. a.
```
subtype Index_Type is Integer range 1..24;
type Float_Array is array (Index_Type) of Float;
```

c.
```
subtype Uppercase is Character range 'A'..'Z';
type Boolean_Array is array (Uppercase) of Boolean;
```

10. Sample(1) is 1
Sample(2) is 1
Sample(3) is 1
Sample(4) is −1
Sample(5) is −1
Sample(6) is −1
Sample(7) is −1
Sample(8) is −1

12. a.
```
Jobs(43).Start.Hour := 18;
```

c.
```
Jobs(12) := (Start => (10, 52, 17),
             Stop  => (11, 31, 0));
```

14. a.
```
type Float_Array is array (Integer range <>) of Float;
```

c.
```
type Boolean_Array is array (Character range <>) of Boolean;
```

18. a. 6
c. 30 (in the array Tickets)
e. Row

21. a.
```
type Teams is (Lions, Tigers, Bears);
```

b.
```
type Team_Record_Array is array (Teams) of Integer;
```

24. a. Two-dimensional array
c. Array of arrays

26. a.
```
type    Index_1 is range -1..3;
subtype Index_2 is Character range 'A'..'Z';
type    Index_3 is range 1..20;
type Three_D_Array is array (Index_1, Index_2, Index_3) of Float;
```

27. So that the Ada compiler can detect any interchanged array indices.

Programming Warm-up Exercises

1.
```
Passing := (Index_Type => True);
```

4.
```
Temp : Natural;
Low  : Index_Type;
High : Index_Type;

Low  := Index_Type'First;
High := Index_Type'Last;
```

```
Swap_Loop:
loop
   exit Swap_Loop when Low >= High;
   Temp          := Scores(Low);
   Scores(Low)   := Scores(High);
   Scores(High) := Temp;
   Low  := Low + 1;
   High := High - 1;
end loop Swap_Loop;
```

9.

```
function Minimum (Grade_List : in Grade_Array) return Score_Range is
   Result : Score_Range;
begin
   Result := Grade_List(Grade_List'First);
   for Index in Grade_List'First + 1 .. Grade_List'Last loop
      if Grade_List(Index) > Result then
         Result := Index;
      end if;
   end loop;
   return Result;
end Minimum;
```

13.

```
function Largest (Table : in Integer_Array) return Integer is
   Result : Integer;
begin
   Result := Table (Table'First(1), Table'First(2));
   for Row in Table'Range(1) loop
      for Column in Table'Range(2) loop
         if Table (Row, Column) > Result then
            Result := Index;
         end if;
      end loop;
   end loop;
   return Result;
end Largest;
```

16.

```
procedue Initialize (Sales : out Sales_Array) is
begin
   for Index_1 in Sales'Range(1) loop
      for Index_2 in Sales'Range(2) loop
         for Index_3 in Sales'Range(3) loop
            Sales(Index_1, Index_2, Index_3) := 0;
         end loop;
      end loop;
   end loop;
end Initialize;
```

Chapter 12

Exam Preparation Exercises

4. a.
```
Name : Customer_Accounts.Name_Rec;
```
   b.
```
package Name_Rec_IO is new Sequential_IO
       (Element_Type => Customer_Accounts.Name_Rec);
```
   c.
```
function "<" (Left  : in Customer_Accounts.Name_Rec;
              Right : in Customer_Accounts.Name_Rec)
                        return Boolean is
begin
   return Left.Account_Number  <  Right.Account_Number;
end "<";
```
6. a.
```
package Color_IO is new Ada.Text_IO.Enumeration_IO
                              (Enum => Pixel.Color_Type);
```
   b.
```
use type Pixel.Color_Type;

First_Color  : Pixel.Color_Type;
Second_Color : Pixel.Color_Type;

procedure Display_Color_Group (Color : in Pixel.Color_Type) is
begin
   Color_IO.Put (Color);
   case Color of
      when Pixel.Primary_Color_Type =>
         Ada.Text_IO.Put_Line (" is a primary color.");
      when Pixel.Secondary_Color_Type =>
         Ada.Text_IO.Put_Line (" is a secondary color.");
      when Pixel.Neutral_Color_Type =>
         Ada.Text_IO.Put_Line (" is a neutral color.");
   end case;
end Display_Color_Group;

Color_IO.Get (First_Color);
Display_Color_Group (First_Color);
Color_IO.Get (Second_Color);
Display_Color_Group (Second_Color);
if First_Color in Pixel.Primary_Color_Type      and
      Second_Color in Pixel.Primary_Color_Type  then
   Ada.Text_IO.Put ("Mixing these colors yields ");
   Color_IO.Put (Item => First_Color + Second_Color);
   Ada.Text_IO.New_Line;
end if;
```
10. b. Fruit and Pear (body)
    c. None
    f. Apple (body) and Banana (body)

12. The use package clause allows you to use any resource defined in the package specification without prefixing. The use type clause allows you to use the operators for a particular type defined in the package specification without prefixing. Because of the loss of documentation, we recommend that you do not use any use package clauses in your programs.

Programming Warm-up Exercises

1.
```
with Vector_ADT;
package Vector_IO is

   procedure Get (Item : out Vector_ADT.Vector);

   procedure Put (Item : in Vector_ADT.Vector;
                  Fore : in Positive;
                  Aft  : in Positive;
                  Exp  : in Positive);
end Vector_IO;
```

5.
```
function "<" (Left : in Vector; Right : in Vector) return Boolean is
   Left_Magnitude  : Component_Type;
   Right_Magnitude : Component_Type;
begin
   Left_Magnitude  := Left  * Left;   -- Dot products used to
   Right_Magnitude := Right * Right;  -- determine magnitudes
   return Left_Magnitude < Right_Magnitude;
end "<";
```

6.
```
function Has_Greater_Than (Item : in Float; List : in Float_Array)
is
   Index : Integer;
begin
   Index := List'First;
   Search_Loop:    -- Search for a larger value than Item
   loop            -- Each iteration, check one value in list
      exit when Index > List'Last  or else  Item > List(Index);
      Index := Index + 1;
   end loop;
   -- If we didn't go off the end of List, we found a larger value
   return Index <= List'Last;
end Has_Greater_Than;
```

Chapter 13

Exam Preparation Exercises

2. False. Both procedures and functions can be recursive.
4. $F(4) = 1$; $F(6) = -1$; $F(5)$ is undefined.
6. An if statement is the control structure that most commonly appears in a recursive procedure.

10. a. EDCBA
    b. Reaching the end of the line

Programming Warm-up Exercises

2.
```
function F (N : in Natural) return Integer is
   Result : Integer;
begin
   if N = 0 then
      Result := 1;
   elsif N = 1 then
      Result := 2;
   elsif N = 2 then
      Result := 3;
   else
      Result := F(N-1) - F(N-2) + F(N-3);
   end if;
   return Result;
end F;
```

4.
```
procedure Line_Print (In_File : in out Ada.Text_IO.File_Type) is
   Ch : Character;
begin
   Line_Loop:
   loop
      exit Line_Loop when Ada.Text_IO.End_Of_File (In_File);
      Char_Loop:
      loop
         exit Char_Loop when Ada.Text_IO.End_Of_Line (In_File);
         Ada.Text_IO.Get (File => In_File, Item => Ch);
         Ada.Text_IO.Put (Ch);
      end loop Char_Loop;
      Ada.Text_IO.Skip_Line (In_File);
      Ada.Text_IO.New_Line;
   end loop Line_Loop;
end Line_Print;
```

8.
```
procedure Halves (N : in Integer) is
begin
   if N >= 0 then
      Ada.Integer_Text_IO.Put (N);
      Ada.Integer_Text_IO.Put (N/2);
      Ada.Text_IO.New_Line;
      Halves (N => N-1);
   end if;
end Halves
```

11.
```
procedure Print (List: Integer_Array) is
begin
   if List'Length > 0 then
      Print (List=> List (List'First + 1 .. List'Last));
      Ada.Integer_Text_IO.Put (Item => List (List'First));
end if;
end Print;
```

Index

K